Daniel Fluharty

Borland C++: The Complete Reference

Herbert Schildt

Osborne **McGraw-Hill**

Berkeley New York St. Louis San Francisco
Auckland Bogotá Hamburg London Madrid
Mexico City Milan Montreal New Delhi Panama City
Paris São Paulo Singapore Sydney
Tokyo Toronto

Osborne **McGraw-Hill**
2600 Tenth Street
Berkeley, California 94710
U.S.A.

For information on translations or book distributors outside the U.S.A., or to arrange bulk purchase discounts for sales promotions, premiums, or fundraisers, please contact Osborne/**McGraw-Hill** at the above address.

Borland C++: The Complete Reference

Copyright © 1997 by The McGraw-Hill Companies. All rights reserved. Printed in the United States of America. Except as permitted under the Copyright Act of 1976, no part of this publication may be reproduced or distributed in any form or by any means, or stored in a database or retrieval system, without the prior written permission of the publisher, with the exception that the program listings may be entered, stored, and executed in a computer system, but they may not be reproduced for publication.

1234567890 DOC 9987

ISBN 0-07-882230-0

Publisher
Brandon A. Nordin

Acquisitions Editor
Wendy Rinaldi

Project Editor
Emily Rader

Associate Project Editor
Heidi Poulin

Editorial Assistant
Ann Sellers

Technical Editor
Greg Guntle

Copy Editors
Dennis Weaver
Linda Medoff

Proofreader
Linda Medoff

Indexer
Sheryl Schildt

Computer Designer
Jani P. Beckwith

Illustrator
Lance Ravella

Cover Design
Adrian Morgan

Quality Control Specialist
Joe Scuderi

Information has been obtained by Osborne/**McGraw-Hill** from sources believed to be reliable. However, because of the possibility of human or mechanical error by our sources, Osborne/**McGraw-Hill**, or others, Osborne/**McGraw-Hill** does not guarantee the accuracy, adequacy, or completeness of any information and is not responsible for any errors or omissions or the results obtained from use of such information.

About the Author

Herb Schildt is the leading authority on the C and C++ languages, an expert Windows programmer, and a master in Java. He has written numerous best-selling Osborne titles, including *C++: The Complete Reference*, *C: The Complete Reference*, *C++ from the Ground Up*, and the recently released *Schildt's Expert C++* and *MFC Programming from the Ground Up*. He is coauthor of the highly acclaimed *Java: The Complete Reference*. He is a member of both the ANSI C and ANSI C++ standardization committees.

Contents

Preface xv

Part I

The C Language

1 An Overview of C 3
The Origins of the C Language . . 3
A Middle-Level Language . . . 3
A Structured Language 5
A Programmer's Language . . . 6
Compilers Versus Interpreters . . 7
The Form of a C Program 8
The Library and Linking 8
Separate Compilation . . . 9
A C Program's Memory Map 10
A Review of Terms 11

2 Variables, Constants, Operators, and Expressions 13
Identifier Names 13
Data Types 14
Type Modifiers 14
Access Modifiers 17
Declaration of Variables 17
Local Variables 18
Formal Parameters 20
Global Variables 20
Storage Class Specifiers 22
extern 23
static Variables 24
static Local Variables . . . 24
static Global Variables . . . 26
Register Variables 27
Assignment Statements 28
Multiple Assignments . . . 28
Type Conversion in Assignments 29
Variable Initializations . . 30
Constants 31
Backslash Character Constants 31
Operators 33
Arithmetic Operators . . . 33

Increment and Decrement 33
Relational and Logical Operators 35
Bitwise Operators 37
The ? Operator 41
The & and * Pointer Operators 41
The sizeof Compile-Time Operator 43
The Comma Operator . . . 44
The . and -> Operators . . 44
[ ] and ( ) 45
Precedence Summary . . . 45
Expressions 46
Type Conversion in Expressions 46
Casts 48
Spacing and Parentheses 48
C Shorthand 49

3 Program Control Statements 51
True and False in C 51
Selection Statements 51
if 52
Nested ifs 53
The if-else-if Ladder 54
The ? Alternative 55
switch 58
Nested switch Statements 61
Loops 62
for 62
for Loop Variations 63
The Infinite Loop 66
for Loops with No Bodies 67
while 67
do/while 69
break 70
exit( ) 71
continue 73
Labels and goto 74

4 Functions 77
The return Statement 77
Returning from a Function 78
Return Values 79
Returning Values from main( ) 80
Scope Rules of Functions 81
Function Arguments 81
Call by Value, Call by Reference 82
Creating a Call by Reference 83
Calling Functions with Arrays 84
Arguments to main( ) 88
Functions Returning Noninteger Values 93
Using Function Prototypes . . . 95
Standard Library Function Prototypes . . . 97
Prototyping Functions That Have No Parameters 98
Returning Pointers 99
Classic Versus Modern Parameter Declarations . . . 100
Recursion 101
Pointers to Functions 103
Implementation Issues 105
Parameters and General-Purpose Functions 106
Efficiency 106

5 Arrays 109
Single-Dimension Arrays . . . 109
Generating a Pointer to an Array 110
Passing Single-Dimension Arrays to Functions 111
Strings 112
Two-Dimensional Arrays . . . 114
Arrays of Strings 118
Multidimensional Arrays . . . 119
Indexing Pointers 120
Allocated Arrays 122

Array Initialization 126
Unsized-Array Initializations 127
A Tic-Tac-Toe Example 129

6 Pointers 133
Pointers Are Addresses 133
Pointer Variables 134
The Pointer Operators 134
Pointer Expressions 136
Pointer Assignments . . 136
Pointer Arithmetic 137
Pointer Comparisons . . 138
Dynamic Allocation and Pointers 140
Understanding const Pointers 142
Pointers and Arrays 143
Pointers to Character Arrays 144
Arrays of Pointers 146
Pointers to Pointers: Multiple Indirection 147
Initializing Pointers 148
Pointers to Functions 150
Problems with Pointers . . . 152

7 Structures, Unions, and User-Defined Types . . . 155
Structures 156
Accessing Structure Members 158
Structure Assignments . . 158
Arrays of Structures 159
An Inventory Example . . 159
Passing Structures to Functions 166
Passing Structure Members to Functions 166
Passing Entire Structures to Functions 167
Structure Pointers 168
Declaring a Structure Pointer 168
Using Structure Pointers 168
Arrays and Structures Within Structures 172
Bit-Fields 172
Unions 175
Enumerations 177
Using sizeof to Ensure Portability 180
typedef 181

8 Input, Output, Streams, and Files 183
C Versus C++ I/O 184
Streams and Files 184
Streams 185
Files 185
Console I/O 187
Reading and Writing Characters 187
Reading and Writing Strings: gets( ) and puts( ) 189
Formatted Console I/O 190
printf( ) 191
scanf( ) 198
The ANSI C File System . . . 205
The File Pointer 206
Opening a File 206
Writing a Character 207
Reading a Character . . . 209
fclose( ) 209
Using fopen( ), getc( ), putc( ), and fclose( ) . . 210
Using feof( ) 211
Two Extended Functions: getw( ) and putw( ) 213
Working with Strings: fgets( ) and fputs( ) . . . 213
fread( ) and fwrite( ) . . . 214
fseek( ) and Random Access I/O 216
fprintf( ) and fscanf( ) . . 218
Erasing Files 222
ferror( ) and rewind( ) . . 222
The Console Connection . . . 223

9 The Preprocessor and Comments 225
#define 226
#error 229
#include 229
Conditional Compilation Directives 230
#if, #else, #elif, and #endif 231
#ifdef and #ifndef 233
#undef 234
Using defined 235
#line 235
#pragma 236
The # and ## Preprocessor Operators 240
Predefined Macro Names . . . 241
Comments 243

Part II

The Borland Function Library

10 Linking, Libraries, and Header Files 247
The Linker 247
Library Files Versus Object Files 249
The ANSI C Standard Library Versus Borland Extensions 249
Header Files 249
Macros in Header Files . . 250

11 I/O Functions 253

12 String, Memory, and Character Functions . . 321

13 Mathematical Functions . . 355

14 Time-, Date-, and System-Related Functions 375

15 Dynamic Allocation 443

16 Directory Functions 467

17 Process Control Functions 485

18 Text and Graphics Functions 495

19 Miscellaneous Functions . . 573

Part III

Borland C++

20 An Overview of C++ . . . 619
The Origins of C++ 619
What Is Object-Oriented Programming? 620
Encapsulation 621
Polymorphism 621
Inheritance 622
Some C++ Fundamentals . . 622
Compiling a C++ Program . . 625
Introducing C++ Classes . . . 625
Function Overloading 629
Operator Overloading 632
Inheritance 632
Constructors and Destructors 636
The C++ Keywords 640
Two New Data Types 640

21 A Closer Look at Classes and Objects 641
Parameterized Constructors . . 641
Friend Functions 645

Default Function Arguments 650
Using Default Arguments Correctly . . 653
Classes and Structures Are Related 654
Unions and Classes Are Related 656
Anonymous Unions . . . 657
Inline Functions 658
Creating Inline Functions Inside a Class 659
Passing Objects to Functions 660
Returning Objects 663
Object Assignment 664
Arrays of Objects 664
Initializing Arrays of Objects 666
Creating Initialized Versus Uninitialized Arrays 668
Pointers to Objects 668

22 Function and Operator Overloading 671
Overloading Constructor Functions 671
Localizing Variables 673
Localizing the Creation of Objects 674
Function Overloading and Ambiguity 676
Finding the Address of an Overloaded Function . . . 679
The this Pointer 680
Operator Overloading 681
friend Operator Functions 688
References 692
Reference Parameters . . 692
Passing References to Objects 695
Returning References . . 696
Independent References 697
Using a Reference to Overload a Unary Operator 699
Overloading [ ] 702
Applying Operator Overloading 705

23 Inheritance, Virtual Functions, and Polymorphism 711
Inheritance and the Access Specifiers 712
Understanding the Access Specifiers 712
Base Class Access Control 714
Constructors and Destructors in Derived Classes 717
Multiple Inheritance 720
Passing Parameters to a Base Class 722
Pointers and References to Derived Types 724
References to Derived Types 726
Virtual Functions 726
Why Virtual Functions? 731
Pure Virtual Functions and Abstract Types 736
Early Versus Late Binding . . 738

24 The C++ I/O Class Library 741
Why C++ Has Its Own I/O System 741
C++ Streams 742
The C++ Predefined Streams 742
The C++ Stream Classes . . . 743
Creating Your Own Inserters and Extractors 743
Creating Inserters 743
Overloading Extractors . . 746
Formatting I/O 748
Formatting Using the ios Member Functions . . . 748
Using Manipulators . . . 753
Creating Your Own Manipulator Functions . . . 755

Creating Parameterless Manipulators 755
Creating Parameterized Manipulators 757
File I/O 760
Opening and Closing a File 760
Reading and Writing Text Files 763
Binary I/O 764
Detecting EOF 767
Random Access 768

25 Array-based I/O 771
The Array-based Classes . . . 771
Creating an Array-based Output Stream 772
Using an Array as Input . . . 774
Using ios Member Functions on Array-based Streams 775
Input/Output Array-based Streams 776
Random Access Within Arrays 777
Using Dynamic Arrays 778
Manipulators and Array-based I/O 779
Custom Extractors and Inserters 780
Uses for Array-based Formatting 783

26 Templates, Exceptions, and RTTI 785
Generic Functions 785
A Function with Two Generic Types 787
Explicitly Overloading a Generic Function . . . 788
Generic Function Restrictions 789
Generic Classes 790
An Example with Two Generic Data Types . . 794
Exception Handling 795
Exception-Handling Fundamentals 795
Using Multiple catch Statements 800
Exception-Handling Options 801
Catching All Exceptions 801
Restricting Exceptions . . 802
Rethrowing an Exception 804
Applying Exception Handling 805
Run-time Type Identification (RTTI) 806
New Casting Operators 808

27 Miscellaneous C++ Topics 813
Dynamic Allocation Using new and delete 813
Allocating Objects 816
Another Way to Watch for Allocation Failure . . 819
Overloading new and delete 820
static Class Members 821
Virtual Base Classes 824
const and volatile Member Functions 828
Using the asm Keyword . . . 829
Linkage Specification 830
The .* and –>* Operators . . . 831
Creating Conversion Functions 833
Copy Constructors 835
Granting Access 838
Using Namespaces 839
Some Recent Changes 840
New Headers 840
Explicit Constructors . . . 841
Using mutable 842
typename 842
The Standard Template Library 842
Differences Between C and C++ 845
Final Thoughts 845

Part IV

The Borland C++ Integrated Development Environment

28 The Integrated Development Environment 849
The IDE Main Window 850
The Menu Bar 851
Exploring the Menu Bar . . . 852
File 852
Edit 853
Search 853
View 853
Project 853
Script 854
Tool 854
Debug 854
Options 854
Window 854
Help 855
Using Context-Sensitive Help 856
The SpeedBar 856
The Status Bar 857
Using SpeedMenus 857
Scripting 857
A Short Word on Creating Projects and Compiling Programs 858

29 Using the Editor 859
Invoking the Editor and Entering Text 859
Deleting Characters, Words, and Lines 861
Moving, Copying, and Deleting Blocks of Text 861
Using the Clipboard 863
More on Cursor Movement . . 864
Find and Replace 864
Saving and Loading Your File 867
Understanding Autoindentation 867
Moving Blocks of Text to and from Disk Files 868
Pair Matching 868
Miscellaneous Commands . . 868
Using the SpeedMenu 869
Changing the Editor Defaults 869
Keyboard Command Summary 869

30 Using Borland C++'s Integrated Debugging Environment 873
Preparing Your Programs for Debugging 873
What Is a Source-Level Debugger? 874
Debugger Basics 874
Single-Stepping 875
Breakpoints 876
Setting Unconditional Source Breakpoints . . . 877
Setting Conditional Source Breakpoints . . . 878
Watching Variables 880
Watched-Expression Format Codes 881
Qualifying a Variable's Name 883
Watching the Stack 885
Evaluating an Expression . . . 886
Modifying a Variable 886
Inspecting a Variable 887
Pausing a Program 887
Using the CPU Window . . . 888
A Debugging Tip 889

Part V

Windows 95 Programming Overview

31 Windows 95 Fundamentals 893
What Is Windows 95? 893
Windows 95 Uses Thread-based Multitasking 894

The Windows 95 Call-based Interface . . 894
Dynamic Link Libraries (DLLs) 895
Windows 95 Versus Windows 3.1 895
User Differences 896
Programming Differences 897
The NT Connection 899
Windows 95 Programs Are Unique 899
How Windows 95 and Your Program Interact 900
Win32: The Windows 95 API 900
The Components of a Window 901
Some Windows 95 Application Fundamentals 902
WinMain( ) 902
The Window Function . . 903
Window Classes 903
The Message Loop 903
Windows Data Types . . 904
A Windows 95 Skeleton . . . 904
Compiling the Skeleton . . 907
A Closer Look at the Skeleton 907
Defining the Window Class 908
Creating a Window . . . 911
The Message Loop 913
The Window Function 914
What About Definition Files? 915
Naming Conventions 915

32 Application Essentials: Messages and Basic I/O 917
Message Boxes 917
Understanding Windows 95 Messages 920
Responding to a Keypress . . 921
Outputting Text to a Window 924
Device Contexts 930
Processing the WM_PAINT Message 930
Generating a WM_PAINT Message 935
Responding to Mouse Messages 938
More About Mouse Messages 942

33 Using Menus 943
Introducing Menus 943
Using Resources 944
Compiling .RC files 944
Creating a Simple Menu 945
Including a Menu in Your Program 948
Responding to Menu Selections 948
A Sample Menu Program . . . 949
A Short Word About Borland's Resource Editor 952
Adding Menu Accelerator Keys 952
Loading the Accelerator Table 955
Dynamically Managing a Menu 958
Adding an Item to a Menu 958
Deleting a Menu Item . . 958
Obtaining a Handle to a Menu 959
Obtaining the Size of a Menu 960
Enabling and Disabling a Menu Item 960
Demonstrating Dynamic Menu Management . . 961
Creating Dynamic Menus . . 966

34 Dialog Boxes 973
Dialog Boxes Use Controls . . 973
Modal Versus Modeless Dialog Boxes 974
Receiving Dialog Box Messages 974

Activating a Dialog Box . . . 975
Deactivating a Dialog Box 975
Creating a Simple Dialog Box 975
The Dialog Box Resource File 976
The Dialog Box Window Function 979
A First Dialog Box Sample Program 979
Adding a List Box 984
List Box Basics 985
Initializing the List Box . . 987
Processing a Selection . . 988
Adding an Edit Box 989
The Entire Modal Dialog Box Program 992
Using a Modeless Dialog Box 998
Creating a Modeless Dialog Box 1000
What Next? 1007

Part VI

A Jump-Start to Java

35 Overview of Java 1011
What Is Java? 1011
Why Java? 1012
Safety 1012
Portability 1013
Java's Magic: The Bytecodes . . 1013
Key Advantages of Java . . . 1014
Simple 1014
Object-Oriented 1014
Robust 1015
Multithreaded 1015
Architecture-Neutral . . 1015
Interpreted and High Performance 1015
Distributed 1016
Dynamic 1016
Differences Between Java and C++ 1016
What Java Removed from C++ 1016
New Features Added by Java 1017
Features That Differ . . . 1018
Java Applications and Applets 1019
Methods Versus Functions . . 1019
A Simple Java Application . . 1019
Entering the Program . . 1019
Compiling and Running a Java Program 1020
A Closer Look at The First Application 1021
A Second Example 1022
Some Java Basics 1024
Java Is a Strongly Typed Language 1024
Java's Built-in Simple Types 1025
String Literals 1026
Type Conversion and Casting 1026
Operators 1027
Control Statements . . . 1027
Class Fundamentals 1028
A Simple Java Class 1029
Declaring Objects 1030
Assigning Object Reference Variables . . 1031
Adding a Method and a Constructor 1032
Arrays 1034
One-Dimensional Arrays 1034
Multidimensional Arrays 1036
Garbage Collection 1037
The finalize( ) Method . . 1038
36 Inheritance, Packages, and Interfaces 1039
Inheritance 1040
When Constructors Are Called 1042
Using super 1043

Using super to Call Superclass Constructors 1043
A Second Use for super 1048
Method Overriding and Dynamic Dispatch 1049
Dynamic Dispatch 1050
Abstract Methods and Classes 1053
Using final 1054
Using final to Prevent Overriding 1054
Using final to Prevent Inheritance 1054
Using final to Create Named Constants . . . 1055
The Object Class 1055
Packages 1055
Defining a Package . . . 1056
Understanding CLASSPATH 1057
A Short Package Example 1057
Importing Packages 1059
The Standard Packages . . 1060
Access Control and Packages 1060
Interfaces 1061
Defining an Interface . . 1062
Implementing an Interface 1062
Interfaces Can Be Extended 1064
Accessing Implementations Through Interface References 1064
Applying Interfaces . . 1064

37 Introducing Applets . . . 1069
A Simple Applet 1069
Compiling and Viewing the Applet 1070
The Applet Class 1073
Applet Architecture 1073
An Applet Skeleton 1074
Order of Applet Initialization and Termination 1075
The update( ) Method . . 1077
Requesting Repainting . . . 1077
Using the Status Window . . 1078
Handling Events 1079
The Event Class 1079
Processing Mouse Events 1079
Handling Keyboard Events 1083
More Events 1084
Things to Explore 1085
Learning More About Java . . 1085

Index 1087

Preface

This book is about Borland C++ version 5. Borland has been making state-of-the-art compilers since the 1980s. Version 5 is their most powerful and full-featured compiler yet. It is known for its speed of compilation and for the efficiency of the code that it produces. Borland C++ is really three compilers rolled into one. First, it is a C compiler. (C is the language upon which C++ is built.) Second, it is a C++ compiler. Finally, it also includes an add-on for Java, the Internet programming language. It can produce programs for a wide variety of targets, including DOS, Windows 95/NT, and Windows 3.1. By any measure, it is one of the finest programming development environments available. The purpose of this book is to help you get the most out of it.

About This Book

This book describes the entire Borland C++ programming environment. As such, it discusses both the C and the C++ languages and their libraries in significant detail. It also provides an introduction to Windows 95 programming using Borland C++ and Borland's latest addition: the Java add-on. This book includes numerous example programs which help illustrate the elements that form each language. It is designed for programmers at all skill levels. If you are just learning to program, this guide makes an excellent companion to any tutorial, providing answers to your specific questions. If you are an experienced C or C++ programmer, this book serves as a handy desk reference.

How This Book Is Organized

As you can surmise given the size of this book, Borland C++ is a large topic. To help bring order to such a vast amount of information, this book is organized into these six parts:

Part 1	The C Language
Part 2	The Borland Function Library
Part 3	Borland C++
Part 4	The Borland C++ Integrated Development Environment
Part 5	Windows 95 Programming Overview
Part 6	A Jump-Start to Java

The organization of this book allows the C programmer to quickly find material related to that language while at the same time letting the C++ programmer find the material appropriate to that language. Further, if you are currently a C programmer and want to become proficient at C++, the organization of this book prevents you from "wading through" reams of information that you already know. You can simply concentrate on the C++ sections of the book.

Conventions Used in This Book

In this book, keywords, operators, function names, and variable names are shown in bold when referenced in text. General forms are shown in italics. Also, when referencing a function name in text, the name is followed by parentheses. In this way, you can easily distinguish a variable name from a function name.

Source Code on the Web

The source code for all of the programs in this book is available at Osborne's Web site (www.osborne.com), free of charge.

Special Thanks

I wish to thank Joseph O'Neil for his help in the preparation of this book.

PART ONE

The C Language

Part 1 of this guide discusses the C language. As you probably know, C++ is built upon the foundation of C. When C++ was invented, the C language was used as the starting point. To C were added several new features and extensions designed to support object-oriented programming (OOP). However, the C-like aspects of C++ were never abandoned. In fact, the ANSI C standard is a *base document* for the ANSI C++ draft standard. Simply put: since C++ is built on C, you cannot program in C++ unless you know how to program in C.

Because C++ is a superset of C, any C++ compiler is, by definition, also a C compiler. And Borland C++ is no exception. Borland C++ allows you to compile both C programs and C++ programs. When used as a C compiler, Borland C++ supports and fully complies with the ANSI standard for C. When used as a C++ compiler, it fully implements the current draft of the ANSI C++ standard.

The material described in Part 1 is applicable to both the C and the C++ languages. The C++-specific features of Borland C++ are detailed in Part 3.

The reason that the C-based features are covered in their own section is to make it easier for the experienced C programmer to learn and quickly find information about C++ without having to "wade through" reams of information about C that he or she already knows. Throughout Part 1, any minor differences between C and C++ are noted.

One last point: Because the programs in Part 1 are C programs, you must compile them as C programs. To do this, just make sure that their file names use the .C (not the .CPP) extension. Whenever Borland C++ compiles a file that has the .C extension, it automatically compiles it as a C, rather than a C++, program.

Chapter One

An Overview of C

This chapter presents an overview of the origins, uses, and philosophy of the C programming language.

The Origins of the C Language

Dennis Ritchie invented and first implemented the C programming language on a DEC PDP-11 that used the UNIX operating system. The language is the result of a development process that started with an older language called BCPL. Martin Richards developed BCPL, which influenced Ken Thompson's invention of a language called B, which led to the development of C in the 1970s.

For many years the de facto standard for C was the version supplied with the UNIX System V operating system. It is described in *The C Programming Language* by Brian Kernighan and Dennis Ritchie (Prentice-Hall, 1978). The growing popularity of computers led to the creation of a large number of C implementations. In what could almost be called a miracle, the source code accepted by most of these implementations was highly compatible. However, because no standard existed, there were discrepancies. To rectify this situation, ANSI established a committee in the beginning of the summer of 1983 to create an ANSI standard for the C language. The standard was finally adopted in December of 1989, and Borland C++ fully implements the resulting ANSI standard for C.

A Middle-Level Language

C is often called a *middle-level computer language*. This does not mean that C is less powerful, harder to use, or less developed than a high-level language such as BASIC or Pascal; nor does it imply that C is similar to, or presents the problems associated with, assembly language. The definition of C as a middle-level language means that it combines elements of high-level languages with the functionalism of assembly language. Table 1-1 shows how C fits into the spectrum of languages.

As a middle-level language, C allows the manipulation of bits, bytes, and addresses—the basic elements with which the computer functions. Despite this fact, C code is very portable. (*Portability* means that it is possible to adapt software written for one type of computer to another.) For example, if a program written for an Apple Macintosh can be moved easily to an IBM PC, that program is portable.

All high-level programming languages support the concept of data types. A *data type* defines a set of values that a variable can store along with a set of operations that can be performed on that variable. Common data types are integer, character, and real. Although C has five basic built-in data types, it is not a strongly typed language like Pascal or Ada. In fact, C will allow almost all type conversions. For example, character and integer types may be freely intermixed in most expressions. Unlike a high-level language, C performs almost no run-time error checking such as verifying array boundaries. These checks are the responsibility of the programmer.

As mentioned, a special feature of C is that it allows the direct manipulation of bits, bytes, words, and pointers. This suits it to system-level programming, where these operations are common. Another important aspect of C is that it has only 32 keywords (27 from the Kernighan and Ritchie standard and 5 added by the ANSI standardization committee), which are the commands that make up the C language. High-level languages typically have several more.

Highest level	Ada
	Modula-2
	Pascal
	COBOL
	FORTRAN
	BASIC
Middle level	C++
	C
	FORTH
	Macro-assembly language
Lowest level	Assembly language

Table 1-1. *C's Place in the World of Languages*

A Structured Language

Although the term *block-structured language* does not strictly apply to C, C is commonly called a structured language because of structural similarities to ALGOL, Pascal, and Modula-2. (Technically, a block-structured language permits procedures or functions to be declared inside other procedures or functions. In this way, the concepts of "global" and "local" are expanded through the use of additional *scope rules,* which govern the "visibility" of a variable or procedure. Since C does not allow the creation of functions within functions, it is not really block-structured.)

The distinguishing feature of a structured language is *compartmentalization* of code and data. Compartmentalization is the language's ability to section off and hide from the rest of the program all information and instructions necessary to perform a specific task. One way of achieving compartmentalization is to use subroutines that employ local (temporary) variables. By using local variables, the programmer can write subroutines so that the events that occur within them cause no side effects in other parts of the program. This capability makes it very easy for C programs to share sections of code. If you develop compartmentalized functions, you only need to know what a function does, not how it does it. Remember that excessive use of global variables (variables known throughout the entire program) may allow bugs to creep into a program by allowing unwanted side effects. (Anyone who has programmed in standard BASIC is well aware of this problem!)

A structured language allows you a variety of programming possibilities. It directly supports several loop constructs, such as **while**, **do-while**, and **for**. In a structured language, the use of **goto** is either prohibited or discouraged. A structured language allows you to indent statements and does not require a strict field concept.

Here are some examples of structured and nonstructured languages:

Structured	**Nonstructured**
Pascal	FORTRAN
Ada	BASIC
C++	COBOL
C	
Modula-2	

Structured languages are newer; nonstructured languages are older. Today it is widely accepted that the clarity of structured languages makes programming and maintenance easier. Indeed, few programmers would seriously consider a nonstructured language for new software development.

The main structural component of C is the function—C's stand-alone subroutine. In C, functions are the building blocks in which all program activity occurs. They allow the separate tasks in a program to be defined and coded separately, thus allowing your programs to be modular. After a function has been created, you can rely on it to work properly in various situations, without creating side effects in other parts of the program. The fact that you can create stand-alone functions is extremely critical in larger projects where one programmer's code must not accidentally affect another's.

Another way to structure and compartmentalize code in C is to use code blocks. A *code block* is a logically connected group of program statements that is treated as a unit. In C, a code block is created by placing a sequence of statements between opening and closing curly braces. In this example,

```
if(x<10) {
  printf("too low, try again");
  reset_counter(-1);
}
```

the two statements after the **if** and between the curly braces are both executed if **x** is less than 10. These two statements together with the braces are a code block. They are a logical unit: One of the statements cannot execute without the other. Code blocks not only allow many algorithms to be implemented with clarity, elegance, and efficiency, but also help the programmer conceptualize the true nature of the routine.

A Programmer's Language

One might respond to the statement "C is a programmer's language" with the question, "Aren't all programming languages for programmers?" The answer is an unqualified "No!" Consider the classic examples of nonprogrammer's languages, COBOL and BASIC. COBOL was designed to enable nonprogrammers to read and, presumably, understand a program. BASIC was created essentially to allow nonprogrammers to program a computer to solve relatively simple problems.

In contrast, C was created, influenced, and field-tested by real working programmers. The end result is that C gives the programmer what the programmer wants: few restrictions, few complaints, block structures, stand-alone functions, and a compact set of keywords. It is truly amazing that by using C, a programmer can achieve nearly the efficiency of assembly code, combined with the structure of ALGOL or Modula-2. It is no wonder that C is one of the most popular languages among topflight professional programmers.

The fact that C can often be used in place of assembly language contributes greatly to its popularity among programmers. Assembly language uses a symbolic representation of the actual binary code that the computer executes. Each assembly language operation maps into a single task for the computer to perform. Although assembly language gives programmers the potential for accomplishing tasks with maximum flexibility and efficiency, it is notoriously difficult to use when developing and debugging a program. Furthermore, since assembly language is unstructured, the final program tends to be spaghetti code—a tangled mess of jumps, calls, and indexes. This lack of structure makes assembly language programs difficult to read, enhance, and maintain. Perhaps more important, assembly language routines are not portable between machines with different central processing units.

Initially, C was used for systems programming. A *systems program* is part of a large class of programs that forms a portion of the operating system of the computer or its support utilities. For example, the following are usually called systems programs:

Operating systems
Interpreters
Editors
Assembly programs
Compilers
Database managers

As C grew in popularity, many programmers began to use it to program all tasks because of its portability and efficiency. Because there are C compilers for almost all computers, it is possible to take code written for one machine and compile and run it on another with few or no changes. This portability saves both time and money. In addition, C compilers tend to produce tighter and faster object code than most other types of compilers.

Perhaps the most significant reason that C is used in all types of programming tasks is that programmers like it! It has the speed of assembly language and the extensibility of FORTH but few of the restrictions of Pascal or Modula-2. Each C programmer can create and maintain a unique library of functions that have been tailored to his or her personality and can be used in many different programs. Because it allows—indeed, encourages—separate compilation, C allows programmers to manage projects easily and minimize duplication of effort. And, of course, it is the language upon which C++ is built.

Compilers Versus Interpreters

The terms *compiler* and *interpreter* refer to the way in which a program is executed. In theory, any programming language can be either compiled or interpreted, but some languages are usually executed one way or the other. For example, BASIC is usually interpreted and C is usually compiled. The way a program is executed is not defined by the language in which it is written. Interpreters and compilers are simply sophisticated programs that operate on your program source code.

An interpreter reads the source code of your program one line at a time, performs the specific instructions contained in that line, and then gets the next line. A compiler reads the entire program and converts it into *object code,* which is a translation of the program source code into a form that can be directly executed by the computer. Object code is also called binary code and machine code. Once a program is compiled, a line of source code is no longer meaningful in the execution of the program.

When you use an interpreter, it must be present each time you wish to run your program. For example, in traditional BASIC you have to execute the BASIC interpreter first and then load your program and type **RUN** each time you want to use it. The BASIC interpreter then examines your program one line at a time for correctness and then executes it. This slow process occurs every time the program runs. By contrast, a compiler converts your program into object code that can be directly executed by your computer. Because the compiler translates your program only once, all you need to do is execute your program directly, usually by the simple process of typing its name. Thus, compilation is a one-time cost, while interpreted code incurs an overhead cost each time a program runs.

Two terms that you will often encounter are *compile time,* which refers to the events that occur during the compilation process, and *run time,* which refers to the events that occur while the program is actually executing. You usually see these terms in discussions of errors, as in the phrases "compile-time errors" and "run-time errors."

The Form of a C Program

Table 1-2 lists the 32 keywords that, combined with the formal C syntax, form the C programming language. Also shown are 12 extended keywords added by Borland which may be included in a C program. Of course, using the extended keywords renders your program nonportable. (Additional keywords are defined for use with C++. See Part 3.)

All C keywords are lowercase. In C, uppercase and lowercase are different: **else** is a keyword; ELSE is not. A keyword may not be used for any other purpose in a C program—that is, it may not serve as a variable or function name.

All C programs consist of one or more functions. The only function that absolutely must be present is called **main( )**, and it is the first function called when program execution begins. In well-written C code, **main( )** outlines what the program does. The outline is composed of function calls. Although **main( )** is technically not part of the C language, treat it as if it were. Don't try to use **main** as the name of a variable, for example.

The general form of a C program is illustrated in Figure 1-1, where **f1( )** through **fN( )** represent user-defined functions.

The Library and Linking

Technically speaking, it is possible to create a useful, functional C program that consists solely of the statements actually created by the programmer. However, this is rarely done because C does not, within the actual definition of the language, provide any method of performing I/O operations. As a result, most programs include calls to various functions contained in C's *standard library*.

The C language defines a standard library that provides functions that perform most commonly needed tasks. When you call a function that is not part of the program you wrote, the compiler "remembers" its name. Later, the *linker* combines

The 32 Keywords as Defined by ANSI Standard C			
auto	double	int	struct
break	else	long	switch
case	enum	register	typedef
char	extern	return	union
const	float	short	unsigned
continue	for	signed	void
default	goto	sizeof	volatile
do	if	static	while
Additional Keywords Added by Borland That Are Allowed in a C Program			
asm	_cs	_ds	_es
_ss	cdecl	far	huge
interrupt	near	pascal	_export

Table 1-2. *A List of the C Keywords*

the code you wrote with the object code already found in the standard library. This process is called *linking*.

The functions that are kept in the library are in *relocatable* format. This means that the memory addresses for the various machine-code instructions have not been absolutely defined; only offset information has been kept. When your program links with the functions in the standard library, these memory offsets are used to create the actual addresses used. There are several technical manuals and books that explain this process in more detail. However, you do not need any further explanation of the actual relocation process to program in C or use Borland C++.

Separate Compilation

Most short C programs are completely contained within one source file. However, as a program gets longer, so does its compile time, and long compile times make for short tempers! Hence, C allows a program to be broken into pieces and contained in many files, and each file can be compiled separately. Once all files have been compiled, they are linked together, along with any library routines, to form the complete object code

```
global declarations

return-type main(parameter list)
{
 statement sequence
}

return-type f1(parameter list)
{
 statement sequence
}

return-type f2(parameter list)
{
 statement sequence
}
.
.
.
return-type fN(parameter list)
{
 statement sequence
}
```

Figure 1-1. *The general form of a C program*

for your program. The advantage of separate compilation is that a change in the code of one file does not necessitate the recompilation of the entire program. On all but the simplest projects, the time saving is substantial.

A C Program's Memory Map

A compiled C program creates and uses four logically distinct regions of memory that serve specific functions. The first region is the memory that actually holds the code of your program. The next region is the memory where global variables are stored. The remaining two regions are the stack and the heap. The *stack* is used for a great many things while your program executes. It holds the return address of function calls, arguments to functions, and local variables. It is also used to save the current state of the CPU. The *heap* is a region of free memory, which your program can use via C's dynamic allocation functions, for things like linked lists and trees.

Although the exact physical layout of each of the four regions of memory differs based on the way you tell Borland C++ to compile your program, the diagram in Figure 1-2 shows conceptually how your C programs appear in memory.

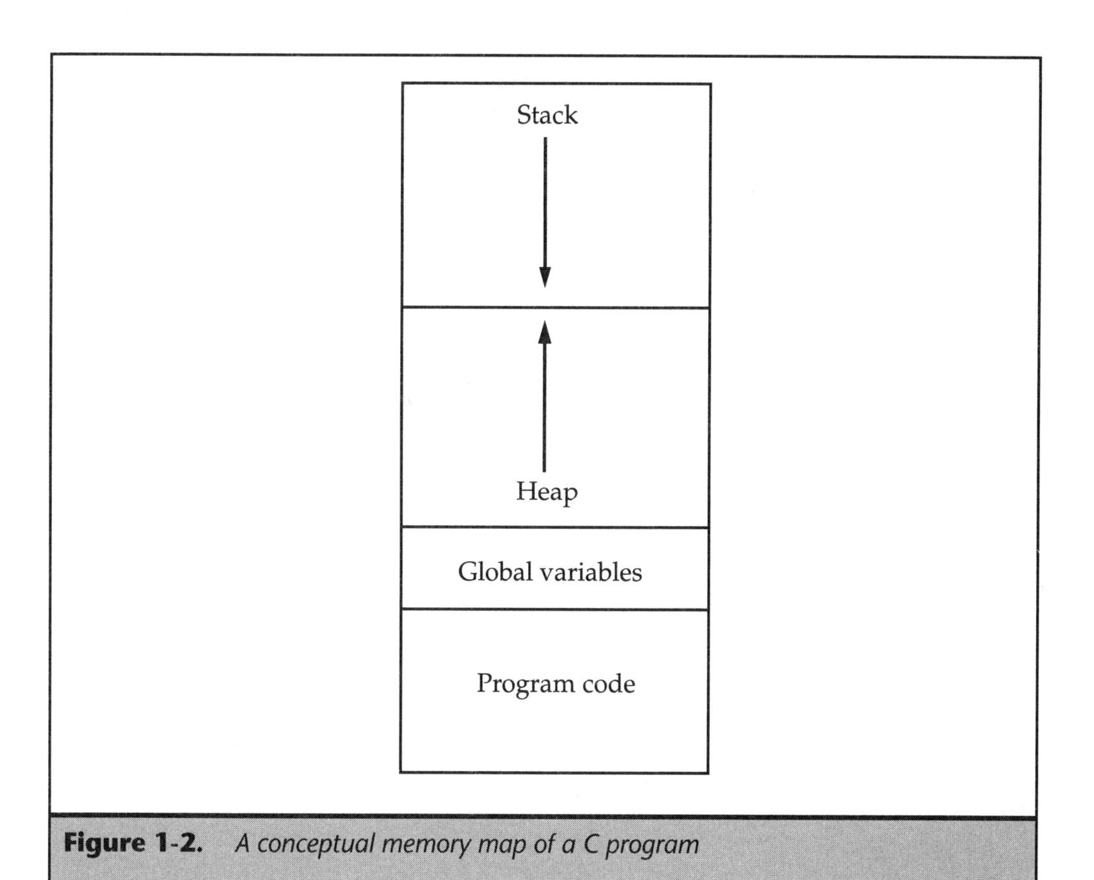

Figure 1-2. *A conceptual memory map of a C program*

A Review of Terms

The terms that follow will be used frequently throughout the remainder of this book. You should be completely familiar with their meanings.

Source code — The text of a program that you can read; commonly thought of as the program. The source code is input into the compiler.

Object code — Translation of the source code of a program into machine code. Object code is the input to the linker.

Linker — A program that links separately compiled functions together into one program. It combines the functions in the standard C library with the code that you wrote. The output of the linker is an executable program.

Library	The file containing the standard functions that can be used by your program. These functions include all I/O operations as well as other useful routines.
Compile time	The events that occur while your program is being compiled. A common occurrence during compile time is a syntax error.
Run time	The events that occur while your program is executing.

Chapter Two

Variables, Constants, Operators, and Expressions

Variables and constants are manipulated by operators to form expressions. These are the atomic elements of the C and C++ languages. This chapter will examine each element closely.

Identifier Names

The names that are used for variables, functions, labels, and various other user-defined objects are called *identifiers.* Identifiers can vary from one to several characters in length. However, in C, only the first 31 characters are guaranteed to be significant. (In C++, all characters are significant.) The first character must be a letter or an underscore, with subsequent characters being either letters, numbers, or the underscore. Here are some examples of correct and incorrect identifier names:

Correct	Incorrect
count	1count
test23	hi!there
high_balance	high..balance

In C, upper- and lowercase are treated differently. Hence, **count**, **Count**, and **COUNT** are three separate identifiers. An identifier cannot be the same as a C keyword, and it should not have the same name as functions that you wrote or that are in the C library.

Data Types

There are five atomic data types in C: character, integer, floating point, double floating point, and valueless. Values of type **char** are used to hold ASCII characters or any 8-bit quantity. Variables of type **int** are used to hold integer quantities. Variables of type **float** and **double** hold real numbers. (Real numbers have both an integer and a fractional component.)

The **void** type has three uses. The first is to declare explicitly a function as returning no value; the second is to declare explicitly a function as having no parameters; the third is to create generic pointers. Each of these uses is discussed in subsequent chapters.

C supports several other types, including structures, unions, bit fields, enumerations, and user-defined types. These are discussed in Chapter 7.

Type Modifiers

Excepting type **void**, the basic data types may have various *modifiers* preceding them. A modifier is used to alter the meaning of the base type to fit the needs of various situations more precisely. The list of modifiers is shown here:

signed
unsigned
long
short

The modifiers **signed**, **unsigned**, **long**, and **short** may be applied to integer base types. You can apply **unsigned** and **signed** to characters. **long** may also be applied to **double**. Table 2-1 shows all allowed combinations that adhere to the ANSI C standard for 16-bit data types, along with their bit widths and ranges as implemented by Borland C++. Table 2-2 shows this information for 32-bit data types.

The use of **signed** on integers is redundant (but allowed) because the default integer declaration assumes a signed number.

The difference between signed and unsigned integers is in the way the high-order bit of the integer is interpreted. If a signed integer is specified, then the compiler will generate code that assumes the high-order bit of an integer is to be used as a *sign flag*.

Type	Bit Width	Range
char	8	–128 to 127
unsigned char	8	0 to 255
signed char	8	–128 to 127
int	16	–32768 to 32767
unsigned int	16	0 to 65535
signed int	16	–32768 to 32767
short int	16	–32768 to 32767
unsigned short int	16	0 to 65535
signed short int	16	–32768 to 32767
long int	32	–2147483648 to 2147483647
unsigned long int	32	0 to 4294967295
signed long int	32	–2147483648 to 2147483647
float	32	3.4E–38 to 3.4E+38
double	64	1.7E–308 to 1.7E+308
long double	80	3.4E–4932 to 1.1E+4932

Table 2-1. *All Possible Combinations of the Basic Types and Modifiers for 16-Bit Word Sizes*

If the sign bit is 0, then the number is positive; if it is 1, then the number is negative. Here is an overly simplified example:

```
 127 in binary is 0 0 0 0 0 0 0 0  0 1 1 1 1 1 1 1
–127 in binary is 1 0 0 0 0 0 0 0  0 1 1 1 1 1 1 1
                  ↑
                  sign bit
```

Type	Bit Width	Range
char	8	–128 to 127
unsigned char	8	0 to 255
signed char	8	–128 to 127
int	32	–2147483648 to 2147483647
unsigned int	32	0 to 4294967295
signed int	32	–2147483648 to 2147483647
short int	16	–32768 to 32767
unsigned short int	16	0 to 65535
signed short int	16	–32768 to 32767
long int	32	–2147483648 to 2147483647
unsigned long int	32	0 to 4294967295
signed long int	32	–2147483648 to 2147483647
float	32	3.4E–38 to 3.4E+38
double	64	1.7E–308 to 1.7E+308
long double	80	3.4E–4932 to 1.1E+4932

Table 2-2. *All Possible Combinations of the Basic Types and Modifiers for 32-Bit Word Sizes*

The reader is cautioned that virtually all computers (including those that run Borland C++) will use *two's complement* arithmetic, which will cause the representation of –127 to appear different than the simplified example just shown. However, the use of the sign bit is the same. A negative number in two's complement form has all bits reversed and one is added to the number. For example, –127 in two's complement appears like this:

```
1 1 1 1 1 1 1 1 1 0 0 0 0 0 0 1
```

Signed integers are important for a great many algorithms, but they only have half the absolute magnitude of their unsigned brothers. For example, here is 32,767:

```
01111111 11111111
```

If the high-order bit were set to 1, the number would then be interpreted as -1. However, if you had declared this to be an **unsigned int**, then when the high-order bit is set to 1, the number becomes 65,535.

Access Modifiers

C has two type modifiers that are used to control the ways in which variables may be accessed or modified. These modifiers are called **const** and **volatile**:

Variables of type **const** may not be changed during execution by your program. For example,

```
const int a;
```

will create an integer variable called **a** that cannot be modified by your program. It can, however, be used in other types of expressions. A **const** variable will receive its value either from an explicit initialization or by some hardware-dependent means. For example, this gives **count** the value of 100:

```
const int count = 100;
```

Aside from initialization, no **const** variable can be modified by your program.

The modifier **volatile** is used to tell the compiler that a variable's value can be changed in ways not explicitly specified by the program. For example, a global variable's address can be passed to the clock routine of the operating system and used to hold the time of the system. In this situation, the contents of the variable are altered without any explicit assignment statements in the program. This is important because the compiler automatically optimizes certain expressions by making the assumption that the content of a variable is unchanging inside that expression. Also, some optimizations may change the order of evaluation of an expression during the compilation process. The **volatile** modifier prevents these changes from occurring.

It is possible to use **const** and **volatile** together. For example, if **0x30** is assumed to be the address of a port that is changed by external conditions only, then the following declaration is precisely what you would want to prevent any possibility of accidental side effects:

```
const volatile unsigned char *port=0x30;
```

Declaration of Variables

All variables must be declared before they are used. The general form of a declaration is shown here:

type variable_list;

Here, *type* must be a valid C data type and *variable_list* may consist of one or more identifier names with comma separators. Some declarations are shown here:

```
int i, j, l;

short int si;

unsigned int ui;

double balance, profit, loss;
```

Remember, in C, the name of a variable has nothing to do with its type.

There are three basic places where variables will be declared: inside functions, in the definition of function parameters, or outside all functions. These variables are called local variables, formal parameters, and global variables.

Local Variables

Variables that are declared inside a function are called *local variables.* In some C literature, these variables may be referred to as *automatic variables* in keeping with C's use of the (optional) keyword **auto** that can be used to declare them. Since the term *local variable* is more commonly used, this guide will continue to use it. Local variables can be referenced only by statements that are inside the block in which the variables are declared. Stated another way, local variables are not known outside their own code block. You should remember that a block of code is begun when an opening curly brace is encountered and terminated when a closing curly brace is found.

One of the most important things to understand about local variables is that they exist only while the block of code in which they are declared is executing. That is, a local variable is created upon entry into its block and destroyed upon exit.

The most common code block in which local variables are declared is the function. For example, consider these two functions:

```
void func1(void)
{
  int x;

  x = 10;
}

void func2(void)
{
  int x;
```

```
  x = -199;
}
```

The integer variable **x** was declared twice, once in **func1( )** and once in **func2( )**. The **x** in **func1( )** has no bearing on, or relationship to, the **x** in **func2( )** because each **x** is only known to the code within the same block as the variable's declaration.

The C language contains the keyword **auto**, which can be used to declare local variables. However, since all nonglobal variables are assumed to be **auto** by default, it is virtually never used.

It is common practice to declare all variables needed within a function at the start of that function's code block. This is done mostly to make it easy for anyone reading the code to know what variables are used. However, it is not necessary to do this because local variables can be declared within any code block. (However, they must be declared at the start of a block, before any "action" statements occur.) To understand how this works, consider the following function:

```
void f(void)
{
  int t;

  scanf("%d", &t);

  if(t==1) {
    char s[80];  /* s exists only inside this block */
    printf("enter name:");
    gets(s);
    process(s);
  }
  /* s is not known here */
}
```

Here, the local variable **s** is known only within the **if** code block. Since **s** is known only within the **if** block, it may not be referenced elsewhere—not even in other parts of the function that contains it.

One reason you might want to declare a variable within its own block instead of at the top of a function is to prevent its accidental misuse elsewhere in the function. In essence, declaring variables inside the blocks of code that actually use them allows you to compartmentalize your code and data into more easily managed units.

Because local variables are destroyed upon exit from the function in which they are declared, they cannot retain their values between function calls. (As you will see shortly, however, it is possible to direct the compiler to retain their values through the use of the **static** modifier.)

Unless otherwise specified, storage for local variables is on the stack. The fact that the stack is a dynamic and changing region of memory explains why local variables cannot, in general, hold their values between function calls.

Formal Parameters

If a function is to use arguments, then it must declare variables that will accept the values of the arguments. These variables are called the *formal parameters* of the function. They behave like any other local variables inside the function. As shown in the following program fragment, their declaration occurs inside the parentheses that follow the function name.

```
/* return 1 if c is part of string s; 0 otherwise */
int is_in(char *s, char c)
{
  while(*s)
    if(*s==c) return 1;
    else s++;

  return 0;
}
```

The function **is_in( )** has two parameters: **s** and **c**. You must tell the compiler what type of variables these are by declaring them as shown above. Once this has been done, they may be used inside the function as normal local variables. Keep in mind that, as local variables, they are also dynamic and are destroyed upon exit from the function.

As with local variables, you may make assignments to a function's formal parameters or use them in any allowable C expression. Even though these variables perform the special task of receiving the value of the arguments passed to the function, they can be used like any other local variable.

Global Variables

Unlike local variables, *global variables* are known throughout the entire program and may be used by any piece of code. Also, they will hold their values during the entire execution of the program. Global variables are created by declaring them outside of any function. They may be accessed by any expression regardless of what function that expression is in.

In the following program, you can see that the variable **count** has been declared outside of all functions. Its declaration comes before the **main( )** function. However, it could have been placed anywhere prior to its first use, as long as it was not in a function. Common practice is to declare global variables at the top of the program.

```
#include <stdio.h>

void func1(void), func2(void);

int count;  /* count is global  */

int main(void)
{
  count = 100;
  func1();
  return 0; /* return success to the system */
}

void func1(void)
{
  func2();
  printf("count is %d", count); /* will print 100 */
}

void func2(void)
{
  int count;

  for(count=1; count<10; count++)
    putchar(' ');
}
```

Looking closely at this program fragment, it should be clear that although neither **main( )** nor **func1( )** has declared the variable **count**, both may use it. However, **func2( )** has declared a local variable called **count**. When **func2( )** references **count**, it will be referencing only its local variable, not the global one. Remember that if a global variable and a local variable have the same name, all references to that name inside the function where the local variable is declared refer to the local variable and have no effect on the global variable. This is a convenient benefit. However, forgetting this can cause your program to act very strangely, even though it "looks" correct.

Storage for global variables is in a fixed region of memory set aside for this purpose by the compiler. Global variables are very helpful when the same data is used in many functions in your program. You should avoid using unnecessary global variables, however, for three reasons:

1. They take up memory the entire time your program is executing, not just when they are needed.

2. Using a global variable where a local variable will do makes a function less general because it relies on something that must be defined outside itself.
3. Using a large number of global variables can lead to program errors because of unknown, and unwanted, side effects.

One of the principal points of a structured language is the compartmentalization of code and data. In C, compartmentalization is achieved through the use of local variables and functions. For example, here are two ways to write **mul( )**—a simple function that computes the product of two integers.

Two Ways to Write mul( )

General	Specific
	int x, y;
int mul(int x, int y)	int mul(void)
{	{
return(x*y);	return(x*y);
}	}

Both functions will return the product of the variables **x** and **y**. However, the generalized, or *parameterized,* version can be used to return the product of *any* two numbers, whereas the specific version can be used to find only the product of the global variables **x** and **y**.

Storage Class Specifiers

There are four storage class specifiers supported by C. They are

```
extern
static
register
auto
```

These tell the compiler how the variable that follows should be stored. The storage specifier precedes the rest of the variable declaration. Its general form is

storage_specifier type var_name;

Each specifier will be examined in turn.

extern

Because C allows separately compiled modules of a large program to be linked together to speed up compilation and aid in the management of large projects, there must be some way of telling all the files about the global variables required by the program. The solution is to declare all of your globals in one file and use **extern** declarations in the other, as shown in Table 2-3.

In File 2, the global variable list was copied from File 1 and the **extern** specifier was added to the declarations. The **extern** specifier tells the compiler that the following variable types and names have been declared elsewhere. In other words, **extern** lets the compiler know what the types and names are for these global variables without actually creating storage for them again. When the two modules are linked, all references to the external variables are resolved.

File 1	File 2

int x, y;
char ch;
 	
main(void)
{
.
.
.
}
 	
void func1(void)
{
    x=23;
}
	extern int x, y;
	extern char ch;
	
	void func22(void)
	{
	    x=y/10;
	}
	
	void func23(void)
	{
	    y=10;
	}

Table 2-3. *Using Global Variables in Separately Compiled Files*

When a declaration creates storage for a variable, it is called a *definition.* **extern** statements are declarations, but not definitions. They simply tell the compiler that a definition exists elsewhere in the program.

There is another, optional use of **extern** that you may occasionally see. When you use a global variable inside a function that is in the same file as the declaration for the global variable, you may elect to declare it as **extern**, although you don't have to and it is rarely done. The following program fragment shows the use of this option:

```
int first, last;  /* global definition of first and last */

int main(void)
{
  extern int first;   /* optional use of the
                         extern declaration */

  /* ... */
}
```

Although **extern** variable declarations can occur inside the same file as the global declaration, they are not necessary. If the C compiler encounters a variable that has not been declared, the compiler checks whether it matches any of the global variables. If it does, the compiler assumes that the global variable is the one being referenced.

static Variables

static variables are permanent variables within their own function or file. They differ from global variables because they are not known outside their function or file, but they maintain their values between calls. This feature makes them very useful when you write generalized functions and function libraries, which may be used by other programmers. Because the effect of **static** on local variables is different from its effect on global ones, they will be examined separately.

static Local Variables

When **static** is applied to a local variable it causes the compiler to create permanent storage for it in much the same way that it does for a global variable. The key difference between a **static** local variable and a global variable is that the **static** local variable remains known only to the block in which it is declared. In simple terms, a **static** local variable is a local variable that retains its value between function calls.

It is very important to the creation of stand-alone functions that **static** local variables are available in C because there are several types of routines that must preserve a value between calls. If **static** variables were not allowed, then globals would have to be used—opening the door to possible side effects. A simple example of how a **static** local variable can be used is illustrated by the **count( )** function in this short program:

```
#include <stdio.h>
#include <conio.h>

int count(int i);

int main(void)
{
  do {
    count(0);
  } while(!kbhit());
  printf("count called %d times", count(1));
  return 0;
}

int count(int i)
{
  static int c=0;

  if(i) return c;
  else c++;
  return 0;
}
```

Sometimes it is useful to know how many times a function has been executed during a program run. While it is certainly possible to use a global variable for this purpose, a better way is to have the function in question keep track of this information itself, as is done by the **count( )** function. In this example, if **count( )** is called with a value of 0, then the counter variable **c** is incremented. (Presumably, in a real application, the function would also perform some other useful processing.) If **count( )** is called with any other value, it returns the number of times it has been called. Counting the number of times a function is called can be useful during the development of a program so that those functions called most frequently can receive the most attention.

Another good example of a function that would require a **static** local variable is a number series generator that produces a new number based on the last one. It is possible for you to declare a global variable for this value. However, each time the function is used in a program, you would have to remember to declare that global variable and make sure that it did not conflict with any other global variables already declared—a major drawback. Also, using a global variable would make this function difficult to place in a function library. The better solution is to declare the variable that holds the generated number to be **static**, as in this program fragment:

```
int series(void)
{
```

```
    static int series_num;

    series_num = series_num+23;
    return(series_num);
}
```

In this example, the variable **series_num** stays in existence between function calls, instead of coming and going the way a normal local variable would. This means that each call to **series( )** can produce a new member of the series based on the last number without declaring that variable globally.

You may have noticed something that is unusual about the function **series( )** as it stands in the example. The static variable **series_num** is never explicitly initialized. This means that the first time the function is called, **series_num** will have the value zero, by default. While this is acceptable for some applications, most series generators will need a flexible starting point. To do this requires that **series_num** be initialized prior to the first call to **series( )**, which can be done easily if **series_num** is a global variable. However, avoiding having to make **series_num** global was the entire point of making it **static** to begin with. This leads to the second use of **static**.

static Global Variables

When the specifier **static** is applied to a global variable, it instructs the compiler to create a global variable that is known only to the *file* in which the **static** global variable is declared. This means that even though the variable is global, other routines in other files may have no knowledge of it or alter its contents directly; thus it is not subject to side effects. For the few situations where a local **static** cannot do the job, you can create a small file that contains only the functions that need the **static** global variable, separately compile that file, and use it without fear of side effects.

To see how a **static** global variable can be used, the series generator example from the previous section is recoded so that a starting "seed" value can be used to initialize the series through a call to a second function called **series_start( )**. The entire file containing **series( )**, **series_start( )**, and **series_num** follows:

```
/* This must all be in one file - preferably by itself */

static int series_num;


int series(void);
void series_start(int seed);

int series(void)
{
  series_num = series_num + 23;
  return(series_num);
```

```
}

/* initialize series_num */
void series_start(int seed)
{
  series_num = seed;
}
```

Calling **series_start( )** with some known integer value initializes the series generator. After that, calls to **series( )** will generate the next element in the series.

The names of **static** local variables are known only to the function or block of code in which they are declared, and the names of **static** global variables are known only to the file in which they reside. This means that if you place the **series( )** and **series_start( )** functions in a separate file, you can use the functions, but you cannot reference the variable **series_num**. It is hidden from the rest of the code in your program. In fact, you may even declare and use another variable called **series_num** in your program (in another file, of course) and not confuse anything. In essence, the **static** modifier allows variables to be known to the functions that need them, without confusing other functions.

static variables enable you to hide portions of your program from other portions. This can be a tremendous advantage when trying to manage a very large and complex program.

Register Variables

C has one last storage specifier that originally applied only to variables of types **int** and **char**. However, the ANSI C standard has broadened its scope. The **register** specifier requests the compiler to store a variable declared with this modifier in a manner that allows the fastest access time possible. For integers and characters, this typically means in the register of the CPU rather than in memory, where normal variables are stored. For other types of variables, the compiler may use any other means to decrease their access time. In fact, it can also simply ignore the request altogether.

In Borland C++, the **register** specifier may be applied to local variables and to the formal parameters in a function. You cannot apply **register** to global variables. Also, because a **register** variable may be stored in a register of the CPU, you cannot obtain the address of a **register** variable. (This restriction applies only to C, and not C++.)

In general, operations on **register** variables occur much faster than on variables stored in main memory. In fact, when the value of a variable is actually held in the CPU, no memory access is required to determine or modify its value. This makes **register** variables ideal for loop control. Here is an example of how to declare a **register** variable of type **int** and use it to control a loop. This function computes the result of $\mathbf{m}^{\mathbf{e}}$ for integers.

```
int int_pwr(register int m, register int e)
{
  register int temp;

  temp = 1;

  for(; e; e--) temp *= m;
   return temp;
}
```

In this example, **m**, **e**, and **temp** are declared to be **register** variables because all are used within the loop. In general practice, **register** variables are used where they will do the most good; that is, in places where many references will be made to the same variable. This is important because not all variables can be optimized for access time.

It is important to understand that the **register** specifier is just a request to the compiler, which the compiler is free to ignore. However, in general, you can count on at least two **register** variables of type **char** or **int** actually being held in a CPU register for any one function. Additional **register** variables will be optimized to the best ability of the compiler.

Assignment Statements

The general form of the *assignment statement* is

variable_name = expression;

where an expression may be as simple as a single constant or as complex as a combination of variables, operators, and constants. Like BASIC and FORTRAN, C uses a single equal sign to indicate assignment (unlike Pascal or Modula-2, which use the := construct). The target, or left part, of the assignment must be a variable, not a function or a constant.

Multiple Assignments

C allows you to assign many variables the same value by using multiple assignments in a single statement. For example, this program fragment assigns **x**, **y**, and **z** the value 0:

```
x = y = z = 0;
```

In professional programs, variables are frequently assigned a common value using this method.

Type Conversion in Assignments

Type conversion refers to the situation in which variables of one type are mixed with variables of another type. When this occurs in an assignment statement, the *type conversion rule* is very easy: The value of the right (expression) side of the assignment is converted to the type of the left side (target variable), as illustrated by this example:

```
int x;
char ch;
float  f;
void func(void)
{
  ch = x;     /* 1 */
  x = f;      /* 2 */
  f = ch;     /* 3 */
  f = x;      /* 4 */
}
```

In line 1, the left, high-order bits of the integer variable **x** are lopped off, leaving **ch** with the lower 8 bits. If **x** had been between 256 and 0 to begin with, then **ch** and **x** would have identical values. Otherwise, the value of **ch** would reflect only the lower order bits of **x**. In line 2, **x** receives the nonfractional part of **f**. In line 3, **f** receives the 8-bit integer value stored in **ch**, converted into floating point format. In line 4, **f** receives the value of integer **x** converted into floating point format.

When converting from integers to characters, long integers to integers, and integers to short integers, the basic rule is that the appropriate amount of high-order bits will be removed. When using 16-bit integers, this means 8 bits will be lost when going from an integer to a character, and 16 bits will be lost when going from a long integer to an integer.

Table 2-4 synopsizes these assignment type conversions. You must remember two important points that can affect the portability of the code you write:

1. The conversion of an **int** to a **float**, or a type **float** to **double**, and so on, will not add any precision or accuracy. These kinds of conversions will only change the form in which the value is represented.
2. Some C compilers (and processors) will always treat a **char** variable as positive, no matter what value it has when converting it to an integer or **float**. Other compilers may treat **char** variable values greater than 127 as negative numbers when converting (as does Borland C++). Generally speaking, you should use **char** variables for characters, and use **int**, **short int**, or **signed char** when needed to avoid a possible portability problem in this area.

To use Table 2-4 to make a conversion not directly shown, simply convert one type at a time until you finish. For example, to convert from a **double** to an **int**, first convert from a **double** to a **float** and then from a **float** to an **int**.

Target Type	Expression Type	Possible Info Loss
signed char	unsigned char	If value > 127, the target will be negative
char	short int	High-order 8 bits
char	int (16 bit)	High-order 8 bits
char	int (32 bit)	High-order 24 bits
short int	int (16 bit)	None
short int	int (32 bit)	High-order 16 bits
int (16 bit)	long int	High-order 16 bits
int (32 bit)	long int	None
float	double	Precision, result rounded
double	long double	Precision, result rounded

Table 2-4. *The Outcome of Common Type Conversions*

If you have used a computer language like Pascal, which prohibits this automatic type conversion, you may think that C is very loose and sloppy. However, keep in mind that C was designed to make the life of the programmer easier by allowing work to be done in C rather than assembler. To do this, C has to allow such type conversions.

Variable Initializations

You can give variables a value at the time they are declared by placing an equal sign and a constant after the variable name. This is called an *initialization*, and its general form is

type variable_name = constant;

Some examples are

```
char ch = 'a';

int first = 0;

float balance = 123.23;
```

Global and **static** global variables are initialized only at the start of the program. Local variables are initialized each time the block in which they are declared is entered. However, **static** local variables are only initialized once—not each time the block is entered. All global and **static** local variables are initialized to zero if no other initializer is specified. Non-**static** local and **register** variables that are not initialized will have indeterminate values.

Constants

Constants in C refer to fixed values that may not be altered by the program. They can be of any data type, as shown in Table 2-5.

C supports one other type of constant in addition to those of the predefined data types. This is a string. All string constants are enclosed between double quotes, such as **"this is a test"**. You must not confuse strings with characters. A single character constant is enclosed by single quotes, such as **'a'**. Because strings are simply arrays of characters, they will be discussed in Chapter 5.

Backslash Character Constants

Enclosing all character constants in single quotes works for most printing characters, but a few, such as the carriage return, are impossible to enter from the keyboard. For this reason, C uses the special backslash character constants, shown in Table 2-6.

You use a backslash code exactly the same way you would any other character. For example,

```
ch = '\t';
printf("this is a test\n");
```

first assigns a tab to **ch** and then prints "this is a test" on the screen followed by a newline.

Data Type	Constant Examples
char	'a' '\n' '9'
int	1 123 21000 –234
long int	35000L –34L
short int	10 –12 90
unsigned int	10000U 987U 40000U
float	123.23F 4.34e –3F
double	123.23 12312.333 –0.9876324

Table 2-5. *Constant Examples for Data Types*

Code	Meaning
\b	Backspace
\f	Form feed
\n	Newline
\r	Carriage return
\t	Horizontal tab
\"	Double quote
\'	Single quote character
\0	Null
\\	Backslash
\v	Vertical tab
\a	Alert
N	Octal constant (where *N* is an octal value)
\x*N*	Hexadecimal constant (where *N* is a hexadecimal value)

Table 2-6. *Backslash Codes*

Operator	Action
–	Subtraction, also unary minus
+	Addition
*	Multiplication
/	Division
%	Modulus division
– –	Decrement
++	Increment

Table 2-7. *Arithmetic Operators*

Operators

C is very rich in built-in operators. An *operator* is a symbol that tells the compiler to perform specific mathematical or logical manipulations. There are three general classes of operators in C: arithmetic, relational and logical, and bitwise. In addition, C has some special operators for particular tasks.

Arithmetic Operators

Table 2-7 lists the *arithmetic operators* allowed in C. The operators **+**, **–**, *****, and **/** all work the same way in C as they do in most other computer languages. They can be applied to almost any built-in data type allowed by C. When **/** is applied to an integer or character, any remainder is truncated; for example, **10/3** equals 3 in integer division.

The modulus division operator **%** also works in C the way it does in other languages. Remember that the modulus division operation yields the remainder of an integer division. However, as such, **%** cannot be used on type **float** or **double**. The following code fragment illustrates its use:

```
int x, y;

x = 10;
y = 3;

printf("%d", x/y);    /* will display 3 */
printf("%d", x%y);    /* will display 1, the remainder of
                         the integer division */

x = 1;
y = 2;

printf("%d %d", x/y, x%y); /*  will display 0 1 */
```

The reason the last line prints a 0 and 1 is because **1/2** in integer division is 0 with a remainder of 1. **1%2** yields the remainder 1.

The unary minus, in effect, multiplies its single operand by –1. That is, any number preceded by a minus sign switches its sign.

Increment and Decrement

C allows two very useful operators not generally found in other computer languages. These are the increment and decrement operators, **++** and **– –**. The operation **++** adds 1 to its operand, and **– –** subtracts 1. Therefore, the following are equivalent operations:

```
x = x + 1;
```

is the same as

```
++x;
```

Also,

```
x = x - 1;
```

is the same as

```
--x;
```

Both the increment and decrement operators may either precede (prefix) or follow (postfix) the operand. For example,

```
x = x + 1;
```

can be written

```
++x;
```

or

```
x++;
```

However, there is a difference when they are used in an expression. When an increment or decrement operator precedes its operand, C performs the increment or decrement operation prior to using the operand's value. If the operator follows its operand, C uses the operand's value before incrementing or decrementing it. Consider the following:

```
x = 10;
y = ++x;
```

In this case, **y** is set to 11. However, if the code had been written as

```
x = 10;
y = x++;
```

y would have been set to 10. In both cases, **x** is set to 11; the difference is when it happens. There are significant advantages in being able to control when the increment or decrement operation takes place.

The precedence of the arithmetic operators is as follows:

highest	+ (unary plus) – (unary minus) ++ ––
	* / %
lowest	+ – (binary operators)

Operators on the same precedence level are evaluated by the compiler from left to right. Of course, parentheses may be used to alter the order of evaluation. Parentheses are treated by C in the same way they are by virtually all other computer languages: They give an operation, or set of operations, a higher precedence level.

Relational and Logical Operators

In the term *relational operator*, the word *relational* refers to the relationships values can have with one another. In the term *logical operator*, the word *logical* refers to the ways these relationships can be connected together using the rules of formal logic. Because the relational and logical operators often work together, they will be discussed together here.

The key to the concepts of relational and logical operators is the idea of *true* and *false*. In C, *true* is any value other than 0. *False* is 0. Expressions that use relational or logical operators will return 0 for false and 1 for true.

Table 2-8 shows the relational and logical operators. The truth table for the logical operators is shown here using 1s and 0s:

<table>
<tr><th>p</th><th>q</th><th>p && q</th><th>p || q</th><th>!p</th></tr>
<tr><td>0</td><td>0</td><td>0</td><td>0</td><td>1</td></tr>
<tr><td>0</td><td>1</td><td>0</td><td>1</td><td>1</td></tr>
<tr><td>1</td><td>1</td><td>1</td><td>1</td><td>0</td></tr>
<tr><td>1</td><td>0</td><td>0</td><td>1</td><td>0</td></tr>
</table>

Both the relational and logical operators are lower in precedence than the arithmetic operators. This means that an expression like **10 > 1+12** is evaluated as if it were written **10 > (1+12)**. The result is, of course, false.

Several operations can be combined in one expression, as shown here:

```
10>5 && !(10<9) || 3<=4
```

which will evaluate true.

The following shows the relative precedence of the relational and logical operators:

```
highest     !
            >  >=  <  <=
            ==  !=
            &&
lowest      ||
```

Relational Operators

Operator	Action
>	Greater than
>=	Greater than or equal
<	Less than
<=	Less than or equal
==	Equal
!=	Not equal

Logical Operators

Operator	Action
&&	AND
||	OR
!	NOT

Table 2-8. *Relational and Logical Operators*

As with arithmetic expressions, it is possible to use parentheses to alter the natural order of evaluation in a relational or logical expression. For example,

```
!1 && 0
```

will be false because the **!** is evaluated first, then the **&&** is evaluated. However, when the same expression is parenthesized as shown here, the result is true.

```
!(1 && 0)
```

Remember, all relational and logical expressions produce a result of either 0 or 1. Therefore, the following program fragment is not only correct, but also prints the number 1 on the display:

```
int x;

x = 100;
printf("%d", x>10);
```

Bitwise Operators

Unlike many other languages, C supports a complete complement of *bitwise operators.* Since C was designed to take the place of assembly language for most programming tasks, it needed the ability to support all (or at least many) operations that can be done in assembler. Bitwise operations are the testing, setting, or shifting of the actual bits in a byte or word, which correspond to C's standard **char** and **int** data types and variants. Bitwise operators cannot be used on type **float**, **double**, **long double**, **void**, or other more complex types. Table 2-9 lists these operators.

The bitwise AND, OR, and NOT (one's complement) are governed by the same truth table as were their logical equivalents, except that they work on a bit-by-bit level. The exclusive OR ^ has the truth table shown here:

p	q	p^q
0	0	0
0	1	1
1	0	1
1	1	0

Operator	Action
&	AND
|	OR
^	Exclusive OR (XOR)
~	One's complement
>>	Shift right
<<	Shift left

Table 2-9. *The Bitwise Operators*

As the table indicates, the outcome of an XOR is true only if exactly one of the operands is true; it is false otherwise.

Bitwise operations most often find application in device drivers, such as modem programs, disk file routines, and printer routines, because the bitwise operations can be used to mask off certain bits, such as parity. (The parity bit is used to confirm that the rest of the bits in the byte are unchanged. It is usually the high-order bit in each byte.)

The bitwise AND is most commonly used to turn bits off. That is, any bit that is 0 in either operand causes the corresponding bit in the outcome to be set to 0. For example, the following function reads a character from the modem port using the function **read_modem( )** and resets the parity bit to 0.

```
char get_char_from_modem(void)
{
  char ch;

  ch = read_modem(); /* get a character from the
                        modem port */

  return(ch & 127);
}
```

Parity is indicated by the eighth bit, which is set to 0 by ANDing it with a byte that has bits 1 through 7 set to 1 and bit 8 set to 0. The expression **ch & 127** means to AND together the bits in **ch** with the bits that make up the number 127. The net result is that the eighth bit of **ch** will be set to 0. In the following example, assume that **ch** had received the character **'A'** and had the parity bit set:

```
        parity bit
        ↓
        11000001        ch containing an 'A' with parity bit set
        01111111        127 in binary
&       ________        do bitwise AND
        01000001        'A' without parity
```

The bitwise OR, as the reverse of AND, can be used to turn bits on. Any bit that is set to 1 in either operand causes the corresponding bit in the outcome to be set to 1. For example, **128 | 3** is

```
        10000000        128 in binary
        00000011        3 in binary
|       ________        bitwise OR
        10000011        result
```

An exclusive OR, usually abbreviated XOR, will turn a bit on only if the bits being compared are different. For example, **127 ^ 120** is

	0 1 1 1 1 1 1 1	127 in binary
	0 1 1 1 1 0 0 0	120 in binary
^	________	bitwise XOR
	0 0 0 0 0 1 1 1	result

In general, bitwise ANDs, ORs, and XORs apply their operations directly to each bit in the variable individually. For this reason, among others, bitwise operators are not usually used in conditional statements the way the relational and logical operators are. For example if **x=7**, then **x && 8** evaluates to true (1), whereas **x & 8** evaluates to false (0).

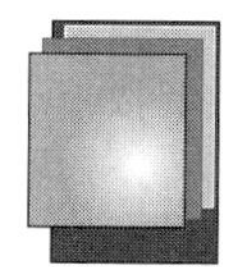

REMEMBER: Relational and logical operators always produce a result that is either 0 or 1, whereas the similar bitwise operations may produce any arbitrary value in accordance with the specific operation. In other words, bitwise operations may create values other than 0 or 1, while the logical operators will always evaluate to 0 or 1.

The shift operators, **>>** and **<<**, move all bits in a variable to the right or left as specified. The general form of the shift right statement is

variable >> number of bit positions

and the shift left statement is

variable << number of bit positions

Remember, a shift is *not* a rotate. That is, the bits shifted off one end *do not* come back around to the other. The bits shifted off are lost, and 0s are brought in. However, a right shift of a negative number shifts in ones. (This maintains the sign bit.)

Bit shift operations can be very useful when decoding external device input, like D/A converters, and reading status information. The bitwise shift operators can also be used to perform very fast multiplication and division of integers. A shift left will effectively multiply a number by 2 and a shift right will divide it by 2, as shown in Table 2-10.

The one's complement operator, **~**, will reverse the state of each bit in the specified variable. That is, all 1's are set to 0, and all 0s are set to 1.

The bitwise operators are used often in cipher routines. If you wished to make a disk file appear unreadable, you could perform some bitwise manipulations on it. One

	x as Each Statement Executes	Value of x
char x;		
x=7;	00000111	7
x=x <<1;	00001110	14
x=x <<3;	01110000	112
x=x <<2;	11000000	192
x=x>>1;	01100000	96
x=x >>2;	00011000	24

Each left shift multiplies by 2. You should notice that information has been lost after x<<2 because a bit was shifted off the end.

Each right shift divides by 2. Notice that subsequent division will not bring back any lost bits.

Table 2-10. *Multiplication and Division with Shift Operators*

of the simplest methods would be to complement each byte by using the one's complement to reverse each bit in the byte as shown here:

Original byte	00101100	
After 1st complement	11010011	same
After 2nd complement	00101100	

Notice that a sequence of two complements in a row always produces the original number. Hence, the first complement would represent the coded version of that byte. The second complement would decode it to its original value.

You could use the **encode( )** function shown here to encode a character:

```
/* A simple cipher function. */
char encode(char ch)
```

```
{
  return(~ch); /* complement it */
}
```

The ? Operator

C has a very powerful and convenient operator that can be used to replace certain statements of the if-then-else form. The ternary operator **?** takes the general form

Exp1 ? *Exp2* : *Exp3*

where *Exp1, Exp2,* and *Exp3* are expressions. Notice the use and placement of the colon.

The **?** operator works like this. *Exp1* is evaluated. If it is true, then *Exp2* is evaluated and becomes the value of the expression. If *Exp1* is false, then *Exp3* is evaluated and its value becomes the value of the expression. For example,

```
x = 10;
y = x>9 ? 100 : 200;
```

In this example, **y** will be assigned the value **100**. If **x** had been less than or equal to 9, **y** would have received the value **200**. The same code written using the **if/else** statement would be

```
x = 10;
if(x>9) y = 100;
else y = 200;
```

The **?** operator will be discussed more fully in Chapter 3 in relationship to C's other conditional statements.

The & and * Pointer Operators

A *pointer* is the memory address of a variable. A pointer variable is a variable that is specifically declared to hold a pointer to an object of its specified type. Knowing a variable's address can be of great help in certain types of routines. Pointers have three main uses in C:

1. They can provide a very fast means of referencing array elements.
2. They allow C functions to modify their calling parameters.
3. They support dynamic data structures, such as linked lists.

These topics and uses will be dealt with in Chapter 6, which is devoted exclusively to pointers. However, the two operators that are used to manipulate pointers will be presented here.

The first pointer operator is **&**. It is a unary operator that returns the memory address of its operand. (Remember that a unary operator only requires one operand.) For example,

```
m = &count;
```

places into **m** the memory address of the variable **count**. This address is the computer's internal location of the variable. It has nothing to do with the *value* of **count**. The operation of the **&** can be remembered as returning the "the address of." Therefore, the above assignment statement could be read as "m receives the address of count."

To better understand the above assignment, assume the variable **count** resides at memory location 2000. Also assume that **count** has a value of 100. After the above assignment, **m** will have the value 2000.

The second operator, *, is the complement of the **&**. It is a unary operator that returns the *value of the variable located at the address that follows.* For example, if **m** contains the memory address of the variable **count**, then

```
q = *m;
```

places the value of **count** into **q**. Following the above example, **q** will have the value 100 because 100 is stored at location 2000, which is the memory address that was stored in **m**. The operation of the * can be remembered as "at address." In this case, the statement could be read as "q receives the value at address m."

Unfortunately, the multiplication sign and the "at address" sign are the same and the bitwise AND and the "address of" sign are the same. These operators have no relationship to each other. Both **&** and * have a higher precedence than all other arithmetic operators except the unary minus, with which they are equal.

Variables that will hold memory addresses, or pointers as they are called in C, must be declared by putting a * in front of the variable name to indicate to the compiler that it will hold a pointer to that type of variable. For example, to declare a character pointer called **ch** you would write

```
char *ch;
```

Here, **ch** is not a character, but rather a pointer to a character—there is a big difference. The type of data that a pointer will be pointing to, in this case **char**, is called the *base type* of the pointer. However, the pointer variable itself is a variable that will be used to hold the address to an object of the base type. Hence, a character pointer (or any pointer for that matter) will be of sufficient size to hold an address as defined by the architecture of the computer on which it is running. The key point to remember is that a pointer should only be used to point to data that is of that pointer's base type.

You can mix both pointer and nonpointer directives in the same declaration statement. For example,

```
int x, *y, count;
```

declares **x** and **count** to be integer types, and **y** to be a pointer to an integer type.

Here, the * and & operators are used to put the value 10 into a variable called **target**:

```
#include <stdio.h>

/* Assignment with * and &. */
int main(void)
{
  int target, source;
  int *m;

  source = 10;
  m = &source;
  target = *m;

  printf("%d", target);

  return 0;
}
```

The sizeof Compile-Time Operator

sizeof is a unary compile-time operator that returns the length, in bytes, of the variable or parenthesized type specifier it precedes. For example,

```
float f;

printf("%f ", sizeof f);
printf("%d", sizeof(int));
```

displays **4 2**. (Assuming 16-bit integers.)

Remember that to compute the size of a type you must enclose the type name in parentheses (like a cast, which is explained later in this chapter). This is not necessary for variable names.

The principal use of **sizeof** is to help generate portable code when that code depends upon the size of the C built-in data types. For example, imagine a database program that needs to store six integer values per record. To make the database program portable to the widest variety of computers, you must not assume that an integer is 2 or 4 bytes; you must determine its actual length using **sizeof**. This being the case, the following routine could be used to write a record to a disk file:

```
/* write a record to a disk file */
void put_rec(FILE *fp, int rec[6])
{
```

```
    int size, num;

    size = sizeof(int) * 6;
    num = fwrite(rec, size, 1, fp);
    if(num!=1) printf("write error");
}
```

The key point of this example is that, coded as shown, **put_rec( )** will compile and run correctly on any computer—including those using 2- or 4-byte integers. Correctly using **sizeof** means that you can use Borland C++ to develop code that will ultimately run in a different environment.

The Comma Operator

The comma operator is used to string together several expressions. The left side of the comma operator will always be evaluated as **void**. This means that the expression on the right side will become the value of the total comma-separated expression. For example,

```
x = (y=3, y+1);
```

first assigns **y** the value 3 and then assigns **x** the value of 4. The parentheses are necessary because the comma operator has a lower precedence than the assignment operator.

Essentially, the comma causes a sequence of operations to be performed. When it is used on the right side of an assignment statement, the value assigned is the value of the last expression of the comma-separated list. Here is another example:

```
y = 10;
x = (y=y-5, 25/y);
```

After execution, **x** will have the value 5 because **y**'s original value of 10 is reduced by 5, and then that value is divided into 25, yielding 5 as the result.

You might think of the comma operator as having the same meaning the word *and* has in normal English when it is used in the phrase "do this and this and this."

The . and -> Operators

The . (dot) operator and the -> (arrow) operator are used to reference individual elements of structures and unions. Structures and unions are aggregate data types that can be referenced under a single name. Unions and structures will be thoroughly covered in Chapter 7, but a short discussion of the operators used with them is given here.

The dot operator is used when operating on an actual structure or union. The arrow operator is used with a pointer to a structure or union. Suppose you were given the structure

```
struct employee {
  char name[80];
  int age;
  float wage;
} emp;

struct tom *p = &emp; /* address of emp into p */
```

To assign the value 123.23 to element **wage** of structure **emp**, you would write

```
emp.wage = 123.23;
```

However, the same assignment using a pointer to structure **emp** would be

```
p->wage = 123.23;
```

[ ] and ( )

In C, parentheses do the expected job of increasing the precedence of the operations inside of them.

Square brackets perform array indexing, and will be discussed fully in Chapter 5. Briefly, given an array, the expression within the square brackets provides an index into that array. For example,

```
#include <stdio.h>

char s[80];

int main(void)
{

   s[3] = 'X';
   printf("%c", s[3]);

  return 0;
}
```

first assigns the value 'X' to the fourth element (remember, all arrays in C begin at 0) of array **s**, and then prints that element.

Precedence Summary

Table 2-11 lists the precedence of all C operators. Note that all operators, except the unary operators and **?**, associate from left to right. The unary operators (*, &, –) and **?** associate from right to left.

Precedence	Operators
Highest	() [] -> .
	! ~ + − ++ −− & * sizeof (type)
	* / %
	+ − (binary)
	<< >>
	< <= > >=
	== !=
	&
	^
	|
	&&
	||
	?:
	= *= /= %= += −= &= ^= |= <<= >>=
Lowest	,

Table 2-11. *Precedence of C Operators*

Expressions

Operators, constants, and variables are the constituents of *expressions*. An expression in C is any valid combination of those pieces. Because most expressions tend to follow the general rules of algebra, they are often taken for granted. However, there are a few aspects of expressions that relate to C specifically and will be discussed here.

Type Conversion in Expressions

When constants and variables of different types are mixed in an expression, they are converted to the same type. The compiler will convert all operands "up" to the type of the largest operand. This is done on an operation-by-operation basis, as described in the following type conversion rules:

1. All **char**s and **short int**s are converted to **int**s. All **float**s are converted to **double**s.
2. For all operand pairs, if one of the operands is a **long double**, the other operand is converted to **long double**.
   Otherwise, if one of the operands is **double**, the other operand is converted to **double**.
   Otherwise, if one of the operands is **long**, the other operand is converted to **long**.
   Otherwise, if one of the operands is **unsigned**, the other operand is converted to **unsigned**.

Once these conversion rules have been applied, each pair of operands will be of the same type and the result of each operation will be the same as the type of both operands. Please note that the second rule has several conditions that must be applied in sequence.

For example, consider the type conversions that occur in Figure 2-1.

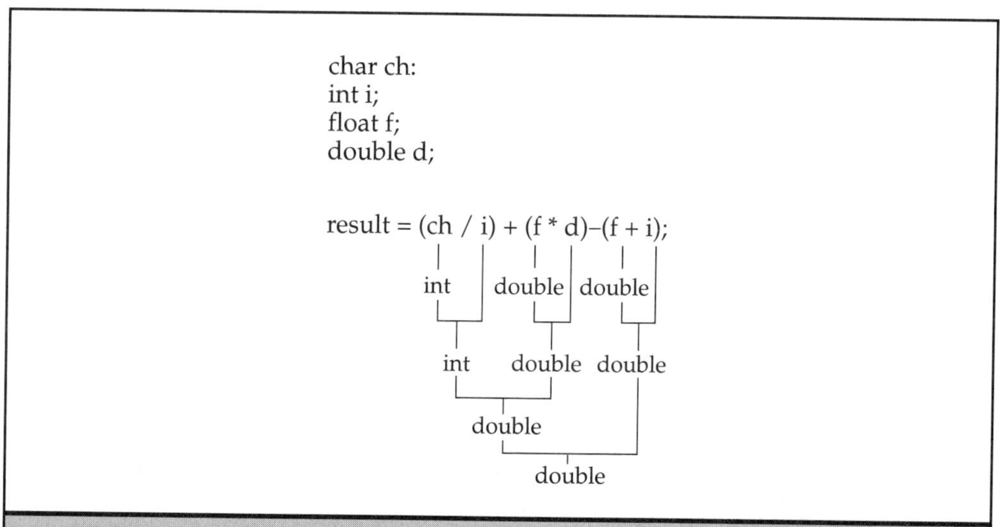

Figure 2-1. *An example of type conversion*

First, the character **ch** is converted to an integer and **float f** is converted to **double**. Then the outcome of **ch/i** is converted to a **double** because **f*d** is **double**. The final result is **double** because, by this time, both operands are **double**.

Casts

It is possible to force an expression to be of a specific type by using a construct called a *cast*. The general form of a cast is

(type) expression

where *type* is one of the standard C data types or a user-defined type. For example, if you wished to make the expression **x/2** be evaluated to type **float** you could write it:

```
(float) x/2
```

Casts are considered operators. As an operator, a cast is unary and has the same precedence as any other unary operator.

Although casts are not usually used a great deal in C programming, there are times when they can be very useful. For example, suppose you wish to use an integer for loop control, yet perform computation on it requiring a fractional part, as in the following program:

```
#include <stdio.h>

/* Print i and i/2 with fractions. */
int main(void)
{
  int i;

  for(i=1; i<=100; ++i )
    printf("%d / 2 is: %f\n", i, (float) i/2);
  return 0;
}
```

Without the cast (**float**), only an integer division would have been performed; but the cast ensures that the fractional part of the answer will be displayed on the screen.

Spacing and Parentheses

To aid readability, an expression in C may have tabs and spaces in it at your discretion. For example, the following two expressions are the same.

```
x=10/y~(127/x);

x = 10 / y ~(127/x);
```

Use of redundant or additional parentheses does not cause errors or slow down the execution of the expression. You are encouraged to use parentheses to clarify the exact order of evaluation, both for yourself and for others who may have to read your program later. For example, which of the following two expressions is easier to read?

```
x=y/3-34*temp&127;
```

```
x = (y/3) - ((34*temp) & 127);
```

C Shorthand

C has a special shorthand that simplifies the coding of a certain type of assignment statement. For example,

```
x = x + 10;
```

can be written, in C shorthand, as

```
x += 10;
```

The operator pair **+=** tells the compiler to assign to **x** the value of **x** plus 10.

This shorthand works for all the binary operators in C (those that require two operands). The general form of the shorthand

var = var operator expression;

is the same as

var operator = expression;

For another example,

```
x = x - 100;
```

is the same as

```
x -= 100;
```

You will see shorthand notation used widely in professionally written C programs and you should become familiar with it.

Chapter Three

Program Control Statements

This chapter discusses C's rich and varied program control statements. These are the mechanisms by which the flow of execution is directed. C defines three specific categories of program control statements: *iteration*, *selection*, and *jump*. The iteration statements are **while**, **for**, and **do/while**. These are also commonly called *loop* statements. The selection statements, also called *conditional* statements, are the **if** and **switch**. The jump statements include the **break**, **continue**, and **goto** statements. (The **return** statement is also, technically, a jump statement because it affects program control. However, its discussion is deferred until the following chapter on functions.) The **exit( )** function is discussed here because it also can affect the flow of a program.

True and False in C

Most program control statements in any computer language, including C, rely on a conditional test that determines what course of action is to be taken. The conditional test produces either a true or false value. Unlike many other computer languages that specify special values for true and false, a true value in C is any nonzero value, including negative numbers. A false value is zero. This approach to true and false is implemented in C primarily because it allows a wide range of routines to be coded very efficiently.

Selection Statements

C supports two types of selection statements: **if** and **switch**. In addition, the **?** operator is an alternative to the **if** in certain circumstances.

if

The general form of the **if** statement is

if(*expression*) *statement;*
else *statement;*

where *statement* may be either a single statement or a block of statements. (Remember that in C a *block* is a group of statements surrounded by braces.) The **else** clause is optional.

The general form of the **if** with blocks of statements is

if(*expression*) {
  statement sequence
}
else {
  statement sequence
}

If the expression is true (anything other than 0), the statement or block that forms the target of the **if** is executed; otherwise, the statement or block that is the target of the **else** is executed. Remember, only the code associated with the **if** or the code that is associated with the **else** executes, never both.

For example, consider the following program, which plays a very simple version of "guess the magic number" game. It prints the message "** Right **" when the player guesses the magic number.

```
#include <stdio.h>

/* Magic number program. */
int main(void)
{
  int magic = 123;   /* magic number */
  int guess;

  printf("Enter your guess: ");
  scanf("%d", &guess);

  if(guess == magic) printf("** Right **");

  return 0;
}
```

This program uses the equality operator to determine whether the player's guess matches the magic number. If it does, the message is printed on the screen.

Taking the magic number program further, the next version illustrates the use of the **else** statement to print a message when the wrong number is tried.

```
#include <stdio.h>

/* Magic number program - improvement 1. */
int main(void)
{
  int magic = 123;  /* magic number */
  int guess;

  printf("Enter your guess: ");
  scanf("%d",&guess);

  if(guess == magic) printf("** Right **");
  else printf(".. Wrong ..");

  return 0;
}
```

Nested ifs

One of the most confusing aspects of **if** statements in any programming language is nested **if**s. A *nested if* is an **if** statement that is the object of either an **if** or an **else**. The reason that nested **if**s are so troublesome is that it can be difficult to know what **else** associates with what **if**. For example:

```
if(x)
  if(y) printf("1");
  else printf("2");
```

To which **if** does the **else** refer?

Fortunately, C provides a very simple rule for resolving this type of situation. In C, the **else** is linked to the closest preceding **if** (at the same scope level) that does not already have an **else** statement associated with it. In this case, the **else** is associated with the **if(y)** statement. To make the **else** associate with the **if(x)** you must use braces to override its normal association, as shown here:

```
if(x) {
  if(y) printf("1");
}
else printf("2");
```

The **else** is now associated with the **if(x)** because it is no longer part of the **if(y)** block. Because of C's scope rules, the **else** now has no knowledge of the **if(y)** statement because they are no longer in the same scope.

A further improvement to the magic number program provides the player with feedback on how close each guess is. This is accomplished by the use of a nested **if**:

```
#include <stdio.h>

/* Magic number program - improvement 2. */
int main(void)
{
  int magic = 123;  /* magic number */
  int guess;

  printf("Enter your guess: ");
  scanf("%d", &guess);

  if(guess == magic) {
    printf("** Right ** ");
    printf("%d is the magic number", magic);
  }
  else {
    printf(".. Wrong .. ");
    if(guess > magic) printf("Too high");
    else printf("Too low");
  }
  return 0;
}
```

The if-else-if Ladder

A common programming construct is the *if-else-if ladder.* It looks like this:

if (*expression*)
 statement;
else if (*expression*)
 statement;
else if (*expression*)
 statement;
.
.
.
else
 statement;

The conditions are evaluated from the top downward. As soon as a true condition is found, the statement associated with it is executed, and the rest of the ladder is bypassed. If none of the conditions are true, the final **else** is executed. The final **else** often acts as a *default condition*; that is, if all other conditional tests fail, the last **else** statement is performed. If the final **else** is not present, then no action takes place if all other conditions are false.

Using an if-else-if ladder, the magic number program becomes

```
#include <stdio.h>

/* Magic number program - improvement 3. */
int main(void)
{
  int magic = 123;  /* magic number */
  int guess;

  printf("Enter your guess: ");
  scanf("%d", &guess);

  if(guess == magic) {
    printf("** Right ** ");
    printf("%d is the magic number", magic);
  }
  else if(guess > magic)
    printf(".. Wrong .. Too High");
  else printf(".. Wrong .. Too low");

  return 0;
}
```

The ? Alternative

The **?** operator can be used to replace **if/else** statements of the general form:

> if(*condition*) *expression*;
> else *expression*;

The key restriction is that the target of both the **if** and the **else** must be a single expression—not another C statement.

The **?** is called a *ternary operator* because it requires three operands and takes the general form

> *Exp1* ? *Exp2* : *Exp3*

where *Exp1*, *Exp2*, and *Exp3* are expressions. Notice the use and placement of the colon.

The value of a **?** expression is determined as follows. *Exp1* is evaluated. If it is true, then *Exp2* is evaluated and becomes the value of the entire **?** expression. If *Exp1* is false, then *Exp3* is evaluated and its value becomes the value of the expression. For example:

```
x = 10;
y = x>9 ? 100 : 200;
```

In this example, **y** is assigned the value 100. If **x** had been less than or equal to 9, **y** would have received the value 200. The same code written using the **if/else** statement would be

```
x = 10;
if(x>9) y = 100;
else y = 200;
```

The use of the **?** operator to replace **if/else** statements is not restricted to assignments. Remember that all functions (except those declared as **void**) can return a value. Hence, it is permissible to use one or more function calls in a C expression. When the function's name is encountered, the function is, of course, executed so that its return value can be determined. Therefore, it is possible to execute one or more function calls using the **?** operator by placing them in the expressions that form the operands.

For example:

```
#include <stdio.h>

int f1(int n), f2(void);

int main(void)
{
  int t;

  printf(": ");
  scanf("%d", &t);
  /* print proper message */
  t ? f1(t)+f2() : printf("Zero Entered");

  return 0;
}

int f1(int n)
{
```

```
  printf("%d ",n);
  return 0;

}

int f2(void)
{
  printf("entered");
  return 0;
}
```

In this simple example, if you enter a 0, the **printf( )** function is called and the "Zero Entered" message appears. If you enter any other number, then both **f1( )** and **f2( )** are executed. It is important to note that the value of the **?** expression is discarded in this example; it is not necessary to assign it to anything. Even though neither **f1( )** nor **f2( )** returns a meaningful value, they cannot be defined as returning **void** because doing so prevents their use in an expression. Therefore, the functions simply return zero.

Using the **?** operator, it is possible to rewrite the magic number program again as shown here:

```
#include <stdio.h>

/* Magic number program - improvement 4. */
int main(void)
{
  int magic = 123;  /* magic number */
  int guess;

  printf("Enter your guess: ");
  scanf("%d", &guess);
  if(guess == magic) {
    printf("** Right ** ");
    printf("%d is the magic number", magic);
  }
  else
    guess > magic ? printf("High") : printf("Low");

  return 0;
}
```

Here, the **?** operator causes the proper message to be displayed based on the outcome of the test **guess > magic**.

switch

Although the if-else-if ladder can perform multiway tests, it is hardly elegant. The code can be very hard to follow and can confuse even its author at a later date. For these reasons, C has a built-in multiple-branch decision statement called **switch**, which successively tests a value against a list of integer or character constants. When a match is found, the statement or statements associated with that value are executed. The general form of the **switch** statement is

```
switch(expression) {
  case constant1:
    statement sequence
    break;
  case constant2:
    statement sequence
    break;
  case constant3:
    statement sequence
    break;
    .
    .
    .
  default:
    statement sequence
}
```

The **default** statement is executed if no matches are found. The **default** is optional and, if not present, no action takes place if all matches fail. When a match is found, the statements associated with that **case** are executed until the **break** statement is reached or, in the case of the **default** (or last **case** if no **default** is present), the end of the **switch** statement is encountered.

There are three important things to know about the **switch** statement:

1. The **switch** differs from the **if** in that **switch** can only test for equality whereas the **if** can evaluate a relational or logical expression.
2. No two **case** constants in the same **switch** can have identical values. Of course, a **switch** statement enclosed by an outer **switch** may have **case** constants that are the same.
3. If character constants are used in the **switch**, they are automatically converted to their integer values.

The **switch** statement is often used to process keyboard commands, such as menu selection. As shown here, the function **menu( )** displays a menu for a spelling checker program and calls the proper procedures:

```
void menu(void)
{
  char ch;

  printf("1. Check Spelling\n");
  printf("2. Correct Spelling Errors\n");
  printf("3. Display Spelling Errors\n");
  printf("Strike Any Other Key to Skip\n");
  printf("      Enter your choice: ");

  ch = getche();  /* read the selection from the keyboard */

  switch(ch) {
    case '1':
      check_spelling();
      break;
    case '2':
      correct_errors();
      break;
    case '3':
      display_errors();
      break;
    default :
      printf("No option selected");
  }
}
```

Technically, the **break** statements are optional inside the **switch** statement. They are used to terminate the statement sequence associated with each constant. If the **break** statement is omitted, execution continues into the next **case**'s statements until either a **break** or the end of the **switch** is reached. You can think of the **case**s as labels. Execution starts at the label that matches and continues until a **break** statement is found or the **switch** ends. For example, the function shown here makes use of the "drop through" nature of the **case**s to simplify the code for a device driver input handler:

```
void inp_handler(void)
{
  int ch, flag;

  ch = read_device(); /* read some sort of device */
  flag = -1;

  switch(ch) {
```

```
    case 1:  /* these cases have common statement */
    case 2:  /* sequences */
    case 3:
      flag = 0;
      break;
    case 4:
      flag = 1;
    case 5:
      error(flag);
      break;
    default:
      process(ch);
  }
}
```

This routine illustrates two facets of the **switch** statement. First, you can have empty conditions. In this case, the first three **case**s all execute the same statements:

```
flag = 0;
break;
```

Second, execution continues into the next **case** if no **break** statement is present. If **ch** matches 4, **flag** is set to 1 and, because there is no **break** statement, execution continues and the statement **error(flag)** is executed. In this case, **flag** has the value 1. If **ch** had matched 5, **error(flag)** would have been called with a **flag** value of –1. The ability to run **case**s together when no **break** is present enables you to create very efficient code because it prevents the unwarranted duplication of code.

It is important to understand that the statements associated with each label are not code blocks but rather *statement sequences.* (Of course, the entire **switch** statement defines a block.) This technical distinction is important only in certain special situations. For example, the following code fragment is in error and will not compile because it is not possible to declare a variable in a statement sequence:

```
/* This is incorrect. */
switch(c) {
  case 1:
    int t;
    .
    .
    .
```

However, a variable could be added as shown here:

```
/* This is correct. */
switch(c) {
```

```
  int t;
  case 1:
    .
    .
    .
```

Of course, it is possible to create a block of code as one of the statements in a sequence and declare a variable within it as shown here:

```
/* This is also correct. */
switch(c) {
  case 1:
    { /* create a block */
      int t;
      .
      .
      .
    }
    .
    .
    .
```

NOTE: The preceding discussion only applies to C, not to C++. In C++, you can declare a variable at any point, including within a statement sequence.

Nested switch Statements

It is possible to have a **switch** as part of the statement sequence of an outer **switch**. Even if the **case** constants of the inner and outer **switch** contain common values, no conflicts will arise. For example, the following code fragment is perfectly acceptable:

```
switch(x) {
  case 1:
    switch(y) {
      case 0: printf("Divide by zero error.");
              break;
      case 1: process(x,y);
    }
    break;
  case 2:
   .
   .
   .
```

Loops

In C, and in all other modern programming languages, loops allow a set of instructions to be performed until a certain condition is reached. This condition may be predefined as in the **for** loop, or open-ended as in the **while** and **do** loops.

for

The general format of C's **for** loop is probably familiar to you because it is found in one form or another in nearly all programming languages. However, in C it has unexpected flexibility and power.

The general form of the **for** statement is

for(*initialization; condition; increment*) *statement;*

The **for** statement allows many variants, but there are three main parts:

1. The *initialization* is usually an assignment statement that is used to set the loop control variable.
2. The *condition* is a relational expression that determines when the loop will exit.
3. The *increment* defines how the loop control variable will change each time the loop is repeated.

These three major sections must be separated by semicolons. The **for** loop continues to execute as long as the condition is true. Once the condition becomes false, program execution resumes on the statement following the **for** loop.

For a simple example, the following program prints the numbers 1 through 100.

```
#include <stdio.h>

int main(void)
{
  int x;

  for(x=1; x<=100; x++) printf("%d ", x);

  return 0;
}
```

In the program, **x** is initially set to 1. Since **x** is less than 100, **printf( )** is called, **x** is increased by 1, and then **x** is tested to see if it is still less than or equal to 100. This process repeats until **x** is greater than 100, at which point the loop terminates. In this example, **x** is the *loop control variable,* which is changed and checked each time the loop repeats.

Here is an example of a **for** loop that iterates multiple statements:

```
for(x=100; x!=65; x-=5) {
  z = sqrt(x);
  printf("The square root of %d, %f", x, z);
}
```

Both the **sqrt( )** and **printf( )** calls are executed until **x** equals 65. Note that the loop is *negative running*: **x** is initialized to 100, and 5 is subtracted from it each time the loop repeats.

An important point about **for** loops is that the conditional test is always performed at the top of the loop. This means that the code inside the loop may not be executed at all if the condition is false to begin with. For example:

```
x = 10;
for(y=10; y!=x; ++y) printf("%d", y);
printf("%d", y);
```

This loop never executes because **x** and **y** are in fact equal when the loop is entered. Because the conditional expression is false, neither the body of the loop nor the increment portion of the loop is executed. Hence, **y** still has the value 10 assigned to it, and the output is only the number 10 printed once on the screen.

for Loop Variations

The preceding discussion described the most common form of the **for** loop. However, several variations are allowed that increase its power, flexibility, and applicability to certain programming situations.

One of the most common variations is achieved by using the comma operator to allow two or more variables to control the loop. (You should recall that the comma operator is used to string together a number of expressions in a "do this and this" fashion. It is described in Chapter 2.) For example, this loop uses the variables **x** and **y** to control the loop, with both variables being initialized inside the **for** statement:

```
for(x=0, y=0; x+y<10; ++x) {
  scanf("%d", &y);
      .
      .
      .
}
```

Here, commas separate the two initialization statements. Each time **x** is incremented, the loop repeats, and **y**'s value is set by keyboard input. Both **x** and **y** must be at the correct value for the loop to terminate. It is necessary to initialize **y** to 0 so that its value is defined prior to the first evaluation of the conditional expression. If **y** were not defined it might, by chance or earlier program usage, contain a 10, thereby making the conditional test false and preventing the loop from executing.

Another example of using multiple loop control variables is found in the **reverse( )** function shown here. The purpose of **reverse( )** is to copy the contents of the first string argument back-to-front into the second string argument. For example, if it is called with "hello" in **s**, upon completion, **r** contains "olleh."

```
/* Copy s into r backwards. */
void reverse(char *s, char *r)
{
  int i, j;

  for(i=strlen(s)-1, j=0; i>=0; j++,i--) r[i] = s[j];
  r[j] = '\0'; /* append null terminator */
}
```

The conditional expression does not necessarily involve simply testing the loop control variable against some target value. In fact, the condition may be any relational or logical statement. This means that you can test for several possible terminating conditions. For example, this function could be used to log a user onto a remote system. The user is given three tries to enter the password. The loop terminates when either the three tries are used up or the correct password is entered.

```
void sign_on(void)
{
  char str[20];
  int x;

  for(x=0; x<3 && strcmp(str,"password"); ++x) {
    printf("enter password please:");
    gets(str);
  }
  if(x==3) hang_up();
}
```

Remember, **strcmp( )** is a standard library function that compares two strings and returns 0 if they match.

Another interesting variation of the **for** loop is created by remembering that each of the three sections of the **for** may consist of any valid C expression. They need not actually have anything to do with what the sections are usually used for. With this in mind, consider the following example:

```
#include <stdio.h>

int readnum(void), prompt(void);
```

```
int sqrnum(int num);

int main(void)
{
  int t;

  for(prompt(); t=readnum(); prompt()) sqrnum(t);
  return 0;
}

int prompt(void)
{
  printf(": ");

  return 0;
}

int readnum(void)
{
  int t;

  scanf("%d", &t);
  return t;
}

int sqrnum(int num)
{
  printf("%d\n", num*num);
  return 0;
}
```

If you look closely at the **for** loop in **main( )**, you will see that each part of the **for** comprises function calls that prompt the user and read a number entered from the keyboard. If the number entered is 0, the loop terminates because the conditional expression is false; otherwise, the number is squared. Thus, in this **for** loop the initialization and increment portions are used in a nontraditional but completely valid sense.

Another interesting trait of the **for** loop is that pieces of the loop definition need not be there. In fact, there need not be an expression present for any of the sections; they are optional. For example, this loop runs until 123 is entered:

```
for(x=0; x!=123; ) scanf("%d", &x);
```

Notice that the increment portion of the **for** definition is blank. This means that each time the loop repeats, **x** is tested to see if it equals 123, but no further action takes place. If, however, you type 123 at the keyboard, the loop condition becomes false and the loop terminates.

It is not uncommon to see the initialization occur outside the **for** statement. This most frequently happens when the initial condition of the loop control variable must be computed by some complex means. For example:

```
gets(s);  /* read a string into s */
if(*s) x = strlen(s); /* get the string's length */


for( ;x<10; ) {
  printf("%d", x);
  ++x;
}
```

Here, the initialization section has been left blank and **x** is initialized before the loop is entered.

The Infinite Loop

One of the most interesting uses of the **for** loop is the creation of the infinite loop. Since none of the three expressions that form the **for** loop are required, it is possible to make an endless loop by leaving the conditional expression empty. For example:

```
for(;;) printf(" this loop will run forever.\n");
```

Although you may have an initialization and increment expression, it is more common among C programmers to use the **for(;;)** with no expressions to signify an infinite loop.

Actually, the **for(;;)** construct does not necessarily create an infinite loop because C's **break** statement, when encountered anywhere inside the body of a loop, causes immediate termination of the loop. (The **break** statement is discussed later in this chapter.) Program control then picks up at the code following the loop, as shown here:

```
for(;;) {
  ch = getchar();   /* get a character */
  if(ch=='A') break;  /* exit the loop */
}

printf("you typed an A");
```

This loop will run until **A** is typed at the keyboard.

for Loops with No Bodies

A statement, as defined by the C syntax, may be empty. This means that the body of the **for** (or any other loop) may also be empty. This fact can be used to improve the efficiency of certain algorithms as well as to create time delay loops.

One of the most common tasks to occur in programming is the removal of spaces from an input stream. For example, a database may allow a query such as "show all balances less than 400." The database needs to have each word of the query fed to it separately, without spaces. That is, the database input processor recognizes "show" but not " show" as a command. The following loop removes any leading spaces from the stream pointed to by **str**:

```
for( ; *str==' '; str++) ;
```

As you can see, there is no body to this loop—and no need for one either.

Time delay loops are often used in programs. The following shows how to create one using **for**:

```
for(t=0; t<SOME_VALUE; t++) ;
```

while

The second iteration statement available in C is the **while**. Its general form is

while(*condition*) *statement;*

where *statement* is either an empty statement, a single statement, or a block of statements that is to be repeated. The *condition* may be any expression, with true being any nonzero value. The loop iterates while the condition is true. When the condition becomes false, program control passes to the line after the loop code.

The following example shows a keyboard input routine that simply loops until **A** is typed:

```
void wait_for_char(void)
{
  char ch;

  ch = '\0';  /* initialize ch */
  while(ch!='A')  ch = getchar();
}
```

First, **ch** is initialized to null. The **while** loop then begins by checking to see if **ch** is not equal to A. Because **ch** was initialized to null beforehand, the test is true and the loop begins. Each time a key is pressed on the keyboard, the test is tried again. Once an **A** is input, the condition becomes false because **ch** equals A, and the loop terminates.

As with the **for** loop, **while** loops check the test condition at the top of the loop, which means that the loop code may not execute at all. This eliminates having to perform a separate conditional test before the loop. A good illustration of this is the function **pad( )**, which adds spaces to the end of a string up to a predefined length. If the string is already at the desired length, no spaces will be added.

```
/* Add spaces to the end of a string. */
void pad(char *s, int length)
{
  int l;
  l = strlen(s);   /* find out how long it is */

  while(l<length) {
    s[l] = ' ';    /* insert a space */
    l++;
  }

  s[l] = '\0';  /* strings need to be
                   terminated in a null */
}
```

The two arguments to **pad( )** are **s**, a pointer to the string to lengthen, and **length**, the desired length of **s**. If the string **s** is already equal to or greater than **length**, the code inside the **while** loop never executes. If **s** is less than **length**, **pad( )** adds the required number of spaces to the string. The **strlen( )** function, which is part of the standard library, returns the length of the string.

Where several separate conditions may be needed to terminate a **while** loop, it is common to have only a single variable forming the conditional expression, with the value of this variable being set at various points throughout the loop. For example:

```
void func1(void)
{
  int working;

  working = 1;   /* i.e., true */

  while(working) {
    working=process1();
    if(working)
      working=process2();
    if(working)
      working=process3();
  }
}
```

Here, any of the three routines may return false and cause the loop to exit.

There need not be any statements at all in the body of the **while** loop. For example,

```
while((ch=getchar()) != 'A') ;
```

simply loops until **A** is typed at the keyboard. If you feel uncomfortable with the assignment inside the **while** conditional expression, remember that the equal sign is really just an operator that evaluates to the value of the right-hand operand.

do/while

Unlike the **for** and **while** loops that test the loop condition at the top of the loop, the **do/while** loop checks its condition at the bottom of the loop. This means that a **do/while** loop always executes at least once. The general form of the **do/while** loop is

do {
  statement sequence;
} while(*condition*);

Although the braces are not necessary when only one statement is present, they are usually used to improve readability and avoid confusion (to the reader, not the compiler) with the **while**.

This **do/while** reads numbers from the keyboard until one is less than or equal to 100.

```
do {
  scanf("%d", &num);
} while(num>100);
```

Perhaps the most common use of the **do/while** is in a menu selection routine. When a valid response is typed, it is returned as the value of the function. Invalid responses cause a reprompt. The following shows an improved version of the spelling checker menu that was developed earlier in this chapter:

```
void menu(void)
{
  char ch;

  printf("1. Check Spelling\n");
  printf("2. Correct Spelling Errors\n");
  printf("3. Display Spelling Errors\n");
  printf("      Enter your choice: ");

  do {
    ch = getche();  /* read the selection from the keyboard */
```

```
      switch(ch) {
        case '1':
          check_spelling();
          break;
        case '2':
          correct_errors();
          break;
        case '3':
          display_errors();
          break;
      }
    } while(ch!='1' && ch!='2' && ch!='3');
}
```

In the case of a menu function, you always want it to execute at least once. After the options have been displayed, the program loops until a valid option is selected.

break

The **break** statement has two uses. The first is to terminate a **case** in the **switch** statement, and is covered earlier in this chapter in the section on the **switch**. The second use is to force immediate termination of a loop, bypassing the normal loop conditional test. This use is examined here.

When the **break** statement is encountered inside a loop, the loop is immediately terminated and program control resumes at the next statement following the loop. For example:

```
#include <stdio.h>

int main(void)
{
  int t;

  for(t=0; t<100; t++) {
    printf("%d ", t);
    if(t==10) break;

  }
  return 0;
}
```

This prints the numbers 0 through 10 on the screen and then terminates because the **break** causes immediate exit from the loop, overriding the conditional test **t<100** built into the loop.

The **break** statement is commonly used in loops in which a special condition can cause immediate termination. For example, here a keypress can stop the execution of the **look_up( )** routine:

```
int look_up(char *name)
{
  char tname[40];
  int loc;

  loc = -1;
  do {
    loc = read_next_name(tname);
    if(kbhit()) break;
  } while(!strcmp(tname, name));
  return loc;
}
```

You might use a function like this to find a name in a database file. If the file is very long and you are tired of waiting, you could strike a key and return from the function early. The **kbhit( )** function returns 0 if no key has been hit; it returns non-0 otherwise.

A **break** will cause an exit from only the innermost loop. For example,

```
for(t=0; t<100; ++t) {
  count = 1;
  for(;;) {
    printf("%d ", count);
    count++;
    if(count==10) break;
  }
}
```

prints the numbers 1 through 10 on the screen 100 times. Each time the **break** is encountered, control is passed back to the outer **for** loop.

A **break** used in a **switch** statement affects only that **switch** and not any loop the **switch** happens to be in.

exit( )

The function **exit( )**, which is found in the standard library, causes immediate termination of the entire program. Because the **exit( )** function stops program execution and forces a return to the operating system, its use is somewhat specific as a program control device, yet a great many C programs rely on it. The **exit( )** function has this general form:

void exit(int *status*);

It uses the **stdlib.h** header file. The value of *status* is returned to the operating system.

exit( ) is traditionally called with an argument of 0 to indicate that termination is normal. Other arguments are used to indicate some sort of error that a higher level process will be able to access. You may also use the predefined macros **EXIT_SUCCESS** and **EXIT_FAILURE** as values for *status*.

A common use of **exit( )** occurs when a mandatory condition for the program's execution is not satisfied. For example, imagine a computer game that requires a special graphics adaptor for its operation. The **main( )** function of this game might look like this:

```
#include <stdlib.h>

int main(void)
{
  if(!special_adaptor()) exit(1);
  play();
  return 0;
}
```

where **special_adaptor( )** is a user-defined function that returns true if the needed adaptor is present. If the card is not in the system, **special_adaptor( )** returns false and the program terminates.

As another example, **exit( )** is used by this version of **menu( )** to quit the program and return to the operating system:

```
void menu(void)
{
  char ch;

  printf("1. Check Spelling\n");
  printf("2. Correct Spelling Errors\n");
  printf("3. Display Spelling Errors\n");
  printf("4. Quit\n");
  printf("      Enter your choice: ");

  do {
    ch = getchar();  /* read the selection from the keyboard */

    switch(ch) {
      case '1':
        check_spelling();
        break;
      case '2':
        correct_errors();
        break;
```

```
      case '3':
        display_errors();
        break;
      case '4':
        exit(0);   /* return to OS */
    }
  } while(ch!='1' && ch!='2' && ch!='3');
}
```

continue

The **continue** statement works somewhat like the **break** statement. But, instead of forcing termination, **continue** forces the next iteration of the loop to take place, skipping any code in between. For example, the following routine displays only positive numbers:

```
do {
  scanf("%d", &x);
  if(x<0) continue;
  printf("%d ", x);
} while(x!=100);
```

In **while** and **do/while** loops, a **continue** statement causes control to go directly to the conditional test and then continue the looping process. In the case of the **for**, first the increment part of the loop is performed, next the conditional test is executed, and finally the loop continues. The previous example could be changed to allow only 100 numbers to be printed, as shown here:

```
for(t=0; t<100; ++t) {
  scanf("%d", &x);
  if(x<0) continue;
  printf("%d ", x);
}
```

In the following example, **continue** is used to expedite the exit from a loop by forcing the conditional test to be performed sooner:

```
void code(void)
{
  char done, ch;

  done = 0;
  while(!done) {
    ch = getchar();
    if(ch=='.') {
```

```
        done = 1;
        continue;
      }
      putchar(ch+1);   /* shift the alphabet one position */
    }
}
```

You could use this function to code a message by shifting all characters one letter higher; for example, 'a' would become ' b'. The function terminates when a period is read, and no further output occurs because the conditional test, brought into effect by **continue**, finds **done** to be true and causes the loop to exit.

Labels and goto

Although **goto** fell out of favor some years ago, it has managed to polish its tarnished image a bit. This book will not judge its validity as a form of program control. It should be stated, however, that there are no programming situations that require its use; it is a convenience that, if used wisely, can be beneficial in certain programming situations. As such, **goto** is not used extensively in this book outside of this section. (In a language like C, which has a rich set of control structures and allows additional control using **break** and **continue**, there is little need for it.) The chief concern most programmers have about the **goto** is its tendency to confuse a program and render it nearly unreadable. However, there are times when the use of the **goto** actually clarifies program flow rather than confuses it.

The **goto** requires a label for operation. A *label* is a valid C identifier followed by a colon. The label must be in the same function as the **goto** that uses it. For example, a loop from 1 to 100 could be written using a **goto** and a label as shown here:

```
x = 1;

loop1:
  x++;
  if(x<100) goto loop1;
```

One good use for the **goto** is to exit from several layers of nesting. For example:

```
for(...) {
  for(...) {
    while(...) {
      if(...) goto stop;
        .
        .
        .
    }
  }
```

```
}
stop:
  printf("error in program\n");
```

Eliminating the **goto** would force a number of additional tests to be performed. A simple **break** statement would not work here because it would only exit from the innermost loop. If you substituted checks at each loop, the code would then look like this:

```
done = 0;
for(...) {
  for(...) {
    while(...) {
      if(...) {
        done = 1;
        break;
      }
      .
      .
      .
    }
    if(done) break;
  }
  if(done) break;
}
```

You should use the **goto** sparingly, if at all. But if the code would be much more difficult to read or if execution speed of the code is critical, by all means use the **goto**.

Chapter Four

Functions

Functions are the building blocks of C in which all program activity occurs. The general form of a function is

type-specifier function_name(*parameter list*)
{
   body of the function
}

The *type-specifier* specifies the type of value that the function returns using the **return** statement. It can be any valid type. If no type is specified, the function is assumed to return an integer result. The *parameter list* is a comma-separated list of variables that receive the values of the arguments when the function is called. A function may be without parameters, in which case the parameter list contains only the keyword **void**.

As just explained, C assumes that a function returns a value of type **int** if no other type specifier is present. This is currently the way C++ works, as well. However, this situation will probably change in the future because the current draft of the ANSI C++ standard has disallowed the integer default. If this feature stands (and it probably will), then each function will need to have an explicit type specifier. For this reason, it is recommended that new code explicitly declare the return type of all functions.

The return Statement

The **return** statement has two important uses. First, it causes an immediate exit from the function it is in. That is, it causes program execution to return to the calling code. Second, it can be used to return a value. Both of these uses are examined here.

Returning from a Function

There are two ways that a function terminates execution and returns to the caller. One way is when the last statement in the function has executed and, conceptually, the function's ending } is encountered. (Of course, the curly brace isn't actually present in the object code, but you can think of it in this way.) For example, this function simply prints a string backward on the screen:

```
void pr_reverse(char *s)
{
  register int t;

  for(t=strlen(s)-1; t > -1; t--) printf("%c", s[t]);
}
```

Once the string has been displayed, there is nothing left for the function to do, so it returns to the place it was when it was called.

However, not many functions use this default method of terminating their execution. Most functions rely on the **return** statement to stop execution, either because a value must be returned or to simplify a function's code and make it more efficient by allowing multiple exit points. It is important to remember that a function may have several **return** statements in it. For example, the function shown here returns either the index of the first occurrence of the substring pointed to by **s1** within the string pointed to by **s2** or –1 if no match is found:

```
int find_substr(char *s1, char *s2)
{
  register int t;
  char *p, *p2;

  for(t=0; s1[t]; t++) {
    p = &s1[t];
    p2 = s2;
    while(*p2 && *p2==*p) {
      p++;
      p2++;
    }
    if(!*p2) return t;
  }
  return -1;
}
```

Notice how the two **return** statements help simplify this function.

Return Values

All functions, except those of type **void**, return a value. This value is explicitly specified by the **return** statement. If a function is not specified as **void**, and if no return value is specified, then an unknown garbage value is returned. As long as a function is not declared as **void** it can be used as an operand in any valid C expression. Therefore, each of the following expressions is valid in C:

```
x = power(y);

if(max(x, y) > 100) printf("greater");

for(ch=getchar(); isdigit(ch); ) ... ;
```

However, a function cannot be the target of an assignment. A statement such as

```
swap(x, y) = 100;   /* incorrect statement */
```

is wrong. The compiler will flag it as an error.

Keep in mind that if a function is declared as **void** it cannot be used in any expression. For example, assume that **f( )** is declared as **void**. The following statements will not compile:

```
int t;

t = f();  /* no value to assign to t */

f()+f();  /* no value to add */
```

Although all functions not of type **void** have return values, when you write programs you generally use three types of functions. The first is simply computational. It is designed specifically to perform operations on its arguments and return a value based on that operation—it is essentially a "pure" function. Examples of this sort of function are the standard library functions **sqr( )** and **sin( )**.

The second type of function manipulates information and returns a value that simply indicates the success or failure of that manipulation. An example is **fwrite( )**, which is used to write information to a disk file. If the write operation is successful, **fwrite( )** returns the number of items successfully written. If an error occurs, the number returned is not equal to the number of items it was requested to write.

The last type of function has no explicit return value. In essence, the function is strictly procedural and produces no value. An example is **srand( )**, which is used to initialize the random-number-generating function **rand( )**. Sometimes, functions that don't produce an interesting result often return something anyway. For example,

printf( ) returns the number of characters written. It would be very unusual to find a program that actually checked this. Therefore, although all functions except those of type **void** return values, you don't necessarily have to use them for anything. A very common question concerning function return values is, "Don't I have to assign this value to some variable since a value is being returned?" The answer is "No." If there is no assignment specified, then the return value is simply discarded. Consider the following program, which uses **mul( )**:

```
#include <stdio.h>

int mul(int a, int b);


int main(void)
{
  int x, y, z;

  x = 10;    y = 20;
  z = mul(x, y);               /* 1 */
  printf("%d", mul(x, y));     /* 2 */
  mul(x, y);                   /* 3 */

  return 0;
}

int mul(int a, int b)
{
  return a*b;
}
```

Line 1 assigns the return value of **mul( )** to **z**. In line 2, the return value is not actually assigned, but it is used by the **printf( )** function. Finally, in line 3, the return value is lost because it is neither assigned to another variable nor used as part of an expression.

Returning Values from main( )

When you use a **return** statement in **main( )**, your program returns a termination code to the calling process (usually to the operating system). The returned value must be an integer. For many operating systems, including DOS, Windows, and OS/2, a return value of 0 indicates that the program terminated normally. All other values indicate that some error occurred.

All the programs in this book return values from **main( )**, although technically this is optional. If you don't specify a **return** value, then an unknown value is returned to the operating system. For this reason, it is a good idea to use an explicit **return** statement.

Scope Rules of Functions

The *scope rules* of a language are the rules that govern whether a piece of code knows about, or has access to, another piece of code or data.

Each function in C is a discrete block of code. A function's code is private to that function and cannot be accessed by any statement in any other function except through a call to that function. (It is not possible, for instance, to use the **goto** to jump into the middle of another function.) The code that makes up the body of a function is hidden from the rest of the program and, unless it uses global variables or data, it can neither affect nor be affected by other parts of the program. In other words, the code and data that are defined within one function cannot interact with the code and data defined in another function because the two functions have a different scope.

Variables that are defined within a function are called *local variables.* A local variable comes into existence when the function is entered and is destroyed upon exit. Therefore, local variables cannot hold their value between function calls. The only exception to this rule is when the variable is declared with the **static** storage-class specifier. This causes the compiler to treat it like a global variable for storage purposes, but still limit its scope to within the function. (Chapter 2 contains a complete discussion of global and local variables.)

All functions in C are at the same scope level. That is, it is not possible to define a function within a function.

Function Arguments

If a function is to use arguments, it must declare variables that accept the values of the arguments. These variables are called the *formal parameters* of the function. They behave like other local variables inside the function and are created upon entry into the function and destroyed upon exit. As shown in the following example, the parameter declaration occurs after the function name and before the function's opening brace:

```
/* return 1 if c is part of string s; 0 otherwise */
int is_in(char *s, char c)
{
  while(*s)
    if(*s==c) return 1;
    else s++;

  return 0;
}
```

The function **is_in( )** has two parameters: **s** and **c**. This function returns 1 if the character **c** is part of the string **s**, and 0 otherwise.

As with local variables, you can make assignments to a function's formal parameters or use them in any allowable C expression. Even though these variables perform the special task of receiving the value of the arguments passed to the function, they can be used like any other local variable.

Call by Value, Call by Reference

In general, subroutines can be passed arguments in one of two ways. The first is *call by value.* This method copies the value of an argument into the formal parameter of the subroutine. Changes made to the parameters of the subroutine have no effect on the variables used to call it.

Call by reference is the second way a subroutine can have arguments passed to it. In this method, the *address* of an argument is copied into the parameter. Inside the subroutine, the address is used to access the actual argument used in the call. This means that changes made to the parameter affect the variable used to call the routine.

With a few exceptions, C uses call by value to pass arguments. This means that you generally cannot alter the variables used to call the function. Consider the following function:

```
#include <stdio.h>

int sqr(int x);

int main(void)
{
  int t=10;

  printf("%d %d", sqr(t), t);
  return 0;
}

int sqr(int x)
{
  x = x*x;
  return x;
}
```

In this example, the value of the argument to **sqr( )**, 10, is copied into the parameter **x**. When the assignment **x=x*x** takes place, the only thing modified is the local variable **x**. The variable **t**, used to call **sqr( )**, still has the value 10. Hence, the output will be "100 10".

Remember that only a copy of the value of the argument is passed to that function. What occurs inside the function has no effect on the variable used in the call.

Creating a Call by Reference

Even though C's parameter-passing convention is call by value, it is possible to cause a call by reference by passing a pointer to the argument. Since this passes the address of the argument to the function, it is then possible to change the value of the argument outside the function.

Pointers are passed to functions just like any other value. Of course, it is necessary to declare the parameters as pointer types. For example, the function **swap( )**, which exchanges the value of its two integer arguments, is shown here:

```
void swap(int *x, int *y)
{
  int temp;

  temp = *x;  /* save the value at address x */
  *x = *y;    /* put y into x */
  *y = temp;  /* put x into y */
}
```

The * operator is used to access the variable pointed to by its operand. (A complete discussion of the * is found in Chapter 2. Also, Chapter 6 deals exclusively with pointers.) Hence, the contents of the variables used to call the function are swapped.

It is important to remember that **swap( )** (or any other function that uses pointer parameters) must be called with the *addresses of the arguments.* The following program shows the correct way to call **swap( )**:

```
#include <stdio.h>

void swap(int *x, int *y);

int main(void)
{
  int x, y;

  x = 10;
  y = 20;
  swap(&x, &y);
  printf("%d %d", x, y);

  return 0;
}
```

In this example, the variable **x** is assigned the value 10, and **y** is assigned the value 20. Then **swap( )** is called with the addresses of **x** and **y**. The unary operator **&** is used to produce the addresses of the variables. Therefore, the addresses of **x** and **y**, not their values, are passed to the function **swap( )**.

Calling Functions with Arrays

Arrays will be covered in detail in Chapter 5. However, the operation of passing arrays as arguments to functions is dealt with here because it is an exception to the standard call by value parameter-passing convention.

When an array is used as an argument to a function, only the address of the array is passed, not a copy of the entire array. When you call a function with an array name, a pointer to the first element in the array is passed to the function. (Remember that in C an array name without any index is a pointer to the first element in the array.) The parameter declaration must be of a compatible pointer type. There are three ways to declare a parameter that is to receive an array pointer. First, it can be declared as an array, as shown here:

```
#include <stdio.h>

void display(int num[10]);

int main(void)  /* print some numbers */
{
  int t[10], i;

  for(i=0; i<10; ++i) t[i]=i;
  display(t);
  return 0;
}

void display(int num[10])
{
  int i;

  for(i=0; i<10; i++) printf("%d ", num[i]);
}
```

Even though the parameter **num** is declared to be an integer array of 10 elements, C automatically converts it to an integer pointer because no parameter can actually receive an entire array. Only a pointer to an array is passed, so a pointer parameter must be there to receive it.

A second way to declare an array parameter is to specify it as an unsized array, as shown here:

```
void display(int num[])
{
```

```
  int i;

  for(i=0; i<10; i++) printf("%d ", num[i]);
}
```

where **num** is declared to be an integer array of unknown size. Since C provides no array boundary checks, the actual size of the array is irrelevant to the parameter (but not to the program, of course). This method of declaration also actually defines **num** as an integer pointer.

The final way that **num** can be declared—and the most common form in professionally written C programs—is as a pointer, as shown here:

```
void display(int *num)
{
  int i;

  for(i=0; i<10; i++) printf("%d ", num[i]);
}
```

This is allowed because any pointer can be indexed using **[ ]** as if it were an array. (Actually, arrays and pointers are very closely linked.)

All three methods of declaring an array parameter yield the same result: a pointer.

On the other hand, an array *element* used as an argument is treated like any other simple variable. For example, the program just examined could have been written without passing the entire array, as shown here:

```
#include <stdio.h>

void display(int num);

int main(void) /* print some numbers */
{
  int t[10], i;

  for(i=0; i<10; ++i) t[i] = i;
  for(i=0; i<10; i++) display(t[i]);

  return 0;
}

void display(int num)
{
  printf("%d ", num);
}
```

As you can see, the parameter to **display( )** is of type **int**. It is not relevant that **display( )** is called by using an array element, because only that one value of the array is passed.

It is important to understand that when an array is used as a function argument, its address is passed to a function. This is an exception to C's call by value parameter-passing convention. This means that the code inside the function operates on and potentially alters the actual contents of the array used to call the function. For example, consider the function **print_upper( )**, which prints its string argument in uppercase:

```
#include <stdio.h>
#include <ctype.h>

void print_upper(char *string);

int main(void)   /* print string as uppercase */
{
  char s[80];

  gets(s);
  print_upper(s);

  return 0;
}

void print_upper(char *string)
{
  register int t;

  for(t=0; string[t]; ++t)  {
    string[t] = toupper(string[t]);
    printf("%c", string[t]);
  }
}
```

After the call to **print_upper( )**, the contents of array **s** in **main( )** are changed to uppercase. If this is not what you want to happen, you could write the program like this:

```
#include <stdio.h>
#include <ctype.h>

void print_upper(char *string);

int main(void)   /* print string as uppercase */
```

```
{
  char s[80];
  gets(s);
  print_upper(s);

  return 0;
}

void print_upper(char *string)
{
  register int t;

  for(t=0; string[t]; ++t)
    printf("%c", toupper(string[t]));
}
```

In this version, the contents of array **s** remain unchanged because its values are not altered.

A classic example of passing arrays to functions is found in the standard library function **gets( )**. Although the **gets( )** in Borland's library is more sophisticated and complex, the function shown in the following example will give you an idea of how it works. To avoid confusion with the standard function, this one is called **xgets( )**.

```
/* A  simplified version of the standard
   gets() library function. */

void xgets(char *s)
{
  register char ch;
  register int t;

  for(t=0; t<79; ) {

    ch = getche();
    switch(ch) {
      case '\r':
        s[t] = '\0'; /* null terminate the string */
        return;
      case '\b':
        if(t>0) t--;
        break;
      default:
        s[t] = ch;
        t++;
    }
```

```
    }
    s[79] = '\0';
}
```

The **xgets( )** function must be called with a character pointer. This, of course, can be the name of a character array, which by definition is a character pointer. Upon entry, **xgets( )** establishes a **for** loop from 0 to 79. This prevents larger strings from being entered at the keyboard. If more than 80 characters are typed, the function returns. Because C has no built-in bounds checking, you should make sure that any array used to call **xgets( )** can accept at least 80 characters. As you type characters on the keyboard, they are entered in the string. If you type a backspace, the counter **t** is reduced by 1. When you enter a carriage return, a null is placed at the end of the string, signaling its termination. Because the actual array used to call **xgets( )** is modified, upon return it will contain the characters typed.

Arguments to main( )

Borland C++ supports three arguments to **main( )**. The first two are the traditional arguments: **argc** and **argv**. These are also the only arguments to **main( )** defined by the ANSI C standard. They allow you to pass command-line arguments to your C program. A *command-line argument* is the information that follows the program's name on the command line of the operating system. For example, when you compile programs using Borland's command-line compiler, you type something like

bcc *program_name*

where *program_name* is the program you wish compiled. The name of the program is passed to the compiler as an argument.

The **argc** parameter holds the number of arguments on the command line and is an integer. It will always be at least 1 because the name of the program qualifies as the first argument. The **argv** parameter is a pointer to an array of character pointers. Each element in this array points to a command-line argument. All command-line arguments are strings; any numbers have to be converted by the program into the proper internal format. The following short program prints "Hello", then your name if you type it directly after the program name:

```
#include <stdio.h>

int main(int argc, char *argv[])
{
  if(argc!=2) {
    printf("You forgot to type your name\n");
    return 1;
  }
```

```
  printf("Hello %s", argv[1]);

  return 0;
}
```

If you title this program **name** and your name is Jon, to run the program you would type **name Jon**. The output from the program would be "Hello Jon". For example, if you were logged into drive A, you would see

```
A>name Jon
Hello Jon
A>
```

after running **name**.

Command-line arguments must be separated by a space or a tab. Commas, semicolons, and the like are not considered separators. For example,

```
run Spot run
```

is composed of three strings, while

```
Herb,Rick,Fred
```

is one string—commas are not legal separators.

If you want to pass a string that contains spaces or tabs as a single argument, you must enclose that string within double quotes. For example, this is a single argument:

```
"this is a test"
```

It is important that you declare **argv** properly. One common method is

```
char *argv[];
```

The empty brackets indicate that it is an array of undetermined length. You can now access the individual arguments by indexing **argv**. For example, **argv[0]** points to the first string, which is always the program's name; **argv[1]** points to the next string, and so on.

A short example using command-line arguments is the following program called **countdown**. It counts down from a value specified on the command line and beeps when it reaches 0. Notice that the first argument containing the number is converted into an integer using the standard function **atoi( )**. If the string "display" is present as the second command-line argument, the count will also be displayed on the screen.

```
/* Countdown program. */

#include <stdio.h>
#include <stdlib.h>
```

```
#include <string.h>

int main(int argc, char *argv[])
{
  int disp, count;

  if(argc<2) {
    printf("You must enter the length of the count\n");
    printf("on the command line. Try again.\n");
    return 1;
  }

  if(argc==3 && !strcmp(argv[2],"display")) disp = 1;
  else disp = 0;

  for(count=atoi(argv[1]); count; --count)
    if(disp) printf("%d ", count);


  printf("%c", '\a');  /* this will ring the bell on most computers */
  return 0;
}
```

Notice that if no arguments are specified, an error message is printed. It is common for a program that uses command-line arguments to issue instructions if an attempt has been made to run it without the proper information being present.

To access an individual character in one of the command strings, you add a second index to **argv**. For example, the following program displays all the arguments with which it was called, one character at a time.

```
#include <stdio.h>

int main(int argc, char *argv[])
{
  int t, i;

  for(t=0; t<argc; ++t) {
    i = 0;
    while(argv[t][i]) {
      printf("%c", argv[t][i]);
      ++i;
    }
    printf(" ");
  }
```

```
  return 0;
}
```

Remember that the first index accesses the string and the second index accesses that character of the string.

You generally use **argc** and **argv** to get initial commands into your program. In theory, you can have up to 32,767 arguments, but most operating systems do not allow more than a few. You normally use these arguments to indicate a file name or an option. Using command-line arguments gives your program a professional appearance and facilitates the program's use in batch files.

If you link the file WILDARGS.OBJ, provided with Borland C++, with your program, command-line arguments like *.EXE automatically expand into any matching file names. (Borland C++ automatically processes the wildcard file name characters and increases the value of **argc** appropriately.) For example, if you link the following program with WILDARGS.OBJ, it tells you how many files match the file name specified on the command line:

```
/* Link this program with WILDARGS.OBJ. */

#include <stdio.h>

int main(int argc, char *argv[])
{
  register int i;

  printf("%d files match specified name\n", argc-1);

  printf("They are: ");

  for(i=1; i<argc; i++)
    printf("%s ", argv[i]);

  return 0;
}
```

If you call this program **WA**, then executing it in the following manner tells you the number of files that have the .EXE extension, and lists their names:

```
C>WA *.EXE
```

In addition to **argc** and **argv**, Borland C++ also allows a third command-line argument called **env**. The **env** parameter tells your program to access the environmental information associated with the operating system. The **env** parameter must follow **argc** and **argv** and is declared like this:

```
char *env[]
```

As you can see, **env** is declared like **argv**. Like **argv**, it is a pointer to an array of strings. Each string is an environmental string defined by the operating system. The **env** parameter does not have a corresponding **argc**-like parameter that tells your program how many environmental strings there are. Instead, the last environmental string is null. The following program displays all the environmental strings currently defined by the operating system:

```
/* This program prints all the environmental
   strings.
*/

#include <stdio.h>

int main(int argc, char *argv[], char *env[])
{
  int t;

  for(t=0; env[t]; t++)
    printf("%s\n", env[t]);

  return 0;
}
```

Notice that even though **argc** and **argv** are not used by this program, they must be present in the parameter list. C does not actually know the names of the parameters. Instead, their usage is determined by the order in which the parameters are declared. In fact, you can call the parameters anything you like. Since **argc**, **argv**, and **env** are traditional names, it is best to use them so anyone reading your program will instantly know that they are arguments to **main( )**.

It is quite common for a program to need to find the value of one specific environmental string. For example, under DOS, Windows, etc., knowing the value of the PATH string allows your program to utilize the currently defined search paths. The following program shows how to find the string that defines the default search paths. It uses the standard library function **strstr( )**, which has this prototype:

char *strstr(const char *_str1_, const char *_str2_);

The **strstr( )** function searches the string pointed to by _str1_ for the first occurrence of the string pointed to by _str2_. If it is found, a pointer to the first occurrence is returned. If no match exists, then **strstr( )** returns null.

```
/* This program searches the environmental
   strings for the one that contains the
   current PATH.
*/
#include <stdio.h>
#include <string.h>


int main(int argc, char *argv[], char *env[])
{
  int t;

  for(t=0; env[t]; t++) {
    if(strstr(env[t], "PATH"))
      printf("%s\n", env[t]);
  }

  return 0;
}
```

Functions Returning Noninteger Values

When the return type of a function is not explicitly declared, it automatically defaults to **int**. (Although this may change in the future.) For many functions, this default is acceptable. However, when a function returns a different data type you must use this two-step process:

1. The function must be given an explicit return type specifier.
2. The compiler must be told the return type of the function before the first call is made to it.

Only in this way can the compiler generate correct code for functions returning noninteger values.

Functions can be declared to return any valid C data type. The method of declaration is similar to that of variables: The type specifier precedes the function name. The type specifier tells the compiler what type of data the function is to return. This information is critical if the program is going to run correctly, because different data types have different sizes and internal representations.

Before you can use a function that returns a noninteger type, its type must be made known to the rest of the program. Unless directed to the contrary, C assumes that a function is going to return an integer value. If the function actually returns some other type, then the compiler will have generated the wrong code for the return value.

In general, the way to inform the compiler about the return type of a function involves using a *forward reference.* A forward reference declares the return type of a function but does not actually define what the function does. The function definition occurs elsewhere in the program.

There are two ways to create a forward reference. The first is the old-style method used by pre-ANSI-standard versions of C and is now obsolete. The second is to use a function prototype (which is the method used in this book). Prototypes were added by the ANSI C standard. The old-style approach is still allowed by the ANSI C standard in order to provide compatibility with older code, but new uses of it are strongly discouraged.

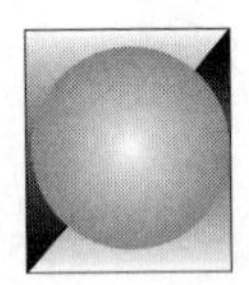

NOTE: C++ does not support the old-style function declaration method. Instead, C++ requires prototypes. The material presented in this section applies only to the C language.

Although outdated, this section briefly describes the old-style function declaration method because many older, existing programs use it. Second, many C programming books and articles published before 1989 use the old-style form. Thus, it is good to be familiar with it. Also, the modern prototype method is essentially an extension of the old-style approach.

The old-style method of informing C about the return type of a function simply declares the return type and name of the function near the top of the program. For example, to tell C that a function called **myfunc( )** returns a **double** value, you would put this declaration near the top of your program:

```
double myfunc();
```

Even if **myfunc( )** has parameters, in this old-style method none are shown within the parentheses. When the compiler reads this line, it knows that **myfunc( )** returns a **double** and generates the correct return code. For example, the following is a correct (although old-style) program:

```
/* This is an old-style program which will generate
   warning messages when compiled. */
#include <stdio.h>
#include <math.h>

double myfunc(); /* forward declaration of myfunc() */

int main(void)
{
  printf("%lf", myfunc(10.0));
  return 0;
}
```

```
double myfunc(double x)
{
  return sqrt(x) * 2.0; /* return sqr root of x * 2 */
}
```

As you can see, even though **myfunc( )** has one parameter, the old-style forward declaration says nothing about it.

While both Borland C++ and the ANSI C standard still allow the preceding function declaration method as a means of telling the compiler about the return type of a function, it should not be used for new code. The reason for this is that the function prototype, which was added by the ANSI committee, provides a much better alternative. And, more importantly, prototypes are *required* for C++ code.

Using Function Prototypes

The ANSI C standard expanded the concept of the forward function declaration. This expanded declaration is called a *function prototype.* Except for the example in the preceding section, every program in this book includes a function prototype for all functions used in the program.

A function prototype performs two special tasks. First, it identifies the return type of the function so that the compiler can generate the correct code for the return data. Second, it specifies the type and number of arguments used by the function. The prototype takes this general form:

type function_name(parameter list);

The prototype normally goes near the top of the program and must appear before any call is made to the function.

In addition to telling the compiler about the return type of the function, function prototypes enable C to provide strong type-checking somewhat similar to that provided by languages such as Pascal. The prototypes allow the compiler to find and report any illegal type conversions between the type of arguments used to call a function and the type definition of its parameters. They also allow the compiler to report when a function is called with too few or too many arguments.

When possible, C automatically converts the type of an argument into the type of the parameter that is receiving it. However, some type conversions are simply illegal. When a function is prototyped, any illegal type conversion will be found and an error message will be issued. As an example, the following program causes an error message to be issued because there is an attempt to call **func( )** with a pointer instead of the **float** required. (It is illegal to transform a pointer into a **float**.)

```
/* This program uses function prototypes to
   enforce strong type checking in the calls
   to func().
```

```
   The program will not compile because of the
   mismatch between the type of the arguments
   specified in the function's prototype and
   the type of arguments used to call the function.
*/

#include <stdio.h>

float func(int x, float y); /* prototype */

int main(void)
{
  int x, *y;

  x = 10;  y = &x;
  func(x, y);  /* type mismatch */
  return 0;
}

float func(int x, float y)
{
  printf("%f", y/(float)x);
  return y/(float) x;
}
```

Using a prototype also allows the compiler to report when the number of arguments used to call a function disagrees with the number of parameters defined by the function. For example, this program will not compile because **func( )** is called with the wrong number of arguments:

```
/*
   The program will not compile because of the
   mismatch between the number of parameters
   specified in the function's prototype and
   the number of arguments used to call the function.
*/

#include <stdio.h>

float func(int x, float y); /* prototype */

int main(void)
{
```

```
  func(2, 2.0, 4);  /* wrong number of args */
  return 0;
}

float func(int x, float y)
{
  printf("%f", y/(float)x);
  return y/(float) x;
}
```

Technically, when you prototype a function, you do not need to include the actual parameter names. For example, both of these are valid prototypes:

```
char func(char *, int);

char func(char *str, int count);
```

However, if you include each parameter name, the compiler uses the names to report any type mismatch errors.

Some functions, such as **printf( )**, can take a variable number of arguments. A variable number of arguments are specified in a prototype using three periods. For example, the prototype to **printf( )** is

int printf(const char **fmt*, . . .);

To create functions with a variable number of arguments, refer to the description of the standard library function **va_arg( )** in Part 2 of this book.

Aside from telling the compiler about a function's return data type, use of function prototypes helps you trap bugs before they occur by preventing a function from being called with invalid arguments. They also help verify that your program is working correctly by not allowing functions to be called with the wrong number of arguments. And, as mentioned, they are also required by C++.

Standard Library Function Prototypes

Any standard library functions used by your program should be prototyped. To accomplish this, you must include the appropriate *header file* for each library function. Header files use the .H extension and are provided along with Borland C++. The header files contain two main elements: any definitions used by the functions and the prototypes for the functions. For example, **stdio.h** is included in almost all programs in this part of the book because it contains the prototype for **printf( )**. If you include the appropriate header file for each library function used in a program, it is possible for the compiler to catch any accidental errors you may make when using them. (Also, when you write a C++ program, all functions must be prototyped.) All of the programs in this book include the appropriate header files. The header files for the functions defined by Borland C++ are discussed in Part 2, when Borland's library functions are described.

Prototyping Functions That Have No Parameters

As you know, a function prototype tells the compiler about the type of data returned by a function as well as the type and number of parameters used by the function. However, since prototypes were not part of the original version of C, a special case is created when you need to prototype a function that takes no parameters. The reason for this is that the ANSI C standard stipulates that when no parameters are included in a function's prototype, no information whatsoever is specified about the type or number of the function's parameters. This is necessary to ensure that older C programs can be compiled by modern compilers, such as Borland C++. When you specifically want to tell the compiler that a function actually takes no parameters, you must use the keyword **void** inside the parameter list. For example, examine this short program:

```
#include <stdio.h>

void display10(void);

int main(void)
{
  display10();

  return 0;
}

void display10(void)
{
  int i;

  for(i=0; i<10; i++)
    printf("%d ", i);
}
```

In this program, the prototype to **display10( )** explicitly tells the compiler that **display10( )** takes no arguments. Since the parameter list of the function must agree with its prototype, the **void** must also be included in the declaration of **display10( )** as well as in its definition later in the program. Assuming the foregoing prototype, Borland C++ will not compile a call to **display10( )** that looks like the following example:

```
display10(100);
```

However, if the **void** had been left out of the parameter list specification, no error would have been reported and the argument would simply have been ignored.

*NOTE: In C++, **f( )** and **f(void)** are equivalent and the preceding discussion does not apply.*

Returning Pointers

Although functions that return pointers are handled in exactly the same way as any other type of function, a few important concepts need to be discussed.

Pointers to variables are *neither* integers *nor* unsigned integers. They are the memory addresses of a certain type of data. The reason for this distinction lies in the fact that when pointer arithmetic is performed, it is relative to the base type—that is, if an integer pointer is incremented it will contain a value that is 2 greater than its previous value (assuming 2-byte integers). More generally, each time a pointer is incremented, it points to the next data item of its type. Since each data type may be of a different length, the compiler must know what type of data the pointer is pointing to in order to make it point to the next data item. (The subject of pointer arithmetic is covered in detail in Chapter 6.)

For example, the following is a function that returns a pointer into a string at the place where a character match was found:

```
char *match(char c, char *s)
{
  register int count;

  count = 0;
  while(c!=s[count] && s[count]) count++;


  return(&s[count]);
}
```

The function **match( )** attempts to return a pointer to the place in a string where the first match with **c** is found. If no match is found, a pointer to the null terminator is returned.

A short program that uses **match( )** is shown here:

```
#include <stdio.h>
#include <conio.h>

char *match(char c, char *s);
```

```
int main(void)
{
  char s[80], *p, ch;

  gets(s);
  ch = getche();
  p = match(ch, s);
  if(p)   /* there is a match */
    printf("%s ", p);
  else
    printf("No match found.");

  return 0;
}
```

This program reads a string and then a character. If the character is in the string, it prints the string from the point of the match. Otherwise, it prints "No match found".

Classic Versus Modern Parameter Declarations

Early versions of C used a different method to declare function parameters, which sometimes is called the *classic* form. The declaration approach used in this book is called the *modern* form. Borland C++ adheres closely to the ANSI standard for C, which supports both forms but *strongly recommends* the modern form. (In fact, it is rare to see new C code that is written using the classic function declarations.) Also, C++ supports only the modern form. However, it is important for you to know the classic form because many older C programs use it.

The classic function parameter declaration consists of two parts: a parameter list, which goes inside the parentheses that follow the function name; and the actual parameter declarations, which go between the closing parentheses and the function's opening curly brace. The general form of the classic parameter definition is shown here:

type function_name(parm1, parm2,. . .parmN)
type parm1;
type parm2;
.
.
.
type parmN;
{
function code
}

For example, this modern declaration:

```
char *f(char *str1, int count, int index)
{
   .
   .
   .
 }
```

will look like this in its classic form:

```
char *f(str1, count, index)
char *str1;
int count, index;
{
   .
   .
   .
 }
```

Notice that in the classic form, more than one parameter can be listed after the type name.

Remember that even though the classic declaration form is outdated, Borland C++ can still correctly compile C programs that use this approach. Therefore, you need not worry if you want to compile a C program that uses classic function declarations. But, C++ programs must use the modern form.

Recursion

In C, functions can call themselves. A function is *recursive* if a statement in the body of the function calls the function that contains it. Sometimes called *circular definition,* recursion is the process of defining something in terms of itself.

A simple example is the function **factr( )**, which computes the factorial of an integer. The factorial of a number *N* is the product of all the whole numbers from 1 to *N*. For example, 3 factorial is $1 \times 2 \times 3$, or 6. Both **factr( )** and its iterative equivalent are shown here:

```
/* Compute the factorial of a number. */
int factr(int n)  /* recursive */
{
  int answer;

  if(n==1) return(1);
  answer = factr(n-1)*n;
```

```
  return(answer);
}

/* Compute the factorial of a number. */
int fact(int n)    /* non-recursive */
{
  int t, answer;

  answer = 1;
  for(t=1; t<=n; t++)
    answer=answer*(t);
  return(answer);
}
```

The operation of the nonrecursive version of **fact( )** should be clear. It uses a loop starting at 1 and ending at the number, and progressively multiplies each number by the moving product.

The operation of the recursive **factr( )** is a little more complex. When **factr( )** is called with an argument of 1, the function returns 1; otherwise, it returns the product of **factr(n–1) * n**. To evaluate this expression, **factr( )** is called with **n–1**. This happens until **n** equals 1 and the calls to the function begin returning.

Computing the factorial of 2, the first call to **factr( )** causes a second call to be made with the argument of **1**. This call returns 1, which is then multiplied by 2 (the original **n** value). The answer is then 2. You might find it interesting to insert **printf( )** statements into **factr( )** to show the level and the intermediate answers of each call.

When a function calls itself, new local variables and parameters are allocated storage on the stack, and the function code is executed with these new variables from its beginning. A recursive call does not make a new copy of the function. Only the arguments are new. As each recursive call returns, the old local variables and parameters are removed from the stack and execution resumes at the point of the function call inside the function. Recursive functions could be said to "telescope" out and back.

The recursive versions of most routines may execute a bit more slowly than the iterative equivalent because of the added function calls; but this is not significant in most cases. Many recursive calls to a function could cause a stack overrun. Because storage for function parameters and local variables is on the stack and each new call creates a new copy of these variables, the stack space could become exhausted. If this happens, a *stack overflow* occurs.

The main advantage to recursive functions is that they can be used to create versions of several algorithms that are clearer and simpler than their iterative equivalents. For example, the QuickSort sorting algorithm is quite difficult to implement in an iterative way. Some problems, especially AI-related ones, also seem to lend themselves to recursive solutions. Finally, some people seem to think recursively more easily than iteratively.

When writing recursive functions, you must have an **if** statement somewhere to force the function to return without the recursive call being executed. If you don't do this, once you call the function, it never returns. This is a very common error when writing recursive functions. Use **printf( )** and **getchar( )** liberally during development so that you can watch what is going on and abort execution if you see that you have made a mistake.

Pointers to Functions

A particularly confusing yet powerful feature of C is the *function pointer*. Even though a function is not a variable, it still has a physical location in memory that can be assigned to a pointer. The address assigned to the pointer is the entry point of the function. This pointer can then be used in place of the function's name. It also allows functions to be passed as arguments to other functions.

To understand how function pointers work, you must understand a little about how a function is compiled and called in C. As each function is compiled, source code is transformed into object code and an entry point is established. When a call is made to a function while your program is running, a machine language "call" is made to this entry point. Therefore, a pointer to a function can also be used to call the function.

The address of a function is obtained by using the function's name without any parentheses or arguments. (This is similar to the way an array's address is obtained by using only the array name without indexes.) For example, consider the following program, paying very close attention to the declarations:

```
#include <stdio.h>
#include <string.h>

void check(char *a, char *b, int (*cmp) (const char *, const char *));

int main(void)
{
  char s1[80], s2[80];
  int  (*p)(const char*, const char*);

  p = strcmp;  /* get address of strcmp() */

  gets(s1);
  gets(s2);

  check(s1, s2, p);
  return 0;
}
```

```
void check(char *a, char *b, int (*cmp) (const char *, const char *))
{
  printf("Testing for equality.\n");
  if(!(*cmp) (a, b)) printf("Equal");
  else printf("Not equal");
}
```

When the function **check( )** is called, two character pointers and one function pointer are passed as parameters. Inside the function **check( )**, the arguments are declared as character pointers and a function pointer. Notice how the function pointer is declared. You should use the same method when declaring other function pointers, except that the return type or parameters of the function can be different. The parentheses around the ***cmp** are necessary for the compiler to interpret this statement correctly.

When you declare a function pointer, you can still provide a prototype to it, as the preceding program illustrates. However, in many cases you won't know the names of the actual parameters, so you can leave them blank or you can use any names you like.

Once inside **check( )**, you can see how the **strcmp( )** function is called.
The statement

```
if(!(*cmp) (a, b)) printf("Equal");
```

performs the call to the function, in this case **strcmp( )**, which is pointed to by **cmp** with the arguments **a** and **b**. This statement also represents the general form of using a function pointer to call the function it points to. The parentheses are necessary around the ***cmp** because of C's precedence rules.

Actually, you can also just use **cmp** directly, if you like, as shown here:

```
if(!cmp(a, b)) printf("Equal");
```

This version also calls the function pointed to by **cmp**, but it uses the normal function syntax. However, using the **(*cmp)** form tips off anyone reading your code that a function pointer is being used to indirectly call a function, instead of calling a function named **cmp**.

It is possible to call **check( )** using **strcmp** directly, as shown here:

```
check(s1, s2, strcmp);
```

This statement would eliminate the need for an additional pointer variable.

You may be asking yourself why anyone would want to write a program this way. In this example, nothing is gained and significant confusion is introduced. However, there are times when it is advantageous to pass arbitrary functions to procedures or to keep an array of functions. The following helps illustrate a use of function pointers. When an interpreter is written, it is common for it to perform function calls to various support routines, such as the sine, cosine, and tangent functions. Instead of having a large **switch** statement listing all of these functions, you can use an array of function pointers, with the proper function selected by its index. You can get the flavor of this type of use by studying the expanded version of the previous example. In this program, **check( )** can be made to check for either alphabetical equality or numeric equality by simply calling it with a different comparison function:

```
#include <stdio.h>
#include <ctype.h>
#include <string.h>
#include <stdlib.h>

void check(char *a, char *b, int (*cmp) (const char *, const char *));

int numcmp(const char *a, const char *b);

int main(void)
{
  char s1[80], s2[80];
  gets(s1);
  gets(s2);

  if(isalpha(*s1))
     check(s1, s2, strcmp);
  else
     check(s1, s2, numcmp);

   return 0;
}

void check(char *a, char *b, int (*cmp) (const char *, const char *))
{
  printf("Testing for equality.\n");
  if(!(*cmp) (a, b)) printf("Equal");
  else printf("Not equal");
}

int numcmp(const char *a, const char *b)
{
  if(atoi(a)==atoi(b)) return 0;
  else return 1;
}
```

Implementation Issues

When you create C functions, you should remember a few important things that affect their efficiency and usability. These issues are the subject of this section.

Parameters and General-Purpose Functions

A general-purpose function is one that is used in a variety of situations, perhaps by many different programmers. Typically, you should not base general-purpose functions on global data. All the information a function needs should be passed to it by its parameters. In the few cases in which this is not possible, you should use **static** variables.

Besides making your functions general-purpose, parameters keep your code readable and less susceptible to bugs caused by side effects.

Efficiency

Functions are the building blocks of C and crucial to the creation of all but the most trivial programs. Nothing said in this section should be construed otherwise. In certain specialized applications, however, you may need to eliminate a function and replace it with *inline code.* Inline code is the equivalent of a function's statements used without a call to that function. Inline code is used instead of function calls only when execution time is critical.

There are two reasons inline code is faster than a function call. First, a "call" instruction takes time to execute. Second, arguments to be passed have to be placed on the stack, which also takes time. For almost all applications, this very slight increase in execution time is of no significance. But if it is, remember that each function call uses time that would be saved if the code in the function were placed inline. For example, below are two versions of a program that prints the square of the numbers from 1 to 10. The inline version runs faster than the other because the function call takes time.

Inline

```
#include <stdio.h>


int main(void)
{
  int x;


  for(x=1; x<11; ++x)
  printf("%d", x*x);
  return 0;
}
```

Function Call

```
#include <stdio.h>
int sqr(int a);

int main(void)
{
  int x

  for(x=1; x<11; ++x)
  printf("%d", sqr(x));
  return 0;
}
int sqr(int a)
{
  return a*a;
}
```

As you create programs, you must always weigh the cost of functions in terms of execution time against the benefits of increased readability and modifiability.

***NOTE:** In C++, the concept of inline functions is expanded and formalized. In fact, inline functions are an important component of the C++ language.*

Chapter Five

Arrays

An *array* is a collection of variables of the same type that are referenced by a common name. A specific element in an array is accessed by an index. In C, all arrays consist of contiguous memory locations. The lowest address corresponds to the first element; the highest address corresponds to the last element. Arrays may have from one to several dimensions.

Arrays and pointers are closely related; a discussion of one usually refers to the other. This chapter focuses on arrays. Chapter 6 looks closely at pointers. You should read both to understand fully these important C/C++ constructs.

Single-Dimension Arrays

The general form of a single-dimension array declaration is

type var_name[*size*];

In C, arrays must be explicitly declared so that the compiler can allocate space for them in memory. Here, *type* declares the base type of the array, which is the type of each element in the array. *size* defines how many elements the array will hold. For a single-dimension array, the total size of an array in bytes is computed as shown here:

total bytes = sizeof(*base type*) * *number of elements*

All arrays have 0 as the index of their first element. Therefore, when you write

```
char p[10];
```

you are declaring a character array that has 10 elements, p[0] through p[9]. For example, the following program loads an integer array with the numbers 0 through 9 and displays them:

```
#include <stdio.h>

int main(void)
{
  int x[10];  /* this reserves 10 integer elements */
  int t;

  for(t=0; t<10; ++t) x[t] = t;

  for(t=0; t<10; ++t) printf("%d ", x[t]);

  return 0;
}
```

In C, there is no bounds checking on arrays. You could overwrite either end of an array and write into some other variable's data, or even into a piece of the program's code. It is the programmer's job to provide bounds checking when it is needed. For example, make certain that the character arrays that accept character input are long enough to accept the longest input.

Single-dimension arrays are essentially lists of information of the same type. For example, Figure 5-1 shows how array **a** appears in memory if it is declared as shown here and starts at memory location 1000:

```
char a[7];
```

Generating a Pointer to an Array

You can generate a pointer to the first element of an array by simply specifying the array name, without any index. For example, given

```
int sample[10];
```

you can generate a pointer to the first element by using the name **sample**, by itself. Thus, this fragment assigns **p** the address of the first element of **sample**:

```
int *p;
int sample[10];

p = sample;
```

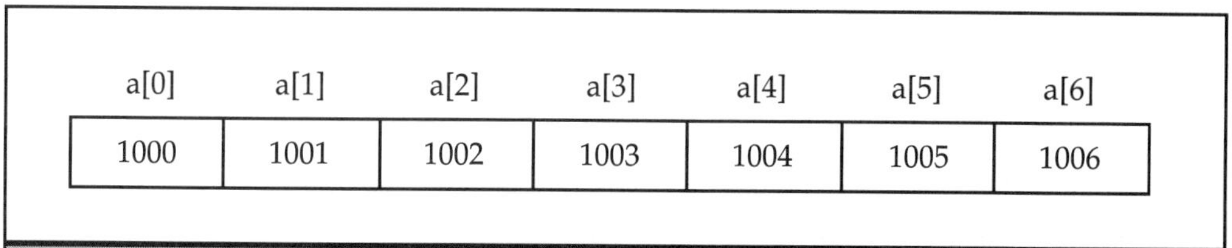

a[0]	a[1]	a[2]	a[3]	a[4]	a[5]	a[6]
1000	1001	1002	1003	1004	1005	1006

Figure 5-1. *A seven-element character array beginning at location 1000*

You can also obtain the address of the first element of an array using the **&** operator. For example, **sample** and **&sample[0]** both produce the same results. However, in professionally written C/C++ code, you will almost never see **&sample[0]**.

Passing Single-Dimension Arrays to Functions

When passing single-dimension arrays to functions, call the function with the array name without any index. This passes the address of the first element of the array to the function. In C, it is not possible to pass the entire array as an argument; a pointer is automatically passed instead. For example, the following fragment passes the address of **i** to **func1( )**:

```
int main(void)
{
  int i[10];

  func1(i);
  .
  .
  .
}
```

If a function is to receive a single-dimension array, you may declare the formal parameter as a pointer, as a sized array, or as an unsized array. For example, to receive **i** into a function called **func1( )**, you could declare **func1( )** as one of these:

```
void func1(int *a)  /* pointer */
{
  .
  .
```

```
    .
}
```

or

```
void func1(int a[10]) /* sized array */
{
    .
    .
    .
}
```

or

```
void func1(int a[]) /* unsized array */
{
    .
    .
    .
}
```

All three methods of declaration tell the compiler that an integer pointer is going to be received. In the first declaration, a pointer is used; in the second, the standard array declaration is employed. In the third declaration, a modified version of an array declaration simply specifies that an array of type **int** of some length is to be received. As far as the function is concerned, it doesn't matter what the length of the array actually is because C performs no bounds checking, anyway. In fact, as far as the compiler is concerned,

```
void func1(int a[32])
{
    .
    .
    .
}
```

also works because the compiler generates code that instructs **func1( )** to receive a pointer—it does not actually create a 32-element array.

Strings

By far the most common use of single-dimension arrays is for character strings. Although C defines no string type, it supports some of the most powerful string manipulation functions found in any language. In C, a string is defined to consist of a character array of any length that is terminated by a null. A null is specified as '\0' and is zero. For this reason it is necessary to declare character arrays to be one character longer than the largest string that they are to hold. For example, if you wished to declare an array **s** that holds a 10-character string, you would write

```
char s[11];
```

This makes room for the null at the end of the string.

Although C does not have a string data type, it still allows string constants. A string constant is a list of characters enclosed between double quotes. For example, here are two string constants:

```
"hello there" "this is a test"
```

It is not necessary to add the null to the end of string constants manually; the C compiler does this for you automatically.

C supports a wide range of string manipulation functions. Some of the most common are **strcpy( )**, **strcat( )**, **strlen( )**, and **strcmp( )**, whose prototypes are shown here:

> char *strcpy(char **s1*, const char **s2*);
> char *strcat(char **s1*, const char **s2*);
> size_t strlen(const char **s1*);
> int strcmp(const char **s1*, const char **s2*);

All of the functions use the **string.h** header file. The **strcpy( )** function copies the string pointed to by *s2* into the one pointed to by *s1*. It returns *s1*. The **strcat( )** function concatenates the string pointed to by *s2* to the one pointed to by *s1*. It also returns *s1*. The **strlen( )** function returns the length of the string pointed to by *s1*. (The **size_t** data type is defined (using **typedef**) as an unsigned integer.) The **strcmp( )** function compares *s1* and *s2*. It returns 0 if the two strings are equal, greater than 0 if the string pointed to by *s1* is greater than the one pointed to by *s2*, and less than zero if the string pointed to by *s1* is less than the string pointed to by *s2*. All comparisons are done lexicographically (according to dictionary order). (These and other string functions are discussed in detail in Part 2 of this book.)

The following program illustrates the use of these string functions:

```
#include <string.h>
#include <stdio.h>

int main(void)
{
  char s1[80], s2[80];

  gets(s1); gets(s2);

  printf("lengths: %d %d\n", strlen(s1), strlen(s2));
```

```
  if(!strcmp(s1, s2)) printf("The strings are equal\n");

  strcat(s1, s2);
  printf("%s\n", s1);

  return 0;
}
```

If this program is run and the strings "hello" and "hello" are entered, the output is

```
lengths: 5 5
The strings are equal
hellohello
```

It is important to remember that **strcmp( )** returns false if the strings are equal, so be sure to use the ! to reverse the condition, as shown in this example, if you are testing for equality.

Two-Dimensional Arrays

C allows multidimensional arrays. The simplest form of the multidimensional array is the two-dimensional array. A two-dimensional array is, in essence, an array of one-dimensional arrays. Two-dimensional arrays are declared using this general form:

type array_name[*2nd dimension size*][*1st dimension size*];

Hence, to declare a two-dimensional integer array **d** of size 10,20, you would write

```
int d[10][20];
```

Pay careful attention to the declaration. Unlike some computer languages, which use commas to separate the array dimensions, C places each dimension in its own set of brackets.

Similarly, to access point 3,5 of array **d**, use

```
d[3][5]
```

In the following example, a two-dimensional array is loaded with the numbers 1 through 12, which it then displays on the screen:

```
#include <stdio.h>

int main(void)
{
  int t,i, num[3][4];
```

```
  /* load numbers */
  for(t=0; t<3; ++t)
    for(i=0; i<4; ++i)
      num[t][i] = (t*4)+i+1;

  /* display numbers */
  for(t=0; t<3; ++t) {
    for(i=0; i<4; ++i)
      printf("%d ", num[t][i]);
    printf("\n");
  }

  return 0;
}
```

In this example, **num[0][0]** has the value 1; **num[0][1]**, the value 2, **num[0][2]** the value 3; and so on. The value of **num[2][3]** is 12.

Two-dimensional arrays are stored in a row-column matrix, where the first index indicates the row and the second indicates the column. This means that the rightmost index changes faster than the leftmost when accessing the elements in the array in the order they are actually stored in memory. See Figure 5-2 for a graphic representation of

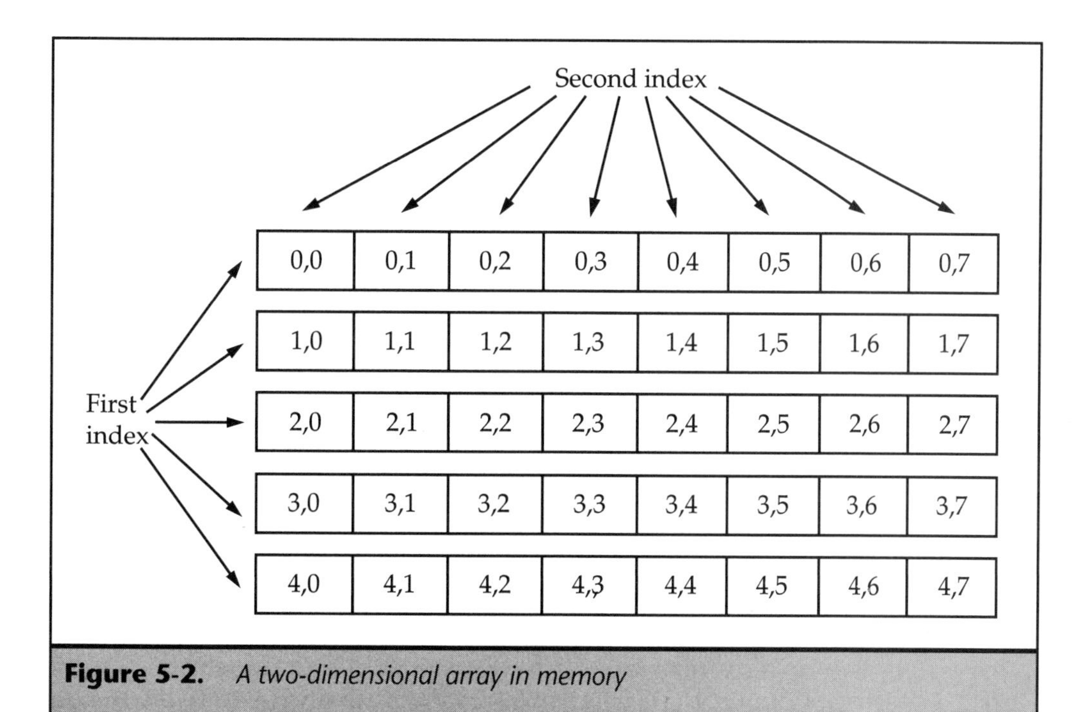

Figure 5-2. *A two-dimensional array in memory*

a two-dimensional array in memory. In essence, the leftmost index can be thought of as a "pointer" to the correct row.

The number of bytes of memory required by a two-dimensional array is computed using the following formula:

bytes = *2nd-dimension* * *1st-dimension* * sizeof (*base-type*)

Therefore, assuming 2-byte integers, an integer array with dimensions 10,5 would have 10×5×2 or 100 bytes allocated.

When a two-dimensional array is used as an argument to a function, a pointer is passed to the first element. However, a function receiving a two-dimensional array as a parameter must minimally define the length of the first dimension, because the compiler needs to know the length of each row if it is to index the array correctly. For example, a function that will receive a two-dimensional integer array with dimensions 5,10 would be declared like this:

```
void func1(int x[][10])
{
   .
   .
   .
}
```

You can specify the second dimension as well, but it is not necessary. The compiler needs to know the first dimension in order to work on statements such as

```
x[2][4]
```

inside the function. If the length of the rows is not known, it is impossible to know where the next row begins.

The short program shown here uses a two-dimensional array to store the numeric grade for each student in a teacher's classes. The program assumes that the teacher has three classes and a maximum of 30 students per class. Notice how the array **grade** is accessed by each of the functions.

```
#include <conio.h>
#include <ctype.h>
#include <stdio.h>
#include <stdlib.h>

#define CLASSES  3
#define GRADES  30
int grade[CLASSES][GRADES];
```

```
void disp_grades(int g[][GRADES]), enter_grades(void);
int get_grade(int num);

int main(void)  /* class grades program */
{
  char ch;

  for(;;) {
    do {
      printf("(E)nter grades\n");
      printf("(R)eport grades\n");
      printf("(Q)uit\n");
      ch = toupper(getche());
    } while(ch!='E' && ch!='R' && ch!='Q');

    switch(ch) {
      case 'E':
        enter_grades();
        break;
      case 'R':
        disp_grades(grade);
        break;
      case 'Q':
        return 0;
    }
  }
}

/* Enter each student's grade. */
void enter_grades(void)
{
  int t, i;

  for(t=0; t<CLASSES; t++) {
    printf("Class # %d:\n", t+1);
    for(i=0; i<GRADES; ++i)
      grade[t][i] = get_grade(i);
  }
}

/* Actually input the grade. */
int get_grade(int num)
{
```

```
  char s[80];

  printf("enter grade for student # %d:\n", num+1);
  gets(s);
  return(atoi(s));
}

/* Display the class grades. */
void disp_grades(int g[][GRADES])
{
  int t, i;

  for(t=0; t<CLASSES; ++t) {
    printf("Class # %d:\n", t+1);
    for(i=0; i<GRADES; ++i)
      printf("grade for student #%d is %d\n",i+1, g[t][i]);
  }
}
```

Arrays of Strings

It is not uncommon in programming to use an array of strings. For example, the input processor to a database may verify user commands against a string array of valid commands. A two-dimensional character array is used to create an array of strings with the size of the left index determining the number of strings and the size of the right index specifying the maximum length of each string. This code fragment declares an array of 30 strings, each having a maximum length of 79 characters:

```
char str_array[30][80];
```

To access an individual string is quite easy: You simply specify only the left index. For example, this statement calls **gets( )** with the third string in **str_array**:

```
gets(str_array[2]);
```

This is functionally equivalent to

```
gets(&str_array[2][0]);
```

but the previous form is much more common in professionally written C code.

To improve your understanding of how string arrays work, study the following short program that uses one as the basis for a very simple text editor.

```
#include <stdio.h>

#define MAX 100
```

```
#define LEN 255

char text[MAX][LEN];

/* A very simple text editor. */
int main(void)
{
  register int t, i, j;

  for(t=0; t<MAX; t++) {
    printf("%d: ", t);
    gets(text[t]);
    if(!*text[t]) break; /* quit on blank line */
  }

  /* this displays the text one character at a time */
  for(i=0; i<t; i++) {
    for(j=0; text[i][j]; j++) printf("%c", text[i][j]);
    printf("%c", '\n');
  }

  return 0;
}
```

This program inputs lines of text until a blank line is entered. Then it redisplays each line. For purposes of illustration, it displays the text one character at a time by indexing the first dimension. However, because each string in the array is null-terminated, the routine that displays the text could be simplified like this:

```
for(i=0; i<t; i++)
    printf("%s\n", text[i]);
```

Multidimensional Arrays

C allows arrays of greater than two dimensions. The general form of a multidimensional array declaration is

type name[*sizeN*]. . .[*size2*][*size1*];

Arrays of more than three dimensions are rarely used because of the large amount of memory required to hold them.

A point to remember about multidimensional arrays is that it takes the computer time to compute each index. This means that accessing an element in a multidimensional array will be slower than accessing an element in a single-dimensional array. For these and other reasons, when large multidimensional arrays are needed, often they are dynamically allocated a portion at a time using C's dynamic allocation functions.

When passing multidimensional arrays into functions, you must declare all but the leftmost dimension. For example, if you declare array **m** as

```
int m[4][3][6][5];
```

then a function, **func1( )**, receiving **m**, could look like

```
int func1(int d[][3][6][5])
{
   .
   .
   .
}
```

Of course, you are free to include the leftmost dimension if you like.

Indexing Pointers

Pointers and arrays are closely related in C. As explained earlier, an array name without an index is a pointer to the first element in the array. For example, given this array,

```
char p[10];
```

the following statements are identical:

```
p

&p[0]
```

Put another way,

```
p == &p[0]
```

evaluates true because the address of the first element of an array is the same as the address of the array.

Conversely, any pointer variable can be indexed as if it were declared to be an array of the base type of the pointer. For example:

```
int *p, i[10];

p = i;
```

```
p[5] = 100;   /* assign using index */

*(p+5) = 100; /* assign using pointer arithmetic */
```

Both assignment statements place the value 100 in the sixth element of **i**. The first statement indexes **p**; the second uses pointer arithmetic. Either way, the result is the same. (Pointers and pointer arithmetic are dealt with in detail in Chapter 6.)

The same holds true for arrays of two or more dimensions. For example, assuming that **a** is a 10-by-10 integer array, these two statements are equivalent:

```
a

&a[0][0]
```

Further, the 0,4 element of **a** may be referenced either by array-indexing, **a[0][4]**, or by the pointer, ***((int *) a+4)**. Similarly, element 1,2 is either **a[1][2]** or ***((int *) a+12)**. In general, for any two-dimensional array,

a[*j*][*k*] is equivalent to *((*type* *) *a*+(*j***rowlength*)+*k*))

where *type* is the base type of the array.

Pointers are sometimes used to access arrays because pointer arithmetic is often a faster process than array-indexing. The gain in speed using pointers is the greatest when an array is being accessed in purely sequential fashion. In this situation, the pointer may be incremented or decremented using C's highly efficient increment and decrement operators. On the other hand, if the array is to be accessed in random order, then the pointer approach may not be much better than array-indexing.

In a sense, a two-dimensional array is like an array of row pointers to arrays of rows. Therefore, using a separate pointer variable is one easy way to access elements within a row of a two-dimensional array. The following function illustrates this technique. It prints the contents of the specified row for the global integer array **num**:

```
int num[10][10];
  .
  .
  .
void pr_row(int j)
{
  int *p, t;

  p = num[j]; /* get address of first element in row j */

  for(t=0; t<10; ++t) printf("%d ", *(p+t));
}
```

This routine can be generalized by making the calling arguments be the row, the row length, and a pointer to the first array element, as shown here:

```
/* General */
void pr_row(int j, int row_dimension, int *p)
{
  int t;

  p = p + (j * row_dimension);
  for(t=0; t<row_dimension; ++t)
    printf("%d ", *(p+t));
}
```

Arrays of greater than two dimensions can be thought of in the same way. For example, a three-dimensional array can be reduced to a pointer to a two-dimensional array, which can be reduced to a pointer to a one-dimensional array. Generally, an *N*-dimensional array can be reduced to a pointer and an *N*-1 dimensional array. This new array can be reduced again using the same method. The process ends when a single-dimension array is produced.

Allocated Arrays

In many programming situations it is impossible to know how large an array will be needed. In addition, many types of programs need to use as much memory as is available, yet still run on machines having only minimal memory. A text editor or a database are examples of this. In these situations, it is not possible to use a predefined array because its dimensions are established at compile time and cannot be changed during execution. The solution is to create a *dynamic array.* A dynamic array uses memory from the region of free memory called the *heap* and is accessed by indexing a pointer to that memory. (Remember that any pointer can be indexed as if it were an array variable.)

In C, you can dynamically allocate and free memory by using the standard library routines **malloc( )**, which allocates memory and returns a **void** * pointer to the start of it, and **free( )**, which returns previously allocated memory to the heap for possible reuse. The prototypes for **malloc( )** and **free( )** are

void *malloc(size_t *num_bytes*);
void free(void **p*);

Both functions use the **stdlib.h** header file. Here, *num_bytes* is the number of bytes requested. As mentioned earlier, the type **size_t** is defined as an unsigned integer. If there is not enough free memory to fill the request, **malloc( )** returns a null. It is important that **free( )** be called only with a valid, previously allocated pointer;

otherwise, damage could be done to the organization of the heap and possibly cause a program crash.

The code fragment shown here allocates 1000 bytes of memory:

```
char *p;

p = malloc(1000); /* get 1000 bytes */
```

Here, **p** points to the first of 1000 bytes of free memory. Notice that no cast is used to convert the **void** pointer returned by **malloc( )** into the desired **char** pointer. Because **malloc( )** returns a **void** pointer, it can be assigned to any other type of pointer and is automatically converted into a pointer of the target type. However, it is important to understand that this automatic conversion *does not* occur in C++. In C++, an explicit type cast is needed when a **void** * pointer is assigned to another type of pointer. Thus, in C++, the preceding assignment must be written as follows:

```
p = (char *) malloc(1000); /* get 1000 bytes */
```

As a general rule, in C++ you must use a type cast when assigning (or otherwise converting) one type of pointer into another. This is one of the fundamental differences between C and C++. Since type casts are needed for C++ and do no harm in C, this book will use them when allocating memory using **malloc( )**.

This example shows the proper way to use a dynamically allocated array to read input from the keyboard using **gets( )**:

```
/* Print a string backwards using dynamic allocation. */

#include <stdlib.h>
#include <stdio.h>
#include <string.h>

int main(void)
{
  char *s;
  register int t;

  s = (char *) malloc(80);

  if(!s) {
    printf("Memory request failed.\n");
    return 1;
  }

  gets(s);
  for(t=strlen(s)-1; t>=0; t--) printf("%c", s[t]);
```

```
  free(s);

  return 0;
}
```

As the program shows, **s** is tested prior to its first use to ensure that a valid pointer is returned by **malloc( )**. This is absolutely necessary to prevent accidental use of a null pointer. (Using a null pointer will often cause a system crash.) Notice how the pointer **s** is indexed as an array to print the string backward.

It is possible to have multidimensional dynamic arrays, but you need to use a function to access them because there must be some way to define the size of all but the leftmost dimension. To do this, a pointer is passed to a function that has its parameter declared with the proper array bounds. To see how this works, study this short example, which builds a table of the numbers 1 through 10 raised to their first, second, third, and fourth powers:

```
#include <stdlib.h>
#include <stdio.h>

int pwr(int a, int b);
void table(int p[5][11]), show(int p[5][11]);

/* This program displays various numbers raised to
   integer powers. */
int main(void)
{
  int *p;

  p = (int *) malloc(55*sizeof(int));

  if(!p) {
    printf("Memory request failed.\n");
    return 1;
  }

  /* here, p is simply a pointer */
  table(p);
  show(p);

  return 0;
}

/* Build a table of numbers. */
void table(int p[5][11]) /* now the compiler thinks that
```

```
                              p is an array */
{
  register int i, j;

  for(j=1; j<11; j++)
    for(i=1; i<5; i++) p[i][j] = pwr(j, i);
}

/* Display the table. */
void show(int p[5][11])
{
  register int i, j;

  printf("%10s %10s %10s %10s\n","N","N^2","N^3","N^4");
  for(j=1; j<11; j++) {
    for(i=1; i<5; i++) printf("%10d ", p[i][j]);
    printf("\n");
  }
}

/* Raise a to the b power. */
int pwr(int a, int b)
{
  register int t=1;

  for(; b; b--) t = t*a;
  return t;
}
```

The output produced by this program is

```
         N        N^2        N^3        N^4
         1          1          1          1
         2          4          8         16
         3          9         27         81
         4         16         64        256
         5         25        125        625
         6         36        216       1296
         7         49        343       2401
         8         64        512       4096
         9         81        729       6561
        10        100       1000      10000
```

As this program illustrates, by defining a function parameter to the desired array dimensions you can "trick" C into handling multidimensional dynamic arrays.

Actually, as far as the compiler is concerned, you have a 5,11 integer array inside the functions **show( )** and **table( )**; the difference is that the storage for the array is allocated manually using the **malloc( )** statement rather than automatically by using the normal array declaration statement. Also, note the use of **sizeof** to compute the number of bytes needed for a 5,11 integer array. This guarantees that the program will work with both 16- and 32-bit integers.

Array Initialization

C allows the initialization of global and local arrays at the time of declaration. The general form of array initialization is similar to that of other variables, as shown here:

type-specifier array_name[*sizeN*]. . .[*size1*] = { *value-list* };

The *value-list* is a comma-separated list of constants that are type-compatible with *type-specifier.* The first constant is placed in the first position of the array, the second constant in the second position, and so on. The last entry in the list is not followed by a comma. Note that a semicolon follows the }. In the following example, a 10-element integer array is initialized with the numbers 1 through 10:

```
int i[10] = {1, 2, 3, 4, 5, 6, 7, 8, 9, 10};
```

This means that **i[0]** has the value 1 and **i[9]** has the value 10.

Character arrays that hold strings allow a shorthand initialization in the form

char *array_name*[*size*] = "*string*";

In this form of initialization, the null terminator is automatically appended to the string. For example, this code fragment initializes **str** to the phrase "hello".

```
char str[6] = "hello";
```

This is the same as writing

```
char str[6] = {'h', 'e', 'l', 'l', 'o', '\0'};
```

Notice that in this version you must explicitly include the null terminator. Because all strings in C end with a null, you must make sure that the array you declare is long enough to include it. This is why **str** is six characters long even though "hello" is only five characters.

Multidimensional arrays are initialized in the same fashion as single-dimensional ones. For example, the following initializes **sqrs** with the numbers 1 through 10 and their squares:

```
int sqrs[10][2] = {
  1, 1,
  2, 4,
  3, 9,
  4, 16,
  5, 25,
  6, 36,
  7, 49,
  8, 64,
  9, 81,
  10, 100
};
```

Here, **sqrs[0][0]** contains 1, **sqrs[0][1]** contains 1, **sqrs[1][0]** contains 2, **sqrs[1][1]** contains 4, and so forth.

When initializing a multidimensional array, you may add braces around the initializers for each dimension. This is called *subaggregate grouping*. For example, here is another way to write the preceding declaration:

```
int sqrs[10][2] = {
  {1, 1},
  {2, 4},
  {3, 9},
  {4, 16},
  {5, 25},
  {6, 36},
  {7, 49},
  {8, 64},
  {9, 81},
  {10, 100}
};
```

When using subaggregate grouping, if you don't supply enough initializers for a given group, the remaining members will be set to zero automatically.

Unsized-Array Initializations

Imagine that you are using an array initialization to build a table of error messages as shown here:

```
char e1[12] = "Read Error\n";
char e2[13] = "Write Error\n";
char e3[18] = "Cannot Open File\n";
```

As you might guess, it is very tedious to manually count the characters in each message to determine the correct array dimensions. It is possible to let C dimension the arrays automatically by using *unsized arrays.* If the size of the array is not specified in an array initialization statement, the C compiler automatically creates an array big enough to hold all the initializers present. Using this approach, the message table becomes

```
char e1[] = "Read Error\n";
char e2[] = "Write Error\n";
char e3[] = "Cannot Open File\n";
```

Given these initializations, this statement

```
printf("%s has length %d\n", e2, sizeof e2);
```

prints

```
write error
has length 13
```

Aside from being less tedious, the unsized-array initialization method allows any of the messages to be changed without fear of accidentally counting the number of characters incorrectly.

Unsized-array initializations are not restricted to only single-dimensional arrays. For multidimensional arrays, you must specify all but the leftmost dimensions in order to allow C to index the array properly. (This is similar to specifying array parameters.) In this way, you can build tables of varying lengths and the compiler automatically allocates enough storage for them. For example, the declaration of **sqrs** as an unsized array is shown here:

```
int sqrs[][2] = {
  1, 1,
  2, 4,
  3, 9,
  4, 16,
  5, 25,
  6, 36,
  7, 49,
  8, 64,
  9, 81,
  10, 100
};
```

The advantage to this declaration over the sized version is that the table may be lengthened or shortened without changing the array dimensions.

A Tic-Tac-Toe Example

This chapter concludes with a longer example that illustrates many of the ways arrays can be manipulated using C.

Two-dimensional arrays are commonly used to simulate board game matrices. Although it is beyond the scope of this book to present a chess or checkers program, a simple tic-tac-toe program can be developed.

The tic-tac-toe matrix is represented using a 3-by-3 character array. You are always "X" and the computer is "O." When you move, an "X" is placed in the specified position of the game matrix. When it is the computer's turn to move, it scans the matrix and puts its "O" in the first empty location of the matrix. (This makes for a fairly dull game—you might find it fun to spice it up a bit!) If the computer cannot find an empty location, it reports a draw game and exits. The game matrix is initialized to contain spaces at the start of the game. The tic-tac-toe program is shown here:

```
#include <stdio.h>
#include <stdlib.h>

/* A simple game of Tic-Tac-Toe. */

#define SPACE  ' '

char matrix[3][3] = {  /* the tic-tac-toe matrix */
  {SPACE, SPACE, SPACE},
  {SPACE, SPACE, SPACE},
  {SPACE, SPACE, SPACE}
};

void get_computer_move(void), get_player_move(void);
void disp_matrix(void);
char check(void);

int main()
{
  char done;

  printf("This is the game of Tic-Tac-Toe.\n");
  printf("You will be playing against the computer.\n");

  done = SPACE;
  do {
    disp_matrix();         /* display the game board */
```

```
    get_player_move();     /* get your move */
    done = check();          /* see if winner */
    if(done!=SPACE) break; /* winner!*/
    get_computer_move();   /* get computer's move */
    done=check();          /* see if winner */
  } while(done==SPACE);
  if(done=='X') printf("You won!\n");
  else printf("I won!!!!\n");
  disp_matrix(); /* show final positions */

  return 0;
}

/* Input the player's move. */
void get_player_move(void)
{
  int x, y;

  printf("Enter coordinates for your X.\n");
  printf("Row? ");
  scanf("%d", &x);
  printf("Column? ");
  scanf("%d", &y);
  x--; y--;
  if(x<0 || y<0 || x>2 || y>2 || matrix[x][y]!=SPACE) {
    printf("Invalid move, try again.\n");
    get_player_move();
  }
  else matrix[x][y]='X';
}

/* Get the computer's move */
void get_computer_move(void)
{
  register int t;
  char *p;

  p = (char *) matrix;
  for(t=0; *p!=SPACE && t<9; ++t) p++;
  if(t==9)  {
    printf("draw\n");
    exit(0); /* game over */
  }
  else *p = 'O';
```

```
}

/* Display the game board. */
void disp_matrix(void)
{
  int t;

  for(t=0; t<3; t++) {
    printf(" %c | %c | %c ", matrix[t][0],
      matrix[t][1], matrix [t][2]);
    if(t!=2) printf("\n---|---|---\n");
  }
   printf("\n");
}

/* See if there is a winner. */
char check(void)
{
  int t;
  char *p;

  for(t=0; t<3; t++) { /* check rows */
    p = &matrix[t][0];
    if(*p==*(p+1) && *(p+1)==*(p+2)) return *p;
  }

  for(t=0; t<3; t++) { /* check columns */
    p = &matrix[0][t];
    if(*p==*(p+3) && *(p+3)==*(p+6)) return *p;
  }

  /* test diagonals */
  if(matrix[0][0]==matrix[1][1] && matrix[1][1]==matrix[2][2])
    return matrix[0][0];

  if(matrix[0][2]==matrix[1][1] && matrix[1][1]==matrix[2][0])
    return matrix[0][2];

  return SPACE;
}
```

The array is initialized to contain spaces because a space is used to indicate to **get_player_move( )** and **get_computer_move( )** that a matrix position is vacant. The fact that spaces are used instead of nulls simplifies the matrix display function

disp_matrix( ) by allowing the contents of the array to be printed on the screen without any translations. Note that the routine **get_player_move( )** is recursive when an invalid location is entered. This is an example of how recursion can be used to simplify a routine and reduce the amount of code necessary to implement a function.

In the main loop, each time a move is entered, the function **check( )** is called. This function determines if the game has been won and by whom. The **check( )** function returns an "X" if you have won, or an "O" if the computer has won. Otherwise, it returns a space. **check( )** works by scanning the rows, the columns, and then the diagonals looking for a winning configuration.

The routines in this example all access the array **matrix** differently. You should study them to make sure that you understand each array operation.

Chapter Six

Pointers

The correct understanding and use of pointers is critical to the creation of most C (and C++) programs for four reasons:

1. Pointers provide the means by which functions can modify their calling arguments.
2. Pointers are used to support C's dynamic allocation system.
3. The use of pointers can improve the efficiency of certain routines.
4. Pointers are commonly used to support certain data structures such as linked lists and binary trees.

In addition to being one of C's strongest features, pointers are also its most dangerous feature. For example, uninitialized or wild pointers can cause the system to crash. Perhaps worse, it is easy to use pointers incorrectly, which causes bugs that are very difficult to find.

Because arrays and pointers are interrelated in C, you will want to examine Chapter 5, which covers arrays.

Pointers Are Addresses

A *pointer* contains a memory address. Most commonly, this address is the location of another variable in memory. If one variable contains the address of another variable, the first variable is said to *point* to the second. For example, if a variable at location 1004 is pointed to by a variable at location 1000, location 1000 will contain the value 1004. This situation is illustrated in Figure 6-1.

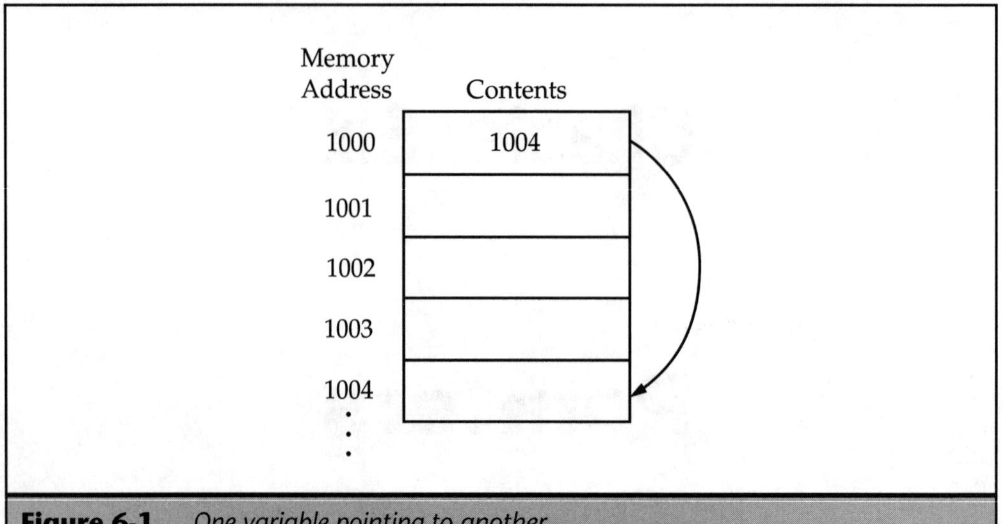

Figure 6-1. *One variable pointing to another*

Pointer Variables

If a variable is going to hold a pointer, it must be declared as such. A pointer declaration consists of a base type, an *, and the variable name. The general form for declaring a pointer variable is

*type *name;*

where *type* is any valid type (the pointer's base type), and *name* is the name of the pointer variable.

The base type of the pointer defines what type of variables the pointer can point to. Technically, any type of pointer can point anywhere in memory, but C assumes that what the pointer is pointing to is an object of its base type. Also, as you will see, all pointer arithmetic is done relative to its base type, so the base type of a pointer is very important.

The Pointer Operators

There are two special pointer operators: * and &. These operators were introduced in Chapter 2. We will take a closer look at them here, beginning with a review of their basic operation.

The & is a unary operator that returns the memory address of its operand.

For example,

```
p = &num;
```

places into **p** the memory address of the variable **num**. This address is the computer's internal location of the variable. It has nothing to do with the value of **num**. The operation of the **&** can be remembered as returning "the address of." Therefore, the preceding assignment statement could be read as "**p** receives the address of **num**."

For example, assume the variable **num** uses memory location 2000 to store its value. Also assume that **num** has a value of 100. Then, after the above assignment, **p** will have the value 2000.

The second operator, *, is the complement of &. It is a unary operator that returns the value of the variable located at the address that follows. For example, if **p** contains the memory address of the variable **num**,

```
q = *p;
```

places the value of **num** into **q**. Following through with this example, **q** has the value 100 because 100 is stored at location 2000, which is the memory address that was stored in **p**. The operation of the * can be remembered as "at address." In this case the statement could be read as "**q** receives the value at address **p**."

The following program illustrates the foregoing discussion:

```
#include <stdio.h>

int main(void)
{
  int num, q;
  int *p;

  num = 100; /* num is assigned 100 */
  p = &num;  /* p receives num's address */
  q = *p;    /* q is assigned num's value
                indirectly through p */

  printf("%d", q); /* prints 100 */

  return 0;
}
```

The above program displays the value 100 on the screen.

Unfortunately, the multiplication sign and the "at address" sign are the same, and the bitwise AND and the "address of " sign are the same. These operators have no relationship to each other. Both & and * have a higher precedence than all other arithmetic operators except the unary minus, with which they are equal.

You must make sure that your pointer variables always point to the correct type of data. For example, when you declare a pointer to be of type **int**, the compiler assumes that any address it holds points to an integer value. Because C allows you to assign any address to a pointer variable, the following code fragment compiles (although the compiler will issue a warning message) but does not produce the desired result:

```
#include <stdio.h>

int main(void)
{
  double x, y;
  int  *p;

  x = 100.123;

  p = &x;
  y = *p;
  printf("%f", y);  /* this will be wrong */

  return 0;
}
```

This does not assign the value of **x** to **y**. Because **p** is declared to be an integer pointer (and assuming 16-bit integers), only 2 bytes of information will be transferred to **y**, not the 8 that normally make up a **double**.

Pointer Expressions

In general, expressions involving pointers conform to the same rules as any other C expression. This section will examine a few special aspects of pointer expressions.

Pointer Assignments

As with any variable, a pointer may be used on the right-hand side of assignment statements to assign its value to another pointer. For example:

```
#include <stdio.h>

int main(void)
{
  int x;
  int *p1, *p2;

  p1 = &x;
  p2 = p1;
```

```
  /* This will display the addresses held by
     p1 and p2. They will be the same.
  */
  printf("%p  %p", p1, p2);

  return 0;
}
```

Here, both **p1** and **p2** will contain the address of **x**.

Pointer Arithmetic

Only two arithmetic operations can be used on pointers: addition and subtraction. To understand what occurs in pointer arithmetic, let **p1** be a pointer to an integer with a current value of 2000 and assume that integers are 2 bytes long. After the expression

```
p1++;
```

the content of **p1** is 2002, not 2001! Each time **p1** is incremented, it points to the next integer. The same is true of decrements. For example,

```
p1--;
```

will cause **p1** to have the value 1998, assuming that it previously was 2000.

Each time a pointer is incremented, it points to the memory location of the next element of its base type. Each time it is decremented, it points to the location of the previous element. In the case of pointers to characters this appears as "normal" arithmetic. However, all other pointers increase or decrease by the length of the data type they point to. Figure 6-2 illustrates this concept.

You are not limited to increment and decrement, however. You may also add or subtract integers to or from pointers. The expression

```
p1 = p1 + 9;
```

makes **p1** point to the ninth element of **p1**'s type beyond the one it is currently pointing to.

Besides addition and subtraction of a pointer and an integer, the only other operation you can perform on a pointer is to subtract it from another pointer. For the most part, subtracting one pointer from another only makes sense when both pointers point to a common object, such as an array. The subtraction then yields the number of elements of the base type separating the two pointer values. Aside from these operations, no other arithmetic operations can be performed on pointers. You cannot multiply or divide pointers; you cannot add pointers; you cannot apply the bitwise shift and mask operators to them; and you cannot add or subtract type **float** or **double** to pointers.

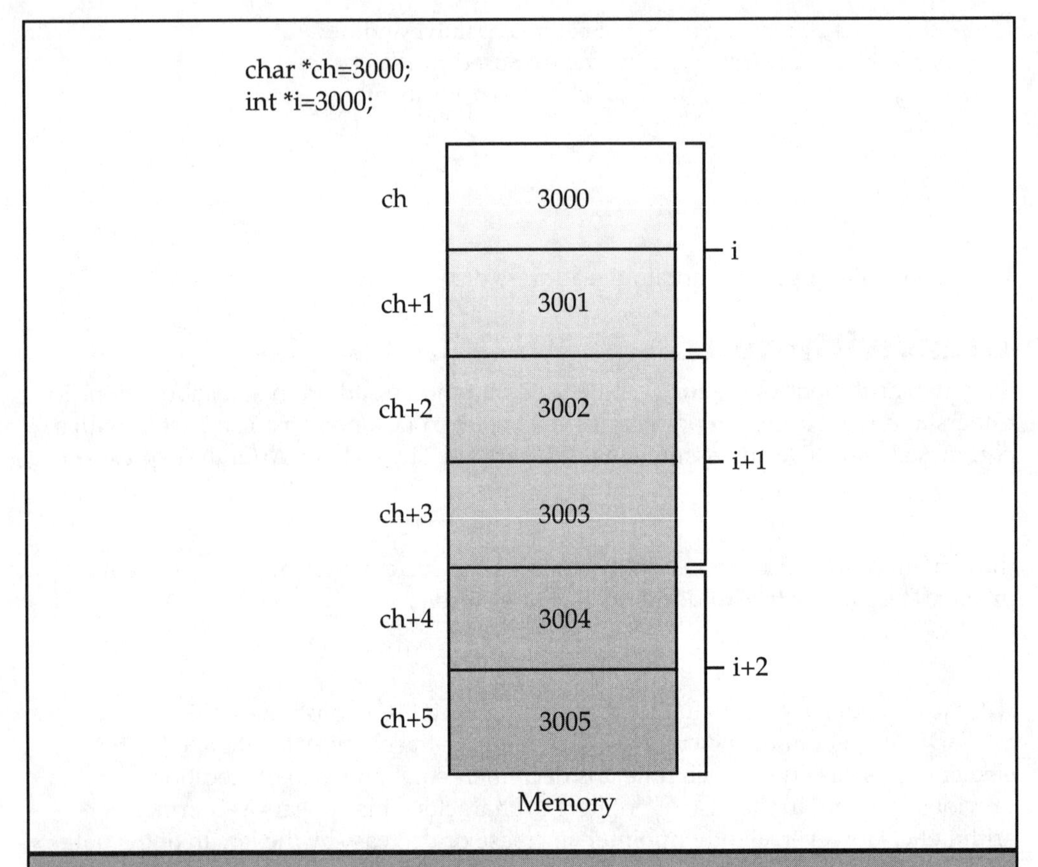

Figure 6-2. *All pointer arithmetic is relative to its base type (assume 16-bit integers)*

Pointer Comparisons

It is possible to compare two pointers in a relational expression. For instance, given the pointers **p** and **q**, the following statement is perfectly valid:

```
if(p<q) printf("p points to lower memory than q\n");
```

Generally, pointer comparisons are used when two or more pointers are pointing to a common object. As an example, imagine that you are constructing a stack routine to hold integer values. A stack is a list that uses "first in, last out" accessing. It is often compared to a stack of plates on a table—the first one set down is the last one to be used. Stacks are used frequently in compilers, interpreters, spreadsheets, and other system-related software. To create a stack, you need two routines: **push( )** and **pop( )**. The **push( )** function puts values on the stack and **pop( )** takes them off. The stack is held in the array **stack**, which is **STCKSIZE** elements long. The variable **tos** holds the memory address of the top of the stack and is used to prevent stack overflows and underflows. Once the stack has been initialized, **push( )** and **pop( )** may be used as a stack for integers. These routines are shown here with a simple **main( )** function to drive them:

```
#include <stdio.h>
#include <stdlib.h>

#define STCKSIZE 50

void push(int i);
int pop(void);

int *p1, *tos, stack[STCKSIZE];

int main(void)
{
  int value;

  p1 =  stack; /* assign p1 the start of stack */
  tos = p1;  /* let tos hold top of stack */

  do {
    printf("Enter a number (-1 to quit, 0 to pop): ");
    scanf("%d", &value);
    if(value!=0) push(value);
    else printf("this is it %d\n", pop());
  } while(value!=-1);
  return 0;
}

void push(int i)
{
  p1++;
  if(p1==(tos + STCKSIZE)) {
    printf("stack overflow");
    exit(1);
  }
  *p1 = i;
}

int pop(void)
{
  if(p1==tos) {
    printf("stack underflow");
```

```
      exit(1);
    }
    p1--;
    return *(p1+1);
}
```

Both the **push( )** and **pop( )** functions perform a relational test on the pointer **p1** to detect limit errors. In **push( )**, **p1** is tested against the end of stack by adding **STCKSIZE** (the size of the stack) to **tos**. In **pop( )**, **p1** is checked against **tos** to be sure that a stack underflow has not occurred.

In **pop( )**, the parentheses are necessary in the **return** statement. Without them, the statement would look like

```
return *p1 + 1;
```

which would return the value at location **p1** plus 1, not the value of the location **p1+1**. You must be very careful to use parentheses to ensure the correct order of evaluation when working with pointers.

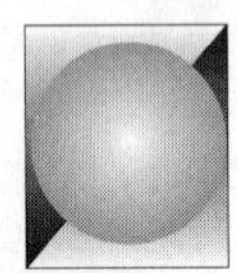

*NOTE: When compiling for a 16-bit target (such as DOS or Windows 3.1), you can declare pointers to be **far**, **near**, or **huge**. These types of pointers are described in Chapter 15.*

Dynamic Allocation and Pointers

Once compiled, all C programs organize the computer's memory into four regions, which hold program code, global data, the stack, and the heap. The heap is an area of free memory that is managed by C's dynamic allocation functions **malloc( )** and **free( )**. These functions were introduced in Chapter 5 in conjunction with arrays. Here, we will examine them further, beginning with a review of their basic operation.

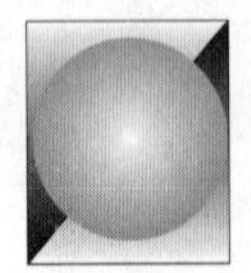

NOTE: Although C++ still supports C's dynamic allocation functions, it also defines its own approach, which is based upon dynamic allocation operators. These are described in Part 3.

The **malloc( )** function allocates memory and returns a pointer to the start of it. The **free( )** function returns previously allocated memory to the heap for possible reuse. The prototypes for **malloc( )** and **free( )** are

void *malloc(size_t *num_bytes*);
void free(void **p*);

Both functions use the **stdlib.h** header file. Here, *num_bytes* is the number of bytes requested. If there is not enough free memory to fill the request, **malloc( )** returns a null. The type **size_t** is defined in **stdlib.h** and specifies an unsigned integer type that is capable of holding the largest amount of memory that may be allocated with a single call to **malloc( )**. It is important that **free( )** be called only with a valid, previously allocated pointer; otherwise, the organization of the heap could be damaged, which might cause a program crash.

The code fragment shown here allocates 25 bytes of memory:

```
char *p;

p = (char *) malloc(25);
```

After the assignment, **p** points to the first of 25 bytes of free memory. The cast to **char *** is not needed for C, but is required for C++ programs. In C, if no type cast is used with **malloc( );** the pointer type is converted automatically to the same type as the pointer variable on the left side of the assignment. In C++, such implicit pointer conversions are disallowed. Although not needed by C, the use of the type casts allow your C code to be compatible with C++, too. As another example, this fragment allocates space for 50 integers. It uses **sizeof** to ensure portability.

```
int *p;

p = (int *) malloc(50*sizeof(int));
```

Since the heap is not infinite, whenever you allocate memory it is imperative to check the value returned by **malloc( )** to make sure that it is not null before using the pointer. Using a null pointer may crash the computer. The proper way to allocate memory and test for a valid pointer is illustrated in this code fragment:

```
int *p;

if((p = (int *) malloc(100))==NULL) {
  printf("Out of memory.\n");
  exit(1);
}
```

The macro NULL is defined in **stdlib.h**. Of course, you can substitute some other sort of error handler in place of **exit( )**. The point is that you do not want the pointer **p** to be used if it is null.

You should include the header file **stdlib.h** at the top of any file that uses **malloc( )** and **free( )** because it contains their prototypes.

Understanding const Pointers

The **const** qualifier was introduced in Chapter 2, where it was used to create variables that could not be changed (by the program) after they were created. However, there is a second use of **const** that relates to pointers. The **const** qualifier can be used to protect the object pointed to by an argument to a function from being modified by that function. That is, when a pointer is passed to a function, that function can modify the actual variable pointed to by the pointer. However, if the pointer is specified as **const** in the parameter declaration, the function code won't be able to modify what it points to. For example, the **sp_to_dash( )** function in the following program prints a dash for each space in its string argument. That is, the string "this is a test" will be printed as "this-is-a-test". The use of **const** in the parameter declaration ensures that the code inside the function cannot modify the object pointed to by the parameter.

```
#include <stdio.h>

void sp_to_dash(const char *str);

int main(void)
{
  sp_to_dash("this is a test");

  return 0;
}

void sp_to_dash(const char *str)
{
  while(*str) {
    if(*str == ' ') printf("%c", '-');
    else printf("%c", *str);
    str++;
  }
}
```

If you had written **sp_to_dash( )** in such a way that the string would be modified, it will not compile. For example, if you had coded **sp_to_dash( )** as follows, you would receive a compile-time error:

```
/* This is wrong. */
void sp_to_dash(const char *str)
{
  while(*str) {
    if(*str == ' ') *str = '-'; /* can't do this */
```

```
    printf("%c", *str);
    str++;
  }
}
```

Many functions in the standard library use **const** in their parameter declarations. Doing so ensures that no changes to the argument pointed to by a parameter will be altered by the function.

Pointers and Arrays

There is a close relationship between pointers and arrays. Consider this fragment:

```
char str[80], *p1;
p1 = str;
```

Here, **p1** has been set to the address of the first array element in **str**. If you wished to access the fifth element in **str**, you could write

```
str[4]
```

or

```
*(p1+4)
```

Both statements return the fifth element. Remember, arrays start at 0, so a 4 is used to index **str**. You add 4 to the pointer **p1** to get the fifth element because **p1** currently points to the first element of **str**. (Remember that an array name without an index returns the starting address of the array, which is the first element.)

In essence, C allows two methods of accessing array elements. This is important because pointer arithmetic can be faster than array-indexing. Since speed is often a consideration in programming, the use of pointers to access array elements is very common in C programs.

To see an example of how pointers can be used in place of array-indexing, consider these two simplified versions of the **puts( )** standard library function—one with array-indexing and one with pointers. The **puts( )** function writes a string to the standard output device:

```
/* Use array. */
int puts(const char *s)
{
  register int t;

  for(t=0; s[t]; ++t) putchar(s[t]);
```

```
  return 1;
}

/* Use pointer. */
int puts(const char *s)
{
  while(*s) putchar(*s++);
  return 1;
}
```

Most professional C/C++ programmers would find the second version easier to read and understand. In fact, the pointer version is the way routines of this sort are commonly written in C.

Pointers to Character Arrays

Many string operations in C are usually performed by using pointers and pointer arithmetic because strings tend to be accessed in a strictly sequential fashion.

For example, here is one version of the standard library function **strcmp( )** that uses pointers:

```
/* Use pointers. */
int strcmp(const char *s1, const char *s2)
{
  while(*s1)
    if(*s1-*s2)
      return *s1-*s2;
    else {
      s1++;
      s2++;
    }
  return 0; /* equal */
}
```

Remember, all strings in C are terminated by a null, which is a false value. Therefore, a statement such as

```
while (*s1)
```

is true until the end of the string is reached. Here, **strcmp( )** returns 0 if **s1** is equal to **s2**. It returns less than 0 if **s1** is less than **s2**; otherwise, it returns greater than 0.

Most string functions resemble **strcmp( )** with regard to the way it uses pointers, especially where loop control is concerned. Using pointers is faster, more efficient, and often easier to understand than using array-indexing.

One common error that sometimes creeps in when using pointers is illustrated by the following program:

```
/* This program is incorrect. */

#include <stdio.h>
#include <string.h>

int main(void)
{
  char *p1, s[80];

  p1 = s;  /* assign p1 the starting address of s */
  do {
    gets(s);  /* read a string */

    /* print the decimal equivalent of each
       character */
    while(*p1) printf(" %d", *p1++);

  } while(strcmp(s, "done"));
  return 0;
}
```

Can you find the error in this program?

The problem is that **p1** is assigned the address of **s** only once—outside the loop. The first time through the loop, **p1** does point to the first character in **s**. However, in the second (and subsequent iterations), it continues from where it left off, because it is not reset to the start of the array **s**. The proper way to write this program is

```
/* This program is correct. */

#include <stdio.h>
#include <string.h>

int main(void)
{
  char *p1, s[80];

  do {
    p1 = s; /* assign p1 the starting address of s */
    gets(s);  /* read a string */

    /* print the decimal equivalent of each
       character */
```

```
    while(*p1) printf(" %d", *p1++);

  } while(strcmp(s, "done"));
  return 0;
}
```

Here, each time the loop iterates, **p1** is set to the start of string **s**.

Arrays of Pointers

Pointers may be arrayed like any other data type. The declaration for an **int** pointer array of size 10 is

```
int *x[10];
```

To assign the address of an integer variable called **var** to the third element of the array, you would write

```
x[2] = &var;
```

To find the value of **var**, you would write

```
*x[2]
```

If you want to pass an array of pointers into a function, you can use the same method used for other arrays—simply call the function with the array name without any indexes. For example, a function that will receive array **x** would look like this:

```
void display_array(int *q[])
{
  int t;

  for(t=0; t<10; t++)
    printf("%d ", *q[t]);
}
```

Remember, **q** is not a pointer to integers, but to an array of pointers to integers. Therefore, it is necessary to declare the parameter **q** as an array of integer pointers as shown here. It may not be declared simply as an integer pointer because that is not what it is.

A common use of pointer arrays is to hold pointers to error messages. You can create a function that outputs a message given its code number, as shown here:

```
void serror(int num)
{
  static char *err[] = {
    "Cannot Open File\n",
```

```
    "Read Error\n",
    "Write Error\n",
    "Media Failure\n"
  };

  printf("%s", err[num]);
}
```

As you can see, **printf( )** inside **serror( )** is called with a character pointer that points to one of the various error messages indexed by the error number passed to the function. For example, if **num** is passed a 2, the message "Write Error" is displayed.

It is interesting to note that the command-line argument **argv** is an array of character pointers.

Pointers to Pointers: Multiple Indirection

The concept of arrays of pointers is straightforward because the indexes keep the meaning clear. However, cases in which one pointer points to another can be very confusing. A pointer to a pointer is a form of *multiple indirection*, or a chain of pointers. Consider Figure 6-3.

In the case of a normal pointer, the value of the pointer is the address of the location that contains the value desired. In the case of a pointer to a pointer, the first pointer contains the address of the second pointer, which contains the address of the location that contains the value desired.

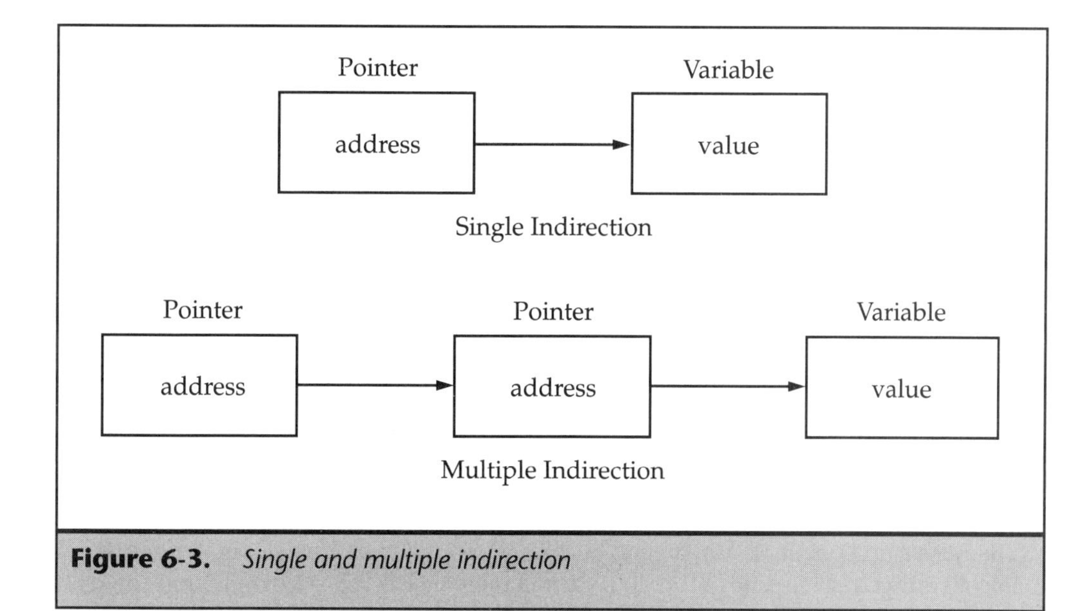

Figure 6-3. *Single and multiple indirection*

Multiple indirection can be carried on to whatever extent desired, but there are few cases where using more than a pointer to a pointer is necessary, or even wise. Excessive indirection is difficult to follow and prone to conceptual errors. (Do not confuse multiple indirection with linked lists, which are used in databases and the like.)

A variable that is a pointer to a pointer must be declared as such. This is done by placing an additional asterisk in front of its name. For example, this declaration tells the compiler that **newbalance** is a pointer to a pointer of type **float**:

```
float **newbalance;
```

It is important to understand that **newbalance** is not a pointer to a floating-point number but rather a pointer to a **float** pointer.

In order to access the target value indirectly pointed to by a pointer to a pointer, the asterisk operator must be applied twice, as is shown in this short example:

```
#include <stdio.h>

int main(void)
{
  int x, *p, **q;

  x = 10;
  p = &x;
  q = &p;

  printf("%d", **q); /* print the value of x */

  return 0;
}
```

Here, **p** is declared as a pointer to an integer, and **q** as a pointer to a pointer to an integer. The call to **printf( )** prints the number 10 on the screen.

Initializing Pointers

After a pointer is declared, but before it has been assigned a value, it may contain an unknown value. If you try to use the pointer prior to giving it a value, you might crash not only your program but also the operating system of your computer—a very nasty type of error!

By convention, a pointer that is pointing nowhere should be given the value null to signify that it points to nothing. However, just because a pointer has a null value does not make it "safe." If you use a null pointer on the left side of an assignment statement, you still risk crashing your program or operating system.

Because a null pointer is assumed to be unused, you can use the null pointer to make many of your pointer routines easier to code and more efficient. For example, you could use a null pointer to mark the end of a pointer array. If this is done, a routine that accesses that array knows that it has reached the end when the null value is encountered. This type of approach is illustrated by the **search( )** function shown here:

```
/* Look up a name. */
int search(char *p[], char *name)
{
  register int t;
  for(t=0; p[t]; ++t)
    if(!strcmp(p[t], name)) return t;

  return -1; /* not found */
}
```

The **for** loop inside **search( )** runs until either a match or a null pointer is found. Because the end of the array is marked with a null, the condition controlling the loop fails when it is reached.

It is common in professionally written C programs to initialize strings. You saw an example of this in the **serror( )** function shown earlier. Another variation on this theme is the following type of string declaration:

```
char *p = "hello world\n";
```

As you can see, the pointer **p** is not an array. The reason this sort of initialization works has to do with the way C operates. All C compilers create what is called a *string table,* which is used internally by the compiler to store the string constants used by the program. Therefore, this declaration statement places the address of "hello world" into the pointer **p**. Throughout the program **p** can be used like any other string. For example, the following program is perfectly valid:

```
#include <stdio.h>
#include <string.h>

char *p = "hello world";

int main(void)
{
  register int t;

  /* print the string forward and backwards */
  printf(p);
  for(t=strlen(p)-1; t>-1; t--) printf("%c", p[t]);
  return 0;
}
```

Pointers to Functions

In Chapter 4, you were introduced to a particularly confusing yet powerful feature of C, the *function pointer*. Even though a function is not a variable, it still has a physical location in memory that can be assigned to a pointer. A function's address is the entry point of the function. Because of this, a function pointer can be used to call a function. In this section, we will take another look at the function pointer.

In certain types of programs, the user can select one option from a long list of possible actions. For example, in an accounting program, you may be presented with a menu that has 20 or more selections. Once the selection has been made, the routine that routes program execution to the proper function can be handled two ways. The most common way is to use a **switch** statement. However, in applications that demand the highest performance, there is a better way. An array of pointers can be created with each pointer in the array containing the address of a function. The selection made by the user is decoded and is used to index into the pointer array, causing the proper function to be executed. This method can be very fast—much faster than the **switch** method.

To see how an array of function pointers can be used as described, imagine that you are implementing a very simple inventory system that is capable of entering, deleting, and reviewing data, as well as exiting to the operating system. If the functions that perform these activities are called **enter( )**, **del( )**, **review( )**, and **quit( )**, respectively, the following fragment correctly initializes an array of function pointers to these functions:

```
void enter(void), del(void), review(void), quit(void);
int menu(void);

void (*options[])(void) = {
  enter,
  del,
  review,
  quit
} ;
```

Pay special attention to the way an array of function pointers is declared. Notice the placement of the parentheses and square brackets.

Although the actual inventory routines are not developed, the following program illustrates the proper way to execute the functions by using the function pointers. Notice how the **menu( )** function automatically returns the proper index into the pointer array:

```
#include <stdlib.h>
#include <stdio.h>
#include <conio.h>
#include <string.h>
```

```
void enter(void), del(void), review(void), quit(void);
int menu(void);

void (*options[])(void) = {
  enter,
  del,
  review,
  quit
} ;

int main(void)
{
  int i;

  i = menu(); /* get user's choice */

  (*options[i])();  /* execute it */
  return 0;

}

int menu(void)
{
  char ch;

  do {

    printf("1. Enter\n");
    printf("2. Delete\n");
    printf("3. Review\n");
    printf("4. Quit\n");
    printf("Select a number: ");
    ch = getche();
    printf("\n");
  } while(!strchr("1234", ch));
  return ch-49; /* convert to an integer equivalent */
}

void enter(void)
{
  printf("In enter.");
}
```

```
void del(void)
{
  printf("In del.");
}

void review(void)
{
  printf("In review.");
}

void quit(void)
{
  printf("In quit.");
  exit(0);
}
```

The program works like this. The menu is displayed, and the user enters the number of the selection desired. Since the number is in ASCII, 49 (the decimal value of 0) is subtracted from it in order to convert it into a binary integer. This value is then returned to **main( )** and is used as an index to **options**, the array of function pointers. Next, the call to the proper function is executed.

Using arrays of function pointers is very common, not only in interpreters and compilers but also in database programs, because often these programs provide a large number of options and efficiency is important.

Problems with Pointers

Nothing will get you into more trouble than a "wild" pointer! Pointers are a mixed blessing. They give you tremendous power and are necessary for many programs. But when a pointer accidentally contains a wrong value, it can be the most difficult bug to track down. The pointer itself is not the problem; the problem is that each time you perform an operation using it, you are reading or writing to some unknown piece of memory. If you read from it, the worst that can happen is that you get garbage. However, if you write to it, you write over other pieces of your code or data. This may not show up until later in the execution of your program, and may lead you to look for the bug in the wrong place. There may be little or no evidence to suggest that the pointer is the problem.

Because pointer errors are such nightmares, you should do your best never to generate one. Toward this end, two of the more common errors are discussed here.

The classic example of a pointer error is the *uninitialized pointer.* For example:

```
/* This program is wrong. */

int main(void)
```

```
{
  int x, *p;

  x = 10;
  *p = x;

  return 0;
}
```

This program assigns the value 10 to some unknown memory location. The pointer **p** has never been given a value; therefore, it contains an indeterminate (i.e., garbage) value. This type of problem often goes unnoticed when your program is very small because the odds are in favor of **p** containing a "safe" address—one that is not in your code, data, stack, heap, or operating system. However, as your program grows, so does the probability of **p** pointing into something vital. Eventually your program stops working. The solution to this sort of trouble is obvious: make sure that a pointer is always pointing at something valid before it is used. Although the mistake is easy to catch in this simple case, frequently uninitialized pointers (or, incorrectly initialized ones) occur in a way that are not as easy to find.

A second common error is caused by a simple misunderstanding of how to use a pointer. For example, this program is fundamentally wrong:

```
#include <stdio.h>

/* This program is wrong. */
int main(void)
{
  int x, *p;

  x = 10;
  p = x;
  printf("%d", *p);

  return 0;
}
```

The call to **printf( )** does not print the value of **x**, which is 10, on the screen. It prints some unknown value because the assignment

```
p = x;
```

is wrong. That statement has assigned the value 10 to the pointer **p**, which was supposed to contain an address, not a value. Fortunately, the error in this program is caught by Borland C++. The compiler issues a warning message that tells you that a nonportable pointer conversion is taking place. This is your clue that a pointer error might have been made—which is the case in this example. To make the program correct, you should write

```
p = &x;
```

Although Borland C++ reported warnings for the mistake in this program, you can't always count on its help. These types of errors can occur in convoluted, roundabout ways that escape detection. So, be careful.

The fact that pointers can cause very tricky bugs if handled incorrectly is no reason to avoid using them. Simply be careful and make sure that you know where each pointer is pointing before using it.

Chapter Seven

Structures, Unions, and User-Defined Types

The C language gives you five ways to create custom data types:

1. The *structure* is a grouping of variables under one name and is called an *aggregate* data type. (The terms "compound" or "conglomerate" are also commonly used.)
2. The *bit-field* is a variation of the structure and allows easy access to individual bits.
3. The *union* enables the same piece of memory to be defined as two or more different types of data.
4. The *enumeration* is a list of symbols.
5. The **typedef** keyword simply creates a new name for an existing type.

Each of these is examined here.

Structures

A *structure* is a collection of variables that are referenced under one name, providing a convenient means of keeping related information together. A *structure declaration* forms a template that may be used to create structure objects. The variables that make up the structure are called *members* of the structure. (Structure members are also commonly referred to as *elements* or *fields*.)

Generally, all the members in the structure are related to each other. For example, the name and address information found in a mailing list is normally represented as a structure. The following code fragment declares a structure template that defines the name and address fields of such a structure. The keyword **struct** tells the compiler that a structure is being declared.

```
struct addr {
  char name[30];
  char street[40];
  char city[20];
  char state[3];
  unsigned long int zip;
};
```

The declaration is terminated by a semicolon because a structure declaration is a statement. Also, the structure name **addr** identifies this particular data structure and is its type specifier. The structure name is often referred to as its *tag*.

At this point, no variable has actually been declared. Only the form of the data has been defined. To declare an actual variable with this structure, you would write

```
struct addr addr_info;
```

This declares a structure variable of type **addr** called **addr_info**. When you declare a structure, you are defining a compound variable type. Not until you declare a variable of that type does one actually exist.

When a structure variable is declared, the compiler automatically allocates sufficient memory to accommodate all of its members. Figure 7-1 shows how **addr_info** appears in memory.

You may also declare one or more variables at the same time that you declare a structure. For example,

```
struct addr {
  char name[30];
  char street[40];
  char city[20];
  char state[3];
  unsigned long int zip;
} addr_info, binfo, cinfo;
```

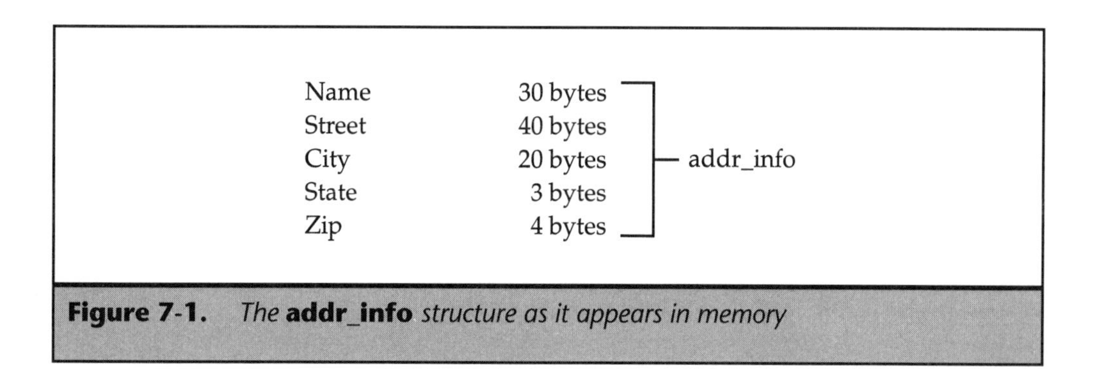

Figure 7-1. *The* **addr_info** *structure as it appears in memory*

declares a structure type called **addr** and declares variables **addr_info**, **binfo**, and **cinfo** of that type.

It is important to understand that each structure variable that you create contains its own copies of the variables that make up the structure. For example, the **zip** field of **binfo** is separate and distinct from the **zip** field in **cinfo**. In fact, the only relationship that **binfo** and **cinfo** have with each other is that they are both instances of the same type of structure. There is no other linkage between the two.

If you need only one structure variable, the structure tag is not needed. This means that

```
struct {
  char name[30];
  char street[40];
  char city[20];
  char state[3];
  unsigned long int zip;
} addr_info;
```

declares one variable named **addr_info** as defined by the structure preceding it.

The general form of a structure declaration is

struct *tag* {
  type variable-name;
  type variable-name;
  type variable-name;
  .
  .
  .
} *structure-variables;*

The *tag* is the type name of the structure—not a variable name. The *structure-variables* is a comma-separated list of variable names. Remember, either *tag* or *structure-variables* is optional, but not both.

Accessing Structure Members

Individual structure members are accessed through the use of the **.** (usually called the "dot") operator. For example, the following code assigns the ZIP code 12345 to the **zip** field of the structure variable **addr_info** declared earlier:

```
addr_info.zip = 12345;
```

The structure variable name followed by a period and the member name references that individual element. All structure members are accessed in the same way. The general form is

structure-name.member-name

Therefore, to print the ZIP code to the screen, you could write

```
printf("%ld", addr_info.zip);
```

This prints the ZIP code contained in the **zip** variable of the structure variable **addr_info**.

In the same fashion, the **addr_info.name** character array can be used with **gets( )**, as shown here:

```
gets(addr_info.name);
```

This passes a character pointer to the start of **name**.

To access the individual characters of **addr_info.name**, you could index **name**. For example, you could print the contents of **addr_info.name** one character at a time by using this code:

```
register int t;

for(t=0; addr_info.name[t]; ++t) putchar(addr_info.name[t]);
```

Structure Assignments

The information contained in one structure can be assigned to another structure of the same type using a single assignment statement. That is, you do not need to assign the value of each member separately. The following program illustrates structure assignments:

```
#include <stdio.h>

int main(void)
{
  struct {
```

```
    int a;
    int b;
  } x, y;

  x.a = 10;
  x.b = 20;

  y = x; /* assign one structure to another */

  printf("Contents of y: %d %d.", y.a, y.b);

  return 0;
}
```

After the assignment, **y.a** and **y.b** will contain the values 10 and 20, respectively.

Arrays of Structures

Perhaps the most common use of structures is in *arrays of structures*. To declare an array of structures, you must first define a structure, and then declare an array variable of that type. For example, to declare a 100-element array of structures of type **addr**, which was declared earlier in this chapter, you would write

```
struct addr addr_info[100];
```

This creates 100 sets of variables that are organized as declared in the structure type **addr**.

To access a specific structure within the **addr_info** array, index the array variable name. For example, to print the ZIP code of the third structure, you would write

```
printf("%ld", addr_info[2].zip);
```

Like all array variables, arrays of structures begin their indexing at zero.

An Inventory Example

To help illustrate how structures and arrays of structures are used, consider a simple inventory program that uses an array of structures to hold inventory information. The functions in this program interact with structures and their members in various ways to illustrate structure usage.

In this example, the information to be stored includes

- Item name
- Cost
- Number on hand

You can define the basic data structure, called **inv**, to hold this information as

```
#define MAX 100

struct inv {
  char item[30];
  float cost;
  int on_hand;
} inv_info[MAX];
```

In the **inv** structure, **item** is used to hold each inventoried item's name. The **cost** member contains the item's cost, and **on_hand** represents the number of items currently available.

The first function needed for the program is **main( )**:

```
int main(void)
{
  char choice;

  init_list(); /* initialize the structure array */
  for(;;) {
    choice = menu_select();
    switch(choice) {
      case 1: enter();
        break;
      case 2: del();
        break;
      case 3: list();
        break;
      case 4: return 0;
    }
  }
}
```

In **main( )**, the call to **init_list( )** prepares the structure array for use by putting a null character into the first byte of each **item** field. The program assumes that a structure is not in use if the **item** field is empty. The **init_list( )** function is defined as follows:

```
/* Initialize the structure array. */
void init_list(void)
{
  register int t;

  for(t=0; t<MAX; ++t) inv_info[t].item[0] = '\0';
}
```

The **menu_select( )** function displays the option messages and returns the user's selection:

```
/* Input the user's selection. */
int menu_select(void)
{
  char s[80];
  int c;

  printf("\n");
  printf("1. Enter an item\n");
  printf("2. Remove an item\n");
  printf("3. List the inventory\n");
  printf("4. Quit\n");
  do {
    printf("\nEnter your choice: ");
    gets(s);
    c = atoi(s);
  } while(c<0 || c>4);
  return c;
}
```

The **enter( )** function prompts the user for input and places the information entered into the next free structure. If the array is full, the message "List Full" is printed on the screen. The function **find_free( )** searches the structure array for an unused element.

```
/* Input the inventory information. */
void enter(void)
{
  int slot;

  slot = find_free();
  if(slot == -1) {
    printf("\nList Full");
    return;
  }

  printf("Enter item: ");
  gets(inv_info[slot].item);

  printf("Enter cost: ");
  scanf("%f", &inv_info[slot].cost);

  printf("Enter number on hand: ");
  scanf("%d%*c",&inv_info[slot].on_hand);
```

```
}

/* Return the index of the first unused array
   location or -1 if no free locations exist.
*/
int find_free(void)
{
  register int t;

  for(t=0; inv_info[t].item[0] && t<MAX; ++t) ;
  if(t == MAX) return -1; /* no slots free */
  return t;
}
```

Notice that **find_free( )** returns a –1 if every structure array variable is in use. This is a "safe" number to use because there cannot be a –1 element of the **inv_info** array.

The **del( )** function requires the user to specify the number of the item that needs to be deleted. The function then puts a null character in the first character position of the **item** field.

```
/* Remove an item from the list. */
void del(void)
{
  register int slot;
  char s[80];

  printf("enter record #: ");
  gets(s);
  slot = atoi(s);
  if(slot >= 0 && slot < MAX) inv_info[slot].item[0] = '\0';
}
```

The final function the program needs is **list( )**. It prints the entire inventory list on the screen.

```
/* Display the list on the screen. */
void list(void)
{
  register int t;

  for(t=0; t<MAX; ++t) {
    if(inv_info[t].item[0]) {
      printf("Item: %s\n", inv_info[t].item);
      printf("Cost: %f\n", inv_info[t].cost);
      printf("On hand: %d\n\n", inv_info[t].on_hand);
```

```
    }
  }
  printf("\n\n");
}
```

The complete listing for the inventory program is shown here. If you have any doubts about your understanding of structures, you should enter this program into your computer and study its execution by making changes and watching their effects.

```
/* A simple inventory program using an array of structures */

#include <stdio.h>
#include <stdlib.h>

#define MAX 100

struct inv {
  char item[30];
  float cost;
  int on_hand;
} inv_info[MAX];

void init_list(void), list(void), del(void);
void enter(void);
int menu_select(void), find_free(void);

int main(void)
{
  char choice;

  init_list(); /* initialize the structure array */
  for(;;) {
    choice = menu_select();
    switch(choice) {
      case 1: enter();
        break;
      case 2: del();
        break;
      case 3: list();
        break;
      case 4: return 0;
    }
  }
}
```

```
/* Initialize the structure array. */
void init_list(void)
{
  register int t;

  for(t=0; t<MAX; ++t) inv_info[t].item[0] = '\0';
}

/* Input the user's selection. */
int menu_select(void)
{
  char s[80];
  int c;

  printf("\n");
  printf("1. Enter an item\n");
  printf("2. Remove an item\n");
  printf("3. List the inventory\n");
  printf("4. Quit\n");
  do {
    printf("\nEnter your choice: ");
    gets(s);
    c = atoi(s);
  } while(c<0 || c>4);
  return c;
}

/* Input the inventory information. */
void enter(void)
{
  int slot;

  slot = find_free();
  if(slot == -1) {
    printf("\nList Full");
    return;
  }

  printf("Enter item: ");
  gets(inv_info[slot].item);

  printf("Enter cost: ");
  scanf("%f", &inv_info[slot].cost);
```

```
  printf("Enter number on hand: ");
  scanf("%d%*c", &inv_info[slot].on_hand);
}

/* Return the index of the first unused array
   location or -1 if no free locations exist.
*/
int find_free(void)
{
  register int t;

  for(t=0; inv_info[t].item[0] && t<MAX; ++t) ;
  if(t == MAX) return -1; /* no slots free */
  return t;
}

/* Remove an item from the list. */
void del(void)
{
  register int slot;
  char s[80];

  printf("enter record #: ");
  gets(s);
  slot = atoi(s);
  if(slot >= 0 && slot < MAX) inv_info[slot].item[0] = '\0';
}

/* Display the list on the screen. */
void list(void)
{
  register int t;

  for(t=0; t<MAX; ++t) {
    if(inv_info[t].item[0]) {
      printf("Item: %s\n", inv_info[t].item);
      printf("Cost: %f\n", inv_info[t].cost);
      printf("On hand: %d\n\n", inv_info[t].on_hand);
    }
  }
  printf("\n\n");
}
```

NOTE: At the time of this writing, when compiling the preceding program using the 16-bit Borland C++ compiler, the floating-point library required by **scanf( )** *is not always properly linked. If you encounter the same problem, there are two fixes that you can use. First, try using the 32-bit compiler. Second, if you add this line to the start of* **main( )**

```
double d = sin(0.5);
```

it will force the floating-point library to be linked. This problem will most likely be corrected with subsequent releases of Borland C++.

Passing Structures to Functions

So far, all structures and arrays of structures used in the examples have been assumed to be either global or defined within the function that uses them. In this section, special consideration will be given to passing structures and their members to functions.

Passing Structure Members to Functions

When you pass a member of a structure to a function, you are actually passing the value of that member to the function. Therefore, you are passing a simple variable. For example, consider this structure:

```
struct fred {
  char x;
  int y;
  float z;
  char s[10];
} mike;
```

Here are examples of each member being passed to a function:

```
func(mike.x);     /* passes character value of x */
func2(mike.y);    /* passes integer value of y */
func3(mike.z);    /* passes float value of z */
func4(mike.s);    /* passes address of string s */
func(mike.s[2]); /* passes character value of s[2] */
```

However, if you wished to pass the address of an individual structure member to achieve call by reference parameter passing, you would place the & operator before the structure name. For example, to pass the address of the elements in the structure **mike**, you would write

```
func(&mike.x);     /* passes address of character x */
func2(&mike.y);    /* passes address of integer y */
```

```
func3(&mike.z);    /* passes address of float z */
func4(mike.s);     /* passes address of string s */
func(&mike.s[2]); /* passes address of character s[2] */
```

Notice that the **&** operator precedes the structure name, not the individual member name. Note also that the array **s** already signifies an address, so that no **&** is required. However, when accessing a specific character in string **s**, as shown in the final example, the **&** is still needed.

Passing Entire Structures to Functions

When a structure is used as an argument to a function, the entire structure is passed using the standard call by value method. This means that any changes made to the contents of the structure inside the function to which it is passed do not affect the structure used as an argument.

When using a structure as a parameter, the most important thing to remember is that the type of the argument must match the type of the parameter. The best way to do this is to define a structure globally and then use its tag name to declare structure variables and parameters as needed. For example:

```
#include <stdio.h>

/* declare a structure type */
struct struct_type {
  int a, b;
  char ch;
} ;

void f1(struct struct_type parm);

int main(void)
{
  struct struct_type arg;  /* declare arg */

  arg.a = 1000;

  f1(arg);

  return 0;
}

void f1(struct struct_type parm)
{
  printf("%d", parm.a);
}
```

This program prints the number 1000 on the screen. As you can see, both **arg** and **parm** are declared to be structures of type **struct_type**.

Structure Pointers

C allows pointers to structures in the same way it does to other types of variables. However, there are some special aspects to structure pointers that you must keep in mind.

Declaring a Structure Pointer

Structure pointers are declared by placing the * in front of a structure variable's name. For example, assuming the previously defined structure **addr**, the following declares **addr_pointer** to be a pointer to data of that type:

```
struct addr *addr_pointer;
```

Using Structure Pointers

To find the address of a structure variable, the **&** operator is placed before the structure's name. For example, given the following fragment,

```
struct bal {
  float balance;
  char name[80];
} person;

struct bal *p;  /* declare a structure pointer */
```

then

```
p = &person;
```

places the address of the structure **person** into the pointer **p**.

To access the members of a structure using a pointer to that structure, you must use the arrow operator. The arrow operator, –>, is formed using a minus sign and a greater-than symbol. For example, to reference the **balance** member using **p**, you would write

```
p->balance
```

To see how structure pointers can be used, examine this simple program that prints the hours, minutes, and seconds on the screen using a software timer. (The timing of the program is adjusted by changing the definition of **DELAY** to fit the speed of your computer.)

```
/* Display a software timer. */

#include <stdio.h>
#include <conio.h>

#define DELAY 128000

struct my_time {
  int hours;
  int minutes;
  int seconds;
} ;

void update(struct my_time *t), display(struct my_time *t);
void mydelay(void);

int main(void)
{
  struct my_time systime;

  systime.hours = 0;
  systime.minutes = 0;
  systime.seconds = 0;

  for(;;) {
    update(&systime);
    display(&systime);
    if(kbhit()) return 0;
  }
}

void update(struct my_time *t)
{
  t->seconds++;
  if(t->seconds==60) {
    t->seconds = 0;
    t->minutes++;
  }
  if(t->minutes==60) {
    t->minutes = 0;
    t->hours++;
  }
```

```
  if(t->hours==24) t->hours = 0;
  mydelay();
}

void display(struct my_time *t)
{
  printf("%02d:", t->hours);
  printf("%02d:", t->minutes);
  printf("%02d\n", t->seconds);
}

void mydelay(void)
{
  long int t;

  for(t=1; t<DELAY; ++t) ;
}
```

A global structure called **my_time** is declared. Inside **main( )**, the structure variable called **systime**, of type **my_time**, is declared and initialized to 00:00:00. This means that **systime** is known directly only to the **main( )** function.

The functions **update( )**, which changes the time, and **display( )**, which prints the time, are passed the address of **systime**. In both functions the argument is declared to be a pointer to a structure of type **my_time**. Inside the functions, each structure element is actually referenced through a pointer. For example, to set the hours back to 0 when 24:00:00 was reached, this statement is used:

```
if(t->hours==24) t->hours = 0;
```

This line of code tells the compiler to take the address of **t** (which points to **systime** in **main( )**) and assign 0 to its **hours** member.

REMEMBER: *Use the dot operator to access structure members when operating on the structure itself. Use the arrow operator when referencing a structure through a pointer.*

As a final example of using structure pointers, the following program illustrates how a general-purpose integer input function can be designed. The function **input_xy( )** allows you to specify the **x** and **y** coordinates at which a prompting message will be displayed and then inputs an integer value. To accomplish these things, it uses the structure **xyinput**.

```
/* A generalized input example using structure pointers. */

#include <stdio.h>
```

```
#include <conio.h>
#include <string.h>

struct xyinput {
  int x, y; /* screen location for prompt */
  char message[80]; /* prompting message */
  int i; /* input value */
} ;

void input_xy(struct xyinput *info);

int main(void)
{
  struct xyinput mess;

  mess.x = 10; mess.y = 10;
  strcpy(mess.message, "Enter an integer: ");

  clrscr();

  input_xy(&mess);

  printf("Your number squared is: %d.", mess.i*mess.i);

  return 0;
}

/* Display a prompting message at the specified location
   and input an integer value.
*/
void input_xy(struct xyinput *info)
{
  gotoxy(info->x, info->y);

  printf(info->message);
  scanf("%d", &info->i);
}
```

The program uses the functions **clrscr( )** and **gotoxy( )** to clear the screen and position the cursor, respectively. Both functions use the **conio.h** header file. A function like **input_xy( )** is useful when your program must input many pieces of information. (In fact, you might want to create several functions like **input_xy( )** that input other types of data.)

Arrays and Structures Within Structures

A member of a structure can be either simple or compound. A simple member is any of the built-in data types, such as integer or character. You have already seen a few compound elements. The character array used in **addr_info** is an example. Other compound data types are single- and multidimensional arrays of the other data types and structures.

A member of a structure that is an array is treated as you might expect from the earlier examples. For example, consider this structure:

```
struct x {
  int a[10][10]; /* 10 x 10 array of ints */
  float b;
} y;
```

To reference integer 3,7 in **a** of structure **y**, you would write

```
y.a[3][7]
```

When a structure is a member of another structure, it is called a nested structure. For example, here the structure **addr** is nested inside **emp**:

```
struct emp {
  struct addr address;
  float wage;
} worker;
```

Here, a structure **emp** has been declared as having two members. The first is the structure of type **addr**, which contains an employee's address. The other is **wage**, which holds the employee's wage. The following code fragment assigns $35,000 to the **wage** element of **worker** and 98765 to the **zip** field of **address**:

```
worker.wage = 35000.00;

worker.address.zip = 98765;
```

As this example shows, the members of each structure are referenced from outermost to innermost (left to right).

Bit-Fields

Unlike most other computer languages, C has a built-in feature, called a *bit-field*, that allows access to a single bit. Bit-fields are useful for a number of reasons. Here are three:

1. If storage is limited, you can store several Boolean (true/false) variables in one byte.
2. Certain device interfaces transmit information encoded into bits within a single byte.
3. Certain encryption routines need to access the bits within a byte.

Although all these functions can be performed using the bitwise operators, a bit-field can add more clarity to your code.

The method C uses to access bits is based on the structure. A bit-field is really just a special type of structure member that defines how long, in bits, the field is to be. The general form of a bit-field declaration is

struct *struct-name* {
  type name1 : *length;*
  type name2 : *length;*
  .
  .
  .
  type nameN : *length;*
}

A bit-field must be declared as either **int**, **unsigned**, or **signed**. Bit-fields of length 1 should be declared as **unsigned** because a single bit cannot have a sign. Bit-fields can be from 1 to 16 bits long for 16-bit environments and from 1 to 32 bits long in 32-bit environments. In Borland C++, the leftmost bit is the most significant bit.

For example, consider the structure definition below:

```
struct device {
  unsigned active : 1;
  unsigned ready : 1;
  unsigned xmt_error : 1;
} dev_code;
```

This structure defines three variables of 1 bit each. The structure variable **dev_code** might be used to decode information from the port of a tape drive, for example. Assuming a hypothetical tape drive, the following code fragment writes a byte of information to the tape and checks for errors using **dev_code** from above:

```
void wr_tape(char c)
{
  while(!dev_code.ready) rd(&dev_code); /* wait */

  wr_to_tape(c); /* write out byte */
```

```
  while(dev_code.active) rd(&dev_code); /* wait until
                                            info is written */

  if(dev_code.xmt_error) printf("Write Error");
}
```

Here, **rd( )** returns the status of the tape drive and **wr_to_tape( )** writes the data.

Figure 7-2 shows what the bit variable **dev_code** looks like in memory.

As you can see from the previous example, each bit-field is accessed using the dot operator. However, if the structure is referenced through a pointer, you must use the –> operator.

You do not have to name each bit-field. This makes it easy to reach the bit you want and pass up unused ones. For example, if the tape drive also returned an end-of-tape flag in bit 5, you could alter structure **device** to accommodate this, as shown here:

```
struct device {
  unsigned active : 1;
  unsigned ready : 1;
  unsigned xmt_error : 1;
  unsigned : 2;
  unsigned EOT : 1;
} dev_code;
```

Bit-fields have certain restrictions. You cannot take the address of a bit-field variable. Bit-field variables cannot be arrayed. You cannot know, from machine to machine, whether the fields will run from right to left or from left to right; any code that uses bit-fields may have machine dependencies.

Finally, it is valid to mix other structure elements with bit-fields. For example,

```
struct emp {
  struct addr address;
  float pay;
  unsigned lay_off:1;    /* lay off or active */
  unsigned hourly:1;     /* hourly pay or wage */
  unsigned deductions:3; /* IRS deductions */
};
```

defines an employee record that uses only 1 byte to hold three pieces of information: the employee's status, whether the employee is salaried, and the number of deductions. Without the use of the bit-field, this information would have taken 3 bytes.

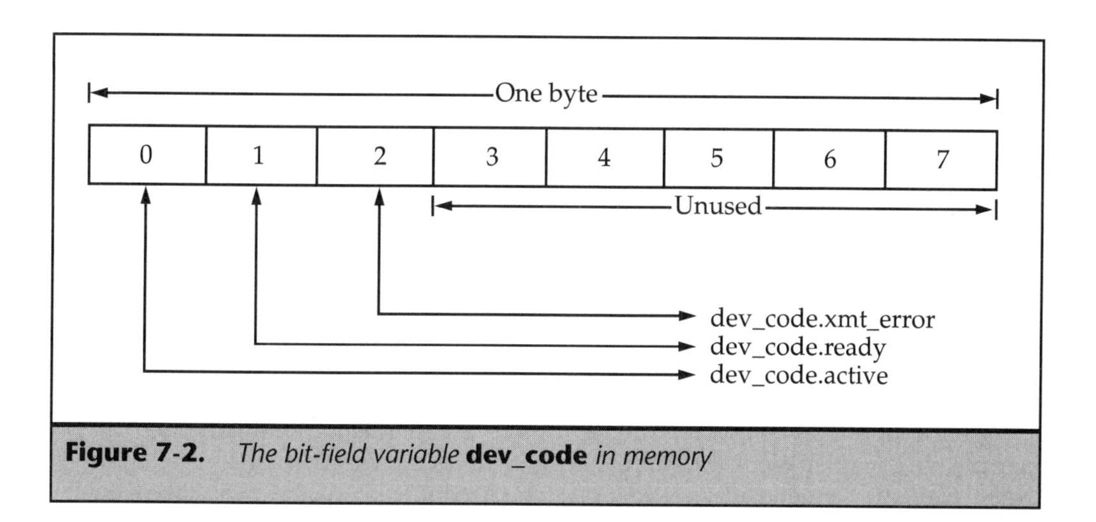

Figure 7-2. *The bit-field variable* **dev_code** *in memory*

Unions

A **union** is a memory location that is shared by several variables that are of different types. The **union** declaration is similar to that of a structure, as shown in this example:

```
union union_type {
  int i;
  char ch;
} ;
```

As with structures, you may declare a variable either by placing its name at the end of the definition or by using a separate declaration statement. To declare a **union** variable **cnvt** of type **union_type** using the definition just given, you would write

```
union union_type cnvt;
```

In **cnvt**, both integer **i** and character **ch** share the same memory location. (Of course, **i** occupies 2 (or 4) bytes and **ch** uses only 1.) Figure 7-3 shows how **i** and **ch** share the same address (assuming 16-bit integers). At any time, you can refer to the data stored in **cnvt** as either an integer or as a character.

When a **union** is declared, the compiler automatically creates a variable large enough to hold the largest variable type in the **union**.

To access a **union** member, use the same syntax that you would use for structures: the dot and arrow operators. If you are operating on the **union** directly, use the dot operator. If the **union** variable is accessed through a pointer, use the arrow operator. For example, to assign the integer 10 to element **i** of **cnvt**, you would write

```
cnvt.i = 10;
```

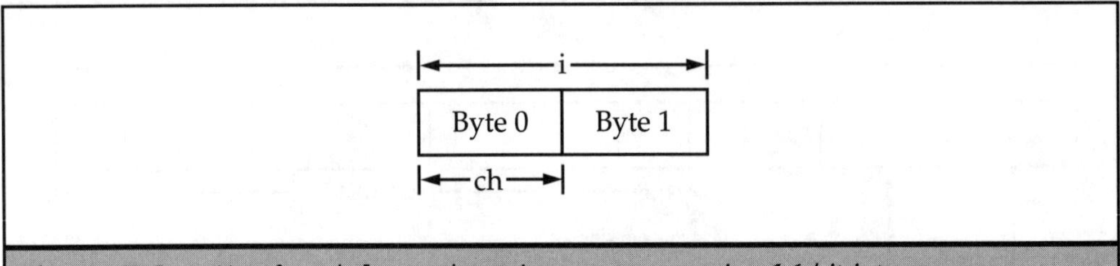

Figure 7-3. *How **i** and **ch** use the union **cnvt**, assuming 16-bit integers*

Using a **union** can help you produce machine-independent (portable) code. Because the compiler keeps track of the actual sizes of the variables that make up the **union**, machine dependencies are reduced. You need not worry about the size of an integer, character, **float**, or whatever.

Unions are used frequently when type conversions are needed because you can refer to the data held in the union in fundamentally different ways. For example, consider the problem of writing an integer to a file. While you can write any type of data (including an integer) to a file using **fwrite( )**, **fwrite( )** is more than is needed for such a simple operation. However, using a **union** you can easily create a function that writes the binary representation of an integer to a file, one byte at a time. Although there are many ways to code such a function, here is one way to do it using a **union**. For the sake of this example, 16-bit integers are assumed. First, a **union** composed of one integer and a 2-byte character array is created:

```
union pw {
  int i;
  char ch[2];
};
```

This **union** will let us access the two bytes that make up an integer as two individual characters. Now, you can use **pw** to create the **write_int( )** function shown in the following program:

```
#include <stdio.h>
#include <stdlib>

union pw {
  int i;
  char ch[2];
};

int write_int(int num, FILE *fp);
```

```
int main()
{
  FILE *fp;

  fp = fopen("test.tmp", "w+");

  if(fp==NULL) {
    printf("Cannot open file.\n");
    exit(1);
  }

  write_int(1000, fp);
  fclose(fp);

  return 0;
}

/* write an integer using union */
int write_int(int num, FILE *fp)
{
  union pw wrd;

  wrd.i = num;
  putc(wrd.ch[0], fp); /* write first half */
  return putc(wrd.ch[1], fp); /* write second half */
}
```

Although called with an integer, **write_int( )** uses the **union** to write both halves of the integer to the disk file one byte at a time.

Enumerations

An *enumeration* is a set of named integer constants that specifies all the legal values that a variable of its type can have. Enumerations are common in everyday life. For example, an enumeration of the coins used in the United States is

penny, nickel, dime, quarter, half-dollar, dollar

Enumerations are defined by using the keyword **enum** to signal the start of an enumeration type. The general form is

enum *tag* { *enumeration-list* } *variable-list*;

Both the enumeration name *tag* and the *variable-list* are optional, but one of them must be present. The *enumeration-list* is a comma-separated list of identifiers. As with structures, the tag is used to declare variables of its type. The following fragment defines an enumeration called **coin** and declares **money** to be of that type:

```
enum coin { penny, nickel, dime, quarter,
            half_dollar, dollar};

enum coin money;
```

Given this definition and declaration, the following types of statements are perfectly valid:

```
money = dime;

if(money==quarter) printf("is a quarter\n");
```

The key point to understand about an enumeration is that each of the symbols stands for an integer value and can be used in any integer expression. For example,

```
printf("The value of quarter is %d ", quarter);
```

is perfectly valid.

Unless initialized otherwise, the value of the first enumeration symbol is 0, the second is 1, and so forth. Therefore,

```
printf("%d %d", penny, dime);
```

displays **0 2** on the screen.

It is possible to specify the value of one or more of the symbols by using an initializer. This is done by following the symbol with an equal sign and an integer value. Whenever an initializer is used, symbols that appear after it are assigned values greater than the previous initialization value. For example, the following assigns the value of 100 to **quarter**.

```
enum coin { penny, nickel, dime, quarter=100,
            half_dollar, dollar};
```

Now, the values of these symbols are

penny	0
nickel	1
dime	2
quarter	100
half_dollar	101
dollar	102

Using initializations, more than one element of an enumeration can have the same value.

A common misconception is that the symbols of an enumeration can be input and output directly, but this is not true. For example, the following code fragment will not perform as desired:

```
/* This will not work. */

money = dollar;

printf("%s", money);
```

Remember that the symbol **dollar** is simply a name for an integer: it is not a string. Hence, it is not possible for **printf( )** to display the string "dollar" using the value in **money**. Likewise, you cannot give an enumeration variable a value using a string equivalent. That is, this code does not work:

```
/* This code will not work. */

money = "penny";
```

Actually, creating code to input and output enumeration symbols is quite tedious (unless you are willing to settle for their integer values). For example, the following code is needed to display, in words, the kind of coins that **money** contains:

```
switch(money) {
  case penny: printf("penny");
     break;
  case nickel: printf("nickel");
     break;
  case dime: printf("dime");
     break;
  case quarter: printf("quarter");
     break;
  case half_dollar: printf("half_dollar");
     break;
  case dollar: printf("dollar");
}
```

Sometimes, it is possible to declare an array of strings and use the enumeration value as an index to translate an enumeration value into its corresponding string. For example, this code also outputs the proper string:

```
char name[][12]={
  "penny",
  "nickel",
```

```
  "dime",
  "quarter",
  "half_dollar",
  "dollar"
};
  .
  .
  .
printf("%s", name[money]);
```

Of course, this works only if no initializations are used, because the string array must be indexed starting at 0.

Since enumeration values must be converted manually to their human-readable string values for human I/O, they are most useful in routines that do not make such conversions. For example, an enumeration is commonly used to define a compiler's symbol table.

Using sizeof to Ensure Portability

You have seen that structures and unions can be used to create variables of varying sizes, and that the actual size of these variables may change from machine to machine. The **sizeof** unary operator is used to compute the size of any variable or type and can help eliminate machine-dependent code from your programs. It is especially useful where structures or unions are concerned.

For the discussion that follows, keep in mind that Borland C++ has the following sizes for these data types:

Type	Size in Bytes
char	1
int (16 bits)	2
int (32 bits)	4
long int	4
float	4
double	8
long double	10

Therefore, assuming 16-bit integers, the following code will print the numbers **1**, **2**, **4**, and **10** on the screen:

```
char ch;
int i;
```

```
float f;

printf("%d", sizeof ch);

printf("%d", sizeof i);

printf("%d", sizeof f);

printf("%d", sizeof(long double));
```

The size of a structure is equal to or greater than the sum of the sizes of its members. For example,

```
struct s {
  char ch;
  int i;
  float f;
} s_var;
```

Here, **sizeof(s_var)** is at least 7 (4+2+1). However, the size of **s_var** might be greater. Depending on what compiler you are using (and what options are set), it is possible that data may be aligned on word (or paragraph) boundaries. This means that the size of an aggregate data type (such as a structure) may be slightly larger than the sum of its parts. Manually adding up the lengths of the structure members, for example, may not yield its correct size. Therefore, for maximum portability, you should always use **sizeof** to determine the size of a structure variable.

Since the **sizeof** operator is a *compile-time* operator, all the information necessary to compute the size of any variable is known at compile time. This is especially meaningful for **union**s because the size of a union is always equal to the size of its largest member. For example, consider the following:

```
union u {
  char ch;
  int i;
  float f;
} u_var;
```

The **sizeof(u_var)** will be 4 bytes long. At run time, it does not matter what **u_var** is *actually* holding; all that matters is the size of the largest variable it can hold, because the **union** must be as large as its largest element.

typedef

C allows you to define new data type names using the **typedef** keyword. You are not actually creating a new data type; you are defining a new name for an existing type.

This process can help make machine-dependent programs more portable; only the **typedef** statements need to be changed. It also can help you document your code by allowing descriptive names for the standard data types. The general form of the **typedef** statement is

typedef *type name;*

where *type* is any existing data type and *name* is the new name for this type. The new name you define is in addition to, not a replacement for, the existing type name.

For example, you could create a new name for **float** by using

```
typedef float balance;
```

This statement tells the compiler to recognize **balance** as another name for **float**. Next you could create a **float** variable using **balance**:

```
balance past_due;
```

Here, **past_due** is a floating-point variable of type **balance**, which is another word for **float**.

You can also use **typedef** to create names for more complex types. For example:

```
typedef struct {
  float due;
  int over_due;
  char name[40];
} client;  /* here client is the new type name */

client clist[NUM_CLIENTS]; /* define array of
                              structures of type client */
```

Using **typedef** can help make your code easier to read and more portable. But remember, you are *not* creating any new data types.

Chapter Eight

Input, Output, Streams, and Files

C does not define any keywords that perform input or output. Instead, I/O is accomplished through the use of library functions. For C programs, Borland C++ supports three I/O systems:

- The ANSI C standard I/O system
- The UNIX-like I/O system
- Several low-level, platform-specific I/O functions

With a few exceptions, this chapter discusses only the ANSI C I/O system. The reason for this is twofold. First, the ANSI C I/O system is the most widely used. Second, it is fully portable to all platforms. The functions that comprise the other two systems are covered in Part 2 of this book.

The purpose of this chapter is to present an overview of the ANSI C I/O system and to illustrate the way its core functions work together. The ANSI C I/O library contains a rich and diverse assortment of I/O routines—more than can be fully covered here. However, the functions presented in this chapter are sufficient for most circumstances.

During this discussion, keep in mind that the prototypes and several predefined types and constants for the ANSI C I/O library functions are found in the file **stdio.h**.

C Versus C++ I/O

Before beginning, it is necessary to answer an important question. Because C forms the foundation for C++, how does C's I/O system relate to the I/O system provided by C++?

C++ supports the entire set of ANSI C I/O functions. Thus, if you will be porting C code to C++ sometime in the future, you will not have to change all of your I/O routines right away. However, C++ also defines its own object-oriented I/O system, which includes both I/O functions and I/O operators, and completely duplicates the functionality of the ANSI C I/O system. If you are writing C++ code, then you should use the C++ I/O system (described in Part 3). For C code, you will need to use the standard C I/O system described in this chapter. However, even if you will be writing mostly C++ code, you will still want to be familiar with the ANSI C I/O system for these three reasons:

- For several years to come, C and C++ will coexist. Also, many programs will be hybrids of both C and C++ code. Further, it will be common for C programs to be "upgraded" into C++ programs. Thus, knowledge of both the C and the C++ I/O system will be necessary. For example, in order to change the C-based I/O functions into C++ object-oriented I/O functions, you will need to know how both the C and C++ I/O systems operate.
- An understanding of the basic principles behind the ANSI C I/O system helps you understand the C++ object-oriented I/O system. (Both share the same general concepts.)
- In certain situations (for example, in very short, "throw-away" programs), it may be easier to use C's non-object-oriented approach to I/O than it is to use the object-oriented I/O defined by C++.

In addition, there is an unwritten rule that any C++ programmer must also be a C programmer. If you don't know how to use the C I/O system, you will be limiting your professional horizons.

Streams and Files

Fundamental to understanding the C (and C++) I/O system are the concepts of *streams* and *files.* The C I/O system supplies a consistent interface to the programmer independent of the actual device being accessed. That is, the C I/O system provides a level of abstraction between the programmer and the hardware. This abstraction is called a *stream*; the actual device is called a *file*. It is important to know how they interact.

Streams

The C I/O system is designed to work with a wide variety of devices, including terminals, disk drives, and so on. Even though each device is different, the I/O system transforms each into a logical device called a *stream*. All streams are similar in behavior. Because streams are largely device-independent, the same function that can write to a disk file can also be used to write to another type of device, such as the console. There are two types of streams: text and binary.

Text Streams

A *text stream* is a sequence of characters. In a text stream, certain character translations may occur as required by the host environment. For example, a newline may be converted to a carriage return/linefeed pair. Therefore, there may not be a one-to-one relationship between the characters that are written or read and those on the external device. Also, because of possible translations, the number of characters written or read may not be the same as those on the external device.

Binary Streams

A *binary stream* is a sequence of bytes that have a one-to-one correspondence to those in the external device. That is, no character translations occur. Also, the number of bytes written or read is the same as the number on the external device. However, an implementation-defined number of null bytes may be appended to a binary stream. These null bytes might be used to pad the information so that it fills a sector on a disk, for example.

Files

In C, a *file* is a logical concept that can be applied to everything from disk files to terminals. A stream is associated with a specific file by performing an *open* operation. Once a file is open, information can be exchanged between it and your program.

Not all files have the same capabilities. For example, a disk file can support random access, but a modem cannot. This illustrates an important point about the C I/O system: All streams are the same but all files are not.

If the file can support random access (also called *position requests*), opening that file initializes the *file position indicator* to the start of the file. As each character is read from or written to the file, the position indicator is incremented, ensuring progression through the file.

The smallest accessible portion of a disk is a *sector*. Information is written to or read from a disk one sector at a time. Thus, even if your program only needs a single byte of data, an entire sector of data will be read. This data is put into a region of memory called a *buffer* until it can be used by your program. When data is output to a disk file, it is buffered until a full sector's worth of information has been accumulated, at which point it is actually physically written to the file.

A stream is disassociated from a specific file using a *close* operation. Closing a stream causes any contents of its associated buffer to be written to the external device (it will be padded, if necessary, to fill out a complete sector). This process is generally called *flushing* the buffer, and it guarantees that no information is accidentally left in the disk buffer. All files are closed automatically when your program terminates normally by **main( )** returning to the operating system or by calling **exit( )**. However, it is better to actually close a file using **fclose( )** as soon as it is no longer needed, because several events can prevent the buffer from being written to the disk file. For example, files are not written if a program terminates through a call to **abort( )**, if it crashes, or if the user turns the computer off before terminating the program.

At the beginning of a program's execution, five predefined text streams are opened. They are **stdin**, **stdout**, **stderr**, **stdaux**, and **stdprn**, and they refer to the standard I/O devices connected to the system, as shown here:

Stream	Device
stdin	Keyboard
stdout	Screen
stderr	Screen
stdaux	First serial port
stdprn	Printer

The first three streams are defined by the ANSI C standard, and any code that uses them is fully portable. The last two are specific to Borland and may not be portable to other compilers. Most operating systems, including Windows and DOS, allow I/O redirection, so routines that read or write to these streams can be redirected to other devices. (Redirection of I/O is the process whereby information that would normally go to one device is rerouted to another device by the operating system.) You should never try explicitly to open or close these files.

Each stream that is associated with a file has a file control structure of type **FILE**. This structure is defined in the header **stdio.h**. You must not make modifications to this structure.

If you are new to programming, C's separation of streams and files may seem unnecessary or contrived. Just remember that its main purpose is to provide a consistent interface. In C, you need only think in terms of streams and use only one file system to accomplish all I/O operations. The C I/O system automatically converts the raw input or output from each device into an easily managed stream.

The remainder of this chapter discusses the standard C I/O system. It does so by dividing it into two parts: console I/O and file I/O. As you will see, these are different sides of the same coin. However, this somewhat artificial distinction makes it easier to discuss them.

Console I/O

Console I/O refers to operations that occur at the keyboard and screen of your computer. Because input and output to the console is such a common affair, a subsystem of the ANSI C I/O file system was created to deal exclusively with console I/O. Technically, these functions direct their operations to the standard input (**stdin**) and standard output (**stdout**) of the system. It is possible to redirect the console I/O to other devices. For simplicity of discussion, however, it is assumed that the console will be the device used since it is the most common.

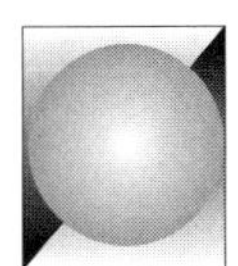

NOTE: Neither the C nor the C++ languages provide built-in support for graphic user interfaces, such as Windows. When performing input or output in a Windows environment, you will need to use special functions defined by Windows itself. For an overview of Windows programming, see Part 5.

Reading and Writing Characters

The simplest of the standard console I/O functions are **getchar( )**, which reads a character from the keyboard, and **putchar( )**, which prints a character to the screen at the current cursor location. However, **getchar( )** has some significant limitations, which are described below. For this reason, most of the time you will substitute **getche( )** when you need to read a character. The **getche( )** function is defined by Borland, not by the ANSI C standard. Although it is a common extension, it may not be nonportable to other environments. **getche( )** waits until a key is pressed and then returns its value. The key pressed is also *echoed* to the screen automatically. The prototypes for **getche( )** and **putchar( )** are shown here:

```
int getche(void);
int putchar(int ch);
```

The **getche( )** function returns the character pressed. The **putchar( )** function returns *ch* if successful, or **EOF** if an error occurs. (**EOF** is a macro defined in **stdio.h** that stands for *end of file.*) Even though *ch* is declared as an integer, only the low-order byte is displayed on the screen. Similarly, even though **getche( )** returns an integer, the low-order byte will contain the character entered at the keyboard. The **getche( )** function requires the **conio.h** header file.

The following program inputs characters from the keyboard and prints them in reverse case. That is, uppercase prints as lowercase, and lowercase as uppercase. The program halts when a period is typed.

```
/* Case Switcher */
#include <conio.h>
#include <stdio.h>
#include <ctype.h>

int main(void) {
  char ch;

  do {
    ch = getche();
    if(islower(ch)) putchar(toupper(ch));
    else putchar(tolower(ch));
  } while (ch!='.'); /* use a period to stop*/
  return 0;
}
```

There are two important alternatives to **getche( )**. The first is **getchar( )**, mentioned earlier, which is the character input function defined by ANSI C. The trouble with **getchar( )** is that it buffers input until a carriage return is entered. The reason for this is that the original UNIX systems line-buffered terminal input—that is, you had to enter a carriage return before anything you had just typed was actually sent to the computer. To be compatible with the UNIX implementation, many C compilers, including Borland, have implemented **getchar( )** so that it line-buffers input. This is quite annoying in today's interactive environments, and the use of **getchar( )** is not recommended. You may want to play with it a little to understand its effect better. However, this guide makes little use of **getchar( )**.

A second, more useful, variation on **getche( )** is **getch( )**, which operates like **getche( )** except that the character you type is not echoed to the screen. You can use this fact to create a rather humorous (if disconcerting) program to run on some unsuspecting user. The program, shown here, displays what appears to be a standard command prompt and waits for input. However, every character the user types is displayed as the next letter in the alphabet. That is, an "A" becomes "B", and so forth. To stop the program, press CTRL-A.

```
/* This program appears to act as a command-prompt gone wild. It
   displays the command prompt but displays every character
   the user types as the next letter in the alphabet.
*/

#include <stdio.h>
#include <conio.h>

int main(void)
{
```

```
  char ch;

  do {
    printf("C>");
    for(;;) {
      ch = getch(); /* read chars without echo */
      if(ch=='\r' || ch==1) {
        printf("\n");
        break;
      }
      putchar(ch+1);
    }
  } while(ch!=1) ; /* exit on control-A */

  return 0;
}
```

While this program is, obviously, just for fun, **getch( )** has many practical uses. For example, you could use it to input a password without echoing the password to the screen.

Reading and Writing Strings: gets( ) and puts( )

On the next step up, in terms of complexity and power, are the functions **gets( )** and **puts( )**. They enable you to read and write strings of characters at the console.

The **gets( )** function reads a string of characters entered at the keyboard and places them at the address pointed to by its character pointer argument. You may type characters at the keyboard until you strike a carriage return. The carriage return does not become part of the string; instead, a null terminator is placed at the end, and **gets( )** returns. In fact, it is impossible to use **gets( )** to obtain a carriage return (**getchar( )** and its variants can, though). Typing mistakes can be corrected by using the BACKSPACE before pressing ENTER. The **gets( )** function has the prototype

char *gets(char **str*);

where *str* is a character array. The **gets( )** function returns a pointer to *str*. The following program reads a string into the array **str** and prints its length:

```
#include <stdio.h>
#include <string.h>

int main(void)
{
  char str[80];
```

```
  gets(str);
  printf("Length is %d", strlen(str));

  return 0;
}
```

There is a potential problem with using **gets( )** that you need to be aware of: Using **gets( )**, it is possible to overrun the boundaries of the array with which it is called. This is because there is no way for **gets( )** to know when it has reached the limit of the array. For example, if you call **gets( )** with an array that is 40 bytes long and then enter 40 or more characters, you will have overrun the array. This will, obviously, cause problems and often lead to a system crash. As an alternative, you can use the **fgets( )** function (described later in this chapter), which allows you to specify a maximum length. The only trouble with **fgets( )** is that it retains the newline character. If you don't want the newline, it must be removed manually. It is possible that in the future, a replacement for **gets( )** will be added to standard C, but for now it is still the easiest way to read a string from the keyboard—just be careful.

The **puts( )** function writes its string argument to the screen followed by a newline. Its prototype is

int puts(const char **str*);

Here, *str* is the string being output. The function returns nonnegative if successful and **EOF** on failure. It recognizes the same backslash codes as **printf( )**, such as **\t** for tab. A call to **puts( )** requires far less overhead than the same call to **printf( )** because **puts( )** outputs only a string of characters; it does not output numbers or do format conversions. It takes up less space and runs faster than **printf( )**. The following statement writes "hello" on the screen:

```
puts("hello");
```

The simplest functions that perform console I/O operations are summarized in Table 8-1.

Formatted Console I/O

The C standard library contains two functions that perform formatted input and output on the built-in data types: **printf( )** and **scanf( )**. The term *formatted* refers to the fact that these functions can read and write data in various formats that are under your control. The **printf( )** function is used to write data to the console; **scanf( )**, its complement, reads data from the keyboard. Both **printf( )** and **scanf( )** can operate on any of the built-in data types, including characters, strings, and numbers.

Function	Operation
getchar( )	Reads a character from the keyboard; waits for carriage return
getche( )	Reads a character with echo; does not wait for carriage return; not defined by ANSI standard C, but a common extension
getch( )	Reads a character without echo; does not wait for carriage return; not defined by ANSI standard C, but a common extension
putchar( )	Writes a character to the screen
gets( )	Reads a string from the keyboard
puts( )	Writes a string to the screen

Table 8-1. *The Basic Console I/O Functions*

printf( )

The **printf( )** function has this prototype:

int printf(const char *fmt_string, . . .);

The first argument, *fmt_string*, defines the way any subsequent arguments are displayed. Often called the *format string*, it consists of two types of items: characters that will be printed on the screen, and format specifiers that define the way arguments that follow the format string are displayed. A format specifier begins with a percent sign and is followed by the format code. The format specifiers are shown in Table 8-2. There must be exactly the same number of arguments as there are format specifiers, and the format specifiers and arguments are matched in order from left to right. For example, this call to **printf( )**

```
printf("Hi %c %d %s", 'c', 10, "there!");
```

displays "Hi c 10 there!". The **printf( )** function returns the number of characters output. It returns **EOF** if an error occurs.

Printing Characters

To print an individual character, use **%c**. This causes its matching argument to be output, unmodified, to the screen.

To print a string, use **%s**.

Code	Format
%c	Character.
%d	Signed decimal integers.
%i	Signed decimal integers.
%e	Scientific notation (lowercase e).
%E	Scientific notation (uppercase E).
%f	Decimal floating point.
%g	Uses %e or %f, whichever is shorter.
%G	Uses %E or %F, whichever is shorter.
%o	Unsigned octal.
%s	String of characters.
%u	Unsigned decimal integers.
%x	Unsigned hexadecimal (lowercase letters).
%X	Unsigned hexadecimal (uppercase letters).
%p	Displays a pointer.
%n	The associated argument is an integer pointer into which the number of characters written so far is placed.
%%	Prints a % sign.

Table 8-2. *The* **printf( )** *Format Specifiers*

Printing Numbers

You may use either **%d** or **%i** to indicate a signed decimal number. These format specifiers are equivalent; both are supported for historical reasons.

To output an unsigned value, use **%u**.

The **%f** format specifier displays numbers in floating point.

The **%e** and **%E** specifiers tell **printf( )** to display a floating point argument in scientific notation. Numbers represented in scientific notation take this general form:

```
x.dddddE+/-yy
```

If you want to display the letter "E" in uppercase, use the **%E** format; otherwise, use **%e**.

You can tell **printf( )** to use either **%f** or **%e** by using the **%g** or **%G** format specifiers. This causes **printf( )** to select the format specifier that produces the shortest output. Where applicable, use **%G** if you want "E" shown in uppercase; otherwise, use **%g**. The following program demonstrates the effect of the **%g** format specifier:

```
#include <stdio.h>

int main(void)
{
  double f;

  for(f=1.0; f<1.0e+10; f=f*10)
    printf("%g ", f);

  return 0;
}
```

It produces the following output:

```
1 10 100 1000 10000 100000 1e+06 1e+07 1e+08 1e+09
```

You can display unsigned integers in octal or hexadecimal format using **%o** and **%x**, respectively. Since the hexadecimal number system uses the letters A through F to represent the numbers 10 through 15, you can display these letters in either upper- or lowercase. For uppercase, use the **%X** format specifier; for lowercase, use **%x**, as shown here:

```
#include <stdio.h>

int main(void)
{
  unsigned num;

  for(num=0; num<255; num++) {
    printf("%o ", num);
    printf("%x ", num);
    printf("%X\n", num);
  }

  return 0;
}
```

Displaying an Address

If you wish to display an address, use **%p**. This format specifier causes **printf( )** to display a machine address in a format compatible with the type of addressing used by the computer. The next program displays the address of **sample**:

```
#include <stdio.h>

int sample;

int main(void)
{
  printf("%p", &sample);

  return 0;
}
```

The %n Specifier

The **%n** format specifier is different from the others. Instead of telling **printf( )** to display something, it causes **printf( )** to load the variable pointed to by its corresponding argument with a value equal to the number of characters that have been output. In other words, the value that corresponds to the **%n** format specifier must be a pointer to a variable. After the call to **printf( )** has returned, this variable will hold the number of characters output, up to the point at which the **%n** was encountered. Examine this program to understand this somewhat unusual format code:

```
#include <stdio.h>

int main(void)
{
  int count;

  printf("this%n is a test\n", &count);
  printf("%d", count);

  return 0;
}
```

This program displays **this is a test** followed by the number 4. The **%n** format specifier is used primarily to enable your program to perform dynamic formatting.

Format Modifiers

Many format specifiers may take modifiers that alter their meaning slightly. For example, you can specify a minimum field width, the number of decimal places, and left justification. The format modifier goes between the percent sign and the format code. These modifiers are discussed next.

The Minimum Field-Width Specifier

An integer placed between the % sign and the format code acts as a *minimum field-width specifier*. This pads the output with spaces to ensure that it reaches a certain minimum length. If the string or number is longer than that minimum, it will still be printed in full. The default padding is done with spaces. If you wish to pad with 0's, place a 0 before the field-width specifier. For example, **%05d** will pad a number of less than five digits with 0's so that its total length is five. The following program demonstrates the minimum field-width specifier:

```
#include <stdio.h>

int main(void)
{
  double item;

  item = 10.12304;

  printf("%f\n", item);
  printf("%10f\n", item);
  printf("%012f\n", item);

  return 0;
}
```

This program produces the following output:

```
10.123040
 10.123040
00010.123040
```

The minimum field-width modifier is most commonly used to produce tables in which the columns line up. For example, the next program produces a table of squares and cubes for the numbers 1 through 19:

```
#include <stdio.h>

int main(void)
{
  int i;

  /* display a table of squares and cubes */
  for(i=1; i<20; i++)
```

```
    printf("%8d %8d %8d\n", i, i*i, i*i*i);

  return 0;
}
```

A sample of its output is shown here:

```
 1        1        1
 2        4        8
 3        9       27
 4       16       64
 5       25      125
 6       36      216
 7       49      343
 8       64      512
 9       81      729
10      100     1000
11      121     1331
12      144     1728
13      169     2197
14      196     2744
15      225     3375
16      256     4096
17      289     4913
18      324     5832
19      361     6859
```

The Precision Specifier

The *precision specifier* follows the minimum field-width specifier (if there is one). It consists of a period followed by an integer. Its exact meaning depends upon the type of data it is applied to.

When you apply the precision specifier to floating-point data using the **%f**, **%e**, or **%E** specifiers, it determines the number of decimal places displayed. For example, **%10.4f** displays a number at least ten characters wide with four decimal places. If you don't specify the precision, a default of six is used.

When the precision specifier is applied to **%g** or **%G**, it specifies the number of significant digits.

Applied to strings, the precision specifier specifies the maximum field length. For example, **%5.7s** displays a string at least five and not exceeding seven characters long. If the string is longer than the maximum field width, the end characters will be truncated.

When applied to integer types, the precision specifier determines the minimum number of digits that will appear for each number. Leading zeros are added to achieve the required number of digits.

The following program illustrates the precision specifier:

```
#include <stdio.h>

int main(void)
{
  printf("%.4f\n", 123.1234567);
  printf("%3.8d\n", 1000);
  printf("%10.15s\n", "This is a simple test.");

  return 0;
}
```

It produces the following output:

```
123.1235
00001000
This is a simpl
```

Justifying Output

By default, all output is right-justified. That is, if the field width is larger than the data printed, the data will be placed on the right edge of the field. You can force output to be left-justified by placing a minus sign directly after the %. For example, **%–10.2f** left-justifies a floating-point number with two decimal places in a 10-character field.

The following program illustrates left justification:

```
#include <stdio.h>

int main(void)
{
  printf("right-justified:%8d\n", 100);
  printf("left-justified:%-8d\n", 100);

  return 0;
}
```

Handling Other Data Types

There are two format modifiers that allow **printf( )** to display **short** and **long** integers. These modifiers may be applied to the **d**, **i**, **o**, **u**, and **x** type specifiers. The **l** (*ell*) modifier tells **printf( )** that a **long** data type follows. For example, **%ld** means that a **long int** is to be displayed. The **h** modifier instructs **printf( )** to display a **short** integer. For instance, **%hu** indicates that the data is of type **short unsigned int**.

The **L** modifier may prefix the floating-point specifiers **e**, **f**, and **g** and indicates that a **long double** follows.

The * and # Modifiers

The **printf( )** function supports two additional modifiers to some of its format specifiers: * and #.

Preceding **g**, **G**, **f**, **E**, or **e** specifiers with a # ensures that there will be a decimal point even if there are no decimal digits. If you precede the **x** or **X** format specifier with a #, the hexadecimal number will be printed with a **0x** prefix. Preceding the **o** specifier with # causes the number to be printed with a leading zero. You cannot apply # to any other format specifiers.

Instead of constants, the minimum field width and precision specifiers may be provided by arguments to **printf( )**. To accomplish this, use an * as a placeholder. When the format string is scanned, **printf( )** will match the * to an argument in the order in which they occur. For example, in Figure 8-1, the minimum field width is 10, the precision is 4, and the value to be displayed is **123.3**.

The following program illustrates both # and *:

```
#include <stdio.h>

int main(void)
{
  printf("%x %#x\n", 10, 10);
  printf("%*.*f", 10, 4, 1234.34);

  return 0;
}
```

scanf( )

The general-purpose console input routine is **scanf( )**. It reads all the built-in data types and automatically converts numbers into the proper internal format. It is somewhat like the reverse of **printf( )**. The general form of **scanf( )** is

int scanf(const char **fmt_string*, . . .);

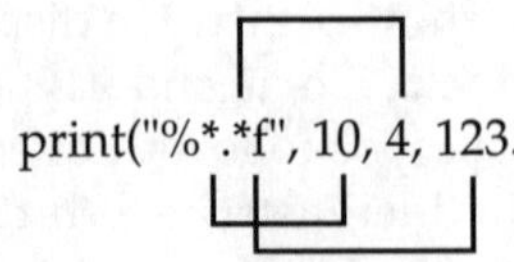

```
print("%*.*f", 10, 4, 123.3);
```

Figure 8-1. *How the * is matched to its value*

The *fmt_string* determines how values are read into the variables pointed to in the argument list.

The format string consists of three classifications of characters:

- Format specifiers
- White-space characters
- Non-white-space characters

The **scanf( )** function returns the number of fields that are input. It returns **EOF** if a premature end of file is reached.

Format Specifiers

The input format specifiers are preceded by a % sign and tell **scanf( )** what type of data is to be read next. These codes are listed in Table 8-3. The format specifiers are matched, in order from left to right, with the arguments in the argument list.

Code	Meaning
%c	Read a single character.
%d	Read a decimal integer.
%i	Read a decimal integer.
%e	Read a floating-point number.
%f	Read a floating-point number.
%g	Read a floating-point number.
%o	Read an octal number.
%s	Read a string.
%x	Read a hexadecimal number.
%p	Read a pointer.
%n	Receives an integer value equal to the number of characters read so far.
%u	Read an unsigned integer.
%[ ]	Scan for a set of characters.

Table 8-3. *The* **scanf( )** *Format Specifiers*

Inputting Numbers

To read a decimal number, use the **%d** or **%i** specifiers. (These specifiers, which do the same thing, are both included for historical reasons.)

To read a floating-point number represented in either standard or scientific notation, use **%e**, **%f**, or **%g**. (Again, these specifiers, which do precisely the same thing, are included for historical reasons.)

You can use **scanf( )** to read integers in either octal or hexadecimal form by using the **%o** and **%x** format commands, respectively. The **%x** may be in either upper- or lowercase. You may enter the letters A through F in upper- or lower-case when entering hexadecimal numbers. The following program reads an octal and a hexadecimal number:

```
#include <stdio.h>

int main(void)
{
  int i, j;

  scanf("%o%x", &i, &j);
  printf("%o %x", i, j);

  return 0;
}
```

The **scanf( )** function stops reading a number when the first nonnumeric character is encountered.

Inputting Unsigned Integers

To input an unsigned integer, use the **%u** format specifier. For example,

```
unsigned num;
scanf("%u", &num);
```

reads an unsigned number and puts its value into **num**.

Reading Individual Characters Using scanf( )

As you learned earlier in this chapter, you can read individual characters using **getchar( )** or a derivative function. You can also use **scanf( )** for this purpose if you use the **%c** format specifier. However, like most implementations of **getchar( )**, **scanf( )** will generally line-buffer input when the **%c** specifier is used. This is the case with Borland C++, too. Line-buffering makes **scanf( )** somewhat troublesome in an interactive environment.

Although spaces, tabs, and newlines are used as field separators when reading other types of data, when reading a single character, white-space characters are read like any other character. For example, with an input stream of "**x y**," this code fragment

```
scanf("%c%c%c", &a, &b, &c);
```

returns with the character **x** in **a**, a space in **b**, and the character **y** in **c**.

Reading Strings

The **scanf( )** function can be used to read a string from the input stream using the **%s** format specifier. The **%s** causes **scanf( )** to read characters until it encounters a white-space character. The characters that are read are put into the character array pointed to by the corresponding argument and the result is null-terminated. As it applies to **scanf( )**, a white-space character is either a space, a newline, a tab, a vertical tab, or a form feed. Unlike **gets( )**, which reads a string until a carriage return is typed, **scanf( )** reads a string until the first white space is entered. This means that you cannot use **scanf( )** to read a string like "this is a test" because the first space terminates the reading process. To see the effect of the **%s** specifier, try this program using the string "hello there":

```
#include <stdio.h>

int main(void)
{
  char str[80];

  printf("Enter a string: ");
  scanf("%s", str);
  printf("Here's your string: %s", str);

  return 0;
}
```

The program responds with only the "hello" portion of the string.

Inputting an Address

To input a memory address, use the **%p** format specifier. This specifier causes **scanf( )** to read an address in the format defined by the architecture of the CPU. For example, this program inputs an address and then displays what is at that memory address:

```
#include <stdio.h>

int main(void)
{
  char *p;

  printf("Enter an address: ");
  scanf("%p", &p);
```

```
  printf("Value at location %p is %c\n", p, *p);

  return 0;
}
```

The %n Specifier

The **%n** specifier instructs **scanf( )** to assign the number of characters read from the input stream at the point at which the **%n** was encountered to the variable pointed to by the corresponding argument.

Using a Scanset

The **scanf( )** function supports a general-purpose format specifier called a scanset. A *scanset* defines a set of characters. When **scanf( )** processes the scanset, it will input characters, as long as those characters are part of the scanset. The characters read will be assigned to the character array that is pointed to by the scanset's corresponding argument. You define a scanset by putting the characters to scan for inside square brackets. The beginning square bracket must be prefixed by a percent sign. For example, the following scanset tells **scanf( )** to read only the characters X, Y, and Z.

```
%[XYZ]
```

When you use a scanset, **scanf( )** continues to read characters and put them into the corresponding character array until it encounters a character that is not in the scanset. Upon return from **scanf( )**, this array will contain a null-terminated string that consists of the characters that have been read. To see how this works, try this program:

```
#include <stdio.h>

int main(void)
{
  int i;
  char str[80], str2[80];

  scanf("%d%[abcdefg]%s", &i, str, str2);
  printf("%d %s %s", i, str, str2);

  return 0;
}
```

Enter **123abcdtye** followed by ENTER. The program will then display **123 abcd tye**. Because the "t" is not part of the scanset, **scanf( )** stops reading characters into **str** when it encounters the "t." The remaining characters are put into **str2**.

You can specify a range inside a scanset using a hyphen. For example, this tells **scanf( )** to accept the characters "A" through "Z".

```
%[A-Z]
```

Technically, the use of the hyphen to describe a range is not defined by the ANSI C standard. However, it is nearly universally accepted.

You can specify more than one range within a scanset. For example, this program reads digits and then letters:

```
/* A scanset example using ranges. */
#include <stdio.h>

int main(void)
{
  char s1[80], s2[80];

  printf("Enter numbers, then some letters");
  scanf("%[0-9]%[a-zA-Z]", s1, s2);
  printf("%s %s", s1, s2);

  return 0;
}
```

You can specify an inverted set if the first character in the set is a caret (^). When the ^ is present, it instructs **scanf( )** to accept any character that *is not* defined by the scanset. Here, the previous program uses the ^ to invert the type of characters the scanset will read:

```
/* A scanset example using inverted ranges. */
#include <stdio.h>

int main(void)
{
  char s1[80], s2[80];

  printf("Enter non-numbers, then some non-letters");
  scanf("%[^0-9]%[^a-zA-Z]", s1, s2);
  printf("%s %s", s1, s2);

  return 0;
}
```

One important point to remember is that the scanset is case-sensitive. Therefore, if you want to scan for both uppercase and lowercase letters, they must be specified individually.

Discarding Unwanted White Space

A white-space character in the control string causes **scanf( )** to skip over one or more white-space characters in the input stream. A white-space character is a space, a tab, a vertical tab, a form feed, or a newline. In essence, one white-space character in the control string causes **scanf( )** to read—but not store—any number (including zero) of white-space characters up to the first non-white-space character.

Non-White-Space Characters in the Control String

A non-white-space character in the control string causes **scanf( )** to read and discard matching characters in the input stream. For example, **"%d,%d"** causes **scanf( )** to read an integer, read and discard a comma, and then read another integer. If the specified character is not found, **scanf( )** terminates. If you wish to read and discard a percent sign, use %% in the control string.

You Must Pass scanf( ) Addresses

All the variables used to receive values through **scanf( )** must be passed by their addresses. This means that all arguments must be pointers to the variables used as arguments. Recall that this is C's way of creating a call by reference, and it allows a function to alter the contents of an argument. For example, to read an integer into the variable **count**, you would use the following **scanf( )** call:

```
scanf("%d", &count);
```

Strings will be read into character arrays, and the array name (without any index) is the address of the first element of the array. So, to read a string into the character array **str**, you would use

```
scanf("%s", str);
```

In this case, **str** is already a pointer and need not be preceded by the **&** operator.

Format Modifiers

As with **printf( )**, **scanf( )** allows a number of its format specifiers to be modified.

The format specifiers can include a maximum field-length modifier. This is an integer, placed between the % and the format specifier, that limits the number of characters read for that field. For example, to read no more than 20 characters into **str**, write

```
scanf("%20s", str);
```

If the input stream is greater than 20 characters, a subsequent call to input begins where this call leaves off. For example, if you enter

ABCDEFGHIJKLMNOPQRSTUVWXYZ

as the response to the **scanf( )** call in this example, only the first 20 characters, or up to the "T," are placed into **str** because of the maximum field-width specifier. This means that the remaining characters, UVWXYZ, have not yet been used. If another **scanf( )** call is made, such as

```
scanf("%s", str);
```

the letters UVWXYZ are placed into **str**. Input for a field may terminate before the maximum field length is reached if a white space is encountered. In this case, **scanf( )** moves on to the next field.

To read a long integer, put an **l** (*ell*) in front of the format specifier. To read a short integer, put an **h** in front of the format specifier. These modifiers can be used with the **d**, **i**, **o**, **u**, and **x** format codes.

By default, the **f**, **e**, and **g** specifiers instruct **scanf( )** to assign data to a **float**. If you put an **l** (*ell*) in front of one of these specifiers, **scanf( )** assigns the data to a **double**. Using an **l** tells **scanf( )** that the variable receiving the data is a **long double**.

Suppressing Input

You can tell **scanf( )** to read a field but not assign it to any variable by preceding that field's format code with an *. For example, given

```
scanf("%d%*c%d", &x, &y);
```

you could enter the coordinate pair **10,10**. The comma would be correctly read but not assigned to anything. Assignment suppression is especially useful when you need to process only a part of what is being entered.

The ANSI C File System

The ANSI C file system is the part of the I/O system that allows you to read and write disk files. It is composed of several interrelated functions. The most common are shown in Table 8-4. The header file **stdio.h** must be included in any program in which these functions are used.

The header file **stdio.h** provides the prototypes for the I/O functions and defines these three types: **size_t**, **fpos_t**, and **FILE**. The **size_t** type is an unsigned integer, as is **fpos_t**. The **FILE** type is discussed in the next section.

stdio.h also defines several macros. The ones relevant to this chapter are **NULL**, **EOF**, **FOPEN_MAX**, **SEEK_SET**, **SEEK_CUR**, and **SEEK_END**. The **NULL** macro defines a null pointer. The **EOF** macro is generally defined as –1 and is the value returned when an input function tries to read past the end of the file. **FOPEN_MAX** defines an integer value that determines the number of files that may be open at any one time. The other macros are used with **fseek( )**, which is the function that performs random access on a file.

Name	Function
fopen( )	Opens a file.
fclose( )	Closes a file.
putc( )	Writes a character to a file.
fputc( )	Same as **putc( )**.
getc( )	Reads a character from a file.
fgetc( )	Same as **getc( )**.
fseek( )	Seeks to a specified byte in a file.
fprintf( )	Is to a file what **printf( )** is to the console.
fscanf( )	Is to a file what **scanf( )** is to the console.
feof( )	Returns true if end of file is reached.
ferror( )	Returns true if an error has occurred.
rewind( )	Resets the file position indicator to the beginning of the file.
remove( )	Erases a file.
fflush( )	Flushes a file.

Table 8-4. *The Most Common ANSI C File System Functions*

The File Pointer

The file pointer is the common thread that unites the ANSI C file system. A *file pointer* is a pointer to information that defines various things about the file, including its name, status, and the current position of the file. In essence, the file pointer identifies a specific disk file and is used by the associated stream to direct the operation of the I/O functions. A file pointer is a pointer variable of type **FILE**. In order to read or write files, your program needs to use file pointers. To obtain a file pointer variable, use a statement like this:

```
FILE *fp;
```

Opening a File

The **fopen( )** function opens a stream for use, links a file with that stream, and then returns a **FILE** pointer to that stream. Most often (always for the purpose of this discussion) the file is a disk file. The **fopen( )** function has this prototype:

FILE *fopen(const char *filename, const char *mode);

where *mode* points to a string containing the desired open status. The legal values for *mode* in Borland C++ are shown in Table 8-5. The *filename* must be a string of characters that provides a valid file name for the operating system and may include a path specification.

The **fopen( )** function returns a pointer of type **FILE**. This pointer identifies the file and is used by most other file system functions. It should never be altered by your code. The function returns a null pointer if the file cannot be opened.

As Table 8-5 shows, a file can be opened in either text or binary mode. In text mode, carriage return linefeed sequences are translated into newline characters on input. On output, the reverse occurs: newlines are translated to carriage return linefeeds. No such translations occur on binary files. When neither a **t** nor a **b** is specified in the *mode* argument, the text/binary status of the file is determined by the value of the global variable defined by Borland, called **_fmode**. By default, **_fmode** is set to **O_TEXT**, which is text mode. When set to **O_BINARY**, then files will be opened in binary mode. (These macros are defined in **fcntl.h**.) Of course, using an explicit **t** or **b** overrides the effects of the **_fmode** variable. Also, **_fmode** is specific to Borland; it is not defined by the ANSI C I/O system.

If you wish to open a file for writing with the name **test**, write

```
fp = fopen("test", "w");
```

where **fp** is a variable of type **FILE ***. However, you usually see it written like this:

```
if((fp = fopen("test", "w"))==NULL) {
  puts("Cannot open file.");
  exit(1);
}
```

This method detects any error in opening a file, such as a write-protected or full disk, before attempting to write to it.

If you use **fopen( )** to open a file for output, then any pre-existing file by that name is erased and a new file started. If no file by that name exists, then one is created. If you want to add to the end of the file, you must use mode **a** (append). If the file does not exist, it will be created. Opening a file for read operations requires an existing file. If no file exists, an error is returned. If a file is opened for read/write operations, it is not erased if it exists; if no file exists, one is created.

Writing a Character

The ANSI C I/O system defines two equivalent functions that output a character: **putc( )** and **fputc( )**. (Actually, **putc( )** is implemented as a macro.) There are two identical functions simply to preserve compatibility with older versions of C. This book uses **putc( )**, but you can use **fputc( )** if you like.

Mode	Meaning
"r"	Open a file for reading. (Opened as text file by default, see discussion.)
"w"	Create a file for writing. (Opened as text file by default, see discussion.)
"a"	Append to a file. (Opened as text file by default, see discussion.)
"rb"	Open a binary file for reading.
"wb"	Create a binary file for writing.
"ab"	Append to a binary file.
"r+"	Open a file for read/write. (Opened as text file by default, see discussion.)
"w+"	Create a file for read/write. (Opened as text file by default, see discussion.)
"a+"	Append or create a file for read/write. (Opened as text file by default, see discussion.)
"r+b"	Open a binary file for read/write.
"w+b"	Create a binary file for read/write.
"a+b"	Append or create a binary file for read/write.
"rt"	Open a text file for reading.
"wt"	Create a text file for writing.
"at"	Append to a text file.
"r+t"	Open a text file for reading.
"w+t"	Create a text file for read/write.
"a+t"	Open or create a text file for read/write.

Table 8-5. *The Legal Values for Mode*

The **putc( )** function is used to write characters to a stream that was previously opened for writing using the **fopen( )** function. The prototype for **putc( )** is

int putc(int *ch*, FILE **fp*);

where *fp* is the file pointer returned by **fopen( )** and *ch* is the character to be output. The file pointer tells **putc( )** which disk file to write to. For historical reasons, *ch* is defined as an **int**, but only the low-order byte is used.

If a **putc( )** operation is a success, it returns the character written. If **putc( )** fails, an **EOF** is returned.

Reading a Character

There are also two equivalent functions that input a character: **getc( )** and **fgetc( )**. Both are defined to preserve compatibility with older versions of C. This book uses **getc( )** (which is actually implemented as a macro), but you can use **fgetc( )** if you like.

The **getc( )** function is used to read characters from a stream opened in read mode by **fopen( )**. The prototype is

int getc(FILE **fp*);

where *fp* is a file pointer of type **FILE** returned by **fopen( )**. For historical reasons, **getc( )** returns an integer, but the high-order byte is 0.

The **getc( )** function returns an **EOF** when the end of the file has been reached. To read a text file to the end, you could use the following code:

```
ch = getc(fp);

while(ch!=EOF) {
  ch = getc(fp);
}
```

fclose( )

The **fclose( )** function is used to close a stream that was opened by a call to **fopen( )**. It writes any data still remaining in the disk buffer to the file and does a formal operating-system–level close on the file. A call to **fclose( )** frees the file control block associated with the stream and makes it available for reuse. There is an operating system limit to the number of open files you can have at any one time, so it may be necessary to close one file before opening another.

The **fclose( )** function has the prototype

int fclose(FILE **fp*);

where *fp* is the file pointer returned by the call to **fopen( )**. A return value of 0 signifies a successful close operation; an **EOF** is returned if an error occurs. Generally, **fclose( )**

will fail only when a diskette has been prematurely removed from the drive or if there is no more space on the diskette.

Using fopen( ), getc( ), putc( ), and fclose( )

The functions **fopen( )**, **getc( )**, **putc( )**, and **fclose( )** comprise a minimal set of file routines. A simple example of using **putc( )**, **fopen( )**, and **fclose( )** is the following program, **ktod**. It simply reads characters from the keyboard and writes them to a disk file until a period is typed. The file name is specified from the command line. For example, if you call this program **ktod**, then typing **ktod test** allows you to enter lines of text into the file called **test**.

```
/* ktod: key to disk. */

#include <stdio.h>

int main(int argc, char *argv[])
{
  FILE *fp;
  char ch;

  if(argc!=2) {
    printf("You forgot to enter the filename.");
    return 1;
  }

  if((fp=fopen(argv[1], "w")) == NULL) {
    printf("Cannot open file.");
    return 1;
  }

  do {
    ch = getchar();
    putc(ch, fp);
  } while (ch!='.');

  fclose(fp);

  return 0;
}
```

The complementary program **dtos** will read any text file and display the contents on the screen. You must specify the name of the file on the command line.

```
/* dtos: disk to screen. */
#include <stdio.h>

int main(int argc, char *argv[])
{
  FILE *fp;
  char ch;

  if(argc!=2) {
    printf("You forgot to enter the filename.");
    return 1;
  }

  if((fp=fopen(argv[1], "r")) == NULL) {
    printf("Cannot open file.");
    return 1;
  }

  ch = getc(fp);   /* read one character */

  while (ch!=EOF) {
    putchar(ch);  /* print on screen */
    ch = getc(fp);
  }

  fclose(fp);

  return 0;
}
```

Using feof( )

As stated earlier, the C file system can also operate on binary data. When a file is opened for binary input, an integer value equal to the **EOF** mark may be read. This would cause **getc( )** to indicate an end-of-file condition even though the physical end of the file had not been reached. To solve this problem, C includes the function **feof( )**, which is used to determine the end of the file when reading binary data. It has this prototype:

int feof(FILE **fp*);

where *fp* identifies the file. The **feof( )** function returns non-0 if the end of the file has been reached; otherwise, 0 is returned. Therefore, the following routine reads a binary file until the end-of-file mark is encountered:

```
while(!feof(fp)) ch = getc(fp);
```

This method can be applied to text files as well as binary files.

The following program copies a file of any type. Notice that the files are opened in binary mode and **feof( )** is used to check for the end of the file.

```
/* This program will copy a file to another. */
#include <stdio.h>

int main(int argc, char *argv[])
{
  FILE *in, *out;
  char ch;

  if(argc!=3) {
    printf("You forgot to enter a filename.");
    return 1;
  }

  if((in=fopen(argv[1], "rb")) == NULL) {
    printf("Cannot open source file.");
    return 1;
  }
  if((out=fopen(argv[2], "wb")) == NULL) {
    printf("Cannot open destination file.");
    return 1;
  }

  /* This code actually copies the file. */
  while(!feof(in)) {
     ch = getc(in);
     if(!feof(in)) putc(ch, out);
  }

  fclose(in);
  fclose(out);

  return 0;
}
```

Two Extended Functions: getw( ) and putw( )

In addition to **getc( )** and **putc( )**, Borland supports two additional buffered I/O functions: **putw( )** and **getw( )**, which you might find useful. (Although these functions are not defined by the ANSI standard, they are included with Borland C++ and are commonly found in most other C compiler libraries.) They are used to read and write integers from and to a disk file. These functions work exactly the same as **putc( )** and **getc( )**, except that instead of reading or writing a single character, they read or write integers. For example, the following code fragment writes an integer to the file pointed to by *fp*:

```
putw(100, fp);
```

Working with Strings: fgets( ) and fputs( )

The C I/O system includes two functions that can read and write strings from and to streams: **fgets( )** and **fputs( )**. Their prototypes are

int fputs(const char **str,* FILE **fp*);
char *fgets(char **str,* int *length,* FILE **fp*);

The function **fputs( )** works much like **puts( )** except that it writes the string to the specified stream. The **fgets( )** function reads a string from the specified stream until either a newline character or *length* –1 characters have been read. If a newline is read, it will be part of the string (unlike **gets( )**). In either case, the resultant string will be null-terminated. The function returns *str* if successful and a null pointer if an error occurs.

As mentioned earlier in this chapter, you may want to use **fgets( )** as an alternative to **gets( )**. To do so, simply specify **stdin** as the file pointer. For example, this program reads up to 79 characters received from standard input:

```
#include <stdio.h>

int main(void)
{
  char s[80];

  printf("Enter a string: ");
  fgets(s, 80, stdin);
  printf("Here is your string: %s", s);

  return 0;
}
```

The advantage of using **fgets( )** over **gets( )** is that you can prevent the input array from being overrun. However, the array may contain the newline character.

fread( ) and fwrite( )

The ANSI C file system provides two functions, **fread( )** and **fwrite( )**, that allow the reading and writing of blocks of data. Their prototypes are

size_t fread(void **buffer*, size_t *num_bytes*, size_t *count*, FILE **fp*);
size_t fwrite(const void **buffer*, size_t *num_bytes*, size_t *count*, FILE **fp*);

In the case of **fread( )**, *buffer* is a pointer to a region of memory that receives the data read from the file. For **fwrite( )**, *buffer* is a pointer to the information to be written to the file. The length of each item, in bytes, to be read or written is specified by *num_bytes*. The argument *count* determines how many items (each being *num_bytes* in length) will be read or written. Finally, *fp* is a file pointer to a previously opened stream.

The **fread( )** function returns the number of items read. This value may be less than *count* if the end of the file is reached or an error occurs. The **fwrite( )** function returns the number of items written. This value will equal *count* unless an error occurs.

As long as the file has been opened for binary data, **fread( )** and **fwrite( )** can read and write any type of information. For example, this program writes a **float** to a disk file:

```
/* Write a floating-point number to a disk file. */
#include <stdio.h>

int main(void)
{
  FILE *fp;
  float f = 12.23;

  if((fp=fopen("test", "wb"))==NULL) {
    printf("Cannot open file.");
    return 1;
  }

  fwrite(&f, sizeof(float), 1, fp);
  fclose(fp);


  return 0;
}
```

As this program illustrates, the buffer can be (and often is) simply a variable.

One of the most useful applications of **fread( )** and **fwrite( )** involves the reading and writing of blocks of data, such as arrays or structures. For example, this fragment writes the contents of the floating-point array **balance** to the file **balance** using a single **fwrite( )** statement. Next, it reads the array, using a single **fread( )** statement, and displays its contents.

```
#include <stdio.h>

int main(void)
{
  register int i;
  FILE *fp;
  float balance[100];

  /* open for write */
  if((fp=fopen("balance", "wb"))==NULL) {
    printf("Cannot open file.");
    return 1;
  }

  for(i=0; i<100; i++) balance[i] = (float) i;

  /* this saves the entire balance array in one step */
  fwrite(balance, sizeof balance, 1, fp);
  fclose(fp);

  /* zero array */
  for(i=0; i<100; i++) balance[i] = 0.0;

  /* open for read */
  if((fp=fopen("balance","rb"))==NULL) {
    printf("cannot open file");
    return 1;
  }

  /* this reads the entire balance array in one step */
  fread(balance, sizeof balance, 1, fp);

  /* display contents of array */
  for(i=0; i<100; i++) printf("%f ", balance[i]);

  fclose(fp);
  return 0;
}
```

Using **fread( )** and **fwrite( )** to read or write complex data is more efficient than using repeated calls to **getc( )** and **putc( )**.

fseek( ) and Random Access I/O

You can perform random read and write operations using the buffered I/O system with the help of **fseek( )**, which sets the file position locator. Its prototype is

int fseek(FILE **fp*, long *num_bytes*, int *origin*);

where *fp* is a file pointer returned by a call to **fopen( )**; *num_bytes*, a long integer, is the number of bytes from *origin* to seek to; and *origin* is one of the following macros (defined in **stdio.h**):

Origin	**Macro Name**
Beginning of file	SEEK_SET
Current position	SEEK_CUR
End of file	SEEK_END

The macros are defined as integer values with **SEEK_SET** being 0, **SEEK_CUR** being 1, and **SEEK_END** being 2. Therefore, to seek *num_bytes* from the start of the file, *origin* should be **SEEK_SET**. To seek from the current position, use **SEEK_CUR**; and to seek from the end of the file, use **SEEK_END**. The **fseek( )** function returns 0 when successful and a nonzero value if an error occurs.

For example, you could use the following code to read the 234th byte in a file called **test**:

```
int func1(void)
{
  FILE *fp;

  if((fp=fopen("test", "rb")) == NULL) {
    printf("Cannot open file.");
    exit(1);
  }

  fseek(fp, 234L, 0);
  return getc(fp);     /* read one character */
                       /* at 234th position */
  }
}
```

Another example that uses **fseek( )** is the following **dump** program, which lets you examine the contents in both ASCII and hexadecimal of any file you choose. You can look at the file in 128-byte "sectors" as you move about the file in either direction. To exit the program, type a **–1** when prompted for the sector. Notice the use of **fread( )** to read the file. At the end-of-file mark, less than **SIZE** number of bytes are likely to be read, so the number returned by **fread( )** is passed to **display( )**. (Remember that **fread( )** returns the number of items actually read.) Enter this program into your computer and study it until you are certain how it works:

```
/* dump: A simple disk look utility using fseek. */
#include <stdio.h>
#include <ctype.h>

#define SIZE 128

void display(int numread);

char buf[SIZE];
void display();

int main(int argc, char *argv[])
{
  FILE *fp;
  int sector, numread;

  if(argc!=2) {
    printf("Usage: dump filename");
    return 1;
  }

  if((fp=fopen(argv[1], "rb"))==NULL) {
    printf("Cannot open file.");
    return 1;
  }

  do {
    printf("Enter sector: ");
    scanf("%d", &sector);
    if(sector >= 0) {
      if(fseek(fp, sector*SIZE, SEEK_SET)) {
        printf("seek error");
      }
      if((numread=fread(buf, 1, SIZE, fp)) != SIZE)
```

```
        printf("EOF reached.");

      display(numread);
    }
  } while(sector>=0);
  return 0;
}

/* Display the contents of a file. */
void display(int numread)
{
  int i, j;

  for(i=0; i<numread/16; i++) {
    for(j=0; j<16; j++) printf("%3X", buf[i*16+j]);
    printf("  ");
    for(j=0; j<16; j++) {
      if(isprint(buf[i*16+j])) printf("%c", buf[i*16+j]);
      else printf(".");
    }
    printf("\n");
  }
}
```

Notice that the library function **isprint( )** is used to determine which characters are printing characters. The **isprint( )** function returns true if the character is printable and false otherwise, and requires the use of the header file **ctype.h**, which is included near the top of the program. A sample output with **dump** used on itself is shown in Figure 8-2.

fprintf( ) and fscanf( )

In addition to the basic I/O functions, the buffered I/O system includes **fprintf( )** and **fscanf( )**. These functions behave exactly like **printf( )** and **scanf( )**, except that they operate with disk files. The prototypes of **fprintf( )** and **fscanf( )** are

int fprintf(FILE **fp*, const char **fmt_string*, . . .);
int fscanf(FILE **fp*, const char **fmt_string*, . . .);

where *fp* is a file pointer returned by a call to **fopen( )**. Except for directing their output to the file defined by *fp*, they operate exactly like **printf( )** and **scanf( )**, respectively.

```
Enter sector: 0
 2F 2A 20 64 75 6D 70 3A 20 41 20 73 69 6D 70 6C  /* dump: A simpl
 65 20 64 69 73 6B 20 6C 6F 6F 6B 20 75 74 69 6C  e disk look util
 69 74 79 20 75 73 69 6E 67 20 66 73 65 65 6B 2E  ity using fseek.
 20 2A 2F  D  A 23 69 6E 63 6C 75 64 65 20 3C 73   */..#include <s
 74 64 69 6F 2E 68 3E  D  A 23 69 6E 63 6C 75 64  tdio.h>..#includ
 65 20 3C 63 74 79 70 65 2E 68 3E  D  A  D  A 23  e <ctype.h>....#
 64 65 66 69 6E 65 20 53 49 5A 45 20 31 32 38  D  define SIZE 128.
  A  D  A 76 6F 69 64 20 64 69 73 70 6C 61 79 28  ...void display(

Enter sector: 1
 69 6E 74 20 6E 75 6D 72 65 61 64 29 3B  D  A  D  int numread);...
  A 63 68 61 72 20 62 75 66 5B 53 49 5A 45 5D 3B  .char buf[SIZE];
  D  A 76 6F 69 64 20 64 69 73 70 6C 61 79 28 29  ..void display()
 3B  D  A  D  A 69 6E 74 20 6D 61 69 6E 28 69 6E  ;....int main(in
 74 20 61 72 67 63 2C 20 63 68 61 72 20 2A 61 72  t argc, char *ar
 67 76 5B 5D 29  D  A 7B  D  A 20 20 46 49 4C 45  gv[])..{..  FILE
 20 2A 66 70 3B  D  A 20 20 69 6E 74 20 73 65 63   *fp;..  int sec
 74 6F 72 2C 20 6E 75 6D 72 65 61 64 3B  D  A  D  tor, numread;...

Enter sector: -1
```

Figure 8-2. *Sample output from the dump program*

To illustrate how useful these functions can be, the following program maintains a simple telephone directory in a disk file. You may enter names and numbers or look up a number given a name.

```
/* A simple telephone directory */

#include <conio.h>
#include <stdlib.h>
#include <stdio.h>
#include <ctype.h>
#include <string.h>

void add_num(void), lookup(void);
char menu(void);
```

```
int main(void)
{
  char choice;

  do {
    choice = menu();
    switch(choice) {
      case 'a': add_num();
        break;
      case 'l': lookup();
        break;
    }
  } while (choice!='q');

  return 0;
}

/* Display menu and get request. */
char menu(void)
{
  char ch;

  do {
    printf("(A)dd, (L)ookup, or (Q)uit: ");
    ch = tolower(getche());
    printf("\n");
  } while(ch != 'q' && ch != 'a' && ch != 'l');

  return ch;
}

/* Add a name and number to the directory. */
void add_num(void)
{
  FILE *fp;
  char name[80];
  int a_code, exchg, num;

  /* open it for append */
  if((fp=fopen("phone","a")) == NULL) {
    printf("Cannot open directory file.");
    exit(1);
```

```
  }

  printf("Enter name and number: ");
  fscanf(stdin, "%s%d%d%d", name, &a_code, &exchg, &num);
  fscanf(stdin, "%*c"); /* remove CR from input stream */

  /* write to file */
  fprintf(fp,"%s %d %d %d\n", name, a_code, exchg, num);

  fclose(fp);
}

/* Find a number given a name. */
void lookup(void)
{
  FILE *fp;
  char name[80], name2[80];
  int a_code, exchg, num;

  /* open it for read */
  if((fp=fopen("phone","r")) == NULL) {
    printf("Cannot open directory file.");
    exit(1);
  }

  printf("name? ");
  gets(name);

  /* look for number */
  while(!feof(fp)) {
    fscanf(fp,"%s%d%d%d", name2, &a_code, &exchg, &num);
    if(!strcmp(name, name2)) {
      printf("%s: (%d) %d-%d\n",name, a_code, exchg, num);
      break;
    }
  }

  fclose(fp);
}
```

Enter this program and run it. After you have entered a couple of names and numbers, examine the file **phone**. As you would expect, it appears just the way it would if the information had been displayed on the screen using **printf( )**.

*NOTE: Although **fprintf( )** and **fscanf( )** are often the easiest way to write and read assorted data to disk files, they are not always the most efficient. Because formatted ASCII data is being written just as it would appear on the screen (instead of in binary), you incur extra overhead with each call. If speed or file size is a concern, you should probably use **fread( )** and **fwrite( )**.*

Erasing Files

The **remove( )** function erases a file. Its prototype is

int remove(const char **filename*);

It returns 0 upon success, non-0 if it fails.

This program uses **remove( )** to erase a file specified by the user:

```
/* A remove() example. */

#include <stdio.h>

int main(void)
{
  char fname[80];

  printf("Name of file to remove: ");
  gets(fname);

  if(remove(fname)) {
    printf("Error removing file");
    return 1;
  }

  else return 0;
}
```

ferror( ) and rewind( )

The **ferror( )** function is used to determine whether a file operation has produced an error. The function **ferror( )** has this prototype:

int ferror(FILE **fp*)

where *fp* is a valid file pointer. It returns true if an error has occurred during the last file operation; it returns false otherwise. Because each file operation sets the error condition, **ferror( )** should be called immediately after each file operation; otherwise, an error may be lost.

The **rewind( )** function resets the file position locator to the beginning of the file specified as its argument. The prototype is

void rewind(FILE *fp*)

where *fp* is a valid file pointer.

The Console Connection

As mentioned at the start of this chapter, whenever a program starts execution, five streams are opened automatically. They are **stdin**, **stdout**, **stderr**, **stdaux**, and **stdprn**. Because these are file pointers, they may be used by any function in the ANSI C I/O system that uses a file pointer. For example, **putchar( )** could be defined as

```
int putchar(int c)
{
  return putc(c, stdout);
}
```

As this example illustrates, C makes little distinction between console I/O and file I/O. In essence, the console I/O functions are simply special versions of their parallel file functions that direct their operations to either **stdin** or **stdout**. The reason they exist is as a convenience to you, the programmer. In general, you may use **stdin**, **stdout**, and **stderr** as file pointers in any function that uses a variable of type **FILE ***.

In environments that allow redirection of I/O, **stdin** and **stdout** can be redirected. This means that they could refer to a device other than the keyboard or screen. For example, consider this program:

```
#include <stdio.h>

int main(void)
{
  char str[80];

  printf("Enter a string: ");
  gets(str);
  printf(str);

  return 0;
}
```

Assume that this program is called TEST. If you execute TEST normally, it displays its prompt on the screen, reads a string from the keyboard, and displays that string on the display. However, either **stdin** or **stdout**, or both, could be redirected to a file. For example, in a DOS or Windows environment, executing TEST like this:

```
TEST > OUTPUT
```

causes the output of TEST to be written to a file called OUTPUT. Executing TEST like this:

```
TEST < INPUT > OUTPUT
```

directs **stdin** to the file called INPUT and sends output to the file called OUTPUT.

As you can see, console I/O and file I/O are really just two slightly different ways of looking at the same thing.

Chapter Nine

The Preprocessor and Comments

The source code for a C (or C++) program can include various instructions to the compiler. Although not actually part of the C language, these *preprocessor directives* expand the scope of its programming environment. This chapter examines the preprocessor. It also examines Borland's built-in macros and some additions made to the preprocessor by Borland C++. The chapter ends with an examination of comments.

ANSI standard C defines the following preprocessor directives:

```
#if
#ifdef
#ifndef
#else
#elif
#endif
#include
#define
#undef
#line
#error
#pragma
```

All preprocessor directives begin with a # sign and each preprocessing directive must be on its own line. For example;

```
/* Will not work! */
#include <stdio.h>  #include <stdlib.h>
```

will not work.

#define

The **#define** directive defines an identifier and a character sequence that will be substituted for the identifier each time it is encountered in the source file. The identifier is called a *macro name* and the replacement process is called *macro substitution*. The general form of the directive is

#define *macro-name character-sequence*

Notice that there is no semicolon in this statement. There can be any number of spaces between the identifier and the character sequence, but once it begins, it is terminated only by a new line.

For example, if you wish to use **TRUE** for the value 1 and **FALSE** for the value 0, then you would declare two macro **#defines**:

```
#define TRUE 1
#define FALSE 0
```

This causes the compiler to substitute a 1 or a 0 each time the name **TRUE** or **FALSE** is encountered in your source file. For example, the following prints "0 1 2" on the screen:

```
printf("%d %d %d", FALSE, TRUE, TRUE+1);
```

Once a macro name has been defined, it can be used as part of the definition of other macro names. For example, this code defines the names **ONE**, **TWO**, and **THREE** to their respective values:

```
#define ONE   1
#define TWO   ONE+ONE
#define THREE ONE+TWO
```

Macro substitution is simply replacing an identifier with its associated string. Therefore, if you wished to define a standard error message, you might write something like this:

```
#define E_MS "Standard error on input.\n"
/* ... */
printf(E_MS);
```

The compiler substitutes the string "Standard error on input." when the identifier **E_MS** is encountered. To the compiler, the **printf( )** statement actually appears to be

```
printf("Standard error on input.\n");
```

No text substitutions occur if the identifier is within a string. For example;

```
#define XYZ this is a test
/* ... */
printf("XYZ");
```

does not print "this is a test", but rather "XYZ".

If the string is longer than one line, you can continue it on the next line by placing a backslash at the end of the line, as shown in this example:

```
#define LONG_STRING "This is a very long \
string that is used as an example."
```

It is common practice among C programmers to use capital letters for defined identifiers. This convention helps anyone reading the program know at a glance that a macro substitution will take place. Also, it is best to put all **#define**s at the start of the file or, perhaps, in a separate include file rather than sprinkling them throughout the program.

The most common use of macro substitutions is to define names for "magic numbers" that occur in a program. For example, you may have a program that defines an array and has several routines that access that array. Instead of "hard coding" the array's size with a constant, it is better to define a name that represents the size and use that name whenever the size of the array is needed. This way, if you need to change the size of the array, you will only need to change the **#define** statement and then recompile. All uses of the name will automatically be updated. For example:

```
#define MAX_SIZE 100
/* ... */
float balance[MAX_SIZE];
/* ... */
float temp[MAX_SIZE];
```

To change the size of both arrays, simply change the definition of **MAX_SIZE**.

The **#define** directive has another powerful feature: the macro name can have arguments. Each time the macro name is encountered, the arguments associated with it are replaced by the actual arguments found in the program. This type of macro is called a *function-like macro*. For example:

```
#include <stdio.h>

#define MIN(a,b)  ((a)<(b)) ? (a) : (b)

int main(void)
{
  int x, y;
```

```
  x = 10;
  y = 20;
  printf("The minimum is: %d", MIN(x, y));

  return 0;
}
```

When this program is compiled, the expression defined by **MIN(a,b)** is substituted, except that **x** and **y** are used as the operands. That is, the **printf( )** statement looks like this after the substitution:

```
printf("The minimum is: %d",((x)<(y)) ? (x) : (y));
```

Be very careful how you define macros that take arguments; otherwise, there can be some surprising results. For example, examine this short program, which uses a macro to determine whether a value is even or odd:

```
/* This program will give the wrong answer. */

#include <stdio.h>

#define EVEN(a) a%2==0 ? 1 : 0

int main(void)
{
  if(EVEN(9+1)) printf("is even");
  else printf("is odd");

  return 0;
}
```

This program will not work correctly because of the way the macro substitution is made. When Borland C++ compiles this program, the **EVEN(9+1)** is expanded to

```
9+1%2==0 ? 1 : 0
```

As you may recall, the % (modulus) operator has higher precedence than the plus operator. This means that the % operation is first performed on the 1 and that result is added to 9, which (of course) does not equal 0. To fix the trouble, there must be parentheses around **a** in the macro definition of **EVEN**, as shown in this corrected version of the program:

```
#include <stdio.h>

#define EVEN(a) (a)%2==0 ? 1 : 0
```

```
int main(void)
{
  if(EVEN(9+1)) printf("is even");
  else printf("is odd");

  return 0;
}
```

Now, the **9+1** is evaluated prior to the modulus operation. In general, it is a good idea to surround macro parameters with parentheses to avoid troubles like the one just described.

The use of macro substitutions in place of real functions has one major benefit: it increases the speed of the code because no overhead for a function call is incurred. However, this increased speed might be paid for with an increase in the size of the program because of duplicated code.

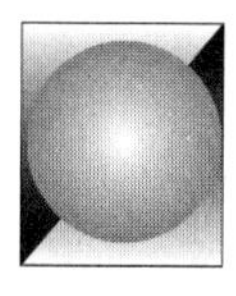

NOTE: Although parameterized macros are a valuable feature, you will see in Part 3 that C++ has a better way of creating inline code that does not rely upon macros.

#error

The **#error** directive forces the compiler to stop compilation when it is encountered. It is used primarily for debugging. The general form of the directive is

#error *error-message*

The *error-message* is not between double quotes. When the compiler encounters this directive, it displays an error message that has the following general form and then terminates compilation:

Fatal: *filename linenum*: Error directive: *error-message*

Here, *filename* is the name of the file in which the **#error** directive was found, *linenum* is the line number of the directive, and *error-message* is the message, itself.

#include

The **#include** directive instructs the compiler to include another source file with the one that contains the **#include** directive. The name of the additional source file must be enclosed between double quotes or angle brackets. For example, these two directives both instruct the compiler to read and compile the header for the standard I/O library functions:

```
#include "stdio.h"
#include <stdio.h>
```

It is valid for included files to have **#include** directives in them. This is referred to as *nested includes.* For example, this program, shown with its include files, includes a file that includes another file:

```
/* The program file: */
#include <stdio.h>

int main(void)
{
  #include "one"

  return 0;
}
```

```
/* Include file ONE: */
printf("This is from the first include file.\n");
#include "two"
```

```
/* Include file TWO: */
printf("This is from the second include file.\n");
```

If explicit path names are specified as part of the file name identifier, only those directories are searched for the included file. Otherwise, if the file name is enclosed in quotes, first the current working directory is searched. If the file is not found, the standard directories are searched.

If no explicit path names are specified and the file name is enclosed by angle brackets, the file is searched for in the standard directories. At no time is the current working directory searched.

Conditional Compilation Directives

There are several directives that allow you to selectively compile portions of your program's source code. This process is called *conditional compilation* and is used widely by commercial software houses that provide and maintain many customized versions of one program.

#if, #else, #elif, and #endif

The general idea behind the **#if** is that if the constant expression following the **#if** is true, the code that is between it and an **#endif** is compiled; otherwise, the code is skipped. The **#endif** is used to mark the end of an **#if** block.

The general form of **#if** is

#if *constant-expression*
 statement sequence
#endif

For example:

```
/* A simple #if example. */
#include <stdio.h>

#define MAX 100
int main(void)
{
#if MAX>99
  printf("Compiled for array greater than 99.\n");
#endif
  return 0;
}
```

This program displays the message on the screen because, as defined in the program, **MAX** is greater than 99. This example illustrates an important point. The expression that follows the **#if** is *evaluated at compile time*. Therefore, it must contain only identifiers that have been previously defined and constants; no variables can be used.

The **#else** works in much the same way as the **else** that forms part of the C language: it establishes an alternative if the **#if** fails. The previous example can be expanded as shown here:

```
/* A simple #if/#else example. */
#include <stdio.h>

#define MAX 10
int main(void)
{
#if MAX>99
  printf("Compiled for array greater than 99.\n");
#else
  printf("Compiled for small array.\n");
#endif
  return 0;
}
```

In this case, **MAX** is defined to be less than 99, so the **#if** portion of the code is not compiled, but the **#else** alternative is. Therefore, the message "Compiled for small array." is displayed.

Notice that the **#else** is used to mark both the end of the **#if** block and the beginning of the **#else** block. This is necessary because there can be only one **#endif** associated with any **#if**.

The **#elif** means "else if " and is used to establish an if-else-if ladder for multiple compilation options. The **#elif** is followed by a constant expression. If the expression is true, that block of code is compiled and no other **#elif** expressions are tested. Otherwise, the next in the series is checked. The general form of the **#elif** is

#if *expression*
  statement sequence
#elif *expression 1*
  statement sequence
#elif *expression 2*
  statement sequence
#elif *expression 3*
  statement sequence
#elif *expression 4*
  .
  .
  .
#elif *expression N*
  statement sequence
#endif

For example, this fragment uses the value of **ACTIVE_COUNTRY** to define the currency sign:

```
#define US 0
#define ENGLAND 1
#define FRANCE 2

#define ACTIVE_COUNTRY US

#if ACTIVE_COUNTRY==US
  char currency[] = "dollar";
#elif ACTIVE_COUNTRY==ENGLAND
  char currency[] = "pound";
#else
  char currency[] = "franc";
#endif
```

#ifs and **#elif**s can be nested. When this occurs, each **#endif**, **#else**, or **#elif** is associated with the nearest **#if** or **#elif**. For example, the following is perfectly valid:

```
#if MAX>100
   #if SERIAL_VERSION
      int port = 198;
   #elif
      int port = 200;
   #endif
#else
   char out_buffer[100];
#endif
```

In Borland C++, you can use the **sizeof** compile-time operator in an **#if** statement. For example, the next fragment determines whether a program is being compiled for small or large arrays.

```
#if (sizeof(char *) == 2)
  printf("Program compiled for small array.");
#else
  printf("Program compiled for large array.");
#endif
```

#ifdef and #ifndef

Another method of conditional compilation uses the directives **#ifdef** and **#ifndef**, which mean "if defined" and "if not defined," respectively, and which refer to macro names. The general form of **#ifdef** is

> #ifdef *macro-name*
> *statement sequence*
> #endif

If the *macro-name* has been previously defined in a **#define** statement, the statement sequence between the **#ifdef** and **#endif** is compiled.

The general form of **#ifndef** is

> #ifndef *macro-name*
> *statement sequence*
> #endif

If *macro-name* is currently undefined by a **#define** statement, the block of code is compiled.

Both the **#ifdef** and **#ifndef** can use an **#else** statement but not the **#elif**. For example,

```
#include <stdio.h>

#define TED 10

int main(void)
{
#ifdef TED
  printf("Hi Ted\n");
#else
  printf("Hi anyone\n");
#endif
#ifndef RALPH
  printf("RALPH not defined\n");
#endif
  return 0;
}
```

prints "Hi Ted" and "RALPH not defined". However, if **TED** were not defined, "Hi anyone" would be displayed, followed by "RALPH not defined".

You can nest **#ifdefs** and **#ifndefs** in the same way as **#ifs**.

#undef

The **#undef** directive is used to undefine a macro name. Its general form is

#undef *macro-name*

For example:

```
#define LEN 100
#define WIDTH 100

char array[LEN][WIDTH];

#undef LEN
#undef WIDTH
/* at this point both LEN and WIDTH are undefined */
```

Both **LEN** and **WIDTH** are defined until the **#undef** statements are encountered.

The principal use of **#undef** is to allow macro names to be localized to only those sections of code that need them.

Using defined

In addition to **#ifdef**, there is a second way to determine if a macro name is defined. You can use the **#if** directive in conjunction with the **defined** compile-time operator. The **defined** operator has this general form:

defined *macro-name*

If *macro-name* is currently defined, then the expression is true. Otherwise, it is false. For example, to determine if the macro **MYFILE** is defined, you can use either of these two preprocessing commands:

```
#if defined MYFILE
```

or

```
#ifdef MYFILE
```

You may also precede **defined** with the **!** to reverse the condition. For example, the following fragment is compiled only if **DEBUG** is not defined.

```
#if !defined DEBUG
  printf("Final version!\n");
#endif
```

One reason for **defined** is that it allows the existence of a macro name to be determined by an **#elif** statement.

#line

The **#line** directive is used to change the contents of **__LINE__** and **__FILE__**, which are predefined macro names. **__LINE__** contains the line number of the line currently being compiled and **__FILE__** contains the name of the file being compiled. The basic form of the **#line** command is

#line *number* "*filename*"

where *number* is any positive integer and the optional *filename* is any valid file identifier. The line number becomes the new value of **__LINE__**. The file name becomes the new value of **__FILE__**. **#line** is primarily used for debugging purposes and special applications.

For example, the following specifies that the line count will begin with 100. The **printf( )** statement displays the number 102 because it is the third line in the program after the **#line 100** statement.

```
#include <stdio.h>

#line 100                      /* reset the line counter */
int main(void)                 /* line 100 */
{                              /* line 101 */
  printf("%d\n", __LINE__);   /* line 102 */

  return 0;
}
```

#pragma

The **#pragma** directive is defined by the ANSI C standard to be an implementation-defined directive that allows various instructions to be given to the compiler. The general form of the **#pragma** directive is

#pragma *name*

where *name* is the name of the **#pragma** directive.

Borland defines these 14 **#pragmas**:

argsused
anon_struct
codeseg
comment
exit
hdrfile
hdrstop
inline
intrinsic
message
option
saveregs
startup
warn

The **argsused** directive must precede a function. It is used to prevent a warning message if an argument to the function that the **#pragma** precedes is not used in the body of the function.

To enable the use of anonymous structures, specify the **anon_struct** directive.

You can specify the segment, class, or group used by a function with the **codeseg** directive.

Using the **comment** directive, you can embed a comment into an output file, such as your program's .obj or .exe file.

The **exit** directive specifies one or more functions that will be called when the program terminates. The **startup** directive specifies one or more functions that will be called when the program starts running. They have these general forms:

#pragma exit *function-name priority*
#pragma startup *function-name priority*

The *priority* is a value between 64 and 255 (the values 0 through 63 are reserved). The priority determines the order in which the functions are called. If no priority is given, it defaults to 100. All startup and exit functions must be declared as shown here:

```
void f(void);
```

The following example defines a startup function called **start( )**.

```
#include <stdio.h>

void start(void);

#pragma startup start 65

int main(void)
{
  printf("In main\n");

  return 0;
}

void start(void)
{
  printf("In start\n");
}
```

The output from this program is shown here:

In start
In main

As this example shows, you must provide a function prototype for all exit and startup functions prior to the **#pragma** statement.

You can specify the name of the file that will be used to hold precompiled headers using the **hdrfile** directive. Its general form is

#pragma hdrfile "*fname*.csm"

where *fname* is the name of the file (the extension must be **.csm**).

The **hdrstop** directive tells Borland C++ to stop precompiling header files.

Another **#pragma** directive is **inline**. It has the general form

#pragma inline

This tells the compiler that inline assembly code is contained in the program. For the fastest compile times, Borland C++ needs to know in advance that inline assembly code is contained in a program.

Using Borland C++, it is possible to tell the compiler to generate inline code instead of an actual function call using the **intrinsic** directive. It has the general form

#pragma intrinsic *func-name*

where *func-name* is the name of the function that you want to inline.

If you check the Inline Intrinsic Function option in the IDE or use the -Oi command-line switch, Borland C++ automatically inlines the following functions:

alloca	memcpy	stpcpy	strcpy	strncpy
fabs	memset	strcat	strlen	strnset
memchr	rotl	strchr	strncat	strrchr
memcmp	rotr	strcmp	strncmp	

You can override the automatic inlining by using this form of the **intrinsic** directive:

#pragma intrinsic -*func-name*

The **message** directive lets you specify a message within your program code that is displayed as a warning when the program is compiled. For example:

```
#include <stdio.h>

#pragma message This will be displayed as a warning.

int main(void)
{
  int i=10;

  printf("This is i: %d\n", i);
#pragma message This is also displayed as a warning.
  return 0;
}
```

When compiled, you will see the two **#pragma** messages displayed as warnings. When using the IDE, they will appear in the standard message window.

The **option** directive allows you to specify command-line options within your program instead of actually specifying them on the command line. It has the general form

#pragma option *option-list*

For example, this causes the program that contains it to be compiled for the large memory model:

```
#pragma option -ml
```

The following options *cannot* be used by the **option** directive:

-B	-c	-D	-e	-E	-F	-h
-l	-M	-o	-P	-Q	-S	-T
-U	-V	-X	-Y			

For some options, the **option** directive must precede all declarations, including function prototypes. For this reason, it is a good idea to make it one of the first statements in your program.

The **saveregs** directive prevents a function declared as **huge** from altering the value of any registers. This directive must immediately precede the function and affects only the function that it precedes.

The **warn** directive allows you to enable or disable various warning messages. It takes the form

#pragma warn *setting*

where *setting* specifies the warning option.

The # and ## Preprocessor Operators

C provides two preprocessor operators: # and ##. These operators are used in conjunction with **#define**.

The # operator causes the argument it precedes to be turned into a quoted string. For example, consider this program:

```
#include "stdio.h"

#define mkstr(s)  # s

int main(void)
{
  printf(mkstr(I like C));

  return 0;
}
```

The C preprocessor turns the line

```
printf(mkstr(I like C));
```

into

```
printf("I like C");
```

The ## operator is used to concatenate two tokens. For example:

```
#include "stdio.h"

#define concat(a, b)  a ## b

int main(void)
{
  int xy = 10;

  printf("%d", concat(x, y));
```

```
  return 0;
}
```

The preprocessor transforms

```
printf("%d", concat(x, y));
```

into

```
printf("%d", xy);
```

If these operators seem strange to you, keep in mind that they are not needed or used in most programs. They exist primarily to allow some special cases to be handled by the preprocessor.

Predefined Macro Names

The ANSI C standard specifies five built-in predefined macro names. They are

__LINE__
__FILE__
__DATE__
__TIME__
__STDC__

Borland C++ defines these additional built-in macros:

__BCOPT__
__BCPLUSPLUS__
__BORLANDC__
__CDECL__
_CHAR_UNSIGNED
__CONSOLE__
_CPPUNWIND
__cplusplus
__DLL__
_M_IX86
__MSDOS__
__MT__
__OVERLAY__
__PASCAL__
__TCPLUSPLUS__
__TEMPLATES__
__TLS__
__TURBOC__

_WCHAR_T
_WCHAR_T_DEFINED
_Windows
__WIN32__

The **__LINE__** and **__FILE__** macros were discussed in the **#line** discussion earlier in this chapter. The others are examined here.

The **__DATE__** macro contains a string in the form *month/day/year* that is the date of the translation of the source file into object code.

The time at which the source code was compiled is contained as a string in **__TIME__**. The form of the string is *hour:minute:second*.

If the macro **__STDC__** is defined, the program was compiled with ANSI C standard compliance checking turned on. If this is not the case, **__STDC__** is undefined.

The **__BCOPT__** is defined if optimization is used.

If you are using Borland C++, the macro **__BCPLUSPLUS__** is defined if you have compiled your program as a C++ program. It is undefined otherwise. Compiling a C++ program also causes **__TCPLUSPLUS__** to be defined. Both these macros contain hexadecimal values that will increase with each new release of the compiler.

__BORLANDC__ contains the current version number (as specified in hexadecimal) of the compiler. For Borland C++ 5, the value is 500.

The **__CDECL__** macro is defined if the standard C calling convention is used—that is, if the Pascal option is not in use. If this is not the case, the macro is undefined (if defined, its value is 1).

If **_CHAR_UNSIGNED** is defined, the default character type is **unsigned**.

When **__CONSOLE__** is defined for the 32-bit compiler, the program is a console application.

If **__CPPUNWIND** is defined as 1, stack unwinding is enabled.

If your program is compiled as a C++ program, **__cplusplus** is defined as 1. Otherwise, it is not defined.

For Borland C++, **__DLL__** is defined as 1 when creating a Windows DLL object file. Otherwise, it is undefined.

The **_M_IX86** macro is always defined.

The **__MSDOS__** macro is defined with the value 1 in all situations when using an MS-DOS version of Borland C/C++.

The **__MT__** macro is defined as 1 only if the multithreaded library is used with the 32-bit compiler.

When a program is compiled using overlays, **__OVERLAY__** is defined as 1. Otherwise, **__OVERLAY__** is undefined.

The **__PASCAL__** macro is defined as 1 only if the Pascal calling conventions are used to compile a program.

For Borland C++, **__TEMPLATES__** is defined as 1 for all versions of these compilers that support templates. This macro applies only to C++ compilation.

When compiling using the 32-bit compiler, **__TLS__** will be defined as nonzero.

__TURBOC__ represents a hexadecimal value that is increased with each new release.

For C++ programs, **_WCHAR_T** and **_WCHAR_T_DEFINED** are defined as 1 to indicate that **wchar_t** is a built-in data type. They are not defined for C programs.

For Borland C++, **_Windows** is defined if your program is compiled for use under Windows.

When using the 32-bit compiler, **__WIN32__** is defined.

For the most part, these built-in macros are used in fairly complex programming environments when several different versions of a program are developed or maintained.

Comments

In C, all comments begin with the character pair /* and end with */. There must be no spaces between the asterisk and the slash. The compiler ignores any text between the beginning and ending comment symbols. For example, this program prints only **hello** on the screen:

```
#include <stdio.h>

int main(void)
{
  printf("hello");
  /* printf("there"); */

  return 0;
}
```

Comments may be placed anywhere in a program as long as they do not appear in the middle of a keyword or identifier. That is, this comment is valid:

```
x = 10+ /* add the numbers */5;
```

while

```
swi/*this will not work*/tch(c) { ...
```

is incorrect because a keyword cannot contain a comment. However, you should not generally place comments in the middle of expressions because it obscures their meaning.

Comments may not be nested. That is, one comment may not contain another comment. For example, this code fragment causes a compile-time error:

```
/* this is an outer comment
  x = y/a;
  /* this is an inner comment - and causes an error */
*/
```

You should include comments whenever they are needed to explain the operation of the code. All but the most obvious functions should have a comment at the top that states what the function does, how it is called, and what it returns.

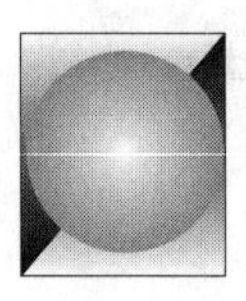

NOTE: *C++ fully supports C-style comments. However, it also allows you to define a single-line comment. Single-line comments begin with a // and end at the end of the line.*

PART TWO

The Borland Function Library

Part 2 examines the function library included with Borland C++. Chapter 10 begins with a discussion of linking, libraries, and header files. Chapters 11 through 19 describe the functions found in the library, with each chapter concentrating on a specific group.

The functions described here are available for use by both C and C++ programs. As you may know, the C++ language also defines a number of class libraries that may only be used by C++ programs. Several of the class libraries are described in Part 3, when C++ is discussed.

Chapter Ten

Linking, Libraries, and Header Files

The creation of a C or C++ compiler involves two major efforts. The first is the construction of the compiler itself. The second is the creation of the function library. Because the Borland library contains so many functions, it is safe to assume that it required a substantial programming effort. (Consider that even a description of these functions requires several hundred pages!) Every C or C++ program relies upon library functions to perform many of the tasks carried out by the program. Because of the fundamental role that the library plays in your program, it is important to have an overview of how the library works. Specifically, you need to understand the job the linker performs, how libraries differ from object files, and the role of header files. These items are examined here.

The Linker

The output of the compiler is a relocatable object file and the output of the linker is an executable file. The role the linker plays is twofold. First, it physically combines the files specified in the link list into one program file. Second, it resolves external references and memory addresses. An external reference is created any time the code in one file refers to code found in another file. This may be through either a function call or a reference to a global variable. For example, when the two files shown here are linked together, file Two's reference to **count** must be resolved. It is the linker that "tells" the code in file Two where **count** will be found in memory.

File One:

```
int count;
void display(void);

int main(void)
{
  count = 10;
  display();
  return 0;
}
```

File Two:

```
#include <stdio.h>
extern int count;

void display(void)
{
  printf("%d", count);
}
```

In a similar fashion, the linker also "tells" file One where the function **display( )** is located so that it may be called.

When the compiler generates the object code for file Two, it substitutes a placeholder for the address of **count** because it has no way of knowing where **count** will be located in memory. The same sort of thing occurs when file One is compiled. The address of **display( )** is not known, so a placeholder is used. This process forms the basis for *relocatable code*. When the files are joined by the linker, the placeholders are replaced with relative addresses.

To better understand relocatable code, you must first understand absolute code. Although it is seldom used today, in the earlier days of computers it was not uncommon for a program to be compiled to run at a specific memory location. When compiled in this way, all addresses are fixed at compile time. Because the addresses are fixed, the program can only be loaded into and executed in exactly one region of memory: the one for which it was compiled. Relocatable code, on the other hand, is compiled in such a way that the address information is not fixed. When making a relocatable object file, the linker assigns the address of each call, jump, or global variable an offset. When the file is loaded into memory for execution, the loader automatically resolves the offsets into addresses that will work for the location in memory into which it is being loaded. This means that a relocatable program can be loaded into and run from many different memory locations.

Library Files Versus Object Files

Although libraries are similar to object files, they have one crucial difference: not all the code in the library is added to your program. When you link a program that consists of several object files, all the code in each object file becomes part of the finished executable program. This happens whether the code is actually used or not. In other words, all object files specified at link time are "added together" to form the program. However, this is not the case with library files.

A library is a collection of functions. Unlike an object file, a library file stores the name of each function, the function's object code, and relocation information necessary to the linking process. When your program references a function contained in a library, the linker looks up that function and adds that code to your program. In this way, only functions that you actually use in your program are added to the executable file.

Since the Borland functions are contained in a library, only those actually used by your program will be included in your program's executable code. (If they were in object files, every program you wrote would be several hundred thousand bytes long!)

The ANSI C Standard Library Versus Borland Extensions

The ANSI C standard has defined both the content and the form of the standard C library. Borland C++ complies with this standard by supplying all functions defined by the ANSI C standard. (At this time, Borland C++ does not supply the wide-character functions added by the 1995 Amendment to the standard. But these are not used by most programmers.) However, to allow the fullest possible use and control of the computer, Borland C++ contains many additional functions that are not defined by ANSI. Such extensions include a complete set of screen and graphics functions for DOS, special 16-bit allocation functions, and directory functions. This book describes both the standard functions and the extended ones added by Borland. As long as you will not be porting the programs you write to a new environment, it is perfectly fine to use these extended functions. However, if ANSI compliance is an issue, then you will want to use only those functions defined by the ANSI C standard.

Header Files

Many functions found in the library work with their own specific data types and structures to which your program must have access. These structures and types are defined in *header files* supplied with the compiler and they must be included (using **#include**) in any file that uses the functions to which they refer. In addition, all functions in the library have their prototypes defined in a header file. This is done for two reasons. First, in C++, all functions must be prototyped. Second, although in C prototyping is an option, its use is strongly suggested because it provides a means of stronger type checking. (Also, it is possible that future versions of the C language will require prototyping.) In a C program, by including the header files that correspond to the standard functions used by your program, you can catch potential type-mismatch errors. For example, including **string.h**, the string functions' header, causes the following code to produce a warning message when compiled:

```
#include <string.h>

char s1[20] = "hello ";
char s2[] = "there.";

int main(void)
{
  int p;

  p = strcat(s1, s2);
  return 0;
}
```

Because **strcat( )** is declared as returning a character pointer in its header file, the compiler can now flag as a possible error the assignment of that pointer to the integer **p**.

Remember: although the inclusion of many header files is technically optional (yet advisable) in C, they must be included in all C++ programs. In the remaining chapters of Part 2, the description of each function will specify its header file.

Borland C++ defines a large number of header files. The header files for Borland C++ are located in its INCLUDE directory. In a standard installation, this will be BC5\INCLUDE. Fortunately, most of the time your program will only need to include a few of the header files. Several of the more commonly used header files supplied with Borland C++ are shown in Table 10-1. Those files defined by the ANSI C standard or used by C++ are so indicated.

Macros in Header Files

Many of the library functions are not actually functions at all but rather parameterized macro definitions contained in a header file. Generally, this is of little consequence, but this distinction will be pointed out when discussing such "functions." If for some reason you wish to avoid the use of a standard macro, you can undefine it using the **#undef** preprocessing directive.

ALLOC.H	Dynamic allocation functions
ASSERT.H	Defines the **assert( )** macro (ANSI C)
BIOS.H	ROM-BIOS functions
CONIO.H	Screen-handling functions
CTYPE.H	Character-handling functions (ANSI C)
DIR.H	Directory-handling functions
DOS.H	DOS interfacing functions
ERRNO.H	Defines error codes (ANSI C)
FCNTL.H	Defines constants used by **open( )** function
FLOAT.H	Defines implementation-dependent, floating-point values (ANSI C)
FSTREAM.H	File I/O class definitions (C++)
GRAPHICS.H	Graphics functions
IO.H	UNIX-like I/O routines
IOMANIP.H	Defines I/O manipulators (C++)
IOSTREAM.H	Defines I/O stream class (C++)
LIMITS.H	Defines various implementation-dependent limits (ANSI C)
LOCALE.H	Country- and language-specific functions (ANSI C)
MATH.H	Various definitions used by the math library (ANSI C)
PROCESS.H	**spawn( )** and **exec( )** functions
SETJMP.H	Nonlocal jumps (ANSI C)
SHARE.H	File sharing
SIGNAL.H	Defines signal values (ANSI C)
STDARG.H	Variable-length argument lists (ANSI C)
STDDEF.H	Defines some commonly used constants (ANSI C)
STDIO.H	Declarations for standard I/O streams (ANSI C)
STDLIB.H	Miscellaneous declarations (ANSI C)
STRING.H	String handling (ANSI C)
STRSTREA.H	Array-based stream I/O classes (C++)
TIME.H	System time functions (ANSI C)

Table 10-1. *Some Commonly Used Header Files*

[illegible]

Chapter Eleven

I/O Functions

Borland's I/O library functions can be grouped into three major categories:

- The ANSI C I/O system
- The UNIX-like I/O system
- Several platform-specific I/O functions.

This chapter describes the functions that comprise the ANSI C I/O system and the UNIX-like I/O system. It also describes some of the platform-specific functions. Other platform-specific functions, such as those for direct screen output and graphics, are described in Chapter 18. The platform-specific functions relate mostly to the DOS environment. They can also be used in a DOS session when running Windows.

For the ANSI C I/O system, the header **stdio.h** is required. For the UNIX-like routines, the header **io.h** is required. The platform-specific functions use headers such as **conio.h** and **dos.h**.

Many of the I/O functions set the predefined global integer variable **errno** to an appropriate error code when an error occurs. This variable is declared in **errno.h**.

NOTE: *The C++ I/O classes, functions, and operators are discussed in Part 3.*

int access(const char *filename, int mode)

Description

The prototype for **access( )** is found in **io.h**.

The **access( )** function belongs to the UNIX-like file system and is not defined by the ANSI C standard. It is used to see if a file exists. It can also be used to tell whether the file is write-protected and if it can be executed. The name of the file in question is pointed to by *filename*. The value of *mode* determines exactly how **access( )** functions. The legal values are

Value	Checks For
0	File existence
1	Executable file
2	Write access
4	Read access
6	Read/write access

The **access( )** function returns 0 if the specified access is allowed; otherwise, it returns –1. Upon failure, the predefined global variable **errno** is set to one of these values:

ENOENT	File not found
EACCES	Access denied

Example

The following program checks to see if the file **TEST.TST** is present in the current working directory:

```
#include <stdio.h>
#include <io.h>

int main(void)
{
  if(!access("TEST.TST", 0))
    printf("File Present");
  else
    printf("File not Found");
  return 0;
}
```

Related Function

chmod( )

int chmod(const char *filename, int mode)

Description

The prototype for **chmod( )** is found in **io.h**.

The **chmod( )** function is not defined by the ANSI C standard. It changes the access mode of the file pointed to by *filename* to that specified by *mode*. The value of *mode* must be one or both of the macros **S_IWRITE** and **S_IREAD**, which correspond to write access and read access, respectively. To change a file's mode to read/write status, call **chmod( )** with *mode* set to **S_IWRITE | S_IREAD**.

The **chmod( )** function returns 0 if successful and –1 if unsuccessful.

Example

This call to **chmod( )** attempts to set the file **TEST.TST** to read/write access:

```
if(!chmod("TEST.TST", S_IREAD | S_IWRITE))
  printf("File set to read/write access.");
```

Related Functions

access( )

int chsize(char handle, long size)

Description

The prototype for **chsize( )** is found in **io.h**.

The **chsize( )** function is not defined by the ANSI C standard. It extends or truncates the file specified by *handle* to the value of *size*.

The **chsize( )** function returns 0 if successful. Upon failure, it returns –1 and **errno** is set to one of the following:

EACCES	Access denied
EBADF	Bad file handle
ENOSPC	Out of space

Example

This call to **chsize( )** attempts to change the size of **TEST.TST**.

```
/*
  Assume that a file associated with handle
```

```
  has been opened.
*/

if(!chsize(handle, 256))
  printf("File size is now 256 bytes.");
```

Related Functions

open( ), close( ), creat( )

void clearerr(FILE *stream)

Description

The prototype for **clearerr( )** is found in **stdio.h**.

The **clearerr( )** function is used to reset the file error flag pointed to by *stream* to 0 (off). The end-of-file indicator is also reset.

The error flags for each stream are initially set to 0 by a successful call to **fopen( )**. Once an error has occurred, the flags stay set until an explicit call to either **clearerr( )** or **rewind( )** is made.

File errors can occur for a wide variety of reasons, many of which are system dependent. The exact nature of the error can be determined by calling **perror( )**, which displays which error has occurred (see **perror( )**).

Example

This program copies one file to another. If an error is encountered, a message is printed and the error is cleared.

```
#include <stdio.h>
#include <stdlib.h>

int main(int argc, char *argv[])  /* copy one file to another */
{
  FILE *in, *out;
  char ch;

  if(argc!=3) {
    printf("You forgot to enter a filename\n");
    exit(0);
  }

  if((in=fopen(argv[1], "rb")) == NULL) {
    printf("Cannot open file.\n");
    exit(0);
  }
  if((out=fopen(argv[2],"wb")) == NULL) {
```

```
      printf("Cannot open file.\n");
      exit(0);
    }

    while(!feof(in)) {
      ch = getc(in);
      if(ferror(in)) {
        printf("Read Error");
        clearerr(in);
      } else {
        if(!feof(in)) putc(ch, out);
        if(ferror(out)) {
          printf("Write Error");
          clearerr(out);
        }
      }
    }
    fclose(in);
    fclose(out);
    return 0;
  }
```

Related Functions

feof( ), ferror( ), perror( )

int close(int fd)
int _rtl_close(int fd)

Description

The prototypes for **close( )** and **_rtl_close( )** are found in **io.h**.

The **close( )** function belongs to the UNIX-like file system and is not defined by the ANSI C standard. When **close( )** is called with a valid file descriptor, it closes the file associated with it and flushes the write buffers if applicable. (File descriptors are created through a successful call to **open( )** or **creat( )** and do not relate to streams or file pointers.)

When successful, **close( )** returns a 0; if unsuccessful, it returns a –1. Although there are several reasons why you might not be able to close a file, the most common is the premature removal of the medium. For example, if you remove a diskette from the drive before the file is closed, an error will result.

The **_rtl_close( )** function works exactly like **close( )**.

Example

This program opens and closes a file using the UNIX-like file system:

```
#include <stdio.h>
#include <fcntl.h>
#include <sys\stat.h>
#include <io.h>
#include <stdlib.h>

int main(int argc, char *argv[])
{
  int fd;

  if((fd=open(argv[1], O_RDONLY))==-1) {
    printf("Cannot open file.");
    exit(1);
  }

  printf("File is existent.\n");

  if(close(fd))
    printf("Error in closing file.\n");
  return 0;
}
```

Related Functions

open( ), creat( ), read( ), write( ), unlink( )

int creat(const char *filename, int pmode)
int _rtl_creat(const char *filename, int attrib)
int creatnew(const char *filename, int attrib)
int creattemp(char *filename, int attrib)

Description

The prototypes for these functions are found in **io.h**.

The **creat( )** function is part of the UNIX-like file system and is not defined by the ANSI C standard. Its purpose is to create a new file with the name pointed to by *filename* and to open it for writing. On success **creat( )** returns a file descriptor that is greater than or equal to 0; on failure it returns a –1. (File descriptors are integers and do not relate to streams or file pointers.)

The value of *pmode* determines the file's access setting, sometimes called its *permission mode*. The value of *pmode* is highly dependent upon the execution environment. For Borland C++, its values can be **S_IWRITE** or **S_IREAD**. If *pmode* is set to **S_IREAD**, a read-only file is created. If it is set to **S_IWRITE**, a writable file is created. You can OR these values together to create a read/write file.

If, at the time of the call to **creat( )**, the specified file already exists, it is erased and all previous contents are lost unless the original file was write-protected.

The **_rtl_creat( )** function works like **creat( )** but uses a DOS/Windows attribute byte. The *attrib* argument may be one of these macros:

FA_RDONLY	Set file to read only
FA_HIDDEN	Make hidden file
FA_SYSTEM	Mark as a system file

The **creatnew( )** function is the same as **_rtl_creat( )**, except that if the file already exists on disk, **creatnew( )** returns an error and does not erase the original file.

The **creattemp( )** function is used to create a unique temporary file. You call **creattemp( )** with *filename* pointing to the path name ending with a backslash. Upon return, *filename* contains the name of a unique file. You must make sure that *filename* is large enough to hold the file name.

In the case of an error in any of these functions, **errno** is set to one of these values:

ENOENT	Path or file does not exist
EMFILE	Too many files are open
EACCES	Access denied
EEXIST	File exists (**creatnew( )** only)

Example

The following code fragment creates a file called **test**:

```
#include <stdio.h>
#include <sys\stat.h>
#include <io.h>
#include <stdlib.h>

int main(void)
{
  int fd;

  if((fd=creat("test", S_IWRITE))==-1) {
    printf("Cannot open file.\n");
```

```
    exit(1);
  }
  .
  .
  .
```

Related Functions

open( ), close( ), read( ), write( ), unlink( ), eof( )

int dup(int handle)
int dup2(int old_handle, int new_handle)

Description

The prototypes for **dup( )** and **dup2( )** are found in **io.h**.

The **dup( )** function returns a new file descriptor that fully describes (i.e., duplicates) the state of the file associated with *handle.* It returns nonnegative on success, –1 on failure.

The **dup2( )** function duplicates *old_handle* as *new_handle.* If there is a file associated with *new_handle* prior to the call to **dup2( )**, it is closed. It returns 0 if successful, –1 when an error occurs. In the case of an error, **errno** is set to one of these values:

EMFILE	Too many files are open
EBADF	Bad file handle

Example

This fragment assigns **fp2** a new file descriptor:

```
FILE *fp, *fp2;
  .
  .
  .
fp2 = dup(fp);
```

Related Functions

close( ), creat( )

int eof(int fd)

Description

The prototype for **eof( )** is found in **io.h**.

The **eof( )** function is part of the UNIX-like file system and is not defined by the ANSI C standard. When called with a valid file descriptor, **eof( )** returns 1 if the end of the file has been reached; otherwise, it returns a 0. If an error has occurred, it returns a –1 and **errno** is set to **EBADF** (bad file number).

Example

The following program displays a text file on the console using **eof( )** to determine when the end of the file has been reached.

```
#include <stdio.h>
#include <io.h>
#include <fcntl.h>
#include <stdlib.h>

int main(int argc, char *argv[])
{
  int fd;
  char ch;

  if((fd=open(argv[1], O_RDWR))==-1) {
    printf("Cannot open file.\n");
    exit(1);
  }

  while(!eof(fd)) {
    read(fd, &ch, 1);  /* read one char at a time */
    printf("%c", ch);
  }

  close(fd);
  return 0;
}
```

Related Functions

open( ), close( ), read( ), write( ), unlink( )

int fclose(FILE *stream)
int fcloseall(void)

Description

The prototypes for **fclose( )** and **fcloseall( )** are found in **stdio.h**.

The **fclose( )** function closes the file associated with *stream* and flushes its buffer. After an **fclose( )**, *stream* is no longer connected with the file and any automatically allocated buffers are deallocated.

If **fclose( )** is successful, a 0 is returned; otherwise, a non-0 number is returned. Trying to close a file that has already been closed is an error.

The **fcloseall( )** function closes all open streams except **stdin**, **stdout**, **stdaux**, **stdprn**, and **stderr**. It is not defined by the ANSI C standard.

Example

The following code opens and closes a file:

```
#include <stdio.h>
#include <stdlib.h>

int main(void)
{
  FILE *fp;

  if((fp=fopen("test", "rb"))==NULL) {
    printf("Cannot open file.\n");
    exit(1);
  }
 .
 .
 .
  if(fclose(fp))
    printf("File close error.\n");
  return 0;
}
```

Related Functions

fopen( ), freopen( ), fflush( )

FILE *fdopen(int handle, char *mode)

Description

The prototype for **fdopen( )** is found in **stdio.h**.

The **fdopen( )** function is not defined by the ANSI C standard. It returns a stream that shares the same file that is associated with *handle*, where *handle* is a valid file descriptor obtained through a call to one of the UNIX-like I/O routines. In essence, **fdopen( )** is a bridge between the ANSI stream-based file system and the UNIX-like file system. The value of *mode* must be the same as that of the mode that originally opened the file.

See **open( )** and **fopen( )** for details.

Related Functions

open( ), fopen( ), creat( )

int feof(FILE *stream)

Description

The prototype for **feof( )** is found in **stdio.h**.

The **feof( )** macro checks the file position indicator to determine if the end of the file associated with *stream* has been reached. A non-0 value is returned if the file position indicator is at the end of the file; a 0 is returned otherwise.

Once the end of the file has been reached, subsequent read operations return **EOF** until either **rewind( )** is called or the file-position indicator is moved using **fseek( )**.

The **feof( )** macro is particularly useful when working with binary files because the end-of-file marker is also a valid binary integer. You must make explicit calls to **feof( )** rather than simply testing the return value of **getc( )**, for example, to determine when the end of the file has been reached.

Example

This code fragment shows the proper way to read to the end of a binary file:

```
/*
  Assume that fp has been opened as a binary file
  for read operations.
*/
while(!feof(fp)) getc(fp);
```

Related Functions

clearerr( ), ferror( ), perror( ), putc( ), getc( )

int ferror(FILE *stream)

Description

The prototype for the **ferror( )** macro is found in **stdio.h**.

The **ferror( )** function checks for a file error on the given *stream*. A return value of 0 indicates that no error has occurred, while a non-0 value indicates an error.

The error flags associated with *stream* stay set until either the file is closed, or **rewind( )** or **clearerr( )** is called.

Use the **perror( )** function to determine the exact nature of the error.

Example

The following code fragment aborts program execution if a file error occurs:

```
/*
  Assume that fp points to a stream opened for write
  operations.
*/
```

```
while(!done) {
  putc(info,fp);
  if(ferror(fp)) {
    printf("File Error\n");
    exit(1);
  }
 .
 .
 .
}
```

Related Functions

clearerr( ), feof( ), perror( )

int fflush(FILE *stream)

Description

The prototype for **fflush( )** is found in **stdio.h**.

If *stream* is associated with a file opened for writing, a call to **fflush( )** causes the contents of the output buffer to be physically written to the file. If *stream* points to an input file, the input buffer is cleared. In either case the file remains open.

A return value of 0 indicates success, while non-0 means a write error has occurred.

All buffers are automatically flushed upon normal termination of the program or when they are full. Closing a file flushes its buffer.

Example

The following code fragment flushes the buffer after each write operation.

```
/*
  Assume that fp is associated with an output file.
*/
 .
 .
 .
fwrite(buf, sizeof(data_type), 1, fp);
fflush(fp);
 .
 .
 .
```

Related Functions

fclose( ), fopen( ), flushall( ), fwrite( )

int fgetc(FILE *stream)

Description

The prototype for **fgetc( )** is found in **stdio.h**.

The **fgetc( )** function returns the next character from the input *stream* from the current position and increments the file-position indicator.

If the end of the file is reached, **fgetc( )** returns **EOF**. However, since **EOF** is a valid integer value, when working with binary files you must use **feof( )** to check for end-of-file. If **fgetc( )** encounters an error, **EOF** is also returned. Again, when working with binary files you must use **ferror( )** to check for file errors.

Example

This program reads and displays the contents of a text file:

```
#include <stdio.h>
#include <stdlib.h>

int main(int argc, char *argv[])
{
  FILE *fp;
  char ch;

  if((fp=fopen(argv[1], "r"))==NULL) {
    printf("Cannot open file.\n");
    exit(1);
  }

  while((ch=fgetc(fp))!=EOF) {
    printf("%c", ch);
  }
  fclose(fp);
  return 0;
}
```

Related Functions

fputc( ), getc( ), putc( ), fopen( )

int fgetchar(void)

Description

The prototype for **fgetchar( )** is found in **stdio.h**.

The **fgetchar( )** macro is defined as **fgetc(stdin)**. Refer to **fgetc( )** for details.

int *fgetpos(FILE *stream, fpos_t *pos)

Description

The prototype for **fgetpos( )** is found in **stdio.h**.

The **fgetpos( )** function stores the current location of the file pointer associated with *stream* in the variable pointed to by *pos*. The type **fpos_t** is defined in **stdio.h**.

If successful, **fgetpos( )** returns 0; upon failure, a value other than 0 is returned and **errno** is set to one of the following values:

EBADF	Bad file stream
EINVAL	Invalid argument

Example

This program uses **fgetpos( )** to display the current file position:

```
#include <stdio.h>
#include <stdlib.h>
int main(int argc, char *argv[])
{
  FILE *fp;
  long l;
  int  i;
  fpos_t *pos;  /* fpos_t is defined in stdio.h */
  pos = &l;

  if((fp=fopen(argv[1], "w+"))==NULL) {
    printf("Cannot open file.\n");
    exit(1);
  }

  for (i=0; i<10; i++)
    fputc('Z', fp);  /* write 10 Z's to the file */
  fgetpos(fp, pos);

  printf("We are now at position %ld in the file.", *pos);
  fclose(fp);
  return 0;
}
```

Related Functions

fsetpos( ), fseek( ), ftell( )

char *fgets(char *str, int num, FILE *stream)

Description

The prototype for **fgets( )** is found in **stdio.h**.

The **fgets( )** function reads up to *num*–1 characters from *stream* and places them into the character array pointed to by *str*. Characters are read until either a newline or an **EOF** is received, or until the specified limit is reached. After the characters have been read, a null is placed in the array immediately after the last character read. A newline character will be retained and will be part of *str*.

If successful, **fgets( )** returns *str*; a null pointer is returned upon failure. If a read error occurs, the contents of the array pointed to by *str* are indeterminate. Because a null pointer is returned when either an error occurs or the end of the file is reached, you should use **feof( )** or **ferror( )** to determine what has actually happened.

Example

This program uses **fgets( )** to display the contents of the text file specified in the first command-line argument:

```
#include <stdio.h>
#include <stdlib.h>

int main(int argc, char *argv[])
{
  FILE *fp;
  char str[128];

  if((fp=fopen(argv[1], "r"))==NULL) {
    printf("Cannot open file.\n");
    exit(1);
  }

  while(!feof(fp)) {
    if(fgets(str, 126, fp))
      printf("%s", str);
  }
  fclose(fp);
  return 0;
}
```

Related Functions

fputs( ), fgetc( ), gets( ), puts( )

long filelength(int handle)

Description

The prototype for **filelength( )** is found in **io.h**.

The **filelength( )** function is not defined by the ANSI C standard. It returns the length, in bytes, of the file associated with the file descriptor *handle.* Remember that the return value is of type **long**. If an error occurs, –1L is returned and **errno** is set to **EBADF**, which means bad file handle.

Example

This fragment prints the length of a file whose file descriptor is **fd**:

```
printf("The file is %ld bytes long.", filelength(fd));
```

Related Function

open( )

int fileno(FILE *stream)

Description

The prototype for the **fileno( )** macro is found in **stdio.h**.

The **fileno( )** function is not defined by the ANSI C standard. It is used to return a file descriptor to the specified stream.

Example

After this fragment has executed, **fd** is associated with the file pointed to by **stream**:

```
FILE *stream;
int fd;

if((stream=fopen("TEST", "r"))==NULL) {
  printf("Cannot open TEST file.");
  exit(1);
}

fd = fileno(stream);
```

Related Function

fdopen( )

int flushall(void)

Description

The prototype for **flushall( )** is found in **stdio.h**. It is not defined by the ANSI C standard.

A call to **flushall( )** causes the contents of all the output buffers associated with file streams to be physically written to their corresponding files and all the input buffers to be cleared. All streams remain open.

The number of open streams is returned.

All buffers are automatically flushed upon normal termination of the program or when they are full. Also, closing a file flushes its buffer.

Example

The following code fragment flushes all buffers after each write operation:

```
/*
  Assume that fp is associated with an output file.
*/
   .
   .
   .
fwrite(buf,sizeof(data_type),1,fp);
flushall();
   .
   .
   .
```

Related Functions

fclose( ), fopen( ), fcloseall( ), fflush( )

FILE *fopen(const char *fname, const char *mode)

Description

The prototype for **fopen( )** is found in **stdio.h**.

The **fopen( )** function opens a file whose name is pointed to by *fname* and returns the stream that is associated with it. The type of operations that are allowed on the file are defined by the value of *mode*. The legal values for *mode* are shown in Table 11-1. The parameter *fname* must be a string of characters that constitutes a valid file name and can include a path specification.

If **fopen( )** is successful in opening the specified file, a **FILE** pointer is returned. If the file cannot be opened, a null pointer is returned.

As Table 11-1 shows, a file can be opened in either text or binary mode. In text mode, carriage return, linefeed sequences are translated to newline characters on input. On output, the reverse occurs: newlines are translated to carriage return, linefeeds. No such translations occur on binary files.

If the *mode* string does not specify either a **b** (for binary) or a **t** (for text), the type of file opened is determined by the value of the built-in global variable **_fmode**. By default, **_fmode** is **O_TEXT**, which means text mode. It can be set to **O_BINARY**, which means binary mode. These macros are defined in **fcntl.h**.

One correct method of opening a file is illustrated by this code fragment:

```
FILE *fp;

if ((fp = fopen("test", "w"))==NULL) {
  printf("Cannot open file.\n");
  exit(1);
}
```

This method detects any error in opening a file, such as a write-protected or full disk, before attempting to write to it. A null, which is 0, is used because no file pointer ever has that value. **NULL** is defined in **stdio.h**.

If you use **fopen( )** to open a file for write operations, any preexisting file by that name is erased, and a new file is started. If no file by that name exists, one is created. If you want to add to the end of the file, you must use mode **a**. If the file does not exist, an error is returned. Opening a file for read operations requires an existing file. If no file exists, an error is returned. Finally, if a file is opened for read/write operations, it is not erased if it exists; however, if no file exists, one is created.

Example

This fragment opens a file called **test** for binary read/write operations:

```
FILE *fp;

if((fp=fopen("test", "r+b"))==NULL) {
  printf("Cannot open file.\n");
  exit(1);
}
```

Related Functions

fclose( ), fread( ), fwrite( ), putc( ), getc( )

Mode	Meaning
"r"	Open a file for reading. (Opened as text file by default, see discussion.)
"w"	Create a file for writing. (Opened as text file by default, see discussion.)
"a"	Append to a file. (Opened as text file by default, see discussion.)
"rb"	Open a binary file for reading.
"wb"	Create a binary file for writing.
"ab"	Append to a binary file.
"r+"	Open a file for read/write. (Open as text file by default, see discussion.)
"w+"	Create a file for read/write. (Open as text file by default, see discussion.)
"a+"	Append or create a file for read/write. (Open as text file by default, see discussion.)
"r+b"	Open a binary file for read/write.
"w+b"	Create a binary file for read/write.
"a+b"	Append or create a binary file for reading.
"rt"	Open a text file for reading.
"wt"	Create a text file for writing.
"at"	Append to a text file.
"r+t"	Open a text file for read/write.
"w+t"	Create a text file for read/write.
"a+t"	Open or create a text file for read/write.

Table 11-1. *Legal Values for Mode*

int fprintf(FILE *stream, const char *format, arg-list)

Description

The prototype for **fprintf( )** is found in **stdio.h**.

The **fprintf( )** function outputs the values of the arguments that make up *arg-list* as specified in the *format* string to the stream pointed to by *stream*. The return value is the number of characters actually printed. If an error occurs, a negative number is returned.

The operations of the format control string and commands are identical to those in **printf( )**; see the **printf( )** function for a complete description.

Example

This program creates a file called **test** and writes the string "this is a test 10 20.01" into the file using **fprintf( )** to format the data:

```
#include <stdio.h>
#include <stdlib.h>

int main(void)
{
  FILE *fp;

  if((fp=fopen("test", "w"))==NULL) {
    printf("Cannot open file.\n");
    exit(1);
  }

  fprintf(fp, "this is a test %d %f", 10, 20.01);

  fclose(fp);
  return 0;
}
```

Related Functions

printf( ), fscanf( )

int fputc(int ch, FILE *stream)

Description

The prototype for **fputc( )** is found in **stdio.h**.

The **fputc( )** function writes the character *ch* to the specified stream at the current file position and then increments the file-position indicator. Even though *ch* is declared to be an **int**, it is converted by **fputc( )** into an **unsigned char**. Because all character arguments are elevated to integers at the time of the call, you generally see character variables used as arguments. If an integer is used, the high-order byte is simply discarded.

The value returned by **fputc( )** is the value of the character written. If an error occurs, **EOF** is returned. For files opened for binary operations, **EOF** may be a valid character, and the function **ferror( )** must be used to determine whether an error has actually occurred.

Example

This function writes the contents of a string to the specified stream:

```
void write_string(char *str, FILE *fp)
{
  while(*str) if(!ferror(fp)) fputc(*str++, fp);
}
```

Related Functions

fgetc( ), fopen( ), fprintf( ), fread( ), fwrite( )

int fputchar(int ch)

Description

The prototype for **fputchar( )** is found in **stdio.h**.

The **fputchar( )** function writes the character *ch* to **stdout**. Even though *ch* is declared to be an **int**, it is converted by **fputchar( )** into an **unsigned char**. Because all character arguments are elevated to integers at the time of the call, you generally see character variables used as arguments. If an integer is used, the high-order byte is simply discarded. A call to **fputchar( )** is the functional equivalent of a call to **fputc(ch, stdout)**.

The value returned by **fputchar( )** is the value of the character written. If an error occurs, **EOF** is returned. For files opened for binary operations, **EOF** may be a valid character and the function **ferror( )** must be used to determine whether an error has actually occurred.

Example

This function writes the contents of a string to **stdout**:

```
void write_string(char *str)
{
  while(*str) if(!ferror(fp)) fputchar(*str++);
}
```

Related Functions

fgetc( ), fopen( ), fprintf( ), fread( ), fwrite( )

int fputs(const char *str, FILE *stream)

Description

The prototype for **fputs( )** is found in **stdio.h**.

The **fputs( )** function writes the contents of the string pointed to by *str* to the specified stream. The null terminator is not written.

The **fputs( )** function returns the last character written on success, **EOF** on failure.

If the stream is opened in text mode, certain character translations may take place. This means that there may not be a one-to-one mapping of the string onto the file. However, if it is opened in binary mode, no character translations occur and a one-to-one mapping exists between the string and the file.

Example

This code fragment writes the string "this is a test" to the stream pointed to by **fp**.

```
fputs("this is a test", fp);
```

Related Functions

fgets( ), gets( ), puts( ), fprintf( ), fscanf( )

size_t fread(void *buf, size_t size, size_t count, FILE *stream)

Description

The prototype for **fread( )** is found in **stdio.h**.

The **fread( )** function reads *count* number of objects—each object being *size* number of characters in length—from the stream pointed to by *stream* and places them in the character array pointed to by *buf*. The file-position indicator is advanced by the number of characters read.

The **fread( )** function returns the number of items actually read. If fewer items are read than are requested in the call, either an error has occurred or the end of the file has been reached. You must use **feof( )** or **ferror( )** to determine what has taken place.

If the stream is opened for text operations, then carriage return, linefeed sequences are automatically translated into newlines.

Example

This program reads ten floating-point numbers from a disk file called **test** into the array **bal**:

```
#include <stdio.h>
#include <stdlib.h>

int main(void)
{
  FILE *fp;
  float bal[10];
```

```
  if((fp=fopen("test", "rb"))==NULL) {
    printf("Cannot open file.\n");
    exit(1);
  }

  if(fread(bal, sizeof(float), 10, fp)!=10) {
    if(feof(fp)) printf("Premature end of file.");
    else printf("File read error.");
  }

  fclose(fp);
  return 0;
}
```

Related Functions

fwrite( ), fopen( ), fscanf( ), fgetc( ), getc( )

FILE *freopen(const char *fname, const char *mode, FILE *stream)

Description

The prototype for **freopen( )** is found in **stdio.h**.

The **freopen( )** function is used to associate an existing stream with a different file. The new file's name is pointed to by *fname*, the access mode is pointed to by *mode*, and the stream to be reassigned is pointed to by *stream*. The string *mode* uses the same format as **fopen( )**; a complete discussion is found in the **fopen( )** description.

When called, **freopen( )** first tries to close a file that is currently associated with *stream*. However, failure to achieve a successful closing is ignored, and the attempt to reopen continues.

The **freopen( )** function returns a pointer to *stream* on success and a null pointer otherwise.

The main use of **freopen( )** is to redirect the system-defined files **stdin**, **stdout**, and **stderr** to some other file.

Example

The program shown here uses **freopen( )** to redirect the stream **stdout** to the file called **OUT**. Because **printf( )** writes to **stdout**, the first message is displayed on the screen and the second is written to the disk file.

```
#include <stdio.h>
#include <stdlib.h>
```

```
int main(void)
{
  FILE *fp;

  printf("This will display on the screen\n");

  if((fp=freopen("OUT", "w", stdout))==NULL) {
    printf("Cannot open file.\n");
    exit(1);
  }

  printf("This will be written to the file OUT");
  fclose(fp);
  return 0;
}
```

Related Functions

fopen( ), fclose( )

int fscanf(FILE *stream, const char *format, arg-list)

Description

The prototype for **fscanf( )** is found in **stdio.h**.

The **fscanf( )** function works exactly like the **scanf( )** function, except that it reads the information from the stream specified by *stream* instead of **stdin**. See the **scanf( )** function for details.

The **fscanf( )** function returns the number of arguments actually assigned values. This number does not include skipped fields. A return value of **EOF** means that an attempt was made to read past the end of the file.

Example

This code fragment reads a string and a **float** number from the stream **fp**:

```
char str[80];
float f;

fscanf(fp, "%s%f", str, &f);
```

Related Functions

scanf( ), fprintf( )

int fseek(FILE *stream, long offset, int origin)

Description

The prototype for **fseek( )** is found in **stdio.h**.

The **fseek( )** function sets the file-position indicator associated with *stream* according to the values of *offset* and *origin*. Its main purpose is to support random I/O operations. The *offset* is the number of bytes from *origin* to make the new position. The *origin* is 0, 1, or 2, with 0 being the start of the file, 1 the current position, and 2 the end of the file. The following macros for *origin* are defined in **stdio.h**:

Name	Origin
SEEK_SET	Beginning of file
SEEK_CUR	Current position
SEEK_END	End of file

A return value of 0 means that **fseek( )** succeeded. A non-0 value indicates failure.

You can use **fseek( )** to move the position indicator anywhere in the file, even beyond the end. However, it is an error to attempt to set the position indicator before the beginning of the file.

The **fseek( )** function clears the end-of-file flag associated with the specified stream. Furthermore, it nullifies any prior **ungetc( )** on the same stream. (See **ungetc( )**.)

Example

The function shown here seeks to the specified structure of type **addr**. Notice the use of **sizeof** both to obtain the proper number of bytes to seek and to ensure portability.

```
struct addr {
  char name[40];
  char street[40];
  char city[40];
  char state[3];
  char zip[10];
} info;

void find(long client_num)
{
  FILE *fp;

  if((fp=fopen("mail", "rb"))==NULL) {
    printf("Cannot open file.\n");
```

```
    exit(1);
  }

  /* find the proper structure */
  fseek(fp, client_num*sizeof(struct addr), 0);

  /* read the data into memory */
  fread(&info, sizeof(struct addr), 1, fp);
  fclose(fp);
}
```

Related Functions

ftell( ), **rewind( )**, **fopen( )**

int fsetpos(FILE *stream, const fpos_t *pos)

Description

The prototype for **fsetpos( )** is found in **stdio.h**.

The **fsetpos( )** function sets the file pointer associated with *stream* to the location pointed to by *pos*. This value was set by a previous call to **fgetpos( )**. The type **fpos_t** is defined in **stdio.h.** It is capable of representing any file location.

If successful, **fsetpos( )** returns 0; upon failure, a value other than 0 is returned, and **errno** is also set to a non-0 value.

Example

This program uses **fsetpos( )** to reset the current file position to an earlier value:

```
#include <stdio.h>
#include <stdlib.h>

int main(int argc, char *argv[])
{
  FILE *fp;
  long l;
  int  i;
  fpos_t *pos;  /* fpos_t is defined in stdio.h */
  pos = &l;

  if((fp=fopen(argv[1], "w+"))==NULL) {
    printf("Cannot open file.\n");
    exit(1);
  }
```

```
  for (i=0; i<10; i++)
    fputc('Y', fp);  /* write 10 Y's to the file */
  fgetpos(fp, pos);

  for (i=0; i<10; i++)
    fputc('Z', fp);  /* write 10 Z's to the file */
  fsetpos(fp, pos);  /* reset to the end of the Y's */

  fputc('A', fp);     /* replace first Z with an A. */
  fclose(fp);
  return 0;
}
```

Related Functions

fgetpos( ), fseek( ), ftell( )

FILE *_fsopen(const char *fname, const char *mode, int shflg)

Description

The prototype for **_fsopen( )** is found in **stdio.h**. You will also need to include **share.h**. This function is not defined by the ANSI C standard.

The **_fsopen( )** function opens a file whose name is pointed to by *fname* and returns a **FILE** pointer to the stream associated with it. The file is opened for shared-mode access using a network. It returns null if the file cannot be opened.

_fsopen( ) is similar to the standard library function **_fopen( )**, except that it is designed for use with networks to manage file sharing. The string pointed to by *mode* determines the type of operations that may be performed on the file. Its legal values are the same as for **fopen( )**. (Refer to **fopen( )** for details.)

The *shflg* parameter determines how file sharing will be allowed. It will be one of the following macros (defined in **share.h**):

shflg	**Meaning**
SH_COMPAT	Compatibility mode
SH_DENYRW	No reading or writing
SH_DENYWR	No writing
SH_DENYRD	No reading
SH_DENYNONE	Allow reading and writing
SH_DENYNO	Allow reading and writing

Example

This call to **_fsopen( )** opens a file called **TEST.DAT** for binary output and denies network input operations:

```
fp=_fsopen("TEST.DAT", "wb", SH_DENYRD);
```

Related Functions

fopen( ), sopen( )

int fstat(int handle, struct stat *statbuf)

Description

The prototype for **fstat( )** is found in **sys\stat.h**.

The function is not defined by the ANSI C standard. The **fstat( )** function fills the structure pointed to by *statbuf* with information on the file associated with the file descriptor *handle.* Information on the contents of **stat** can be found in the file **sys\stat.h**.

Upon successfully filling the **stat** structure, 0 is returned. On error, –1 is returned and **errno** is set to **EBADF**.

Example

The following example opens a file, fills the **stat** structure, and prints out one of its fields:

```
#include <stdio.h>
#include <sys\stat.h>
#include <stdlib.h>

int main(void)
{
  FILE *fp;
  struct stat buff;

  if((fp=fopen("test", "rb"))==NULL) {
    printf("Cannot open file.\n");
    exit(1);
  }

  /* fill the stat structure */
  fstat(fileno(fp), &buff);

  printf("Size of the file is: %ld\n", buff.st_size);
  fclose(fp);
  return 0;
}
```

Related Functions

stat( ), access( )

long ftell(FILE *stream)

Description

The prototype for **ftell( )** is found in **stdio.h**.

The **ftell( )** function returns the current value of the file-position indicator for the specified stream. This value is the number of bytes the indicator is from the beginning of the file.

The **ftell( )** function returns –1L when an error occurs. If the stream is incapable of random seeks—if it is the console, for instance—the return value is undefined.

Example

This code fragment returns the current value of the file-position indicator for the stream pointed to by **fp**:

```
long i;
if((i=ftell(fp))==-1L) printf("A file error has occurred.\n");
```

Related Function

fseek( )

size_t fwrite(const void *buf, size_t size, size_t count, FILE *stream)

Description

The prototype for **fwrite( )** is found in **stdio.h**.

The **fwrite( )** function writes *count* number of objects—each object being *size* number of characters in length—to the stream pointed to by *stream* from the character array pointed to by *buf.* The file-position indicator is advanced by the number of characters written.

The **fwrite( )** function returns the number of items actually written, which, if the function is successful, equals the number requested. If fewer items are written than are requested, an error has occurred.

If the stream is opened for text operations, then newline characters are automatically translated into carriage return, linefeed sequences when the file is written.

Example

This program writes a **float** to the file **test**. Notice that **sizeof** is used both to determine the number of bytes in a **float** variable and to ensure portability.

```
#include <stdio.h>
#include <stdlib.h>

int main(void)
{
  FILE *fp;
  float f=12.23;

  if((fp=fopen("test", "wb"))==NULL) {
    printf("Cannot open file.\n");
    exit(1);
  }

  fwrite(&f, sizeof(float), 1, fp);

  fclose(fp);
  return 0;
}
```

Related Functions

fread( ), fscanf( ), getc( ), fgetc( )

int getc(FILE *stream)

Description

The prototype for **getc( )** is found in **stdio.h**.

The **getc( )** macro returns the next character from the current position in the input *stream* and increments the file-position indicator. The character is read as an **unsigned char** that is converted to an integer.

If the end of the file is reached, **getc( )** returns **EOF**. However, since **EOF** is a valid integer value, when working with binary files you must use **feof( )** to check for the end of the file. If **getc( )** encounters an error, **EOF** is also returned. Remember that if you are working with binary files you must use **ferror( )** to check for file errors.

Example

This program reads and displays the contents of a text file:

```
#include <stdio.h>
#include <stdlib.h>

int main(int argc, char *argv[])
{
```

```
  FILE *fp;
  char ch;

  if((fp=fopen(argv[1], "r"))==NULL) {
    printf("Cannot open file.\n");
    exit(1);
  }

  while((ch=getc(fp))!=EOF)
    printf("%c", ch);

  fclose(fp);
  return 0;
}
```

Related Functions

fputc( ), fgetc( ), putc( ), fopen( )

int getch(void)
int getche(void)

Description

The prototypes for **getch( )** and **getche( )** are found in **conio.h**.

The **getch( )** function returns the next character read from the console but does not echo that character to the screen.

The **getche( )** function returns the next character read from the console and echoes that character to the screen.

Neither function is defined by the ANSI C standard.

Example

This fragment uses **getch( )** to read the user's menu selection for a spelling checker program.

```
do {
  printf("1: Check spelling\n");
  printf("2: Correct spelling\n");
  printf("3: Look up a word in the dictionary\n");
  printf("4: Quit\n");

  printf("\nEnter your selection: ");
  choice = getch();
} while(!strchr("1234", choice));
```

Related Functions

getc( ), **getchar( )**, **fgetc( )**

int getchar(void)

Description

The prototype for **getchar( )** is found in **stdio.h**.

The **getchar( )** macro returns the next character from **stdin**. The character is read as an **unsigned char** that is converted to an integer. If the end-of-file marker is read, **EOF** is returned.

The **getchar( )** macro is functionally equivalent to **getc(stdin)**.

Example

This program reads characters from **stdin** into the array **s** until a carriage return is entered and then displays the string.

```
#include <stdio.h>

int main(void)
{
  char s[256], *p;

  p = s;

  while((*p++=getchar())!='\n') ;
  *p = '\0';   /* add null terminator */
  printf(s);
  return 0;
}
```

Related Functions

fputc( ), **fgetc( )**, **putc( )**, **fopen( )**

char *gets(char *str)

Description

The prototype for **gets( )** is found in **stdio.h**.

The **gets( )** function reads characters from **stdin** and places them into the character array pointed to by *str*. Characters are read until a newline or an **EOF** is reached. The newline character is not made part of the string but is translated into a null to terminate the string.

If successful, **gets( )** returns *str*; if unsuccessful, it returns a null pointer. If a read error occurs, the contents of the array pointed to by *str* are indeterminate. Because a null pointer is returned when either an error has occurred or the end of the file is reached, you should use **feof( )** or **ferror( )** to determine what has actually happened.

There is no limit to the number of characters that **gets( )** will read; it is the programmer's job to make sure that the array pointed to by *str* is not overrun.

Example

This program uses **gets( )** to read a file name:

```
#include <stdio.h>
#include <stdlib.h>

int main(void)
{
  FILE *fp;
  char fname[128];

  printf("Enter filename: ");
  gets(fname);

  if((fp=fopen(fname, "r"))==NULL) {
    printf("Cannot open file.\n");
    exit(1);
  }

 .
 .
 .
  fclose(fp);
  return 0;
}
```

Related Functions

fputs( ), fgetc( ), fgets( ), puts( )

int getw(FILE *stream)

Description

The prototype for **getw( )** is found in **stdio.h**.

The **getw( )** function is not defined by the ANSI C standard.

The **getw( )** function returns the next integer from *stream* and advances the file-position indicator appropriately.

Because the integer read may have a value equal to **EOF**, you must use **feof( )** or **ferror( )** to determine when the end-of-file marker is reached or an error has occurred.

Example

This program reads integers from the file **inttest** and displays their sum.

```
#include <stdio.h>
#include <stdlib.h>

int main(void)
{
  FILE *fp;
  int sum = 0;

  if((fp=fopen("inttest", "rb"))==NULL) {
    printf("Cannot open file.\n");
    exit(1);
  }

  while(!feof(fp))
    sum = getw(fp)+sum;

  printf("The sum is %d", sum);
  fclose(fp);
  return 0;
}
```

Related Functions

putw( ), fread( )

int isatty(int handle)

Description

The prototype for **isatty( )** is found in **io.h**.

The function **isatty( )** is not defined by the ANSI C standard. It returns non-0 if *handle* is associated with a character device that is a terminal, console, printer, or serial port; otherwise, it returns 0.

Example

This fragment reports whether the device associated with **fd** is a character device:

```
if(isatty(fd)) printf("is a character device");
else printf("is not a character device");
```

Related Function

open( )

int lock(int handle, long offset, long length)

Description

The prototype for **lock( )** is found in **io.h**.

The **lock( )** function is not defined by the ANSI C standard. It is used to lock a region of a file, thus preventing another program from using it until the lock is removed. To unlock a file use **unlock( )**. These functions provide control for file sharing in network environments.

The file to be locked is associated with *handle.* The portion of the file to be locked is determined by the starting *offset* from the beginning of the file and the *length.*

If **lock( )** is successful, 0 is returned. Upon failure, –1 is returned.

Example

This fragment locks the first 128 bytes of the file associated with **fd**:

```
lock(fd, 0, 128);
```

Related Functions

unlock( ), sopen( )

int locking(int handle, int mode, long length)

Description

The prototype for **locking( )** is in **io.h**. You must also include **sys\locking.h**.

The **locking( )** function is not defined by the ANSI C standard. It is used to lock a region of a shared file when using a network. Locking the file prevents other users from accessing it.

The *mode* parameter must be one of these macros:

Mode	Meaning
LK_LOCK	Lock the specified region. If the locking request fails, retry ten times, once each second.
LK_RLCK	Same as LK_LOCK.
LK_NBLCK	Lock the specified region. If the locking request fails, perform no retries.
LK_NBRLCK	Same as LK_NBLCK.
LK_UNLCK	Unlock the specified region.

The handle of the file to lock is specified in *handle.* The file will be locked (or unlocked) beginning with the current position and extending *length* number of bytes.

The **locking( )** function returns 0 if successful and –1 otherwise. On failure, **errno** is set to one of these values:

EBADF	Bad file handle
EACCESS	Access denied
EDEADLOCK	File cannot be locked
EINVAL	Invalid argument

Example

This call to **locking( )** unlocks 10 bytes in the file described by **fd**:

```
if(locking(fd, LK_UNLOCK, 10)) {
  // process error
}
```

Related Functions

lock( ), sopen( )

long lseek(int handle, long offset, int origin)

Description

The prototype for **lseek( )** is found in **io.h**.

The **lseek( )** function is part of the UNIX-like I/O system and is not defined by the ANSI C standard.

The **lseek( )** function sets the file-position indicator to the location specified by *offset* and *origin* for the file specified by *handle.*

How **lseek( )** works depends on the values of *origin* and *offset.* The *origin* may be 0, 1, or 2. The following chart explains how the *offset* is interpreted for each *origin* value:

Origin	Effect of Call to lseek( )
0	Count the offset from the start of the file
1	Count the offset from the current position
2	Count the offset from the end of the file

The following macros are defined in **io.h**. They can be used for a value of *origin* in order of 0 through 2.

SEEK_SET
SEEK_CUR
SEEK_END

The **lseek( )** function returns *offset* on success. Therefore, **lseek( )** will be returning a **long** integer. Upon failure, a –1L is returned and **errno** is set to one of these values:

EBADF	Bad file number
EINVAL	Invalid argument

Example

The example shown here allows you to examine a file one sector at a time using the UNIX-like I/O system. You will want to change the buffer size to match the sector size of your system.

```
#include <stdio.h>
#include <fcntl.h>
#include <sys\stat.h>
#include <io.h>
#include <stdlib.h>

#define BUF_SIZE  128

/* read buffers using lseek() */
int main(int argc, char *argv[])
{
  char buf[BUF_SIZE+1], s[10];
  int fd, sector;

  buf[BUF_SIZE+1] = '\0'; /* null terminate buffer for printf */
  if((fd=open(argv[1], O_RDONLY | O_BINARY))==-1) { /* open for write */
    printf("Cannot open file.\n");
    exit(0);
  }
  do {
    printf("Buffer: ");
    gets(s);

    sector = atoi(s); /* get the sector to read */

    if(lseek(fd, (long)sector*BUF_SIZE,0)==-1L)
      printf("Seek Error\n");

    if(read(fd, buf, BUF_SIZE)==0) {
      printf("Read Error\n");
    }
    else {
```

```
      printf("%s\n", buf);
    }
  } while(sector > 0);
  close(fd);
  return 0;
}
```

Related Functions

read( ), write( ), open( ), close( )

int open(const char *filename, int access, unsigned mode)
int _rtl_open(const char *filename, int access)

Description

The prototypes for **open( )** and **_rtl_open( )** are found in **io.h**.

The **open( )** function is part of the UNIX-like I/O system and is not defined by the ANSI C standard.

Unlike the buffered I/O system, the UNIX-like system does not use file pointers of type **FILE**, but rather file descriptors of type **int**. The **open( )** function opens a file with the name *filename* and sets its access mode as specified by *access*. You can think of *access* as being constructed of a base mode of operation plus modifiers. The following base modes are allowed.

Base	Meaning
O_RDONLY	Open for read only
O_WRONLY	Open for write only
O_RDWR	Open for read/write

After selecting one of these values, you may OR it with one or more of the following access modifiers:

Access Modifier	Meaning
O_NDELAY	Not used; included for UNIX compatibility
O_APPEND	Causes the file pointer to be set to the end of the file before each write operation
O_CREAT	If the file does not exist, creates it with its attribute set to the value of *mode*

Access Modifier	Meaning
O_TRUNC	If the file exists, truncates it to length 0 but retains its file attributes
O_EXCL	When used with O_CREAT, will not create output file if a file by that name already exists
O_BINARY	Opens a binary file
O_TEXT	Opens a text file

The *mode* argument is only required if the **O_CREAT** modifier is used. In this case, *mode* may be one of three values:

Mode	Meaning
S_IWRITE	Write access
S_IREAD	Read access
S_IWRITE | S_IREAD	Read/write access

A successful call to **open( )** returns a positive integer that is the file descriptor associated with the file. A return value of –1 means that the file cannot be opened, and **errno** is set to one of these values:

ENOENT	File does not exist
EMFILE	Too many open files
EACCES	Access denied
EINVACC	Access code is invalid

The function **_rtl_open( )** accepts a larger number of modifiers for the *access* parameter if executing under DOS 3.*x* or greater or Windows. These additional values are

Access Modifier	Meaning
O_NOINHERIT	File not passed to child programs
SH_COMPAT	Other open operations that use SH_COMPAT are allowed
SH_DENYRW	Only the current file descriptor has access to the file
SH_DENWR	Only read access to the file allowed
SH_DENYRD	Only write access to the file allowed
SH_DENYNO	Allow other sharing options except SH_COMPAT

Example

You will usually see the call to **open( )** like this:

```
if((fd=open(filename, mode)) == -1)  {
  printf("Cannot open file.\n");
  exit(1);
}
```

Related Functions

close( ), read( ), write( )

void perror(const char *str)

Description

The prototype for **perror( )** is found in **stdio.h**.

The **perror( )** function maps the value of the global **errno** onto a string and writes that string to **stderr**. If the value of *str* is not null, the string is written first, followed by a colon and then the proper error message, as determined by the value of **errno**.

Example

This program purposely generates a domain error by calling **asin( )** with an out-of-range argument. The output is "Program Error Test: Math argument".

```
#include <stdio.h>
#include <math.h>
#include <errno.h> /* contains declaration for errno */

int main(void)
{
  /* this will generate a domain error */
  asin(10.0);
  if(errno==EDOM)
    perror("Program Error Test");
  return 0;
}
```

Related Function

ferror( )

int printf(const char *format, arg-list)

Description

The prototype for **printf( )** is found in **stdio.h**.

The **printf( )** function writes to **stdout** the arguments that make up *arg-list* under the control of the string pointed to by *format*.

The string pointed to by *format* contains two types of items. The first type consists of characters that will be printed on the screen. The second type contains format specifiers that define the way the arguments are displayed. A format specifier consists of a percent sign followed by the format code. The format commands are shown in Table 11-2. There must be exactly the same number of arguments as there are format specifiers, and the format specifiers and arguments are matched in order. For example, this **printf( )** call:

```
printf("Hi %c %d %s", 'c', 10, "there!");
```

displays "Hi c 10 there!".

Code	Format
%c	Character.
%d	Signed decimal integers.
%i	Signed decimal integers.
%e	Scientific notation (lowercase e).
%E	Scientific notation (uppercase E).
%f	Decimal floating point.
%g	Uses %e or %f, whichever is shorter (if %g, uses lowercase e).
%G	Uses %E or %f, whichever is shorter (if %G, uses uppercase E).
%o	Unsigned octal.
%s	String of characters.
%u	Unsigned decimal integers.
%x	Unsigned hexadecimal (lowercase letters).
%X	Unsigned hexadecimal (uppercase letters).
%p	Displays a pointer.
%n	Associated argument is a pointer to an integer into which is placed the number of characters written so far.
%%	Prints a % sign.

Table 11-2. **printf( )** *Format Commands*

If there are insufficient arguments to match the format commands, the output is undefined. If there are more arguments than format commands, the remaining arguments are discarded.

The **printf( )** function returns the number of characters actually printed. A negative return value indicates an error.

The format commands may have modifiers that specify the field width, the precision, and a left-justification flag. An integer placed between the percent sign and the format command acts as a *minimum field-width specifier*, padding the output with blanks or zeros to ensure that it is a minimum length. If the string or number is greater than that minimum, it will be printed in full. The default padding is done with spaces. For numeric values, if you wish to pad with zeros, place a zero before the field-width specifier. For example, **%05d** pads a number of less than five digits with zeros so that its total length is five digits.

The effect of the *precision modifier* depends upon the type of format command being modified. To add a precision modifier, place a decimal point followed by the precision after the field-width specifier. For **e**, **E**, and **f** formats, the precision modifier determines the number of decimal places printed. For example, **%10.4f** displays a number at least ten characters wide with four decimal places. However, when used with the **g** or **G** specifier, the precision determines the maximum number of significant digits displayed.

When the precision modifier is applied to integers, it specifies the minimum number of digits that will be displayed. (Leading zeros are added, if necessary.)

When the precision modifier is applied to strings, the number following the period specifies the maximum field length. For example, **%5.7s** displays a string that is at least five characters long and does not exceed seven. If the string is longer than the maximum field width, the end characters are truncated.

By default, all output is right justified. That is, if the field width is larger than the data printed, the data will be placed on the right edge of the field. You can force the information to be left justified by placing a minus sign directly after the percent sign. For example, **%–10.2f** left justifies a floating-point number with two decimal places in a ten-character field.

There are two format specifiers that allow **printf( )** to display **short** and **long** integers. These specifiers may be applied to the **d**, **i**, **o**, **u**, **x**, and **X** type specifiers. The **l** specifier tells **printf( )** that a **long** data type follows. For example, **%ld** means that a **long int** is to be displayed. The **h** specifier instructs **printf( )** to display a **short int**. Therefore, **%hu** indicates that the data is of type **short unsigned int**.

Although nonstandard (and not needed), the **l** modifier may also prefix the floating-point specifiers **e**, **E**, **f**, **g**, and **G** and indicates that a **double** follows. **L** is used to indicate a **long double**.

The **n** format causes the number of characters written so far to be put into the integer variable pointed to by the argument corresponding to the **n** specifier. For example, this code fragment displays the number **15** after the line **this is a test**.

```
int i;

printf("this is a test %n", &i);
printf("%d", i);
```

The **#** has a special meaning when used with some **printf( )** format specifiers. Preceding a **g**, **G**, **f**, **e**, or **E** specifier with a **#** ensures that the decimal point will be present even if there are no decimal digits. If you precede the **x** format specifier with a **#**, the hexadecimal number will be printed with a **0x** prefix. When used with the **o** specifier, it causes a leading 0 to be printed. The **#** cannot be applied to any other format specifiers.

The minimum field-width and precision specifiers may be provided by arguments to **printf( )** instead of by constants. To accomplish this, use an * as a placeholder. When the format string is scanned, **printf( )** will match * to arguments in the order in which they occur.

Example

This program displays the output shown in its comments:

```
#include <stdio.h>

int main(void)
{
  /* This prints "this is a test" left-justified
     in a 20-character field.
  */
  printf("%-20s", "this is a test");

  /* This prints a float with 3 decimal places in a
     10-character field. The output will be "    12.235".
  */
  printf("%10.3f", 12.234657);
  return 0;
}
```

Related Functions

scanf( ), **fprintf( )**

int putc(int ch, FILE *stream)

Description

The prototype for **putc( )** is found in **stdio.h**.

The **putc( )** macro writes the character contained in the least significant byte of *ch* to the output stream pointed to by *stream*. Because character arguments are elevated to integers at the time of the call, you can use character variables as arguments to **putc( )**.

If successful, **putc( )** returns the character written; it returns **EOF** if an error occurs. If the output stream has been opened in binary mode, **EOF** is a valid value for *ch*. This means that you must use **ferror( )** to determine whether an error has occurred.

Example

The following loop writes the characters in string **str** to the stream specified by **fp**. The null terminator is not written.

```
for(; *str; str++) putc(*str, fp);
```

Related Functions

fgetc( ), fputc( ), getchar( ), putchar( )

int putch(int ch)

Description

The prototype for **putch( )** is in **conio.h**. This function is not defined by the ANSI C standard.

The **putch( )** function displays the character specified in *ch* on the screen. This function writes directly to the screen and not to **stdout**. Therefore, no character translations are performed and no redirection will occur.

If successful, **putch( )** returns *ch*. On failure, **EOF** is returned.

Example

This outputs the character X to the screen:

```
putch('X');
```

Related Function

putchar( )

int putchar(int ch)

Description

The prototype for **putchar( )** is found in **stdio.h**.

The **putchar( )** macro writes the character contained in the least significant byte of *ch* to **stdout**. It is functionally equivalent to **putc(ch, stdout)**. Because character arguments are elevated to integers at the time of the call, you can use character variables as arguments to **putchar( )**.

If successful, **putchar( )** returns the character written; if an error occurs it returns **EOF**. If the output stream has been opened in binary mode, **EOF** is a valid value for *ch*. This means that you must use **ferror( )** to determine if an error has occurred.

Example

The following loop writes the characters in string **str** to **stdout**. The null terminator is not written.

```
for(; *str; str++) putchar(*str);
```

Related Functions

fputchar( ), **putc( )**

int puts(const char *str)

Description

The prototype for **puts( )** is found in **stdio.h**.

The **puts( )** function writes the string pointed to by *str* to the standard output device. The null terminator is translated to a newline.

The **puts( )** function returns a newline if successful and an **EOF** if unsuccessful.

Example

The following writes the string "this is an example" to **stdout**.

```
#include <stdio.h>
#include <string.h>

int main(void)
{
  char str[80];

  strcpy(str, "this is an example");
  puts(str);
  return 0;
}
```

Related Functions

putc( ), **gets( )**, **printf( )**

int putw(int i, FILE *stream)

Description

The prototype for **putw( )** is in **stdio.h**. The **putw( )** function is not defined by the ANSI C standard and may not be fully portable.

The **putw( )** function writes the integer *i* to *stream* at the current file position and increments the file-position pointer appropriately.

The **putw( )** function returns the value written. A return value of **EOF** means an error has occurred in the stream if it is in text mode. Because **EOF** is also a valid integer value, you must use **ferror( )** to detect an error in a binary stream.

Example

This code fragment writes the value 100 to the stream pointed to by **fp**:

```
putw(100, fp);
```

Related Functions

getw( ), printf( ), fwrite( )

int read(int fd, void *buf, unsigned count)
int _rtl_read(int fd, void *buf, unsigned count)

Description

The prototypes for **read( )** and **_rtl_read( )** are found in **io.h**.

Neither the **read( )** nor the **_rtl_read( )** function is defined by the ANSI C standard. The **read( )** function is part of the UNIX-like I/O system. The **_rtl_read( )** function is specific to Borland C++ and the DOS/Windows operating system.

The **read( )** function reads *count* number of bytes from the file described by *fd* into the buffer pointed to by *buf*. The file-position indicator is incremented by the number of bytes read. If the file is opened in text mode, character translations may take place.

The return value is the number of bytes actually read. This number will be smaller than *count* if an end-of-file marker is encountered or an error occurs before *count* number of bytes have been read. A value of –1 is returned if an error occurs, and a value of 0 is returned if an attempt is made to read at end-of-file. If an error occurs, then **errno** is set to one of these values:

EACCES	Access denied
EBADF	Bad file number

The difference between **read( )** and **_rtl_read( )** is that **read( )** removes carriage returns and returns **EOF** when a CTRL-Z is read from a text file. The **_rtl_read( )** function does not perform these actions.

Example

This program reads the first 100 bytes from the file **TEST.TST** into the array **buffer**:

```
#include <stdio.h>
#include <io.h>
```

```
#include <fcntl.h>
#include <stdlib.h>

int main(void)
{
  int fd;
  char buffer[100];

  if((fd=open("TEST.TST", O_RDONLY))==-1) {
    printf("Cannot open file.\n");
    exit(1);
  }

  if(read(fd, buffer, 100)!=100)
    printf("Possible read error.");
  return 0;
}
```

Related Functions

open( ), close( ), write( ), lseek( )

int remove(const char *fname)

Description

The prototype for **remove( )** is found in **stdio.h**.

The **remove( )** function erases the file specified by *fname*. It returns 0 if the file was successfully deleted and –1 if an error occurred. If an error occurs, then **errno** is set to one of these values:

ENOENT	File does not exist
EACCES	Access denied

Example

This program removes the file specified on the command line:

```
#include <stdio.h>

int main(int argc, char *argv[])
{
  if(remove(argv[1])==-1)
    printf("Remove Error");
  return 0;
}
```

Related Function

rename( )

int rename(const char *oldfname, const char *newfname)

Description

The prototype for **rename( )** is found in **stdio.h**.

The **rename( )** function changes the name of the file specified by *oldfname* to *newfname*. The *newfname* must not match any existing directory entry.

The **rename( )** function returns 0 if successful and non-0 if an error has occurred. If an error occurs, then **errno** is set to one of these values:

ENOENT	File does not exist
EACCES	Access denied
ENOTSAM	Device not the same

Example

This program renames the file specified as the first command-line argument to that specified by the second command-line argument. Assuming the program is called **change**, a command line consisting of "change this that" will change the name of a file called **this** to **that**.

```
#include <stdio.h>

int main(int argc, char *argv[])
{
  if(rename(argv[1], argv[2])!=0)
    printf("Rename Error");
  return 0;
}
```

Related Function

remove( )

void rewind(FILE *stream)

Description

The prototype for **rewind( )** is found in **stdio.h**.

The **rewind( )** function moves the file-position indicator to the start of the specified stream. It also clears the end-of-file and error flags associated with *stream.* It returns 0 if successful and non-0 otherwise.

Example

This function reads the stream pointed to by **fp** twice, displaying the file each time:

```
void re_read(FILE *fp)
{
  /* read once */
  while(!feof(fp)) putchar(getc(fp));

  rewind(fp);

  /* read twice */
  while(!feof(fp)) putchar(getc(fp));
}
```

Related Function

fseek( )

int _rtl_chmod (const char *filename, int get_set, int attrib)

Description

The prototype for **_rtl_chmod( )** is found in **io.h**.

The **_rtl_chmod( )** function is not defined by the ANSI C standard. It is used to read or set the attribute byte associated with the file pointed to by *filename* as allowed by DOS or Windows. If *get_set* is 0, **_rtl_chmod( )** returns the current file attribute and *attrib* is not used. If *get_set* is 1, the file attribute is set to the value of *attrib.* The *attrib* argument can be one of these macros:

FA_RDONLY	Set file to read only
FA_HIDDEN	Make hidden file
FA_SYSTEM	Mark as a system file
FA_LABEL	Make volume label
FA_DIREC	Make directory
FA_ARCH	Mark as archive

The **_rtl_chmod( )** function returns the file attribute if successful. Upon failure, it returns a –1 and sets **errno** to either **ENOENT**, if the file does not exist, or **EACCES**, if access to the file is denied.

Example

This line of code sets the file **TEST.TST** to read only.

```
if(_rtl_chmod("TEST.TST", 1, FA_RDONLY)==FA_RDONLY)
  printf("File set to read-only mode.");
```

Related Functions

chmod( ), access( )

int scanf(const char *format, arg-list)

Description

The prototype for **scanf( )** is in **stdio.h**. The **scanf( )** function is a general-purpose input routine that reads the stream **stdin**. It can read all the built-in data types and automatically convert them into the proper internal format. It is much like the reverse of **printf( )**.

The control string pointed to by *format* consists of three types of characters:

- Format specifiers
- White-space characters
- Non-white-space characters

The format specifiers are preceded by a percent sign and tell **scanf( )** what type of data is to be read next. These codes are listed in Table 11-3. For example, **%s** reads a string while **%d** reads an integer.

The format string is read left to right and the format codes are matched, in order, with the arguments that make up the argument list.

A white-space character in the control string causes **scanf( )** to skip over one or more white-space characters in the input stream. A white-space character is a space, a tab, or a newline. In essence, one white-space character in the control string causes **scanf( )** to read, but not store, any number (including zero) of white-space characters up to the first non-white-space character.

A non-white-space character causes **scanf( )** to read and discard a matching character. For example, **"%d,%d"** causes **scanf( )** to read an integer, read and discard a comma, and then read another integer. If the specified character is not found, **scanf( )** terminates.

All the variables used to receive values through **scanf( )** must be passed by their addresses. This means that all arguments must be pointers to the variables used as arguments. This is C's way of creating a call by reference, and it allows a function to

Code	Meaning
%c	Read a single character.
%d	Read a decimal integer.
%i	Read a decimal integer.
%e	Read a floating-point number.
%f	Read a floating-point number.
%g	Read a floating-point number.
%o	Read an octal number.
%s	Read a string.
%x	Read a hexadecimal number.
%p	Read a pointer.
%n	Receives an integer value equal to the number of characters read so far.
%u	Read an unsigned integer.
%[]	Scan for a set of characters.
%%	Read a % sign.

Table 11-3. scanf( ) *Format Codes*

alter the contents of an argument. For example, to read an integer into the variable **count**, you would use the following **scanf( )** call:

```
scanf("%d", &count);
```

Strings are read into character arrays, and the array name, without any index, is the address of the first element of the array. So, to read a string into the character array **address**, use

```
scanf("%s", address);
```

In this case, **address** is already a pointer and need not be preceded by the **&** operator.

The input data items must be separated by spaces, tabs, or newlines. Punctuation such as commas, semicolons, and the like do not count as separators. This means that

```
scanf("%d%d", &r, &c);
```

accepts an input of **10 20**, but fails with **10,20**. The **scanf( )** format specifiers are matched in order with the variables receiving the input in the argument list.

An * placed after the % and before the format specifier reads data of the specified type but suppresses its assignment. Thus,

```
scanf("%d%*c%d", &x, &y);
```

given the input **10/20** places the value 10 into **x**, discards the division sign, and gives **y** the value 20.

The format commands can specify a maximum field-length modifier. This is an integer placed between the % and the format specifier that limits the number of characters read for any field. For example, if you wish to read no more than 20 characters into **address**, you would write

```
scanf("%20s", address);
```

If the input stream were greater than 20 characters, a subsequent call to input would begin where this call left off. Input for a field may terminate before the maximum field length is reached if a white space is encountered. In this case, **scanf( )** moves on to the next field.

Although spaces, tabs, and newlines are used as field separators, they are read like any other character when reading a single character. For example, with an input stream of **x y**,

```
scanf("%c%c%c", &a, &b, &c);
```

returns with the character **x** in **a**, a space in **b**, and the character **y** in **c**.

Be careful: Any other characters in the control string—including spaces, tabs, and newlines—are used to match and discard characters from the input stream. Any character that matches is discarded. For example, given the input stream **10t20**,

```
scanf("%st%s", &x, &y);
```

places 10 into **x** and 20 into **y**. The **t** is discarded because of the **t** in the control string.

Another feature of **scanf( )** is called a *scanset*. A scanset defines a set of characters that will be read by **scanf( )** and assigned to the scanset's corresponding character array. You define a scanset by putting inside square brackets the characters you want to scan for. The beginning square bracket must be prefixed by a percent sign. For example, this scanset tells **scanf( )** to read only the characters **A**, **B**, and **C**:

```
%[ABC]
```

The argument corresponding to the scanset must be a pointer to a character array. When you use a scanset, **scanf( )** continues to read characters and put them into the array until a character that is not part of the scanset is encountered. (That is, a scanset reads only matching characters.) Upon return from **scanf( )**, the array will contain a null-terminated string.

You can specify an inverted set if the first character in the set is a ^ . When the ^ is present, it instructs **scanf( )** to accept any character that *is not* defined by the scanset.

You can specify a range using a hyphen. For example, this tells **scanf( )** to accept the letters "A" through "Z":

```
%[A-Z]
```

Remember that the scanset is case sensitive. Therefore, if you want to scan for both upper- and lowercase letters, you must specify them individually.

The **scanf( )** function returns a number equal to the number of fields that were successfully assigned values. This number does not include fields that were read but not assigned because the * modifier was used to suppress the assignment. **EOF** is returned if an error occurs before the first field is assigned.

When using Borland C++ in a 16-bit environment, you can override the default memory model used to compile your program by explicitly specifying the size of each pointer used in a call to **scanf( )**. To specify a **near** pointer, use the **N** modifier. To specify a **far** pointer, use the **F** modifier. (You cannot use the **N** modifier if your program was compiled for the **huge** memory model.)

Example

The operation of the following **scanf( )** statements are explained in their comments.

```
char str[80];
int i;

/* read a string and an integer */
scanf("%s%d", str, &i);

/* read up to 79 chars into str */
scanf("%79s", str);

/* skip the integer between the two strings */
scanf("%s%*d%s", str, &i, str);
```

Related Functions

printf( ), fscanf( )

void setbuf(FILE *stream, char *buf)

Description

The prototype to **setbuf( )** is found in **stdio.h**.

The **setbuf( )** function is used either to specify the buffer the specified stream will use or, if called with *buf* set to null, to turn off buffering. If a programmer-defined buffer is to be specified, it must be **BUFSIZ** characters long. **BUFSIZ** is defined in **stdio.h.**

The **setbuf( )** function returns no value.

Example

This following fragment associates a programmer-defined buffer with the stream pointed to by **fp**:

```
char buffer[BUFSIZ];
   .
   .
   .
setbuf(fp,buffer);
```

Related Functions

fopen( ), fclose( ), setvbuf( )

int setmode(int handle, int mode)

Description

The prototype to **setmode( )** is found in **io.h**.

The **setmode( )** function is not defined by the ANSI C standard. It is used to reset the mode of an already open file given its file descriptor and the new mode desired. The only valid modes are **O_BINARY** and **O_TEXT**.

It returns 0 on success, –1 on error. If an error occurs, **errno** is set to **EINVAL** (invalid argument).

Example

This line of code sets the file associated with **fd** to text-only operation.

```
setmode(fd, O_TEXT)
```

Related Functions

open( ), creat( )

int setvbuf(FILE *stream, char *buf, int mode, size_t size)

Description

The prototype for **setvbuf( )** is found in **stdio.h**.

The **setvbuf( )** function allows the programmer to specify the buffer, its size, and its mode for the specified stream. The character array pointed to by *buf* is used as *stream*'s buffer for I/O operations. The size of the buffer is set by *size*, and *mode* determines how buffering will be handled. If *buf* is null, no buffering takes place.

The legal values of *mode* are **_IOFBF**, **_IONBF**, and **_IOLBF**. These are defined in **stdio.h**. When the mode is set to **_IOFBF**, full buffering takes place. This is the default setting. When set to **_IONBF**, the stream is unbuffered regardless of the value *buf*. If *mode* is **_IOLBF**, the stream is line-buffered, which means that the buffer is flushed each time a newline character is written for output streams; for input streams an input request reads all characters up to a newline. In either case, the buffer is also flushed when full.

The value of *size* must be greater than 0 and less than 32,768.

The **setvbuf( )** function returns 0 on success, non-0 on failure.

Example

This fragment sets the stream **fp** to line-buffered mode with a buffer size of 128:

```
#include <stdio.h>
char buffer[128];
  .
  .
  .
setvbuf(fp, buffer, _IOLBF, 128);
```

Related Function

setbuf( )

int sopen(const char *filename, int access, int shflag, int mode)

Description

The prototype for **sopen( )** is found in **io.h**. The **sopen( )** macro is part of the UNIX-like file system.

The **sopen( )** macro opens a file for shared-mode access using a network. It is defined as

open(*filename*, (*access* | *shflag*), *mode*)

The **sopen( )** macro opens a file with the name *filename* and sets its access mode as specified by *access* and its share mode as specified by *shflag*. You can think of *access* as being constructed of a base mode of operation plus modifiers. The following base modes are allowed:

Base	Meaning
O_RDONLY	Open for read only
O_WRONLY	Open for write only
O_RDWR	Open for read/write

After selecting one of these values, you may OR it with one or more of the following access modifiers:

Modifiers	Meaning When Set
O_NDELAY	Not used; included for UNIX compatibility.
O_APPEND	Causes the file pointer to be set to the end of the file before each write operation.
O_CREAT	If the file does not exist, it is created with its attribute set to the value of *mode*.
O_TRUNC	If the file exists, it is truncated to length 0 but retains its file attributes.
O_EXCL	When used with **O_CREAT**, will not create output file if a file by that name already exists.
O_NOINHERIT	Child programs do not inherit the file.
O_BINARY	Opens a binary file.
O_TEXT	Opens a text file.

The *shflag* argument defines the type of sharing allowed on this file and can be one of these values:

shflag	Meaning
SH_COMPAT	Compatibility mode
SH_DENYRW	No read or write
SH_DENYWR	No write
SH_DENYRD	No read
SH_DENYNONE	Allow read/write
SH_DENYNO	Allow read/write

The *mode* argument is only required if the **O_CREAT** modifier is used. In this case, *mode* can be one of these values:

Mode	Meaning
S_IWRITE	Write access
S_IREAD	Read access
S_IWRITE | S_IREAD	Read/write access

A successful call to **sopen( )** returns a positive integer that is the file descriptor associated with the file. A return value of –1 means that the file cannot be opened, and **errno** will be set to one of these values:

ENOENT	File does not exist
EMFILE	Too many open files
EACCES	Access denied
EINVACC	Invalid access code

Example

You will usually see the call to **sopen( )** like this:

```
if((fd=sopen(filename, access, shflag, mode)) ==-1)  {
  printf("Cannot open file.\n");
  exit(1);
}
```

Related Functions

open( ), _rtl_open( ), close( )

int sprintf(char *buf, const char *format, arg-list)

Description

The prototype for **sprintf( )** is found in **stdio.h**.

The **sprintf( )** function is identical to **printf( )**, except that the output generated is placed into the array pointed to by *buf*. See the **printf( )** function.

The return value is equal to the number of characters actually placed into the array.

Example

After this code fragment executes, **str** holds **one 2 3**:

```
char str[80];
sprintf(str, "%s %d %c", "one", 2, '3');
```

Related Functions

printf( ), fsprintf( )

int sscanf(char *buf, const char *format, arg-list)

Description

The prototype for **sscanf( )** is found in **stdio.h**.

The **sscanf( )** function is identical to **scanf( )**, except that data is read from the array pointed to by *buf* rather than **stdin**. See **scanf( )**.

The return value is equal to the number of fields that were actually assigned values. This number does not include fields that were skipped through the use of the * format-command modifier. A value of 0 means that no fields were assigned, and **EOF** indicates that a read was attempted at the end of the string.

Example

This program prints the message "hello 1" on the screen:

```
#include <stdio.h>

int main(void)
{
  char str[80];
  int i;

  sscanf("hello 1 2 3 4 5", "%s%d", str, &i);
  printf("%s %d", str, i);
  return 0;
}
```

Related Functions

scanf( ), fscanf( )

int stat(char *filename, struct stat *statbuf)

Description

The prototype for **stat( )** is found in **sys\stat.h**.

The **stat( )** function fills the structure pointed to by *statbuf* with information on the file associated with *filename*. The **stat** structure is defined in **sys\stat.h**.

Upon successfully filling the **stat** structure, 0 is returned. If unsuccessful, –1 is returned and **errno** is set to **ENOENT**.

Example

The following example opens a file, fills the **stat** structure, and prints out one of its fields:

```
#include <stdio.h>
#include <sys\stat.h>
#include <stdlib.h>

int main(void)
{
  FILE *fp;
  struct stat buff;

  if((fp=fopen("test", "rb"))==NULL) {
    printf("Cannot open file.\n");
    exit(1);
  }

  /* fill the stat structure */
  stat("test", &buff);

  printf("Size of the file is: %ld\n", buff.st_size);
  fclose(fp);
  return 0;
}
```

Related Functions

fstat( ), access( )

long tell(int fd)

Description

The prototype for **tell( )** is found in **io.h**.

The **tell( )** function is part of the UNIX-like I/O system and is not defined by the ANSI C standard.

The **tell( )** function returns the current value of the file-position indicator associated with the file descriptor *fd*. This value is the number of bytes the position indicator is from the start of the file. A return value of –1L indicates an error and **errno** is set to EBADF (bad file handle).

Example

This fragment prints the current value of the position indicator for the file described by **fd**:

```
long pos;
   .
   .
   .
pos = tell(fd);
printf("Position indicator is %ld bytes from the start", pos);
```

Related Functions

lseek( ), open( ), close( ), read( ), write( )

FILE *tmpfile(void)

Description

The prototype for the **tmpfile( )** function is found in **stdio.h**.

The **tmpfile( )** function opens a temporary file for update and returns a pointer to the stream. The function automatically uses a unique file name to avoid conflicts with existing files.

The **tmpfile( )** function returns a null pointer on failure; otherwise, it returns a pointer to the stream.

The temporary file created by **tmpfile( )** is automatically removed when the file is closed or when the program terminates.

Example

This fragment creates a temporary working file:

```
FILE *temp;

if(!(temp=tmpfile())) {
  printf("Cannot open temporary work file.\n");
  exit(1);
}
```

Related Function

tmpnam( )

char *tmpnam(char *name)

Description

The prototype for **tmpnam( )** is found in **stdio.h**.

The **tmpnam( )** function is defined by the ANSI C standard. It generates a unique file name and stores it in the array pointed to by *name.* The main purpose of **tmpnam( )**

is to generate a temporary file name that is different from any other file name in the directory.

The function may be called up to **TMP_MAX** times, defined in **stdio.h**. Each time it generates a new temporary file name.

A pointer to *name* is returned. If *name* is null, a pointer to an internal string is returned.

Example

This program displays three unique temporary file names:

```
#include <stdio.h>

int main(void)
{
  char name[40];
  int i;
  for(i=0; i<3; i++) {
    tmpnam(name);
    printf("%s ", name);
  }
  return 0;
}
```

Related Function

tmpfile( )

int ungetc(int ch, FILE *stream)

Description

The prototype for **ungetc( )** is found in **stdio.h**.

The **ungetc( )** function returns the character specified by the low-order byte of *ch* back into the input *stream.* This character is then returned by the next read operation on *stream.* A call to **fflush( )** or **fseek( )** undoes an **ungetc( )** operation and discards the character put back.

Only one character can be put back between subsequent read operations.

You cannot unget an **EOF**.

A call to **ungetc( )** clears the end-of-file flag associated with the specified stream. The value of the file-position indicator for a text stream is undefined until all pushed-back characters are read, in which case it is the same as it was prior to the first **ungetc( )** call. For binary streams, each **ungetc( )** call decrements the file-position indicator.

The return value is equal to *ch* on success and **EOF** on failure.

Example

This function reads words from the input stream pointed to by **fp**. The terminating character is returned to the stream for later use. For example, given input of **count/10**, the first call to **read_word( )** returns **count** and puts the **/** back on the input stream.

```
void read_word(FILE *fp, char *token)
{

  while(isalpha(*token=getc(fp))) token++;

  ungetc(fp, *token);
}
```

Related Function

getc( )

int ungetch(int ch)

Description

The prototype for **ungetch( )** is in **conio.h**. This function is not defined by the ANSI C standard. It cannot be used in Windows programs.

The **ungetch( )** function returns the character specified in the low-order byte of *ch* back into the console input buffer. This character is then returned by the next call to a console input function. Only one character can be put back between subsequent input operations.

The return value is equal to *ch* on success and **EOF** on failure.

Example

This program inputs a key, displays it, returns it to the input buffer, and reads and displays it again:

```
#include <stdio.h>
#include <conio.h>

int main()
{
  char ch;

  ch = getch(); // get keypress
  putch(ch); // show the key
  ungetch(ch);  // return to buffer
  ch = getch(); // get same key again
  putch(ch); // show the key again
```

```
  return 0;
}
```

Related Function

ungetc( )

int unlink(const char *fname)

Description

The prototype to **unlink( )** is found in **dos.h**.

The **unlink( )** function is part of the UNIX-like I/O system and is not defined by the ANSI C standard.

The **unlink( )** function removes the specified file from the directory. It returns 0 on success and –1 on failure and sets **errno** to one of the following values:

Error	Meaning
ENOENT	Invalid path or file name
EACCES	Access denied

Example

This program deletes the file specified as the first command-line argument:

```
#include <stdio.h>
#include <dos.h>

int main(int argc, char *argv[])
{
  if(unlink(argv[1])==-1)
    printf("Cannot remove file.");
  return 0;
}
```

Related Functions

open( ), close( )

int unlock(int handle, long offset, long length)

Description

The prototype for **unlock( )** is found in **io.h**.

The **unlock( )** function is not defined by the ANSI C standard. It is used to unlock a portion of a locked file, thus allowing another program to use it until a new lock is placed on the file. To lock a file, use **lock( )**. These functions provide control for file sharing in network environments.

The file to be unlocked is associated with *handle.* The portion of the file to be unlocked is determined by the starting *offset* from the beginning of the file and the *length.*

If **unlock( )** is successful, 0 is returned. If it is unsuccessful, –1 is returned.

Example

This fragment unlocks the first 128 bytes of the file associated with **fd**:

```
unlock(fd, 0, 128);
```

Related Functions

lock( ), sopen( )

int vprintf(const char *format, va_list arg_ptr) int vfprintf(FILE *stream, const char *format, va_list arg_ptr) int vsprintf(char *buf, const char *format, va_list arg_ptr)

Description

The prototypes for these functions require the files **stdio.h** and **stdarg.h**.

The functions **vprintf( )**, **vfprintf( )**, and **vsprintf( )** are functionally equivalent to **printf( )**, **fprintf( )**, and **sprintf( )**, respectively, except that the argument list has been replaced by a pointer to a list of arguments. This pointer must be of type **va_list**, which is defined in **stdarg.h**. See the proper related function. Also see **va_arg( )**, **va_start( )**, and **va_end( )** in Chapter 19 for further information.

Example

This fragment shows how to set up a call to **vprintf( )**. The call to **va_start( )** creates a variable-length argument pointer to the start of the argument list. This pointer must be used in the call to **vprintf( )**. The call to **va_end( )** clears the variable-length argument pointer.

```
#include <stdio.h>
#include <stdarg.h>

void print_message(char *, ...);

int main(void)
```

```
{
  print_message("Cannot open file %s","test");
  return 0;
}

void print_message( char *format, ...)
{
  va_list ptr; /* get an arg ptr */

  /* initialize ptr to point to the first argument after the
     format string
  */
  va_start(ptr, format);
  /* print out message */
  vprintf(format, ptr);
  va_end(ptr);
}
```

Related Functions

va_list( ), va_start( ), va_end( )

int vscanf(const char *format, va_list arg_ptr)
int vfscanf(FILE *stream, const char *format, va_list arg_ptr)
int vsscanf(const char *buf, const char *format, va_list arg_ptr)

Description

The prototypes for these functions require the files **stdio.h** and **stdarg.h**.

The functions **vscanf( )**, **vfscanf( )**, and **vsscanf( )** are functionally equivalent to **scanf( )**, **fscanf( )**, and **sscanf( )**, respectively, except that the argument list has been replaced by a pointer to a list of arguments. This pointer must be of type **va_list**, which is defined in **stdarg.h**. See the proper related function. Also see **va_arg( )**, **va_start( )**, and **va_end( )** in Chapter 19 for further information.

Example

This fragment shows how to set up a call to **vscanf( )**. The program reads two integers entered by the user. The call to **va_start( )** creates a variable-length argument pointer to the start of the argument list. It is this pointer that must be used in the call to **vscanf( )** that read the integers. The call to **va_end( )** clears the variable-length argument pointer.

```
#include <stdio.h>
#include <stdarg.h>

void read_int(int num, ...);

int main(void)
{
  int a, b;
  read_int(2, &a, &b);
  printf("%d %d", a, b);

  return 0;
}

void read_int(int num, ...)
{
  va_list ptr; /* get an arg ptr */

  /* initialize ptr to point to the first argument after the
     format string
  */
  va_start(ptr, num);

  printf("Enter %d integers: ", num);
  /* read ints */
  vscanf("%d %d", ptr);

  va_end(ptr);
}
```

Related Functions

va_list( ), va_start( ), va_end( )

int write(int handle, void *buf, int count)
int _rtl_write(int handle, void *buf, int count)

Description

The prototypes for **write( )** and **_rtl_write( )** are found in **io.h**.

The **write( )** function is part of the UNIX-like I/O system and is not defined by the ANSI C standard.

The **write( )** function writes *count* number of bytes to the file described by *handle* from the buffer pointed to by *buf*. The file-position indicator is incremented by the number of bytes written. If the file is opened in text mode, linefeeds are automatically expanded to carriage return, linefeed combinations. However, **_rtl_write( )** does not perform this expansion.

The return value is the number of bytes actually written. This number may be smaller than *count* if an error is encountered. A value of –1 means an error has occurred, and **errno** is set to one of these values:

Value	Meaning
EACCES	Access denied
EBADF	Bad file number

Example

This program writes the 100 bytes from **buffer** to the file **test**.

```
#include <studio.h>
#include <io.h>
#include <fcntl.h>
#include <stdlib.h>

int main(void)
{
  int fd;
  char buffer[100];

  if((fd=open("test", O_WRONLY))==-1) {
    printf("Cannot open file.\n");
    exit (1);
  }

  gets(buffer);

  if(write(fd, buffer, 100) !=100)
    printf("Write Error");
  close(fd);

  return 0;
}
```

Related Functions

read( ), close( ), lseek( )

Chapter Twelve

String, Memory, and Character Functions

The Borland library has a rich and varied set of string-, memory-, and character-handling functions. As they relate to these functions, a string is a null-terminated array of characters, memory is a block of contiguous RAM, and a character is a single byte value. The string functions require the header file **string.h** to provide their prototypes. The memory manipulation functions use **mem.h**, but several may also use **string.h**. The character functions use **ctype.h** as their header file.

Because C/C++ has no bounds checking on array operations, it is the programmer's responsibility to prevent an array overflow. Technically, if an array has overflowed, its behavior is undefined. In a practical sense, overflowing an array means that your program will seriously malfunction.

In C/C++, a *printable character* is one that can be displayed on a terminal. These are the characters between a space (0x20) and tilde (0xFE). *Control characters* have values between (0) and (0x1F), as well as DEL (0x7F). The ASCII characters are between 0 and 0x7F.

The character functions are declared to take an integer argument. While this is true, only the low-order byte is used by the function. Therefore, you are free to use a character argument because it is automatically elevated to **int** at the time of the call.

Most of the functions described in this chapter are defined by the ANSI C standard and are fully portable. The major exception to this is that Borland includes several FAR versions of many string functions. These will be discussed along with their normal versions. (The FAR versions are not defined by the ANSI C standard.) These functions apply only to 16-bit environments.

Several functions use the **size_t** data type. This type is defined in the various header files used by the functions described here and is an unsigned integer type.

int isalnum(int ch)

Description

The prototype for **isalnum( )** is found in **ctype.h**.

The **isalnum( )** macro returns non-0 if its argument is either a letter of the alphabet (upper- or lowercase) or a digit. If the character is not alphanumeric, 0 is returned.

Example

This program checks each character read from **stdin** and reports all alphanumeric ones:

```
#include <ctype.h>
#include <stdio.h>

int main(void)
{
  char ch;

  for(;;) {
    ch = getchar();
    if(ch==' ') break;
    if(isalnum(ch)) printf("%c is alphanumeric\n", ch);
  }
  return 0;
}
```

Related Functions

isalpha( ), isdigit( ), iscntrl( ), isgraph( ), isprint( ), ispunct( ), isspace( )

int isalpha(int ch)

Description

The prototype for **isalpha( )** is found in **ctype.h**.

The **isalpha( )** macro returns non-0 if *ch* is a letter of the alphabet (upper- or lowercase); otherwise, it returns 0.

Example

This program checks each character read from **stdin** and reports all those that are letters of the alphabet:

```
#include <ctype.h>
#include <stdio.h>

int main(void)
{
  char ch;

  for(;;) {
    ch = getchar();
    if(ch==' ') break;
    if(isalpha(ch)) printf("%c is a letter\n", ch);
  }
  return 0;
}
```

Related Functions

isalnum( ), isdigit( ), iscntrl( ), isgraph( ), isprint( ), ispunct( ), isspace( )

int isascii(int ch)

Description

The prototype for **isascii( )** is found in **ctype.h** and is not defined by the ANSI C standard.

The **isascii( )** macro returns non-0 if *ch* is in the range 0 through 0x7F; otherwise, it returns 0.

Example

This program checks each character read from **stdin** and reports all those that are defined by ASCII:

```
#include <ctype.h>
#include <stdio.h>

int main(void)
{
  char ch;

  for(;;) {
    ch = getchar();
    if(ch==' ') break;
    if(isascii(ch)) printf("%c is ASCII defined\n", ch);
  }
  return 0;
}
```

Related Functions

isalnum( ), isdigit( ), iscntrl( ), isgraph( ), isprint( ), ispunct( ), isspace( )

int iscntrl(int ch)

Description

The prototype for **iscntrl( )** is found in **ctype.h**.

The **iscntrl( )** macro returns non-0 if *ch* is between 0 and 0x1F or is equal to 0x7F (DEL); otherwise, it returns 0.

Example

This program checks each character read from **stdin** and reports all those that are control characters:

```
#include <ctype.h>
#include <stdio.h>

int main(void)
{
  char ch;

  for(;;) {
    ch = getchar();
    if(ch==' ') break;
    if(iscntrl(ch)) printf("%c is a control character\n", ch);
  }
  return 0;
}
```

Related Functions

isalnum( ), isdigit( ), isalpha( ), isgraph( ), isprint( ), ispunct( ), isspace( )

int isdigit(int ch)

Description

The prototype for **isdigit( )** is found in **ctype.h**.

The **isdigit( )** macro returns non-0 if *ch* is a digit, that is, 0 through 9; otherwise, it returns 0.

Example

This program checks each character read from **stdin** and reports all those that are digits:

```
#include <ctype.h>
#include <stdio.h>

int main(void)
{
  char ch;

  for(;;) {
    ch = getchar();
    if(ch==' ') break;
    if(isdigit(ch)) printf("%c is a digit\n", ch);
  }
  return 0;
}
```

Related Functions

isalnum( ), iscntrl( ), isalpha( ), isgraph( ), isprint( ), ispunct( ), isspace( )

int isgraph(int ch)

Description

The prototype for **isgraph( )** is found in **ctype.h**.

The **isgraph( )** macro returns non-0 if *ch* is any printable character other than a space; otherwise, it returns 0. Printable characters are in the range 0x21 through 0x7E.

Example

This program checks each character read from **stdin** and reports all those that are printable characters:

```
#include <ctype.h>
#include <stdio.h>

int main(void)
{
  char ch;

  for(;;) {
    ch = getchar();
    if(ch==' ') break;
    if(isgraph(ch)) printf("%c is a printing character\n", ch);
  }
  return 0;
}
```

Related Functions

isalnum( ), iscntrl( ), isalpha( ), isdigit( ), isprint( ), ispunct( ), isspace( )

int islower(int ch)

Description

The prototype for **islower( )** is found in **ctype.h**.

The **islower( )** macro returns non-0 if *ch* is a lowercase letter ("a" through "z"); otherwise, it returns 0.

Example

This program checks each character read from **stdin** and reports all those that are lowercase letters:

```
#include <ctype.h>
#include <stdio.h>

int main(void)
{
  char ch;

  for(;;) {
    ch = getchar();
    if(ch==' ') break;
    if(islower(ch)) printf("%c is lowercase\n", ch);
  }
  return 0;
}
```

Related Function

isupper( )

int isprint(int ch)

Description

The prototype for **isprint( )** is found in **ctype.h**.

The **isprint( )** macro returns non-0 if *ch* is a printable character, including a space; otherwise, it returns 0. The printable characters are in the range 0x20 through 0x7E.

Example

This program checks each character read from **stdin** and reports all those that are printable:

```
#include <ctype.h>
#include <stdio.h>

int main(void)
{
  char ch;

  for(;;) {
    ch = getchar();
    if(ch==' ') break;
    if(isprint(ch)) printf("%c is printable\n", ch);
  }
  return 0;
}
```

Related Functions

isalnum( ), iscntrl( ), isalpha( ), isdigit( ), isgraph( ), ispunct( ), isspace( )

int ispunct(int ch)

Description

The prototype for **ispunct( )** is found in **ctype.h**.

The **ispunct( )** macro returns non-0 if *ch* is a punctuation character or a space; otherwise, it returns 0.

Example

This program checks each character read from **stdin** and reports all those that are punctuation:

```
#include <ctype.h>
#include <stdio.h>

int main(void)
{
  char ch;

  for(;;) {
    ch = getchar();
    if(ch==' ') break;
    if(ispunct(ch)) printf("%c is punctuation\n", ch);
  }
  return 0;
}
```

Related Functions

isalnum( ), iscntrl( ), isalpha( ), isdigit( ), isgraph( ), isspace( )

int isspace(int ch)

Description

The prototype for **isspace( )** is found in **ctype.h**.

The **isspace( )** macro returns non-0 if *ch* is a space, carriage return, horizontal tab, vertical tab, form feed, or newline character; otherwise, it returns 0.

Example

This program checks each character read from **stdin** and reports all those that are white-space characters:

```
#include <ctype.h>
#include <stdio.h>

int main(void)
{
  char ch;

  for(;;) {
    ch = getchar();
    if(ch=='.') break;
    if(isspace(ch)) printf("%c is white-space\n", ch);
  }
  return 0;
}
```

Related Functions

isalnum( ), iscntrl( ), isalpha( ), isdigit( ), isgraph( ), ispunct( )

int isupper(ch)

Description

The prototype for **isupper( )** is found in **ctype.h**.

The **isupper( )** macro returns non-0 if *ch* is an uppercase letter ("A" through "Z"); otherwise, it returns 0.

Example

This program checks each character read from **stdin** and reports all those that are uppercase letters:

```
#include <ctype.h>
#include <stdio.h>

int main(void)
{
  char ch;

  for(;;) {
    ch = getchar();
    if(ch==' ') break;
    if(isupper(ch)) printf("%c is upper-case\n", ch);
  }
  return 0;
}
```

Related Function

islower( )

int isxdigit(int ch)

Description

The prototype for **isxdigit( )** is found in **ctype.h**.

The **isxdigit( )** macro returns non-0 if *ch* is a hexadecimal digit; otherwise, it returns 0. A hexadecimal digit will be in one of these ranges: "A" through "F", "a" through "f ", or "0" through "9".

Example

This program checks each character read from **stdin** and reports all those that are hexadecimal digits:

```
#include <ctype.h>
#include <stdio.h>

int main(void)
{
  char ch;

  for(;;) {
    ch = getchar();
    if(ch==' ') break;
    if(isxdigit(ch)) printf("%c is hexadecimal \n", ch);
  }
  return 0;
}
```

Related Functions

isalnum( ), iscntrl( ), isalpha( ), isdigit( ), isgraph( ), isspace( ), ispunct( )

void *memccpy(void *dest, const void *source, int ch, size_t count)
void far * far _fmemccpy(void far *dest, const void far *source, int ch, size_t count)

Description

The prototype for **memccpy( )** is found in both **string.h** and **mem.h** and is not defined by the ANSI C standard.

The **memccpy( )** function copies the contents of the memory pointed to by *source* into the memory pointed to by *dest*. The copy operation stops either when *count* number of bytes have been copied or after the first occurrence of *ch* has been copied. It returns a pointer to the end of *dest* if *ch* is found or null if *ch* is not part of *source*.

_fmemccpy( ) is the FAR version of **memccpy( )**.

Example

After this fragment has executed, the word "hello" will be in array **out** because the space is used to terminate the copy operation:

```
char str[20], out[20];

strcpy(str, "hello there");

memccpy(out, str,' ', 20);
```

Related Functions

memcpy( ), strcpy( )

void *memchr(const void *buffer, int ch, size_t count)
void far * far _fmemchr(const void far *buffer, int ch, size_t count)

Description

The prototype for the **memchr( )** function is found in both **string.h** and **mem.h**.

The **memchr( )** function searches *buffer* for the first occurrence of *ch* in the first *count* characters.

The **memchr( )** function returns a pointer to the first occurrence of *ch* in *buffer*, or a null pointer if *ch* is not found.

_fmemchr( ) is the FAR version of **memchr( )**.

Example

This program prints " is a test" on the screen:

```
#include <stdio.h>
#include <string.h>

int main(void)
{
  void *p;

  p = memchr("this is a test", ' ', 14);
  printf((char *) p);
  return 0;
}
```

Related Functions

memmove( ), memcpy( )

int memcmp(const void *buf1, const void *buf2, size_t count)
int memicmp(const void *buf1, const void *buf2, size_t count)
int far _fmemcmp(const void far *buf1, const void far *buf2, size_t count)
int far _fmemicmp(const void far *buf1, const void far *buf2, size_t count)

Description

The prototype for the **memcmp( )** function is found in both **string.h** and **mem.h**. The **memicmp( )** function is not defined by the ANSI C standard.

The **memcmp( )** function compares the first *count* characters of the arrays pointed to by *buf1* and *buf2*. The comparison is done lexicographically.

The **memcmp( )** function returns an integer that is interpreted as indicated here:

Value	Meaning
Less than 0	*buf1* is less than *buf2*
0	*buf1* is equal to *buf 2*
Greater than 0	*buf1* is greater than *buf2*

The **memicmp( )** function is identical to **memcmp( )**, except that case is ignored when comparing letters.

_fmemcmp( ) and **_fmemicmp( )** are the FAR versions of these functions.

Example

This program shows the outcome of a comparison of its two command-line arguments:

```
#include <stdio.h>
#include <string.h>

int main(int argc, char *argv[])

{
  int outcome;
  size_t len, l1, l2;

  /* find the length of shortest */
  len = (l1=strlen(argv[1]))<(l2=strlen(argv[2])) ? l1:l2;

  outcome = memcmp(argv[1], argv[2], len);
  if(!outcome) printf("equal");
  else if(outcome<0) printf("First less than second.\n");
  else printf("First greater than second\n");
  return 0;
}
```

Related Functions

memcpy( ), memchr( ), strcmp( )

void *memcpy(void *dest, const void *source, size_t count)
void far * far _fmemcpy(void far *dest, const void far *source, size_t count)

Description

The prototype for **memcpy( )** is found in both **string.h** and **mem.h**.

The **memcpy( )** function copies *count* characters from the array pointed to by *source* into the array pointed to by *dest*. If the arrays overlap, the behavior of **memcpy( )** is undefined.

The **memcpy( )** function returns a pointer to *dest*.

_fmemcpy( ) is the FAR version of this function.

Example

This program copies the contents of **buf1** into **buf2** and displays the result:

```
#include <stdio.h>
#include <string.h>
#define SIZE 80

int main(void)
{
  char buf1[SIZE], buf2[SIZE];

  strcpy(buf1, "When, in the course of...");
  memcpy(buf2, buf1, SIZE);
  printf(buf2);
  return 0;
}
```

Related Function

memmove( )

void *memmove(void *dest, const void *source, size_t count)
void far * far _fmemmove(void far *dest, const void far *source, size_t count)

Description

The prototype for **memmove( )** is found in both **string.h** and **mem.h**.

The **memmove( )** function copies *count* characters from the array pointed to by *source* into the array pointed to by *dest*. If the arrays overlap, the copy takes place correctly, placing the correct contents into *dest* but leaving *source* modified.

The **memmove( )** function returns a pointer to *dest*.

_fmemmove( ) is the equivalent FAR version of **memmove( )**.

Example

This program copies the contents of *str1* into *str2* and displays the result:

```
#include <stdio.h>
#include <string.h>

int main(void)
{
  char str1[40], str2[40];
```

```
  strcpy(str1, "Born to code in C/C++.");
  memmove(str2, str1, strlen(str1));
  printf(str2);
  return 0;
}
```

Related Functions

memcpy( ), movedata( ), movmem( )

void *memset(void *buf, int ch, size_t count)
void far * far _fmemset(void far *buf, int ch, size_t count)

Description

The prototype for **memset( )** is found in both **string.h** and **mem.h**.

The **memset( )** function copies the low-order byte of *ch* into the first *count* characters of the array pointed to by *buf*. It returns *buf*.

The most common use of **memset( )** is to initialize a region of memory to some known value.

_fmemset( ) is the FAR version of this function.

Example

This fragment first initializes to null the first 100 bytes of the array pointed to by *buf* and then sets the first 10 bytes to 'X' and displays the string "XXXXXXXXXX":

```
memset(buf, '\0', 100);
memset(buf, 'X', 10);
printf((char *) buf);
```

Related Functions

memcpy( ), memcmp( ), memmove( )

void movedata(unsigned sourceseg, unsigned sourceoff, unsigned destseg, unsigned destoff, size_t count)

Description

The prototype for **movedata( )** is found in both **string.h** and **mem.h**. The **movedata( )** function is not defined by the ANSI C standard.

The **movedata( )** function copies *count* characters from the memory at location *sourceseg:sourceoff* into the memory location *destseg:destoff*. The **movedata( )** function works regardless of which memory model is selected.

Example

This program copies the first 25 bytes of the data segment into the array **buff**.

```
#include <stdio.h>
#include <string.h>
#include <dos.h>

int main(void)
{
  char buff[25];

  movedata(_DS, 0, FP_SEG(buff), FP_OFF(buff), 25);
  return 0;
}
```

Related Functions

memcpy( ), movmem( ), memmove( )

void movmem(const void *source, void *dest, unsigned count)
void _fmovmem(const void far *source, void far *dest, unsigned count)

Description

The prototype for **movmem( )** is found in **mem.h**. The function **movmem( )** is not defined by the ANSI C standard.

The **movmem( )** function copies *count* characters from the array pointed to by *source* into the array pointed to by *dest*. If the arrays overlap, the copy takes place correctly, placing the correct contents into *dest* but leaving *source* modified.

The **movmem( )** function is equivalent to the **memmove( )** function, except that the **movmem( )** function has no return value and is not defined by the ANSI C standard. **_fmovmem( )** is the equivalent FAR version of **movmem( )**.

Related Functions

memcpy( ), movedata( ), memmove( )

void setmem(void *buf, unsigned count, char ch)

Description

The prototype for **setmem( )** is found in **mem.h**. The **setmem( )** function is not defined by the ANSI C standard.

The **setmem( )** function copies *ch* into the first *count* characters of the array pointed to by *buf*.

The **setmem( )** function is equivalent to the **memset( )** function except that the **setmem( )** function has no return value and is not defined by the ANSI C standard.

Related Functions

memcpy( ), memset( ), memmove( )

char *stpcpy(char *str1, const char *str2)

Description

The prototype for **stpcpy( )** is found in **string.h** and is not defined by the ANSI C standard.

The **stpcpy( )** function is used to copy the contents of *str2* into *str1*. *str2* must be a pointer to a null-terminated string. The **stpcpy( )** function returns a pointer to the end of *str1*.

Example

The following code fragment copies "hello" into string **str**:

```
char str[8];
stpcpy(str, "hello");
```

Related Function

strcpy( )

char *strcat(char *str1, const char *str2)
char far * far _fstrcat(char far *str1, const char *str2)

Description

The prototype for **strcat( )** is found in **string.h**.

The **strcat( )** function concatenates a copy of *str2* to *str1* and terminates *str1* with a null. The null terminator originally ending *str1* is overwritten by the first character of *str2*. The string *str2* is untouched by the operation.

The **strcat( )** function returns *str1*.

Remember that no bounds checking takes place, so it is the programmer's responsibility to ensure that *str1* is large enough to hold both its original contents and the contents of *str2*.

_fstrcat( ) is the FAR version of this function.

Example

This program appends the first string read from **stdin** to the second. For example, assuming the user enters "hello" and "there", the program prints "therehello".

```
#include <stdio.h>
#include <string.h>

int main(void)
{
  char s1[80], s2[80];

  gets(s1);
  gets(s2);

  strcat(s2, s1);
  printf(s2);
  return 0;
}
```

Related Functions

strchr( ), **strcmp( )**, **strcpy( )**

char *strchr(const char *str, int ch)
char far * far _fstrchr(const char far *str, int ch)

Description

The prototype for **strchr( )** is found in **string.h**.

The **strchr( )** function returns a pointer to the first occurrence of *ch* in the string pointed to by *str*. If no match is found, it returns a null pointer.

_fstrchr( ) is the FAR version of this function.

Example

This program prints the string " is a test":

```
#include <stdio.h>
#include <string.h>

int main(void)
```

```
{
  char *p;

  p = strchr("this is a test", ' ');
  printf(p);
  return 0;
}
```

Related Functions

strpbrk( ), strstr( ), strtok( ), strspn( )

int strcmp(const char *str1, const char *str2)

Description

The prototype for the **strcmp( )** function is found in **string.h**.

The **strcmp( )** function lexicographically compares two null-terminated strings and returns an integer based on the outcome, as shown here:

Value	Meaning
Less than 0	*str1* is less than *str2*
0	*str1* is equal to *str2*
Greater than 0	*str1* is greater than *str2*

Example

The following function can be used as a password-verification routine. It returns 0 on failure and 1 on success.

```
int password()
{
  char s[80];

  printf("Enter password: ");
  gets(s);

  if(strcmp(s, "pass")) {
    printf("Invalid password.\n");
    return 0;
  }
  return 1;
}
```

Related Functions

strchr( ), strcpy( ), strncmp( )

int strcoll(char *str1, char *str2)

Description

The prototype for the **strcoll( )** function is found in **string.h**.

The **strcoll( )** function is equivalent to the **strcmp( )** function. Please refer to **strcmp( )** for a description.

Related Functions

strncmp( ), stricmp( )

char *strcpy(char *str1, const char *str2)

Description

The prototype for **strcpy( )** is found in **string.h**.

The **strcpy( )** function is used to copy the contents of *str2* into *str1*; *str2* must be a pointer to a null-terminated string. The **strcpy( )** function returns a pointer to *str1*.

If *str1* and *str2* overlap, the behavior of **strcpy( )** is undefined.

Example

The following code fragment copies "hello" into string **str**.

```
char str[80];
strcpy(str, "hello");
```

Related Functions

strchr( ), strcmp( ), memcpy( ), strncmp( )

size_t strcspn(const char *str1, const char *str2)
size_t far _fstrcspn(const char far *str1, const char far *str2)

Description

The prototype for the **strcspn( )** function is found in **string.h**.

The **strcspn( )** function returns the length of the initial substring of the string pointed to by *str1* that is made up of only those characters not contained in the string pointed to by *str2*. Stated differently, **strcspn( )** returns the index of the first character in the string pointed to by *str1* that matches any of the characters in the string pointed to by *str2*.

_fstrcspn( ) is the FAR version of this function.

Example

This program prints the number 8:

```
#include <stdio.h>
#include <string.h>

int main(void)
{
  int len;

  len = strcspn("this is a test", "ab");
  printf("%d", len);
  return 0;
}
```

Related Functions

strpbrk( ), strstr( ), strtok( ), strrchr( )

char *strdup(const char *str)
char far * far _fstrdup(const char far *str)

Description

The prototype for **strdup( )** is found in **string.h**. The **strdup( )** function is not defined by the ANSI C standard.

The **strdup( )** function allocates enough memory, via a call to **malloc( )**, to hold a duplicate of the string pointed to by *str* and then copies that string into the allocated region and returns a pointer to it.

_fstrdup( ) is the FAR version of this function.

Example

This fragment duplicates the string **str**.

```
char str[80], *p;

strcpy(str, "this is a test");

p = strdup(str);
```

Related Function
strcpy( )

char *_strerror(const char *str)

Description
The prototype for the **_strerror( )** function is found in **stdio.h** and **string.h**.

The **_strerror( )** function lets you display your own error message followed by a colon and the most recent error message generated by the program. It returns a pointer to the entire string.

The **_strerror( )** function is not defined by the ANSI C standard.

Example
This fragment prints a message stating that the function called **swap( )** encountered an error:

```
void swap()
{
  /* ... */
  if(error) printf(_strerror("Error in swap."));
```

Related Functions
perror( ), **strerror( )**

char *strerror(int num)

Description
The prototype for the **strerror( )** function is found in **stdio.h** and **string.h**.

The **strerror( )** function returns a pointer to the error message associated with an error number.

Example
This fragment prints the error message associated with the global variable **errno** if an error has occurred.

```
if(errno) printf(strerror(errno));
```

Related Functions
perror( ), **_strerror( )**

int stricmp(const char *str1, const char *str2)
int strcmpi(const char *str1, const char *str2)
int far _fstricmp(const char far *str1, const char far *str2)

Description

The prototypes for the **stricmp( )** function and **strcmpi( )** macro are found in **string.h**. Neither of these are defined by the ANSI C standard.

The **stricmp( )** function lexicographically compares two null-terminated strings while ignoring case; **strcmpi( )** is a macro that translates to a **stricmp( )** call.

Both functions return an integer based on the outcome, as shown here:

Value	Meaning
Less than 0	*str1* is less than *str2*
0	*str1* is equal to *str2*
Greater than 0	*str1* is greater than *str2*

_fstricmp( ) is the FAR version of this **stricmp( )**.

Example

The following function compares the two file names specified on the command line to determine if they are the same:

```
#include <stdio.h>
#include <string.h>

int main(int argc, char *argv[])
{
  if(!stricmp(argv[1], argv[2]))
    printf("The filenames are the same.\n");
  else
    printf("The filenames differ.\n");

  return 0;
}
```

Related Functions

strnchr( ), strcmp( ), strncpy( )

size_t strlen(const char *str)
size_t _fstrlen(const char far *str)

Description

The prototype for **strlen( )** is found in **string.h**.

The **strlen( )** function returns the length of the null-terminated string pointed to by *str*. The null is not counted.

_fstrlen( ) is the FAR version of **strlen( )**.

Example

This code fragment prints the number 5 on the screen:

```
strcpy(s, "hello");
printf("%d", strlen(s));
```

Related Functions

strchr( ), **strcmp( )**, **memcpy( )**, **strncmp( )**

char *strlwr(char *str)
char far * far _fstrlwr(char far *str)

Description

The prototype for **strlwr( )** is found in **string.h**. The **strlwr( )** function is not defined by the ANSI C standard.

The **strlwr( )** function converts the string pointed to by *str* to lowercase. It returns *str*.

_fstrlwr( ) is the FAR version of this function.

Example

This program prints "this is a test" on the screen:

```
#include <stdio.h>
#include <string.h>

int main(void)
{
  char s[80];

  strcpy(s, "THIS IS A TEST");
```

```
  strlwr(s);

  printf(s);

  return 0;
}
```

Related Function

strupr( )

char *strncat(char *str1, const char *str2, size_t count)
char far * far _fstrncat(char far *str1, const char far *str2, size_t count)

Description

The prototype for the **strncat( )** function is found in **string.h**.

The **strncat( )** function concatenates no more than *count* characters of the string pointed to by *str2* to the string pointed to by *str1* and terminates *str1* with a null. The null terminator originally ending *str1* is overwritten by the first character of *str2*. The string *str2* is untouched by the operation.

The **strncat( )** function returns *str1*.

Remember, no bounds checking takes place, so it is the programmer's responsibility to ensure that *str1* is large enough to hold both its original contents and those of *str2*.

_fstrncat( ) is the FAR version of this function.

Example

This program appends the first string read from **stdin** to the second and prevents an array overflow from occurring in *str1*. For example, if the user enters "hello" and "there", the program prints "therehello":

```
#include <stdio.h>
#include <string.h>

int main(void)
{
  char s1[80], s2[80];
  size_t len;

  gets(s1);
  gets(s2);
```

```
    /* compute how many chars will actually fit */
    len = 79-strlen(s2);

    strncat(s2, s1, len);
    printf(s2);
    return 0;
}
```

Related Functions

strnchr( ), strncmp( ), strncpy( ), strcat( )

int strncmp(const char *str1, const char *str2, size_t count)
int strnicmp(const char *str1, const char *str2, size_t count)
int strncmpi(const char *str1, const char *str2, size_t count)
int far _fstrncmp(const char far *str1, const char far *str2, size_t count)
int far _fstrnicmp(const char far *str1, const char far *str2, size_t count)

Description

The prototypes for the **strncmp( )** and **strnicmp( )** functions, and the **strncmpi( )** macro are found in **string.h**. Of these, only **strncmp( )** is defined by the ANSI C standard.

The **strncmp( )** function lexicographically compares no more than *count* characters from the two null-terminated strings. The functions **strnicmp( )** and **strncmpi( )** perform the same comparison while ignoring case; **strncmpi( )** is a macro that translates to a **strnicmp( )** call.

All three functions return an integer based on the outcome, as shown here:

Value	Meaning
Less than 0	*str1* is less than *str2*
0	*str1* is equal to *str2*
Greater than 0	*str1* is greater than *str2*

If there are fewer than *count* characters in either string, the comparison ends when the first null is encountered.

_fstrncmp( ) is the FAR version of **strncmp( )**.

_fstrnicmp( ) is the FAR version of **strnicmp( )**.

Example

The following function compares the first eight characters of the two file names specified on the command line to determine if they are the same:

```
#include <stdio.h>
#include <string.h>

int main(int argc, char *argv[])
{
  if(!strnicmp(argv[1], argv[2], 8))
    printf("The filenames are the same.\n");
  else
    printf("The filenames differ.\n");
  return 0;
}
```

Related Functions

strnchr( ), strcmp( ), strncpy( )

char *strncpy(char *dest, const char *source, size_t count)
char far * far _fstrncpy(char far *dest, const char far *source, size_t count)

Description

The prototype for **strncpy( )** is found in **string.h**.

The **strncpy( )** function is used to copy up to *count* characters from the string pointed to by *source* into the string pointed to by *dest*. The *source* must be a pointer to a null-terminated string. The **strncpy( )** function returns a pointer to *dest*.

If *dest* and *source* overlap, the behavior of **strncpy( )** is undefined.

If the string pointed to by *source* has fewer than *count* characters, nulls are appended to the end of *dest* until *count* characters have been copied.

Alternately, if the string pointed to by *source* is longer than *count* characters, the resulting string pointed to by *dest* is not null-terminated.

_fstrncpy( ) is the FAR version of **strncpy( )**.

Example

The following code fragment copies at most 79 characters of *str1* into *str2*, thus ensuring that no array boundary overflow will occur:

```
char str1[128], str2[80];
gets(str1);
strncpy(str2, str1, 79);
```

Related Functions

strchr( ), **strncmp( )**, **memcpy( )**, **strncat( )**

char *strnset(char *str, int ch, size_t count)
char far * far _fstrnset(char far *str, int ch, size_t count)

Description

The prototype for **strnset( )** is found in **string.h**.

The **strnset( )** function sets the first *count* characters in the string pointed to by *str* to the value of *ch*. It returns *str*.

_fstrnset( ) is the FAR version of this function.

Example

This fragment sets the first 10 characters of *str* to the value **x**:

```
strnset(str, 'x', 10);
```

Related Function

strset( )

char *strpbrk(const char *str1, const char *str2)
char far * far _fstrpbrk(const char far *str1, const char far *str2)

Description

The prototype for **strpbrk( )** is found in **string.h**.

The **strpbrk( )** function returns a pointer to the first character in the string pointed to by *str1* that matches any character in the string pointed to by *str2*. The null terminators are not included. If there are no matches, a null pointer is returned.

_fstrpbrk( ) is the FAR version of this function.

Example

This program prints the message "s is a test" on the screen:

```
#include <stdio.h>
#include <string.h>

int main(void)
{
  char *p;

  p = strpbrk("this is a test", " absj");
  printf(p);
  return 0;
}
```

Related Functions

strrchr( ), strstr( ), strtok( ), strspn( )

char *strrchr(const char *str, int ch)
char far * far _fstrrchr(const char far *str, int ch)

Description

The prototype for **strrchr( )** is found in **string.h**.

The **strrchr( )** function returns a pointer to the last occurrence of the low-order byte of *ch* in the string pointed to by *str*. If no match is found, it returns a null pointer.

_fstrrchr( ) is the FAR version of this function.

Example

This program prints the string "is a test":

```
#include <stdio.h>
#include <string.h>

int main(void)
{
  char *p;

  p = strrchr("this is a test", 'i');
  printf(p);
  return 0;
}
```

Related Functions
strpbrk( ), **strstr( )**, **strtok( )**, **strspn( )**

char *strrev(char *str)
char far * far _fstrrev(char far *str)

Description
The prototype for **strrev( )** is found in **string.h**. The **strrev( )** function is not defined by the ANSI C standard.

The **strrev( )** function reverses all characters, except the null terminator, in the string pointed to by *str*. It returns *str*.

_fstrrev( ) is the FAR version of this function.

Example
This program prints "hello" backward on the screen:

```
#include <stdio.h>
#include <string.h>

char s[] = "hello";

main(void)
{
  strrev(s);

  printf(s);

  return 0;
}
```

Related Function
strset( )

char *strset(char *str, int ch)
char far * far _fstrset(char far *str, int ch)

Description
The prototype for **strset( )** is found in **string.h**. The **strset( )** function is not defined by the ANSI C standard.

The **strset( )** function sets all characters in the string pointed to by *str* to the value of *ch*. It returns **str**.

_fstrset( ) is the FAR version of this function.

Example

This fragment fills the string *str* with the value **x**.

```
strset(str, 'x');
```

Related Function

strnset( )

size_t strspn(const char *str1, const char *str2)
size_t far _fstrspn(const char far *str1, const char far *str2)

Description

The **strspn( )** function returns the length of the initial substring of the string pointed to by *str1* that is made up of only those characters contained in the string pointed to by *str2*. Stated differently, **strspn( )** returns the index of the first character in the string pointed to by *str1* that does not match any of the characters in the string pointed to by *str2*.

_fstrspn( ) is the FAR version of this function.

Example

This program prints the number 8:

```
#include <stdio.h>
#include <string.h>

int main(void)
{
  int len;

  len = strspn("this is a test", "siht ");
  printf("%d",len);
  return 0;
}
```

Related Functions

strpbrk( ), strstr( ), strtok( ), strrchr( )

char *strstr(const char *str1, const char *str2) char far * far _fstrstr(const char far *str1, const char far *str2)

Description

The prototype for **strstr( )** is found in **string.h**.

The **strstr( )** function returns a pointer to the first occurrence in the string pointed to by *str1* of the string pointed to by *str2* (except *str2* 's null terminator). It returns a null pointer if no match is found.

_fstrstr( ) is the FAR version of this function.

Example

This program displays the message "is is a test":

```
#include <stdio.h>
#include <string.h>

int main(void)
{
  char *p;

  p = strstr("this is a test", "is");
  printf(p);
  return 0;
}
```

Related Functions

strpbrk( ), strspn( ), strtok( ), strrchr( ), strchr( ), strcspn( )

char *strtok(char *str1, const char *str2) char far * far _fstrtok(char far *str1, const char far *str2)

Description

The prototype for **strtok( )** is in **string.h**.

The **strtok( )** function returns a pointer to the next token in the string pointed to by *str1*. The characters making up the string pointed to by *str2* are the delimiters that determine the token. A null pointer is returned when there is no token to return.

The first time **strtok( )** is called, *str1* is actually used in the call. Subsequent calls use a null pointer for the first argument. In this way the entire string can be reduced to its tokens.

It is important to understand that the **strtok( )** function modifies the string pointed to by *str1*. Each time a token is found, a null is placed where the delimiter was found. In this way **strtok( )** continues to advance through the string.

It is possible to use a different set of delimiters for each call to **strtok( )**.

_fstrtok( ) is the FAR version of this function.

Example

This program tokenizes the string "The summer soldier, the sunshine patriot" with spaces and commas as the delimiters. The output is
"The | summer | soldier | the | sunshine | patriot".

```
#include <stdio.h>
#include <string.h>

int main(void)
{
  char *p;

  p = strtok("The summer soldier, the sunshine patriot"," ");
  printf(p);
  do {
    p=strtok('\0', ", ");
    if(p) printf("|%s", p);
  } while(p);
  return 0;
}
```

Related Functions

strpbrk( ), strspn( ), strtok( ), strrchr( ), strchr( ), strcspn( )

char *strupr(char *str)
char far * far _fstrupr(char far *str)

Description

The prototype for **strupr( )** is found in **string.h**. The **strupr( )** function is not defined by the ANSI C standard.

The **strupr( )** function converts the string pointed to by *str* to uppercase. It returns *str*.

_fstrupr( ) is the FAR version of this function.

Example

This program prints "THIS IS A TEST" on the screen:

```
#include <stdio.h>
#include <string.h>

int main(void)
{
  char s[80];

  strcpy(s, "this is a test");

  strupr(s);

  printf(s);

  return 0;
}
```

Related Function

strlwr( )

size_t strxfrm(char *dest, const char *source, size_t count)

Description

The prototype for **strxfrm( )** is found in **string.h**.

The **strxfrm( )** function is used to copy up to *count* characters from the string pointed to by *source* into the string pointed to by *dest*. The *source* must be a pointer to a null-terminated string. In the process, any country-related items are transformed into the proper format for the current country. The **strxfrm( )** function returns the length of the string pointed to by *dest*.

The **strxfrm( )** function is similar to the **strncpy( )** function.

Related Functions

strncpy( ), movedata( ), memcpy( ), strncat( )

int tolower(int ch)
int _tolower(int ch)

Description

The prototype for **tolower( )** and the definition of the macro **_tolower( )** are found in **ctype.h**. The **_tolower( )** macro is not defined by the ANSI C standard.

The **tolower( )** function returns the lowercase equivalent of *ch* if *ch* is an uppercase letter; otherwise, it returns *ch* unchanged. The **_tolower( )** macro is equivalent, but should only be used when *ch* is an uppercase letter; otherwise, the results are undefined.

Example

This code fragment displays a "q".

```
putchar(tolower('Q'));
```

Related Function

toupper( )

int toupper(int ch)
int _toupper(int ch)

Description

The prototype for **toupper( )** and the macro **_toupper( )** are found in **ctype.h**. The **_toupper( )** macro is not defined by the ANSI C standard.

The **toupper( )** function returns the uppercase equivalent of *ch* if *ch* is a letter; otherwise, it returns *ch* unchanged. The **_toupper( )** macro is equivalent, but should only be used when *ch* is a lowercase letter; otherwise, the results are undefined.

Example

This displays an "A".

```
putchar(toupper('a'));
```

Related Function

tolower( )

Chapter Thirteen

Mathematical Functions

The ANSI C standard defines 22 mathematical functions that fall into the following categories:

- Trigonometric functions
- Hyperbolic functions
- Exponential and logarithmic functions
- Miscellaneous

Borland implements all of these functions and includes several of its own. Many of the functions added by Borland are **long double** versions of the standard functions. These Borland-specific functions are also discussed here.

All the math functions require the header **math.h** to be included in any program using them. In addition to declaring the math functions, this header defines three macros called **EDOM**, **ERANGE**, and **HUGE_VAL**. If an argument to a math function is not in the domain for which it is defined, an implementation-defined value is returned and the global **errno** is set equal to **EDOM**. If a routine produces a result that is too large to be represented, an overflow happens. This causes the routine to return **HUGE_VAL** and **errno** is set to **ERANGE**, indicating a range error. (If the function returns a **long double**, then it returns **_LHUGE_VAL**.) If an underflow happens, the routine returns 0 and sets **errno** to **ERANGE**.

double acos(double arg)
long double acosl(long double arg)

Description

The prototype for **acos( )** is in **math.h**.

The **acos( )** function returns the arc cosine of *arg*. The argument to **acos( )** must be in the range –1 to 1; otherwise, a domain error occurs. The return value is in the range 0 to π and is in radians.

acosl( ) is the **long double** version of this function.

Example

This program prints the arc cosines, in one-tenth increments, of the values –1 through 1:

```
#include <stdio.h>
#include <math.h>

int main(void)
{
  double val = -1.0;

  do {
    printf("arc cosine of %f is %f\n", val, acos(val));
    val += 0.1;
  } while(val <= 1.0);
  return 0;
}
```

Related Functions

asin( ), atan( ), atan2( ), sin( ), cos( ), tan( ), sinh( ), cosh( ), tanh( )

double asin(double arg)
long double asinl(long double arg)

Description

The prototype for **asin( )** is in **math.h**.

The **asin( )** function returns the arc sine of *arg*. The argument to **asin( )** must be in the range –1 to 1; otherwise, a domain error occurs. Its return value is in the range –π/2 to π/2 and is in radians.

asinl( ) is the **long double** version of this function.

Example

This program prints the arc sines, in one-tenth increments, of the values –1 through 1:

```
#include <stdio.h>
#include <math.h>

int main(void)
{
  double val = -1.0;

  do {
    printf("arc sine of %f is %f\n", val, asin(val));
    val += 0.1;
  } while(val <= 1.0);
  return 0;
}
```

Related Functions

atan( ), atan2( ), sin( ), cos( ), tan( ), sinh( ), cosh( ), tanh( )

double atan(double arg)
long double atanl(long double arg)

Description

The prototype for **atan( )** is in **math.h**.

The **atan( )** function returns the arc tangent of *arg*. The return value is in radians and in the range $-\pi/2$ to $\pi/2$.

atanl( ) is the **long double** version of this function.

Example

This program prints the arc tangents, in one-tenth increments, of the values –1 through 1.

```
#include <stdio.h>
#include <math.h>

int main(void)
{
  double val = -1.0;

  do {
```

```
    printf("arc tangent of %f is %f\n", val, atan(val));
    val += 0.1;
  } while(val <= 1.0);
  return 0;
}
```

Related Functions

asin( ), acos( ), atan2( ), tan( ), cos( ), sin( ), sinh( ), cosh( ), tanh( )

double atan2(double y, double x)
long double atan2l(long double y, long double x)

Description

The prototype for **atan2( )** is in **math.h**.

The **atan2( )** function returns the arc tangent of *y/x*. It uses the signs of its arguments to compute the quadrant of the return value. The return value is in radians and in the range $-\pi$ to π.

atan2l( ) is the **long double** version of this function.

Example

This program prints the arc tangents, in one-tenth increments of *y*, from –1 through 1:

```
#include <stdio.h>
#include <math.h>

int main(void)
{
  double y = -1.0;

  do {
    printf("atan2 of %f is %f\n", y, atan2(y, 1.0));
    y += 0.1;
  } while(y <= 1.0);
  return 0;
}
```

Related Functions

asin( ), acos( ), atan( ), tan( ), cos( ), sin( ), sinh( ), cosh( ), tanh( )

double cabs(struct complex znum)
long double cabsl(struct _complexl znum)

Description

The prototype for **cabs( )** is in **math.h**. This macro is not defined by the ANSI C standard.

The **cabs( )** macro returns the absolute value of a complex number. The structure **complex** is defined as

```
struct complex {
    double x;
    double y;
};
```

If an overflow occurs, **HUGE_VAL** is returned and **errno** is set to **ERANGE** (out of range).

cabsl( ) is the **long double** version of this macro and **_complexl** is the **long double** equivalent of **complex**.

Example

This code prints the absolute value of a complex number that has a real part equal to 1 and an imaginary part equal to 2:

```
#include <stdio.h>
#include <math.h>

int main(void)
{
  struct complex z;

  z.x = 1;
  z.y = 2;

  printf("%f", cabs(z));
  return 0;
}
```

Related Function

abs( )

double ceil(double num)
long double ceill(long double num)

Description

The prototype for **ceil( )** is in **math.h**.

The **ceil( )** function returns the smallest integer (represented as a **double**) not less than *num*. For example, given 1.02, **ceil( )** returns 2.0. Given –1.02, **ceil( )** returns –1.

ceill( ) is the **long double** version of **ceil( )**.

Example

This fragment prints the value "10" on the screen:

```
printf("%f", ceil(9.9));
```

Related Functions

floor( ), fmod( )

double cos(double arg)
long double cosl(long double arg)

Description

The prototype for **cos( )** is in **math.h**.

The **cos( )** function returns the cosine of *arg*. The value of *arg* must be in radians. The return value is in the range –1 to 1.

cosl( ) is the **long double** version of this function.

Example

This program prints the cosines, in one-tenth increments, of the values –1 through 1:

```
#include <stdio.h>
#include <math.h>

int main(void)
{
  double val = -1.0;

  do {
    printf("cosine of %f is %f\n", val, cos(val));
    val += 0.1;
  } while(val <= 1.0);
  return 0;
}
```

Related Functions

asin( ), **acos( )**, **atan2( )**, **atan( )**, **tan( )**, **sin( )**, **sinh( )**, **cosh( )**, **tanh( )**

double cosh(double arg)
long double coshl(long double arg)

Description

The prototype for **cosh( )** is in **math.h**.

The **cosh( )** function returns the hyperbolic cosine of *arg*.

coshl( ) is the **long double** version of this function.

Example

This program prints the hyperbolic cosines, in one-tenth increments, of the values –1 through 1:

```
#include <stdio.h>
#include <math.h>

int main(void)
{
  double val = -1.0;

  do {
    printf("hyperbolic cosine of %f is %f\n", val, cosh(val));
    val += 0.1;
  } while(val <= 1.0);
  return 0;
}
```

Related Functions

asin( ), **acos( )**, **atan2( )**, **atan( )**, **tan( )**, **cos( )**, **sin( )**, **tanh( )**

double exp(double arg)
long double expl(long double arg)

Description

The prototype for **exp( )** is in **math.h**.

The **exp( )** function returns the natural logarithm *e* raised to the *arg* power.

expl( ) is the **long double** version of **exp( )**.

Example

This fragment displays the value of *e* (rounded to 2.718282).

```
printf("Value of e to the first: %f", exp(1.0));
```

Related Function

log( )

double fabs(double num)
long double fabsl(long double num)

Description

The prototype for **fabs( )** is in **math.h**.

The **fabs( )** function returns the absolute value of *num*.

fabsl( ) is the **long double** version of this function.

Example

This program prints "1.0 1.0" on the screen:

```
#include <stdio.h>
#include <math.h>

int main(void)
{
  printf("%1.1f %1.1f", fabs(1.0), fabs(-1.0));
  return 0;
}
```

Related Function

abs( )

double floor(double num)
long double floorl(long double num)

Description

The prototype for **floor( )** is in **math.h**.

The **floor( )** function returns the largest integer (represented as a **double**) that is not greater than *num*. For example, given 1.02, **floor( )** returns 1.0. Given -1.02, **floor( )** returns –2.0.

floorl( ) is the **long double** version of this function.

Example

This fragment prints "10" on the screen:

```
printf("%f", floor(10.9));
```

Related Function
fmod( )

double fmod(double x, double y)
long double fmodl(long double x, long double y)

Description
The prototype for **fmod( )** is in **math.h**.

The **fmod( )** function returns the remainder of *x/y*.

fmodl( ) is the **long double** version of this function.

Example
This program prints "1.0" on the screen, which represents the remainder of 10/3:

```
#include <stdio.h>
#include <math.h>

int main(void)
{
  printf("%1.1f", fmod(10.0, 3.0));
  return 0;
}
```

Related Functions
ceil( ), floor( ), fabs( )

double frexp(double num, int *exp)
long double frexpl(long double num, int *exp)

Description
The prototype for **frexp( )** is in **math.h**.

The **frexp( )** function decomposes the number *num* into a mantissa in the range 0.5 to less than 1, and an integer exponent such that $num = mantissa * 2^{exp}$. The mantissa is returned by the function, and the exponent is stored at the variable pointed to by *exp*.

frexpl( ) is the **long double** version of this function.

Example
This code fragment prints "0.625" for the mantissa and "4" for the exponent:

```
int e;
double f;
```

```
f = frexp(10.0, &e);
printf("%f %d", f, e);
```

Related Function

ldexp( )

double hypot(double x, double y)
long double hypotl(long double x, long double y)

Description

The prototype for **hypot( )** is in **math.h**. This function is not defined by the ANSI C standard.

The **hypot( )** function returns the length of the hypotenuse of a right triangle given the lengths of the other two sides.

hypotl( ) is the **long double** version of this function.

Example

This code fragment prints the value "2.236068":

```
printf("%f", hypot(2, 1));
```

double ldexp(double num, int exp)
long double ldexpl(long double num, int exp)

Description

The prototype for **ldexp( )** is in **math.h**.

The **ldexp( )** function returns the value of *num* * 2^{exp}. If overflow occurs, HUGE_VAL is returned.

ldexpl( ) is the **long double** version of this function.

Example

This program displays the number "4":

```
#include <stdio.h>
#include <math.h>

int main(void)
{
  printf("%f", ldexp(1, 2));
  return 0;
}
```

Related Functions

frexp( ), modf( )

double log(double num)
long double logl(long double num)

Description

The prototype for **log( )** is in **math.h**.

The **log( )** function returns the natural logarithm for *num*. A domain error occurs if *num* is negative and a range error occurs if the argument is 0.

logl( ) is the **long double** version of this function.

Example

This program prints the natural logarithms for the numbers 1 through 10:

```
#include <stdio.h>
#include <math.h>

int main(void)
{
  double val = 1.0;

  do {
    printf("%f %f\n", val, log(val));
    val++;
  } while (val < 11.0);
  return 0;
}
```

Related Function

log10( )

double log10(double num)
long double log10l(long double num)

Description

The prototype for **log10( )** is in **math.h**.

The **log10( )** function returns the base 10 logarithm for *num*. A domain error occurs if *num* is negative, and a range error occurs if the argument is 0.

log10l( ) is the **long double** version of this function.

Example

This program prints the base 10 logarithms for the numbers 1 through 10:

```
#include <stdio.h>
#include <math.h>

int main(void)
{
  double val = 1.0;

  do {
    printf("%f %f\n", val, log10(val));
    val++;
  } while (val < 11.0);
  return 0;
}
```

Related Function

log( )

int _matherr(struct exception *err)
int _matherrl(struct _exceptionl *err)

Description

The prototype for **_matherr( )** is in **math.h**. This function is not defined by the ANSI C standard.

The **_matherr( )** function allows you to create custom math error handling routines. The function must perform as follows. When the **_matherr( )** function can resolve a problem, it returns non-zero and no message is printed. Also, the **errno** built-in variable is not altered. However, if **_matherr( )** cannot resolve the problem, it returns zero, the appropriate error message is printed, and the value of **errno** is changed. By default, Borland C++ provides a version of **_matherr( )** that returns zero.

The **_matherr( )** function is called with an argument of type **exception**, which is shown here.

```
struct exception {
  int type;
  char *name;
  double arg1, arg2;
  double retval;
};
```

The **type** element holds the type of the error that occurred. Its value will be one of the following values.

Symbol	**Meaning**
DOMAIN	Domain error
SING	Result is a singularity
OVERFLOW	Overflow error
UNDERFLOW	Underflow error
TLOSS	Total loss of significant digits

The **name** element holds a pointer to a string that holds the name of the function in which the error took place. The **arg1** and **arg2** elements hold the arguments to the function that caused the error. If the function only takes one argument, it will be in **arg1**. Finally, **retval** holds the default return value for **_matherr( )**. You can return a different value.

_matherrl is used with the **long double** math functions. The structure **_exceptionl** is the same as **_exception** except that the elements **arg1**, **arg2**, and **retval** are of type **long double**.

double modf(double num, double *i) long double modfl(long double num, long double *i)

Description

The prototype for **modf( )** is in **math.h**.

The **modf( )** function decomposes *num* into its integer and fractional parts. It returns the fractional portion and places the integer part in the variable pointed to by *i*.

modfl( ) is the **long double** version of this function.

Example

This fragment prints "10" and "0.123" on the screen:

```
double i;
double f;

f = modf(10.123, &i);
printf("%f %f", i, f);
```

Related Functions

frexp( ), ldexp( )

double poly(double x, int n, double c[ ])
long double polyl(long double x, int n, long double c[ ])

Description

The prototype for **poly( )** is in **math.h**. This function is not defined by the ANSI C standard.

The **poly( )** function evaluates a polynomial in *x* of degree *n* with coefficients *c[0]* through *c[n]* and returns the result. For example, if *n*=3, the polynomial evaluated is

$$c[3]x^3 + c[2]x^2 + c[1]x + c[0]$$

polyl( ) is the **long double** version of this function.

Example

This program prints 47 on the screen.

```
#include <stdio.h>
#include <math.h>

int main(void)
{
  double c[2];

  c[1] = 2;
  c[0] = 45;

  printf("%f", poly(1, 2, c));
  return 0;
}
```

Related Function

hypot( )

double pow(double base, double exp)
long double powl(long double base, long double exp)

Description

The prototype for **pow( )** is in **math.h**.

The **pow( )** function returns *base* raised to the *exp* power ($base^{exp}$). An overflow produces a range error. Domain errors may also occur.

powl( ) is the **long double** version of this function.

Example

This program prints the first 11 powers of 12.

```
#include <stdio.h>
#include <math.h>

int main(void)
{
  double x=12.0, y=0.0;

  do {
    printf("%f\n", pow(x, y));
    y++;
  } while(y<11);
  return 0;
}
```

Related Functions

exp( ), log( ), sqrt( ), pow10( )

double pow10(int n)
long double pow10l(int n)

Description

The prototype for **pow10( )** is in **math.h**. This function is not defined by the ANSI C standard.

The **pow10( )** function returns 10 raised to the power *n*. Overflow and underflow are the only possible errors.

pow10l( ) is the **long double** version of this function.

Example

This program prints the first 11 powers of 10:

```
#include <stdio.h>
#include <math.h>

int main(void)
{
  int x=0;
```

```
  while(x < 11)
    printf("%f\n", pow10(x++));
  return 0;
}
```

Related Functions

exp( ), log( ), sqrt( ), pow( )

double sin(double arg)
long double sinl(long double arg)

Description

The prototype for **sin( )** is in **math.h**.

The **sin( )** function returns the sine of *arg*. The value of *arg* must be in radians. **sinl( )** is the **long double** version of this function.

Example

This program prints the sines, in one-tenth increments, of the values –1 through 1:

```
#include <stdio.h>
#include <math.h>

int main(void)
{
  double val = -1.0;

  do {
    printf("sine of %f is %f\n", val, sin(val));
    val += 0.1;
  } while(val <= 1.0);
  return 0;
}
```

Related Functions

asin( ), acos( ), atan2( ), atan( ), tan( ), cos( ), sinh( ), cosh( ), tanh( )

double sinh(double arg)
long double sinhl(long double arg)

Description

The prototype for **sinhl( )** is in **math.h**.

The **sinh( )** function returns the hyperbolic sine of *arg*.
sinhl( ) is the **long double** version of this function.

Example

This program prints the hyperbolic sines, in one-tenth increments, of the values –1 through 1.

```
#include <stdio.h>
#include <math.h>

int main(void)
{
  double val = -1.0;

  do {
    printf("hyperbolic sine of %f is %f\n", val, sinh(val));
    val += 0.1;
  } while(val <= 1.0);
    return 0;
}
```

Related Functions

asin( ), acos( ), atan2( ), atan( ), tan( ), cos( ), tanh( ), cosh( )

double sqrt(double num)
long double sqrtl(long double num)

Description

The prototype for **sqrt( )** is in **math.h**.

The **sqrt( )** function returns the square root of *num*. If called with a negative argument, a domain error occurs.

sqrtl( ) is the **long double** version of this function.

Example

This fragment prints "4" on the screen:

```
printf("%f", sqrt(16.0));
```

Related Functions

exp( ), log( ), pow( )

double tan(double arg)
long double tanl(long double arg)

Description

The prototype for **tan( )** is in **math.h**.

The **tan( )** function returns the tangent of *arg*. The value of *arg* must be in radians. **tanl( )** is the **long double** version of this function.

Example

This program prints the tangent, in one-tenth increments, of the values –1 through 1:

```
#include <stdio.h>
#include <math.h>

int main(void)
{
  double val = -1.0;

  do {
    printf("tangent of %f is %f\n", val, tan(val));
    val += 0.1;
  } while(val <= 1.0);
  return 0;
}
```

Related Functions

asin( ), atan( ), atan2( ), cos( ), sin( ), sinh( ), cosh( ), tanh( )

double tanh(double arg)
long double tanhl(long double arg)

Description

The prototype for **tanh( )** is in **math.h**.

The **tanh( )** function returns the hyperbolic tangent of *arg*. **tanhl( )** is the **long double** version of this function.

Example

This program prints the hyperbolic tangent, in one-tenth increments, of the values –1 through 1:

```
#include <stdio.h>
#include <math.h>
```

```
int main(void)
{
  double val = -1.0;

  do {
    printf("Hyperbolic tangent of %f is %f\n", val, tanh(val));
    val += 0.1;
  } while(val <= 1.0);
  return 0;
```

Related Functions

asin( ), atan( ), atan2( ), cos( ), sin( ), cosh( ), sinh( )

Chapter Fourteen

Time-, Date-, and System-Related Functions

This chapter covers those functions that in one way or another are more system sensitive than others. Of the functions defined by the ANSI C standard, these include the time and date functions, which relate to the system by using its time and date information.

Also discussed in this chapter is a category of functions that allow a lower level of system control than is normal. None of these functions is defined by the ANSI C standard because each operating environment is different. However, Borland C++ provides extensive DOS and BIOS interfacing functions. These functions only apply for 16-bit programs written for DOS (or a DOS session when running Windows). As you may know, Windows provides its own, very large set of interfacing functions, called the Windows API (Application Programming Interface). These functions are not described here because they are not provided by Borland. However, an overview of Windows programming is presented in Part 5.

The functions that deal with the system time and date require the header file **time.h** for their prototypes. This header also defines two types. The type **time_t** is capable of representing the system time and date as a long integer. This is referred to as the *calendar time*. The structure type **tm** holds the date and time broken down into its elements. The **tm** structure is defined as shown here:

```
struct tm {
  int tm_sec;    /* seconds, 0-59 */
  int tm_min;    /* minutes, 0-59 */
```

```
  int tm_hour;  /* hours, 0-23 */
  int tm_mday;  /* day of the month, 1-31 */
  int tm_mon;   /* months since Jan, 0-11 */
  int tm_year;  /* years from 1900 */
  int tm_wday;  /* days since Sunday, 0-6 */
  int tm_yday;  /* days since Jan 1, 0-365 */
  int tm_isdst; /* daylight saving time indicator */
};
```

The value of **tm_isdst** will be positive if daylight saving time is in effect, 0 if it is not in effect, and negative if there is no information available. This form of the time and date is called the *broken-down time.*

Borland C++ also includes some nonstandard time and date functions that bypass the normal time and date system and interface more closely with DOS. The functions use structures of either type **time** or **date**, which are defined in **dos.h**. Their declarations are shown here.

```
struct date {
  int da_year; /* year */
  char da_day; /* day of month */
  char da_mon; /* month, Jan=1 */
};

struct time {
  unsigned char ti_min;  /* minutes */
  unsigned char ti_hour; /* hours */
  unsigned char ti_hund; /* hundredths of seconds */
  unsigned char ti_sec;  /* seconds */
};
```

The DOS interfacing functions require the header **dos.h**. The file **dos.h** defines a union, called **REGS**, that corresponds to the registers of the 8086 family of CPUs and is used by some of the system interfacing functions. It is defined as the union of two structures to allow each register to be accessed by either word or byte. Because Borland C++ can compile code for both 16-bit and 32-bit environments, the definition of the register structures and union are somewhat complicated in order to accomodate both modes. However, for the functions described in this chapter, only the 16-bit versions are needed. The 16-bit equivalents of these structures are shown here.

```
struct WORDREGS
{
  unsigned int ax, bx, cx, dx, si, di, cflag, flags;
};

struct BYTEREGS
```

```
{
  unsigned char al, ah, bl, bh, cl, ch, dl, dh;
};

union REGS {
  struct WORDREGS x;
  struct BYTEREGS h;
};
```

Also defined in **dos.h** is the structure type **SREGS**, which is used by some functions to set the segment registers. Its 16-bit equivalent is defined as shown here.

```
struct SREGS     {
  unsigned int es, cs, ss, ds;
};
```

Several of the functions described here interface directly to the ROM-BIOS—the lowest level of the operating system. These functions require the header **bios.h**.

A few functions require predefined structures that have not been discussed. Definitions for these structures will be described as needed.

Microsoft Compatibility Functions

Borland C++ includes several redundant DOS and BIOS interface functions. Although Borland C++ defines its own complete set of DOS and BIOS interface functions, it also supplies versions of these functions that are compatible with Microsoft C++. The Microsoft versions all begin with **_dos** or **_bios**. Aside from portability issues, it doesn't matter which versions you use.

You will also find some other apparently redundant functions with slightly different names. Again, the reason for this is to provide compatibility with Microsoft C++. In general, the Microsoft versions of these functions begin with an underscore. For example, **enable( )** is a Borland function and **_enable( )** is the name of the Microsoft version included for compatibility.

int absread(int drive, int numsects, long sectnum, void *buf)
int abswrite(int drive, int numsects, long sectnum, void *buf)

Description

The prototypes for **absread( )** and **abswrite( )** are in **dos.h**. These functions are not defined by the ANSI C standard.

The functions **absread( )** and **abswrite( )** perform absolute disk read and write operations, respectively. They bypass the logical structure of the disk and ignore files or directories. Instead they operate on the disk at the sector specified in *sectnum.* The drive is specified in *drive* with drive A being equal to 0. The number of sectors to read or write is specified in *numsects* and the information is read into or from the region of memory pointed to by *buf.*

Upon success, these functions return 0; they return non-0 on failure. When a failure occurs, the built-in variable **errno** is set to the error value returned by DOS. You will need DOS technical documentation to determine the nature of any error that occurs.

You must use great caution when calling **abswrite( )** because it is very easy to corrupt the disk directory or a file.

Example

This program displays the contents of the specified disk sector.

```
#include <stdio.h>
#include <dos.h>
#include <stdlib.h>

int main(void)
{
  char buf[2048];
  int sector, i;

  for(;;) {
    printf("\nEnter sector: ");
    scanf("%d", &sector);
    if(sector==-1) return 0;
    absread(2, 1, sector, buf); /* read drive c */
    for(i=0; i<512; i++) {
      printf("%c ", buf[i]);
      if(!(i%16)) {
        printf("\n");
      }
    }
  }
}
```

Related Functions

read( ), fread( ), write( ), fwrite( )

char *asctime(const struct tm *ptr)

Description

The prototype for **asctime( )** is in **time.h**.

The **asctime( )** function returns a pointer to a string representing the information stored in the structure pointed to by *ptr* that is converted into the following form:

day month date hours:minutes:seconds year

For example:

Wed Jun 19 12:05:34 1999

The structure pointer passed to **asctime( )** is generally obtained from either **localtime( )** or **gmtime( )**.

The buffer used by **asctime( )** to hold the formatted output string is a statically allocated character array and is overwritten each time the function is called. If you wish to save the contents of the string, it is necessary to copy it elsewhere.

Example

This program displays the local time defined by the system:

```
#include <stdio.h>
#include <time.h>

int main(void)
{
  struct tm *ptr;
  time_t lt;

  lt = time(NULL);
  ptr = localtime(&lt);
  printf(asctime(ptr));
  return 0;
}
```

Related Functions

localtime( ), gmtime( ), time( ), ctime( )

int bdos(int fnum, unsigned dx, unsigned al)
int bdosptr(int fnum, void *dsdx, unsigned al)

Description

The prototypes for **bdos( )** and **bdosptr( )** are in **dos.h**. These functions are not defined by the ANSI C standard.

The **bdos( )** function is used to access the DOS system call specified by *fnum*. It first places the values *dx* into the DX register and *al* into the AL register and then executes an INT 0x21 instruction.

If you will be passing a pointer argument to DOS, use the **bdosptr( )** function instead of **bdos( )**. Although for the tiny, small, and medium memory models, the two functions are operationally equivalent, when the larger memory models are used, 32-bit pointers are required. When this is the case, the pointer will be passed in DS:DX.

Both the **bdos( )** and **bdosptr( )** functions return the value of the AX register, which is used by DOS to return information.

Example

This program reads characters directly from the keyboard, bypassing all of C's I/O functions, until a "q" is typed:

```
/* Do raw keyboard reads. */
#include <dos.h>

int main(void)
{
  char ch;

  while((ch=bdos(1, 0, 0))!='q') ;
  /* ... */
  return 0;
}
```

Related Functions

intdos( ), intdosx( )

int bioscom(int cmd, char byte, int port)
unsigned _bios_serialcom(int cmd, int port, char byte)

Description

The prototypes for **bioscom( )** and **_bios_serialcom( )** are in **bios.h**. These functions are not defined by the ANSI C standard.

The **bioscom( )** and **_bios_serialcom( )** functions are used to manipulate the RS232 asynchronous communication port specified in *port*. Their operation is determined by the value of *cmd*, whose values are shown here, along with their macro equivalents defined in **bios.h**.

cmd	Macro	Meaning
0	_COM_INIT	Initialize the port
1	_COM_SEND	Send a character
2	_COM_RECEIVE	Receive a character
3	_COM_STATUS	Return the port status

Before using the serial port you will probably want to initialize it to something other than its default setting. To do this, set *cmd* equal to 0. The exact way the port will be set up is determined by the value of *byte*, which is encoded with initialization parameters as shown here:

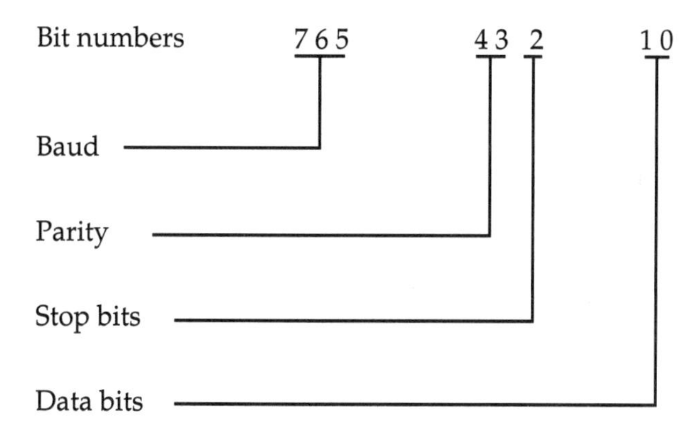

The baud is encoded as shown here:

Baud	Bit Pattern
9600	1 1 1
4800	1 1 0
2400	1 0 1
1200	1 0 0
600	0 1 1
300	0 1 0

Baud	Bit Pattern
150	0 0 1
110	0 0 0

The parity bits are encoded as shown here:

Parity	Bit Pattern
No parity	0 0
Odd	0 1
Even	1 1

The number of stop bits is determined by bit 2 of the serial port initialization byte. If it is 1, two stop bits are used; otherwise, one stop bit is used. Finally, the number of data bits is set by the code in bits 1 and 0 of the initialization byte. Of the four possible bit patterns, only two are valid. If bits 1 and 0 contain the pattern 1 0, 7 data bits are used. If they contain 1 1, then 8 data bits are used.

For example, if you want to set the port to 9600 baud, even parity, 1 stop bit, and 8 data bits, you would use this bit pattern:

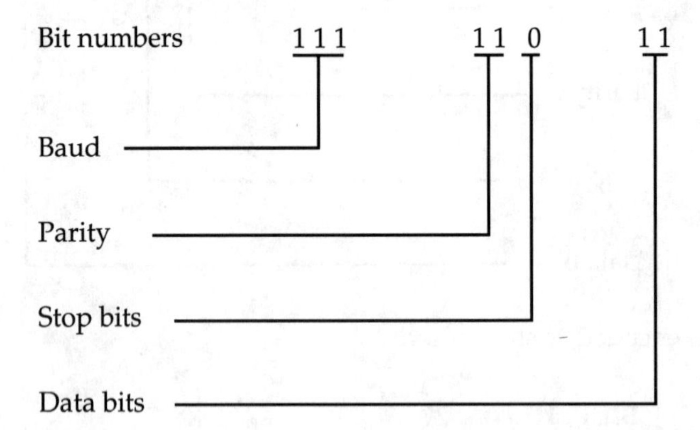

In decimal, this works out to 251.

The return value of **bioscom( )** and **_bios_serialcom( )** is always a 16-bit quantity. The high-order byte contains the status bits and they have the following values:

Meaning When Set	Bit
Data ready	0
Overrun error	1
Parity error	2
Framing error	3
Break-detect error	4
Transfer holding register empty	5
Transfer shift register empty	6
Time-out error	7

If *cmd* is set to 0, 1, or 3, the low-order byte is encoded as shown here:

Meaning When Set	Bit
Change in clear-to-send	0
Change in data-set-ready	1
Trailing-edge ring detector	2
Change inline signal	3
Clear-to-send	4
Data-set-ready	5
Ring indicator	6
Line signal detected	7

When *cmd* has a value of 2, the lower order byte contains the value received by the port.

Example

This initializes port 0 to 9600 baud, even parity, 1 stop bit, and 8 data bits:

```
bioscom(0, 251, 0);
```

Related Function

bioskey( )

int biosdisk(int cmd, int drive, int head, int track, int sector, int nsects, void *buf)

Description

The prototype for **biosdisk( )** is in **bios.h**. This function is not defined by the ANSI C standard.

The **biosdisk( )** function performs BIOS-level disk operations using interrupt 0x13. These operations ignore the logical structure of the disk, including files. All operations take place on sectors.

The drive affected is specified in *drive* with 0 corresponding to A, 1 to B, and so on for floppy drives. The first fixed disk is drive 0x80, the second 0x81, and so on. The part of the disk that is operated on is specified in *head, track,* and *sector.* This function returns the outcome of the operation. You should refer to a PC technical reference manual for details of the operation and options of the BIOS-level disk routines. Keep in mind that direct control of the disk requires thorough and intimate knowledge of both the hardware and DOS. It is best avoided except in unusual situations.

Related Functions

absread( ), abswrite( ), _bios_disk( )

unsigned _bios_disk(unsigned cmd, struct diskinfo_t *info)

Description

The prototype for **_bios_disk( )** is in **bios.h**. This function is not defined by the ANSI C standard.

The **_bios_disk( )** function performs BIOS-level disk operations using interrupt 0x13. These operations ignore the logical structure of the disk, including files. All operations take place on sectors.

The **diskinfo_t** structure looks like this:

```
struct diskinfo_t {
  unsigned drive;
  unsigned head;
  unsigned track;
  unsigned sector;
  unsigned nsectors;
  void far *buffer;
};
```

The drive affected is specified in *drive* with 0 corresponding to A, 1 to B, and so on for floppy drives. The first fixed disk is drive 0x80, the second 0x81, and so on. The part of the disk that is operated on is specified in *head, track,* and *sector.* The *nsector* field specifies the number of sectors to read or write and *buffer* points to a buffer that will hold information written to or read from the disk. This function returns the outcome of the operation. You should refer to a PC reference manual for details of the operation and options of the BIOS-level disk routines. Keep in mind that direct control of the disk requires thorough and intimate knowledge of the hardware, as well as DOS and BIOS. It is best avoided except in unusual situations.

Related Functions

absread( ), abswrite( ), biosdisk( )

int biosequip(void)
unsigned _bios_equiplist(void)

Description

The prototypes for **biosequip( )** and **_bios_equiplist( )** are found in **bios.h**. These functions are not defined by the ANSI C standard.

Both **biosequip( )** and **_bios_equiplist( )** functions return a list of the equipment installed in the computer encoded as a 16-bit value. This value is encoded as shown here:

Bit	Equipment
0	Must boot from the floppy drive
1	80x87 math coprocessor installed
2, 3	Motherboard RAM size 0 0: 16K 0 1: 32K 1 0: 48K 1 1: 64K
4, 5	Initial video mode 0 0: unused 0 1: 40x25 BW, color adapter 1 0: 80x25 BW, color adapter 1 1: 80x25, monochrome adapter
6, 7	Number of floppy drives 0 0: one 0 1: two 1 0: three 1 1: four
8	0 if DMA chip installed; 1 otherwise

Bit	Equipment
9, 10, 11	Number of serial ports 0 0 0: zero 0 0 1: one 0 1 0: two 0 1 1: three 1 0 0: four 1 0 1: five 1 1 0: six 1 1 1: seven
12	Game adapter installed
13	Serial printer installed
14, 15	Number of printers 0 0: zero 0 1: one 1 0: two 1 1: three

Example

This program displays the number of floppy drives installed in the computer:

```
#include <stdio.h>
#include <bios.h>

int main(void)
{
  unsigned eq;

  eq = biosequip();

  eq >>= 6; /* shift bits 6 and 7 into lowest position */

  printf("number of disk drives: %d", (eq & 3) + 1);

  return 0;
}
```

Related Function

bioscom( )

int bioskey(int cmd)
unsigned _bios_keybrd(unsigned cmd)

Description

The prototypes for **bioskey( )** and **_bios_keybrd( )** are in **bios.h**. These functions are not defined by the ANSI C standard. The **bios.h** file also contains several macros that can be used as parameters to these functions.

The **bioskey( )** and **_bios_keybrd( )** functions perform direct keyboard operations. The value of *cmd* determines what operation is executed.

If *cmd* is 0 or the macro **_KEYBRD_READ**, both functions return the next key struck on the keyboard. (They will wait until a key is pressed.) Both return a 16-bit quantity that consists of two different values. The low-order byte contains the ASCII character code if a "normal" key is pressed. It will contain 0 if a "special" key is pressed. Special keys include the arrow keys, the function keys, and the like. The high-order byte contains the position code of the key.

If *cmd* is 1 or the macro **_KEYBRD_READY**, both functions check to see if a key has been pressed. They return the value of the key pressed (–1 for CTRL-BRK), which is non-0 if a key has been pressed; 0 otherwise. In no situation is the keystroke removed from the keyboard buffer.

When *cmd* is 2 or the macro **_KEYBRD_SHIFTSTATUS**, the shift status is returned. The status of the various keys that shift a state are encoded into the low-order part of the return value as shown here:

Bit	Meaning
0	Right SHIFT pressed
1	Left SHIFT pressed
2	CTRL key pressed
3	ALT pressed
4	SCROLL LOCK on
5	NUM LOCK on
6	CAPS LOCK on
7	INS on

For **_bios_keybrd( )** only: If *cmd* is **_NKEYBRD_READ**, the function reads the position codes for extended keyboards. If *cmd* is **_NKEYBRD_READY**, additional keys are checked on extended keyboards. Finally, if *cmd* is **_NKEYBRD_SHIFTSTATUS**, then the following status information is also returned in the high-order byte of the return value, as shown here:

Bit	Meaning
8	Left CTRL pressed
9	Left ALT pressed
10	Right CTRL pressed
11	Right ALT pressed
12	SCROLL LOCK pressed
13	NUM LOCK pressed
14	CAPS LOCK pressed
15	SYS REQ pressed

Example

This fragment generates random numbers until a key is pressed:

```
while(!bioskey(1)) rand();
```

Related Functions

getche( ), kbhit( )

int biosmemory(void)
unsigned _bios_memsize(void)

Description

The prototypes for **biosmemory( )** and **_bios_memsize( )** are in **bios.h**. These functions are not defined by the ANSI C standard.

The **biosmemory( )** and **_bios_memsize( )** functions return the amount of memory (in units of 1K) installed in the system that is usable by DOS. Thus, the maximum value reported by these functions is 640K.

Example

This program reports the amount of memory in the system:

```
#include <stdio.h>
#include <bios.h>

int main(void)
{
  printf("%dK bytes of ram", biosmemory());

  return 0;
}
```

Related Function

biosequip( )

int biosprint(int cmd, int byte, int port) unsigned _bios_printer(int cmd, int port, int byte)

Description

The prototypes for **biosprint( )** and **_bios_printer( )** are in **bios.h**. These functions are not defined by the ANSI C standard.

The **biosprint( )** and **_bios_printer( )** functions control the printer port specified in *port*. If *port* is 0, then LPT1 is used; if *port* is 1, LPT2 is accessed, and so on. The exact function performed is contingent upon the value of *cmd*. The legal values for *cmd* are shown here, along with macro equivalents defined in **bios.h**.

Value	Macro	Meaning
0	_PRINTER_WRITE	Print the character in *byte*.
1	_PRINTER_INIT	Initialize the printer *port*.
2	_PRINTER_STATUS	Return the status of the port.

These functions return printer port status as encoded into the low-order byte of the return value as shown here:

Bit	Meaning
0	Time-out error
1	Unused
2	Unused
3	I/O error
4	Printer selected
5	Out-of-paper error
6	Acknowledge
7	Printer not busy

Example

This fragment prints the string "hello" on the printer connected to LPT1:

```
char p[]="hello";

while(*p) biosprint(0, *p++, 0);
```

Related Function

bioscom( )

long biostime(int cmd, long newtime)

Description

The prototype for **biostime( )** is in **bios.h**. This function is not defined by the ANSI C standard.

The **biostime( )** function reads or sets the system clock. Its value is 0 at midnight and increases until reset at midnight again or manually set to some value. If *cmd* is 0, **biostime( )** returns the current timer value, in clock ticks. If *cmd* is 1, the timer is set to the value of *newtime*, specified in clock ticks.

Example

This program prints the current value of the timer:

```
#include <stdio.h>
#include <bios.h>

int main(void)
{
  printf("The current timer value is %ld", biostime(0,0));
  return 0;
}
```

Related Functions

time( ), ctime( ), _bios_timeofday( )

unsigned _bios_timeofday(int cmd, long *newtime)

Description

The prototype for **_bios_timeofday( )** is in **bios.h**. This function is not defined by the ANSI C standard.

The **_bios_timeofday( )** function reads or sets the system clock. If *cmd* is 0, then the function reads the current time. If *cmd* is 1, then the time is set. (You may also use the macros **_TIME_GETCLOCK** and **_TIME_SETCLOCK**, respectively, for this parameter.)

When setting the clock, the new time, in clock ticks, is passed in the variable pointed to by *newtime*. There is no meaningful return value when setting the time.

When reading the system time, the variable pointed to by *newtime* will contain the system time, in clock ticks, after the function has returned. The function returns 1 if the timer has not been read since midnight. It returns 0 otherwise.

Example

This resets the system timer:

```
_bios_timeofday(_TIME_SETCLOCK, 0L);
```

Related Functions

time( ), biostime( )

void _chain_intr(void (interrupt far *newintr)( ))

Description

The prototype for **_chain_intr( )** is in **dos.h**. This function is not defined by the ANSI C standard.

The **_chain_intr( )** function is primarily for use in DOS TSR (Terminate and Stay Resident) programs and interrupt handlers. It is used to pass control from a currently executing interrupt handler or TSR to another. The address of the new interrupt handler or TSR is specified in *newintr*. The new interrupt handler uses the registers that are on the stack, not the current state of the registers at the time of the call to **_chain_intr( )**.

The reason **_chain_intr( )** is often used with TSRs is that it facilitates the inclusion of a new TSR in a chain of existing TSRs or interrupt handlers.

Because of the complex nature of TSRs and interrupt handlers, no example is given.

Related Functions

getvect( ), setvect( )

clock_t clock(void)

Description

The prototype for **clock( )** is in **time.h**.

The **clock( )** function returns the amount of time elapsed since the program that called **clock( )** started running. If a clock is not available, –1 is returned. To convert the return value to seconds, divide it by the macro **CLK_TCK**.

Example

This program times the number of seconds that it takes for the empty **for** loop to go from 0 to 500000:

```
#include <stdio.h>
#include <time.h>

int main(void)
{
  clock_t start, stop;
  unsigned long t;

  start = clock();
  for(t=0; t<500000L; t++);
  stop = clock();
  printf("Loop required %f seconds",
         (stop - start) / CLK_TCK);

  return 0;
}
```

Related Functions

localtime( ), gmtime( ), time( ), asctime( )

struct COUNTRY *country(int countrycode, struct COUNTRY *countryptr)

Description

The prototype for **country( )** is in **dos.h**. This function is not defined by the ANSI C standard.

The **country( )** function sets several country-dependent items, such as the currency symbol and the way the date and time are displayed.

The structure **COUNTRY** is defined like this:

```
struct COUNTRY {
  int co_date;         /* date format */
  char co_curr[5];     /* currency symbol */
  char co_thsep[2];    /* thousand separator */
  char co_desep[2];    /* decimal separator */
  char co_dtsep[2];    /* date separator */
  char co_tmsep[2];    /* time separator */
  char co_currstyle;   /* currency style */
  char co_digits;      /* significant digits in currency */
```

```
  char co_time;       /* format of time */
  long co_case;       /* case map */
  char so_dasep[2];   /* data separator */
  char co_fill[10];   /* filler */
};
```

If *countrycode* is set to 0, the country-specific information is put in the structure pointed to by *countryptr.* If *countrycode* is non-0, the country-specific information is set to the value of the structure pointed to by *countryptr.*

The value of **co_date** determines the date format. If it is 0, U.S. style (month, day, year) format is used. If it is 1, the European style (day, month, year) is used. Finally, if it is 2, the Japanese style (year, month, day) is used.

The way currency is displayed is determined by the value of **co_currstyle**. The legal values for **co_currstyle** are shown here.

Value	Meaning
0	Currency symbol immediately precedes the value.
1	Currency symbol immediately follows the value.
2	Currency symbol precedes the value with a space between the symbol and the value.
3	Currency symbol follows the value with a space between the symbol and the value.

The function returns a pointer to the *countryptr* argument.

Example

This program displays the currency symbol:

```
#include <stdio.h>
#include <dos.h>

int main(void)
{
  struct COUNTRY c;

  country(0, &c);

  printf(c.co_curr);

  return 0;
}
```

char *ctime(const time_t *time)

Description

The prototype for **ctime( )** is in **time.h**.

The **ctime( )** function returns a pointer to a string of the form

day month date hours:minutes:seconds year

given a pointer to the calendar time. The calendar time is generally obtained through a call to **time( )**. The **ctime( )** function is equivalent to

```
asctime(localtime(time))
```

The buffer used by **ctime( )** to hold the formatted output string is a statically allocated character array and is overwritten each time the function is called. If you wish to save the contents of the string, it is necessary to copy it elsewhere.

Example

This program displays the local time defined by the system:

```
#include <stdio.h>
#include <time.h>
#include <stddef.h>

int main(void)
{
  time_t lt;

  lt = time(NULL);
  printf(ctime(&lt));
  return 0;
}
```

Related Functions

localtime( ), gmtime( ), time( ), asctime( )

void ctrlbrk(int (*fptr)(void))

Description

The prototype for **ctrlbrk( )** is in **dos.h**. This function is not defined by the ANSI C standard.

The **ctrlbrk( )** function is used to replace the control-break handler called by DOS with the one pointed to by *fptr*. This routine is called each time the CTRL-BRK key combination is pressed. A control-break generates an interrupt 0x23.

Borland C++ automatically replaces the old control-break handler when your program exits.

The new control-break routine should return non-0 if the program is to continue running. If it returns 0, the program will be terminated.

Example

This program prints the numbers 0 to 31,999 unless the CTRL-BRK key is pressed, which causes the program to abort.

```
#include <stdio.h>
#include <dos.h>

int break_handler(void);

int main(void)
{
  register int i;

  ctrlbrk(break_handler);

  for(i=0; i<32000; i++)  printf("%d ", i);

  return 0;
}

break_handler(void)
{
  printf("This is the new break handler.");
  return 0;
}
```

Related Function

geninterrupt( )

void delay(unsigned time)

Description

The prototype for **delay( )** is in **dos.h**. This function is not defined by the ANSI C standard.

The **delay( )** function halts program execution for *time* number of milliseconds.

Example

This program displays a message and beeps twice:

```
#include <stdio.h>
#include <dos.h>

int main(void)
{
  printf("beep beep ");

  sound(500);
  delay(600);
  nosound();
  delay(300);
  sound(500);
  delay(600);
  nosound();

  return 0;
}
```

Related Function

sleep( )

double difftime(time_t time2, time_t time1)

Description

The prototype for **difftime( )** is in **time.h**.

The **difftime( )** function returns the difference, in seconds, between *time1* and *time2*. That is, it returns *time2–time1*.

Example

This program times the number of seconds that it takes for the empty **for** loop to go from 0 to 500,000:

```
#include <stdio.h>
#include <time.h>
#include <stddef.h>

int main(void)
{
  time_t start,end;
```

```
  long unsigned int t;

  start = time(NULL);
  for(t=0; t<500000L; t++) ;
  end = time(NULL);
  printf("Loop required %f seconds", difftime(end, start));

  return 0;
}
```

Related Functions

localtime( ), gmtime( ), time( ), asctime( )

void disable(void)
void _disable(void)

Description

The prototypes for **disable( )** and **_disable( )** are in **dos.h**. These macros are not defined by the ANSI C standard.

The **disable( )** and **_disable( )** macros disable interrupts. The only interrupt that they allow is the NMI (nonmaskable interrupt). Use this function with care because many devices in the system use interrupts.

Related Functions

enable( ), geninterrupt( )

unsigned _dos_close(int fd)

Description

The prototype for **_dos_close( )** is in **dos.h**. This function is not defined by the ANSI C standard.

The **_dos_close( )** function closes the file specified by the file descriptor *fd*. The file must have been opened using a call to **_dos_creat( )**, **_dos_open( )**, or **_dos_creatnew( )**. The function returns 0 if successful. Otherwise, non-0 is returned and **errno** is set to **EBADF** (bad file descriptor).

Example

This fragment closes the file associated with the file descriptor **fd**:

```
_dos_close(fd);
```

Related Functions

_dos_creat( ), _dos_open( )

unsigned _dos_creat(const char *fname, unsigned attr, int *fd)
unsigned _dos_creatnew(const char *fname, unsigned attr, int *fd)

Description

The prototypes for **_dos_creat( )** and **_dos_creatnew( )** are in **dos.h**. These functions are not defined by the ANSI C standard.

The **_dos_creat( )** function creates a file by the name pointed to by *fname* with the attributes specified by *attr*. It returns a file descriptor to the file in the integer pointed to by *fd*. If the file already exists, it will be erased. The **_dos_creatnew( )** function is the same as **_dos_creat( )**, except that if the file already exists, it will not be erased and **_dos_creatnew( )** will return an error.

The valid values for *attr* are shown here. (The macros are defined in **dos.h**.)

Macro	Meaning
_A_NORMAL	Normal file
_A_RDONLY	Read-only file
_A_HIDDEN	Hidden file
_A_SYSTEM	System file
_A_VOLID	Volume label
_A_SUBDIR	Subdirectory
_A_ARCH	Archive byte set

Both functions return 0 if successful and non-0 on failure. On failure, **errno** will contain one of these values: **ENOENT** (file not found), **EMFILE** (too many open files), **EACCES** (access denied), or **EEXIST** (file already exists).

Example

This fragment opens a file called TEST.TST for output:

```
int fd;

if(_dos_creat("test.tst", _A_NORMAL, &fd))
  printf("Cannot open file.\n");
```

Related Function

_dos_open( )

int dosexterr(struct DOSERROR *err)

Description

The prototype for **dosexterr( )** is in **dos.h**. This function is not defined by the ANSI C standard.

The **dosexterr( )** function fills the structure pointed to by *err* with extended error information when a DOS call fails. The **DOSERROR** structure is defined like this:

```
struct DOSERROR {
  int de_exterror; /* error code */
  char de_class;    /* class of error */
  char de_action   /* suggested action */
  char de_locus;   /* location of error */
};
```

For the proper interpretation of the information returned by DOS, refer to the DOS technical reference manual.

Related Function

ferror( )

void _dos_getdate(struct dosdate_t *d)
void _dos_gettime(struct dostime_t *t)

Description

The prototypes for **_dos_getdate( )** and **_dos_gettime( )** are in **dos.h**. These functions are not defined by the ANSI C standard.

The **_dos_getdate( )** function returns the DOS system date in the structure pointed to by *d*. The **_dos_gettime( )** function returns the DOS system time in the structure pointed to by *t*.

The **dosdate_t** structure is defined like this:

```
struct dosdate_t {
  unsigned char day;
  unsigned char month;
  unsigned int year;
  unsigned char dayofweek;  /* Sunday is 0 */
};
```

The **dostime_t** structure is defined as shown here:

```
struct dostime_t {
  unsigned char hour;
  unsigned char minute;
```

```
  unsigned char second;
  unsigned char hsecond; /* hundredths of second */
};
```

Example

This displays the system time and date:

```
#include <stdio.h>
#include <dos.h>

int main(void)
{
  struct dosdate_t d;
  struct dostime_t t;

  _dos_getdate(&d);
  _dos_gettime(&t);

  printf("Time and date: %d:%d:%d, %d/%d/%d",
         t.hour, t.minute, t.second, d.month, d.day,
         d.year);

  return 0;
}
```

Related Functions

_dos_settime( ), **_dos_setdate( )**

unsigned _dos_getdiskfree(unsigned char drive, struct diskfree_t *dfptr)

Description

The prototype for **_dos_getdiskfree( )** is in **dos.h**. This function is not defined by the ANSI C standard.

The **_dos_getdiskfree( )** function returns the amount of free disk space in the structure pointed to by *dfptr* for the drive specified by *drive*. The drives are numbered from 1 beginning with A. You can specify the default drive by giving *drive* the value 0. The **diskfree_t** structure is defined like this:

```
struct diskfree_t {
  unsigned total_clusters;
  unsigned avail_clusters;
```

```
  unsigned sectors_per_cluster;
  unsigned bytes_per_sector;
};
```

The function returns 0 if successful. If an error occurs, it returns non-0 and **errno** is set to **EINVAL** (invalid drive).

Example

This program prints the number of free clusters available for use on drive C:

```
#include <dos.h>
#include <stdio.h>

int main(void)
{
  struct diskfree_t p;

  _dos_getdiskfree(3, &p); /* drive C */

  printf("Number of free clusters is %d.",
          p.avail_clusters);

  return 0;
}
```

Related Function

getdfree( )

void _dos_getdrive(unsigned *drive)

Description

The prototype for **_dos_getdrive( )** is in **dos.h**. This function is not defined by the ANSI C standard.

The **_dos_getdrive( )** function returns the number of the currently logged in disk drive in the integer pointed to by *drive*. Drive A is encoded as 1, drive B as 2, and so on.

Example

This fragment displays the current disk drive:

```
unsigned d;

_dos_getdrive(&d);
printf("drive is %c", d-1+'A');
```

Related Function

_dos_setdrive( )

unsigned _dos_getfileattr(const char *fname, unsigned *attrib)

Description

The prototype for **_dos_getfileattr( )** is in **dos.h**. This function is not defined by the ANSI C standard.

The **_dos_getfileattr( )** returns the attribute of the file specified by *fname* in the unsigned integer pointed to by *attrib,* which may be one or more of these values. (The macros are defined in **dos.h**.)

Macro	**Meaning**
_A_NORMAL	Normal file
_A_RDONLY	Read-only file
_A_HIDDEN	Hidden file
_A_SYSTEM	System file
_A_VOLID	Volume label
_A_SUBDIR	Subdirectory
_A_ARCH	Archive byte set

The **_dos_getfileattr( )** function returns 0 if successful; it returns non-0 otherwise. If failure occurs, **errno** is set to **ENOENT** (file not found).

Example

This fragment determines if the file TEST.TST is a normal file:

```
unsigned attr;

if(_dos_getfileattr("test.tst", &attr))
  printf("file error");

if(attr & _A_NORMAL) printf("File is normal.\n");
```

Related Function

_dos_setfileattr( )

unsigned _dos_getftime(int fd, unsigned *fdate, unsigned *ftime)

Description

The prototype for **_dos_getftime( )** is in **dos.h**. This function is not defined by the ANSI C standard.

The function **_dos_getftime( )** returns the time and date of creation for the file associated with file descriptor *fd* in the integers pointed to by *ftime* and *fdate*. The file must have been opened using **_dos_open( )**, **_dos_creatnew( )**, or **_dos_creat( )**.

The bits in the object pointed to by *ftime* are encoded as shown here:

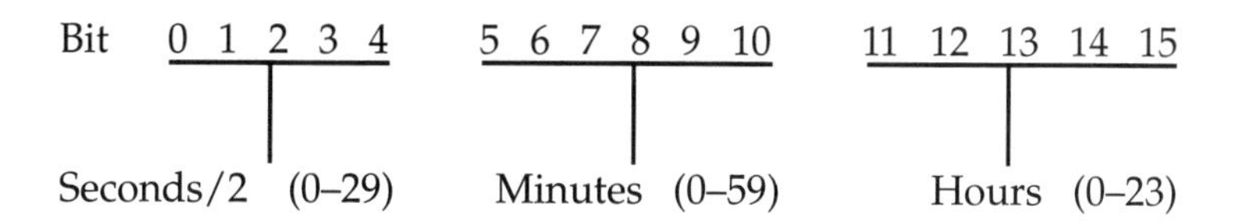

The bits in the object pointed to by *fdate* are encoded like this:

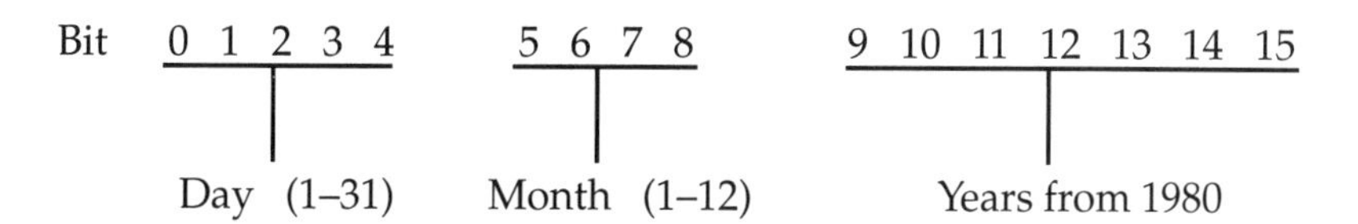

As indicated, the year is represented as the number of years from 1980. Therefore, if the year is 2000, the value of bits 9 through 15 will be 20. The **_dos_getftime( )** function returns 0 if successful. If an error occurs, non-0 is returned and **errno** is set to **EBADF** (bad file handle).

Example

This program prints the year the file TEST.TST was created:

```
#include <io.h>
#include <dos.h>
#include <fcntl.h>
#include <stdio.h>
#include <stdlib.h>

int main(void)
{
```

```
  struct {
    unsigned day: 5;
    unsigned month: 4;
    unsigned year: 7;
  } d;

  unsigned t;
  int fd;

  if(_dos_open("TEST.TST", O_RDONLY, &fd)) {
    printf("Cannot open file.\n");
    exit(1);
  }

  _dos_getftime(fd, (unsigned *) &d, &t);

  printf("Date of creation: %u", d.year+1980);

  return 0;
}
```

Related Function

_dos_setftime( )

void interrupt (far *_dos_getvect(unsigned intr))( )

Description

The prototype for **_dos_getvect( )** is in **dos.h**. This function is not defined by the ANSI C standard.

The **_dos_getvect( )** function returns the address of the interrupt service routine associated with the interrupt specified in *intr.* This value is returned as a **far** pointer.

Example

This fragment returns the address of the print screen function, which is associated with interrupt 5:

```
void interrupt (*p)();

p = _dos_getvect(5);
```

Related Function

setvect( )

unsigned _dos_open(const char *fname, unsigned mode, int *fd)

Description

The prototype for **_dos_open( )** is in **dos.h**. This function is not defined by the ANSI C standard.

The **_dos_open( )** function opens the file whose name is pointed to by *fname* in the mode specified by *mode* and returns a file descriptor to the file in the integer pointed to by *fd*.

The foundation values for the *mode* parameter are shown below. (These macros are defined in **dos.h**.)

Value	Meaning
O_RDONLY	Read only
O_WRONLY	Write only
O_RDWR	Read/write

You may add the following file-sharing attributes to *mode* by ORing them with the foundation value. (These macros are defined in **share.h**.)

Value	Meaning
SH_COMPAT	Compatibility mode only
SH_DENYNO	Allow reading and writing
SH_DENYRD	Deny reading
SH_DENYRW	Deny reading and writing
SH_DENYWR	Deny writing

You may also specify that the file cannot be inherited by a child process by ORing the macro **O_NOINHERIT**. This macro is defined in **fcntl.h**.

The **_dos_open( )** function returns 0 if successful and non-0 on failure. If an error occurs, **errno** is set to one of these values:

Value	Meaning
EACCES	Access denied
EINVACC	Invalid access attempted (for example, trying to read a file opened for write operations)

Value	Meaning
EMFILE	Too many open files
ENOENT	File not found

Example

This fragment opens a file called TEST.TST for read/write operations:

```
int fd;

if(_dos_open("test.tst", O_RDWR, &fd))
   printf("Error opening file.");
```

Related Functions

_dos_creat( ), _dos_creatnew( ), _dos_close( )

unsigned _dos_read(int fd, void far *buf, unsigned count, unsigned *numread)

Description

The prototype for **_dos_read( )** is in **dos.h**. This function is not defined by the ANSI C standard.

The **_dos_read( )** function reads up to *count* bytes from the file specified by the file descriptor *fd* into the buffer pointed to by *buf*. The number of bytes actually read are returned in *numread*, which may be less than *count* if the end of the file is reached before the specified number of bytes have been input. The file must have been opened using a call to **_dos_creat( )**, **_dos_creatnew( )**, or **_dos_open( )**. Also, **_dos_read( )** treats all files as binary.

Upon success, **_dos_read( )** returns 0; non-0 on failure. On failure, **errno** is set to either **EACCES** (access denied) or **EBADF** (bad file handle). Also, when a failure occurs, the return value is determined by DOS and you will need DOS technical documentation to determine the exact nature of the error, if one should occur.

Example

This fragment reads up to 128 characters from the file described by *fd*:

```
int fd;
unsigned count
char *buf[128];
.
.
.
```

```
if(_dos_read(fd, buf, 128, &count))
  printf("Error reading file.\n");
```

Related Function

_dos_write( )

unsigned _dos_setdate(struct dosdate_t *d)
unsigned _dos_settime(struct dostime_t *t)

Description

The prototypes for **_dos_setdate( )** and **_dos_settime( )** are in **dos.h**. These functions are not defined by the ANSI C standard.

The **_dos_setdate( )** function sets the DOS system date as specified in the structure pointed to by *d*. The **_dos_settime( )** function sets the DOS system time as specified in the structure pointed to by *t*.

The **dosdate_t** structure is defined like this:

```
struct dosdate_t {
  unsigned char day;
  unsigned char month;
  unsigned int year;
  unsigned char dayofweek;   /* Sunday is 0 */
};
```

The **dostime_t** structure is defined as shown here:

```
struct dostime_t {
  unsigned char hour;
  unsigned char minute;
  unsigned char second;
  unsigned char hsecond; /* hundredths of second */
};
```

Both functions return 0 if successful. On failure they return a non-0 DOS error code and **errno** is set to **EINVAL** (invalid time or date).

Example

The following program sets the system time to 10:10:10.0.

```
struct dostime_t t;

t.hour = 10;
t.minute  = 10;
t.second  = 10;
```

```
t.hsecond = 0;

_dos_settime(&t);
```

Related Functions

_dos_gettime( ), _dos_getdate( )

void _dos_setdrive(unsigned drive, unsigned *num)

Description

The prototype for **_dos_setdrive( )** is in **dos.h**. This function is not defined by the ANSI C standard.

The **_dos_setdrive( )** function changes the current disk drive to the one specified by *drive*. Drive A corresponds to 1, drive B to 2, and so on. The number of drives in the system is returned in the integer pointed to by *num*.

Example

This fragment makes drive B the current drive:

```
unsigned num;

_dos_setdrive(2, &num);
```

Related Function

_dos_getdrive( )

unsigned _dos_setfileattr(const char *fname, unsigned attrib)

Description

The prototype for **_dos_setfileattr( )** is in **dos.h**. This function is not defined by the ANSI C standard.

The **_dos_setfileattr( )** sets the attributes of the file specified by *fname* to that specified by *attrib*, which must be one (or more) of these values. When using more than one, OR them together. (The macros are defined in **dos.h**.)

Macro	Meaning
_A_NORMAL	Normal file
_A_RDONLY	Read-only file

Macro	Meaning
_A_HIDDEN	Hidden file
_A_SYSTEM	System file
_A_VOLID	Volume label
_A_SUBDIR	Subdirectory
_A_ARCH	Archive byte set

The **_dos_setfileattr( )** function returns 0 if successful; it returns non-0 otherwise. If failure occurs, **errno** is set to **ENOENT** (invalid file).

Example

This fragment sets the file TEST.TST to read only:

```
unsigned attr;

attr = _A_RDONLY;

if(_dos_setfileattr("test.tst", attr))
  printf("File Error");
```

Related Function

_dos_getfileattr( )

unsigned _dos_setftime(int fd, unsigned fdate, unsigned ftime)

Description

The prototype for **_dos_setftime( )** is in **dos.h**. This function is not defined by the ANSI C standard.

The **_dos_setftime( )** sets the date and time of the file specified by *fd*, which must be a valid file descriptor obtained through a call to **_dos_open( )**, **_dos_creat( )**, or **_dos_creatnew( )**.

The bits in *ftime* are encoded as shown here:

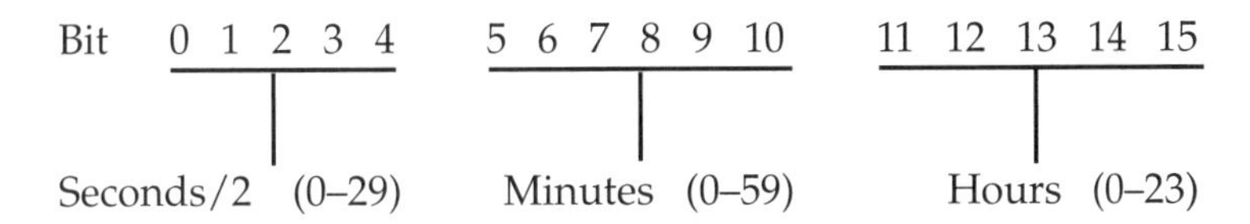

The bits in *fdate* are encoded like this:

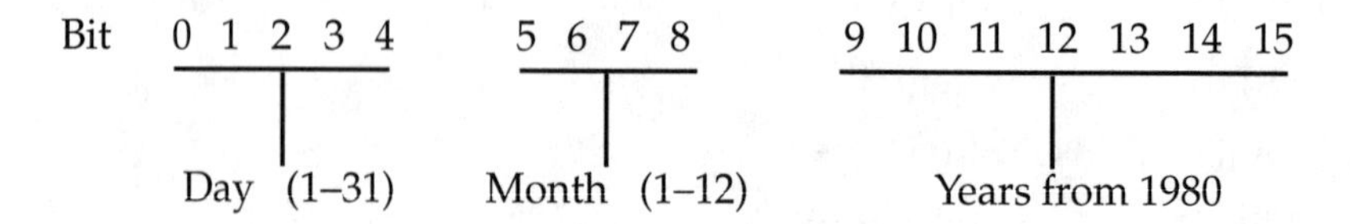

As indicated, the year is represented as the number of years from 1980. Therefore, to set the year to 2000, the value of bits 9 through 15 must be 20. The **_dos_setftime( )** function returns 0 if successful. If an error occurs, non-0 is returned and **errno** is set to **EBADF** (bad file handle).

Example

This changes the year of the file's creation date to 2000:

```
#include <stdio.h>
#include <io.h>
#include <dos.h>
#include <fcntl.h>
#include <stdlib.h>

int main(void)
{
  struct dt {
    unsigned day: 5;
    unsigned month: 4;
    unsigned year: 7;
  } ;

  union {
    struct dt date_time;
    unsigned u;
  } d;

  unsigned t;
  int fd;

  if(_dos_open("TEST.TST", O_RDONLY, &fd)) {
    printf("Cannot open file.\n");
    exit(1);
  }
```

```
  _dos_getftime(fd, &d.u, &t);
  d.date_time.year = 20;

  _dos_setftime(fd, d.u, t);

  return 0;
}
```

Related Function

_dos_getftime( )

void _dos_setvect(unsigned intr, void interrupt (far *isr)( ))

Description

The prototype for **_dos_setvect( )** is in **dos.h**. This function is not defined by the ANSI C standard.

The **_dos_setvect( )** puts the address of the interrupt service routine pointed to by *isr* into the vectored interrupt table at the location specified by *intr.*

Because of the specialized nature of rerouting interrupt vectors, no example is shown.

Related Function

getvect( )

long dostounix(struct date *d, struct time *t)

Description

The prototype for **dostounix( )** is in **dos.h**. This function is not defined by the ANSI C standard.

The function **dostounix( )** returns the system time as returned by **gettime( )** and **getdate( )** into a form compatible with the UNIX time format, which is also compatible with the ANSI standard's format.

Example

See **getdate( )** for an example.

Related Functions

unixtodos( ), ctime( ), time( )

unsigned _dos_write(int fd, void far *buf, unsigned count, unsigned *numwritten)

Description

The prototype for **_dos_write( )** is in **dos.h**. This function is not defined by the ANSI C standard.

The **_dos_write( )** function writes up to *count* bytes to the file specified by the file descriptor *fd* from the buffer pointed to by *buf*. The number of bytes actually written are returned in *numwritten,* which may be less than requested if the disk becomes full. All files are treated as binary and no character translations will occur.

Upon success, **_dos_write( )** returns 0; it returns non-0 on failure. The return value is determined by DOS and you will need DOS technical documentation to determine the nature of the error, if one should occur. Also, if an error occurs, **errno** will be set to either **EACCES** (Access denied) or **EBADF** (Bad file handle).

Example

This fragment writes 128 characters from the file described by *fd*:

```
int fd;
unsigned count
char *buf[128];
.
.
.
if(_dos_write(fd, buf, 128, &count))
  printf("Error writing file.");
```

Related Function

_dos_read( )

void enable(void)
void _enable(void)

Description

The prototypes for **enable( )** and **_enable( )** are in **dos.h**. These functions are not defined by the ANSI C standard.

The **enable( )** and **_enable( )** functions enable interrupts.

Related Functions

disable( ), geninterrupt( )

unsigned FP_OFF(void far *ptr)
unsigned FP_SEG(void far *ptr)

Description

The prototypes for **FP_OFF( )** and **FP_SEG( )** are in **dos.h**. These macros are not defined by the ANSI C standard.

The **FP_OFF( )** macro returns the offset portion of the far pointer *ptr*. The **FP_SEG( )** macro returns the segment of the far pointer *ptr*.

Example

This program prints the segment and offset of the far pointer **ptr**:

```
#include <stdio.h>
#include <dos.h>
#include <stdlib.h>

int main(void)
{
  char far *ptr;

  ptr = (char far *) malloc(100);

  printf("segment:offset of ptr: %u %u", FP_SEG(ptr),
         FP_OFF(ptr));

  return 0;
}
```

Related Function

MK_FP( )

void ftime(struct timeb *time)

Description

The prototype for **ftime( )** is in **sys\timeb.h**. This function is not defined by the ANSI C standard.

The **ftime( )** function fills the **timeb** structure with system time information. Specifically, it retrieves the elapsed time in seconds since January 1, 1970 (GMT), the fractional part of any elapsed second in milliseconds, the difference between GMT and local time in minutes, and whether daylight saving time is in effect.

The **timeb** structure looks like this:

```
struct timeb {
  long time; /* time in seconds from Jan. 1, 1970 */
  short millitm; /* milliseconds */
  short timezone; /* difference between GMT and local time */
  short dstflag; /* non-0 if daylight saving time is in effect */
};
```

Example

This program displays the number of seconds that have elapsed since January 1, 1970, Greenwich mean time:

```
#include <stdio.h>
#include <sys\timeb.h>

int main(void)
{
  struct timeb lt;

  ftime(&lt);
  printf("%ld seconds %d milliseconds.",lt.time,lt.millitm);
  return 0;
}
```

Related Functions

localtime( ), gmtime( ), ctime( ), asctime( )

void geninterrupt(int intr)

Description

The prototype for **geninterrupt( )** is in **dos.h**. This function is not defined by the ANSI C standard.

The **geninterrupt( )** macro generates a software interrupt. The number of the interrupt generated is determined by the value of *intr.*

Example

This generates interrupt 5, the print screen function:

```
#include <dos.h>

int main(void)
{
  geninterrupt(5); /* print screen function */
  return 0;
}
```

Related Functions

enable( ), disable( )

int getcbrk(void)

Description

The prototype for **getcbrk( )** is in **dos.h**. This function is not defined by the ANSI C standard.

The **getcbrk( )** function returns 0 if extended control-break checking is off and 1 if extended control-break checking is on. When extended control-break checking is off, the only time DOS checks to see if the CTRL-BRK key combination has been pressed is when console, printer, or auxiliary communication devices are performing I/O operations. When the extended checking is on, the control-break combination is checked for by each DOS call.

Example

This prints the current state of control-break checking:

```
printf("The current cbrk setting is %d", getcbrk());
```

Related Function

setcbrk( )

void getdate(struct date *d)
void gettime(struct time *t)

Description

The prototypes for **getdate( )** and **gettime( )** are in **dos.h**. These functions are not defined by the ANSI C standard.

The **getdate( )** function fills the **date** structure pointed to by *d* with the DOS form of the current system date. The **gettime( )** function fills the **time** structure pointed to by *t* with the DOS form of the current system time.

Example

This converts the DOS version of time and date into the form that can be used by the standard ANSI C time and date routines and displays the time and date on the screen:

```
#include <stdio.h>
#include <time.h>
#include <dos.h>

int main(void)
```

```
{
  time_t t;
  struct time dos_time;
  struct date dos_date;
  struct tm *local;

  getdate(&dos_date);
  gettime(&dos_time);

  t = dostounix(&dos_date, &dos_time);
  local = localtime(&t);
  printf("time and date: %s", asctime(local));

  return 0;
}
```

Related Functions

settime( ), setdate( )

void getdfree(unsigned char drive, struct dfree *dfptr)

Description

The prototype for **getdfree( )** is in **dos.h**. This function is not defined by the ANSI C standard.

The **getdfree( )** function assigns information about the amount of free disk space to the structure pointed to by *dfptr* for the drive specified by *drive*. The drives are numbered from 1 beginning with drive A. You can specify the default drive by calling **getdfree( )** with a value of 0. The **dfree** structure is defined like this:

```
struct dfree {
  unsigned df_avail; /* unused clusters */
  unsigned df_total; /* total number of clusters */
  unsigned df_bsec;  /* number of bytes per sector */
  unsigned df_sclus; /* number of sectors per cluster */
};
```

If an error occurs, the **df_sclus** field is set to –1.

Example

This program prints the number of free clusters available for use on drive C:

```
#include <stdio.h>
#include <dos.h>
```

```
int main(void)
{
  struct dfree p;

  getdfree(3, &p); /* drive C */

  printf("Number of free clusters is %d.", p.df_avail);

  return 0;
}
```

Related Functions
getfat( ), _dos_getdiskfree( )

char far *getdta(void)

Description
The prototype for **getdta( )** is in **dos.h**. This function is not defined by the ANSI C standard.

The **getdta( )** function returns a pointer to the disk transfer address (DTA). A **far** pointer is returned because you cannot assume, in all circumstances, that the disk transfer address will be located within the data segment of your program.

Example
This assigns the DTA to the **far** pointer **ptr**:

```
char far *ptr;

ptr = getdta();
```

Related Function
setdta( )

void getfat(unsigned char drive, struct fatinfo *fptr)
void getfatd(struct fatinfo *fptr)

Description
The prototypes for **getfat( )** and **getfatd( )** are in **dos.h**. These functions are not defined by the ANSI C standard.

The **getfat( )** function returns various information about the disk in *drive*, which is gathered from that drive's file allocation table (FAT). If the value of *drive* is 0, the default drive is used. Otherwise, 1 is used for drive A, 2 for B, and so on. The structure pointed to by *fptr* is loaded with the information from the FAT. The structure **fatinfo** is defined as

```
struct fatinfo {
  char fi_sclus;      /* number of sectors per cluster */
  char fi_fatid;      /* FAT ID */
  unsigned fi_nclus; /* total number of clusters */
  int fi_bysec;       /* number of bytes per sector */
};
```

The **getfatd( )** function is the same as **getfat( )**, except that the default drive is always used.

Example

This program displays the total storage capacity, in bytes, of the default drive:

```
#include <stdio.h>
#include <dos.h>

int main(void)
{
  long total;
  struct fatinfo p;

  getfat(0, &p);

  total = (long) p.fi_sclus * (long) p.fi_nclus *
          (long) p.fi_bysec;

  printf("Total storage capacity: %ld.", total);

  return 0;
}
```

Related Function

getdfree( )

int getftime(int handle, struct ftime *ftptr)

Description

The prototype for **getftime( )** is in **io.h**. This function is not defined by the ANSI C standard.

The function **getftime( )** returns time and date of creation for the file associated with *handle*. The information is loaded into the structure pointed to by *ftptr*. The bit-field structure **ftime** is defined like this:

```
struct ftime {
  unsigned ft_tsec:  5; /* seconds */
  unsigned ft_min:   6; /* minutes */
  unsigned ft_hour:  5; /* hours */
  unsigned ft_day:   5; /* days */
  unsigned ft_month: 4; /* month */
  unsigned ft_year:  7; /* year from 1980 */
};
```

The **getftime( )** function returns 0 if successful. If an error occurs, –1 is returned and **errno** is set to **EINVFNC** (invalid function number), **EBADF** (bad file number), or **EACCES** (access denied).

Example

This program prints the year the file TEST.TST was created:

```
#include <stdio.h>
#include <io.h>
#include <dos.h>
#include <fcntl.h>
#include <stdlib.h>

int main(void)
{
  struct ftime p;
  int fd;

  if((fd=open("TEST.TST", O_RDONLY))==-1) {
    printf("Cannot open file.\n");
   exit(1);
  }

  getftime(fd, &p);

  printf("%d", p.ft_year + 1980);

  return 0;
}
```

Related Functions

open( ), _dos_open( )

unsigned getpsp(void)

Description

The prototype for **getpsp( )** is in **dos.h**. This function is not defined by the ANSI C standard.

The **getpsp( )** function returns the segment of the program segment prefix (PSP). This function works only with DOS version 3.0 or later.

The PSP is also set in the global variable **_psp**, which may be used with versions of DOS more recent than 2.0.

Related Function

biosdisk( )

void interrupt(*getvect(int intr))( )

Description

The prototype for **getvect( )** is in **dos.h**. This function is not defined by the ANSI C standard.

The **getvect( )** function returns the address of the interrupt service routine associated with the interrupt specified in *intr*. This value is returned as a **far** pointer.

Example

This fragment returns the address of the print screen function, which is associated with interrupt 5:

```
void interrupt (*p)(void);

p = getvect(5);
```

Related Function

setvect( )

int getverify(void)

Description

The prototype for **getverify( )** is in **dos.h**. This function is not defined by the ANSI C standard.

The **getverify( )** function returns the status of the DOS verify flag. When this flag is on, all disk writes are verified against the output buffer to ensure that the data was properly written. If the verify flag is off, no verification is performed.

If the verify flag is off, 0 is returned; otherwise, 1 is returned.

Example

This program prints the value of the DOS verify flag:

```
#include <stdio.h>
#include <dos.h>

int main(void)
{
  printf("The verify flag is set to %d.", getverify());

  return 0;
}
```

Related Function

setverify( )

struct tm *gmtime(const time_t *time)

Description

The prototype for **gmtime( )** is in **time.h**.

The **gmtime( )** function returns a pointer to the broken-down form of *time* in the form of a **tm** structure. The time is represented in Greenwich mean time. The *time* value is generally obtained through a call to **time( )**.

The structure used by **gmtime( )** to hold the broken-down time is statically allocated and is overwritten each time the function is called. If you wish to save the contents of the structure, it is necessary to copy it elsewhere.

Example

This program prints both the local time and the Greenwich mean time of the system:

```
#include <stdio.h>
#include <time.h>
#include <stddef.h>

/* print local and GM time */
int main(void)
{
  struct tm *local, *gm;
  time_t t;

  t = time(NULL);
  local = localtime(&t);
```

```
  printf("Local time and date: %s", asctime(local));
  gm = gmtime(&t);
  printf("Greenwich mean time and date: %s", asctime(gm));

  return 0;
}
```

Related Functions

localtime( ), time( ), asctime( )

void harderr(int (*handler)( ))
void _harderr(int (far *handler)( ))
void hardresume(int code)
void _hardresume(int code)
void hardretn(int code)
void _hardretn(int code)

Description

The prototypes for **harderr( )**, **_harderr( )**, **hardresume( )**, **_hardresume( )**, **hardretn( )**, and **_hardretn( )** are in **dos.h**. These functions are not defined by the ANSI C standard.

The functions **harderr( )** and **_harderr( )** allow you to replace DOS's default hardware error handler with one of your own. The function is called with the address of the function that is to become the new error-handling routine. It will be executed each time an interrupt 0x24 occurs.

For **harderrr( )**, the error-handling function pointed to by *handler* must have the following prototype:

void *err_handler*(int *errnum*, int *ax*, int *bp*, int *si*);

Here, *errnum* is DOS's error code and *ax*, *bp*, and *si* contain the values of the AX, BP, and SI registers. If *ax* is nonnegative, a disk error has occurred. When this is the case, ANDing *ax* with 0xFF yields the number of the drive that failed with drive A being equal to 0. If *ax* is negative, a device failed. You must consult a DOS technical reference guide for complete interpretation of the error codes. The *bp* and *si* registers contain the address of the device driver for the device that sustained the error.

When using **_harderr( )**, the error handler pointed to by *handler* must be a FAR function and have this prototype:

void far *err_handler*(unsigned *err*, unsigned *errnum*, unsigned far **devptr*)

Here, *err* receives a code that indicates what device has failed. If *err* is nonnegative, a disk error has occurred. When this is the case, ANDing *err* with 0xFF yields the number of the drive that failed with drive A being equal to 0. If *err* is negative, a device failed. You must consult a DOS technical reference guide for complete interpretation of the error codes. The *errnum* value is the actual device error code passed to the handler. The contents of *devptr* contain the address of the device driver that sustained the error.

There are two very important rules that you must follow when creating your own error handlers. First, the interrupt handler must not use any of the standard or UNIX-like I/O functions. Attempting to do so will crash the computer. Second, you may use only DOS calls numbers 1 through 12.

The error interrupt handler can exit in one of two ways. First, the **hardresume( )** (and **_hardresume( )**) function causes the handler to exit to DOS, returning the value of *code*. Second, the handler can return to the program via a call to **hardretn( )** (or **_hardretn( )**) with a return value of *code*. For **hardresume( )** and **_hardresume( )**, the value returned must be one of the following. (The macro equivalents are defined in **dos.h**.)

Value	Macro	Meaning
0	_HARDERR_IGNORE	Ignore
1	_HARDERR_RETRY	Retry
2	_HARDERR_ABORT	Abort
3	_HARDERR_FAIL	Fail

Due to the complex nature of interrupt service functions, no example is shown.

Related Function

geninterrupt( )

int inp(unsigned port)
int inport(int port)
unsigned inpw(unsigned port)
unsigned char inportb(int port)

Description

The prototypes for **inp( )**, **inport( )**, **inpw( )**, and **inportb( )** are in **dos.h**. These functions are not defined by the ANSI C standard.

The **inport( )** and **inpw( )** functions return the word value read from the port specified in *port*.

The **inportb( )** and **inp( )** macros return a byte read from the specified port.

Example

The following fragment reads a word from port 1:

```
unsigned int i;

i = inport(1);
```

Related Functions

outport( ), outportb( ), outp( ), outpw( )

int int86(int int_num, union REGS *in_regs, union REGS *out_regs)
int int86x(int int_num, union REGS *in_regs, union REGS *out_regs, struct SREGS *segregs)

Description

The prototypes for **int86( )** and **int86x( )** are in **dos.h**. These functions are not defined by the ANSI C standard.

The **int86( )** function is used to execute a software interrupt specified by *int_num*. The contents of the union *in_regs* are first copied into the registers of the processor and then the proper interrupt is executed.

Upon return, the union *out_regs* contains the values of the registers that the CPU has upon return from the interrupt. If the carry flag is set, an error has occurred. The value of the AX register is returned.

The **int86x( )** copies the values of *segregs–>ds* into the DS register and *segregs–>es* into the ES register. This allows programs compiled for the large data model to specify which segments to use during the interrupt.

REGS and **SREGS** are defined in the header **dos.h**.

Example

The **int86( )** function is often used to call ROM routines in the PC. For example, this function executes an INT 0x10, function code 0, that causes the video mode to be set to the value specified by the argument **mode**:

```
#include <dos.h>

/* Set the video mode */
void set_mode(char mode)
{
  union REGS in, out;

  in.h.al = mode;
```

```
  in.h.ah = 0;  /* set mode function number */

  int86(0x10, &in, &out);
}
```

Related Functions

intdos( ), bdos( )

int intdos(union REGS *in_regs, union REGS *out_regs)
int intdosx(union REGS *in_regs, union REGS *out_regs, struct SREGS *segregs)

Description

The prototypes for **intdos( )** and **intdosx( )** are in **dos.h**. These functions are not defined by the ANSI C standard.

The **intdos( )** function is used to access the DOS system call specified by the contents of the union pointed to by *in_regs*. It executes an INT 0x21 instruction and places the outcome of the operation in the union pointed to by *out_regs*. The **intdos( )** function returns the value of the AX register that is used by DOS to return information. Upon return, if the carry flag is set, an error has occurred.

The **intdos( )** function is used to access those system calls that either require arguments in registers other than only DX and/or AL or that return information in a register other than AX.

The union **REGS** defines the registers of the 8088/86 family of processors and is found in the **dos.h** header file.

For **intdosx( )**, the value of *segregs* specifies the DS and ES registers. This is principally for use in programs compiled using the large data models.

Example

This program reads the time directly from the system clock, bypassing all of C's time functions:

```
#include <stdio.h>
#include <dos.h>

int main(void)
{
  union REGS in, out;

  in.h.ah = 0x2c;  /* get time function number */
```

```
  intdos(&in, &out);
  printf("time is %.2d:%.2d:%.2d", out.h.ch, out.h.cl, out.h.dh);

  return 0;
}
```

Related Functions

bdos( ), int86( )

void intr(int intr_num, struct REGPACK *reg)

Description

The prototype for **intr( )** is in **dos.h**. This function is not defined by the ANSI C standard.

The **intr( )** function executes the software interrupt specified by *intr_num*. It provides an alternative to the **int86( )** function, but does not contain any expanded functionality.

The values of the registers in the structure pointed to by *reg* are copied into the CPU registers before the interrupt occurs. After the interrupt returns, the structure contains the values of the registers as set by the interrupt service routine. The structure **REGPACK** is defined as shown here:

```
struct REGPACK {
  unsigned r_ax, r_bx, r_cx, r_dx;
  unsigned r_bp, r_si, r_di, r_ds, r_es;
  unsigned r_flags;
};
```

Any registers not used by the interrupt are ignored.

Example

This program prints the screen using interrupt 5, the print screen interrupt:

```
/* Print the screen. */
#include <dos.h>

int main(void)
{
  struct REGPACK r;

  intr(5, &r);

  return 0;
}
```

Related Functions

int86( ), intdos( )

int ioctl(int device, int cmd, void *dx, void *cx)

Description

The prototype for **ioctl( )** is in **io.h**. This function is not defined by the ANSI C standard.

The **ioctl( )** function is essentially a UNIX-based function that Borland compilers include for compatibility, although the parameters supported by Borland are not portable to UNIX or vice versa. It executes a call to DOS function 0x44, which controls the device specified by *device*. Refer to a DOS technical reference manual for details of its operation.

The function returns the outcome of the 0x44 DOS function.

int kbhit(void)

Description

The prototype for **kbhit( )** is in **conio.h**. This function is not defined by the ANSI C standard.

The **kbhit( )** function returns true if a key has been pressed on the keyboard. It returns 0 otherwise. In no situation is the key removed from the input buffer.

Example

This fragment loops until a key is pressed:

```
while(!kbhit());  /* wait for keypress */
```

Related Functions

bioskey( ), _bios_keybrd( )

void keep(unsigned char status, unsigned size)
void _dos_keep(unsigned char status, unsigned size)

Description

The prototypes for **keep( )** and **_dos_keep( )** are in **dos.h**. These functions are not defined by the ANSI C standard.

The **keep( )** and **_dos_keep( )** functions execute an interrupt 0x31, which causes the current program to terminate, but stay resident. The value of *status* is returned to DOS as a return code. The size of the program that is to stay resident is specified in *size*. The rest of the memory is freed for use by DOS.

Because the subject of TSR programs is quite complex, no example is presented here.

Related Function

geninterrupt( )

struct tm *localtime(const time_t *time)

Description

The prototype for **localtime( )** is in **time.h**

The **localtime( )** function returns a pointer to the broken-down form of *time* in the form of a **tm** structure. The time is represented in local time. The *time* value is generally obtained through a call to **time( )**.

The structure used by **localtime( )** to hold the broken-down time is statically allocated and is overwritten each time the function is called. To save the contents of the structure, it is necessary to copy it elsewhere.

Example

This program prints both the local time and the Greenwich mean time of the system:

```
#include <stdio.h>
#include <time.h>
#include <stddef.h>

/* Print local and Greenwich mean time. */
int main(void)
{
  struct tm *local, *gm;
  time_t t;

  t = time(NULL);
  local = localtime(&t);
  printf("Local time and date: %s", asctime(local));
  gm = gmtime(&t);
  printf("Greenwich mean time and date: %s", asctime(gm));

  return 0;
}
```

Related Functions

gmtime( ), time( ), asctime( )

time_t mktime(struct tm *p)

Description

The prototype for **mktime( )** is in **time.h**.

The **mktime( )** function converts the time pointed to by *p* into calendar time.

The **mktime( )** returns the time as a value of type **time_t**. If no time information is available, then –1 is returned.

Example

This program displays the day of the week for the given year, month, and day:

```
#include <stdio.h>
#include <time.h>

int main(void)
{
  struct tm t;

  t.tm_year = 90;  /* year 1990    */
  t.tm_mon  =  1;  /* month - 1 */
  t.tm_mday =  7;
  mktime(&t);
  printf("The day of the week is %d", t.tm_wday);

  return 0;
}
```

Related Functions

localtime( ), **time( )**, **asctime( )**

void far *MK_FP(unsigned seg, unsigned off)

Description

The prototype for **MK_FP( )** is in **dos.h**. This macro is not defined by the ANSI C standard.

The **MK_FP( )** macro returns a **far** pointer given the segment *seg* and the offset *off*.

Example

This returns the appropriate **far** pointer given a segment value of 16 and an offset of 101:

```
void far *p;

p = MK_FP(16, 101);
```

Related Functions

FP_OFF( ), FP_SEG( )

void outport(int port, int word)
unsigned outpw(unsigned port, unsigned word)
void outportb(int port, unsigned char byte)
int outp(unsigned port, int byte)

Description

The prototypes for **outport( )**, **outpw( )**, **outportb( )**, and **outp( )** and are in **dos.h**. These functions are not defined by the ANSI C standard.

The **outport( )** and **outpw( )** functions output the value of *word* to the port specified in *port*.

The macros **outportb( )** and **outp( )** output the specified *byte* to the specified *port*.

The **outp( )** and **outpw( )** functions return the value sent to the port.

Example

This fragment writes the value 0xFF to port 0x10:

```
outport(0x10, 0xFF);
```

Related Functions

inport( ), inportb( ), inp( ), inpw( )

char *parsfnm(const char *fname, struct fcb *fcbptr, int option)

Description

The prototype for **parsfnm( )** is in **dos.h**. This function is not defined by the ANSI C standard.

The **parsfnm( )** function converts a file name contained in a string pointed to by *fname* into the form required by the file control block (FCB) and places it into the one pointed to by *fcbptr*. This function is frequently used with command-line arguments.

The function uses DOS function 0x29. The *option* parameter is used to set the AL register prior to the call to DOS. Refer to a DOS programmer's manual for complete information on the 0x29 function. The **fcb** structure is defined as

```
struct  fcb  {
  char fcb_drive;      /* Drive: 0 = default, 1 = A, 2 = B */
  char fcb_name[8];    /* Filename */
  char fcb_ext[3];     /* File extension */
  short fcb_curblk;    /* Number of block */
  short fcb_recsize;   /* Size of logical record in bytes */
  long fcb_filsize;    /* Size of file in bytes */
  short fcb_date;      /* Date of last write */
  char fcb_resv[10];   /* Reserved */
  char fcb_currec;     /* Record currently in block */
  long fcb_random;     /* Random record number */
};
```

If the call to **parsfnm( )** is successful, a pointer to the next byte after the file name is returned. If there is an error, 0 is returned.

Related Function

fopen( )

int peek(unsigned seg, unsigned offset)
char peekb(unsigned seg, unsigned offset)
void poke(unsigned seg, unsigned offset, int word)
void pokeb(unsigned seg, unsigned offset, char byte)

Description

The prototypes for **peek( )**, **peekb( )**, **poke( )**, and **pokeb( )** are in **dos.h**. These macros are not defined by the ANSI C standard.

The **peek( )** macro returns the 16-bit value at the location in memory pointed to by *seg:offset*.

The **peekb( )** macro returns the 8-bit value at the location in memory pointed to by *seg:offset*.

The **poke( )** macro stores the 16-bit value of *word* at the address pointed to by *seg:offset*.

The **pokeb( )** macro stores the 8-bit value of *byte* at the address pointed to by *seg:offset*.

Example

The following program displays the value of the byte stored at location 0000:0100.

```
#include <stdio.h>
#include <dos.h>

int main(void)
{
  printf("%d", peekb(0, 0x0100));
  return 0;
}
```

Related Functions

FP_OFF( ), FP_SEG( ), MK_FP( )

int randbrd(struct fcb *fcbptr, int count)
int randbwr(struct fcb *fcbptr, int count)

Description

The prototypes for **randbrd( )** and **randbwr( )** are in **dos.h**. These functions are not defined by the ANSI C standard.

The **randbrd( )** function reads *count* number of records into the memory at the current disk transfer address. The actual records read are determined by the values of the structure pointed to by *fcbptr.* The **fcb** structure is defined as

```
struct  fcb  {
  char fcb_drive;      /* Drive: 0 = default, 1 = A, 2 = B */
  char fcb_name[8];    /* Filename */
  char fcb_ext[3];     /* File extension */
  short fcb_curblk;    /* Number of block */
  short fcb_recsize;   /* Size of logical record in bytes */
  long fcb_filsize;    /* Size of file in bytes */
  short fcb_date;      /* Date of last write */
  char fcb_resv[10];   /* Reserved */
  char fcb_currec;     /* Record currently in block */
  long fcb_random;     /* Random record number */
};
```

The **randbrd( )** function uses DOS function 0x27 to accomplish its operation. Refer to a DOS programmer's guide for details.

The **randbwr( )** function writes *count* records to the file associated with the **fcb** structure pointed to by *fcbptr*. The **randbwr( )** uses DOS function 0x28 to accomplish its operation. Refer to a DOS programmer's guide for details.

The following values are returned by the functions.

Value	Meaning
0	All records successfully transferred.
1	EOF encountered but the last record transferred is complete.
2	Too many records, but those records transferred are complete.
3	EOF encountered and the last record is incomplete. (Applies to **randbrd( )** only.)

Related Function

parsfnm( )

void segread(struct SREGS *sregs)

Description

The prototype for **segread( )** is in **dos.h**. This function is not defined by the ANSI C standard.

The **segread( )** function copies the current values of the segment registers into the structure of type **SREGS** pointed to by *sregs*. This function is intended for use by the **intdosx( )** and **int86x( )** functions. Refer to these functions for further information.

int setcbrk(int cb)

Description

The prototype for **setcbrk( )** is in **dos.h**. This function is not defined by the ANSI C standard.

The **setcbrk( )** function turns extended control-break checking on and off. If *cb* is 1, extended control-break checking is turned on; if it is 0, extended control-break checking is turned off. When extended control-break checking is off, the only time DOS checks to see if the CTRL-BRK key combination has been pressed is when performing standard I/O operations. When extended checking is on, the control-break combination is checked for each time a DOS function is accessed.

The **setcbrk( )** function returns *cb*.

Example

This program toggles extended control-break checking:

```
#include <stdio.h>
#include <dos.h>

int main(void)
```

```
{
  if (getcbrk() == 0)
     setcbrk(1);
  else
     setcbrk(0);

  printf("BREAK is %s", (getcbrk()) ? "on" : "off");
  return 0;
}
```

Related Functions

getcbrk( ), enable( ), disable( )

void setdate(struct date *d)
void settime(struct time *t)

Description

The prototypes for **setdate( )** and **settime( )** are in **dos.h**. These functions are not defined by the ANSI C standard.

The **setdate( )** function sets the DOS system date as specified in the structure pointed to by *d*. The **settime( )** function sets the DOS system time as specified in the structure pointed to by *t*.

Example

The following program sets the system time to 10:10:10.0.

```
struct time t;

t.ti_hour = 10;
t.ti_min  = 10;
t.ti_sec  = 10;
t.ti_hund = 0;

settime(&t);
```

Related Functions

gettime( ), getdate( )

void setdta(char far *dta)

Description

The prototype for **setdta( )** is in **dos.h**. This function is not defined by the ANSI C standard.

The **setdta( )** function sets the disk transfer address (DTA) to that specified by *dta.*

Example

The following fragment sets the disk transfer address to location A000:0000.

```
char far *p;

p = MK_FP(0xA000, 0)
setdta(p);
```

Related Function

getdta( )

int setftime(int handle, struct ftime *t)

Description

The prototype to **setftime( )** is found in **io.h**. This function is not defined by the ANSI C standard.

The **setftime( )** function is used to set the date and time associated with a disk file. It changes the date and time of the file linked to *handle* using the information found in the structure pointed to by *t*. The **ftime** structure is shown here:

```
struct ftime {
  unsigned ft_tsec:  5; /* seconds */
  unsigned ft_min:   6; /* minutes */
  unsigned ft_hour:  5; /* hours */
  unsigned ft_day:   5; /* days */
  unsigned ft_month: 4; /* month */
  unsigned ft_year:  7; /* year from 1980 */
}
```

Since a file's date and time are generally used to indicate the time of the file's last modification, you should use **setftime( )** carefully.

If **setftime( )** is successful, 0 is returned. If an error occurs, –1 is returned and **errno** is set to one of the following:

Value	Meaning
EINVFNC	Invalid function number
EACCES	Access denied
EBADF	Bad file handle

Example

This line of code sets the file to the date and time specified in the **ftime** structure:

```
setftime(fd, &t);
```

Related Function

getftime( )

void setvect(int intr, void interrupt(*isr)( ))

Description

The prototype for **setvect( )** is in **dos.h**. This function is not defined by the ANSI C standard.

The **setvect( )** function puts the address of the interrupt service routine, pointed to by *isr*, into the vectored interrupt table at the location specified by *intr*.

Related Function

getvect( )

void setverify(int value)

Description

The prototype for **setverify( )** is in **dos.h**. This function is not defined by the ANSI C standard.

The **setverify( )** function sets the state of the DOS verify flag. When this flag is on, all disk writes are verified against the output buffer to ensure that the data was properly written. If the verify flag is off, no verification is performed.

To turn on the verify flag, call **setverify( )** with *value* set to 1. Set *value* to 0 to turn it off.

Example

This program turns on the DOS verify flag:

```
#include <stdio.h>
#include <dos.h>

int main(void)
{
  printf("Turning the verify flag on.");
  setverify(1);

  return 0;
}
```

Related Function

getverify( )

void sleep(unsigned time)

Description

The prototype for **sleep( )** is in **dos.h**. This function is not defined by the ANSI C standard.

The **sleep( )** function suspends program execution for *time* number of seconds.

Example

This program waits 10 seconds between messages:

```
#include <stdio.h>
#include <dos.h>

int main(void)
{
  printf("hello");

  sleep(10);

  printf(" there");

  return 0;
}
```

Related Functions

time( ), delay( )

int stime(time_t *t)

Description

The prototype for **stime( )** is in **time.h**. This function is not defined by the ANSI C standard.

The **stime( )** function sets the current system time to the value pointed to by *t*. This value must specify the time as the number of seconds since January 1, 1970, Greenwich mean time.

The **stime( )** function always returns 0.

Example

This program sets the time to January 1, 1970:

```
#include <stdio.h>
#include <time.h>

int main(void)
{
  time_t t;

  t = 0;
  stime(&t);
  return 0;
}
```

Related Functions

settime( ), gettime( ), time( )

char *_strdate(char *buf)
char *_strtime(char *buf)

Description

The prototypes for **_strdate( )** and **_strtime( )** are in **time.h**. These functions are not defined by the ANSI C standard.

The **_strdate( )** function converts the system date into a string and copies it into the character array pointed to by *buf*. The date will have the form *MM/DD/YY*. The array pointed to by *buf* must be at least 9 characters long. **_strdate( )** returns *buf*.

The **_strtime( )** function converts the system time into a string and copies it into the array pointed to *buf*. The time will have this form: *HH:MM:SS*. The array pointed to by *buf* must be at least 9 characters long. **_strtime( )** returns a pointer to *buf*.

Example

This program displays the current system time and date:

```
#include <stdio.h>
#include <time.h>

int main(void)
{
  char str[9];

  _strtime(str);
  printf("Time: %s", str);

  _strdate(str);
```

```
  printf(", Date: %s", str);

  return 0;
}
```

Related Functions

time( ), clock( )

size_t strftime(char *str, size_t maxsize, char const *fmt, const struct tm *time)

Description

The prototype for **strftime( )** is in **time.h**. It stores time and date information, along with other information, into the string pointed to by *str* according to the format commands found in the string pointed to by *fmt* and using the time specified in *time.* A maximum of *maxsize* characters will be placed into *str.*

The **strftime( )** function works a little like **sprintf( )** in that it recognizes a set of format commands that begin with the percent sign (%) and it places its formatted output into a string. The format commands are used to specify the exact way various time and date information is represented in *str.* Any other characters found in the format string are placed into *str* unchanged. The time and date displayed are in local time. The format commands are shown in Table 14-1. Notice that many of the commands are case sensitive.

The **strftime( )** function returns the number of characters placed in the string pointed to by *str,* or 0 if an error occurs.

Example

Assuming that **ltime** points to a structure that contains 10:00:00 AM, Jan 2, 1994, then this fragment will print "It is now 10 AM".

```
strftime(str, 100, "It is now %H %p", ltime)
printf(str);
```

Related Functions

time( ), localtime( ), gmtime( )

time_t time(time_t *time)

Description

The prototype for **time( )** is in **time.h**.

The **time( )** function returns the current calendar time of the system.

Command	Replaced By
%a	Abbreviated weekday name
%A	Full weekday name
%b	Abbreviated month name
%B	Full month name
%c	Standard date and time string
%d	Day-of-month as decimal (1–31)
%H	Hour, range (0–23)
%I	Hour, range (1–12)
%j	Day-of-year as decimal (1–366)
%m	Month as decimal (1–12)
%M	Minute as decimal (0–59)
%p	Locale's equivalent of AM or PM
%S	Second as decimal (0–61)
%U	Week-of-year, Sunday being first day (0–52)
%w	Weekday as decimal (0–6, Sunday being 0)
%W	Week-of-year, Monday being first day (0–53)
%x	Standard date string
%X	Standard time string
%y	Year in decimal without century (00–99)
%Y	Year including century as decimal
%Z	Time zone name
%%	The percent sign

Table 14-1. *The ANSI-Defined* strftime( ) *Format Commands*

The **time( )** function can be called either with a null pointer or with a pointer to a variable of type **time_t**. If the latter is used, then the argument is also assigned the calendar time.

Example

This program displays the local time defined by the system:

```
#include <stdio.h>
#include <time.h>

int main(void)
{
  struct tm *ptr;
  time_t lt;

  lt = time(NULL);
  ptr = localtime(&lt);
  printf(asctime(ptr));

  return 0;
}
```

Related Functions

localtime( ), gmtime( ), strftime( ), ctime( )

void tzset(void)

Description

The prototype for **tzset( )** is in **time.h**. This function is not defined by the ANSI C standard.

The **tzset( )** function sets Borland C++'s built-in variables **_daylight** (daylight saving time indicator), **_timezone** (time zone number), and **_tzname** (time zone name) using the environmental variable **TZ**. Since the ANSI C standard time functions provide complete access and control over the system time and date, there is no reason to use **tzset( )**. The **tzset( )** function is included for UNIX compatibility.

void unixtodos(long utime, struct date *d, struct time *t)

Description

The prototype for **unixtodos( )** is in **dos.h**. This function is not defined by the ANSI C standard.

The **unixtodos( )** function converts the UNIX-like time format into a DOS format. The UNIX and ANSI standard time formats are the same. The *utime* argument holds the UNIX time format. The structures pointed to by *d* and *t* are loaded with the corresponding DOS date and time.

Example

This converts the time contained in **timeandday** into its corresponding DOS format:

```
struct time t;
struct date d;

unixtodos(timeandday, &d, &t)
```

Related Function

dostounix( )

Chapter Fifteen

Dynamic Allocation

There are two primary ways that your program can store information in the main memory of the computer. The first uses *global* and *local variables*—including arrays, structures, and classes. In the case of global and static local variables, the storage is fixed throughout the run time of your program. For local variables, storage is allocated on the stack. Although these variables are implemented efficiently in Borland C++, they require the programmer to know in advance the amount of storage needed for every situation.

The second way information can be stored is through the use of Borland C++'s dynamic allocation system. In this method, storage for information is allocated from the free memory area as it is needed and returned to free memory when it has served its purpose. The free memory region lies between your program's permanent storage area and the stack. This region, called the *heap,* is used to satisfy a dynamic allocation request.

One advantage to using dynamically allocated memory to hold data is that the same memory can be used for several different things in the course of a program's execution. Because memory can be allocated for one purpose and freed when that use has ended, it is possible for another part of the program to use the same memory for something else at a different time. Another advantage of dynamically allocated storage is that it enables the creation of linked lists, binary trees, and other dynamic data structures.

At the core of C's dynamic allocation system are the functions **malloc( )** and **free( )**, which are part of the standard library. Each time a **malloc( )** memory request is made, a portion of the remaining free memory is allocated. Each time a **free( )** memory release call is made, memory is returned to the system.

NOTE: C++ also defines two dynamic allocation operators called new and delete. These are discussed in Part 3 of this book. For C++ code, you will normally use the allocation operators and not the functions described in this chapter.

The ANSI C standard defines only four functions for the dynamic allocation system: **calloc( )**, **malloc( )**, **free( )**, and **realloc( )**. However, Borland C++ contains several other dynamic allocation functions. Some of these additional functions are necessary to support the segmented architecture of the 8086 family of processors when operating in 16-bit mode. (This is the mode used by DOS and Windows 3.1, for example.) The 16-bit, segmented memory model also requires three nonstandard pointer type modifiers called **near**, **far**, and **huge**. When compiling code for the modern, 32-bit model, memory is flat and you will normally use only the four standard allocation functions. (Memory models and pointer type modifiers are described in the following section.)

The ANSI C standard specifies that the header information necessary to its dynamic allocation functions is in **stdlib.h**. However, Borland C++ lets you use either **stdlib.h** or **alloc.h**. This guide uses **stdlib.h** because it is portable. Some of the other dynamic allocation functions require the headers **alloc.h**, **malloc.h**, or **dos.h**. You should pay special attention to which header file is used with each function.

Understanding Memory Models

As you may know, modern CPUs, such as the 80486 and Pentium, are enhanced and expanded versions of the 8086 processor. The 8086 is the 16-bit processor for which DOS was designed. All subsequent processors, including the newer 32-bit ones, have retained the 16-bit mode of operation for purposes of compatibility. Thus, modern 32-bit processors have two basic modes of operation: 32 bit and 16 bit.

When running in 32-bit mode, such as that used by Windows NT or Windows 95, the memory space is flat. That is, these operating systems use the *flat memory model*. In this model, addresses run smoothly and consecutively from zero to the top of whatever amount of memory is installed in the computer. Thus, memory is addressed as you would intuitively expect. However, this is not the case for 16-bit operation.

When operating in 16-bit, segmented mode (sometimes called DOS-compatibility mode), the 8086 family of processors view memory as a collection of 64K chunks, each called a *segment*. Each byte of memory is defined by its segment address (held in a segment register of the CPU) and its offset (held in another register) within that segment. Both the segment and offset use 16-bit values. When a memory address lies within the current segment, only the 16-bit offset need be loaded to specify that address. However, if the memory address lies outside the current segment, both the 16-bit segment and the 16-bit offset need to be loaded. Thus, when accessing memory within the current segment, the compiler can treat a pointer or a call or jump instruction as a 16-bit object. When accessing memory outside the current segment, the compiler must treat a pointer or call or jump instruction as a 32-bit entity.

When using the 16-bit segmented model, the value in the segment register is in units of 16 (or paragraphs). The offset is in units of bytes. Segmented addresses are written using this form: *seg:offset*. For example, 1FAB:0933. Here, the segment is 1FAB and the offset is 0933. As you might have surmised, there is not a one-to-one mapping of a location in memory to its segment:offset address. For example, 0000:0010 specifies the same location as 0001:0000. Forgetting this fact can lead to troubles.

Given the segmented nature of the 8086 family when operating in 16-bit compatibility mode, you can organize memory into one of these six models (shown in order of increasing execution time):

Model	Description
Tiny	All segment registers are set to the same value and all addressing is done using 16 bits. This means that the code, data, and stack must all fit within the same 64K segment. Fastest program execution.
Small	All code must fit in one 64K segment and all data must fit in a second 64K segment. All pointers are 16 bits. As fast as tiny model.
Medium	All data must fit in one 64K segment, but the code may use multiple segments. All pointers to data are 16 bits, but all jumps and calls require 32-bit addresses. Quick access to data, slower code execution.
Compact	All code must fit in one 64K segment, but the data may use multiple segments. However, no single static data item can exceed 64K. All pointers to data are 32 bits, but jumps and calls may use 16-bit addresses. Slow access to data, faster code execution.
Large	Both code and data may use multiple segments. All pointers are 32 bits. However, no single static data item can exceed 64K. Slower program execution.
Huge	Both code and data may use multiple segments. All pointers are 32 bits. A single static data item can exceed 64K. Slowest program execution.

As you might guess, it is much faster to access memory via 16-bit pointers rather than 32-bit pointers because half as many bits need to be loaded into the CPU for each memory reference.

far, near, and huge Pointers

Occasionally, you will need to use a pointer that is different from the default provided by the memory model you have choosen for your program. Borland C++ allows pointers of either 16 or 32 bits to be explicitly created by the program, thus overriding the default model. One way this occurs is when a program requires a lot of data for one specific operation. In such cases, a **far** pointer is created and the memory is allocated using a nonstandard version of **malloc( )** that allocates memory from outside the default data segment. In this way, all other memory accesses remain fast and execution time does not suffer as much as it would if a larger model were used. The reverse can also happen: A program that uses a larger model may establish a **near** pointer to a piece of frequently accessed memory to enhance performance. You may also declare **huge** pointers, which are essentially **far** pointers that are normalized for pointer comparisons. The **huge** modifier is used only for data, not for functions.

Be aware of potential problems with **far** pointers. First, pointer arithmetic affects only the offset and can cause "wraparound." This means that when a **far** pointer with the value 0000:FFFF is incremented, its new value will be 0000:0000, not 1000:0000. The value of the segment is never changed. Second, two **far** pointers should not be used in a relational expression because only their offsets will be checked. It is possible to have two different pointers actually point to the same physical address but have different segments and offsets. However, you can compare a **far** pointer against the null pointer. In general, if you need to compare **far** pointers, you must use **huge** pointers. **huge** pointers do not "wrap around" and are normalized to allow comparisons.

In Borland C++, **far** can also be specified as **_far** or **__far**, **near** can be specified as **_near** or **__near**, and **huge** can be specified as **_huge** or **__huge**.

Borland's Segment Specifiers

In addition to **far**, **near**, and **huge**, Borland C++ supports these four addressing modifiers: **_cs**, **_ds**, **_ss**, and **_es**. When these type modifiers are applied to a pointer's declaration they cause the pointer to become a 16-bit offset into the specified segment. That is, given this statement,

```
int _es *ptr;
```

ptr contains a 16-bit offset into the extra segment.

Borland C++ also includes the **_seg** modifier, which creates pointers that are 16 bits long and contain only the segment address. The offset is assumed to be 0. There are several restrictions to **_seg** pointers. You cannot increment or decrement them. In an expression that adds or subtracts an integer value from a **_seg** pointer, a **far** pointer is generated. When dereferencing a **_seg** pointer, it is converted into a **far** pointer. You can add a **near** pointer to a **_seg** pointer and the result is a **far** pointer.

Keep in mind that the **near**, **far**, **huge**, **_es**, **_cs**, **_ds**, **_ss**, and **_seg** modifiers are not defined by the ANSI C standard or by C++. Thus, they are not portable. Further, because nearly all new code is being written for the 32-bit, flat addressing model, the use of these modifiers will become increasingly rare. However, a large amount of legacy code still exists that uses the 16-bit segmented memory model.

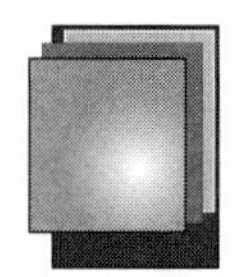

REMEMBER: The 16-bit, segmented memory models are becoming a thing of the past. Most new code that you write will use the 32-bit, flat addressing model.

void *alloca(size_t size)

Description

The prototype for **alloca( )** is in **malloc.h**. This function is not defined by the ANSI C standard.

The **alloca( )** function allocates *size* bytes of memory from the system stack (not the heap) and returns a character pointer to it. A null pointer is returned if the allocation request cannot be honored.

Memory allocated using **alloca( )** is automatically released when the function that called **alloca( )** returns. This means that you should never use a pointer generated by **alloca( )** as an argument to **free( )**.

NOTE: For technical reasons, to ensure that the stack is not corrupted, any function that executes a call to alloca( ) must contain at least one local variable that is assigned a value.

Example

The following allocates 80 bytes from the stack using **alloca( )**.

```
#include <malloc.h>
#include <stdio.h>
#include <stdlib.h>

int main(void)
{
  int i=10;
  char *str;

  if(!(str = (char *) alloca(80))) {
    printf("Allocation error.");
    exit(1);
  }
  /* ... */
  return 0;
}
```

Related Function

malloc( )

int allocmem(unsigned size, unsigned *seg)

Description

The prototype for **allocmem( )** is in **dos.h**. This function is not defined by the ANSI C standard.

The **allocmem( )** function executes a DOS 0x48 function call to allocate a paragraph-aligned block of memory. It puts the segment address of the block into the unsigned integer pointed to by *seg*. The *size* argument specifies the number of paragraphs to be allocated. (A paragraph is 16 bytes.)

If the requested memory can be allocated, a –1 is returned. If insufficient free memory exists, no assignment is made to the unsigned integer pointed to by *seg*, and the size of the largest available block is returned. Also, **errno** is set to **ENOMEM** (insufficient memory).

Example

This fragment allocates 100 paragraphs of memory:

```
unsigned i;
unsigned s;

i = 0;

if((i=allocmem(100, &s)==-1) printf("Allocation successful.");
else
  printf("Allocation failed, only %u paragraphs available.", i);
```

Related Functions

freemem( ), setblock( ), _dos _allocmem( )

int brk(void *eds)

Description

The prototype for **brk( )** is in **alloc.h**. This function is not defined by the ANSI C standard.

The **brk( )** function dynamically changes the amount of memory for use by the data segment. If successful, the end of the data segment is set to *eds* and 0 is returned. If unsuccessful, –1 is returned and **errno** is set to **ENOMEM** (insufficient memory).

Because the application of **brk( )** is highly specialized, no example is presented here.

Related Function

sbrk( )

void *calloc(size_t num, size_t size)

Description

The prototype for **calloc( )** is in **stdlib.h**.

The **calloc( )** function returns a pointer to the allocated memory. The amount of memory allocated is equal to *num*size* where *size* is in bytes. That is, **calloc( )** allocates sufficient memory for an array of *num* objects of *size* bytes.

The **calloc( )** function returns a pointer to the first byte of the allocated region. If there is not enough memory to satisfy the request, a null pointer is returned. It is always important to verify that the return value is not a null pointer before attempting to use the pointer.

Example

This function returns a pointer to a dynamically allocated array of 100 **float**s:

```
#include <stdlib.h>
#include <stdio.h>

float *get_mem(void)
{
  float *p;

  p = (float *) calloc(100, sizeof(float));
  if(!p) {
    printf("Allocation failure.");
    exit(1);
  }
  return p;
}
```

Related Functions

malloc( ), realloc( ), free( )

unsigned coreleft(void) /* small data models */
unsigned long coreleft(void) /* large data models */

Description

The prototype for **coreleft( )** is in **alloc.h**. This function is not defined by the ANSI C standard.

The **coreleft( )** function returns the number of bytes of unused memory left on the heap. For programs compiled using a small memory model, the function returns an **unsigned** integer. For programs compiled using a large data model, **coreleft( )** returns an **unsigned long** integer.

Example

This program displays the size of the heap when compiled for a small data model:

```
#include <alloc.h>
#include <stdio.h>

int main(void)
{
  printf("The size of the heap is %u", coreleft());
  return 0;
}
```

Related Function

malloc( )

unsigned _dos_allocmem(unsigned size, unsigned *seg)

Description

The prototype for **_dos_allocmem( )** is in **dos.h**. This function is not defined by the ANSI C standard.

The **_dos_allocmem( )** function executes a DOS 0x48 function call to allocate a paragraph-aligned block of memory. It puts the segment address of the block into the unsigned integer pointed to by *seg*. The *size* argument specifies the number of paragraphs to be allocated. (A paragraph is 16 bytes.)

If successful, **_dos_allocmem( )** returns 0. If the requested memory cannot be allocated, the appropriate DOS error code is returned and the size of the largest available block (in paragraphs) is put into the **unsigned** integer pointed to by *seg*. On failure, **errno** is also set to **ENOMEM** (insufficient memory).

Example

This fragment allocates 100 paragraphs of memory.

```
unsigned i;
unsigned s;

i = 0;

if(!_dos_allocmem(100, &s)) printf("Allocation successful.");
else
  printf("Failure - only %u paragraphs available", i);
```

Related Functions

_dos_freemem( ), _dos_setblock( )

int _dos_freemem(unsigned seg)

Description

The prototype for **_dos_freemem( )** is in **dos.h**. This function is not defined by the ANSI C standard.

The **_dos_freemem( )** function frees the block of memory whose first byte is at the segment specified by *seg*. This memory must have been previously allocated using **_dos_allocmem( )**. The function returns 0 on success. Upon failure, the DOS error code is returned and **errno** is set to **ENOMEM** (insufficient memory).

Example

This illustrates how to allocate and free memory using **_dos_allocmem( )** and **_dos_freemem( )**.

```
unsigned i;

if(_dos_allocmem(some, &i))
  printf("Allocation error.");
  /* ... */

_dos_freemem(i); /* free memory */
```

Related Functions

_dos_allocmem( ), _dos_setblock( )

unsigned _dos_setblock(unsigned size, unsigned seg, unsigned *max)

Description

The prototype for **_dos_setblock( )** is in **dos.h**. This function is not defined by the ANSI C standard.

The **_dos_setblock( )** function changes the size of the block of memory whose segment address is *seg*. The new size *size* is specified in paragraphs (16 bytes). The block of memory must have been previously allocated using **_dos_allocmem( )**.

If successful, **_dos_setblock( )** returns 0. However, if the size adjustment cannot be made, **_dos_setblock( )** returns a DOS error code and sets the unsigned integer pointed to by *max* to the size (in paragraphs) of the largest block that can be allocated. Also, on failure, **errno** is set to **ENOMEM** (insufficient memory).

Example

This attempts to resize the block of memory whose segment address is in **seg** to 100 paragraphs.

```
unsigned max;
if(_dos_setblock(100, seg, &max)) printf("Resize error.");
```

Related Functions

_dos_allocmem( ), _dos_freemem( )

void far *farcalloc(unsigned long num, unsigned long size)

Description

The prototype for **farcalloc( )** is in **alloc.h**. This function is not defined by the ANSI C standard.

The **farcalloc( )** function is the same as **calloc( )**, except that memory is allocated from outside the current data segment using the far heap.

See **calloc( )** for additional details.

unsigned long farcoreleft(void)

Description

The prototype for **farcoreleft( )** is in **alloc.h**. This function is not defined by the ANSI C standard.

The function **farcoreleft( )** returns the number of bytes of free memory left in the far heap.

Example

This program prints the number of bytes of available memory left in the far heap:

```
#include <alloc.h>
#include <stdio.h>

int main(void)
{
  printf("Far heap free memory: %ld", farcoreleft());
  return 0;
}
```

Related Function

coreleft( )

void farfree(void far *ptr)

Description

The prototype for **farfree( )** is in **alloc.h**. This function is not defined by the ANSI C standard.

The function **farfree( )** is used to release memory allocated from the far heap via a call to **farmalloc( )** or **farcalloc( )**.

You must use great care to call **farfree( )** only with a valid pointer into the far heap. Doing otherwise will corrupt the far heap. You cannot free a far heap pointer with the **free( )** function or a regular heap pointer with **farfree( )**.

Example

This program allocates and then frees a 100-byte region in the far heap:

```
#include <alloc.h>

int main(void)
{
  char far *p;

  p = (char far *) farmalloc(100);

  /* only free it if there was no allocation error */
  if(p) farfree(p);
  return 0;
}
```

Related Function

free( )

void far *farmalloc(unsigned long size)

Description

The prototype for **farmalloc( )** is in **alloc.h**. This function is not defined by the ANSI C standard.

The **farmalloc( )** function returns a pointer into the far heap that is the first byte in a region of memory *size* bytes long. It is the same as **malloc( )**, except that the far heap is used instead of the heap within the default data segment.

See **malloc( )** for further details.

void far *farrealloc(void far *ptr, unsigned long newsize)

Description

The prototype for **farrealloc( )** is in **alloc.h**. This function is not defined by the ANSI C standard.

The **farrealloc( )** function resizes the block of memory previously allocated from the far heap and pointed to by *ptr* to the new size specified in *newsize*. It is functionally equivalent to **realloc( )**, except that it operates on the far heap instead of the heap within the default data segment.

See **realloc( )** for further details.

void free(void *ptr)

Description

The prototype for **free( )** is in **stdlib.h**.

The **free( )** function returns the memory pointed to by *ptr* back to the heap. This makes the memory available for future allocation.

It is imperative that **free( )** be called only with a pointer that was previously allocated using one of these dynamic allocation system functions: **malloc( )**, **realloc( )**, or **calloc( )**. Using an invalid pointer in the call most likely will destroy the memory-management mechanism and cause a system crash.

Example

This program first allocates room for strings entered by the user and then frees them:

```
#include <stdlib.h>
#include <stdio.h>
```

```
int main(void)
{
  char *str[100];
  int i;

  for(i=0; i<100; i++) {
    if((str[i]=(char *)malloc(128))==NULL) {
      printf("Allocation error.");
      exit(0);
    }
    gets(str[i]);
  }

  /* now free the memory */
  for(i=0; i<100; i++) free(str[i]);
  return 0;
}
```

Related Functions

malloc( ), realloc( ), calloc( )

int freemem(unsigned seg)

Description

The prototype for **freemem( )** is in **dos.h**. This function is not defined by the ANSI C standard.

The **freemem( )** function frees the block of memory whose first byte is at *seg*. This memory must have been previously allocated using **allocmem( )**. The function returns 0 on success. On failure, it returns –1 and **errno** is set to **ENOMEM** (insufficient memory).

Example

This fragment illustrates how to allocate and free memory using **allocmem( )** and **freemem( )**:

```
unsigned i;

if(allocmem(some, &i)!=-1)
  printf("Allocation error.");
else
  freemem(i);
```

Related Functions

allocmem( ), setblock( ), _dos_freemem( )

int heapcheck(void)
int farheapcheck(void)

Description

The prototypes for **heapcheck( )** and **farheapcheck( )** are in **alloc.h**. These functions are not defined by the ANSI C standard, and are specific to Borland C++.

The **heapcheck( )** and **farheapcheck( )** functions examine the heap for errors. The **heapcheck( )** function checks the normal heap, and the **farheapcheck( )** function checks the far heap. Both functions return one of these values:

Value	Meaning
_HEAPOK	No errors
_HEAPEMPTY	No heap present
_HEAPCORRUPT	Error found in the heap

Example

This fragment illustrates how to check the heap for errors:

```
if(heapcheck() == _HEAPOK)
  printf("Heap is correct.");
else
  printf("Error in heap.");
```

Related Functions

heapwalk( ), heapchecknode( )

int heapcheckfree(unsigned fill)
int farheapcheckfree(unsigned fill)

Description

The prototypes for **heapcheckfree( )** and **farheapcheckfree( )** are in **alloc.h**. These functions are not defined by the ANSI C standard and are specific to Borland C++.

The **heapcheckfree( )** and **farheapcheckfree( )** functions verify that the free area is filled with the specified value *fill*. The **heapcheckfree( )** function checks the normal heap and the **farheapcheckfree( )** function checks the far heap. Both functions return one of these values:

Value	Meaning
_HEAPOK	No errors
_HEAPEMPTY	No heap present

Value	Meaning
_HEAPCORRUPT	Error found in the heap
_BADVALUE	A value other than *fill* was found

Example

The following code illustrates how to check the heap for the specified value after filling the heap with that value.

```
int status;

heapfillfree(1);
status = heapcheckfree(1)

if(status == _HEAPOK)
  printf("Heap is filled correctly.\n");
else
  if(status == _BADVALUE)
    printf("Heap not filled with correct value.\n");
```

Related Functions

heapfillfree( ), **heapcheckknode( )**

int heapchecknode(void *ptr)
int farheapchecknode(void far *ptr)

Description

The prototypes for **heapchecknode( )** and **farheapchecknode( )** are in **alloc.h**. These functions are not defined by the ANSI C standard, and are specific to Borland C++.

The **heapchecknode( )** and **farheapchecknode( )** functions check the status of a single node in the heap pointed to by *ptr*. The **heapchecknode( )** function checks the normal heap and **farheapchecknode( )** checks the far heap. Both functions return one of these values:

Value	Meaning
_BADNODE	The specified node could not be located
_FREEENTRY	The specified node is free memory
_HEAPCORRUPT	Error found in the heap
_HEAPEMPTY	No heap present
_USEDENTRY	The specified node is being used

If either function is called with a pointer to a node that has been freed, **_BADNODE** could be returned because adjacent free memory is sometimes merged.

Example

The following code illustrates how to check a node on the heap.

```
#include <stdio.h>
#include <stdlib.h>
#include <alloc.h>

int main(void)
{
  char *ptr;
  int status;

  if((ptr = (char *) malloc(10)) == NULL)
    exit(1);

  status = heapchecknode(ptr);

  if(status == _USEDENTRY)
    printf("Node is being used.\n");
  else
    printf("Error in heap.\n");

  free(ptr);
  return 0;
}
```

Related Functions

heapcheck( ), heapcheckfree( )

int _heapchk(void)

Description

The prototype for **_heapchk( )** is in **malloc.h**. This function is not defined by the ANSI C standard.

The **_heapchk( )** function checks the heap. It returns one of these values.

Value	Meaning
_HEAPOK	No errors
_HEAPEMPTY	No heap present
_HEAPBADNODE	Error found in the heap

Related function

heapcheck( )

int heapfillfree(unsigned fill)
int farheapfillfree(unsigned fill)

Description

The prototypes for **heapfillfree( )** and **farheapfillfree( )** are in **alloc.h**. These functions are not defined by the ANSI C standard and are specific to Borland C++.

The **heapfillfree( )** and **farheapfillfree( )** functions fill the free blocks of memory in the heap with *fill*. The **heapfillfree( )** function operates on the normal heap and **farheapfillfree( )** works with the far heap. You may want to use one of these functions to give allocated memory a known initial value.

Both functions return one of these values:

Value	Meaning
_HEAPOK	No errors
_HEAPEMPTY	No heap present
_HEAPCORRUPT	Error found in the heap

Example

This code illustrates how to fill the heap with a desired value:

```
int status;

status = heapfillfree(0);
if(status == _HEAPOK)
  printf("Heap is correct.");
else
  printf("Error in heap.");
```

Related Functions

heapcheckfree( ), _heapset( )

int _heapmin(void)

Description

The prototype for **_heapmin( )** is in **malloc.h**. This function is not defined by the ANSI C standard.

The **_heapmin( )** function releases unallocated portions of the heap so that it can be used by other processes. That is, it "minimizes" the heap. It returns 0 if successful and –1 on failure.

Related Functions

freemem( ), free( )

int _heapset(unsigned fill)

Description

The prototype for **_heapset( )** is in **malloc.h**. This function is not defined by the ANSI C standard.

The **_heapset( )** function fills unallocated blocks of memory in the heap with *fill*. (Only the low-order byte of *fill* is used.) The function returns one of these values.

Value	**Meaning**
_HEAPOK	No errors
_HEAPEMPTY	No heap present
_HEAPBADNODE	Error found in the heap

Related Functions

heapcheckfree( ), heapfillfree( )

int heapwalk(struct heapinfo *hinfo)
int farheapwalk(struct farheapinfo *hinfo)
int _rtl_heapwalk(_HEAPINFO *hinfo)

Description

The prototypes for **heapwalk( )** and **farheapwalk( )** are in **alloc.h**. The prototype for **_rtl_heapwalk( )** is in **malloc.h**. These functions are not defined by the ANSI C standard, and are specific to Borland C++.

The **heapwalk( )** and **farheapwalk( )** functions fill the structure pointed to by *hinfo*. Each call to **heapwalk( )** or **farheapwalk( )** steps to the next node in the heap and returns information on that node. When there are no more nodes on the heap, **_HEAPEND** is returned. If there is no heap, **_HEAPEMPTY** is returned. Each time a valid block is examined, **_HEAPOK** is returned.

The **heapwalk( )** function operates on the normal heap and the **farheapwalk( )** function works with the far heap.

The **heapinfo** and **farheapinfo** structures contain three fields: a pointer to a block, the size of the block, and a flag that is set if the block is being used. These structures are shown here:

```
struct farheapinfo {
  void huge *ptr; /* pointer to block */
  unsigned long size; /* size of block, in bytes */
  int in_use; /* set if block is in use */
};

struct heapinfo {
  void *ptr; /* pointer to block */
  unsigned int size; /* size of block, in bytes */
  int in_use; /* set if block is in use */
};
```

On the first call to either function, you must set the *ptr* field to **NULL** before the first call to **heapwalk( )** or **farheapwalk( )**.

Because of the way Borland C++ organizes the dynamic allocation system, the size of an allocated block of memory is slightly larger than the amount requested when it is allocated.

These functions assume the heap is not corrupted. Always call **heapcheck( )** or **farheapcheck( )** before beginning a walk through the heap.

The **_rtl_heapwalk( )** function is similar to **heapwalk( )**, except that it uses the following structure.

```
typedef struct _heapinfo {
  int *_pentry; /* pointer to block */
  int *__pentry; /* pointer to block */
  size_t _size; /* size of block */
  int _useflag; /* contains _USEDENTRY if block is in use --
                   contains _FREEENTRY if not in use */
} _HEAPINFO;
```

In addition to the values returned by **heapwalk( )**, **_rtl_heapwalk( )** can also return **_HEAPBADNODE** (error found in heap) or **_HEAPBADPTR** (**_pentry** is invalid).

Example

This program walks through the heap, printing the size of each allocated block:

```
#include <stdio.h>
#include <stdlib.h>
#include <alloc.h>
```

```
int main(void)
{
  struct heapinfo hinfo;
  char *p1, *p2;

  if((p1 = (char *) malloc(80)) == NULL)
    exit(1);

  if((p2 = (char *) malloc(20)) == NULL)
    exit(1);

  if(heapcheck() < 0) { /* always check heap before walk */
    printf("Heap corrupt.");
    exit(1);
  }

  hinfo.ptr = NULL;  /* set ptr to null before first call */

  /* examine first block */
  if(heapwalk(&hinfo) == _HEAPOK)
    printf("Size of p1's block is %d\n", hinfo.size);

  /* examine second block */
  if(heapwalk(&hinfo) == _HEAPOK)
    printf("Size of p2's block is %d\n", hinfo.size);

  free(p1);
  free(p2);
  return 0;
}
```

Related Function

heapcheck( )

void *malloc(size_t size)

Description

The prototype for **malloc( )** is in **stdlib.h**.

The **malloc( )** function returns a pointer to the first byte of a region of memory *size* bytes long that has been allocated from the heap. If there is insufficient memory in the heap to satisfy the request, **malloc( )** returns a null pointer. It is always important to verify that the return value is not a null pointer before attempting to use the pointer. Attempting to use a null pointer usually causes a system crash.

Example

This function allocates sufficient memory to hold structures of type **addr**:

```
#include <stdlib.h>

struct addr {
  char name[40];
  char street[40];
  char city[40];
  char state[3];
  char zip[10];
 };
  .
  .
  .
struct addr *get_struct(void)
{
  struct addr *p;

  if(!(p=(struct addr *)malloc(sizeof(addr)))) {
    printf("Allocation error.");
    exit(0);
  }
  return p;
}
```

Related Functions

free( ), realloc( ), calloc( )

void *realloc(void *ptr, size_t newsize)

Description

The prototype for **realloc( )** is in **stdlib.h**.

The **realloc( )** function changes the size of the allocated memory pointed to by *ptr* to that specified by *newsize*. The value of *newsize*, specified in bytes, can be greater or less than the original. A pointer to the memory block is returned because it may be necessary for **realloc( )** to move the block to increase its size. If this occurs, the contents of the old block are copied into the new block and no information is lost.

If there is not enough free memory in the heap to allocate *newsize* bytes, a null pointer is returned.

Example

The following program allocates 17 characters of memory, copies the string "this is 16 chars" into them, and then uses **realloc( )** to increase the size to 18 in order to place a period at the end.

```
#include <stdlib.h>
#include <stdio.h>
#include <string.h>

int main(void)
{
  char *p;

  p = (char *) malloc(17);
  if(!p) {
    printf("Allocation error.");
    exit(1);
  }

  strcpy(p, "This is 16 chars");

  p = (char *) realloc(p,18);
  if(!p) {
    printf("Allocation error.");
    exit(1);
  }

  strcat(p, ".");

  printf(p);

  free(p);

  return 0;
}
```

Related Functions

free( ), malloc( ), calloc( )

void *sbrk(int amount)

Description

The prototype for **sbrk( )** is in **alloc.h**. This function is not defined by the ANSI C standard.

The **sbrk( )** function increments (or decrements if a negative value is used) the amount of memory allocated to the data segment by *amount* number of bytes. If successful, it returns a pointer to the old break address. Otherwise, it returns –1 and **errno** is set to **ENOMEM** (insuficient memory).

Because the use of **sbrk( )** is highly specialized, no example is given.

Related Function

brk( )

int setblock(unsigned seg, unsigned size)

Description

The prototype for **setblock( )** is in **dos.h**. This function is not defined by the ANSI C standard.

The **setblock( )** function changes the size of the block of memory whose segment address is *seg* to *size,* which is specified in paragraphs (16 bytes). The block of memory must have been previously allocated using **allocmem( )**.

If the size adjustment cannot be made, **setblock( )** returns the largest block that can be allocated. On success, it returns –1.

Example

This fragment attempts to resize to 100 paragraphs the block of memory whose segment address is in **seg**:

```
if(setblock(seg, 100)!=-1) printf("Resize error.");
```

Related Functions

allocmem( ), freemem( ), _dos_setblock( )

Chapter Sixteen

Directory Functions

Borland C++ has a number of directory-manipulation functions in its library. Although none of these functions is defined by the ANSI C standard or by C++, they are included to allow easy access to directories.

int chdir(const char *path)

Description

The prototype for **chdir( )** is in **dir.h**. This function is not defined by the ANSI C standard.

The **chdir( )** function makes the directory whose path name is pointed to by *path* the current directory. The path name may include a drive specifier. The directory must exist.

If successful, **chdir( )** returns 0.

If unsuccessful, it returns –1 and sets **errno** to **ENOENT** (invalid path name).

Example

This fragment makes the WP\FORMLETdirectory on drive C the current working directory:

```
chdir("C:\\WP\\FORMLET");
```

Related Functions

mkdir( ), rmdir( )

int _chdrive(int drivenum)

Description

The prototype for **_chdrive( )** is in **direct.h**. This function is not defined by the ANSI C standard.

The **_chdrive( )** function changes the currently logged in drive to the one specified by *drivenum*, with A being 1, B being 2, and so on.

The **_chrdrive( )** function returns 0 if successful; otherwise, –1 is returned.

Example

This changes the currently logged in drive to C:

```
_chdrive(3); /* switch to drive C */
```

Related Functions

setdrive( ), getdrive( )

int closedir(DIR *ptr)
DIR *opendir(char *dirname)
struct dirent *readdir(DIR *ptr)
void rewinddir(DIR *ptr)

Description

The prototypes for **closedir( )**, **opendir( )**, **readdir( )**, and **rewinddir( )** are found in **dirent.h**. These functions are not defined by the ANSI C standard. These functions are included for UNIX compatibility.

The **opendir( )** function opens a directory stream and returns a pointer to a structure of type **DIR**, which maintains information about the directory. You should not modify the contents of this structure. The **closedir( )** function closes the directory stream pointed to by *ptr.*

The **readdir( )** function returns the name of the next file in the directory. That is, **readdir( )** reads the contents of the directory a file at a time. The parameter *ptr* must point to a directory stream opened by **opendir( )**. The **dirent** structure is defined as shown here for DOS:

```
struct dirent
{
  char d_name[13];
};
```

Therefore, **d_name** contains the name of the next file in the directory after a call to **readdir( )** has returned. For Windows 95/NT, the length of **d_name** is 260. For OS/2, it is 256.

The **rewinddir( )** function causes the directory pointed to by *ptr* (and previously obtained using **opendir( )**) to return to the start (that is, to the first entry in the specified directory). This allows the directory to be reread.

The **closedir( )** function returns 0 if successful; it returns –1 otherwise. On failure, it also sets **errno** to **EBADF** (invalid directory). The **opendir( )** function returns null if the directory cannot be opened and **errno** is set to either **ENOENT** (directory not found) or **ENOMEM** (insufficient memory). The **readdir( )** function returns null when the end of the directory is reached.

Because these functions are primarily included for compatibility with UNIX (and better ways exist under DOS/Windows/OS2 to access directories), no examples are given.

Related Functions

findfirst( ), findnext( )

unsigned _dos_findfirst(const char *fname, int attr, struct find_t *ptr)
unsigned _dos_findnext(struct find_t *ptr)

Description

The prototypes for **_dos_findfirst( )** and **_dos_findnext( )** are in **dos.h**. These functions are not defined by the ANSI C standard.

The **_dos_findfirst( )** function searches for the first file name that matches that pointed to by *fname*. The file name may include both a drive specifier and a path name. Also, the file name may include the wildcard characters * and ?. If a match is found, the structure pointed to by *ptr* is filled with information about the file.

The **find_t** structure is defined like this:

```
struct find_t {
  char reserved[21];/* used by DOS */
  char attrib;      /* attribute of file */
  unsigned wr_time; /* last time file was written to */
  unsigned wr_date; /* last date file was written to */
  long size;        /* size in bytes */
  char name[13];    /* filename */
};
```

The *attrib* parameter determines what type of files will be found by **_dos_findfirst( )**. The *attrib* can be one or more of the following macros (defined in **dos.h**):

Macro	Meaning
_A_NORMAL	Normal file
_A_RDONLY	Read-only file
_A_HIDDEN	Hidden file
_A_SYSTEM	System file
_A_VOLID	Volume label
_A_SUBDIR	Subdirectory
_A_ARCH	Archive bit set

The **_dos_findnext( )** function continues a search started by **_dos_findfirst( )**. The buffer pointed to by *ptr* must be the one used in the call to **_dos_findfirst( )**.

Both the **_dos_findfirst( )** and **_dos_findnext( )** functions return 0 on success and non-0 on failure or when no more matches are found. On failure, **errno** will be set to **ENOENT** (file not found).

Example

This program displays all normal files and their sizes in the current directory with a .C extension:

```
#include <dos.h>
#include <stdio.h>

int main(void)
{
  struct find_t f;
  register int done;

  done = _dos_findfirst("*.c", _A_NORMAL, &f);
  while(!done) {
    printf("%s %ld\n", f.name, f.size);
    done = _dos_findnext(&f);
  }
  return 0;
}
```

Related Functions

findfirst( ), findnext( )

int findfirst(const char *fname, struct ffblk *ptr, int attrib)
int findnext(struct ffblk *ptr)

Description

The prototypes for **findfirst( )** and **findnext( )** are in **dir.h**. However, you also need to include the **dos.h** header, which contains macros that can be used as values for *attrib*. These functions are not defined by the ANSI C standard.

The **findfirst( )** function searches for the first file name that matches that pointed to by *fname*. The file name may include both a drive specifier and a path name. The file name may also include the wildcard characters * and ?. If a match is found, the structure pointed to by *ptr* is filled with information about the file.

The **ffblk** structure is defined like this for DOS and Windows 3.1:

```
struct ffblk {
  char ff_reserved[21]; /* reserved */
  char ff_attrib;       /* attributes of file */
  unsigned ff_ftime;    /* creation time */
  unsigned ff_fdate;    /* creation date */
  long ff_fsize;        /* size in bytes */
  char ff_name[13];     /* file name */
};
```

The **ffblk** structure is defined like this for Windows NT/95:

```
struct ffblk {
  long ff_reserved;          /* reserved */
  long ff_fsize;             /* size in bytes */
  unsigned long ff_attrib;   /* attributes of file */
  unsigned short ff_ftime;   /* creation time */
  unsigned short ff_fdate;   /* creation date */
  char ff_name[256];         /* file name */
};
```

The *attrib* parameter determines the type of files to be found by **findfirst( )**. If *attrib* is 0, all types of files that match the desired file name are acceptable. To cause a more selective search, *attrib* can be one of the following macros:

Macro	Meaning
FA_RDONLY	Read-only file
FA_HIDDEN	Hidden file
FA_SYSTEM	System file
FA_LABEL	Volume label
FA_DIREC	Subdirectory
FA_ARCH	Archive bit set

The **findnext( )** function continues a search started by **findfirst( )**.

Both the **findfirst( )** and **findnext( )** functions return 0 on success and –1 on failure. On failure, **errno** is set to **ENOENT** (file name not found). **_doserrno** is set to either **ENMFILE** (no more files in directory) or **ENOENT**.

Example

This program displays all files with a .C extension (and their sizes) in the current working directory:

```
#include <stdio.h>
#include <dos.h>
#include <dir.h>

int main(void)
{
  struct ffblk f;
  register int done;

  done = findfirst("*.c", &f, 0);
  while(!done) {
    printf("%s %ld\n", f.ff_name, f.ff_fsize);
    done = findnext(&f);
  }
  return 0;
}
```

Related Function

fnmerge( )

void fnmerge(char *path, const char *drive, const char *dir, const char *fname, const char *ext)
int fnsplit(const char *path, char *drive, char *dir, char *fname, char *ext)

Description

The prototypes for **fnmerge( )** and **fnsplit( )** are in **dir.h**. These functions are not defined by the ANSI C standard.

The **fnmerge( )** function constructs a file name from the specified individual components and puts that name into the string pointed to by *path*. For example, if *drive* is C:, *dir* is \BCC\, *fname* is TEST, and *ext* is .C, the file name produced is C:\BCC\TEST.C.

The **fnsplit( )** decomposes the file name pointed to by *path* into its component parts. The array size needed for each parameter is shown here, along with a macro defined in **dir.h** that can be used in place of the actual number:

Parameter	Size for DOS and Windows 3.1	Size for Windows 95/NT	Macro Name
path	80	260	MAXPATH
drive	3	3	MAXDRIVE
dir	66	256	MAXDIR
fname	9	256	MAXFILE
ext	5	256	MAXEXT

The **fnsplit( )** function puts the colon after the drive specifier in the string pointed to by *drive*. It puts the period preceding the extension into the string pointed to by *ext*. Leading and trailing backslashes are retained.

The two functions **fnmerge( )** and **fnsplit( )** are complementary—the output from one can be used as input to the other.

The **fnsplit( )** function returns an integer that has five flags encoded into it. The flags have these macro names associated with them (defined in **dir.h**):

Macro Name	Meaning When Set
EXTENSION	Extension present
FILENAME	File name present
DIRECTORY	Directory path present
DRIVE	Drive specifier present
WILDCARDS	One or more wildcard characters present

To determine if a flag is set, AND the flag macro with the return value and test the result. If the result is 1, the flag is set; otherwise, it is cleared.

Example

This program illustrates how **fnmerge( )** encodes a file name. Its output is "C:TEST.C":

```
#include <stdio.h>
#include <dir.h>

int main(void)
{
  char path[MAXPATH];
  fnmerge(path, "C:", "", "TEST", ".C");
  printf(path);
  return 0;
}
```

Related Functions

findfirst( ), findnext( )

char *_fullpath(char *fpath, const char *rpath, int len)

Description

The prototype for **_fullpath( )** is in **stdlib.h**. This function is not defined by the ANSI C standard.

The **_fullpath( )** function constructs a full path name given a relative path name. The relative path name is pointed to by *rpath*. The full path name is put into the array pointed to by *fpath*. The size of the array pointed to by *fpath* is specified by *len*. If *fpath* is null, then an array will be dynamically allocated. (In this case, the array must be freed manually using **free( )**.)

The **_fullpath( )** function returns a pointer to *fpath*, or null if an error occurs.

Example

This program displays the full path to the \INCLUDE directory:

```
#include <stdio.h>
#include <stdlib.h>

int main(void)
{
```

```
  char fpath[80];

  _fullpath(fpath, "\\INCLUDE", 80);

  printf("Full path: %s\n", fpath);

  return 0;
}
```

Related Functions

_makepath( ), mkdir( ), getcwd( )

int getcurdir(int drive, char *dir)

Description

The prototype for **getcurdir( )** is in **dir.h**. This function is not defined by the ANSI C standard.

The **getcurdir( )** function copies the name of the current working directory of the drive specified in *drive* into the string pointed to by *dir*. A 0 value for *drive* specifies the default drive. For drive A, use 1; for B, use 2; and so on.

The string pointed to by *dir* must be at least **MAXDIR** bytes in length. **MAXDIR** is a macro defined in **dir.h**. The directory name will not contain the drive specifier and will not include leading backslashes.

The **getcurdir( )** function returns 0 if successful, –1 on failure.

Example

The following program prints the current directory on the default drive:

```
#include <stdio.h>
#include <dir.h>

int main(void)
{
  char dir[MAXDIR];

  getcurdir(0, dir);
  printf("Current directory is %s", dir);
  return 0;
}
```

Related Function

getcwd( )

char *getcwd(char *dir, int len)

Description

The prototype for **getcwd( )** is in **dir.h**. This function is not defined by the ANSI C standard.

The **getcwd( )** function copies the full path name (up to *len* characters) of the current working directory into the string pointed to by *dir.* An error occurs if the full path name is longer than *len* characters. The **getcwd( )** function returns a pointer to *dir.*

If **getcwd( )** is called with *dir*'s value being null, **getcwd( )** automatically allocates a buffer using **malloc( )** and returns a pointer to this buffer. You can free the memory allocated by **getcwd( )** using **free( )**.

On failure, **getcwd( )** returns null and **errno** is set to **ENODEV** (nonexistent device), **ENOMEM** (insufficient memory), or **ERANGE** (out of range).

Example

This program prints the full path name of the current working directory:

```
#include <stdio.h>
#include <dir.h>

int main(void)
{
  char dir[MAXDIR];

  getcwd(dir, MAXDIR);
  printf("Current directory is %s", dir);
  return 0;
}
```

Related Function

getcurdir( )

char *_getdcwd(int drive, char *path, int len)

Description

The prototype for **_getdcwd( )** is in **direct.h**. This function is not defined by the ANSI C standard.

The **_getdcwd( )** function obtains the path name of the current directory of the drive specified by *drive,* with A being 1, B being 2, and so on. (The default drive is specified as 0.) It copies the path name into the array pointed to by *path.* The size of *path* is specified by *len.* If *path* is null, then an array will be dynamically allocated. (In this case, the array must be freed manually using **free( )**.)

The **_getdcwd( )** function returns *path*. On failure, a null pointer is returned and **errno** contains either **ENOMEM** (insufficient memory) or **ERANGE** (path name exceeds array size).

Example

This program displays the current directory of drive D:

```
#include <stdio.h>
#include <direct.h>

int main(void)
{
  char path[80];

  _getdcwd(4, path, 80);

  printf("Current directory of drive D is %s\n", path);

  return 0;
}
```

Related Functions

mkdir( ), chdir( ), _fullpath( )

int getdisk(void)

Description

The prototype for **getdisk( )** is in **dir.h**. This function is not defined by the ANSI C standard.

The **getdisk( )** function returns the number of the current drive. Drive A corresponds to 0, drive B is 1, and so on.

Example

This program displays the name of the current drive:

```
#include <stdio.h>
#include <dir.h>

int main(void)
{
  printf("Current drive is %c", getdisk()+'A');
  return 0;
}
```

Related Functions

setdisk( ), **getcwd( )**

int _getdrive(void)

Description

The prototype for **_getdrive( )** is in **direct.h**. This function is not defined by the ANSI C standard.

The **_getdrive( )** function returns the number of the current drive, with A being 1, B being 2, and so on.

Example

This statement displays the number of the current drive:

```
printf("Current drive is %d.", _getdrive());
```

Related Function

getcwd( )

void _makepath(char *pname, const char *drive, const char *directory, const char *fname, const char *extension)

Description

The prototype for **_makepath( )** is in **stdlib.h**. This function is not defined by the ANSI C standard.

The **_makepath( )** function constructs a full path name from the elements specified in its parameters and places the result in the array pointed to by *pname*. The drive is specified in the string pointed to by *drive*. The directory (and any subdirectories) are specified in the string pointed to by *directory*. The file name is pointed to by *fname* and the extension is pointed to by *extension*. Any of these strings may be empty.

Example

This program constructs a full path name from its elements. Next, it displays the path and then dissects it into its components using **_splitpath( )**, which is the complement to **_makepath( )**.

```
#include <stdio.h>
#include <stdlib.h>
```

```
int main(void)
{
  char fpath[80];
  char fname[9];
  char dir[64];
  char drive[3];
  char ext[5];

  _makepath(fpath, "B:", "MYDIR", "MYFILE", "DAT");
  printf("%s\n", fpath);

  _splitpath(fpath, drive, dir, fname, ext);
  printf("%s %s %s %s\n", drive, dir, fname, ext);

  return 0;
}
```

Related Functions

_splitpath( ), fnmerge( ), fnsplit( )

int mkdir(const char *path)

Description

The prototype for **mkdir( )** is in **dir.h**. This function is not defined by the ANSI C standard.

The **mkdir( )** function creates a directory using the path name pointed to by *path.*

The **mkdir( )** function returns 0 if successful. If unsuccessful, it returns –1 and sets **errno** to either **EACCESS** (access denied) or **ENOENT** (invalid path name).

Example

This program creates a directory called FORMLET:

```
#include <dir.h>

int main(void)
{
  mkdir("FORMLET");
  return 0;
}
```

Related Function

rmdir( )

char *mktemp(char *fname)

Description

The prototype for **mktemp( )** is in **dir.h**. This function is not defined by the ANSI C standard.

The **mktemp( )** function creates a unique file name and copies it into the string pointed to by *fname*. When you call **mktemp( )**, the string pointed to by *fname* must contain six "X"s followed by a null terminator. The **mktemp( )** function transforms that string into a unique file name. It does not create the file, however.

If successful, **mktemp( )** returns a pointer to *fname*; otherwise, it returns a null.

Example

This program displays a unique file name:

```
#include <stdio.h>
#include <dir.h>

char fname[7] = "XXXXXX";

int main(void)
{
  mktemp(fname);
  printf(fname);
  return 0;
}
```

Related Functions

findfirst( ), findnext( )

int rmdir(const char *path)

Description

The prototype for **rmdir( )** is in **dir.h**. This function is not defined by the ANSI C standard.

The **rmdir( )** function removes the directory whose path name is pointed to by *path*. To be removed, a directory must be empty, must not be the current directory, and must not be the root.

If **rmdir( )** is successful, 0 is returned. Otherwise, –1 is returned and **errno** is set to either **EACCESS** (access denied) or **ENOENT** (invalid path name).

Example

This removes the directory called FORMLET:

```
#include <stdio.h>
#include <dir.h>
int main(void)
{
  if(!rmdir("FORMLET")) printf("FORMLET removed\n");
  return 0;
}
```

Related Function

mkdir( )

char *searchpath(const char *fname)

Description

The prototype for **searchpath( )** is in **dir.h**. This function is not defined by the ANSI C standard.

The **searchpath( )** function tries to find the file whose name is pointed to by *fname* using the PATH environmental variable. If it finds the file, it returns a pointer to the entire path name. This string is statically allocated and is overwritten by each call to **searchpath( )**. If the file cannot be found, a null is returned.

Example

This program displays the path name for the file BCC.EXE:

```
#include <stdio.h>
#include <dir.h>

int main(void)
{
  printf(searchpath("BCC.EXE"));
  return 0;
}
```

Related Function

mktemp( )

int setdisk(int drive)

Description

The prototype for **setdisk( )** is in **dir.h**. This function is not defined by the ANSI C standard.

The **setdisk( )** function sets the current drive to that specified by *drive.* Drive A corresponds to 0, drive B to 1, and so on. It returns the total number of drives in the system.

Example

This program switches to drive A and reports the total number of drives in the system:

```
#include <stdio.h>
#include <dir.h>

int main(void)
{
  printf("%d drives", setdisk(0));
  return 0;
}
```

Related Function

getdisk( )

void _splitpath(const char *fpath, char *drive, char *directory, char *fname, char *extension)

Description

The prototype for **_splitpath( )** is in **stdlib.h**. This function is not defined by the ANSI C standard.

The **_splitpath( )** function dissects the full path name specified in the string pointed to by *fpath.* The drive letter is put in the string pointed to by *drive.* The directory (and any subdirectories) is put in the string pointed to by *directory*. The file name is put in the string pointed to by *fname* and the extension is put in the string pointed to by *extension.* The minimum size of the arrays pointed to by these parameters is shown here.

Parameter	Size for DOS and Windows 3.1	Size for Windows 95/NT	Macro Name
drive	3	3	_MAX_DRIVE
directory	66	256	_MAX_DIR
fname	9	256	_MAX_FILE
extension	5	256	_MAX_EXT

Example

This program displays the elements of the full path B:\MYDIR\MYFILE.DAT:

```
#include <stdio.h>
#include <stdlib.h>

int main(void)
{
  char fname[9];
  char dir[64];
  char drive[3];
  char ext[5];

  _splitpath("B:\\MYDIR\\MYFILE.DAT", drive, dir, fname, ext);

  printf("%s %s %s %s\n", drive, dir, fname, ext);

  return 0;
}
```

Related Functions

_makepath( ), fnsplit( ), fnmerge( )

Chapter Seventeen

Process Control Functions

This chapter covers a number of functions that are used to control the way a program executes, terminates, or invokes the execution of another program. Aside from **abort( )**, **atexit( )**, and **exit( )**, none of the functions described here is defined by the ANSI C standard or C++. However, all allow your program greater flexibility in its execution.

The process control functions have their prototypes in **process.h**. However, those functions defined by the ANSI standard also have their prototypes in the **stdlib.h** header file.

void abort(void)

Description

The prototype for **abort( )** is in **process.h** and **stdlib.h**.

The **abort( )** function causes immediate termination of a program. No files are flushed. It returns a value of 3 to the calling process (usually the operating system).

The primary use of **abort( )** is to prevent a runaway program from closing active files.

Example

This program terminates if the user enters an "A":

```
#include <process.h>
#include <conio.h>
```

```
int main(void)
{
  for(;;)
    if(getch()=='A') abort();
  return 0;
}
```

Related Functions

exit( ), atexit( )

int atexit(void (*func)(void))

Description

The prototype for **atexit( )** is in **stdlib.h**.

The **atexit( )** function establishes the function pointed to by *func* as the function to be called upon normal program termination. That is, the specified function is called at the end of a program run. The act of establishing the function is referred to as *registration* by the ANSI C standard.

The **atexit( )** function returns 0 if the function is registered as the termination function, and non-0 otherwise.

Up to 32 termination functions can be established. They are called in the reverse order of their establishment: first in, last out.

Example

This program prints "hello there" on the screen:

```
#include <stdio.h>
#include <stdlib.h>

/* Example using atexit(). */
int main(void)
{
  void done();

  if(atexit(done)) printf("Error in atexit().");
  return 0;
}

void done()
{
  printf("Hello there!");
}
```

Related Functions

exit( ), abort( )

void _c_exit(void)
void _cexit(void)

Description

The prototypes for **_c_exit( )** and **_cexit( )** are in **process.h**. These functions are defined by the ANSI C standard.

The **_c_exit( )** function performs the same actions as **_exit( )**.

The **_cexit( )** function performs the same actions as **exit( )**, except that the program is not terminated. However, all files are closed and all buffers are flushed and any termination functions are executed.

Example

This statement performs program shutdown procedures, except that the program is not terminated:

```
_cexit();
```

Related Functions

exit( ), _exit( ), atexit( )

int execl(char *fname, char *arg0, . . ., char *argN, NULL)
int execle(char *fname, char *arg0, . . ., char *argN, NULL, char *envp[ ])
int execlp(char *fname, char *arg0, . . ., char *argN, NULL)
int execlpe(char *fname, char *arg0, . . ., char *argN, NULL, char *envp[ ])
int execv(char *fname, char *arg[ ])
int execve(char *fname, char *arg[ ], char *envp[ ])
int execvp(char *fname, char *arg[ ])
int execvpe(char *fname, char *arg[ ], char *envp[ ])

Description

The prototypes for these functions are in **process.h**. These functions are not defined by the ANSI C standard.

The **exec** group of functions is used to execute another program. This other program, called the *child process,* is loaded over the one that contains the **exec** call. The name of the file that contains the child process is pointed to by *fname.* Any arguments to the child process are pointed to either individually by *arg0* through *argN* or by the array *arg[ ].* An environment string must be pointed to by *envp[ ].* (The arguments are pointed to by **argv** in the child process.)

If no extension or period is part of the string pointed to by *fname,* a search is first made for a file by that name. If that fails, the .EXE extension is added and the search is tried again. If that fails, the .COM extension is added and the search is tried again. When an extension is specified, only an exact match will satisfy the search. Finally, if a period but no extension is present, a search is made for only the file specified by the left side of the file name.

The exact way the child process is executed depends on which version of **exec** you use. You can think of the **exec** function as having different suffixes that determine its operation. A suffix can consist of either one or two characters.

Functions that have a **p** in the suffix search for the child process in the directories specified by the PATH command. If a **p** is not in the suffix, only the current directory is searched.

An **l** in the suffix specifies that pointers to the arguments to the child process will be passed individually. Use this method when passing a fixed number of arguments. Notice that the last argument must be **NULL**. (**NULL** is defined in **stdio.h**.)

A **v** in the suffix means that pointers to the arguments to the child process will be passed in an array. This is the way you must pass arguments when you do not know in advance how many there will be or when the number of arguments may change during the execution of your program. Typically, the end of the array is signaled by a null pointer.

An **e** in the suffix specifies that one or more environmental strings will be passed to the child process. The *envp* parameter is an array of string pointers. Each string pointed to by the array must have the form

environment-variable = value

The last pointer in the array must be **NULL**. If the first element in the array is **NULL**, the child retains the same environment as the parent.

It is important to remember that files open at the time of an **exec** call are also open in the child program.

When successful, the **exec** functions return no value. On failure, they return –1 and set **errno** to one of the following values:

Macro	**Meaning**
EACCES	Access to child process file denied
EMFILE	Too many open files

Macro	Meaning
ENOENT	File not found
ENOEXEC	Format of **exec** is invalid
ENOMEM	Not enough free memory to load child process

Example

The first of the following programs invokes the second, which displays its arguments. Remember, both programs must be in separate files.

```
/* First file - parent */

#include <stdio.h>
#include <process.h>
#include <stdlib.h>

int main(void)
{
  execl("test.exe", "test.exe", "hello", "10", NULL);
  return 0;
}


/* Second file - child */
#include <stdio.h>
#include <stdlib.h>

int main(int argc, char *argv[])
{
  printf("This program is executed with these command line ");
  printf("arguments: ");
  printf(argv[1]);
  printf(" %d", atoi(argv[2]));
  return 0;
}
```

Related Function

spawn( )

void exit(int status)
void _exit(int status)

Description

The prototypes for **exit( )** and **_exit( )** are in **process.h** and **stdlib.h**.

The **exit( )** function causes immediate, normal termination of a program. The value of *status* is passed to the calling process. By convention, if the value of *status* is 0, normal program termination is assumed. A non-0 value can be used to indicate an implementation-defined error. You can also use the macros **EXIT_SUCCESS** and **EXIT_FAILURE** as values for *status*. They indicate normal and abnormal termination, respectively. Calling **exit( )** flushes and closes all open files and calls any program termination functions registered using **atexit( )**.

The **_exit( )** program does not close any files, flush any buffers, or call any termination functions. This function is not defined by the ANSI C standard.

Example

This function performs menu selection for a mailing list program. If Q is pressed, the program is terminated.

```
char menu(void)
{
  char ch;

  do {
    printf("Enter names (E)");
    printf("Delete name (D)");
    printf("Print (P)");
    printf("Quit (Q)");
  } while(!strchr("EDPQ", toupper(ch));
  if(ch=='Q') exit(0);
  return ch;
}
```

Related Functions

atexit( ), abort( )

int spawnl(int mode, char *fname, char *arg0, . . ., char *argN, NULL)
int spawnle(int mode, char *fname, char *arg0, . . ., char *argN, NULL, char *envp[ ])
int spawnlp(int mode, char *fname, char *arg0, . . ., char *argN, NULL)
int spawnlpe(int mode, char *fname, char *arg0, . . ., char *argN, NULL, char *envp[ ])
int spawnv(int mode, char *fname, char *arg[ ])
int spawnve(int mode, char *fname, char *arg[ ], char *envp[ ])
int spawnvp(int mode, char *fname, char *arg[ ])
int spawnvpe(int mode, char *fname, char *arg[ ], char *envp[ ])

Description

The prototypes for these functions are in **process.h**. These functions are not defined by the ANSI C standard.

The **spawn** group of functions is used to execute another program. This other program, the *child process,* does not necessarily replace the parent program (unlike the child process executed by the **exec** group of functions). The name of the file that contains the child process is pointed to by *fname.* The arguments to the child process, if any, are pointed to either individually by *arg0* through *argN* or by the array *arg[ ].* If you pass an environment string, it must be pointed to by *envp[ ].* (The arguments will be pointed to by **argv** in the child process.) The *mode* parameter determines how the child process will be executed. It can have one of these values (defined in **process.h**):

Macro	Execution Mode
P_WAIT	Suspends parent process until the child has finished executing.
P_NOWAIT	Executes both the parent and the child concurrently. The ID of the child process is returned to the parent. (This mode is not implemented for 16-bit Windows or DOS.)

Macro	Execution Mode
P_NOWAITO	Same as P_NOWAIT, except that the child process ID is not returned to the parent.
P_DETACH	Same as P_NOWAITO, except that the child executes as a background process.
P_OVERLAY	Replaces the parent process in memory.

If you use the **P_WAIT** option, when the child process terminates, the parent process is resumed at the line after the call to **spawn**.

If no extension or period is part of the string pointed to by *fname*, a search is made for a file by that name. If that fails, then an .EXE extension is tried. If that fails, the .COM extension is added and the search is tried again. If that fails, then a .BAT extension is tried. If an extension is specified, only an exact match satisfies the search. If a period but no extension is present, a search is made for only the file specified by the left side of the file name.

The exact way the child process is executed depends on which version of **spawn** you use. You can think of the **spawn** function as having different suffixes that determine its operation. A suffix can consist of either one or two characters.

Those functions that have a **p** in the suffix search for the child process in the directories specified by the PATH command. If a **p** is not in the suffix, only the current directory is searched.

An **l** in the suffix specifies that pointers to the arguments to the child process will be passed individually. Use this method when passing a fixed number of arguments. Notice that the last argument must be **NULL**. (**NULL** is defined in **stdio.h**.)

A **v** in the suffix means that pointers to the arguments to the child process will be passed in an array. This is the way you must pass arguments when you do not know in advance how many there will be or when the number of arguments may change during the execution of your program. Typically, the end of the array is signaled by a null pointer.

An **e** in the suffix specifies that one or more environmental strings will be passed to the child process. The *envp[ ]* parameter is an array of string pointers. Each string pointed to by the array must have the form:

environment-variable = value

The last pointer in the array must be **NULL**. If the first element in the array is **NULL**, the child retains the same environment as the parent.

It is important to remember that files open at the time of a **spawn** call are also open in the child process.

When successful, the spawned functions return 0. On failure, they return –1 and set **errno** to one of the following values:

Macro	Meaning
EINVAL	Bad argument
E2BIG	Too many arguments
ENOENT	File not found
ENOEXEC	Format of **spawn** is invalid
ENOMEM	Not enough free memory to load child process

A spawned process can spawn another process. The level of nested spawns is limited by the amount of available RAM and the size of the programs.

Example

The first of the following programs invokes the second, which displays its arguments and invokes a third program. After the third program terminates, the second is resumed. When the second program terminates, the parent program is resumed. Remember that the three programs must be in separate files.

```
/* Parent process */
#include <stdio.h>
#include <process.h>

int main(void)
{
  printf("In parent\n");
  spawnl(P_WAIT, "test.exe", "test.exe", "hello", "10", NULL);
  printf("In parent\n");
  return 0;
}
```

```
/* First child */
#include <stdio.h>
#include <stdlib.h>
#include <process.h>

int main(int argc, char *argv[])
{
  printf("First child process executing ");
  printf("with these command line arguments: ");
  printf(argv[1]);
  printf(" %d\n", atoi(argv[2]));
  spawnl(P_WAIT, "test2.exe", NULL);
```

```
  printf("In first child process.\n");
  return 0;
}


/* Second child */
#include <stdio.h>
int main(void)
{
  printf("In second child process.\n");
  return 0;
}
```

Related Function

exec( )

Chapter Eighteen

Text and Graphics Functions

The ANSI C standard doesn't define any text or graphics functions, mainly because the capabilities of diverse hardware environments preclude standardization across a wide range of machines. However, Borland C++ provides extensive screen and graphics support systems for a 16-bit, DOS-based PC environment. If you will be using DOS and not be porting your code to a different compiler, you should feel free to use them. Note that none of the functions described in this chapter relate to or can be used for Windows programming. Graphical output in Windows is accomplished through the use of API (Application Program Interface) functions provided by Windows. The functions described in this chapter relate only to DOS (or a DOS session run under Windows). The prototypes and header information for the text-handling functions are in **conio.h**. The prototypes and related information for the graphics system are in **graphics.h**. None of the functions described in this chapter are defined by the ANSI C standard or C++.

The graphics system requires that the **graphics.lib** library be linked with your program. If you are using the command-line compiler, you need to include its name on the command line. For example, if your program is called **test** and you are using the command-line compiler, your command line should look like this:

```
bcc test graphics.lib
```

If you use the integrated development environment, you must remember to add **graphics.lib** to your project. Frankly, for 16-bit DOS programs, it is usually easier to simply use the command-line compiler.

Central to both the text and graphics functions is the concept of the *window*, the active part of the screen within which output is displayed. A window can be as large as the entire screen, as it is by default, or as small as your specific needs require. Borland C++ uses slightly different terminology between the text and graphics systems to help keep the two systems separate. The text functions refer to *windows*; the graphics system refers to *viewports*. However, the concept is the same. In general, all output is contained within the active window. That is, output that would extend beyond the boundaries of a window or viewport is automatically clipped.

When using graphics, your program must first initialize the graphics system by calling **initgraph( )**. When your program has finished using graphics, it must call **closegraph( )** or **restorecrtmode( )**. The sample programs demonstrate how to initialize and close
the graphics subsystem.

It is important to understand that most of the text and graphics functions are window (viewport) relative. For example, the **gotoxy( )** cursor location function sends the cursor to the specified *x,y* position relative to the window, not the screen.

One last point: When the screen is in a text mode, the upper left corner is location 1,1. In a graphics mode, the upper left corner is 0,0.

void far arc(int x, int y, int start, int end, int radius)

Description

The prototype for **arc( )** is in **graphics.h**.

The **arc( )** function draws an arc from *start* to *end* (given in degrees), along the invisible circle centered at *x,y*, with the radius *radius*. The color of the arc is determined by the current drawing color.

Example

This code draws an arc from 0 to 90 degrees on an imaginary circle located at 100,100 with the radius 20:

```
#include <graphics.h>
#include <conio.h>

int main(void)
{
  int driver, mode;

  driver = DETECT; /* autodetect */
  mode = 0;
  initgraph(&driver, &mode, "c:\\bc5\\bgi");

  setcolor(WHITE);
  arc(100, 100, 0, 90, 20);
```

```
  getch(); /* wait until keypress */
  restorecrtmode();

  return 0;
}
```

Related Functions

circle( ), ellipse( ), getarccoords( )

void far bar(int left, int top, int right, int bottom)
void far bar3d(int left, int top, int right, int bottom, int depth, int topflag)

Description

The prototypes for **bar( )** and **bar3d( )** are in **graphics.h**.

The **bar( )** function draws a rectangular bar that has its upper left corner defined by *left,top* and its lower right corner defined by *right,bottom*. The bar is filled with the current fill pattern and color. (You set the current fill pattern and color using **setfillpattern( )**.) The bar is not outlined.

The **bar3d( )** function is the same as **bar( )** except that it produces a three-dimensional bar of *depth* pixels. The bar is outlined in the current drawing color. This means that if you want a two-dimensional bar that is outlined, use **bar3d( )** with a depth of 0. If *topflag* is non-0, a top is added to the bar; otherwise, the bar has no top.

Example

This program draws a two-dimensional and a three-dimensional bar:

```
#include <graphics.h>
#include <conio.h>

int main(void)
{
  int driver, mode;
  driver = DETECT; /* autodetect */
  mode = 0;
  initgraph(&driver, &mode, "c:\\bc5\\bgi");

  /* display a green 2-d bar */
  setfillstyle(SOLID_FILL, GREEN);
  bar(100, 100, 120, 200);

  /* now show a red 3-d bar */
  setfillstyle(SOLID_FILL, RED);
```

```
  bar3d(200, 100, 220, 200, 10, 1);

  getch();
  restorecrtmode();
  return 0;
}
```

Related Function

rectangle( )

void far circle(int x, int y, int radius)

Description

The prototype for **circle( )** is in **graphics.h**.

The **circle( )** function draws a circle centered at *x,y* with radius *radius* (expressed in pixels) in the current drawing color.

Example

This program draws five concentric circles at location 200,200:

```
#include <graphics.h>
#include <conio.h>

int main(void)
{
  int driver, mode;
  driver = DETECT; /* autodetect */
  mode = 0;
  initgraph(&driver, &mode, "c:\\bc5\\bgi");

  circle(200, 200, 20);
  circle(200, 200, 30);
  circle(200, 200, 40);
  circle(200, 200, 50);
  circle(200, 200, 60);

  getch();
  restorecrtmode();
  return 0;
}
```

Related Functions

arc( ), ellipse( )

void far cleardevice(void)
void far clearviewport(void)

Description

The prototypes for **cleardevice( )** and **clearviewport( )** are in **graphics.h**.

The **cleardevice( )** function clears the screen and resets the current position (CP) to 0,0. This function is used only with the graphics screen modes.

The **clearviewport( )** function clears the current viewport and resets the current position (CP) to 0,0. After **clearviewport( )** has executed, the viewport no longer exists.

Example

This program creates a viewport, writes some text into it, and then clears it:

```
#include <graphics.h>
#include <conio.h>

void box(int, int, int, int, int);

int main(void)
{
  int driver, mode;

  driver = DETECT; /* autodetect */
  mode = 0;
  initgraph(&driver, &mode, "c:\\bc5\\bgi");

  /* frame the screen for perspective */
  box(0, 0, 639, 349, WHITE);

  setviewport(20, 20, 200, 200, 1);
  box(0, 0, 179, 179, RED);

  outtext("this is a test of the viewport");

  outtextxy(20, 10, "press a key");
  getch();
  /* clear the current viewport but not the entire screen */
  clearviewport();

  getch();
  restorecrtmode();
  return 0;
}
```

```
/* Draw a box given the coordinates of its two corners. */
void box(int startx, int starty, int endx, int endy,
         int color)
{
  setcolor(color);
  line(startx, starty, startx, endy);
  line(startx, starty, endx, starty);
  line(endx, starty, endx, endy);
  line(endx, endy, startx, endy);
}
```

Related Function

getviewsettings( )

void far closegraph(void)

Description

The prototype for **closegraph( )** is in **graphics.h**.

The **closegraph( )** function deactivates the graphics environment, which includes returning to the system memory that was used to hold the graphics drivers and fonts. This function should be used when your program uses both graphics and nongraphics output. It also returns the system video mode to what it was prior to the call to **initgraph( )**. You may also use **restorecrtmode( )** in place of **closegraph( )** if your program is terminating. In this case, any allocated memory is automatically freed.

Example

This fragment turns off the graphics system:

```
closegraph();
cprintf("this is not in graphics");
```

Related Function

initgraph( )

void clreol(void)
void clrscr(void)

Description

The prototypes for **clreol( )** and **clrscr( )** are in **conio.h**.

The **clreol( )** function clears from the current cursor position to the end of the line in the active text window. The cursor position remains unchanged.

The **clrscr( )** function clears the entire active text window and locates the cursor in the upper left corner (1,1).

Example

This program illustrates **clreol( )** and **clrscr( )**:

```
#include <conio.h>

int main(void)
{
  register int i;

  gotoxy(10, 10);
  cprintf("This is a test of the clreol() function.");
  getch();
  gotoxy(10, 10);
  clreol();

  for(i=0; i<20; i++) cprintf("Hello there\n\r");
  getch();

  /* clear the screen */
  clrscr();
  return 0;
}
```

Related Functions

delline( ), window( )

int cprintf(const char *fmt, . . .)

Description

The prototype for **cprintf( )** is in **conio.h**.

The **cprintf( )** function works like the **printf( )** function except that it writes to the current text window instead of **stdout**. Its output may not be redirected and it automatically prevents the boundaries of the window from being overrun. See the **printf( )** function for details.

The **cprintf( )** function does not translate the newline (\n) into the linefeed, carriage return pair as does the **printf( )** function, so it is necessary to explicitly put the carriage return (\r) where desired.

The **cprintf( )** function returns the number of characters actually printed. A negative return value indicates that an error has taken place.

Example

This program displays the output shown in its comments:

```
#include <conio.h>

int main(void)
{
  /* This prints "this is a test" left justified
     in 20 character field.
  */
  cprintf("%-20s", "this is a test");

  /* This prints a float with 3 decimal places in a 10
     character field. The output will be "    12.235".
  */
  cprintf("%10.3f\n\r", 12.234657);
  return 0;
}
```

Related Functions

cscanf( ), cputs( )

int cputs(const char *str)

Description

The prototype for **cputs( )** is in **conio.h**.

The **cputs( )** function outputs the string pointed to by *str* to the current text window. Its output cannot be redirected, and it automatically prevents the boundaries of the window from being overrun.

It returns the last character written if successful and **EOF** if unsuccessful.

Example

This program creates a window and uses **cputs( )** to write a line longer than will fit in the window. The line is automatically wrapped at the end of the window instead of spilling over into the rest of the screen.

```
#include <conio.h>

void border(int, int, int, int);

int main(void)
{
  clrscr();
  /* create first window */
```

```
  window(3, 2, 40, 9);
  border(3, 2, 40, 9);
  gotoxy(1,1);
  cputs("This line will be wrapped at the end of the window.");
  getche();
  return 0;
}

/* Draws a border around a text window. */
void border(int startx, int starty, int endx, int endy)
 {
  register int i;

  gotoxy(1, 1);
  for(i=0; i<=endx-startx; i++)
    putch('-');

  gotoxy(1, endy-starty);
  for(i=0; i<=endx-startx; i++)
    putch('-');

  for(i=2; i<endy-starty; i++) {
    gotoxy(1, i);
    putch('|');
    gotoxy(endx-startx+1, i);
    putch('|');
  }
}
```

Related Functions

cprintf( ), **window( )**

int cscanf(char *fmt, . . .)

Description

The prototype for **cscanf( )** is in **conio.h**.

The **cscanf( )** function works like the **scanf( )** function except that it reads the information from the console instead of **stdin**. It cannot be redirected. See the **scanf( )** function for details.

The **cscanf( )** function returns the number of arguments that are actually assigned values. This number does not include skipped fields. The **cscanf( )** function returns the value **EOF** if an attempt is made to read past end-of-file.

Example

This code fragment reads a string and a **float** number from the console:

```
char str[80];
float f;

cscanf("%s%f", str, &f);
```

Related Functions

scanf( ), cprintf( ), sscanf( )

void delline(void)

Description

The prototype for **delline( )** is in **conio.h**.

The **delline( )** function deletes the line in the active window that contains the cursor. All lines below the deleted line are moved up to fill the void. Remember that if the current window is smaller than the entire screen, only the text inside the window is affected.

Example

This program prints 24 lines on the screen and then deletes line 3:

```
#include <conio.h>

int main(void)
{
  register int i;

  clrscr();

  for(i=0; i<24; i++) cprintf("line %d\n\r", i);
  getch();
  gotoxy(1, 3);
  delline();

  getch();
  return 0;
}
```

Related Functions

clreol( ), insline( )

void far detectgraph(int far *driver, int far *mode)

Description

The prototype for **detectgraph( )** is in **graphics.h**.

The **detectgraph( )** function determines what type of graphics adapter, if any, the computer contains. If the system has a graphics adapter, **detectgraph( )** returns the number of the appropriate graphics driver for the adapter in the integer pointed to by *driver*. It sets the variable pointed to by *mode* to the highest resolution supported by the adapter. If no graphics hardware is in the system, the variable pointed to by *driver* contains a –2.

You can use **detectgraph( )** to determine what type of videographics hardware is in the system.

Example

This fragment tests for the presence of a video adapter:

```
int driver, mode;
detectgraph(&driver, &mode);

if(driver==-2) {
  cprintf("No graphics adapter in the system.\n");
  exit(1);
}
```

Related Function

initgraph( )

void far drawpoly(int numpoints, int far *points)

Description

The prototype for **drawpoly( )** is in **graphics.h**.

The **drawpoly( )** function draws a polygon using the current drawing color. The number of endpoints in the polygon is equal to *numpoints*. Since each point consists of both *x* and *y* coordinates, the integer array pointed to by *points* must be at least as large as two times the number of points. Within this array, each point is defined by its *x,y* coordinate pair with the *x* coordinate first.

Example

This program draws the polygon defined in the array **shape**:

```
#include <graphics.h>
#include <conio.h>
```

```
int main(void)
{
  int driver, mode;
  int shape[10] = { /* five points * 2 */
    10, 10,
    100, 80,
    200, 200,
    350, 90,
    0, 0
  };

  driver = DETECT; /* autodetect */
  mode = 0;
  initgraph(&driver, &mode, "c:\\bc5\\bgi");

  drawpoly(5, shape);
  getch();
  restorecrtmode();
  return 0;
}
```

Related Functions

fillpoly( ), line( ), circle( )

void far ellipse(int x, int y, int start, int end, int xr, int yr)

Description

The prototype for **ellipse( )** is in **graphics.h**.

The **ellipse( )** function draws an ellipse in the current drawing color. The center of the ellipse is at *x,y*. The length of the *x* and *y* radii are specified by *xr* and *yr*. The amount of the ellipse actually displayed is determined by the values for *start* and *end*, which are specified in degrees. If *start* equals 0 and *end* equals 360, the entire ellipse is shown.

Example

This program draws an egg-shaped ellipse on the screen:

```
#include <graphics.h>
#include <conio.h>

int main(void)
{  int driver, mode;
```

```
  driver = DETECT; /* autodetect */
  mode = 0;
  initgraph(&driver, &mode, "c:\\bc5\\bgi");

  ellipse(100, 100, 0, 360, 80, 40);

  getch();
  restorecrtmode();
  return 0;
}
```

Related Functions

circle( ), **arc( )**

void far fillellipse(int x, int y, int xr, int yr)

Description

The prototype for **fillellipse( )** is in **graphics.h**.

The **fillellipse( )** function draws and fills an ellipse using the current fill color and pattern. The outline of the ellipse is drawn in the current drawing color. The center of the ellipse is at *x,y*. The length of the *x* and *y* radii are specified by *xr* and *yr*.

Example

This program draws an egg-shaped ellipse on the screen and fills it using the default fill color and pattern.

```
#include <graphics.h>
#include <conio.h>

int main(void)
{
  int driver, mode;

  driver = DETECT; /* autodetect */
  mode = 0;
  initgraph(&driver, &mode, "c:\\bc5\\bgi");

  fillellipse(100, 100, 80, 40);

  getch();
  restorecrtmode();
  return 0;
}
```

Related Functions

fillpoly( ), **ellipse( )**, **floodfill( )**

void far fillpoly(int numpoints, int far *points)

Description

The prototype for **fillpoly( )** is in **graphics.h**.

The **fillpoly( )** function first draws the object, in the current drawing color, consisting of *numpoints* points defined by the *x,y* coordinates in the array pointed to by *points*. (See **drawpoly( )** for details on the construction of a polygon.) It then proceeds to fill the object using the current fill pattern and color. The fill pattern can be set by calling **setfillpattern( )**.

Example

This program fills a triangle with magenta interleaving:

```
#include <graphics.h>
#include <conio.h>

int main(void)
{
  int driver, mode;

  int shape[] = {
    100, 100,
    100, 200,
    200, 200,
    100, 100
  };

  driver = DETECT; /* autodetect */
  mode = 0;
  initgraph(&driver, &mode, "c:\\bc5\\bgi");

  setfillstyle(INTERLEAVE_FILL, MAGENTA);
  fillpoly(4, shape);

  getch();
  restorecrtmode();
  return 0;
}
```

Related Function

floodfill( )

void far floodfill(int x, int y, int border)

Description

The prototype for **floodfill( )** is in **graphics.h**.

The **floodfill( )** function fills an object with the current fill color and pattern given the coordinates of any point within that object and the color of the border of the object (the color of the lines or arcs that make up the object). You must make sure that the object you are filling is completely enclosed. If it isn't, the area outside the shape will also be filled. The background color is used by default, but you can change the way objects are filled using **setfillstyle( )**.

Example

This program uses **floodfill( )** to fill an ellipse with magenta cross-hatching:

```
#include <graphics.h>
#include <conio.h>

int main(void)
{
  int driver, mode;

  driver = DETECT; /* autodetect */
  mode = 0;
  initgraph(&driver, &mode, "c:\\bc5\\bgi");

  ellipse(100, 100, 0, 360, 80, 40);

  setfillstyle(XHATCH_FILL, MAGENTA);
  floodfill(100, 100, WHITE);

  getch();
  restorecrtmode();
  return 0;
}
```

Related Function

fillpoly( )

void far getarccoords(struct arccoordstype far *coords)

Description

The prototype for **getarccoords( )** is in **graphics.h**.

The **getarccoords( )** function fills the structure pointed to by *coords* with coordinates related to the last call to **arc( )**. The **arccoordstype** structure is defined as

```
struct arccoordstype {
  int x, y;
  int xstart, ystart, xend, yend;
};
```

Here, **x** and **y** are the center of the imaginary circle about which the arc is drawn. The starting and ending *x,y* coordinates are stored in **xstart, ystart** and **xend, yend**.

Example

This program draws a quarter of a circle about point 100,100 and then connects a line between the arc's endpoints:

```
#include <graphics.h>
#include <conio.h>

int main(void)
{
  int driver, mode;
  struct arccoordstype ac;

  driver = DETECT; /* autodetect */
  mode = 0;
  initgraph(&driver, &mode, "c:\\bc5\\bgi");

  arc(100, 100, 0, 90, 100);

  /* now, draw a line between the endpoints of the arc */
  getarccoords(&ac);   /* get the coordinates */
  line(ac.xstart, ac.ystart, ac.xend, ac.yend);

  getch();
  restorecrtmode();
  return 0;
}
```

Related Functions
line( ), pieslice( )

void far getaspectratio(int far *xasp, int far *yasp)

Description
The prototype for **getaspectratio( )** is in **graphics.h**.

The **getaspectratio( )** function copies the *x* aspect ratio into the variable pointed to by *xasp* and the *y* aspect ratio into the variable pointed to by *yasp*. You can manipulate these aspect ratios to alter the way objects are displayed on the screen.

Example
This fragment prints the aspect ratios:

```
int xasp, yasp;

getaspectratio(&xasp, &yasp);

cprintf("X,Y aspect ratios %d %d", xasp, yasp);
```

Related Functions
setaspectratio( ), circle( )

int far getbkcolor(void)

Description
The prototype for **getbkcolor( )** is in **graphics.h**.

The **getbkcolor( )** function returns the current background color. The values and their corresponding macros (defined in **graphics.h**) are shown here:

Macro	Integer Equivalent
BLACK	0
BLUE	1
GREEN	2
CYAN	3
RED	4
MAGENTA	5
BROWN	6

Macro	Integer Equivalent
LIGHTGRAY	7
DARKGRAY	8
LIGHTBLUE	9
LIGHTGREEN	10
LIGHTCYAN	11
LIGHTRED	12
LIGHTMAGENTA	13
YELLOW	14
WHITE	15

Example

This fragment displays the current background color:

```
cprintf("background color is %d", getbkcolor());
```

Related Function

setbkcolor( )

int far getcolor(void)

Description

The prototype for **getcolor( )** is in **graphics.h**.

The **getcolor( )** function returns the current drawing color.

Example

This fragment displays the current drawing color:

```
cprintf("drawing color is %d", getcolor());
```

Related Function

setcolor( )

struct palettetype *far getdefaultpalette(void)

Description

The prototype for **getdefaultpalette( )** is in **graphics.h**.

The **getdefaultpalette( )** function returns the default palette defined by the graphics driver used in the call to **initgraph( )**. The structure of **palettetype** is defined in **graphics.h** as

```
struct palettetype {
  unsigned char size;
  signed char colors[MAXCOLORS + 1];
};
```

Example

This code illustrates a call to **getdefaultpalette( )**:

```
struct palettetype far *p;
p = getdefaultpalette();
```

Related Functions

setpalette( ), getpalette( )

char *far getdrivername(void)

Description

The prototype for **getdrivername( )** is in **graphics.h**.

The **getdrivername( )** function returns the name of the current graphics driver. The name is a string held in a statically allocated character array. The contents of this array are overwritten each time you call the function. If you wish to save the contents of the array, you must copy the string elsewhere.

Example

This program displays the name of the current driver:

```
#include <graphics.h>
#include <conio.h>

int main(void)
{
  int driver, mode;
  char *name;
  driver = DETECT; /* autodetect */
  mode = 0;
  initgraph(&driver, &mode, "c:\\bc5\\bgi");

  name = getdrivername();

  outtextxy(10, 10, name);
```

```
  getch();
  restorecrtmode();
  return 0;
}
```

Related Functions

initgraph( ), getmodename( )

void far getfillpattern(char far *pattern)

Description

The prototype for **getfillpattern( )** is in **graphics.h**.

The **getfillpattern( )** function fills the array pointed to by *pattern* with the 8 bytes that make up the current fill pattern. The array must be at least 8 bytes long. The pattern is arranged as an 8-bit by 8-byte pattern.

Example

This program displays the bytes that make up the current fill pattern:

```
#include <stdio.h>
#include <graphics.h>
#include <conio.h>

int main(void)
{
  int driver, mode;
  char f[8], num[10];
  int i;

  driver = DETECT; /* autodetect */
  mode = 0;
  initgraph(&driver, &mode, "c:\\bc5\\bgi");
  getfillpattern((char far *) &f);

  /* display each byte in fill pattern */
  for(i=0; i<8; i++) {
    sprintf(num, "%d ", f[i]);
    outtext(num);
  }

  getch();
  restorecrtmode();
```

```
  return 0;
}
```

Related Functions

setfillpattern( ), setfillstyle( )

void far getfillsettings(struct fillsettingstype far *info)

Description

The prototype for **getfillsettings( )** is in **graphics.h**.

The **getfillsettings( )** function fills the structure pointed to by *info* with the number of the fill pattern and the color currently in use. The **fillsettingstype** structure is defined in **graphics.h** as

```
struct fillsettingstype {
  int pattern;
  int color;
};
```

The values for **pattern** are shown here along with their macro equivalents (defined in **graphics.h**):

Macro	**Value**	**Meaning**
EMPTY_FILL	0	Fill with background color
SOLID_FILL	1	Fill with solid color
LINE_FILL	2	Fill with lines
LTSLASH_FILL	3	Fill with light slashes
SLASH_FILL	4	Fill with slashes
BKSLASH_FILL	5	Fill with backslashes
LTBKSLASH_FILL	6	Fill with light backslashes
HATCH_FILL	7	Fill with light hatching
XHATCH_FILL	8	Fill with hatching
INTERLEAVE_FILL	9	Fill with interleaving
WIDE_DOT_FILL	10	Fill with widely spaced dots
CLOSE_DOT_FILL	11	Fill with closely spaced dots
USER_FILL	12	Fill with custom pattern

The color will be one of the colors valid in the video mode currently in use.

Example

This fragment reads the current fill pattern and color:

```
struct fillsettingstype p;

getfillsettings(&p);
```

Related Function

setfillsettings( )

int far getgraphmode(void)

Description

The prototype for **getgraphmode( )** is in **graphics.h**.

The **getgraphmode( )** function returns the current graphics mode. The value returned does *not* correspond to the actual value BIOS associates with the active video mode. Instead, the value returned is relative to the current video driver. The value returned will be one of these values, as defined in **graphics.h**:

Macro	Value	Resolution
CGAC0	0	320 × 200
CGAC1	1	320 × 200
CGAC2	2	320 × 200
CGAC3	3	320 × 200
CGAHI	4	640 × 200
MCGAC0	0	320 × 200
MCGAC1	1	320 × 200
MCGAC2	2	320 × 200
MCGAC3	3	320 × 200
MCGAMED	4	640 × 200
MCGAHI	5	640 × 480
EGALO	0	640 × 200
EGAHI	1	640 × 350
EGA64LO	0	640 × 200
EGA64HI	1	640 × 350

Macro	Value	Resolution
EGAMONOHI	3	640 × 350
HERCMONOHI	0	720 × 348
ATT400C0	0	320 × 200
ATT400C1	1	320 × 200
ATT400C2	2	320 × 200
ATT400C3	3	320 × 200
ATT400MED	4	640 × 200
ATT400HI	5	640 × 400
VGALO	0	640 × 200
VGAMED	1	640 × 350
VGAHI	2	640 × 480
PC3270HI	0	720 × 350
IBM8514HI	1	1024 × 768
IBM8514LO	0	640 × 480

Example

This fragment displays the number of the current graphics mode relative to the active graphics driver:

```
printf("graphics mode is %d", getgraphmode());
```

Related Function

setgraphmode( )

void far getimage(int left, int top, int right, int bottom, void far *buf)

Description

The prototype for **getimage( )** is in **graphics.h**.

The **getimage( )** function copies the portion of the graphics screen with upper left corner coordinates *left,top* and lower right corner coordinates *right,bottom* into the region of memory pointed to by *buf*.

To determine the number of bytes needed to store an image, use the **imagesize( )** function. An image stored using **getimage( )** can be written to the screen using the **putimage( )** function.

Example

This program copies a rectangle with two diagonal lines to other screen locations:

```
/* This program demonstrates how a graphics image can be
   moved using getimage(), imagesize(), and putimage().
*/
#include <conio.h>
#include <graphics.h>
#include <stdlib.h>
void box(int, int, int, int, int);

int main(void)
{
  int driver, mode;
  unsigned size;
  void *buf;

  driver = DETECT; /* autodetect */
  mode = 0;
  initgraph(&driver, &mode, "c:\\bc5\\bgi");

  box(20, 20, 200, 200, 15);
  setcolor(RED);
  line(20, 20, 200, 200);
  setcolor(GREEN);
  line(20, 200, 200, 20);
  getch();

  /* move the image */

  /* first, get the image's size */
  size = imagesize(20, 20, 200, 200);
  if(size != 0xffff) { /* alloc memory for the image */
    buf = malloc(size);
    if(buf) {
      getimage(20, 20, 200, 200, buf);
      putimage(100, 100, buf, COPY_PUT);
      putimage(300, 50, buf, COPY_PUT);
    }
  }
  outtext("Press a key.");
  getch();
  restorecrtmode();
  return 0;
```

```
}

/* Draw a box given the coordinates of its two corners. */
void box(int startx, int starty, int endx, int endy,
         int color)
{
  setcolor(color);

  line(startx, starty, startx, endy);
  line(startx, starty, endx, starty);
  line(endx, starty, endx, endy);
  line(endx, endy, startx, endy);
}
```

Related Functions

putimage( ), imagesize( )

void far getlinesettings(struct linesettingstype far *info)

Description

The prototype for **getlinesettings( )** is in **graphics.h**.

The **getlinesettings( )** function fills the structure pointed to by *info* with the current line style. The structure **linesettingstype** is defined as

```
struct linesettingstype {
  int linestyle;
  unsigned upattern;
  int thickness;
};
```

The **linestyle** element holds the style of the line. It will be one of these enumerated values (defined in **graphics.h**):

Value	Meaning
SOLID_LINE	Unbroken line
DOTTED_LINE	Dotted line
CENTER_LINE	Centered line (dash-dot-dash)
DASHED_LINE	Dashed line
USERBIT_LINE	User-defined line

If **linestyle** is equal to **USERBIT_LINE**, the 16-bit pattern in **upattern** determines how the line appears. Each bit in the pattern corresponds to one pixel. If that bit is set, the pixel is turned on; otherwise, it is turned off.

The **thickness** element will have one of these values:

Value	Meaning
NORM_WIDTH	Line is 1 pixel wide
THICK_WIDTH	Line is 3 pixels wide

Example

This fragment reads the current line settings:

```
struct linesettingstype info;

getlinesettings(&info);
```

Related Function

setlinestyle( )

int far getmaxcolor(void)

Description

The prototype for **getmaxcolor( )** is in **graphics.h**.

The **getmaxcolor( )** function returns the largest valid color value for the current video mode. For example, in four-color CGA mode, this number will be 3. (The color values for this mode are 0 through 3.)

Example

This program displays the largest valid color value:

```
#include <stdio.h>
#include <graphics.h>
#include <conio.h>

int main(void)
{
  int driver, mode;

  driver = DETECT; /* autodetect */
  mode = 0;
  initgraph(&driver, &mode, "c:\\bc5\\bgi");

  printf("largest color: %d", getmaxcolor());
```

```
  getch();
  restorecrtmode();
  return 0;
}
```

Related Functions

getbkcolor( ), **getpalette( )**

int far getmaxmode(void)

Description

The prototype for **getmaxmode( )** is in **graphics.h**.

The **getmaxmode( )** function returns the maximum mode available for the current graphics driver.

Example

This fragment illustrates a call to **getmaxmode( )**:

```
int mode;
mode = getmaxmode();
```

Related Function

getmoderange( )

int far getmaxx(void)
int far getmaxy(void)

Description

The prototypes for **getmaxx( )** and **getmaxy( )** are in **graphics.h**.

The **getmaxx( )** function returns the largest valid *x* value for the current graphics mode.

The **getmaxy( )** function returns the largest valid *y* value for the current graphics mode.

Example

This code displays the maximum *x* and *y* coordinates supported by the graphics hardware in the system:

```
#include <stdio.h>
#include <graphics.h>
#include <conio.h>

int main(void)
{
  int driver, mode;
```

```
  driver = DETECT; /* autodetect */
  mode = 0;
  initgraph(&driver, &mode, "c:\\bc5\\bgi");

  printf("max X,Y: %d,%d", getmaxx(), getmaxy());
  getch();
  restorecrtmode();
  return 0;
}
```

Related Function

getmaxcolor( )

char *far getmodename(int mode)

Description

The prototype for **getmodename( )** is in **graphics.h**.

The **getmodename( )** function returns the name of the specified mode. The value of *mode* is obtained in the call to **initgraph( )** or **getgraphmode( )**.

Example

This program displays the name of the current mode:

```
#include <graphics.h>
#include <conio.h>
int main(void)
{
  int driver, mode;
  char *name;
  driver = DETECT; /* autodetect */
  mode = 0;
  initgraph(&driver, &mode, "c:\\bc5\\bgi");

  name = getmodename(mode);   /* default mode */

  outtextxy(10, 10, name);

  getch();
  restorecrtmode();
  return 0;
}
```

Related Functions

initgraph( ), getdrivername( )

void far getmoderange(int driver, int far *lowmode, int far *himode)

Description

The prototype for **getmoderange( )** is in **graphics.h**.

The **getmoderange( )** function determines the lowest and highest modes supported by the graphics driver specified by *driver* and puts these values at the variables pointed to by *lowmode* and *himode,* respectively. The valid macros for *driver* are shown here (they are defined in **graphics.h**):

CGA
MCGA
EGA
EGA64
EGAMONO
IBM8514
HERCMONO
ATT400
VGA
PC3270

Example

This program displays the video mode range for the graphics hardware currently installed in the system:

```
#include <stdio.h>
#include <graphics.h>
#include <conio.h>

int main(void)
{
  int driver, mode;
  int high, low;

  driver = DETECT; /* autodetect */
  mode = 0;
  initgraph(&driver, &mode, "c:\\bc5\\bgi");

  getmoderange(driver, &low, &high);
```

```
    printf("mode range: %d - %d", low, high);
    getch();
    restorecrtmode();
    return 0;
}
```

Related Function

getgraphmode( )

void far getpalette(struct palettetype far *pal)

Description

The prototype for **getpalette( )** is in **graphics.h**.

The **getpalette( )** function loads the structure pointed to by *pal* with the current palette. The **palettetype** structure is defined as

```
struct palettetype {
  unsigned char size;
  signed char colors[MAXCOLORS + 1];
};
```

The **size** element holds the number of colors available in the current palette. The **colors** array holds the values for the colors available in the palette. The following colors, along with their macro names, are shown here.

CGA codes (background only):

Macro	Value
BLACK	0
BLUE	1
GREEN	2
CYAN	3
RED	4
MAGENTA	5
BROWN	6
LIGHTGRAY	7
DARKGRAY	8
LIGHTBLUE	9
LIGHTGREEN	10

Macro	Value
LIGHTCYAN	11
LIGHTRED	12
LIGHTMAGENTA	13
YELLOW	14
WHITE	15

EGA and VGA:

Macro	Value
EGA_BLACK	0
EGA_BLUE	1
EGA_GREEN	2
EGA_CYAN	3
EGA_RED	4
EGA_MAGENTA	5
EGA_BROWN	20
EGA_LIGHTGRAY	7
EGA_DARKGRAY	56
EGA_LIGHTBLUE	57
EGA_LIGHTGREEN	58
EGA_LIGHTCYAN	59
EGA_LIGHTRED	60
EGA_LIGHTMAGENTA	61
EGA_YELLOW	62
EGA_WHITE	63

Example

This program prints the number of colors supported by the default video mode:

```
#include <stdio.h>
#include <graphics.h>
#include <conio.h>
```

```
int main(void)
{
  int driver, mode;
  struct palettetype p;

  driver = DETECT; /* autodetect */
  mode = 0;
  initgraph(&driver, &mode, "c:\\bc5\\bgi");
  getpalette(&p);
  printf("number of colors in palette: %d", p.size);
  getch();
  restorecrtmode();
  return 0;
}
```

Related Function

setpalette( )

int far getpalettesize(void)

Description

The prototype for **getpalettesize( )** is in **graphics.h**.

The **getpalettesize( )** function returns the number of colors in the current palette.

Example

This program prints the number of colors in the current default palette:

```
#include <graphics.h>
#include <conio.h>
#include <stdio.h>

int main(void)
{
  int driver, mode;
  int num;
  char buff[100];

  driver = DETECT; /* autodetect */
  mode = 0;
  initgraph(&driver, &mode, "c:\\bc5\\bgi");

  num = getpalettesize();
  sprintf(buff, "Number of colors in palette: %d", num);
```

```
  outtextxy(10, 10, buff);

  getch();
  restorecrtmode();
  return 0;
}
```

Related Functions

setpalette( ), getpalette( )

unsigned far getpixel(int x, int y)

Description

The prototype for **getpixel( )** is in **graphics.h**.

The **getpixel( )** function returns the color of the pixel located at the specified *x,y* position.

Example

This fragment puts the value of the color at location 10,20 into the variable **color**:

```
color = getpixel(10, 20);
```

Related Function

putpixel( )

int gettext(int left, int top, int right, int bottom, void *buf)

Description

The prototype for **gettext( )** is in **conio.h**.

The **gettext( )** function copies the text from a rectangle with upper left corner coordinates *left,top* and lower right corner coordinates *right,bottom* into the buffer pointed to by *buf*. The coordinates are screen, not window, relative.

The amount of memory needed to hold a region of the screen is computed by the formula num_bytes = rows × columns × 2. The reason you must multiply the number of rows times the number of columns by 2 is that each character displayed on the screen requires 2 bytes of storage: 1 for the character itself and 1 for its attributes.

The function returns 1 on success and 0 on failure.

Example

This fragment copies a region of the screen into the memory pointed to by **buf**:

```
buf = malloc(10 * 10 *2);

gettext(10, 10, 20, 20, buf);
```

Related Functions

puttext( ), movetext( )

void gettextinfo(struct text_info *info)

Description

The prototype for **gettextinfo( )** is in **conio.h**.

The **gettextinfo( )** function obtains the current text settings and returns them in the structure pointed to by *info*. The **text_info** structure is declared as shown here:

```
struct text_info {
  unsigned char winleft;       /* upper left   */
  unsigned char wintop;        /* coordinates */
  unsigned char winright;      /* lower right */
  unsigned char winbottom;     /* coordinates */
  unsigned char attribute;     /* current attributes */
  unsigned char normattr;      /* normal attributes */
  unsigned char currmode;      /* active video mode */
  unsigned char screenheight;  /* screen */
  unsigned char screenwidth;   /* dimensions */
  unsigned char curx;          /* current X and */
  unsigned char cury;          /* Y cursor location */
};
```

Example

This fragment obtains the current text settings:

```
struct text_info i;
gettextinfo(&i);
```

Related Functions

textmode( ), gettextsettings( )

void far gettextsettings(struct textsettingstype far *info)

Description

The prototype for **gettextsettings( )** is in **graphics.h**.

The **gettextsettings( )** function loads the structure pointed to by *info* with information about the current graphics text settings. The structure **textsettingstype** is defined in **graphics.h** and is shown here:

```
struct textsettingstype {
  int font;        /* font type */
  int direction; /* horizontal or vertical */
  int charsize;  /* size of characters */
  int horiz;       /* horizontal justification */
  int vert;        /* vertical justification */
};
```

The **font** element will contain one of these values:

Value	**Font**
0	Default 8 × 8 bit-mapped font
1	Stroked triplex font
2	Stroked small font
3	Stroked sans serif font
4	Stroked gothic font
5	Stroked script font
6	Stroked simplex script font
7	Stroked triplex script font
8	Stroked complex font
9	Stroked European font
10	Stroked bold font

The **direction** element must be set to either **HORIZ_DIR** (the default) for horizontal text or **VERT_DIR** for vertical text. The **charsize** element is a multiplier used to scale the size of the output text. The value of **horiz** and **vert** indicate how text will be justified. They will be one of the following values:

Macro	**Meaning**
LEFT_TEXT	Left justify
CENTER_TEXT	Center horizontally
RIGHT_TEXT	Right justify
BOTTOM_TEXT	Bottom justify

Macro	Meaning
CENTER_TEXT	Center vertically
TOP_TEXT	Top justify

Example

This fragment reads the current text settings:

```
struct textsettingstype t;

gettextsettings(&t);
```

Related Function

settextstyle( )

void far getviewsettings(struct viewporttype far *info)

Description

The prototype for **getviewsettings( )** is in **graphics.h**.

The **getviewsettings( )** function loads information about the current viewport into the structure pointed to by *info*. The structure **viewporttype** is defined as

```
struct viewporttype {
  int left, top, right, bottom;
  int clip;
};
```

The fields **left**, **top**, **right**, and **bottom** hold the coordinates of the upper left and lower right corners of the viewport. When **clip** is 0, there is no clipping of output that overruns the viewport boundaries. Otherwise, clipping is performed to prevent boundary overrun.

Example

This fragment prints the dimensions of the current viewpoint:

```
struct viewporttype info;

getviewsettings(&info);

printf("View port is %dx%x by %dx%d", info.left, info.right,
       info.top, info.bottom);
```

Related Function

setviewport( )

int far getx(void)
int far gety(void)

Description

The prototypes for **getx( )** and **gety( )** are in **graphics.h**.

The functions **getx( )** and **gety( )** return the current position's (CP's) *x* and *y* location on the graphics screen. The CP is the location at which the next graphics output will take place.

Example

This fragment displays the CP's current location:

```
printf("CP's loc: %d, %d", getx(), gety());
```

Related Function

moveto( )

void gotoxy(int x, int y)

Description

The prototype for **gotoxy( )** is in **conio.h**.

The **gotoxy( )** function sends the text screen cursor to the location specified by *x,y*. If either or both of the coordinates are invalid, no action takes place.

Example

This program prints **X**s diagonally across the screen:

```
#include <conio.h>

int main(void)
{
  register int i, j;

  clrscr();

  /* print diagonal Xs */
  for(i=1, j=1; j<24; i+=3, j++) {
    gotoxy(i, j);
    cprintf("X");
  }
```

```
    getche();
    clrscr();
    return 0;
}
```

Related Functions

wherex( ), wherey( )

void far graphdefaults(void)

Description

The prototype for **graphdefaults( )** is in **graphics.h**.

The **graphdefaults( )** function resets the graphics system to its default settings. Specifically, the entire screen becomes the viewport with the CP (current position) located at 0,0. The palette, drawing color, and background color are reset; the fill style, fill pattern, text font, and justification are returned to their original values.

Example

This fragment resets the graphics system:

```
graphdefaults();
```

Related Functions

initgraph( ), setpalette( )

char *far grapherrormsg(int errcode)

Description

The prototype for **grapherrormsg( )** is in **graphics.h**.

The **grapherrormsg( )** function returns a pointer to the error message that corresponds to *errcode*. The error code is obtained by a call to **graphresult( )**.

See **graphresult( )** for details of the error conditions.

Example

This fragment displays the outcome of the last graphics operation:

```
printf("%s", grapherrormsg(graphresult()));
```

Related Function

graphresult( )

void far _graphfreemem(void far *ptr, unsigned size)
void far *far _graphgetmem(unsigned size)

Description

The prototypes for **_graphfreemem( )** and **_graphgetmem( )** are in **graphics.h**.

The **_graphgetmem( )** function is called by the graphics system to allocate memory for the graphics drivers and other graphics system needs. The **_graphfreemem( )** function frees this memory.

These functions should not generally be called directly by your programs.

int far graphresult(void)

Description

The prototype for **graphresult( )** is in **graphics.h**.

The **graphresult( )** function returns a value that represents the outcome of the last graphics operation. This value will be one of the following enumerated values:

Name	Value	Meaning
grOk	0	Successful
grNoInitGraph	–1	No driver installed
grNotDetected	–2	No graphics hardware in system
grFileNotFound	–3	Driver file not found
grInvalidDriver	–4	Invalid driver file
grNoLoadMem	–5	Not enough memory
grNoScanMem	–6	Insufficient memory for scan fill
grNoFloodMem	–7	Insufficient memory for flood fill
grFontNotFound	–8	Font file not found
grNoFontMem	–9	Insufficient memory for font
grInvalidMode	–10	Invalid mode
grError	–11	General graphics error
grIOerror	–12	I/O error
grInvalidFont	–13	Font file invalid
grInvalidFontNum	–14	Font number invalid
grInvalidVersion	–18	Version number invalid

Use **grapherrormsg( )** to display a graphics error message given its error number.

Example

This fragment displays the outcome of the last graphics operation:

```
printf("%s", grapherrormsg(graphresult()));
```

Related Function

grapherrormsg( )

void highvideo(void)

Description

The prototype for **highvideo( )** is in **conio.h**.

After a call to **highvideo( )**, characters written to the screen are displayed in high-intensity video. This function works only for text screens.

Example

This fragment turns on high-intensity output:

```
highvideo();
```

Related Functions

lowvideo( ), normvideo( )

unsigned far imagesize(int left, int top, int right, int bottom)

Description

The prototype for **imagesize( )** is in **graphics.h**.

The **imagesize( )** function returns the number of bytes of storage necessary to hold a portion of the screen with upper left corner coordinates *left,top* and lower right corner coordinates *right,bottom*. This function is generally used in conjunction with **getimage( )**. The **imagesize( )** function works only in graphics modes.

Example

This fragment determines the number of bytes needed to hold a graphics image at the specified location:

```
unsigned size;

size = imagesize(10, 10, 100, 100);
```

Related Function

getimage( )

void far initgraph(int far *driver, int far *mode, char far *path)

Description

The prototype for **initgraph( )** is in **graphics.h**.

The **initgraph( )** function is used to initialize the graphics system and to load the appropriate graphics driver. The **initgraph( )** function loads into memory a graphics driver that corresponds to the number pointed to by *driver.* Without a graphics driver loaded into memory, no graphics functions can operate. The video mode used by the graphics functions is specified by an integer pointed to by *mode.* Finally, a path to the driver can be specified in the string pointed to by *path.* If no path is specified, the current working directory is searched.

The graphics drivers are contained in .BGI files, which must be available on the system. However, you need not worry about the actual name of the file because you only have to specify the driver by its number. The header **graphics.h** defines several macros that you can use for this purpose. They are shown here:

Macro	Equivalent
DETECT	0
CGA	1
MCGA	2
EGA	3
EGA64	4
EGAMONO	5
IBM8514	6
HERCMONO	7
ATT400	8
VGA	9
PC3270	10

When you use **DETECT**, **initgraph( )** automatically detects the type of video hardware present in the system and selects the video mode with the greatest resolution. In this case, *driver* will contain the video driver when the function returns.

The value of *mode* must be one of the graphics modes shown here. Notice that the value pointed to by *mode* is not the same as the value recognized by the BIOS routine that actually sets the mode. Instead, the value used to call BIOS to initialize a video mode is created by **initgraph( )** using both the driver and the mode.

Driver	Mode	Equivalent	Resolution
CGA	CGAC0	0	320 × 200
	CGAC1	1	320 × 200
	CGAC2	2	320 × 200
	CGAC3	3	320 × 200
	CGAHI	4	640 × 200
MCGA	MCGAC0	0	320 × 200
	MCGAC1	1	320 × 200
	MCGAC2	2	320 × 200
	MCGAC3	3	320 × 200
	MCGAMED	4	640 × 200
	MCGAHI	5	640 × 480
EGA	EGALO	0	640 × 200
	EGAHI	1	640 × 350
EGA64	EGA64LO	0	640 × 200
	EGA64HI	1	640 × 350
EGAMONO	EGAMONOHI	3	640 × 350
HERC	HERCMONOHI	0	720 × 348
ATT400	ATT400C0	0	320 × 200
	ATT400C1	1	320 × 200
	ATT400C2	2	320 × 200
	ATT400C3	3	320 × 200
	ATT400MED	4	640 × 200
	ATT400HI	5	640 × 400
VGA	VGALO	0	640 × 200
	VGAMED	1	640 × 350
	VGAHI	2	640 × 480

Driver	Mode	Equivalent	Resolution
PC3270	PC3270HI	0	720 × 350
IBM8514	IBM8514HI	1	1024 × 768
	IBM8514LO	0	640 × 480

Example

This fragment uses **initgraph( )** to autodetect the graphics hardware and to select the mode of greatest resolution:

```
int driver, mode;

driver = DETECT; /* autodetect */
mode = 0;
initgraph(&driver, &mode, "");
```

Related Function

getgraphmode( )

void insline(void)

Description

The prototype for **insline( )** is in **conio.h**.

The **insline( )** function inserts a blank line at the current cursor position. All lines below the cursor move down. This function is for text mode only, and it operates relative to the current text window.

Example

The following program illustrates the use of **insline( )**:

```
#include <conio.h>

int main(void)
{
  register int i;

  clrscr();

  for(i=1; i<24; i++) {
    gotoxy(1, i);
    cprintf("This is line %d\n\r", i);
  }
  getche();
```

```
  gotoxy(1, 10);
  insline();
  getch();
  return 0;
}
```

Related Function

delline( )

int far installuserdriver(char far *drivername, int huge (*func)(void))

Description

The prototype for **installuserdriver( )** is in **graphics.h**.

The **installuserdriver( )** function allows you to install third-party BGI drivers. The *drivername* parameter specifies the driver name. The *func* parameter is a pointer to the function that provides autodetection of the required hardware for the installed driver. This parameter is optional and, if not used, **func** must be NULL.

The **installuserdriver( )** function returns the graphics driver's value, which you can then use to call **initgraph( )**.

Example

The following fragment assumes you have acquired a new BGI driver named **newdriver.bgi**:

```
int driver, mode;

driver = installuserdriver("newdriver", NULL);
mode = 0;
initgraph(&driver, &mode, "");
```

Related Function

installuserfont( )

int far installuserfont(char far *fontname)

Description

The prototype for **installuserfont( )** is in **graphics.h**.

The **installuserfont( )** function allows you to install third-party, stroked-character fonts. The parameter *fontname* is a pointer to the name of the file that contains the font.

The **installuserfont( )** function returns the ID number associated with the font, which can then be used in a call to **settextstyle( )** to activate the font. If the font table is full, **grError** is returned and the new font cannot be loaded. (Up to 20 fonts can be loaded at a time.)

Example

This fragment loads a .CHR font file named **newfont.chr**:

```
int fontnumber;

fontnumber = installuserfont("newfont.chr");
settextstyle(fontnumber, HORIZ_DIR, 1);
```

Related Function

installuserdriver( )

void far line(int startx, int starty, int endx, int endy)
void far lineto(int x, int y);
void far linerel(int deltax, int deltay)

Description

The prototypes for **line( )**, **lineto( )**, and **linerel( )** are in **graphics.h**.

The **line( )** function draws a line in the current drawing color from *startx,starty* to *endx,endy*. The current position is unchanged.

The **lineto( )** function draws a line in the current drawing color from the current position (CP) to *x,y* and locates the CP at *x,y*.

The **linerel( )** function draws a line from the CP to the location that is *deltax* units away in the *x* direction and *deltay* units away in the *y* direction. The CP is moved to the new location.

Example

This program illustrates the line functions:

```
#include <graphics.h>
#include <conio.h>

int main(void)
{
  int driver, mode;

  driver = DETECT; /* autodetect */
  mode = 0;
  initgraph(&driver, &mode, "c:\\bc5\\bgi");

  line(100, 100, 200, 200);
```

```
  lineto(100, 50);

  linerel(30, 40);

  getch();
  restorecrtmode();
  return 0;
}
```

Related Functions

circle( ), drawpoly( )

void lowvideo(void)

Description

The prototype for **lowvideo( )** is in **conio.h**.

After a call to **lowvideo( )**, characters written to the screen are displayed in low-intensity video. This function works only for text screens.

Example

This fragment turns on low-intensity output:

```
lowvideo();
```

Related Functions

highvideo( ), normvideo( )

void far moverel(int deltax, int deltay)

Description

The prototype for **moverel( )** is in **graphics.h**.

The **moverel( )** function advances the CP on a graphics screen by the magnitudes of *deltax* and *deltay*.

Example

If the CP is at location 10,10 prior to execution of the following statement, it will be at 20,30 after the statement executes:

```
moverel(10, 20);
```

Related Function

moveto( )

int movetext(int left, int top, int right, int bottom, int newleft, int newtop)

Description

The prototype for **movetext( )** is in **conio.h**.

The **movetext( )** function moves the portion of a text screen with the upper left corner at *left,top* and lower right corner at *right,bottom* to the region of the screen that has *newleft,newtop* as the coordinates of its upper left corner. This function is screen, not window, relative.

The **movetext( )** function returns 0 if one or more coordinates are out of range and non-0 otherwise.

Example

This fragment moves the contents of the rectangle with upper left corner coordinates of 1,1 and lower right corner coordinates of 8,8 to 10,10:

```
movetext(1, 1, 8, 8, 10, 10);
```

Related Function

gettext( )

void far moveto(int x, int y)

Description

The prototype for **moveto( )** is in **graphics.h**.

The **moveto( )** function moves the CP (current position) to the location specified by *x,y* relative to the current viewport.

The **moveto( )** graphics function corresponds to the text **gotoxy( )** function in operation.

Example

This fragment moves the CP to location 100,100:

```
moveto(100, 100);
```

Related Function

moverel( )

void normvideo(void)

Description

The prototype for **normvideo( )** is in **conio.h**.

After a call to **normvideo( )**, characters written to the screen are displayed in normal-intensity video. This function works only for text screens.

Example

This fragment turns on normal-intensity output:

```
normvideo();
```

Related Functions

highvideo( ), lowvideo( )

void far outtext(const char far *str)
void var outtextxy(int x, int y, const char *str)

Description

The prototypes for **outtext( )** and **outtextxy( )** are in **graphics.h**.

The **outtext( )** function displays a text string on a graphics mode screen at the current position using the active text settings (direction, font, size, and justification). If the active direction is horizontal, the CP (current position) is increased by the length of the string; otherwise, no change is made in the CP. In graphics modes, there is no visible cursor, but the current position on the screen is maintained as if there were an invisible cursor.

The **outtextxy( )** function is similar to **outtext( )**, except that it displays the string beginning at the location specified by *x,y*. These coordinates are relative to the current viewport.

To change the style of the text, refer to **settextstyle( )**.

Example

This program illustrates the use of **outtext( )** and **outtextxy( )**:

```
#include <graphics.h>
#include <conio.h>

int main(void)
{
  int driver, mode;
  int i;

  driver = DETECT; /* autodetect */
  mode = 0;
  initgraph(&driver, &mode, "c:\\bc5\\bgi");

  /* write two lines at CP */
```

```
  outtext("this is an example ");
  outtext("another line");

  /* use "cursor" positioning */
  for(i=100; i<200; i+=8) outtextxy(200, i, "hello");

  getch();
  restorecrtmode();
  return 0;
}
```

Related Function

settextstyle( )

void far pieslice(int x, int y, int start, int end, int radius)

Description

The prototype for **pieslice( )** is in **graphics.h**.

The **pieslice( )** function draws a pie slice, using the current drawing color, covering an angle equal to *end–start.* The beginning and ending points of the angle are specified in degrees. The center of the "circle" that the slice is "cut" from is at *x,y* and has a radius equal to *radius.* The slice is filled with the current fill pattern and color.

Example

This program prints a full circle of pie slices, each 45 degrees wide and each in a different color (this program requires EGA or VGA):

```
#include <graphics.h>
#include <conio.h>

int main(void)
{
  int driver, mode;
  int i, start, end;

  driver = DETECT; /* autodetect */
  mode = 0;
  initgraph(&driver, &mode, "c:\\bc5\\bgi");

  /* demonstrate pieslice() */

  start = 0; end = 45;
  for(i=0; i<8; i++) {
```

```
      setfillstyle(SOLID_FILL, i);
      pieslice(300, 200, start, end, 100);
      start += 45;
      end += 45;
    }

    getch();
    restorecrtmode();
    return 0;
}
```

Related Functions

arc( ), circle( )

void far putimage(int x, int y, void far *buf, int op)

Description

The prototype for **putimage( )** is in **graphics.h**.

The **putimage( )** function copies an image previously saved (by using **getimage( )**) in the memory location pointed to by *buf* to the screen beginning at location *x,y*. The value of *op* determines exactly how the image is written to the screen. Its valid enumerated values are

Name	Value	Meaning
COPY_PUT	0	Copy as is
XOR_PUT	1	Exclusive-OR with destination
OR_PUT	2	OR with destination
AND_PUT	3	AND with destination
NOT_PUT	4	Invert source image

Example

The following program demonstrates the **getimage( )**, **imagesize( )**, and **putimage( )** functions:

```
/* This program demonstrates how a graphics image can be
   moved using getimage(), imagesize(), and putimage().
*/
  #include <conio.h>
  #include <graphics.h>
  #include <stdlib.h>
```

```
void box(int, int, int, int, int);

int main(void)
{
  int driver, mode;
  unsigned size;
  void *buf;

  driver = DETECT; /* autodetect */
  mode = 0;
  initgraph(&driver, &mode, "c:\\bc5\\bgi");

  box(20, 20, 200, 200, 15);

  setcolor(RED);
  line(20, 20, 200, 200);
  setcolor(GREEN);
  line(20, 200, 200, 20);
  getch();

  /* move the image */

  /* first, get the image's size */
  size = imagesize(20, 20, 200, 200);
  if(size != 0xffff) { /* alloc memory for the image */
    buf = malloc(size);
    if(buf) {
      getimage(20, 20, 200, 200, buf);
      putimage(100, 100, buf, COPY_PUT);
      putimage(300, 50, buf, COPY_PUT);
    }
  }
  outtext("press a key");
  getch();
  restorecrtmode();
  return 0;
}

/* Draw a box given the coordinates of its two corners. */
void box(int startx, int starty, int endx, int endy,
         int color)
{
  setcolor(color);
```

```
  rectangle(startx, starty, endx, endy);
}
```

Related Functions

getimage( ), imagesize( )

void far putpixel(int x, int y, int color)

Description

The prototype for **putpixel( )** is in **graphics.h**.

The **putpixel( )** function writes the color specified by *color* to the pixel at location *x,y*.

Example

This fragment makes the pixel at location 10,20 green, assuming that green is supported by the current video mode:

```
putpixel(10, 20, GREEN);
```

Related Function

getpixel( )

int puttext(int left, int top, int right, int bottom, void *buf)

Description

The prototype for **puttext( )** is in **conio.h**.

The **puttext( )** function copies text previously saved by **gettext( )** from the buffer pointed to by *buf* into the region with upper left and lower right corners specified by *left,top* and *right,bottom*.

The **puttext( )** function uses screen-absolute, not window-relative, coordinates. It returns 0 if the coordinates are out of range, non-0 otherwise.

Example

This fragment copies a region of the screen into the memory pointed to by *buf* and puts that text in a new location:

```
buf = malloc(10 * 10 *2);
gettext(10, 10, 20, 20, buf);
puttext(0, 0, 30, 30, buf);
```

Related Functions

gettext( ), movetext( )

void far rectangle(int left, int top, int right, int bottom)

Description

The prototype for **rectangle( )** is in **graphics.h**.

The **rectangle( )** function draws a box as defined by the coordinates *left,top* and *right,bottom* in the current drawing color.

Example

This program draws some sample rectangles:

```
#include <graphics.h>
#include <conio.h>

int main(void)
{
  int driver, mode;

  driver = DETECT; /* autodetect */
  mode = 0;
  initgraph(&driver, &mode, "c:\\bc5\\bgi");

  rectangle(100, 100, 300, 300);
  rectangle(150, 90, 34, 300);
  rectangle(0, 0, 2, 2);

  getch();
  restorecrtmode();
  return 0;
}
```

Related Functions

bar( ), bar3d( ), line( )

int registerbgidriver(void (*driver)(void))
int registerbgifont(void (*font)(void))

Description

The prototypes for **registerbgidriver( )** and **registerbgifont( )** are in **graphics.h**.

These functions are used to notify the graphics system that either a graphics driver or a font, or both, have been linked in and there is no need to look for a corresponding disk file.

The actual registration process is somewhat difficult, and you should consult your user manual for details as they relate to your version of Borland C++.

void far restorecrtmode(void)

Description

The prototype for **restorecrtmode( )** is in **graphics.h**.

The **restorecrtmode( )** function restores the screen to the mode that it had prior to the call to **initgraph( )**.

Example

This fragment restores the screen to its original video mode:

```
restorecrtmode();
```

Related Function

initgraph( )

void far sector(int x, int y, int start, int end, int xr, int yr)

Description

The prototype for **sector( )** is in **graphics.h**.

The **sector( )** function draws an elliptical pie slice using the current drawing color and fills it using the current fill color and fill pattern. The slice covers an angle equal to *end–start.* The beginning and ending points of the angle are specified in degrees using the Cartesian coordinate plane, as shown in Figure 18-1. The center of the "ellipse" that the slice is "cut" from is at *x,y.* It has horizontal and vertical radii equal to *xr* and *yr.*

Example

This program prints a full ellipse of pie slices, each 45 degrees wide and each in a different color:

```
#include <graphics.h>
#include <conio.h>

int main(void)
{
  int driver, mode;
  int i, start, end;
```

```
  driver = DETECT; /* autodetect */
  mode = 0;
  initgraph(&driver, &mode, "c:\\bc5\\bgi");

  /* demonstrate sector() */

  start = 0; end = 45;
  for(i=0; i<8; i++) {
    setfillstyle(SOLID_FILL, i);
    sector(300, 200, start, end, 100, 200);
    start += 45;
    end += 45;
  }

  getch();
  restorecrtmode();
  return 0;
}
```

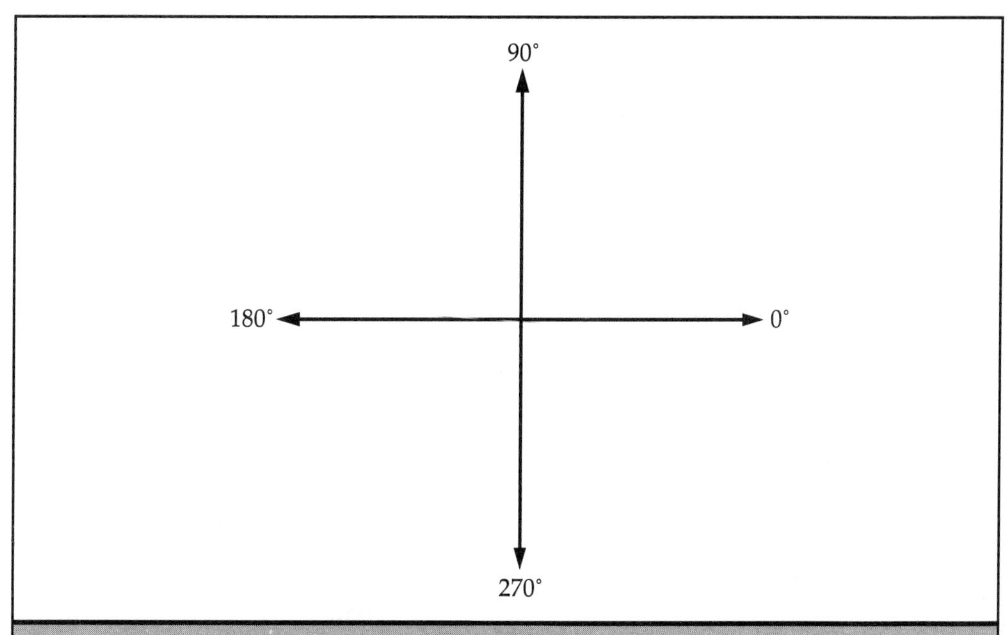

Figure 18-1. *The Cartesian coordinate plane*

Related Functions

pieslice( ), ellipse( ), fillellipse( )

void far setactivepage(int page)

Description

The prototype for **setactivepage( )** is in **graphics.h**.

The **setactivepage( )** function determines the video page that will receive the output of the graphics functions. Borland C++ uses video page 0 by default. If you call **setactivepage( )** with another page, subsequent graphics output is written to the new page, not necessarily the one currently displayed. In graphics modes, only the EGA, VGA, and Hercules adapters support multiple pages. However, even for these adapters, not all modes have multiple pages.

Example

This fragment makes page 1 the active page:

```
setactivepage(1);
```

Related Function

setvisualpage( )

void far setallpalette(struct palettetype far *pal)

Description

The prototype for **setallpalette( )** is in **graphics.h**.

The **setallpalette( )** function changes all the colors in an EGA/VGA palette. The structure **palettetype** is defined as

```
struct palettetype {
  unsigned char size;
  signed char colors[MAXCOLORS+1];
};
```

You must set *size* to the number of colors in the palette of the currently active graphics mode, and set each element of *colors* to its corresponding color. (Refer to **setpalette( )** for the valid colors for the various video adapters.) To leave a specific color unchanged, use the value –1.

If you call **setallpalette( )** with incorrect values, no change to the current palette takes place.

Example

This fragment changes the 16-color palette for an EGA/VGA adapter to the first 16 colors:

```
struct palettetype p;
int i;

for(i=0; i<16; i++) p.colors[i] = i;
p.size = 16;

setallpalette(&p);
```

Related Function

setpalette( )

void far setaspectratio(int xaspect, int yaspect)

Description

The prototype for **setaspectratio( )** is in **graphics.h**.

The **setaspectratio( )** function sets the *x* aspect ratio to the value pointed to by *xaspect* and the *y* aspect ratio to the value pointed to by *yaspect*. By default, the aspect ratios of the graphics system are set so that circles are round. However, you can manipulate the aspect ratios to alter the shape of objects that are displayed on the screen. (The **getaspectratio( )** function is used to get the current aspect ratios.)

Example

This fragment increases the *y* aspect ratio and prints the values of both the *x* and *y* aspect ratios:

```
int xaspect, yaspect;

getaspectratio(&xaspect, &yaspect);
yaspect += 1;
setaspectratio(&xaspect, &yaspect);

cprintf("X,Y aspect ratios are now %d %d",
        xaspect, yaspect);
```

Related Function

getaspectratio( )

void far setbkcolor(int color)

Description

The prototype for **setbkcolor( )** is in **graphics.h**.

The **setbkcolor( )** function changes the background color to the color specified in *color.* The valid values for *color* are

Number	**Macro Name**
0	BLACK
1	BLUE
2	GREEN
3	CYAN
4	RED
5	MAGENTA
6	BROWN
7	LIGHTGRAY
8	DARKGRAY
9	LIGHTBLUE
10	LIGHTGREEN
11	LIGHTCYAN
12	LIGHTRED
13	LIGHTMAGENTA
14	YELLOW
15	WHITE

Example

This program sets the background to light gray before drawing some rectangles:

```
#include <graphics.h>
#include <conio.h>

int main(void)
{
  int driver, mode;

  driver = DETECT; /* autodetect */
  mode = 0;
  initgraph(&driver, &mode, "c:\\bc5\\bgi");

  setbkcolor(LIGHTGRAY);
```

```
  rectangle(100, 100, 300, 300);
  rectangle(150, 90, 34, 300);
  rectangle(0, 0, 2, 2);

  getch();
  restorecrtmode();
  return 0;
}
```

Related Function

setcolor( )

void far setcolor(int color)

Description

The prototype for **setcolor( )** is in **graphics.h**.

The **setcolor( )** function sets the current drawing color to the color specified by *color*. For the valid colors for each video adapter, refer to **setpalette( )**.

Example

Assuming an EGA/VGA adapter, this program prints 16 line segments in 16 different colors (the first is the same color as the background):

```
#include <graphics.h>
#include <conio.h>

int main(void)
{
  int driver, mode;
  int i;

  driver = DETECT; /* autodetect */
  mode = 0;
  initgraph(&driver, &mode, "c:\\bc5\\bgi");

  moveto(0, 200);

  for(i=0; i<16; i++) {
    setcolor(i);
    linerel(20, 0);
  }

  getch();
```

```
  restorecrtmode();
  return 0;
}
```

Related Function

setpalette( )

void far setfillpattern(char far *pattern, int color)

Description

The prototype for **setfillpattern( )** is in **graphics.h**.

The **setfillpattern( )** function sets the fill pattern used by various functions, such as **floodfill( )**, to the pattern pointed to by *pattern.* The array must be at least 8 bytes long. The pattern is arranged as an 8-bit by 8-byte pattern. When a bit is on, the color specified by *color* is displayed; otherwise, the background color is used.

Example

This program creates an unusual fill pattern and uses it to fill a rectangle:

```
#include <graphics.h>
#include <conio.h>

int main(void)
{
  int driver, mode;
  /* define a fill pattern */
  char p[8] = {1, 2, 3, 4, 5, 6, 7};

  driver = DETECT; /* autodetect */
  mode = 0;
  initgraph(&driver, &mode, "c:\\bc5\\bgi");

  setcolor(GREEN);
  rectangle(100, 200, 200, 300);

  setfillpattern(p, RED);
  floodfill(150, 250, GREEN);

  getch();
  restorecrtmode();
  return 0;
}
```

Related Function
setfillstyle( )

void far setfillstyle(int pattern, int color)

Description
The prototype for **setfillstyle( )** is in **graphics.h**.

The **setfillstyle( )** function sets the style and color of the fill used by various graphics functions. The value of *color* must be valid for the current video mode. The values for *pattern* are shown here along with their macro equivalents (defined in **graphics.h**):

Macro	Value	Meaning
EMPTY_FILL	0	Fill with background color
SOLID_FILL	1	Fill with solid color
LINE_FILL	2	Fill with lines
LTSLASH_FILL	3	Fill with light slashes
SLASH_FILL	4	Fill with slashes
BKSLASH_FILL	5	Fill with backslashes
LTBKSLASH_FILL	6	Fill with light backslashes
HATCH_FILL	7	Fill with light hatching
XHATCH_FILL	8	Fill with hatching
INTERLEAVE_FILL	9	Fill with interleaving
WIDE_DOT_FILL	10	Fill with widely spaced dots
CLOSE_DOT_FILL	11	Fill with closely spaced dots
USER_FILL	12	Fill with custom pattern

You define a custom fill pattern using **setfillpattern( )**.

Example
This program fills a box using **LINE_FILL** in the color red:

```
#include <graphics.h>
#include <conio.h>

int main(void)
{
  int driver, mode;
```

```
  driver = DETECT; /* autodetect */
  mode = 0;
  initgraph(&driver, &mode, "c:\\bc5\\bgi");

  setcolor(GREEN);
  rectangle(100, 200, 200, 300);

  setfillstyle(LINE_FILL, RED);
  floodfill(150, 250, GREEN);

  getch();
  restorecrtmode();
  return 0;
}
```

Related Function

setfillpattern( )

unsigned far setgraphbufsize(unsigned size)

Description

The prototype for **setgraphbufsize( )** is in **graphics.h**.

The **setgraphbufsize( )** function is used to set the size of the buffer used by many of the graphics functions. You generally do not need to use this function. If you do use it, you must call it before **initgraph( )**. This function returns the size of the previous buffer.

Related Function

_getgraphmem( )

void far setgraphmode(int mode)

Description

The prototype for **setgraphmode( )** is in **graphics.h**.

The **setgraphmode( )** function sets the current graphics mode to that specified by *mode*, which must be a valid mode for the graphics driver.

Example

This fragment sets a VGA adapter to VGAHI mode:

```
/* after graphics system has been initialized */
setgraphmode(VGAHI);
```

Related Function

getmoderange( )

void far setlinestyle(int style, unsigned pattern, int width)

Description

The prototype for **setlinestyle( )** is in **graphics.h**.

The **setlinestyle( )** function determines the way a line looks when drawn with any graphics function that draws lines.

The *style* element holds the style of the line. It will be one of these enumerated values (defined in **graphics.h**):

Value	Meaning
SOLID_LINE	Unbroken line
DOTTED_LINE	Dotted line
CENTER_LINE	Centered line (dash-dot-dash)
DASHED_LINE	Dashed line
USERBIT_LINE	User-defined line

If *style* is equal to **USERBIT_LINE**, the 16-bit pattern in *pattern* determines how the line appears. Each bit in the pattern corresponds to one pixel. If that bit is set, the pixel is turned on; otherwise, it is turned off.

The *width* element will have one of these values:

Value	Meaning
NORM_WIDTH	Line is 1 pixel wide
THICK_WIDTH	Line is 3 pixels wide

The value of *pattern* is important only if **USERBIT_LINE** is the value of *style.* When it is, each bit in *pattern* that is set will cause a pixel to be turned on. Each 0 bit causes a pixel to be turned off. The pattern then repeats as necessary.

Example

This program displays the built-in line styles:

```
#include <graphics.h>
#include <conio.h>

int main(void)
{
```

```
  int driver, mode;
  int i;

  driver = DETECT; /* autodetect */
  mode = 0;
  initgraph(&driver, &mode, "c:\\bc5\\bgi");

  for(i=0; i<4; i++) {
    setlinestyle(i, 0, 1);
    line(i*50, 100, i*50+50, 100);
  }

  getch();
  restorecrtmode();
  return 0;
}
```

Related Function

setfillstyle( )

void far setpalette(int index, int color)

Description

The prototype for **setpalette( )** is in **graphics.h**.

The **setpalette( )** function changes the colors displayed by the video system. The operation of this function is a little difficult to understand at first. Essentially, it associates the value of *color* with an index into a table that Borland C++ uses to map the color actually shown on the screen with the color being requested. The values for the *color* codes are shown here.

CGA codes (background only):

Macro	Value
BLACK	0
BLUE	1
GREEN	2
CYAN	3
RED	4
MAGENTA	5
BROWN	6

Macro	Value
LIGHTGRAY	7
DARKGRAY	8
LIGHTBLUE	9
LIGHTGREEN	10
LIGHTCYAN	11
LIGHTRED	12
LIGHTMAGENTA	13
YELLOW	14
WHITE	15

EGA and VGA:

Macro	Value
EGA_BLACK	0
EGA_BLUE	1
EGA_GREEN	2
EGA_CYAN	3
EGA_RED	4
EGA_MAGENTA	5
EGA_BROWN	20
EGA_LIGHTGRAY	7
EGA_DARKGRAY	56
EGA_LIGHTBLUE	57
EGA_LIGHTGREEN	58
EGA_LIGHTCYAN	59
EGA_LIGHTRED	60
EGA_LIGHTMAGENTA	61
EGA_YELLOW	62
EGA_WHITE	63

Only the background color can be changed for CGA modes. The background color is always index 0. For CGA modes, this code changes the background color to green:

```
setpalette(0, GREEN);
```

EGA modes can display 16 colors at a time. You can use **setpalette( )** to map a color onto one of the 16 different indexes.

Example

This fragment sets the value of color 5 to cyan:

```
setpalette(5, EGA_CYAN);
```

Related Function

setcolor( )

void far setrgbpalette(int color, int r, int g, int b)

Description

The prototype for **setrgbpalette( )** is in **graphics.h**.

The **setrgbpalette( )** function changes the colors displayed by the video system. It is for use with graphics systems that support RGB displays, such as the IBM 8514 and VGA, only.

The *color* parameter must be a valid entry in the current palette. The other three parameters (*r, g,* and *b*) correspond to the desired red, green, and blue settings of the palette entry. You can mix different proportions of these colors (that is, you specify a color mix for each entry in the palette). The values of *r, g,* and *b* must be in the range 0 through 31. (Only the upper 6 most significant bits of the lower byte are used.)

Example

This fragment sets the 15th color to equal amounts of red, green, and blue:

```
setrgbpalette(15, 16, 16, 16);
```

Related Functions

setpalette( ), getpalette( )

void far settextjustify(int horiz, int vert)

Description

The prototype for **settextjustify( )** is in **graphics.h**.

The **settextjustify( )** function sets the way text is aligned relative to the CP (current position). The values of *horiz* and *vert* determine the effect of **settextjustify( )**, as shown here (the macros are defined in **graphics.h**):

Macro	Value	Meaning
LEFT_TEXT	0	CP at left
CENTER_TEXT	1	CP in the center
RIGHT_TEXT	2	CP at right
BOTTOM_TEXT	0	CP at the bottom
TOP_TEXT	2	CP at the top

The default settings are **LEFT_TEXT** and **TOP_TEXT**.

Example

This fragment places the CP on the right:

```
settextjustify(RIGHT_TEXT, TOP_TEXT);
```

Related Function

settextstyle( )

void far settextstyle(int font, int direction, int size)

Description

The prototype for **settextstyle( )** is in **graphics.h**.

The **settextstyle( )** function sets the active font used by the graphics text output functions. It also sets the direction and size of the characters.

The *font* parameter determines the type of font used. The default is the hardware-defined 8 × 8 bit-mapped font. You can give *font* one of these values (the macros are defined in **graphics.h**):

Macro	Value	Font
DEFAULT_FONT	0	Default 8 × 8 bit-mapped font
TRIPLEX_FONT	1	Stroked triplex font
SMALL_FONT	2	Stroked small font
SANS_SERIF_FONT	3	Stroked sans serif font

Macro	Value	Font
GOTHIC_FONT	4	Stroked gothic font
SCRIPT_FONT	5	Stroked script font
SIMPLEX_FONT	6	Stroked simplex script font
TRIPLEX_SCR_FONT	7	Stroked triplex script font
COMPLEX_FONT	8	Stroked complex font
EUROPEAN_FONT	9	Stroked European font
BOLD_FONT	10	Stroked bold font

The direction in which the text is displayed—either left to right or bottom to top—is determined by the value of *direction,* which can be either **HORIZ_DIR** (0) or **VERT_DIR** (1).

The *size* parameter is a multiplier that increases the character size. It can have a value of 0 through 10.

Example

The following program illustrates the use of the **settextstyle( )** function:

```
/* Demonstrate some different text fonts and sizes. */

#include <graphics.h>
#include <conio.h>

int main(void)
{
  int driver, mode;

  driver = DETECT; /* autodetect */
  mode = 0;
  initgraph(&driver, &mode, "c:\\bc5\\bgi");

  outtext("Normal ");

  /* Gothic font, twice normal size */
  settextstyle(GOTHIC_FONT, HORIZ_DIR, 2);
  outtext("Gothic ");

  /* Triplex font, twice normal size */
  settextstyle(TRIPLEX_FONT, HORIZ_DIR, 2);
  outtext("Triplex ");
```

```
  /* Sans serif font, 7 times normal size*/
  settextstyle(SANS_SERIF_FONT, HORIZ_DIR, 7);
  outtext("Sans serif");
  getch();
  restorecrtmode();
  return 0;
}
```

Related Function

settextjustify( )

void far setusercharsize(int mulx, int divx, int muly, int divy)

Description

The prototype for **setusercharsize( )** is in **graphics.h**.

The **setusercharsize( )** function specifies multipliers and divisors that scale the size of graphics stroked fonts. In essence, after a call to **setusercharsize( )**, each character displayed on the screen has its default size multiplied by *mulx/divx* for its *x* dimension and *muly/divy* for its *y* dimension.

Example

This code writes text in both normal and large letters:

```
#include <graphics.h>
#include <conio.h>

int main(void)
{
  int driver, mode;

  driver = DETECT; /* autodetect */
  mode = 0;
  initgraph(&driver, &mode, "c:\\bc5\\bgi");

  outtext("normal ");
  settextstyle(TRIPLEX_FONT, HORIZ_DIR, USER_CHAR_SIZE);

  /* make very big letters */
  setusercharsize(5, 1, 5, 1);
  outtext("big");
```

```
  getch();
  restorecrtmode();
  return 0;
}
```

Related Function

gettextsettings( )

void far setviewport(int left, int top, int right, int bottom, int clip)

Description

The prototype for **setviewport( )** is in **graphics.h**.

The **setviewport( )** function creates a new viewport using the upper left and lower right corner coordinates specified by *left*, *top*, *right*, and *bottom*. If *clip* is 1, output is automatically clipped at the edge of the viewport and prevented from spilling into other parts of the screen. If *clip* is 0, no clipping takes place.

Example

This fragment creates a viewport with corners at 10,10 and 40,40 with clipping:

```
setviewport(10, 10, 40, 40, 1);
```

Related Function

clearviewport( )

void far setvisualpage(int page)

Description

The prototype for **setvisualpage( )** is in **graphics.h**.

For some video modes, there is enough memory in video adapters to have two or more complete screens' worth of information stored at the same time. The RAM that holds the information displayed on the screen is called a *page*. Borland C++ uses page 0 by default. However, you can use any of the video pages supported by your hardware, switching between them as desired. Although only one screen of data can be displayed at one time, it is occasionally useful to build an image as a background task in a page that is not currently displayed so that it is ready when needed without delay. To activate the image, simply switch to that display page. This method is particularly useful in cases where complex images take a long time to construct. To support this sort of approach, Borland C++ supplies the functions **setactivepage( )** and **setvisualpage( )**.

The **setactivepage( )** function determines the video page to which output of Borland C++'s graphics functions is directed. If you call **setactivepage( )** with a different page than is currently being displayed, subsequent graphics output is written to the new page, not necessarily the one currently displayed. To actually display a different page, use the **setvisualpage( )** function. For example, to display video page 1 you would call **setvisualpage( )** with an argument of 1.

Example

This fragment selects page 1 to be displayed:

```
setvisualpage(1);
```

Related Function

setactivepage( )

void far setwritemode(int wmode)

Description

The prototype for **setwritemode( )** is in **graphics.h**.

The **setwritemode( )** function determines how **line( )**, **linerel( )**, **lineto( )**, **rectangle( )**, and **drawpoly( )** display their output on the screen. The value of *wmode* must be one of these two macros (defined in **graphics.h**): **COPY_PUT** or **XOR_PUT**. Calling **setwritemode( )** using **COPY_PUT** causes subsequent output to overwrite any image on the screen. However, if you call **setwritemode( )** using **XOR_PUT**, subsequent output is XORed with any pre-existing image. The advantage of using the **XOR_PUT** mode is that you can restore the original screen by outputting the same object a second time.

Example

This program illustrates the **setwritemode( )** function:

```
#include <graphics.h>
#include <conio.h>

int main(void)
{
  int driver, mode;

  driver = DETECT; /* autodetect */
  mode = 0;
  initgraph(&driver, &mode, "c:\\bc5\\bgi");

  setwritemode(COPY_PUT);  /* set for overwrite */
  setcolor(BLUE);
  rectangle(10, 10, 100, 100);
  getch();
```

```
    setwritemode(XOR_PUT);   /* set for combining */

    setcolor(RED);
    rectangle(30, 30, 80, 80); /* draw inside first rectangle */
    getch();

    rectangle(30, 30, 80, 80); /* now erase it */
    getch();

    restorecrtmode();
    return 0;
}
```

Related Function

setlinestyle( )

void textattr(int attr)

Description

The prototype for **textattr( )** is in **conio.h**.

The **textattr( )** function sets both the foreground and background colors in a text screen at one time. The value of *attr* represents an encoded form of the color information, as shown here.

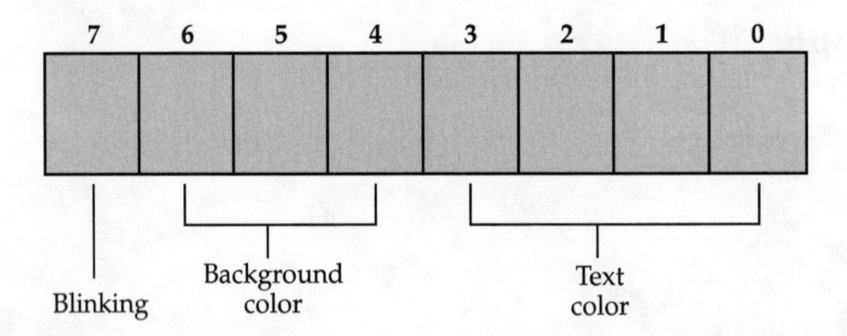

If bit 7 is set, the text blinks. Bits 6 through 4 determine the background color. Bits 3 through 0 set the color for the text. The easiest way to encode the background color into the attribute byte is to multiply the number of the color you desire by 16 and then OR that with the text color. For example, to create a green background with blue text you would use **GREEN * 16 | BLUE**. To cause the text to blink, OR the text color, background color, and **BLINK** (128) together.

Example

This fragment displays the text in blinking red with a blue background:

```
textattr(RED | BLINK | BLUE*16);
```

Related Functions

textbackground( ), textcolor( )

void textbackground(int color)

Description

The prototype for **textbackground( )** is in **conio.h**.

The **textbackground( )** function sets the background color of a text screen. A call to **textbackground( )** affects only the background color of subsequent write operations. The valid colors are shown here along with their macro names (defined in **conio.h**):

Macro	Integer Equivalent
BLACK	0
BLUE	1
GREEN	2
CYAN	3
RED	4
MAGENTA	5
BROWN	6
LIGHTGRAY	7

The new background color takes effect after the call to **textbackground( )**. The background of characters currently on the screen is not affected.

Example

This fragment sets the background color of a text screen to cyan:

```
textbackground(CYAN);
```

Related Function

textcolor( )

void textcolor(int color)

Description

The prototype of **textcolor( )** is in **conio.h**.

The **textcolor( )** function sets the color in which characters are displayed in a text screen. It can also be used to specify blinking characters. The valid values for *color* are shown here, along with their macro names (defined in **conio.h**):

Macro	Integer Equivalent
BLACK	0
BLUE	1
GREEN	2
CYAN	3
RED	4
MAGENTA	5
BROWN	6
LIGHTGRAY	7
DARKGRAY	8
LIGHTBLUE	9
LIGHTGREEN	10
LIGHTCYAN	11
LIGHTRED	12
LIGHTMAGENTA	13
YELLOW	14
WHITE	15
BLINK	128

The color of characters on the screen is not changed by **textcolor( )**; it affects only those written after **textcolor( )** has executed.

Example

This fragment displays subsequent output in blinking characters:

```
textcolor(BLINK);
```

Related Function

textattr( )

int far textheight(char far *str)

Description

The prototype for **textheight( )** is in **graphics.h**.

The **textheight( )** function returns the height, in pixels, of the string pointed to by *str* relative to the current font and size.

Example

This program displays the number 8 for the text height:

```
#include <stdio.h>
#include <graphics.h>
#include <conio.h>

int main(void)
{
  int driver, mode;

  driver = DETECT; /* autodetect */
  mode = 0;
  initgraph(&driver, &mode, "c:\\bc5\\bgi");

  printf("height: %d", textheight("hello"));

  getch();
  restorecrtmode();
  return 0;
}
```

Related Function

textwidth( )

void textmode(int mode)

Description

The prototype for **textmode( )** is in **conio.h**.

The **textmode( )** function is used to change the video mode of a text screen. The argument *mode* must be one of the values shown in the following table. You can use either the integer value or the macro name (the macros are defined in **conio.h**):

Macro Name	Integer Equivalent	Description
BW40	0	40-column black and white
C40	1	40-column color
BW80	2	80-column black and white
C80	3	80-column color
MONO	7	80-column monochrome
C4350	64	43-line EGA or 50-line VGA
LASTMODE	–1	Previous mode

After a call to **textmode( )**, the screen is reset and all text screen attributes are returned to their default settings.

Example

This fragment puts the video hardware into 80-column color mode:

```
textmode(C80);
```

Related Function

gettextinfo( )

int far textwidth(char far *str)

Description

The prototype for **textwidth( )** is in **graphics.h**.

The **textwidth( )** function returns the width, in pixels, of the string pointed to by *str* relative to the current font and size.

Example

This program displays 40 as the pixel length of the string "hello":

```
#include <stdio.h>
#include <graphics.h>
#include <conio.h>

int main(void)
{
  int driver, mode;

  driver = DETECT; /* autodetect */
  mode = 0;
```

```
  initgraph(&driver, &mode, "c:\\bc5\\bgi");

  printf("width: %d", textwidth("hello"));

  getch();
  restorecrtmode();
  return 0;
}
```

Related Function

textheight( )

int wherex(void)
int wherey(void)

Description

The prototypes for **wherex( )** and **wherey( )** are in **conio.h**.

The **wherex( )** and **wherey( )** functions return the current *x* and *y* cursor coordinates relative to the current text window.

Example

This fragment loads the variables **xpos** and **ypos** with the current *x,y* coordinates:

```
int xpos, ypos;

xpos = wherex();
ypos = wherey();
```

Related Function

gotoxy( )

void window(int left, int top, int right, int bottom)

Description

The prototype for **window( )** is in **conio.h**.

The **window( )** function is used to create a rectangular text window with upper left and lower right coordinates specified by *left,top* and *right,bottom*. If any coordinate is invalid, **window( )** takes no action. Once a call to **window( )** has been successfully completed, all references to location coordinates are interpreted relative to the window, not the screen.

Example

This fragment creates a window and writes a line of text at location 2,3 inside that window:

```
window(10, 10, 60, 15);
gotoxy(2, 3);
cprintf("at location 2, 3");
```

Related Function

clrscr( )

Chapter Nineteen

Miscellaneous Functions

The functions discussed in this chapter are those that don't fit easily in any other category. They include various conversions, variable-length argument processing, sorting, and random number generators.

Many of the functions covered here require the use of the header **stdlib.h**. This header defines two types, **div_t** and **ldiv_t**, which are the types of the structures returned by **div( )** and **ldiv( )**, respectively. Also defined are **size_t**, which is the unsigned value that is returned by **sizeof**, and **wchar_t**, which is the data type of wide (16-bit) characters. These macros are also defined:

Macro	Meaning
NULL	A null pointer
RAND_MAX	The maximum value that can be returned by the **rand( )** function
EXIT_FAILURE	The value returned to the calling process if program termination is unsuccessful
EXIT_SUCCESS	The value returned to the calling process if program termination is successful
MB_CUR_MAX	Maximum number of bytes in a multibyte character

Different header files will be discussed in the descriptions of the functions that require them.

int abs(int num)

Description

The prototype for **abs( )** is in both **stdlib.h** and **math.h**. For maximum portability, use **stdlib.h**.

The **abs( )** function returns the absolute value of the integer *num*.

Example

This function converts a user-entered number into its absolute value:

```
#include <stdio.h>
#include <stdlib.h>

int get_abs()
{
  char num[80];

  gets(num);

  return abs(atoi(num));
}
```

Related Function

labs( )

void assert(int exp)

Description

The prototype for **assert( )** is in **assert.h**.

The **assert( )** macro writes error information to **stderr** and aborts program execution if the expression *exp* evaluates to 0. Otherwise, **assert( )** does nothing. The output of the function is in this general form:

Assertion failed: *exp*, file <*file* >, line <*linenum* >

The **assert( )** macro is generally used to help verify that a program is operating correctly; the expression is devised so that it evaluates true only when no errors have taken place.

It is not necessary to remove the **assert( )** statements from the source code once a program is debugged because if the macro **NDEBUG** is defined (as anything) before the **assert.h** header file is included, the **assert( )** macros are ignored.

Example

This code fragment is used to test whether the data read from a serial port is ASCII (that is, that it does not use the 7th bit):

```
.
.
.
ch = read_port();
assert(!(ch & 128)); /* check bit 7 */
.
.
.
```

Related Function

abort( )

double atof(const char *str)
long double _atold(const char *str)

Description

The prototypes for **atof( )** and **_atold( )** are in **stdlib.h** and **math.h**. For compatibility with the ANSI C standard, use **stdlib.h**.

The **atof( )** function converts the string pointed to by *str* into a **double** value. The string must contain a valid floating-point number. If this is not the case, 0 is returned and **errno** is set to **ERANGE**.

The number can be terminated by any character that cannot be part of a valid floating-point number. This includes white space, punctuation (other than periods), and characters other than "E" or "e". This means that if **atof( )** is called with "100.00HELLO", the value 100.00 is returned.

_atold( ) is the **long double** version of **atof( )**.

Example

This program reads two floating-point numbers and displays their sum:

```
#include <stdio.h>
#include <stdlib.h>

int main(void)
{
  char num1[80], num2[80];
```

```
  printf("Enter first number: ");
  gets(num1);
  printf("Enter second number: ");
  gets(num2);
  printf("The sum is: %f", atof(num1)+atof(num2));
  return 0;
}
```

Related Functions

atoi( ), atol( )

int atoi(const char *str)

Description

The prototype for **atoi( )** is in **stdlib.h**.

The **atoi( )** function converts the string pointed to by *str* into an **int** value. The string must contain a valid integer number. If this is not the case, 0 is returned.

The number can be terminated by any character that cannot be part of an integer number. This includes white space, punctuation, and other nondigit characters. This means that if **atoi( )** is called with **123.23**, the integer value 123 is returned and the 0.23 ignored.

Example

This program reads two integer numbers and displays their sum:

```
#include <stdio.h>
#include <stdlib.h>

int main(void)
{
  char num1[80], num2[80];

  printf("Enter first number: ");
  gets(num1);
  printf("Enter second number: ");
  gets(num2);
  printf("The sum is: %d", atoi(num1)+atoi(num2));
  return 0;
}
```

Related Functions

atof( ), atol( )

long atol(const char *str)

Description

The prototype for **atol( )** is in **stdlib.h**.

The **atol( )** function converts the string pointed to by *str* into a **long int** value. The string must contain a valid **long** integer number. If this is not the case, 0 is returned.

The number can be terminated by any character that cannot be part of an integer number. This includes white space, punctuation, and other nondigit characters. This means that if **atol( )** is called with **123.23**, the integer value 123 is returned and the 0.23 ignored.

Example

This program reads two **long** integer numbers and displays their sum:

```
#include <stdio.h>
#include <stdlib.h>

int main(void)
{
  char num1[80], num2[80];

  printf("Enter first number: ");
  gets(num1);
  printf("Enter second number: ");
  gets(num2);
  printf("The sum is: %ld", atol(num1)+atol(num2));
  return 0;
}
```

Related Functions

atof( ), atoi( )

void *bsearch(const void *key, const void *base, size_t num, size_t size, int (*compare)(const void *, const void *))

Description

The prototype for **bsearch( )** is in **stdlib.h**.

The **bsearch( )** function performs a binary search on the sorted array pointed to by *base* and returns a pointer to the first member that matches the key pointed to by *key*. The number of elements in the array is specified by *num*, and the size (in bytes) of each element is described by *size*.

The type **size_t** is defined as an **unsigned int** in **stdlib.h**.

The function pointed to by *compare* compares an element of the array with the key. The form of the *compare* function must be

int *func_name*(const void **arg1*, const void **arg2*)

It must return the following values:

If *arg1* is less than *arg2*, return less than 0.

If *arg1* is equal to *arg2*, return 0.

If *arg1* is greater than *arg2*, return greater than 0.

The array must be sorted in ascending order with the lowest address containing the lowest element.

If the array does not contain the key, a null pointer is returned.

Example

This program reads characters entered at the keyboard and determines whether they belong to the alphabet:

```
#include <stdio.h>
#include <stdlib.h>
#include <ctype.h>

char *alpha="abcdefghijklmnopqrstuvwxyz";
int comp(const void *, const void *);

int main(void)
{
  char ch;
  char *p;

  do {
    printf("Enter a character: ");
    scanf("%c%*c", &ch);
    ch = tolower(ch);
    p = (char *) bsearch(&ch, alpha, 26, 1, comp);
    if(p) printf("is in alphabet\n");
    else printf("is not in alphabet\n");
  } while(p);
```

```
  return 0;
}

/* Compare two characters. */
int comp(const void *ch, const void *s)
{
  return *(char *)ch - *(char *)s;
}
```

Related Function

qsort( )

unsigned int _clear87(void)

Description

The prototype for **_clear87( )** is in **float.h**. This function is not defined by the ANSI C standard.

The **_clear87( )** function resets the 80x87 hardware floating-point coprocessor's status word. The function returns the previous status word.

You must have an 80x87 math coprocessor installed in your system in order to use any of the 80x87-based functions.

Related Function

_status87( )

unsigned int _control87(unsigned fpword, unsigned fpmask)

Description

The prototype for **_control87( )** is in **float.h**. This function is not defined by the ANSI C standard.

The **_control87( )** function returns or modifies the value of the 80x87 control word that controls the behavior of the chip. You must have an 80x87 math coprocessor installed in the computer before using this function.

The parameter *fpmask* determines which bits of the control word will be modified. Each bit in *fpmask* corresponds with each bit in *fpword* and the bits in the floating-point control word. If the bit in *fpmask* is non-0, the control word at the corresponding bit position is set to the value of the corresponding position in *fpword.*

The **_control87( )** function returns the modified control word. However, if *fpmask* contains 0, the control word is unchanged and the current value of the control word is returned.

For a complete description of what each bit controls, consult the header file **float.h**.

Related Functions
_clear87( ), _fpreset( )

div_t div(int numerator, int denominator)

Description
The prototype for **div( )** is in **stdlib.h**.

The **div( )** function returns the quotient and the remainder of the operation *numerator/denominator.*

The structure type **div_t** is defined in **stdlib.h** and has these two fields:

```
int quot;   /* the quotient */
int rem;    /* the remainder */
```

Example
This program displays the quotient and the remainder of 10/3:

```
#include <stdio.h>
#include <stdlib.h>

int main(void)
{
  div_t n;

  n = div(10,3);

  printf("Quotient and remainder: %d %d\n", n.quot, n.rem);

  return 0;
}
```

Related Function
ldiv( )

char *ecvt(double value, int ndigit, int *dec, int *sign)

Description
The prototype for **ecvt( )** is in **stdlib.h**. This function is not defined by the ANSI C standard.

The **ecvt( )** function converts *value* into a string *ndigit* long. After the call, the value of the variable pointed to by *dec* indicates the position of the decimal point. If the decimal point is to the left of the number, the number pointed to by *dec* is negative. The decimal point is not actually stored in the string. If *value* is positive, *sign* is 0. If the number is negative, *sign* is non-0.

The **ecvt( )** function returns a pointer to a static data area that holds the string representation of the number.

Example

This call converts the number 10.12 into a string:

```
int decpnt, sign;
char *out;

out = ecvt(10.12, 5, &decpnt, &sign);
```

Related Functions

fcvt( ), gcvt( )

void _ _emit_ _(unsigned char arg, . . .)

Description

The prototype for **_ _emit_ _( )** is in **dos.h**. This function is not defined by the ANSI C standard.

The **_ _emit_ _( )** function is used to insert one or more values directly into the executable code of your program at the point at which **_ _emit_ _( )** is called. These values generally will be x86 machine instructions. If a value fits into a byte, it is treated as a byte quantity. Otherwise, it is treated as a word quantity. You can only pass **_ _emit_ _( )** byte or word values.

You must be an expert assembly language programmer to use **_ _emit_ _( )**. If you insert incorrect values, your program will crash.

char *fcvt(double value, int ndigit, int *dec, int *sign)

Description

The prototype for **fcvt( )** is in **stdlib.h**. This function is not defined by the ANSI C standard.

The **fcvt( )** function is the same as **ecvt( )**, except that the output is rounded to the number of digits specified by *ndigit*.

The **fcvt( )** function returns a pointer to a static data area that holds the string representation of the number.

Example

This call converts the number 10.12 into a string:

```
int decpnt, sign;
char *out;

out = fcvt(10.12, 5, &decpnt, &sign);
```

Related Functions

ecvt( ), gcvt( )

void _fpreset(void)

Description

The prototype for **_fpreset( )** is in **float.h**. This function is not defined by the ANSI C standard.

The **_fpreset( )** function resets the floating-point arithmetic system. You may need to reset the floating-point routines after a **system( )**, **exec( )**, **spawn( )**, or **signal( )** function executes. Refer to the user manuals for specific details.

Example

This fragment ensures that the floating-point arithmetic routines are reset after **system( )** returns:

```
/* compute and print payroll checks */
system("payroll");

_fpreset();
```

Related Function

_status87( )

char *gcvt(double value, int ndigit, char *buf)

Description

The prototype for **gcvt( )** is in **stdlib.h**. This function is not defined by the ANSI C standard.

The **gcvt( )** function converts *value* into a string *ndigit* long. The converted string output is stored in the array pointed to by *buf* in FORTRAN F-format, if possible. If not, it uses the E-format as defined for **printf( )**. A pointer to *buf* is returned.

Example

This call converts the number 10.12 into a string:

```
char buf[80];

gcvt(10.12, 5, buf);
```

Related Functions

fcvt( ), ecvt( )

char *getenv(const char *name)

Description

The prototype for **getenv( )** is in **stdlib.h**.

The **getenv( )** function returns a pointer to environmental information associated with the string pointed to by *name* in the environmental information table. The string returned must never be changed by the program.

The environment of a program can include such things as path names and devices online. The exact meaning of this data is defined by the operating system.

If a call is made to **getenv( )** with an argument that does not match any of the environmental data, a null pointer is returned.

Example

Assuming that a specific compiler maintains environmental information on the devices connected to the system, the following fragment returns a pointer to the list of devices:

```
.
.
.
p = getenv("DEVICES");
.
.
.
```

Related Functions

putenv( ), system( )

char *getpass(const char *str)

Description

The prototype for **getpass( )** is in **conio.h**. This function is not defined by the ANSI C standard.

After displaying the prompt *str* on the screen, the **getpass( )** function returns a pointer to a null-terminated string of not more than eight characters. This string is statically allocated by **getpass( )** and is overwritten each time the function is called. If you want to save the string, you must copy it elsewhere. Keystrokes are not echoed when the password is entered.

Example

This function waits until the proper password is entered:

```
#include <conio.h>
#include <string.h>
void pswd (char *pw)

{
  char *input;

  do {
    input=getpass("Enter your password:");
  }while (!strcmp("starbar", input));

  printf("You're in!");
}
```

unsigned getpid(void)

Description

The prototype for **getpid( )** is in **process.h**. This function is not defined by the ANSI C standard.

The **getpid( )** function returns the process ID number associated with a program.

Example

This fragment displays the process ID number:

```
printf("This process ID of this program is %d\n", getpid());
```

Related Function

getpsp( )

char *itoa(int num, char *str, int radix)

Description

The prototype for **itoa( )** is in **stdlib.h**. This function is not defined by the ANSI C standard.

The **itoa( )** function converts the integer *num* into its string equivalent and places the result in the string pointed to by *str.* The base of the output string is determined by *radix,* which can be in the range 2 through 36.

The **itoa( )** function returns a pointer to *str.* There is no error return value. Be sure to call **itoa( )** with a string of sufficient length to hold the converted result. The maximum length needed is 17 bytes.

Example

This program displays the value of 1423 in hexadecimal (58F):

```
#include <stdio.h>
#include <stdlib.h>

int main(void)
{
  char p[17];

  itoa(1423, p, 16);

  printf(p);

  return 0;
}
```

Related Functions

atoi( ), sscanf( )

long labs(long num)

Description

The prototype for **labs( )** is in **stdlib.h** and **math.h**. For the ANSI C standard compatibility, use **stdlib.h**.

The **labs( )** function returns the absolute value of the **long int** *num*.

Example

This function converts the user-entered numbers into their absolute values:

```
#include <stdio.h>
#include <stdlib.h>
long int get_labs()
{
  char num[80];

  gets(num);

  return labs(atol(num));
}
```

Related Function

abs( )

ldiv_t ldiv(long numerator, long denominator)

Description

The prototype for **ldiv( )** is in **stdlib.h**.

The **ldiv( )** function returns the quotient and the remainder of the operation *numerator/denominator.*

The structure type **ldiv_t** is defined in **stdlib.h** and has these two fields:

```
long quot;   /* the quotient */
long rem;    /* the remainder */
```

Example

This program displays the quotient and the remainder of 100000L/3L:

```
#include <stdio.h>
#include <stdlib.h>

int main(void)
{
  ldiv_t n;

  n = ldiv(100000L,3L);

  printf("Quotient and remainder: %ld %ld.\n", n.quot, n.rem);

  return 0;
}
```

Related Function

div( )

void *lfind(const void *key, const void *base, size_t *num, size_t size, int (*compare)(const void *, const void *))

void *lsearch(const void *key, void *base, size_t *num, size_t size, int (*compare)(const void *, const void *))

Description

The prototypes for **lfind( )** and **lsearch( )** are in **stdlib.h**. These functions are not defined by the ANSI C standard.

The **lfind( )** and **lsearch( )** functions perform a linear search on the array pointed to by *base* and return a pointer to the first element that matches the key pointed to by *key*. The number of elements in the array is pointed to by *num*, and the size (in bytes) of each element is described by *size*.

The function pointed to by *compare* compares an element of the array with the key. The form of the *compare* function must be

int *func_name*(const void **arg1*, const void **arg2*)

It must return the following values:

If *arg1* does not equal *arg2*, return non-0.

If *arg1* is equal to *arg2*, return 0.

The array being searched does not have to be sorted.

If the array does not contain the key, a null pointer is returned.

The difference between **lfind( )** and **lsearch( )** is that if the item being searched for does not exist in the array, **lsearch( )** adds it to the end of the array; **lfind( )** does not.

Example

This program reads characters entered at the keyboard and determines whether they belong to the alphabet:

```
#include <stdlib.h>
#include <ctype.h>
#include <stdio.h>

char *alpha="abcdefghijklmnopqrstuvwxyz";

int comp(const void *, const void *);

int main(void)
{
  char ch;
  char *p;
  size_t num=26;

  do {
    printf("Enter a character: ");
    scanf("%c%*c", &ch);
    ch = tolower(ch);
    p = (char *) lfind(&ch, alpha, &num, 1, comp);
```

```
    if(p) printf("is in alphabet\n");
    else printf("is not in alphabet\n");
  } while(p);
  return 0;
}

/* Compare two characters. */
int comp(const void *ch, const void *s)
{
  return *(char *)ch - *(char *)s;
}
```

Related Function

qsort( )

struct lconv *localeconv(void)

Description

The prototype for **localeconv( )** is in **locale.h**. It returns a pointer to a structure of type **lconv**, which contains various country-specific environmental information relating to the way numbers are formatted. The **lconv** structure is organized as shown here:

```
struct lconv {
  char *decimal_point;      /* decimal point character
                               for non-monetary values */
  char *thousands_sep;      /* thousands separator
                               for non-monetary values */
  char *grouping;           /* specifies grouping for
                               non-monetary values */
  char int_curr_symbol;     /* international currency symbol */
  char *currency_symbol;    /* local currency symbol */
  char *mon_decimal_point; /* decimal point character
                               for monetary values */
  char *mon_thousands_sep; /* thousands separator
                               for monetary values */
  char *mon_grouping;       /* specifies grouping for
                               monetary values */
  char *positive_sign;      /* positive value indicator
                               for monetary values */
  char *negative_sign;      /* negative value indicator
                               for monetary values */
  char int_frac_digits;     /* number of digits displayed
                               to the right of the decimal
                               point for monetary values
```

```
                              displayed using international
                              format */
  char frac_digits;        /* number of digits displayed
                              to the right of the decimal
                              point for monetary values
                              displayed using local format */
  char p_cs_precedes;      /* 1 if currency symbol precedes
                              positive value,
                              0 if currency symbol
                              follows value */
  char p_sep_by_space;     /* 1 if currency symbol is
                              separated from value by a
                              space, 0 otherwise */
  char n_cs_precedes;      /* 1 if currency symbol precedes
                              a negative value, 0 if
                              currency symbol follows value */
  char n_sep_by_space;     /* 1 if currency symbol is
                              separated from a negative
                              value by a space, 0 if
                              currency symbol follows value */
  char p_sign_posn;        /* indicates position of positive
                              value symbol */
  char n_sign_posn;        /* indicates position of negative
                              value symbol */
}
```

Related Function

setlocale( )

void longjmp(jmp_buf envbuf, int val)

Description

The prototype for **longjmp( )** is in **setjmp.h**.

The **longjmp( )** instruction causes program execution to resume at the point of the last call to **setjmp( )**. These two functions create a way to jump between functions.

The **longjmp( )** function operates by resetting the stack to the state defined in *envbuf*, which must have been set by a prior call to **setjmp( )**. This causes program execution to resume at the statement following the **setjmp( )** invocation. That is, the computer is "tricked" into thinking that it never left the function that called **setjmp( )**. (As a somewhat graphic explanation, the **longjmp( )** function "warps" across time and (memory) space to a previous point in your program without having to perform the normal function-return process.)

The buffer *envbuf* is of type **jmp_buf**, which is defined in the header **setjmp.h**. The buffer must have been set through a call to **setjmp( )** prior to calling **longjmp( )**.

The value of *val* becomes the return value of **setjmp( )** and can be interrogated to determine where the long jump came from. The only value not allowed is 0.

It is important to understand that the **longjmp( )** function must be called before the function that called **setjmp( )** returns. If not, the result is technically undefined. (Actually, a crash will almost certainly occur.)

By far, the most common use of **longjmp( )** is to return from a deeply nested set of routines when a catastrophic error occurs.

Example

This program prints "1 2 3":

```
#include <stdio.h>
#include <setjmp.h>

jmp_buf ebuf;
void f2(void);

int main(void)
{
  char first=1;
  int i;

  printf("1 ");
  i = setjmp(ebuf);
  if(first) {
    first =! first;
    f2();
    printf("this will not be printed");
  }
  printf("%d", i);
  return 0;
}

void f2(void)
{
  printf("2 ");
  longjmp(ebuf, 3);
}
```

Related Function

setjmp( )

char *ltoa(long num, char *str, int radix)
char *ultoa(unsigned long num, char *str, int radix)

Description

The prototype for **ltoa( )** and **ultoa( )** are in **stdlib.h**. These functions are not defined by the ANSI C standard.

The **ltoa( )** function converts the long integer *num* into its string equivalent and places the result in the string pointed to by *str.* The base of the output string is determined by *radix,* which must be in the range 2 through 36. The **ultoa( )** function performs the same conversion, but on an **unsigned long** integer.

The **ltoa( )** and **ultoa( )** functions return a pointer to *str.* There is no error return value. Be sure *str* is of sufficient length to hold the converted result. The longest array you need is 34 bytes.

Example

This program displays the value of 1423 in hexadecimal (58F):

```
#include <stdio.h>
#include <stdlib.h>

int main(void)
{
  char p[34];

  ltoa(1423, p, 16);

  printf(p);

  return 0;
}
```

Related Functions

itoa( ), sscanf( )

unsigned long _lrotl(unsigned long l, int i)
unsigned long _lrotr(unsigned long l, int i)

Description

The prototypes for **_lrotl( )** and **_lrotr( )** are in **stdlib.h**. These functions are not defined by the ANSI C standard.

The **_lrotl( )** and **_lrotr( )** functions rotate the bits of the long value *l*, *i* number of bits to the left or right, respectively, and return the result. When a rotate is performed, bits rotated off one end are inserted onto the other end. For example, given the value

1111 0000 0000 1111 1111 0000 1010 0101

rotating it left by one bit produces the value

1110 0000 0001 1111 1110 0001 0100 1011

Example

The following program shows the effect of left and right rotation:

```
#include <stdio.h>
#include <stdlib.h>

int main(void)
{
  unsigned long l = 1;

  printf("1 rotated left 2 bits = %ld\n", _lrotl(l,2));
  printf("1 rotated right 2 bits = %ld\n", _lrotr(l,2));

  return 0;
}
```

Related Functions

_rotl( ), _rotr( )

max(x,y)
min(x,y)

Description

The **max( )** and **min( )** macros are defined in **stdlib.h**. They are not defined by the ANSI C standard.

The **max( )** macro returns the larger of the two values and the **min( )** returns the smaller of the two values. The **max( )** and **min( )** macros return the same type as passed to them; both arguments passed must be of the same type.

Example

This program illustrates the **min( )** and **max( )** macros:

```
#include <stdlib.h>
#include <stdio.h>

int main (void)
{
  printf("max of 10, 20 is %d\n", max (10, 20));
  printf("min of 10, 20 is %d\n", min (10, 20));

  return 0;
}
```

int mblen(const char *str, size_t size)

Description

The prototype for **mblen( )** is in **stdlib.h**.

This function returns the length of a multibyte character pointed to by *str*. Only the first *size* number of characters are examined.

If *str* is null, then **mblen( )** determines if multibyte characters have state-dependent encodings. In this case, it returns nonzero if they do and zero if they do not.

Example

This statement displays the length of the multibyte character pointed to by **mb**:

```
printf("%d", mblen(mb, 2));
```

Related Functions

mbtowc( ), wctomb( )

size_t mbstowcs(wchar_t *out, const char *in, size_t size)

Description

The prototype for **mbstowcs( )** is in **stdlib.h**.

The **mbstowcs( )** converts the multibyte string pointed to by *in* into a wide character string and puts that result in the array pointed to by *out*. Only *size* number of bytes will be stored in *out*.

The **mbstowcs( )** function returns the number of multibyte characters that are converted. If an error occurs, the function returns –1.

Example

This statement converts the first four characters in the multibyte string pointed to by **mb** and puts the result in **wstr**:

```
mbstowcs(wstr, mb, 4);
```

Related Functions

wcstombs( ), mbtowc( )

int mbtowc(wchar_t *out, const char *in, size_t size)

Description

The prototype for **mbtowc( )** is in **stdlib.h**.

The **mbtowc( )** function converts the multibyte character in the array pointed to by *in* into its wide character equivalent and puts that result in the array pointed to by *out*. Only *size* number of characters will be examined.

This function returns the number of bytes that are put into *out*. If an error occurs, –1 is returned.

If *in* is null, then **mbtowc( )** returns non-0 if multibyte characters have state dependencies. If they do not, 0 is returned.

Example

This statement converts the multibyte character in **mbstr** into its equivalent wide character and puts the result in the object pointed to by **wstr**. (Only the first 2 bytes of **mbstr** are examined.)

```
mbtowc(wstr, mbstr, 2);
```

Related Functions

mblen( ), wctomb( )

void nosound(void)

Description

The prototype for **nosound( )** is in **dos.h**. This function is not defined by the ANSI C standard.

The **nosound( )** function turns off the PC's speaker. This function normally follows a call to the **sound( )** function.

Example

This program makes the speaker beep and then stop:

```
#include <dos.h>

int main(void)
{
  sound(1000);
  sleep(2);
  nosound();

  return 0;
}
```

Related Function

sound( )

int cdecl far _OvrInitEms(unsigned handle, unsigned page, unsigned num)
int cdecl far _OvrInitExt(unsigned long address, unsigned long len)

Description

The prototypes for **_OvrInitEms( )** and **_OvrInitExt( )** are in **dos.h**. These functions are not defined by the ANSI C standard. These functions are for DOS only.

The **_OvrInitEms( )** function prepares the expanded memory of the computer, if it exists, so that it can be used by the overlay manager. The value of *handle* must be a valid EMS handle. Or, it may be 0, in which case the overlay manager simply allocates its own memory. The value of *page* is only meaningful when *handle* is non-0, in which case it specifies the first page of memory to use for swapping. The value of *len* specifies the number of pages to be used by the overlay manager. This function returns 0 if successful and non-0 otherwise.

The **_OvrInitExt( )** function prepares the extended memory of the computer, if it exists, so that it can be used by the overlay manager. The value of *address* determines the beginning address of extended memory to use. If *address* is 0, then the function will determine the beginning address of extended memory. The value of *len* determines how many bytes of memory may be used. If this value is 0, then the overlay manager is free to use all of extended memory. This function returns 0 if successful and non-0 if an error occurs.

Example

This program initializes all of extended memory for use by the overlay manager:

```
#include <dos.h>
#include <stdio.h>

int main(void)
{
  int result;

  result = _OvrInitExt(NULL, 0);
  if(result)
    printf("Cannot use extended memory for overlays.");

  return 0;
}
```

int putenv(const char *evar)

Description

The prototype for **putenv( )** is in **stdlib.h**. This function is not defined by the ANSI C standard.

The **putenv( )** function defines an environmental variable. It returns 0 if successful and –1 if unsuccessful. Refer to **getenv( )** and to your operating system manual for information about environmental variables.

Related Function

getenv( )

void qsort(void *base, size_t num, size_t size, int (*compare) (const void *, const void *))

Description

The prototype for **qsort( )** is in **stdlib.h**.

The **qsort( )** function sorts the array pointed to by *base* using a *quicksort,* a general-purpose sorting algorithm (developed by C.A.R. Hoare). Upon termination, the array is sorted. The number of elements in the array is specified by *num,* and the size (in bytes) of each element is described by *size.*

The function pointed to by *compare* compares an element of the array with the key. The form of the *compare* function must be

int *func_name*(const void **arg1,* const void **arg2*)

It must return the following values:

If *arg1* is less than *arg2,* return less than 0.

If *arg1* is equal to *arg2,* return 0.

If *arg1* is greater than *arg2,* return greater than 0.

The array is sorted into ascending order with the lowest address containing the lowest element.

Example

This program sorts a list of integers and displays the result:

```
#include <stdio.h>
#include <stdlib.h>

int num[10] = {
  1,3,6,5,8,7,9,6,2,0
};

int comp(const int *, const int *);

int main(void)
{
  int i;

  printf("Original array: ");
  for(i=0; i<10; i++) printf("%d ",num[i]);
  printf("\n");

  qsort(num, 10, sizeof(int),
        (int(*)(const void *, const void *)) comp);

  printf("Sorted array: ");
  for(i=0; i<10; i++) printf("%d ", num[i]);

  return 0;
}

/* compare the integers */
int comp(const int *i, const int *j)
{
  return *i - *j;
}
```

Related Function

bsearch( )

int raise(int signal)

Description

The prototype for **raise( )** is in **signal.h**. The **raise( )** function sends the signal specified by *signal* to the currently executing program.

The following signals are defined in **signal.h**:

Macro	**Meaning**
SIGABRT	Termination error
SIGBREAK	User pressed CTRL-Break
SIGFPE	Floating-point error
SIGILL	Bad instruction
SIGINT	User pressed CTRL-C
SIGSEGV	Illegal memory access
SIGTERM	Terminate program
SIGUSR1, SIGUSR2, SIGUSR3	User-defined signals

On success, **raise( )** returns 0.

You will often use this function in conjunction with the **signal( )** function.

Example

This program raises the **SIGTERM** signal, which causes **myhandler( )** to be executed:

```
#include <signal.h>
#include <stdio.h>
#include <stdlib.h>

void myhandler(int);

int main(void)
{
  signal(SIGTERM, myhandler);
  raise(SIGTERM);
  printf("This line will not be executed.\n");
  return 0;
}
```

```
void myhandler(int notused)
{
  printf("Program terminated.\n");
  exit(1);
}
```

Related Function

signal( )

int rand(void)

Description

The prototype for **rand( )** is in **stdlib.h**.

The **rand( )** function generates a sequence of pseudorandom numbers. Each time it is called, it returns an integer between 0 and **RAND_MAX**.

Example

This program displays ten pseudorandom numbers:

```
#include <stdio.h>
#include <stdlib.h>

int main(void)
{
  int i;

  for(i=0; i<10; i++)
    printf("%d ", rand());
  return 0;
}
```

Related Function

srand( )

int random(int num)
void randomize(void)

Description

The prototypes for **random( )** and **randomize( )** are in **stdlib.h**. These functions are not defined by the ANSI C standard.

The **random( )** macro returns a random number in the range 0 through *num* –1.

The **randomize( )** macro initializes the random number generator to some random value. It uses the **time( )** function, so you should include **time.h** in any program that uses **randomize( )**.

Example

This program prints ten random numbers between 0 and 24:

```
#include <time.h>
#include <stdio.h>
#include <stdlib.h>

int main(void)
{
  int i;

  randomize();

  for(i=0; i<10; i++) printf("%d ", random(25));

  return 0;
}
```

Related Functions

rand( ), srand( )

unsigned short _rotl(unsigned short val, int num)
unsigned short _rotr(unsigned short val, int num)

Description

The prototypes for **_rotl( )** and **_rotr( )** are in **stdlib.h**. These functions are not defined by the ANSI C standard.

The **_rotl( )** and **_rotr( )** functions rotate the bits of the value *val, num* number of bits to the left or right, respectively, and return the result. When a rotate is performed, bits rotated off one end are inserted onto the other end. For example, given the value

1111 0000 0000 1111

rotating it left by one bit produces the value

1110 0000 0001 1111

Example

The following program prints the value of 64 after it is rotated left and it is rotated right:

```
#include <stdio.h>
#include <stdlib.h>

int main(void)
{
  unsigned val = 64;

  printf("Rotated left 2 bits = %d\n", _rotl(val,2));
  printf("Rotated right 2 bits = %d\n", _rotr(val,2));

  return 0;
}
```

Related Functions

_lrotl( ), _lrotr( )

void _setcursortype(int type)

Description

The prototype for **_setcursortype( )** is in **conio.h**. This function is not defined by the ANSI C standard.

The **_setcursortype( )** function changes how the cursor is displayed. It can be called with one of three macros (defined in **conio.h**). Calling **_setcursortype( )** with **_NOCURSOR** turns off the cursor. Using **_SOLIDCURSOR** makes a block cursor, and **_NORMALCURSOR** creates an underscore cursor.

Example

This fragment changes the cursor type to a block:

```
_setcursortype(_SOLIDCURSOR);
```

Related Function

setcolor( )

int setjmp(jmp_buf envbuf)

Description

The prototype for **setjmp( )** is in **setjmp.h**.

The **setjmp( )** function saves the contents of the system stack in the buffer *envbuf* for later use by **longjmp( )**.

The **setjmp( )** function returns zero upon invocation. However, when **longjmp( )** executes, it passes an argument (always nonzero) to **setjmp( )**, which appears to be **setjmp( )**'s return value.

See **longjmp( )** for additional information.

Example

This program prints "1 2 3":

```
#include <stdio.h>
#include <setjmp.h>

jmp_buf ebuf;
void f2(void);

int main(void)
{
  char first=1;
  int i;

  printf("1 ");
  i = setjmp(ebuf);
  if(first) {
    first =! first;
    f2();
    printf("this will not be printed");
  }
  printf("%d", i);
  return 0;
}

void f2(void)
{
  printf("2 ");
  longjmp(ebuf, 3);
}
```

Related Function

longjmp( )

void _searchenv(const char *fname, const char *ename, char *fpath)

Description

The prototype for **_searchenv( )** is in **stdlib.h**. The function is not defined by the ANSI C standard.

The **_searchenv( )** searches for the file whose name is pointed to by *fname* using the path defined by the environmental name pointed to by *ename*. If the file is found, its full path is put into the string pointed to by *fpath*.

Example

This program searches for the specified file using the specified path. If it finds the file, it displays the full path:

```
#include <stdlib.h>
#include <stdio.h>

int main(int argc, char *argv[])
{
  char fpath[64];

  if(argc!=3) {
    printf("Usage: FINDFILE <fname> <ename>");
    return 1;
  }

  _searchenv(argv[1], argv[2], fpath);

  /* fpath will contain path if file is found */
  if(*fpath) printf("Path: %s", fpath);

  return 0;
}
```

Related Function

searchpath( )

char *setlocale(int type, const char *locale)

Description

The prototype for **setlocale( )** is in **locale.h**. This function allows certain parameters that are sensitive to the geopolitical location of a program's execution to be queried or set. For example, in Europe, the comma is used in place of the decimal point.

If *locale* is null, then **setlocale( )** returns a pointer to the current localization string. Otherwise, **setlocale( )** attempts to use the specified localization string to set the locale parameters as specified by *type*.

At the time of the call, *type* must be one of the following macros:

LC_ALL
LC_COLLATE
LC_CTYPE
LC_MONETARY
LC_NUMERIC
LC_TIME

LC_ALL refers to all localization categories. **LC_COLLATE** affects the operation of the **strcoll( )** function. **LC_CTYPE** alters the way the character functions work. **LC_MONETARY** determines the monetary format. **LC_NUMERIC** changes the decimal-point character for formatted input/output functions. Finally, **LC_TIME** determines the behavior of the **strftime( )** function.

The **setlocale( )** function returns a pointer to a string associated with the *type* parameter. It returns null if an error occurs.

The following locales are currently supported: German, French, English (Great Britain), and English (United States).

Related Functions

localeconv( ), time( ), strcoll( ), strftime( )

void (*set_new_handler(void (* newhand)( )))( )

Description

The prototype for **set_new_handler( )** is in **new.h**. This function is not defined by the ANSI C standard.

The **set_new_handler( )** function allows you to determine which function is called when a **new** memory allocation request fails. The address of this function is passed in *newhand*. To deactivate your function and return to the default processing of allocation request failures, call **set_new_handler( )** with *newhand* being **NULL**.

In general, you should not use this function. Its use is highly specialized and no example is given.

Related Functions

getvect( ), setvect( )

void (*signal (int signal, void (*sigfunc) (int func)))(int)

Description

The prototype for **signal( )** is in **signal.h**.

The **signal( )** function tells Borland C++ to execute the function pointed to by *sigfunc* if *signal* is received.

The value for *func* must be one of the following macros, defined in **signal.h**, or the address of a function you created:

Macro	**Meaning**
SIG_DFL	Use default signal handling
SIG_IGN	Ignore the signal

If you create your own function, it is executed each time the specified signal is received.

The following signals are defined in **signal.h**. These are the values that can be given to *signal.*

Macro	**Meaning**
SIGABRT	Termination error
SIGBREAK	User pressed CTRL-Break
SIGFPE	Floating-point error
SIGILL	Bad instruction
SIGINT	User pressed CTRL-C
SIGSEGV	Illegal memory access
SIGTERM	Terminate program
SIGUSR1, SIGUSR2, SIGUSR3	User-defined signals

On success, **signal( )** returns the address of the previously defined function for the specified signal. On error, **SIG_ERR** is returned, and **errno** is set to **EINVAL**.

Example

This line causes the function **myint( )** to be called if CTRL-C is pressed:

```
signal(SIGINT, myint);
```

Related Function

raise( )

void sound(unsigned freq)

Description

The prototype for **sound( )** is in **dos.h**. This function is not defined by the ANSI C standard.

The **sound( )** function causes a tone of *freq* frequency to be sounded on the computer's speaker. The frequency is specified in hertz. The tone continues to be produced until a call to **nosound( )** is made.

Example

This program beeps at 440Hz for one second:

```
#include <dos.h>

int main(void)
{
  sound(440);
  sleep(1);
  nosound();

  return 0;
}
```

Related Function

nosound( )

void srand(unsigned seed)

Description

The prototype for **srand( )** is in **stdlib.h**.

The **srand( )** function is used to set a starting point for the sequence generated by **rand( )**. (The **rand( )** function returns pseudorandom numbers.)

The **srand( )** function allows multiple program runs using different sequences of pseudorandom numbers.

Example

This program uses the system time to initialize the **rand( )** function randomly by using **srand( )**:

```
#include <stdio.h>
#include <stdlib.h>
#include <time.h>

/* Seed rand with the system time
   and display the first 100 numbers.
*/
int main(void)
{
  int i, stime;
  long  ltime;

  /* get the current calendar time */

  ltime = time(NULL);
  stime = (unsigned int) ltime/2;
  srand(stime);
  for(i=0; i<10; i++) printf("%d ", rand());
  return 0;
}
```

Related Function

rand( )

unsigned int _status87(void)

Description

The prototype for **_status87( )** is in **float.h**. This function is not defined by the ANSI C standard.

The **_status87( )** function returns the value of the floating-point status word. You must have an 80x87 math coprocessor installed in the computer before using this function.

Related Functions

_clear87( ), **_fpreset( )**

double strtod(const char *start, char **end)
long double _strtold(const char *start, char **end)

Description

The **strtod( )** function converts the string representation of a number stored in the string pointed to by *start* into a **double** and returns the result. Its prototype is in **stdlib.h**.

The **strtod( )** function works as follows: First, any leading white space in the string pointed to by *start* is stripped. Next, each character that makes up the number is read. Any character that cannot be part of a floating-point number stops the process. This includes white space, punctuation other than periods, and characters other than "E" or "e". Finally, *end* is set to point to the remainder, if any, of the original string. This means that if **strtod( )** is called with **100.00 Pliers**, the value 100.00 is returned and *end* points to the space that precedes "Pliers".

If a conversion error occurs, **strtod( )** returns either **HUGE_VAL** for overflow, or **–HUGE_VAL** for underflow. If no conversion could take place, 0 is returned.

_strtold( ) is the **long double** version of this function.

Example

This program reads floating-point numbers from a character array:

```
#include <stdio.h>
#include <stdlib.h>
#include <ctype.h>

int main(void)
{
  char *end, *start="100.00 pliers 200.00 hammers";

  end = start;
  while(*start) {
    printf("%f, ",strtod(start, &end));
    printf("Remainder: %s\n", end);
    start = end;
    /* move past the non-digits */
    while(!isdigit(*start) && *start) start++;
  }
  return 0;
}
```

The output is

```
100.00000, Remainder: pliers 200.00 hammers
200.00000, Remainder: hammers
```

Related Function

atof( )

long strtol(const char *start, char **end, int radix) unsigned long strtoul(const char *start, char **end, int radix)

Description

The prototypes for **strtol( )** and **strtoul( )** are in **stdlib.h**.

The **strtol( )** function converts the string representation of a number stored in the string pointed to by *start* into a **long int** and returns the result. The **strtoul( )** function performs the same conversion, but the result is an **unsigned long**. The base of the number is determined by *radix*. If *radix* is 0, the base is determined by rules that govern constant specification. If *radix* is other than 0, it must be in the range 2 through 36.

The **strtol( )** and **strtoul( )** functions work as follows: First, any leading white space in the string pointed to by *start* is stripped. Next, each character that makes up the number is read. Any character that cannot be part of a **long** integer number stops this process. This includes white space, punctuation, and nondigit characters. Finally, *end* is set to point to the remainder, if any, of the original string. This means that if **strtol( )** is called with **100 Pliers**, the value 100L is returned and *end* points to the space that precedes "Pliers".

If a conversion error occurs, the return value is **LONG_MAX** for overflow, or **LONG_MIN** for underflow, or **ULONG_MAX** for **strtoul( )**. If no conversion could take place, 0 is returned.

Example

This function reads base 10 numbers from standard input and returns their **long** equivalents:

```
#include <stdio.h>
#include <stdlib.h>

long int read_long()
{
  char start[80], *end;

  printf("Enter a number: ");
  gets(start);
  return strtol(start, &end, 10);
}
```

Related Function

atol( )

void swab(char *source, char *dest, int num)

Description

The prototype for **swab( )** is in **stdlib.h**. This function is not defined by the ANSI C standard.

The **swab( )** function copies *num* bytes from the string pointed to by *source* into the string pointed to by *dest,* switching the position of each even/odd pair of bytes as it goes.

Example

This fragment prints "iH":

```
char dest[3];

swab("Hi", dest, 2);
printf(dest);
```

int system(const char *str)

Description

The prototype for **system( )** is in **stdlib.h**.

The **system( )** function passes the string pointed to by *str* as a command to the command processor of the operating system and returns the exit status of the command. A command processor must be present to execute the command.

Example

This program displays the contents of the current working directory:

```
#include <stdlib.h>

int main(void)
{
  system("dir");
  return 0;
}
```

Related Functions

spawn( ), exec( )

int toascii(int ch)

Description

The prototype for **toascii( )** is in **ctype.h**. This function is not defined by the ANSI C standard.

The **toascii( )** function clears all but the lower 7 bits in *ch* and returns the result.

Example

This fragment clears all but the lower 7 bits of the character input from the keyboard:

```
int ch;

ch = getche():

ch = toascii(ch);
```

Related Functions

tolower( ), toupper( )

unsigned umask(unsigned access)

Description

The prototype for **umask( )** is in **io.h**. This function is not defined by the ANSI C standard.

The **umask( )** function modifies the access attribute of a file opened by either **open( )** or **creat( )**. The attribute specified in *access* is removed from the access attribute. The *access* parameter must be one of these two values (which may also be ORed together):

Macro	Meaning
S_IWRITE	File is writable
S_IREAD	File is readable

The **umask( )** function returns the previous access permission mask.

Example

This statement causes subsequent files to be opened as write-only:

```
umask(S_IREAD);
```

Related Functions

creat( ), open( ), fopen( )

int utime(char *fname, struct utimbuf *t)

Description

The prototype for **utime( )** is in **utime.h**. This function is not defined by the ANSI C standard.

The **utime( )** function changes the creation (or last modification) time of the file whose name is pointed to by *fname*. The new time is specified by the structure pointed to by *t*. The **utimbuf** structure is defined like this:

```
struct utimbuf {
  time_t actime;
  time_t modtime;
};
```

For DOS, **actime** is not relevant. If *t* is null, then the file's creation time is set to the current system time.

The **utime( )** function returns 0 if successful. If an error occurs, –1 is returned and **errno** is set to one of these values:

Macro	Meaning
EACCES	Access denied
EMFILE	Too many files are open
ENOENT	Nonexistent file

Example

This program sets the specified file's creation time to the current time of the system. (This is a simple version of the common TOUCH utility program.)

```
#include <utime.h>
#include <stdio.h>

int main(int argc, char *argv[])
{
  if(argc!=2) {
    printf("Usage: SETTIME <fname>");
```

```
    return 1;
  }

  /* set to current system time */
  utime(argv[1], NULL);

  return 0;
}
```

Related Functions

time( ), asctime( ), gmtime( )

void va_start(va_list argptr, last_parm)
void va_end(va_list argptr)
type va_arg(va_list argptr, type)

Description

The prototypes for these macros are in **stdarg.h**.

The **va_arg( )**, **va_start( )**, and **va_end( )** macros work together to allow a variable number of arguments to be passed to a function. The most common example of a function that takes a variable number of arguments is **printf( )**. The type **va_list** is defined by **stdarg.h**.

The general procedure for creating a function that can take a variable number of arguments is as follows: The function must have at least one known parameter, but can have more, prior to the variable parameter list. The rightmost known parameter is called the *last_parm*. The name of the *last_parm* is used as the second parameter in a call to **va_start( )**. Before any of the variable-length parameters can be accessed, the argument pointer *argptr* must be initialized through a call to **va_start( )**. After that, parameters are returned via calls to **va_arg( )** with *type* being the type of the next parameter. Finally, once all the parameters have been read and prior to returning from the function, a call to **va_end( )** must be made to ensure that the stack is properly restored. If **va_end( )** is not called, a program crash is very likely.

Example

This program uses **sum_series( )** to return the sum of a series of numbers. The first argument contains a count of the number of arguments to follow. In this example, the first five elements of the following series are summed:

$$\frac{1}{2} + \frac{1}{4} + \frac{1}{8} + \frac{1}{16} \cdots + \frac{1}{2^n}$$

The output displayed is "0.968750".

```
/* Variable length argument example - sum a series.*/

#include <stdio.h>
#include <stdarg.h>

double sum_series(int, ...);

int main(void)
{
  double d;

  d = sum_series(5, 0.5, 0.25, 0.125, 0.0625, 0.03125);

  printf("Sum of series is %f\n",d);

  return 0;

}

double sum_series(int num, ...)
{
  double sum = 0.0, t;
  va_list argptr;

  /* initialize argptr */
  va_start(argptr, num);

  /* sum the series */
  for(; num; num--) {
   t = va_arg(argptr,double);
   sum += t;
  }

  /* do orderly shutdown */
  va_end(argptr);
  return sum;
}
```

Related Function

vprintf( )

size_t wcstombs(char *out, const wchar_t *in, size_t size)

Description

The prototype for **wcstombs( )** is in **stdlib.h**.

The **wcstombs( )** converts the wide character string pointed to by *in* into its multibyte equivalent and puts the result in the string pointed to by *out*. Only the first *size* bytes of *in* are converted. Conversion stops before that if the null terminator is encountered.

If successful, **wcstombs( )** returns the number of bytes converted. On failure, –1 is returned.

Related Functions

wctomb( ), mbstowcs( )

int wctomb(char *out, wchar_t in)

Description

The prototype for **wctomb( )** is in **stdlib.h**.

The **wctomb( )** converts the wide character in *in* into its multibyte equivalent and puts the result in the string pointed to by *out*. The array pointed to by *out* must be at least **MB_CUR_MAX** characters long.

If successful, **wctomb( )** returns the number of bytes contained in the multibyte character. On failure, –1 is returned.

If *out* is NULL, then **wctomb( )** returns non-0 if the multibyte character has state-dependencies and 0 if it does not.

Related Functions

wcstombs( ), mbtowc( )

PART THREE

Borland C++

Part 3 of this book examines C++. C++ is essentially a superset of C, so everything you already know about C is applicable to C++. Many of the concepts embodied in C++ will be new, but don't worry—you are starting from a firm base. Remember: Knowledge of the C language is prerequisite to learning C++. If you don't already know C, you must take some time to learn it.

Chapter Twenty

An Overview of C++

Put simply, C++ is an *object-oriented* programming language. The object-oriented features of C++ are interrelated, so it is important to have a general understanding of these features before attempting to learn the details. The purpose of this chapter is to provide an overview of the key concepts embodied in C++. The rest of Part 3 closely examines specific C++ features.

The Origins of C++

C++ is an expanded version of C. C is flexible yet powerful, and it has been used to create some of the most important software products of the past several years. However, when a project exceeds a certain size, C reaches its limits. Depending on the project, a program of 25,000 to 100,000 lines becomes hard to manage because it is difficult to grasp as a totality. Beginning in 1979, while working at Bell Laboratories at Murray Hill, New Jersey, Bjarne Stroustrup addressed this problem by adding several extensions to the C language. Initially called "C with Classes," the name was changed to C++ in 1983.

Most additions made to C by Stroustrup support object-oriented programming, sometimes referred to as OOP. (A brief explanation of object-oriented programming follows in the next section.) Stroustrup states that some of C++'s object-oriented features were inspired by another object-oriented language, Simula67. Therefore, C++ represents the blending of two powerful programming methods.

Since the advent of C++, it has gone through three major revisions, one in 1985 and another in 1989. The third revision occurred when work began on the ANSI standard for C++. The first draft of the proposed standard was created on January 25, 1994. The ANSI C++ committee (of which I am a member) has kept virtually all of the features first defined by Stroustrup and has added several new ones as well. The standardization process is typically a slow one, and C++ is no exception. At the time of this writing, the C++ standard is still in draft form and has yet to be finalized. Therefore, keep in mind that C++ is still a "work in progress," and that some features may be "fine-tuned." However, the version of C++ implemented by Borland is stable and in general compliance with the current form of the draft ANSI C++ standard.

When he invented C++, Stroustrup knew that it was important to maintain the original spirit of C—including its efficiency, flexibility, and the philosophy that the programmer (not the language) is in charge—while at the same time adding support for object-oriented programming. As you will see, this goal was largely accomplished. C++ provides the programmer with the freedom and control of C coupled with the power of objects. The object-oriented features in C++, to use Stroustrup's words, "allow programs to be structured for clarity, extensibility, and ease of maintenance without loss of efficiency."

Although C++ was initially designed to aid in the management of very large programs, it is in no way limited to this use. In fact, the object-oriented attributes of C++ can be effectively applied to virtually any programming task. It is not uncommon to see C++ used for projects such as editors, databases, personal file systems, and communication programs. Also, because C++ shares C's efficiency, high-performance systems software can be constructed using C++.

What Is Object-Oriented Programming?

Object-oriented programming is a way of approaching the job of programming. Programming methodologies have changed dramatically since the invention of the computer in order to accommodate the increasing complexity of programs. For example, when computers were first invented, programming was done by toggling in the binary machine instructions using the front panel. As long as programs were just a few hundred instructions long, this approach worked. As programs grew, assembly language was invented so that a programmer could deal with larger, increasingly complex programs using symbolic representations of the machine instructions.

Eventually, high-level languages were introduced that gave the programmer more tools with which to handle complexity. The first widely used language was FORTRAN. While FORTRAN was a very impressive first step, it is hardly a language that encourages clear and easily understood programs.

The 1960s gave birth to *structured* programming—the method encouraged by languages such as C and Pascal. For the first time, with structured languages it was possible to write moderately complex programs fairly easily. However, even using structured programming methods, once a project reaches a certain size, its complexity becomes too difficult for a programmer to manage.

At each milestone in the development of programming, methods were created to allow the programmer to deal with increasingly greater complexity. Each step of the way, the new approach took the best elements of the previous methods and moved forward. Today, many projects are near or at the point where the structured approach no longer works. To solve this problem, object-oriented programming was invented.

Object-oriented programming takes the best ideas of structured programming and combines them with powerful, new concepts that encourage you to look at the task of programming in a new light. Object-oriented programming allows you to easily decompose a problem into subgroups of related parts. Then, you can translate these subgroups into self-contained units called objects.

All object-oriented programming languages have three things in common: encapsulation, polymorphism, and inheritance. Let's look at these concepts now.

Encapsulation

Encapsulation is the mechanism that binds together code and data and that keeps both safe from outside interference or misuse. Further, it is encapsulation that allows the creation of an object. Put simply, an *object* is a logical entity that encapsulates both data and the code that manipulates that data. Within an object, some of the code and/or data may be private to the object and inaccessible to anything outside the object. In this way, an object provides a significant level of protection against some other, unrelated part of the program accidentally modifying or incorrectly using the private members of the object.

For all intents and purposes, an object is a variable of a user-defined type. It may seem strange at first to think of an object, which links both code and data, as a variable. However, in object-oriented programming, this is precisely the case. When you define an object, you are implicitly creating a new data type.

Polymorphism

Object-oriented programming languages support *polymorphism*, which is characterized by the phrase "one interface, multiple methods." In simple terms, polymorphism is the attribute that allows one interface to be used with a general class of actions. The specific action selected is determined by the exact nature of the situation. A real-world example of polymorphism is a thermostat. No matter what type of furnace your house has (gas, oil, electric, etc.) the thermostat works the same way. In this case, the thermostat (which is the interface) is the same no matter what type of furnace (method) you have. For example, if you want a 70-degree temperature, you set the thermostat to 70 degrees. It doesn't matter what type of furnace actually provides the heat.

This same principle can also apply to programming. For example, you might have a program that defines three different types of stacks. One stack is used for integer values, one for character values, and one for floating-point values. Because of polymorphism, you can create two sets of functions called **push( )** and **pop( )**—one set for each type of data. The general concept (interface) is that of pushing and popping data onto and from a stack. The functions define the specific ways (methods) this is done for each type of data. When you push data on the stack, it is the type of the data that will determine which specific version of the **push( )** function will be called.

Polymorphism helps reduce complexity by allowing the same interface to be used to specify a general class of actions. It is the compiler's job to select the *specific action* (i.e., method) as it applies to each situation. You, the programmer, don't need to do this selection manually. You need only remember and utilize the general interface.

The first object-oriented programming languages were interpreters, so polymorphism was supported at runtime. However, because C++ is a compiled language, polymorphism is supported at both runtime and compile time.

Inheritance

Inheritance is the process by which one object can acquire the properties of another object. This is important because it supports the concept of classification. If you think about it, most knowledge is made manageable by hierarchical classifications. For example, a Red Delicious apple is part of the *apple* class, which in turn is part of the *fruit* class, which is under the larger *food* class. Without the use of classifications, each object would have to define all of its characteristics explicitly. Using classifications, an object need only define those qualities that make it unique within its class. It is the inheritance mechanism that makes it possible for one object to be a specific instance of a more general case.

Some C++ Fundamentals

Since C++ is a superset of C, most C programs are C++ programs as well. (There are a few minor differences between C and C++ that will prevent certain types of C programs from being compiled by a C++ compiler. These differences will be discussed in Chapter 27.) You can write C++ programs that look just like C programs, but you won't be taking full advantage of C++'s capabilities. Further, most C++ programmers use a style and certain features that are unique to C++. Since it is important to use C++ to its full potential, this section introduces a few of these features before moving on to the "meat" of C++.

Let's begin with an example. Examine this C++ program:

```
#include <iostream.h>
#include <stdio.h>

int main()
{
  int i;
  char str[80];

  cout << "I like Borland C++.\n";  // this is a single-line comment
  /* you can still use C-style comments, too */

  printf("You can use printf(), but most C++ programs don't.\n");
```

```
  // input a number using >>
  cout << "Enter a number: ";
  cin >> i;

  // now, output a number using <<
  cout << "Your number is " << i << "\n";

  // read a string
  cout << "Enter a string: ";
  cin >> str;
  // print it
  cout << str;

  return 0;
}
```

As you can see, this program looks different from the average C program. The header file, **iostream.h**, is defined by C++ and is used to support C++ I/O operations. The only reason **stdio.h** is included is because of the **printf( )** statement. **stdio.h** is not needed if your C++ program uses only I/O operations specific to C++.

One of the first things you will notice is that the declaration of **main( )** is defined

```
int main()
```

rather than the

```
int main(void)
```

that many of the programs in the preceding parts of this book have used. The reason for this is that in C++, an empty parameter list is the same as one specified as **void**. That is, the preceding two ways to declare **main( )** are the same as far as C++ is concerned. In C++, the use of **void** to indicate an empty parameter list is still permitted, but it is redundant. Since it is not needed, none of the C++ programs shown in this part of the book will use **void** to indicate an empty parameter list.

The following line introduces several C++ features:

```
cout << "I like Borland C++.\n";  // this is a single line comment
```

The statement

```
cout << "I like Borland C++.\n";
```

displays "I like Borland C++." on the screen followed by a carriage return, linefeed combination. In C++, the **<<** has an expanded role. It is still the left-shift operator, but when it is used as shown in this example, it is also an output operator. The word **cout** is an identifier that is linked to the screen. Like C, C++ supports I/O redirection, but for the sake of discussion we can assume that **cout** refers to the screen. You can use **cout** and the << to output any of the built-in data types plus strings of characters.

It is important to note that you can still use **printf( )** (as the program illustrates) or any of C's other I/O functions, but most programmers feel that using **cout <<** is more in the spirit of C++. More generally, a C++ program can use any library function supported by Borland C++—including those defined by C. (These functions are described in Part 2 of this book.) However, in cases where C++ provides an alternative approach, it should usually be used instead of a C-like library function (although there is no rule that enforces this).

In the preceding line of code, a C++ comment follows the output expression. In C++, comments are defined two ways. A C-like comment works the same in C++ as it does in C. However, in C++ you can also define a *single-line comment* using //. When you start a comment using //, whatever follows is ignored by the compiler until the end of the line is reached. In general, use C-like comments when creating multiline comments and single-line comments otherwise.

Next, the program prompts the user for a number. The number is read from the keyboard using this statement:

```
cin >> i;
```

In C++, the >> operator retains its right-shift meaning, but when used as shown, it is an input operator that causes **i** to be given a value read from the keyboard. The identifier **cin** refers to the keyboard. In general, you can use **cin >>** to load a variable of any of the basic data types or a string.

Although not illustrated by the program, you are free to use any of C's input functions, such as **scanf( )**, instead of using **cin >>**. However, as with **cout**, the vast majority of programmers feel that **cin >>** is more in the spirit of C++.

Another interesting line in the program is shown here:

```
cout << "Your number is " << i << "\n";
```

This code displays the following phrase (assuming **i** has the value 100):

```
Your number is 100
```

followed by a carriage return and line feed. In general, you can run together as many << output operations as you want.

The rest of the program demonstrates how you can read and write a string using **cin >>** and **cout <<**. When inputting a string, **cin >>** stops reading when the first white-space character is encountered. This is similar to the way the standard C function **scanf( )** works when inputting a string.

Compiling a C++ Program

Borland C++ can compile both C and C++ programs. In general, if a program ends in .CPP, it is compiled as a C++ program. If it ends in .C, it is compiled as a C program. Therefore, the simplest way to cause Borland C++ to compile your C++ program as a C++ program is to give it the .CPP extension.

If you don't want to give your C++ program the .CPP extension, you must either specify the -P option when using the command line or you must change the default settings of the integrated development environment. To do this, first select the **Options** menu, then the **Tools** option. A dialog box titled "Tools" appears. Double-click on the **CppCompile** entry in the list box. A second dialog box titled "Tool Options" appears. Click on the **Advanced** button. A third dialog box titled "Tool Advanced Options" appears. At the bottom of this dialog box, you will see a text field labeled "Default For:". This is where you can specify that the integrated environment should compile .C files as C++ programs.

Introducing C++ Classes

The **class** is at the root of C++. Before you can create an object in C++, you must first define its general form using the keyword **class**. A class defines a new data type that links code and data. A **class** is similar syntactically to a structure. However, a **class** may also include functions as well as data. As an example, this **class** defines a type called **queue**, which will be used to implement a queue.

```
// This creates the class queue.
class queue {
  int q[100];
  int sloc, rloc;
public:
  void init();
  void qput(int i);
  int qget();
};
```

A **class** can contain private as well as public parts. By default, all items defined in the **class** are private. For example, the variables **q**, **sloc**, and **rloc** are private, meaning they cannot be accessed by any function that is not a member of the **class**. This is how encapsulation is achieved—access to certain items of data may be tightly controlled by keeping them private. Although not shown in this example, you can also define private functions, which can only be called by other members of the **class**.

To make parts of a **class** public (accessible to other parts of your program), you must declare them after the **public** keyword. All variables or functions defined after **public** are accessible by all other functions in the program. Generally, the rest of your program accesses an object through its **public** functions. Although you can have **public** variables, you should try to limit or eliminate their use. Instead, you should make all data private and control access to it through **public** functions. Thus, public functions provide the interface to your class's private data. This helps preserve encapsulation. One other point: Notice that the **public** keyword is followed by a colon.

The functions **init( )**, **qput( )**, and **qget( )** are called *member functions* because they are part of the **class queue**. The variables **sloc, rloc**, and **q** are called *member variables* (or *data members*). Only member functions have access to the private members of the **class** in which they are declared. Thus, only **init( )**, **qput( )**, and **qget( )** have access to **sloc**, **rloc**, and **q**.

Once you have defined a **class**, you can create an object of that type using the **class** name. In essence, the **class**'s name becomes a new data type specifier. For example, this code creates an object called **intqueue** of type **queue**:

```
queue intqueue;
```

You can also create objects when defining a **class** by putting the variable names after the closing curly brace, in exactly the same way as you do with a structure.

The general form of a **class** declaration is

class *class-name* {
    private data and functions
public:
    public data and functions
} *object-list;*

Of course, the *object-list* may be empty.

Inside the declaration of **queue**, prototypes to the member functions are used. In C++, when you need to tell the compiler about a function, you must use its full prototype form. Further, in C++, all functions must be prototyped. Prototypes are not optional, as they are in C.

When it comes time to actually code a function that is a member of a class, you must tell the compiler to which class the function belongs. For example, here is one way to code the **qput( )** function:

```
void queue::qput(int i)
{
  if(sloc==99) {
    cout << "Queue is full.\n";
    return;
  }
```

```
  sloc++;
  q[sloc] = i;
}
```

The :: is called the *scope resolution operator.* Essentially, it tells the compiler that this version of **qput( )** belongs to the **queue** class. Or, put differently, that this **qput( )** is in **queue**'s scope. In C++, several different **class**es can use the same function names. The compiler knows which function belongs to which class because of the scope resolution operator and the **class** name.

To call a member function from a part of your program that is not a member of the **class**, you must use an object's name and the dot operator. For example, this fragment calls **init( )** for object **a**:

```
queue a, b;

a.init();
```

It is very important to understand that **a** and **b** are two separate objects. This means that initializing **a** does not cause **b** to be initialized. The only relationship **a** has with **b** is that they are objects of the same type. Further, **a**'s copies of **sloc**, **rloc**, and **q** are completely separate from **b**'s.

Only when a member function is called by code that does not belong to the **class** must the object name and the dot operator be used. Otherwise, one member function can call another member function directly, without using the dot operator. Also, a member function can refer directly to member variables without the use of the dot operator.

The program shown here demonstrates all the pieces of the **queue** class:

```
#include <iostream.h>

// This creates the class queue.
class queue {
  int q[100];
  int sloc, rloc;
public:
  void init();
  void qput(int i);
  int qget();
};

void queue::init()
{
  rloc = sloc = 0;
}
```

```
void queue::qput(int i)
{
  if(sloc==99) {
    cout << "Queue is full.\n";
    return;
  }
  sloc++;
  q[sloc] = i;
}

int queue::qget()
{
  if(rloc == sloc) {
    cout << "Queue underflow.\n";
    return 0;
  }
  rloc++;
  return q[rloc];
}

int main()
{
  queue a, b;  // create two queue objects

  a.init();
  b.init();

  a.qput(10);
  b.qput(19);

  a.qput(20);
  b.qput(1);

  cout << a.qget() << " ";
  cout << a.qget() << " ";
  cout << b.qget() << " ";
  cout << b.qget() << "\n";

  return 0;
}
```

Remember that the private parts of an object are accessible only by functions that are members of that object. For example, the statement

```
a.rloc = 0;
```

could not be in the **main( )** function of the previous program because **rloc** is private.

*NOTE: By convention, in most C programs the **main( )** function is the first function in the program. However, in the **queue** program the member functions of **queue** are defined before the **main( )** function. While there is no rule that dictates this (they could be defined anywhere in the program), this is the most common approach used when writing C++ code. (In fact, classes and the member functions associated with them are usually contained in a header file.)*

Function Overloading

One way that C++ achieves polymorphism is through the use of *function overloading*. In C++, two or more functions can share the same name as long as their parameter declarations are different. In this situation, the functions that share the same name are said to be *overloaded*. For example, consider this program:

```
#include <iostream.h>

// sqr_it is overloaded three ways
int sqr_it(int i);
double sqr_it(double d);
long sqr_it(long l);

int main()
{
  cout << sqr_it(10) << "\n";

  cout << sqr_it(11.0) << "\n";

  cout << sqr_it(9L) << "\n";

  return 0;
}

int sqr_it(int i)
{
  cout << "Inside the sqr_it() function that uses ";
  cout << "an integer argument.\n";

  return i*i;
}
```

```
double sqr_it(double d)
{
  cout << "Inside the sqr_it() function that uses ";
  cout << "a double argument.\n";

  return d*d;
}

long sqr_it(long l)
{
  cout << "Inside the sqr_it() function that uses ";
  cout << "a long argument.\n";

  return l*l;
}
```

This program creates three similar but different functions called **sqr_it( )**, each of which returns the square of its argument. As the program illustrates, the compiler knows which function to use in each case because of the type of the argument. The value of overloaded functions is that they allow related sets of functions to be accessed using a common name. In a sense, function overloading lets you create a generic name for an operation; the compiler resolves which function is actually needed to perform the operation.

Function overloading is important because it can help manage complexity. To understand how, consider this example. Borland C++ contains the functions **itoa( )**, **ltoa( )**, and **ultoa( )** in its standard library. Collectively, these functions convert different types of numbers (integers, long integers, and unsigned integers) into their string equivalents. Even though these functions perform almost identical actions, in C three different names must be used to represent these tasks, which makes the situation more complex than it actually is. Even though the underlying concept of each function is the same, the programmer has three things to remember. However, in C++ it is possible to use the same name, such as **numtoa( )**, for all three functions. Thus, the name **numtoa( )** represents the *general action* that is being performed. It is left to the compiler to choose the *specific* version for a particular circumstance; the programmer need only remember the general action being performed. Therefore, by applying polymorphism, three things to remember are reduced to one. If you expand the concept, you can see how polymorphism can help you manage very complex programs.

A more practical example of function overloading is illustrated by the following program. C and C++ do not contain any library functions that prompt the user for input and then wait for a response. However, this program creates three functions called **prompt( )** that perform this task for data of types **int**, **double**, and **long**:

```
#include <iostream.h>

void prompt(char *str, int *i);
void prompt(char *str, double *d);
void prompt(char *str, long *l);

int main()
{
  int i;
  double d;
  long l;

  prompt("Enter an integer: ", &i);
  prompt("Enter a double: ", &d);
  prompt("Enter a long: ", &l);

  cout << i << " " << d << " " << l;

  return 0;
}

void prompt(char *str, int *i)
{
  cout << str;
  cin >> *i;
}

void prompt(char *str, double *d)
{
  cout << str;
  cin >> *d;
}

void prompt(char *str, long *l)
{
  cout << str;
  cin >> *l;
}
```

You can use the same name to overload unrelated functions, but you should not. For example, you could use the name **sqr_it( )** to create functions that return the square of an **int** and the square root of a **double**. However, these two operations are fundamentally different and applying function overloading in this manner defeats its purpose. In practice, you should only overload closely related operations.

Operator Overloading

Another way that polymorphism is achieved in C++ is through *operator overloading.* For example, in C++ you can use the << and >> operators to perform console I/O operations. This is possible because in the **iostream.h** header file, these operators are overloaded. When an operator is overloaded, it takes on an additional meaning relative to a certain class. However, it still retains all of its old meanings.

In general, you can overload C++'s operators by defining what they mean relative to a specific class. For example, think back to the **queue** class developed earlier in this chapter. It is possible to overload the **+** operator relative to objects of type **queue** so that it appends the contents of one queue to another. However, the **+** still retains its original meaning relative to other types of data.

Because operator overloading is, in practice, somewhat more complicated than function overloading, examples are deferred until Chapter 22, when the subject is covered in detail.

Inheritance

Inheritance is one of the major traits of an object-oriented programming language. In C++, inheritance is supported by allowing one class to incorporate another class into its declaration. Inheritance allows a hierarchy of classes to be built, moving from most general to most specific. The process involves first defining a *base class*, which defines those qualities common to all objects to be derived from the base. The base class represents the most general description. The classes derived from the base are usually referred to as *derived classes.* A derived class includes all features of the generic base class and then adds qualities specific to itself. To demonstrate how this process works, the next example creates classes that categorize different types of vehicles.

To begin, here is a class, called **road_vehicle**, that very broadly defines vehicles that travel on the road. It stores the number of wheels a vehicle has and the number of passengers it can carry:

```
class road_vehicle {
  int wheels;
  int passengers;
public:
  void set_wheels(int num);
  int get_wheels();
  void set_pass(int num);
  int get_pass();
};
```

We can now use this broad definition of a road vehicle to define specific types of vehicles. For example, this declares a class called **truck** using **road_vehicle**:

```
class truck : public road_vehicle {
  int cargo;
public:
  void set_cargo(int size);
  int get_cargo();
  void show();
};
```

Notice how **road_vehicle** is inherited. The general form for inheritance is

> class *new-class-name* : *access inherited-class* {
>   // *body of new class*
> }

Here, *access* is optional, but if present it must be either **public** or **private**. You will learn more about these options in Chapter 23. For now, all inherited classes will use **public**, which means that all the **public** elements of the ancestor are also **public** in the class that inherits it. Therefore, in the example, members of the class **truck** have access to the member functions of **road_vehicle** just as if they had been declared inside **truck**. However, the member functions of **truck** *do not* have access to the private parts of **road_vehicle**.

The following program illustrates inheritance by creating two subclasses of **road_vehicle**: **truck** and **automobile**:

```
#include <iostream.h>

class road_vehicle {
  int wheels;
  int passengers;
public:
  void set_wheels(int num);
  int get_wheels();
  void set_pass(int num);
  int get_pass();
};

class truck : public road_vehicle {
  int cargo;
public:
  void set_cargo(int size);
  int get_cargo();
```

```
  void show();
};

enum type {car, van, wagon};

class automobile : public road_vehicle {
  enum type car_type;
public:
  void set_type(enum type t);
  enum type get_type();
  void show();
};

void road_vehicle::set_wheels(int num)
{
  wheels = num;
}

int road_vehicle::get_wheels()
{
  return wheels;
}

void road_vehicle::set_pass(int num)
{
  passengers = num;
}

int road_vehicle::get_pass()
{
  return passengers;
}

void truck::set_cargo(int num)
{
  cargo = num;
}

int truck::get_cargo()
{
  return cargo;
}

void truck::show()
```

```
{
  cout << "Wheels: " << get_wheels() << "\n";
  cout << "Passengers: " << get_pass() << "\n";
  cout << "Cargo capacity in cubic feet: " << cargo << "\n";
}

void automobile::set_type(enum type t)
{
  car_type = t;
}

enum type automobile::get_type()
{
  return car_type;
}

void automobile::show()
{
  cout << "Wheels: " << get_wheels() << "\n";
  cout << "Passengers: " << get_pass() << "\n";
  cout << "Type: ";
  switch(get_type()) {
    case van: cout << "Van\n";
      break;
    case car: cout << "Car\n";
      break;
    case wagon: cout << "Wagon\n";
  }
}

int main()
{
  truck t1, t2;
  automobile c;

  t1.set_wheels(18);
  t1.set_pass(2);
  t1.set_cargo(3200);

  t2.set_wheels(6);
  t2.set_pass(3);
  t2.set_cargo(1200);

  t1.show();
```

```
  t2.show();

  c.set_wheels(4);
  c.set_pass(6);
  c.set_type(van);
  c.show();

  return 0;
}
```

As this program illustrates, the major advantage of inheritance is that you can create a base classification that can be incorporated into more specific classes. In this way, each object can represent its own classification precisely.

Notice that both **truck** and **automobile** include member functions called **show( )**, which display information about each object. This is another aspect of polymorphism. Since each **show( )** is linked with its own class, the compiler can easily tell which one to call in any circumstance.

Constructors and Destructors

It is not unusual for some part of an object to require initialization before it can be used. For example, think back to the **queue** class developed earlier in this chapter. Before **queue** could be used, the variables **rloc** and **sloc** had to be set to 0 using the function **init( )**. Because the requirement for initialization is so common, C++ allows objects to initialize themselves when they are created. This automatic initialization is performed through the use of a constructor function.

A *constructor function* is a special function that is a member of a class and has the same name as that class. For example, here is how the **queue** class looks when converted to use a constructor function for initialization:

```
// This creates the class queue.
class queue {
  int q[100];
  int sloc, rloc;
public:
  queue();  // constructor
  void qput(int i);
  int qget();
};
```

Notice that the constructor **queue( )** has no return type specified. In C++, constructor functions cannot return values.

The **queue( )** function is coded like this:

```
// This is the constructor function.
queue::queue()
{
  sloc = rloc = 0;
  cout << "Queue initialized.\n";
}
```

Keep in mind that the message "queue initialized" is output as a way to illustrate the constructor. In actual practice, most constructor functions will not output or input anything. They will simply perform various initializations.

An object's constructor is automatically called when the object is created. This means that it is called when the object's declaration is executed. There is an important distinction between a C-like declaration statement and a C++ declaration. In C, variable declarations are, loosely speaking, passive and resolved mostly at compile time. Put differently, in C, variable declarations are not thought of as being executable statements. However, in C++, variable declarations are active statements that are, in fact, executed at run time. One reason for this is that an object declaration may need to call a constructor, thus causing the execution of a function. Although this difference may seem subtle and largely academic at this point, it has some important implications relative to variable initialization, as you will see later.

An object's constructor is called once for global or **static** local objects. For local objects, the constructor is called each time the object declaration is encountered.

The complement of the constructor is the *destructor.* In many circumstances, an object needs to perform some action or actions when it is destroyed. Local objects are created when their block is entered and destroyed when the block is left. Global objects are destroyed when the program terminates. There are many reasons why a destructor function may be needed. For example, an object may need to deallocate memory that it had previously allocated. In C++, it is the destructor function that handles deactivation. The destructor has the same name as the constructor but it is preceded by a ~. The following is an example of **queue** that uses constructor and destructor functions. (Keep in mind that the **queue** class does not require a destructor, so the one shown here is just for illustration.)

```
// This creates the class queue.
class queue {
  int q[100];
  int sloc, rloc;
public:
  queue();  // constructor
  ~queue(); // destructor
  void qput(int i);
  int qget();
};
```

```
// This is the constructor function.
queue::queue()
{
  sloc = rloc = 0;
  cout << "Queue initialized.\n";
}

// This is the destructor function.
queue::~queue()
{
  cout << "Queue destroyed.\n";
}
```

To see how constructors and destructors work, here is a new version of the sample program from earlier in this chapter:

```
#include <iostream.h>

// This creates the class queue.
class queue {
  int q[100];
  int sloc, rloc;
public:
  queue();  // constructor
  ~queue(); // destructor
  void qput(int i);
  int qget();
};

// This is the constructor function.
queue::queue()
{
  sloc = rloc = 0;
  cout << "Queue initialized.\n";
}

// This is the destructor function.
queue::~queue()
{
  cout << "Queue destroyed.\n";
}

void queue::qput(int i)
{
```

```
  if(sloc==99) {
    cout << "Queue is full.\n";
    return;
  }
  sloc++;
  q[sloc] = i;
}

int queue::qget()
{
  if(rloc == sloc) {
    cout << "Queue underflow.\n";
    return 0;
  }
  rloc++;
  return q[rloc];
}

int main()
{
  queue a, b;  // create two queue objects

  a.qput(10);
  b.qput(19);

  a.qput(20);
  b.qput(1);

  cout << a.qget() << " ";
  cout << a.qget() << " ";
  cout << b.qget() << " ";
  cout << b.qget() << "\n";

  return 0;
}
```

This program displays the following:

```
Queue initialized.
Queue initialized.
10 20 19 1
Queue destroyed.
Queue destroyed.
```

The C++ Keywords

Borland C++ includes all of the keywords defined by C and adds those shown in Table 20-1. Remember that you cannot use any of the keywords as names for variables or functions. Also, the keyword **__rtti** is specific to Borland and not defined by the draft ANSI C++ standard.

Two New Data Types

In looking at the list of keywords in Table 20-1, you may have noticed the addition of two new built-in types: **bool** and **wchar_t**. The **bool** data type is capable of holding a Boolean value. Objects of type **bool** may have only the values **true** and **false.** The values **true** and **false** are also keywords that are part of the C++ language. Values of type **bool** are automatically elevated to integers when used in a non-Boolean expression. Although C++ defines the **bool** data type, it still fully supports the fundamental concept of nonzero values being true and zero being false.

The type **wchar_t** holds wide characters. Wide characters are typically 16-bit values. They are used to represent the character sets of languages that have more than 255 characters. The **wchar_t** is supported in C as a defined type using **typdef**. In C++, it has become a keyword.

Now that you have been introduced to many of C++'s major features, the remaining chapters in this section will examine C++ in detail.

asm	mutable	this
bool	namespace	throw
catch	new	true
class	operator	try
const_cast	private	typeid
delete	protected	typename
dynamic_cast	public	using
explicit	reinterpret_cast	virtual
false	__rtti	wchar_t
friend	static_cast	
inline	template	

Table 20-1. *The Borland C++ Keywords*

Chapter Twenty-One

A Closer Look at Classes and Objects

Classes and objects are two of C++'s most important features. This chapter examines them and related issues in detail.

Parameterized Constructors

It is possible to pass arguments to constructor functions. Typically, these arguments are used to help initialize an object when it is created. To create a parameterized constructor, simply add parameters to it the way you would to any other function. When you define the constructor's body, use the parameters to initialize the object. For example, it is possible to enhance the **queue** class that ended the previous chapter to accept an argument that will act as the queue's ID number. First, **queue** is changed to look like this:

```
// This creates the class queue.
class queue {
  int q[100];
  int sloc, rloc;
  int who; // holds the queue's ID number
public:
  queue(int id);  // parameterized constructor
  ~queue(); // destructor
```

```
  void qput(int i);
  int qget();
};
```

The variable **who** is used to hold an ID number that identifies the queue. Its value is determined by the argument passed to **id** when an object of type **queue** is created. The **queue( )** constructor function now looks like this:

```
// This is the constructor function.
queue::queue(int id)
{
  sloc = rloc = 0;
  who = id;
  cout << "Queue " << who << " initialized.\n";
}
```

To pass an argument to the constructor function, you must specify its value when an object is declared. C++ supports two ways to accomplish this. The first method is shown here:

```
queue a = queue(101);
```

This calls the **queue** class' constructor directly, passing the value 101 to it. The object returned by the constructor is assigned to **a**.

The second method is shorter and more to the point. In this method, the argument or arguments must follow the object's name and be enclosed in parentheses. This code accomplishes the same thing as the previous declaration:

```
queue a(101);
```

Since this method is used by virtually all C++ programmers, it is used by this book nearly exclusively.

The general form of passing arguments to constructor functions is

class-type obj(*arg-list*);

Here, *arg-list* is a comma-separated list of arguments that are passed to the constructor.

The following version of the **queue** program demonstrates passing arguments to constructor functions:

```
#include <iostream.h>

// This creates the class queue.
class queue {
  int q[100];
  int sloc, rloc;
```

```
  int who; // holds the queue's ID number
public:
  queue(int id);  // parameterized constructor
  ~queue(); // destructor
  void qput(int i);
  int qget();
};

// This is the constructor function.
queue::queue(int id)
{
  sloc = rloc = 0;
  who = id;
  cout << "Queue " << who << " initialized.\n";
}

// This is the destructor function.
queue::~queue()
{
  cout << "Queue " << who << " destroyed.\n";
}

void queue::qput(int i)
{
  if(sloc==99) {
    cout << "Queue is full.\n";
    return;
  }
  sloc++;
  q[sloc] = i;
}

int queue::qget()
{
  if(rloc == sloc) {
    cout << "Queue underflow.\n";
    return 0;
  }
  rloc++;
  return q[rloc];
}

int main()
{
```

```
  queue a(1), b(2);  // create two queue objects

  a.qput(10);
  b.qput(19);

  a.qput(20);
  b.qput(1);

  cout << a.qget() << " ";
  cout << a.qget() << " ";
  cout << b.qget() << " ";
  cout << b.qget() << "\n";

  return 0;
}
```

This program produces the following output:

```
Queue 1 initialized.
Queue 2 initialized.
10 20 19 1
Queue 2 destroyed.
Queue 1 destroyed.
```

As you can see by looking at **main( )**, the queue associated with **a** is given the ID number 1, and the queue associated with **b** is given the number 2.

Although the **queue** example only passes a single argument when an object is created, it is possible to pass several. For example, here, objects of type **widget** are passed two values:

```
#include <iostream.h>

class widget {
  int i;
  int j;
public:
  widget(int a, int b);
  void put_widget();
} ;

widget::widget(int a, int b)
{
  i = a;
  j = b;
```

```
}

void widget::put_widget()
{
  cout << i << " " << j << "\n";
}

int main()
{
  widget x(10, 20), y(0, 0);

  x.put_widget();
  y.put_widget();

  return 0;
}
```

This program displays

```
10 20
0 0
```

Friend Functions

It is possible for a nonmember function to have access to the private members of a class by declaring it as a **friend** of the class. For example, here **frd( )** is declared to be a **friend** of the class **cl**:

```
class cl {
   .
   .
   .
public:
  friend void frd();
   .
   .
   .
};
```

As you can see, the keyword **friend** precedes the entire function declaration.

One reason that **friend** functions are allowed in C++ is to accommodate situations in which, for the sake of efficiency, two classes must share the same function. To see an example, consider a program that defines two classes called **line** and **box**. The class **line** contains all necessary data and code to draw a horizontal dashed line of any specified length, beginning at a specified *x,y* coordinate using a specified color. The

box class contains all code and data to draw a box at the specified upper left and lower right coordinates in a specified color. Both classes use the **same_color( )** function to determine whether a line and a box are drawn in the same color. These classes are declared as shown here:

```
class line;

class box {
  int color; // color of box
  int upx, upy; // upper left corner
  int lowx, lowy; // lower right corner
public:
  friend int same_color(line l, box b);
  void set_color(int c);
  void define_box(int x1, int y1, int x2, int y2);
  void show_box();
} ;

class line {
  int color;
  int startx, starty;
  int len;
public:
  friend int same_color(line l, box b);
  void set_color(int c);
  void define_line(int x, int y, int l);
  void show_line();
} ;
```

The **same_color( )** function, which is a member of neither class but a **friend** of both, returns true if both the **line** object and the **box** object, which form its arguments, are drawn in the same color; it returns non-0 otherwise. The **same_color( )** function is defined as

```
// Return true if line and box have same color.
int same_color(line l, box b)
{
  if(l.color==b.color) return 1;
  return 0;
}
```

As you can see, the **same_color( )** function needs access to the private parts of both **line** and **box** to perform its task efficiently. Being a **friend** of each class grants it this access privilege. Further, notice that because **same_color( )** is not a member, no scope resolution operator or class name is used in its definition. (Keep in mind that **public** interface functions can be created to return the colors of both **line** and **box**, and any function could have compared their colors. However, such an approach requires extra function calls, which in some cases is inefficient.)

Notice the empty declaration of **line** at the start of the **class** declarations. Since **same_color( )** in **box** refers to **line** before **line** is declared, **line** must be forward referenced. If this is not done, the compiler will not know what **line** is when encountered in the declaration of **box**. In C++, a forward reference to a class is simply the keyword **class** followed by the type name of the class.

Here is a program that demonstrates the **line** and **box** classes and illustrates how a **friend** function can access the private members of a class. (This program must be run under DOS or a DOS session under Windows.)

```
#include <iostream.h>
#include <conio.h>

class line;

class box {
  int color; // color of box
  int upx, upy; // upper left corner
  int lowx, lowy; // lower right corner
 public:
  friend int same_color(line l, box b);
  void set_color(int c);
  void define_box(int x1, int y1, int x2, int y2);
  void show_box();
} ;

class line {
  int color;
  int startx, starty;
  int len;
public:
  friend int same_color(line l, box b);
  void set_color(int c);
  void define_line(int x, int y, int l);
  void show_line();
} ;

// Return true if line and box have same color.
int same_color(line l, box b)
{
  if(l.color==b.color) return 1;
  return 0;
```

```
}

void box::set_color(int c)
{
  color = c;
}

void line::set_color(int c)
{
  color = c;
}

void box::define_box(int x1, int y1, int x2, int y2)
{
  upx = x1;
  upy = y1;
  lowx = x2;
  lowy = y2;
}

void box::show_box()
{
  int i;

  textcolor(color);

  gotoxy(upx, upy);
  for(i=upx; i<=lowx; i++) cprintf("-");

  gotoxy(upx, lowy-1);
  for(i=upx; i<=lowx; i++) cprintf("-");

  gotoxy(upx, upy);
  for(i=upy; i<=lowy; i++) {
    cprintf("|");
    gotoxy(upx, i);
  }

  gotoxy(lowx, upy);
  for(i=upy; i<=lowy; i++) {
    cprintf("|");
    gotoxy(lowx, i);
  }
}
```

```
void line::define_line(int x, int y, int l)
{
  startx = x;
  starty = y;
  len = l;
}

void line::show_line()
{
  int i;

  textcolor(color);

  gotoxy(startx, starty);

  for(i=0; i<len; i++) cprintf("-");
}

int main()
{
  box b;
  line l;

  b.define_box(10, 10, 15, 15);
  b.set_color(3);
  b.show_box();

  l.define_line(2, 2, 10);
  l.set_color(2);
  l.show_line();

  if(!same_color(l, b)) cout << "Not the same.\n";
  cout << "\nPress a key.";
  getch();

  // now, make line and box the same color
  l.define_line(2, 2, 10);
  l.set_color(3);
  l.show_line();

  if(same_color(l, b)) cout << "Are the same color.\n";

  return 0;
}
```

There are two important restrictions that apply to **friend** functions. First, a derived class does not inherit **friend** functions. Second, **friend** functions may not have a storage-class specifier. That is, they may not be declared as **static** or **extern**.

Default Function Arguments

C++ allows a function to assign a default value to a parameter when no argument corresponding to that parameter is specified in a call to that function. The default value is specified in a manner syntactically similar to a variable initialization. For example, this declares **f( )** as taking one integer variable that has a default value of 1:

```
void f(int i = 1)
{
  .
  .
  .
}
```

Now, **f( )** can be called one of two ways, as these examples show:

```
f(10);  // pass an explicit value
f();   // let function use default
```

The first call passes the value 10 to **i**. The second call gives **i** the default value 1.

Default arguments in C++ enable a programmer to manage greater complexity. In order to handle the widest variety of situations, a function frequently contains more parameters than are required for its most common use. When using default arguments, you need only specify arguments that are not the defaults in that particular situation.

To better understand the reason for default arguments, let's develop a practical example. One useful function, called **xyout( )**, is shown here:

```
//Output a string at specified X,Y location.
void xyout(char *str, int x = 0, int y = 0)
{
  if(!x) x = wherex();
  if(!y) y = wherey();
  gotoxy(x, y);
  cout << str;
}
```

This function displays the string pointed to by **str** beginning at the *x,y* location defined by **x** and **y**. However, if neither **x** nor **y** are specified, the string is output at the current text mode *x,y* location. (You can think of this function as an advanced version of **puts( )**.) The functions **wherex( )**, **wherey( )**, and **gotoxy( )** are part of Borland C++'s library. The **wherex( )** and **wherey( )** functions return the current *x* and *y* coordinates, respectively. The current *x* and *y* coordinates define where the following output operation will begin. The **gotoxy( )** function moves the cursor to the specified *x,y* location. (Chapter 18 discusses the screen control functions in depth.)

The following short program demonstrates how to use **xyout( )**. (This program must be run under DOS or a DOS session in Windows.)

```
#include <iostream.h>
#include <conio.h>

void xyout(char *str, int x=0, int y=0)
{
  if(!x) x = wherex();
  if(!y) y = wherey();
  gotoxy(x, y);
  cout << str;
}

int main()
{
  xyout("hello", 10, 10);
  xyout(" there");
  xyout("I like C++", 40);  // this is still on line 10

  xyout("This is on line 11.\n", 1, 11);
  xyout("This follows on line 12.\n");
  xyout("This follows on line 13.");

  return 0;
}
```

Look closely at how **xyout( )** is called inside **main( )**. This program produces output similar to that shown in Figure 21-1. As this program illustrates, although it is sometimes

```
         hello there                   I like C++
This is on line 11.
This follows on line 12.
This follows on line 13.
```

Figure 21-1. *Sample output from the* **xyout( )** *program*

useful to specify the exact location where text will be displayed, often, you can simply continue on from the point at which the last output occurred. By using default arguments, you can use the same function to accomplish both goals—there is no need for two separate functions.

Notice that in **main( )**, **xyout( )** is called with three, two, or one arguments. When called with only one argument, both **x** and **y** default. However, when called with two arguments, only **y** defaults. There is no way to call **xyout( )** with **x** defaulting and **y** being specified. More generally, when a function is called, all arguments are matched to their respective parameters in order from left to right. Once all existing arguments have been matched, any remaining default arguments are used.

When creating functions that have default argument values, the default values must be specified only once, and this must be the first time the function is declared within the file. For example, if **xyout( )** is defined after **main( )**, the default arguments must be declared in **xyout( )**'s prototype, but the values are not repeated in **xyout( )**'s definition. The following program illustrates this:

```
#include <iostream.h>
#include <conio.h>

void xyout(char *str, int x = 0, int y = 0);

int main()
{
  xyout("hello", 10, 10);
  xyout(" there");
  xyout("I like C++", 40);  // this is still on line 10

  xyout("This is on line 11.\n", 1, 11);
  xyout("This follows on line 12.\n");
  xyout("This follows on line 13.");

  return 0;
}

/* Since x and y's defaults have already been specified
   in xyout()'s prototype, they cannot
   be repeated here.
*/
void xyout(char *str, int x, int y)
{
  if(!x) x = wherex();
  if(!y) y = wherey();
  gotoxy(x, y);
  cout << str;
}
```

If you try specifying new or even the same default values in **xyout( )**'s definition, the compiler will display an error and not compile your program.

Even though default arguments cannot be redefined, each version of an overloaded function can specify different default arguments.

When defining parameters, it is important to understand that all parameters that take default values must appear to the right of those that do not. That is, you cannot specify a nondefaulting parameter once you have defined a parameter that takes a default value. For example, it would have been incorrect to define **xyout( )** as

```
// wrong!
void xyout(int x = 0, int y = 0, char *str)
```

Here is another incorrect attempted use of default parameters:

```
// wrong !
int f(int i, int j=10, int k)
```

Once the default parameters begin, no nondefaulting parameter may occur in the list.

You can also use default parameters in an object's constructor function. For example, here is a slightly different version of the **queue( )** constructor function, shown earlier in this chapter:

```
/* This is the constructor function that uses
   a default value. */
queue::queue(int id=0)
{
  sloc = rloc = 0;
  who = id;
  cout << "Queue " << who << " initialized.\n";
}
```

In this version, if an object is declared without any initializing values, **id** defaults to 0. For example,

```
queue a, b(2);
```

creates two objects, **a** and **b**. The **id** value of **a** is 0 and **b** is 2.

Using Default Arguments Correctly

Although default arguments can be very powerful tools when used correctly, they can be misused. Default arguments should allow a function to perform its job efficiently and easily while still allowing considerable flexibility. Toward this end, all default arguments should represent the way the function is used most of the time. For example, using a default argument makes sense if the default value is used 90 percent of the time. However, if a common value occurs in only 10 percent of the calls, and the rest of the time the arguments corresponding to that parameter vary widely, it may not be a good idea to provide a default argument. When there is no single value that is normally associated with a parameter, there is no reason for a default argument. In fact, declaring default arguments when there is insufficient basis destructures your code because it misleads and confuses anyone reading your program. Where, between 10 and 90 percent, you should elect to use a default argument is, of course, subjective. But 51 percent seems a reasonable break point.

One other important guideline you should follow when using default arguments is this: No default argument should cause a harmful or destructive action. Put differently, the accidental use of a default argument should not cause a catastrophe.

Classes and Structures Are Related

In C++, the **struct** has some expanded capabilities compared to its C counterpart. In C++, **class**es and **struct**s are closely related. In fact, with one exception, they are interchangeable because the C++ **struct** can include data and the code that manipulates that data in the same way that a **class** can. Structures may also contain constructor and destructor functions. The only difference is that by default the members of a **class** are **private** while, by default, the members of a **struct** are **public**. According to the formal C++ syntax, a **struct** defines a class type. Consider this program:

```
#include <iostream.h>

struct cl {
  int get_i(); // these are public
  void put_i(int j); // by default
private:
  int i;
} ;

int cl::get_i()
{
  return i;
}

void cl::put_i(int j)
{
  i = j;
}

int main()
{
  cl s;
```

```
  s.put_i(10);
  cout << s.get_i();

  return 0;
}
```

This simple program defines a structure type called **cl** in which **get_i( )** and **put_i( )** are **public** and **i** is **private**. Notice that a **struct** uses the keyword **private** to introduce the **private** members of the structure.

The following program shows an equivalent program using a **class** instead of **struct**.

```
#include <iostream.h>

class cl {
  int i; // private by default
public:
  int get_i();
  void put_i(int j);
} ;

int cl::get_i()
{
  return i;
}

void cl::put_i(int j)
{
  i = j;
}

int main()
{
  cl s;

  s.put_i(10);
  cout << s.get_i();

  return 0;
}
```

For the most part, C++ programmers use **class** when defining an object that contains both code and data. They use **struct** when defining a data-only object. (That is, **struct** is usually used in a way that is compatible with C-style structures.) However, from time to time you will see C++ code that uses the expanded abilities of structures.

Unions and Classes Are Related

Just as structures and classes are related in C++, unions are also related to classes. A union is essentially a structure in which all elements are stored in the same location. A union can contain constructor and destructor functions as well as member and **friend** functions. Like a structure, **union** members are public by default. For example, the following program uses a union to display the characters that make up the low- and high-order bytes of a short integer (which is 2 bytes long for both 16-bit and 32-bit environments):

```
#include <iostream.h>

union u_type {
  u_type(short int a);  // public by default
  void showchars();
  short int i;
  char ch[2];
};

// constructor
u_type::u_type(short int a)
{
  i = a;
}

// Show the characters that comprise a short int.
void u_type::showchars()
{
  cout << ch[0] << " ";
  cout << ch[1] << "\n";
}

int main()
{
  u_type u(1000);

  u.showchars();

  return 0;
}
```

It is important to understand that, like a structure, a union declaration in C++ defines a class type. This means that the principles of encapsulation are preserved.

There are several restrictions that must be observed when you use C++ unions. First, a **union** cannot inherit any other classes of any type. Further, a **union** cannot be a base **class**. A **union** cannot have virtual member functions. (Virtual functions are discussed in Chapter 23.) No **static** variables can be members of a **union**. A **union** cannot have as a member any object that overloads the = operator. Finally, no object can be a member of a **union** if the object has constructor or destructor functions.

Anonymous Unions

One interesting variation of C++ unions not available in C is the anonymous union. An *anonymous union* is a union that has neither a tag name nor any objects specified in its declaration. The names of the members of the union are accessed directly without using either the dot or arrow operator. Here is a short example using an anonymous union:

```
#include <iostream.h>

int main()
{
  // This declares an anonymous union.
  union {  // no tag name
    int i;
    char ch[2];
  } ;  // no variables specified

  /* Now reference i and ch without referencing
     a union name or dot or arrow operators.
  */
  i = 88;
  cout << i << " " << ch[0];

  return 0;
}
```

Anonymous unions have some restrictions. For obvious reasons, the names of the members of an anonymous union must be different from all other identifiers in the scope of the union. (That is, the member names must not conflict with other identifiers within the union's scope.) Also, global anonymous unions must be specified as **static**. Anonymous unions may not contain member functions. Finally, anonymous unions cannot include **private** or **protected** members.

Remember, just because C++ gives unions greater power and flexibility does not mean that you have to use it. In cases where you simply need a C-style union, you are free to use one in that manner. However, in cases where you can encapsulate a union along with the routines that manipulate it, you add considerable structure to your program.

Inline Functions

Although it does not pertain specifically to object-oriented programming, one very important C++ feature not found in C is the *inline function*. An inline function is a function whose code is expanded inline at the point at which it is called instead of actually being called. This is much like a parameterized function-like macro in C, but more flexible. There are two ways to create an inline function. The first is to use the **inline** modifier. For example, to create an inline function called **f** that returns an **int** and takes no parameters, you must declare it like this:

```
inline int f()
{
  // ...
}
```

The general form of **inline** is

inline *function_declaration*

The **inline** modifier precedes all other aspects of a function's declaration.

The reason for inline functions is efficiency. Every time a function is called, a series of instructions must be executed to set up the function call, including pushing any arguments onto the stack and returning from the function. In some cases, many CPU cycles are used to perform these procedures. However, when a function is expanded inline, no such overhead exists, and the overall speed of your program increases. However, in cases where the inline function is large, the overall size of your program also increases. For this reason, the best inline functions are those that are very small. Larger functions should be left as normal functions.

As an example, the following program uses **inline** to inline the calls to **get_i( )** and **put_i( )**:

```
#include <iostream.h>

class cl {
  int i;
public:
  int get_i();
  void put_i(int j);
} ;

inline int cl::get_i()
{
  return i;
}
```

```
inline void cl::put_i(int j)
{
  i = j;
}

int main()
{
  cl s;

  s.put_i(10);
  cout << s.get_i();

  return 0;
}
```

If you compile this version of the program and compare it to a compiled version of the program in which **inline** is removed, the inline version is several bytes smaller. Also, calls to **get_i( )** and **put_i( )** will execute faster. Remember, however, that if **get_i( )** and **put_i( )** had been very large functions, then the inline version of the program would have been larger than its noninline version. However, it would still have run faster.

It is important to understand that, technically, **inline** is a *request*, not a *command*, to the compiler to generate inline code. There are various situations that can prevent the compiler from complying with the request. For example, some compilers will not inline a function if it contains a loop, a **switch**, or a **goto**. Borland C++ will not inline functions that use an exception or that have a parameter of a class type that defines a destructor. It will also not inline functions that return objects that contain destructors.

Creating Inline Functions Inside a Class

The second way to create an inline function is to define the code to a function *inside* a **class** declaration. Any function that is defined inside a **class** declaration is automatically made into an inline function, if possible. It is not necessary to precede its declaration with the keyword **inline**. For example, the previous program can be rewritten as shown here:

```
#include <iostream.h>

class cl {
  int i;
public:
  // automatic inline functions
  int get_i() { return i; }
  void put_i(int j) { i = j; }
} ;
```

```
int main()
{
  cl s;

  s.put_i(10);
  cout << s.get_i();

  return 0;
}
```

Notice the way the function code is arranged. For very short functions, this arrangement reflects common C++ style. However, you could also write them as shown here:

```
class cl {
  int i;
public:
  // automatic inline functions
  int get_i()
  {
    return i;
  }

  void put_i(int j)
  {
     i = j;
  }
} ;
```

In professionally written C++ code, short functions like those illustrated in the example are commonly defined inside the **class** declaration. This convention is followed in most of the C++ examples in this book.

Passing Objects to Functions

Objects may be passed to functions in just the same way that any other type of variable can. Objects are passed to functions through the use of the standard call-by-value mechanism. This means that a copy of an object is made when it is passed to a function. However, the fact that a copy is created means, in essence, that another object is created. This raises the question of whether the object's constructor function is executed when the copy is made and whether the destructor function is executed when the copy is destroyed. The answer to these two questions may surprise you. To begin, here is an example:

```
#include <iostream.h>

class myclass {
  int i;
public:
  myclass(int n);
  ~myclass();
  void set_i(int n) {i=n;}
  int get_i() {return i;}
};

myclass::myclass(int n)
{
  i = n;
  cout << "Constructing " << i << "\n";
}

myclass::~myclass()
{
  cout << "Destroying " << i << "\n";
}

void f(myclass ob);

int main()
{
  myclass o(1);

  f(o);
  cout << "This is i in main: ";
  cout << o.get_i() << "\n";

  return 0;
}

void f(myclass ob)
{
  ob.set_i(2);

  cout << "This is local i: " << ob.get_i();
  cout << "\n";
}
```

This program produces this output:

```
Constructing 1
This is local i: 2
Destroying 2
This is i in main: 1
Destroying 1
```

Notice that two calls to the destructor function are executed, but only one call is made to the constructor function. As the output illustrates, the constructor function is not called when the copy of **o** (in **main( )**) is passed to **ob** (within **f( )**). The reason that the constructor function is not called when the copy of the object is made is easy to understand. When you pass an object to a function, you want the current state of that object. If the constructor is called when the copy is created, initialization will occur, possibly changing the object. Thus, the constructor function cannot be executed when the copy of an object is generated in a function call.

Although the constructor function is not called when an object is passed to a function, it is necessary to call the destructor when the copy is destroyed. (The copy is destroyed like any other local variable, when the function terminates.) Remember, the copy of the object *does* exist as long as the function is executing. This means that the copy could be performing operations that will require a destructor function to be called when the copy is destroyed. For example, it is perfectly valid for the copy to allocate memory that must be freed when it is destroyed. For this reason, the destructor function must be executed when the copy is destroyed.

To summarize: When a copy of an object is generated because it is passed to a function, the object's constructor function is not called. However, when the copy of the object inside the function is destroyed, its destructor function is called.

By default, when a copy of an object is made, a bitwise copy occurs. This means that the new object is an exact duplicate of the original. The fact that an exact copy is made can, at times, be a source of trouble. Even though objects are passed to functions by means of the normal call-by-value parameter passing mechanism that, in theory, protects and insulates the calling argument, it is still possible for a side effect to occur that may affect, or even damage, the object used as an argument. For example, if an object used as an argument allocates memory and frees that memory when it is destroyed, then its local copy inside the function will free the same memory when its destructor is called. This will leave the original object damaged and effectively useless. As you will see later in this book, it is possible to prevent this type of problem by defining the copy operation relative to your own classes by creating a special type of constructor called a *copy constructor*. (See Chapter 27.)

Returning Objects

A function may return an object to the caller. For example, this is a valid C++ program:

```
#include <iostream.h>

class myclass {
  int i;
public:
  void set_i(int n) {i=n;}
  int get_i() {return i;}
};

myclass f();  // return object of type myclass

int main()
{
  myclass o;

  o = f();

  cout << o.get_i() << "\n";

  return 0;
}

myclass f()
{
  myclass x;

  x.set_i(1);
  return x;
}
```

When an object is returned by a function, a temporary object is automatically created, which holds the return value. It is this object that is actually returned by the function. After the value has been returned, this object is destroyed. The destruction of this temporary object may cause unexpected side effects in some situations. For example, if the object returned by the function has a destructor that frees dynamically allocated memory, that memory will be freed even though the object that is receiving the return value is still using it. As you will see later in this book, there are ways to overcome this problem that involve overloading the assignment operator and defining a copy constructor.

Object Assignment

Assuming that both objects are of the same type, you can assign one object to another. This causes the data of the object on the right side to be copied into the data of the object on the left. For example, this program displays **99**:

```
#include <iostream.h>

class myclass {
  int i;
public:
  void set_i(int n) {i=n;}
  int get_i() {return i;}
};

int main()
{
  myclass ob1, ob2;

  ob1.set_i(99);
  ob2 = ob1; // assign data from ob1 to ob2

  cout << "this is ob2's i: " << ob2.get_i();

  return 0;
}
```

By default, all data from one object is assigned to the other by use of a bit-by-bit copy. However, it is possible to overload the assignment operator and define some other assignment procedure (see Chapter 22).

Arrays of Objects

You can create arrays of objects in the same way that you create arrays of any other data types. For example, the following program establishes a class called **display** that holds information about various display adapters that can be attached to a PC. Specifically, it contains the number of colors that can be displayed and the type of video adapter. Inside **main( )**, an array of three **display** objects is created, and the objects that make up the elements of the array are accessed using the normal indexing procedure.

```
// An example of arrays of objects

#include <iostream.h>

enum disp_type {mono, cga, ega, vga};

class display {
  int colors;  // number of colors
  enum disp_type dt; // display type
public:
  void set_colors(int num) {colors = num;}
  int get_colors() {return colors;}
  void set_type(enum disp_type t) {dt = t;}
  enum disp_type get_type() {return dt;}
} ;

char names[4][5] = {
  "mono",
  "cga",
  "ega",
  "vga"
} ;

int main()
{
  display monitors[3];
  register int i;

  monitors[0].set_type(mono);
  monitors[0].set_colors(1);

  monitors[1].set_type(cga);
  monitors[1].set_colors(4);

  monitors[2].set_type(ega);
  monitors[2].set_colors(16);

  for(i=0; i<3; i++) {
    cout << names[monitors[i].get_type()] << " ";
    cout << "has " << monitors[i].get_colors();
    cout << " colors" << "\n";
  }
```

```
  return 0;
}
```

This program produces the following output:

```
mono has 1 colors
cga has 4 colors
ega has 16 colors
```

Although not related to arrays of objects, notice how the two-dimensional character array **names** is used to convert between an enumerated value and its equivalent character string. In all enumerations that do not contain explicit initializations, the first constant has the value 0, the second 1, and so on. Therefore, the value returned by **get_type( )** can be used to index the **names** array, causing the appropriate name to be printed.

Multidimensional arrays of objects are indexed in precisely the same way as arrays of other types of data.

Initializing Arrays of Objects

If a class defines a parameterized constructor, you may initialize each object in an array by specifying an initialization list like you do for other types of arrays. However, the exact form of the initialization list will be decided by the number of parameters required by the object's constructor function. For objects whose constructors take only one parameter, you can simply specify a list of initial values using the normal array-initialization syntax. Each value in the list is passed, in order, to the constructor function as each element in the array is created. For example, here is a program that initializes an array:

```
#include <iostream.h>

class cl {
  int i;
public:
  cl(int j) {i=j;}  // constructor
  int get_i() {return i;}
};

int main()
{
  cl ob[3] = {1, 2, 3};  // initializers
  int i;

  for(i=0; i<3; i++)
    cout << ob[i].get_i() << "\n";
```

```
  return 0;
}
```

This program displays the numbers **1**, **2**, and **3** on the screen.

If an object's constructor requires two or more arguments, then you will have to use the slightly different initialization form shown here:

```
#include <iostream.h>

class cl {
  int h;
  int i;
public:
  cl(int j, int k) { h=j; i=k; } // constructor
  int get_i() {return i;}
  int get_h() {return h;}
};

int main()
{
  cl ob[3] = {
    cl(1, 2),
    cl(3, 4),
    cl(5, 6)
  };  // initializers

  int i;

  for(i=0; i<3; i++) {
    cout << ob[i].get_h();
    cout << ", ";
    cout << ob[i].get_i() << "\n";
  }

  return 0;
}
```

In this example, **cl**'s constructor has two parameters and therefore requires two arguments. This means that the "shorthand" initialization format cannot be used. Instead, use the "long form" shown in the example. (Of course, you may use the long form in cases where the constructor requires only one argument, too. It is just that the short form is easier to use when only one argument is required.)

Creating Initialized Versus Uninitialized Arrays

A special case occurs if you intend to create both initialized and uninitialized arrays of objects. Consider the following **class**:

```
class cl {
  int i;
public:
  cl(int j) {i=j;}
  int get_i() {return i;}
};
```

Here, the constructor function defined by **cl** requires one parameter. This implies that any array declared of this type must be initialized. That is, it precludes this array declaration:

```
cl a[9]; // error, constructor requires initializers
```

The reason that this statement isn't valid (as **cl** is currently defined) is that it implies that **cl** has a parameterless constructor because no initializers are specified. However, as it stands, **cl** does not have a parameterless constructor. Because there is no valid constructor that corresponds to this declaration, the compiler will report an error. To solve this problem, you need to overload the constructor function, adding one that takes no parameters. In this way, arrays that are initialized and those that are not initialized are both allowed. (Overloading constructors is discussed in detail in Chapter 22.) For example, here is an improved version of **cl**:

```
class cl {
  int i;
public:
  cl() {i=0;}  // called for non-initialized arrays
  cl(int j) {i=j;}  // called for initialized arrays
  int get_i() {return i;}
};
```

Given this **class**, both of the following statements are permissible:

```
cl a1[3] = {3, 5, 6}; // initialized

cl a2[34]; // uninitialized
```

Pointers to Objects

In C, you can access a structure directly or through a pointer to that structure. Similarly, in C++ you can refer to an object either directly (as has been the case in all preceding examples) or by using a pointer to that object. Pointers to objects are among C++'s most important features.

To access a member of an object when using the actual object itself, you use the dot (**.**) operator. To access a specific member of an object when using a pointer to the object, you must use the arrow operator (–>). The use of the dot and arrow operators for objects is the same as their use for structures and unions.

You declare an object pointer using the same declaration syntax as you do for any other type of data. The following program creates a simple class called **P_example**, and defines an object of that class called **ob** and a pointer for an object of type **P_example** called **p**. It then illustrates how to access **ob** directly and indirectly using a pointer:

```
// A simple example using an object pointer.

#include <iostream.h>

class P_example {
  int num;
public:
  void set_num(int val) {num = val;}
  void show_num();
};

void P_example::show_num()
{
  cout << num << "\n";
}

int main()
{
  P_example ob, *p; // declare an object and pointer to it

  ob.set_num(1); // access ob directly

  ob.show_num();

  p = &ob; // assign p the address of ob
  p->show_num();  // access ob using pointer

  return 0;
}
```

Notice that the address of **ob** is obtained using the **&** (address of) operator in the same way the address is obtained for any type of variable.

When a pointer is incremented or decremented, it is increased or decreased in such a way that it will always point to the next element of its base type. The same thing occurs when a pointer to an object is incremented or decremented: the next object is pointed to. The following example modifies the preceding program so that **ob** is a two-element array of type **P_example**. Notice how **p** is incremented and decremented to access the two elements in the array:

```
// Incrementing an object pointer
#include <iostream.h>

class P_example {
  int num;
public:
  void set_num(int val) {num = val;}
  void show_num();
};

void P_example::show_num()
{
  cout << num << "\n";
}

int main()
{
  P_example ob[2], *p;

  ob[0].set_num(10);  // access objects directly
  ob[1].set_num(20);

  p = &ob[0];  // obtain pointer to first element
  p->show_num(); // show value of ob[0] using pointer

  p++;  // advance to next object
  p->show_num(); // show value of ob[1] using pointer

  p--;  // retreat to previous object
  p->show_num(); // again show value of ob[0]

  return 0;
}
```

The output from this program is 10, 20, 10.

Chapter Twenty-Two

Function and Operator Overloading

Chapter 20 introduced two of C++'s most important features, function and operator overloading. This chapter explores these topics in detail. In the course of the discussion, other related topics are also examined.

Overloading Constructor Functions

Although they perform a unique service, constructor functions are not much different from other types of functions and they too can be overloaded. As the last example in the preceding chapter showed, to overload a class' constructor function, simply declare the various forms it will take. As you will see, in many cases there is a significant advantage to be gained by providing overloaded constructors.

Let's begin with an example. The following program declares a class called **timer** that acts as a countdown timer (such as a darkroom timer). When an object of type **timer** is created, it is given an initial time value. When the **run( )** function is called, the timer counts down to 0 and then rings the bell. In this example, the constructor is overloaded to allow the time to be specified in seconds as either an integer or a string, or in minutes and seconds by specifying two integers.

This program makes use of the **clock( )** library function, which returns the number of system clock ticks since the program began running. Dividing this value by the macro **CLK_TCK** converts the return value of **clock( )** into seconds. Both the prototype for **clock( )** and the definition of **CLK_TCK** are found in the header file **time.h**.

```
#include <iostream.h>
#include <stdlib.h>
#include <time.h>

class timer{
  int seconds;
public:
  // seconds specified as a string
  timer(char *t) { seconds = atoi(t); }

  // seconds specified as integer
  timer(int t) { seconds = t; }

  // time specified in minutes and seconds
  timer(int min, int sec) { seconds = min*60 + sec; }

  void run();
} ;

void timer::run()
{
  clock_t t1, t2;

  t1 = t2 = clock()/CLK_TCK;
  while(seconds) {
    if(t1/CLK_TCK+1 <= (t2=clock())/CLK_TCK) {
       seconds--;
       t1 = t2;
    }
  }
  cout << "\a"; // ring the bell
}

int main()
{
  timer a(10), b("20"), c(1, 10);

  a.run(); // count 10 seconds
  b.run(); // count 20 seconds
  c.run(); // count 1 minute, 10 seconds

  return 0;
}
```

As you can see, when **a**, **b**, and **c** are created inside **main( )** they are given initial values using the three different methods supported by the overloaded constructor functions. Each approach causes the appropriate constructor to be used and initializes all three variables properly.

In the program just shown, you may see little value in overloading a constructor function because you could simply decide on a single way to specify the time. However, if you were creating a library of classes for someone else to use, you might want to supply constructors for the most common forms of initialization, allowing the programmer to choose the most appropriate form for his or her application. The next section shows another advantage that is gained by overloading a constructor function.

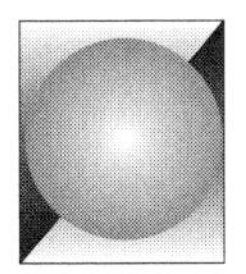

NOTE: C++ defines a special type of overloaded constructor, called a copy constructor, that allows you to determine how objects are copied under certain circumstances. Copy constructors are discussed later in this book.

Localizing Variables

Before continuing with the discussion of overloaded constructors, an important difference between the way local variables may be declared in C versus the way they can be declared in C++ needs to be explained. In C, you must declare all local variables used within a block at the start of that block. You cannot declare a variable in a block after an "action" statement has occurred. For example, in C, this fragment is incorrect:

```
/* Incorrect in C */
void f()
{
  int i;

  i = 10;

  int j;
  /* ... */
}
```

Because the statement **i=10** falls between the declaration of **i** and that of **j**, a C compiler will flag an error and refuse to compile this function. However, in C++ this fragment is perfectly acceptable and will compile without error. In C++, a local variable can be declared at any point within a block. Furthermore, it is known only to code that comes after it within that block.

Here is another example that shows how local variables can be declared anywhere within a block when using C++:

```
#include <iostream.h>
#include <string.h>
```

```
int main()
{
  int i;
  i = 10;

  int j = 100; // perfectly legal in C++

  cout << i*j << "\n";

  cout << "Enter a string: ";
  char str[80];  // also legal in C++
  cin >> str;

  // display the string in reverse order
  int k;  // in C++, declare k where it is needed
  k = strlen(str);
  k--;
  while(k>=0) {
    cout << str[k];
    k--;
  }

  return 0;
}
```

As this program illustrates, in C++ you can declare local variables anywhere within a block of code. Since much of the philosophy behind C++ is the encapsulation of code and data, it makes sense that you can declare variables close to where they are used instead of only at the beginning of the block. Here, the declarations of **i** and **j** are separated simply for illustration. However, you can see how the localization of **k** to its relevant code helps encapsulate that routine. Declaring variables close to the point where they are used helps you avoid accidental side effects. This feature of C++ is also helpful when creating objects, as the next section illustrates.

Localizing the Creation of Objects

The fact that local variables can be declared at any point within a block of code has significant implications for the creation of objects. In real-world programs, you often need to create objects that are initialized using values known only during the execution of your program. Being able to create an object after those values are known can be quite helpful because it prevents you from having to first create an uninitialized object and then, later, set its values.

To see the advantages of declaring local objects near their point of first use, consider this version of the **timer** program. In it, two objects, **b** and **c**, are constructed using information furnished at run time, just prior to their use. It also further illustrates the benefit of overloading constructors to accept different forms of initializations.

```
#include <iostream.h>
#include <stdlib.h>
#include <time.h>

class timer{
  int seconds;
public:
  // seconds specified as a string
  timer(char *t) { seconds = atoi(t); }

  // seconds specified as integer
  timer(int t) { seconds = t; }

  // time specified in minutes and seconds
  timer(int min, int sec) { seconds = min*60 + sec; }

  void run();
} ;

void timer::run()
{
  clock_t t1, t2;

  t1 = t2 = clock()/CLK_TCK;
  while(seconds) {
    if(t1/CLK_TCK+1 <= (t2=clock())/CLK_TCK) {
       seconds--;
       t1 = t2;
    }
  }
  cout << "\a"; // ring the bell
}
int main()
{
  timer a(10);
  a.run();

  cout << "Enter number of seconds: ";
  char str[80];
  cin >> str;
  timer b(str); // initialize at runtime using a string
```

```
  b.run();

  cout << "Enter minutes and seconds: ";
  int min, sec;
  cin >> min >> sec;
  timer c(min, sec);  /* initialize at runtime
                         using minutes and seconds */
  c.run();

  return 0;
}
```

As you can see, object **a** is constructed using an integer constant. However, objects **b** and **c** are constructed using information entered by the user. Thus, they are not declared until that information is known. Also, both **b** and **c** are constructed using the type of data available at the point of their creation. For **b**, this is a string representing seconds. For **c**, this is two integers describing minutes and seconds. By allowing various initialization formats, you need not perform any unnecessary conversions from one form to another when initializing an object. You also more easily allow objects to be constructed near their point of first use.

Function Overloading and Ambiguity

When overloading functions, it is possible to produce a type of error with which you may not be familiar. You can create a situation in which the compiler is unable to choose between two (or more) overloaded functions. When this happens, the situation is said to be *ambiguous*. Ambiguous statements are errors, and programs containing ambiguity will not compile.

By far, the main cause of ambiguity involves C++'s automatic type conversions. C++ automatically attempts to convert the arguments used to call a function into the type of arguments expected by the function. For example, consider this fragment:

```
int myfunc(double d);
 .
 .
 .
cout << myfunc('c');  // not an error, conversion applied
```

As the comment indicates, this is not an error because C++ automatically converts the character **c** into its **double** equivalent. In C++, very few type conversions of this sort are actually disallowed. Although automatic type conversions are convenient, they are also a prime cause of ambiguity. For example, consider the following program:

```
#include <iostream.h>
```

```
float myfunc(float i);
double myfunc(double i);

int main()
{
  cout << myfunc(10.1) << " "; // unambiguous, calls myfunc(double)
  cout << myfunc(10);  // ambiguous

  return 0;
}

float myfunc(float i)
{
  return i;
}

double myfunc(double i)
{
  return -i;
}
```

Here, **myfunc( )** is overloaded so that it can take arguments of either type **float** or type **double**. In the unambiguous line, **myfunc(double)** is called because, unless explicitly specified as **float**, all floating-point constants in C++ are automatically of type **double**. Hence, that call is unambiguous. However, when **myfunc( )** is called by using the integer 10, ambiguity is introduced because the compiler has no way of knowing whether it should be converted to a **float** or to a **double**. This causes an error message to be displayed, and the program will not compile.

As the preceding example illustrates, it is not the overloading of **myfunc( )** relative to **double** and **float** that causes the ambiguity. Rather, it is the specific call to **myfunc( )** using an indeterminate type of argument that causes the confusion. Put differently, the error is not caused by the overloading of **myfunc( )**, but by the specific invocation.

Here is another example of ambiguity caused by C++'s automatic type conversions:

```
#include <iostream.h>

char myfunc(unsigned char ch);
char myfunc(char ch);

int main()
{
  cout << myfunc('c');  // this calls myfunc(char)
  cout << myfunc(88) << " "; // ambiguous
```

```
  return 0;
}

char myfunc(unsigned char ch)
{
  return ch-1;
}

char myfunc(char ch)
{
  return ch+1;
}
```

In C++, **unsigned char** and **char** are *not* inherently ambiguous. However, when **myfunc( )** is called by using the integer 88, the compiler does not know which function to call. That is, should 88 be converted into a **char** or an **unsigned char**?

Another way you can cause ambiguity is by using default arguments in overloaded functions. To see how, examine this program:

```
#include <iostream.h>

int myfunc(int i);
int myfunc(int i, int j=1);

int main()
{
  cout << myfunc(4, 5) << " ";  // unambiguous
  cout << myfunc(10);  // ambiguous

  return 0;
}

int myfunc(int i)
{
  return i;
}

int myfunc(int i, int j)
{
  return i*j;
}
```

Here, in the first call to **myfunc( )**, two arguments are specified; therefore, no ambiguity is introduced and **myfunc(int i, int j)** is called. However, when the second call to **myfunc( )** is made, ambiguity occurs because the compiler does not know whether to call the version of **myfunc( )** that takes one argument or to apply the default to the version that takes two arguments.

Finding the Address of an Overloaded Function

As you know, in C you can assign the address of a function to a pointer and then call that function through the pointer. The same feature also exists in C++. However, because of function overloading, this process is a little more complex. To understand why, first consider this statement, which assigns the address of some function called **myfunc( )** to a pointer called **p**:

```
p = myfunc;
```

If this is part of a C program, then there is one and only one function called **myfunc( )**, and the compiler has no difficulty assigning its address to **p**. However, if this statement is part of a C++ program, then **myfunc( )** might be overloaded. Assuming that it is, how does the compiler know which function's address to assign to **p**? The answer is that it depends upon how **p** is declared. For example, consider this program:

```
#include <iostream.h>

int myfunc(int a);
int myfunc(int a, int b);

int main()
{
  int (*fp)(int a);   // pointer to int xxx(int)

  fp = myfunc;   // points to myfunc(int)

  cout << fp(5);

  return 0;
}

int myfunc(int a)
{
  return a;
}

int myfunc(int a, int b)
{
```

```
  return a*b;
}
```

As the program illustrates, **fp** is declared as a pointer to a function that returns an integer and that takes one integer argument. C++ uses this information to select the **myfunc(int a)** version of **myfunc( )**. Had **fp** been declared like this:

```
int (*fp)(int a, int b);
```

then **fp** would have been assigned the address of the **myfunc(int a, int b)** version of **myfunc( )**.

To review: When you assign the address of an overloaded function to a function pointer, it is the declaration of the pointer that determines which function's address is assigned. Further, the declaration of the function pointer must exactly match one and only one of the overloaded function's declarations.

The this Pointer

Before moving on to operator overloading, it is necessary for you to learn about another of C++'s keywords, **this**, which is an essential ingredient for many overloaded operators.

Each time a member function is called, it is automatically passed a pointer to the object that invoked it. You can access this pointer using **this**. The **this** pointer is an *implicit* parameter to all member functions. (**friend** functions do not have a **this** pointer.) For example, given

```
ob.f();
```

the function **f( )** is automatically passed a **this** pointer, which points to **ob**.

As you know, a member function can access the data of its class directly. For example, given the following class:

```
class cl {
  int i;
  // ...
};
```

a member function can assign **i** the value 10 using this statement:

```
i = 10;
```

Actually, this statement is shorthand for the statement

```
this->i = 10;
```

To see how the **this** pointer works, examine this short program:

```
#include <iostream.h>

class cl {
  int i;
public:
  void load_i(int val) { this->i = val; } // same as i = val
  int get_i() { return this->i; } // same as return i
} ;

int main()
{
  cl o;

  o.load_i(100);
  cout << o.get_i();

  return 0;
}
```

This program displays the number 100.

While the preceding example is trivial—in fact, no one would actually use the **this** pointer in this way—the following section shows one reason why the **this** pointer is so important.

Operator Overloading

A feature of C++ that is related to function overloading is *operator overloading*. With very few exceptions, most of C++'s operators can be given special meanings relative to specific classes. For example, a class that defines a linked list might use the **+** operator to add an object to the list. Another class might use the **+** operator in an entirely different way. When an operator is overloaded, none of its original meaning is lost. It simply means that a new operation relative to a specific class is defined. Therefore, overloading the **+** to handle a linked list does not cause its meaning relative to integers (that is, addition) to be changed.

Operator functions will usually be either members or **friend**s of the class for which they are being used. Although very similar, there are some differences between the way a member operator function is overloaded and the way a **friend** operator function is overloaded. In this section, only member functions will be overloaded. Later in this chapter, you will see how to overload **friend** operator functions.

To overload an operator, you must define what that operation means relative to the class that it is applied to. To do this you create an **operator** function, which defines its action. The general form of a member **operator** function is

type classname::operator#(*arg-list*)
{
  // *operation defined relative to the class*
}

Here, the operator that you are overloading is substituted for the # and *type* is the type of value returned by the specified operation. To facilitate its use in larger expressions, the return value of an operator often is of the same type as the class for which the operator is being overloaded. (Although it could be of any type you choose.) The specific nature of *arg-list* is determined by several factors, as you will soon see.

To see how operator overloading works, let's start with a simple example that creates a class called **three_d** that maintains the coordinates of an object in three-dimensional space. This program overloads the + and = operators relative to the **three_d** class:

```
#include <iostream.h>

class three_d {
  int x, y, z; // 3-d coordinates
public:
  three_d operator+(three_d t);
  three_d operator=(three_d t);

  void show() ;
  void assign(int mx, int my, int mz);
} ;

// Overload the +.
three_d three_d::operator+(three_d t)
{
  three_d temp;

  temp.x = x+t.x;
  temp.y = y+t.y;
  temp.z = z+t.z;
  return temp;
}

// Overload the =.
three_d three_d::operator=(three_d t)
{
  x = t.x;
```

```
  y = t.y;
  z = t.z;
  return *this;
}

// Show X, Y, Z coordinates.
void three_d::show()
{
  cout << x << ", ";
  cout << y << ", ";
  cout << z << "\n";
}

// Assign coordinates.
void three_d::assign(int mx, int my, int mz)
{
  x = mx;
  y = my;
  z = mz;
}

int main()
{
  three_d a, b, c;

  a.assign(1, 2, 3);
  b.assign(10, 10, 10);

  a.show();
  b.show();

  c = a+b;  // now add a and b together
  c.show();

  c = a+b+c; // add a, b and c together
  c.show();

  c = b = a;  // demonstrate multiple assignment
  c.show();
  b.show();

  return 0;
}
```

This program produces the following output:

```
1, 2, 3
10, 10, 10
11, 12, 13
22, 24, 26
1, 2, 3
1, 2, 3
```

As you examine this program, you may be surprised to see that both operator functions have only one parameter each, even though they overloaded binary operations. This is because when a binary operator is overloaded using a member function, only one argument is explicitly passed to it. The other argument is implicitly passed using the **this** pointer. Thus, in the line

```
temp.x = x + t.x;
```

the **x** refers to **this–>x**, which is the **x** associated with the object that invoked the operator function. In all cases, it is the object on the left side of an operation that causes the call to the operator function. The object on the right side is passed to the function.

In general, when using a member function, no parameters are needed when overloading a unary operator, and only one parameter is required when overloading a binary operator. (You cannot overload the **?** ternary operator.) In either case, the object that causes the activation of the operator function is implicitly passed through the **this** pointer.

To understand how operator overloading works, let's examine the preceding program carefully, beginning with the overloaded operator **+**. When two objects of type **three_d** are operated on by the **+** operator, the magnitudes of their respective coordinates are added together, as shown in the **operator+( )** function associated with this class. Notice, however, that this function does not modify the value of either operand. Instead, an object of type **three_d**, which contains the result of the operation, is returned by the function. To understand why the **+** operation does not change the contents of either object, think about the standard arithmetic **+** operation as applied like this: 10+12. The outcome of this operation is 22, but neither 10 nor 12 are changed by it. Although there is no rule that states that an overloaded operator cannot alter the value of one of its operands, it usually makes sense for the overloaded operator to stay consistent with its original meaning. Further, relative to the **three_d** class, we don't want the **+** to alter the contents of an operand.

Another key point about how the **+** operator is overloaded is that it returns an object of type **three_d**. Although the function could have returned any valid C++ type, the fact that it returns a **three_d** object allows the **+** operator to be used in more complicated expressions, such as **a+b+c**. Here, **a+b** generates a result that is of type **three_d**. This value can then be added to **c**. Had any other type of value been generated by **a+b**, it could not have been added to **c**.

In contrast to the **+** operator, the assignment operator does, indeed, cause one of its arguments to be modified. (This is, after all, the very essence of assignment.) Since the **operator=( )** function is called by the object that occurs on the left side of the assignment, it is this object that is modified by the assignment operation. However, even the assignment operation must return a value because in C++ (as well as C), the assignment operation produces the value that occurs on the right side. Thus, to allow statements like

```
a = b = c = d;
```

it is necessary for **operator =( )** to return the object pointed to by **this**, which will be the object that occurs on the left side of the assignment statement. Doing so allows a chain of assignments to be made.

You can also overload unary operators, such as **++** or **– –**. As stated earlier, when overloading a unary operator using a member function, no object is explicitly passed to the operator function. Instead, the operation is performed on the object that generates the call to the function through the implicitly passed **this** pointer. For example, here is an expanded version of the previous example program that defines the increment operation for objects of type **three_d**:

```
#include <iostream.h>

class three_d {
  int x, y, z; // 3-d coordinates
public:
  three_d operator+(three_d op2);  // op1 is implied
  three_d operator=(three_d op2);  // op1 is implied
  three_d operator++(); // op1 is also implied here

  void show() ;
  void assign(int mx, int my, int mz);
} ;

// Overload the +.
three_d three_d::operator+(three_d op2)
{
  three_d temp;

  temp.x = x+op2.x;  // these are integer additions
  temp.y = y+op2.y;  // and the + retains its original
  temp.z = z+op2.z;  // meaning relative to them
  return temp;
}
```

```
// Overload the =.
three_d three_d::operator=(three_d op2)
{
  x = op2.x; // these are integer assignments
  y = op2.y; // and the = retains its original
  z = op2.z; // meaning relative to them
  return *this;
}

// Overload a unary operator.
three_d three_d::operator++()
{
  x++;
  y++;
  z++;
  return *this;
}

// Show X, Y, Z coordinates.
void three_d::show()
{
  cout << x << ", ";
  cout << y << ", ";
  cout << z << "\n";
}

// Assign coordinates.
void three_d::assign(int mx, int my, int mz)
{
  x = mx;
  y = my;
  z = mz;
}

int main()
{
  three_d a, b, c;

  a.assign(1, 2, 3);
  b.assign(10, 10, 10);

  a.show();
  b.show();
```

```
  c = a+b;  // now add a and b together
  c.show();

  c = a+b+c; // add a, b and c together
  c.show();

  c = b = a;  // demonstrate multiple assignment
  c.show();
  b.show();

  ++c;  // increment c
  c.show();
  return 0;
}
```

In early versions of C++, it was not possible to determine whether an overloaded **++** or **– –** preceded or followed its operand. For example, assuming some object called **O**, these two statements were identical:

```
O++;

++O;
```

However, later versions of C++ provide a means of differentiating between a prefix or postfix increment or decrement operation. To accomplish this, your program must define two versions of the **operator++( )** function. One is defined as shown in the foregoing program. The other is declared like this:

```
loc operator++(int x);
```

If the **++** precedes its operand, then the **operator++( )** function is called. If the **++** follows its operand, then the **operator++(int x)** is called and **x** has the value 0.

The action of an overloaded operator as applied to the class for which it is defined need not have any relationship to that operator's default use with C++'s built-in types. For example, the **<<** and **>>** as applied to **cout** and **cin** have little in common with the same operators applied to integer types. However, for the purpose of structure and readability of your code, an overloaded operator should reflect, when possible, the spirit of the operator's original use. For example, the **+** relative to **three_d** is conceptually similar to the **+** relative to integer types. There is little benefit, for example, in defining the **+** operator relative to a particular class in such a way that it acts more like you would expect the || operator to perform. While you can give an overloaded operator any meaning you like, it is best, for clarity, to relate its new meaning to its original meaning.

Some restrictions to overloading operators also apply. First, you cannot alter the precedence of any operator. Second, you cannot alter the number of operands required by the operator, although your **operator( )** function could choose to ignore an operand. Finally, except for the =, overloaded operators are inherited by any derived classes. Each class must define explicitly its own overloaded = operator if one is needed. Of course, a derived class is free to overload any operator relative to itself—including those overloaded by its base class.

The only operators you cannot overload are

```
. :: .* ?
```

friend Operator Functions

It is possible for an operator function to be a **friend** of a class rather than a member. As you learned earlier in this chapter, since **friend** functions are *not* members of a class, they do not have the implied argument **this**. Therefore, when a **friend** is used to overload an operator, both operands are passed when overloading binary operators and a single operand is passed when overloading unary operators. The only operators that cannot use **friend** functions are =, ( ), [ ], and –>. The rest can use either member or **friend** functions to implement the specified operation relative to its class. For example, here is a modified version of the preceding program using a **friend** instead of a member function to overload the + operator:

```
#include <iostream.h>

class three_d {
  int x, y, z; // 3-d coordinates
public:
  friend three_d operator+(three_d op1, three_d op2);
  three_d operator=(three_d op2);   // op1 is implied
  three_d operator++(); // op1 is implied here, too

  void show() ;
  void assign(int mx, int my, int mz);
} ;

// This is now a friend function.
three_d operator+(three_d op1, three_d op2)
{
  three_d temp;

  temp.x = op1.x + op2.x;  // these are integer additions
  temp.y = op1.y + op2.y;  // and the + retains its original
  temp.z = op1.z + op2.z;  // meaning relative to them
  return temp;
}
```

```
// Overload the =.
three_d three_d::operator=(three_d op2)
{
  x = op2.x; // these are integer assignments
  y = op2.y; // and the = retains its original
  z = op2.z; // meaning relative to them
  return *this;
}

// Overload a unary operator.
three_d three_d::operator++()
{
  x++;
  y++;
  z++;
  return *this;
}

// Show X, Y, Z coordinates.
void three_d::show()
{
  cout << x << ", ";
  cout << y << ", ";
  cout << z << "\n";
}

// Assign coordinates.
void three_d::assign(int mx, int my, int mz)
{
  x = mx;
  y = my;
  z = mz;
}
int main()
{
  three_d a, b, c;

  a.assign(1, 2, 3);
  b.assign(10, 10, 10);

  a.show();
  b.show();
```

```
  c = a+b;  // now add a and b together
  c.show();

  c = a+b+c; // add a, b and c together
  c.show();

  c = b = a;  // demonstrate multiple assignment
  c.show();
  b.show();

  ++c;  // increment c
  c.show();

  return 0;
}
```

As you can see by looking at **operator+( )**, now both operands are passed to it. The left operand is passed in **op1** and the right operand in **op2**.

In many cases, there is no benefit to using a **friend** function instead of a member function when overloading an operator. However, there is one situation in which you must use a **friend** function. As you know, a pointer to an object that invokes a member operator function is passed in **this**. In the case of binary operators, the object on the left invokes the function. This works as long as the object on the left defines the specified operation. For example, assuming an object called **O**, which has assignment and addition defined for it, this is a valid statement:

```
O = O + 10; // will work
```

Since the object **O** is on the left of the **+** operator, it invokes its overloaded operator function, which (presumably) is capable of adding an integer value to some element of **O**. However, this statement doesn't work:

```
O = 10 + O; // won't work
```

The reason this statement does not work is that the object on the left of the **+** operator is an integer, which is a built-in type for which no operation involving an integer and an object of **O**'s type is defined.

You can use built-in types on the left side of an operation if the **+** is overloaded using two **friend** functions. In this case, the operator function is explicitly passed both arguments and it is invoked like any other overloaded function, based upon the types of its arguments. One version of the **+** operator function handles *object+integer* and the other handles *integer+object*. Overloading the **+** (or any other binary operator) using a

friend allows a built-in type to occur on the left or right side of the operator. The following program shows how to accomplish this:

```
#include <iostream.h>

class CL {
public:
  int count;
  CL operator=(int i);
  friend CL operator+(CL ob, int i);
  friend CL operator+(int i, CL ob);
};

CL CL::operator=(int i)
{
  count = i;
  return *this;
}

// This handles ob + int.
CL operator+(CL ob, int i)
{
  CL temp;

  temp.count = ob.count + i;
  return temp;
}

// This handles int + ob.
CL operator+(int i, CL ob)
{
  CL temp;

  temp.count = ob.count + i;
  return temp;
}

int main()
{
  CL obj;
  obj = 10;
```

```
  cout << obj.count << " "; // outputs 10

  obj = 10 + obj; // add object to integer
  cout << obj.count << " "; // outputs 20

  obj = obj + 12; // add integer to object
  cout << obj.count;        // outputs 32

  return 0;
}
```

As you can see, the **operator+( )** function is overloaded twice to accommodate the two ways in which an integer and an object of type **CL** can occur in the addition operation.

Although you can use a **friend** function to overload a unary operator, such as **++**, you first need to know about another feature of C++, the reference, which is the subject of the next section.

References

C++ contains a feature that is related to the pointer. This feature is called a reference. A *reference* is essentially an implicit pointer that acts as another name for an object.

Reference Parameters

By default, C and C++ pass arguments to a function using call-by-value. Passing an argument using call-by-value causes a copy of that argument to be used by the function and prevents the argument used in the call from being modified by the function. In C (and optionally in C++), when a function needs to be able to alter the values of the variables used as arguments, the parameters must be explicitly declared as pointer types and the function must operate on the calling variables using the * pointer operator. For example, the following program implements a function called **swap( )**, which exchanges the values of its two integer arguments:

```
#include <iostream.h>

void swap(int *a, int *b);

int main()
{
  int x, y;

  x = 99;
  y = 88;
```

```
  cout << x << " " << y << "\n";

  swap(&x, &y); // exchange their values

  cout << x << " " << y << "\n";

  return 0;
}

// C-like, explicit pointer version of swap().
void swap(int *a, int *b)
{
  int t;

  t = *a;
  *a = *b;
  *b = t;
}
```

When calling **swap( )**, the variables used in the call must be preceded by the **&** operator in order to produce a pointer to each argument. This is the way that a call-by-reference is generated in C. However, even though C++ still allows this syntax, it supports a cleaner, more transparent method of generating a call-by-reference using a *reference parameter*.

In C++, it is possible to tell the compiler to automatically generate a call-by-reference rather than a call-by-value for one or more parameters of a particular function. This is accomplished by preceding the parameter name in the function's declaration by the **&**. For example, here is a function called **f( )** that takes one reference parameter of type **int**:

```
void f(int &f)
{
  f = rand(); // this modifies the calling argument
}
```

Notice that the statement

```
f = rand() ;
```

does not use the * pointer operator. When you declare a reference parameter, the C++ compiler automatically knows that it is an implicit pointer and dereferences it for you.

Each time **f( )** is called, it is automatically passed the *address* of its argument. For example, given this fragment,

```
int val;

f(val);  // get random value
printf("%d", val);
```

the address of **val**, not its value, is passed to **f( )**. Thus, **f( )** can modify the value of **val**. Notice that it is not necessary to precede **val** with the **&** operator when **f( )** is called. The compiler automatically passes **val**'s address.

To see reference parameters in actual use, the **swap( )** function is rewritten using references. Look carefully at how **swap( )** is declared and called:

```
#include <iostream.h>

void swap(int &a, int &b); // declare as reference parameters

int main()
{
  int x, y;

  x = 99;
  y = 88;

  cout << x << " " << y << "\n";

  swap(x, y); // exchange their values

  cout << x << " " << y << "\n";

  return 0;
}

/* Here, swap() is defined as using call-by-reference,
   not call-by-value. */
void swap(int &a, int &b)
{
  int t;

  t = a;
  a = b;  // this swaps x
  b = t;  // this swaps y
}
```

Again, notice that by making **a** and **b** reference parameters, there is no need to precede the arguments of **swap( )** with the **&** operator or to apply the * inside **swap( )** when the values are exchanged. In fact, it would be an error to do so. Remember that the compiler automatically generates the addresses of the arguments used to call **swap( )** and automatically dereferences **a** and **b**.

There are several restrictions that apply to reference variables:

- You cannot reference a reference variable. That is, you cannot take its address.
- You cannot create arrays of references.
- You cannot create a pointer to a reference.
- References are not allowed on bit-fields.

Passing References to Objects

In Chapter 21 it was explained that when an object is passed as an argument to a function, a copy of that object is made. Further, when the copy is made, that object's constructor function is *not* called. (Rather, an exact copy of the calling argument is made.) However, when the function terminates, the copy's destructor *is* called. If for some reason you do not want a copy to be made or the destructor function to be called, simply pass the object by reference. When you pass by reference, no copy of the object is made. This means that no object used as a parameter is destroyed when the function terminates, and the parameter's destructor is not called. For example, try this program:

```
#include <iostream.h>

class cl {
  int id;
public:
  int i;
  cl(int i);
  ~cl();
  void neg(cl &o) {o.i = -o.i;}
};

cl::cl(int num)
{
  cout << "Constructing " << num << "\n";
  id = num;
}

cl::~cl()
{
  cout << "Destructing " << id << "\n";
}

int main()
```

```
{
  cl o(1);

  o.i = 10;
  o.neg(o);

  cout << o.i << "\n";

  return 0;
}
```

Here is the output of this program:

```
Constructing 1
-10
Destructing 1
```

As you can see, only one call is made to **cl**'s destructor function. Had **o** been passed by value, a second object would have been created inside **neg( )** and the destructor would have been called a second time when that object was destroyed at the time **neg( )** terminated.

When passing parameters by reference, remember that changes to the object inside the function affect the calling object.

Returning References

A function may return a reference. This has the rather startling effect of allowing a function to be used on the left side of an assignment statement! For example, consider this simple program:

```
#include <iostream.h>

char &replace(int i);  // return a reference

char s[80] = "Hello There";

int main()
{

  replace(5) = 'X'; // assign X to space after Hello

  cout << s;

  return 0;
}
```

```
char &replace(int i)
{
  return s[i];
}
```

This program replaces the space between **Hello** and **There** with an **X**. That is, the program displays **HelloXthere**. Take a look at how this is accomplished.

As shown, **replace( )** is declared as returning a reference to a character array. As **replace( )** is coded, it returns a reference to the element of **s** that is specified by its argument **i.** The reference returned by **replace( )** is then used in **main( )** to assign to that element the character **X**.

Independent References

Even though references are included in C++ primarily to support call-by-reference parameter passing and to act as a return value from a function, it is possible to declare a stand-alone reference variable. This is called an *independent reference*. However, independent reference variables are seldom a good idea because they tend to confuse and destructure your program. With these reservations in mind, we will take a short look at them here.

Since a reference variable must point to some object, an independent reference must be initialized when it is declared. Generally, this means that it will be assigned the address of a previously declared variable. Once this is done, the reference variable can be used anywhere that the variable it references can. In fact, there is virtually no distinction between the two. For example, consider this program:

```
#include <iostream.h>

int main()
{
  int j, k;
  int &i = j; // independent reference to j

  j = 10;

  cout << j << " " << i; // outputs 10 10

  k = 121;
  i = k; // copies k's value into j -- not k's address

  cout << "\n" << j;  // outputs 121

  return 0;
}
```

This program displays the following output:

```
10 10
121
```

The address pointed to by the reference variable **i** is fixed and cannot be changed. Thus, when the statement **i = k** is evaluated, it is **k**'s value that is copied into **j** (referenced by **i**), not its address. For another example, **i++** does *not* cause **i** to point to a new address. Instead, **k** is increased by 1. Remember that references are not pointers.

You can also use an independent reference to point to a constant. For example, the following is valid:

```
int &i = 100;
```

A Matter of Style

When declaring pointer and reference variables, some C++ programmers use a unique coding style that associates the * or the & with the type name and not the variable. For example, here are two functionally equivalent declarations:

```
int& p; // & associated with type
int &p; // & associated with variable
```

Associating the * or & with the type name reflects the desire of some programmers for C++ to contain a separate pointer or reference type. However, the trouble with associating the & or * with the type name rather than the variable is that, according to the formal C++ syntax, neither the & nor the * is distributive over a list of variables. Thus, misleading declarations are easily created. For example, the following declaration creates *one, not two*, integer pointers. Here, **b** is declared as an integer (not an integer pointer) because, as specified by the C++ syntax, when used in a declaration, the * (or &) is linked to the individual variable that it precedes, not to the type that it follows:

```
int* a, b;
```

The trouble with this declaration is that the visual message suggests that both **a** and **b** are pointer types, even though, in fact, only **a** is a pointer. This visual confusion not only misleads novice C++ programmers, but occasionally old pros, too.

It is important to understand that as far as the C++ compiler is concerned, it doesn't matter whether you write **int *p** or **int* p**. Thus, if you prefer to associate the * or & with the type rather than the variable, feel free to do so. However, to avoid confusion, this book will continue to associate the * and the & with the variables that they modify rather than their types.

In this case, Borland C++ generates a temporary object that has the value 100 and **i** references that object.

As stated earlier, in general it is not a good idea to use independent references because they are not necessary and tend to confuse your code.

Using a Reference to Overload a Unary Operator

Now that you have learned about references, you will see how to use them to allow a **friend** function to overload a unary operator. To begin, think back to the original version of the overloaded **++** operator relative to the **three_d** class. It is shown here for your convenience:

```
// Overload a unary operator.
three_d three_d::operator++()
{
  x++;
  y++;
  z++;
  return *this;
}
```

As you know, each member function has as an implicit argument a pointer to itself that is referred to inside the member function using the keyword **this**. For this reason, when overloading a unary operator using a member function, no argument is explicitly declared. The only argument needed in this situation is the implicit pointer to the object that activated the call to the overloaded operator function. Since **this** is a pointer to the object, any changes made to the object's data affect the object that generates the call to the operator function. Unlike member functions, a **friend** function does not receive a **this** pointer and therefore cannot reference the object that activated it. Thus, trying to create a **friend operator++( )** function as shown here does not work:

```
// THIS WILL NOT WORK
three_d operator++(three_d op1)
{
 op1.x++;
 op1.y++;
 op1.z++;
 return op1;
}
```

This function does not work because only a *copy* of the object that activated the call to **operator++( )** is passed to the function in parameter **op1**. Thus, the changes inside **operator++( )** do not affect the object that generated the call.

The way to use a **friend** when overloading a unary **++** or **– –** is to use a reference parameter. In this way, the compiler knows in advance that it must generate the address of the invoking object when it calls the operator function. This allows the operand to be changed. Here is the entire **three_d** program, using a **friend operator++( )** function:

```
// This version uses a friend operator++() function.
#include <iostream.h>

class three_d {
  int x, y, z; // 3-d coordinates
public:
  friend three_d operator+(three_d op1, three_d op2);
  three_d operator=(three_d op2);  // op1 is implied
  // use a reference to overload the ++
  friend three_d operator++(three_d &op1);

  void show() ;
  void assign(int mx, int my, int mz);
} ;

// This is now a friend function.
three_d operator+(three_d op1, three_d op2)
{
  three_d temp;

  temp.x = op1.x + op2.x;  // these are integer additions
  temp.y = op1.y + op2.y;  // and the + retains its original
  temp.z = op1.z + op2.z;  // meaning relative to them
  return temp;
}

// Overload the =.
three_d three_d::operator=(three_d op2)
{
  x = op2.x; // these are integer assignments
  y = op2.y; // and the = retains its original
  z = op2.z; // meaning relative to them
  return *this;
}

/* Overload a unary operator using a friend function.
   This requires the use of a reference parameter. */
three_d operator++(three_d &op1)
{
```

```
  op1.x++;
  op1.y++;
  op1.z++;
  return op1;
}

// Show X, Y, Z coordinates.
void three_d::show()
{
  cout << x << ", ";
  cout << y << ", ";
  cout << z << "\n";
 }

// Assign coordinates.
void three_d::assign(int mx, int my, int mz)
{
  x = mx;
  y = my;
  z = mz;
}

int main()
{
  three_d a, b, c;
  a.assign(1, 2, 3);
  b.assign(10, 10, 10);

  a.show();
  b.show();

  c = a+b;  // now add a and b together
  c.show();

  c = a+b+c; // add a, b and c together
  c.show();

  c = b = a;  // demonstrate multiple assignment
  c.show();
  b.show();

  ++c;  // increment c
  c.show();
```

```
   return 0;
}
```

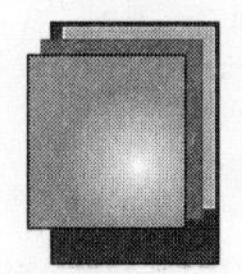

REMEMBER: In general, you should use member functions to implement overloaded operators. friend functions are allowed in C++ mostly to handle some special-case situations.

Overloading [ ]

Aside from the few operators mentioned earlier, you can overload any other C++ operator. Most of the time you will only need to overload the standard operators, such as the arithmetic, relational, or logical. However, there is one rather "exotic" operator that is often useful to overload: [ ], the array subscripting operator. In C++, the [ ] is considered a binary operator when you are overloading it. The [ ] must be overloaded by a member function. You cannot use a **friend** function. The general form of an **operator[ ]( )** function is as shown here:

```
type class-name::operator[ ](int i)
{
// . . .
}
```

Technically, the parameter does not have to be of type **int**, but an **operator[ ]( )** function is typically used to provide array subscripting, and as such, an integer value is generally used.

Given an object called **O**, the expression

```
O[3]
```

translates into this call to the **operator[ ]( )** function:

```
operator[](3)
```

That is, the value of the expression within the subscripting operator is passed to the **operator[ ]( )** function in its explicit parameter. The **this** pointer will point to **O**, the object that generated the call.

In the following program, **atype** declares an array of three integers. Its constructor function initializes each member of the array to the specified values. The overloaded **operator[ ]( )** function returns the value of the array as indexed by the value of its parameter.

```
#include <iostream.h>
```

```
class atype {
  int a[3];
public:
  atype(int i, int j, int k) {
    a[0] = i;
    a[1] = j;
    a[2] = k;
  }
  int operator[](int i) {return a[i];}
};

int main()
{
  atype ob(1, 2, 3);

  cout << ob[1];  // displays 2

  return 0;
}
```

You can design the **operator[ ]( )** function in such a way that the **[ ]** can be used on both the left and right sides of an assignment statement. To do this, simply specify the return value of **operator[ ]( )** as a reference. The following program makes this change and shows its use:

```
#include <iostream.h>

class atype {
  int a[3];
public:
  atype(int i, int j, int k) {
    a[0] = i;
    a[1] = j;
    a[2] = k;
  }
  int &operator[](int i) {return a[i];}
};

int main()
{
  atype ob(1, 2, 3);

  cout << ob[1];  // displays 2
  cout << " ";
```

```
  ob[1] = 25;  // [] on left of =

  cout << ob[1];  // now displays 25

  return 0;
}
```

Because **operator[ ]( )** now returns a reference to the array element indexed by **i,** it can be used on the left side of an assignment to modify an element of the array. (Of course, it may still be used on the right side as well.)

One advantage to being able to overload the **[ ]** operator is that it allows a means of implementing safe array indexing in C++. As you know, in C++ it is possible to overrun (or underrun) an array boundary at run time without generating a run-time error message.

However, if you create a class that contains the array, and allow access to that array only through the overloaded **[ ]** subscripting operator, then you can intercept an out-of-range index. For example, this program adds a range check to the preceding program and proves that it works:

```
// A safe array example.
#include <iostream.h>
#include <stdlib.h>

class atype {
  int a[3];
public:
  atype(int i, int j, int k) {
    a[0] = i;
    a[1] = j;
    a[2] = k;
  }
  int &operator[](int i);
};

// Provide range checking for atype.
int &atype::operator[](int i)
{
  if(i<0 || i> 2) {
    cout << "Boundary Error\n";
    exit(1);
  }
  return a[i];
}
```

```
int main()
{
  atype ob(1, 2, 3);

  cout << ob[1];  // displays 2
  cout << " ";

  ob[1] = 25;  // [] appears on left
  cout << ob[1];  // displays 25

  ob[3] = 44; // generates runtime error, 3 is out-of-range
  return 0;
}
```

In this program, when the statement

```
ob[3] = 44;
```

executes, the boundary error is intercepted by **operator[ ]( )**, and the program is terminated before any damage can be done. (In actual practice, some sort of error-handling function would be called to deal with the out-of-range condition; the program would not have to terminate.)

Applying Operator Overloading

This chapter concludes by developing another, more practical example of operator overloading that implements a string type. As you know, C++ implements strings as null-terminated character arrays and not as a built-in type of their own. This approach makes strings powerful, elegant, and efficient. However, there are many times when you need to use a string, but don't need an extremely high level of efficiency or power. In these cases, working with normal, null-terminated strings can become a tiresome chore. However, using C++ it is possible to define a string class that trades a little efficiency for a big gain in ease of use.

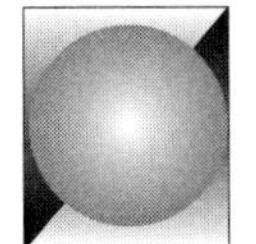

*NOTE: At the time of this writing, the ANSI C++ standardization committee is in the process of defining a standard string class. Borland C++ currently includes a string class of its own, called **string**. The purpose of this section is not to develop an alternative to these classes. Instead, it is to present an example that illustrates how easily a new data type can be integrated into your C++ programming environment and to show off the power of operator overloading. The development of a string class is the quintessential example.*

To begin, the following class declares the type **str_type**:

```
#include <iostream.h>
#include <string.h>

class str_type {
  char string[80];
public:
  str_type(char *str = "\0") { strcpy(string, str); }


  str_type operator+(str_type str); // concatenate
  str_type operator=(str_type str); // assign

  // output the string
  void show_str() { cout << string; }
} ;
```

As you can see, **str_type** declares one 80-character array in its private portion. For the sake of this example, no string can be longer than 79 bytes. The class has one constructor function that can be used to initialize the array **string** with a specific value or assign it a null string in the absence of any initializer. It also declares two overloaded operators that perform concatenation and assignment. Finally, it declares the function **show_str( )**, which outputs **string** to the screen. The overloaded operator functions are shown here:

```
// Concatenate two strings.
str_type str_type::operator+(str_type str) {
  str_type temp;

  strcpy(temp.string, string);
  strcat(temp.string, str.string);
  return temp;
}

// Assign one string to another.
str_type str_type::operator=(str_type str) {
  strcpy(string, str.string);
  return *this;
}
```

Given these definitions, the following **main( )** illustrates their use:

```
int main()
{
  str_type a("Hello "), b("There"), c;
```

```
  c = a + b;

  c.show_str();

  return 0;
}
```

This program outputs "Hello There" on the screen. It first concatenates **a** with **b** and then assigns this value to **c**.

Keep in mind that both the = and the + are defined only for objects of type **str_type**. For example, this statement is invalid because it tries to assign object **a** a normal, quoted C++ string:

```
a = "this is currently wrong";
```

However, the **str_type** class can be enhanced to allow such a statement. To expand the types of operations supported by the **str_type** class so that you can assign normal C++ strings to **str_type** objects or concatenate a C++ string with a **str_type** object, you need to overload the + and = operations a second time. First, the class declaration is changed, as shown here:

```
class str_type {
  char string[80];
public:
  str_type(char *str = "\0") { strcpy(string, str); }

  str_type operator+(str_type str); // concatenate objects
  str_type operator+(char *str);  /* concatenate object with
                                     a string */

  str_type operator=(str_type str); /* assign object to
                                       object */
  char *operator=(char *str); // assign string to object

  void show_str() { cout << string; }
} ;
```

Next, the overloaded **operator+( )** and **operator =( )** are implemented, as shown here:

```
// Assign a string to an object.
str_type str_type::operator=(char *str)
{
  str_type temp;
```

```
  strcpy(string, str);
  strcpy(temp.string, string);
  return temp;
}

// Add a string to an object.
str_type str_type::operator+(char *str)
{
  str_type temp;

  strcpy(temp.string, string);
  strcat(temp.string, str);
  return temp;
}
```

Look carefully at these functions. Notice that the right-side argument is not an object of type **str_type** but rather a pointer to a character array—that is, a normal string in C++. However, notice that both functions return an object of type **str_type**. Although the functions could, in theory, have returned some other type, it makes the most sense to return an object since the targets of these operations are also objects. The advantage to defining string operations that accept normal C++ strings as the right-side operand is that it allows some statements to be written in a natural way. For example, these are now valid statements:

```
str_type a, b, c;

a = "hi there";  // assign an object a string

c = a + " George";  // concatenate an object with a string
```

The following program incorporates the additional meanings for the + and = operations and illustrates their uses:

```
// Expanding the string type.
#include <iostream.h>
#include <string.h>

class str_type {
  char string[80];
public:
  str_type(char *str = "\0") { strcpy(string, str); }

  str_type operator+(str_type str);
  str_type operator+(char *str);
```

```
  str_type operator=(str_type str);
  str_type operator=(char *str);

  void show_str() { cout << string; }
} ;

str_type str_type::operator+(str_type str) {
  str_type temp;

  strcpy(temp.string, string);
  strcat(temp.string, str.string);
  return temp;
}

str_type str_type::operator=(str_type str) {
  strcpy(string, str.string);
  return *this;
}

str_type str_type::operator=(char *str)
{
  str_type temp;

  strcpy(string, str);
  strcpy(temp.string, string);
  return temp;
}

str_type str_type::operator+(char *str)
{
  str_type temp;

  strcpy(temp.string, string);
  strcat(temp.string, str);
  return temp;
}

int main()
{
  str_type a("Hello "), b("There"), c;

  c = a + b;

  c.show_str();
```

```
  cout << "\n";

  a = "to program in because";
  a.show_str();
  cout << "\n";

  b = c = "C++ is fun";

  c = c+" "+a+" "+b;
  c.show_str();

  return 0;
}
```

This program displays the following on the screen:

```
Hello There
to program in because
C++ is fun to program in because C++ is fun
```

On your own, try creating other string operations. For example, you might try defining the – so that it performs a substring deletion. For example, if object **A**'s string is "This is a test" and object **B**'s string is "is", then **A-B** yields "th a test". In this case, all occurrences of the substring are removed from the original string.

Chapter Twenty-Three

Inheritance, Virtual Functions, and Polymorphism

As you know, two of the cornerstones of object-oriented programming (OOP) are inheritance and polymorphism. Inheritance is important because it allows the creation of hierarchical classifications. Using inheritance, you can create a general class that defines traits common to a set of related items. This class may then be inherited by other, more specific classes, each adding only those things that are unique to the derived class.

Inheritance is also important for another reason: it is used to support run-time polymorphism. Polymorphism is sometimes characterized by the phrase "one interface, multiple methods." This means that a general class of operations can be accessed in the same fashion even though the specific actions associated with each operation may differ.

In C++, polymorphism is supported both at run time and at compile time. Operator and function overloading are examples of compile-time polymorphism. However, as powerful as operator and function overloading are, they cannot perform all tasks required by a true, object-oriented language. Therefore, C++ also allows run-time polymorphism through the use of derived classes (i.e., inheritance) and virtual functions, both of which are discussed in this chapter.

This chapter begins with a closer look at inheritance.

Inheritance and the Access Specifiers

In this section, we will explore the interplay between C++'s access specifiers and inheritance. Before beginning, let's review terminology. A class that is inherited by another class is called the *base class.* Sometimes it is also referred to as the *parent class.* The class that does the inheriting is called the *derived class,* or the *child class.* This book uses the terms *base* and *derived* because they are the traditional terms.

Understanding the Access Specifiers

In C++, a class can categorize its members into three classifications: **public**, **private**, or **protected**. A **public** member can be accessed by any other function in the program. A **private** member can be accessed only by member or **friend** functions of its class. A **protected** member is similar to a **private** member, except where inheritance is concerned.

When one class inherits another class, all **public** members of the base class become **public** members of the derived class and are therefore accessible to the derived class. However, all **private** members of the base class remain private to that class and are inaccessible to the derived class. For example, in the following fragment:

```
class X {
  int i;
  int j;
public:
  void get_ij();
  void put_ij();
} ;

class Y : public X {
  int k;
public:
  int get_k();
  void make_k();
} ;
```

class **Y** inherits and can access **X**'s **public** functions **get_ij( )** and **put_ij( )** but cannot access **i** or **j** because they are **private** to **X**. In all cases, a **private** member remains private to the class in which it is declared. Thus, **private** members cannot participate in inheritance.

The fact that private members cannot be inherited gives rise to an interesting question: What if you want to keep a member private, but allow its use by derived classes? The answer is the keyword **protected**. A **protected** member acts just like a **private** one except for one important difference. When a **protected** member is inherited, the derived class has access to it. Thus, specifying a member as **protected** allows you to make it available within a class hierarchy but prevent its access from outside that hierarchy. For example:

```
class X {
protected:
  int i;
  int j;
public:
  void get_ij();
  void put_ij();
} ;

class Y : public X {
  int k;
public:
  int get_k();
  void make_k();
} ;
```

Here, **Y** has access to **i** and **j** even though they are still inaccessible to the rest of the program. When you make an element **protected**, you restrict its access, but you allow this access to be inherited. When a member is **private**, access is not inherited.

One other point about the **private**, **protected**, and **public** keywords is that they can appear in any order and any number of times in the declaration of a class. For example, this code is perfectly valid:

```
class my_class {
protected:
  int i;
  int j;
public:
  void f1();
  void f2();
protected:
  int a;
public:
  int b;
} ;
```

However, it is usually considered good form to have only one heading for each access specifier inside each **class** or **struct** declaration.

Base Class Access Control

How a base class is inherited by a derived class affects the access status of the inherited members. As you know, the general form for inheriting a class is

```
class class-name : access class-name {
   .
   .
   .
};
```

Here, *access* determines how the base class is inherited and it must be **private**, **public**, or **protected**. (It can also be omitted, in which case **public** is assumed if the base class is a structure, or **private** if the base class is a class.) If *access* is **public**, all **public** and **protected** members of the base class become **public** and **protected** members of the derived class, respectively. If *access* is **private**, all **public** and **protected** members of the base class become **private** members of the derived class. If *access* is **protected**, all **public** and **protected** members of the base class become **protected** members of the derived class. To understand the ramifications of these conversions, let's work through an example. Consider the following program:

```
#include <iostream.h>

class X {
protected:
  int i;
  int j;
public:
  void get_ij() {
    cout << "Enter two numbers: ";
    cin >> i >> j;
  }
  void put_ij() { cout << i << " " << j << "\n"; }
} ;

// In Y, i and j of X become protected members.
class Y : public X {
  int k;
public:
  int get_k() { return k; }
  void make_k() { k = i*j; }
} ;

/* Z has access to i and j of X, but not to
```

```
   k of Y, since it is private. */
class Z : public Y {
public:
  void f();
} ;

// i and j are accessible here
void Z::f()
{
  i = 2; // ok
  j = 3; // ok
}

int main()
{
  Y var;
  Z var2;

  var.get_ij();
  var.put_ij();

  var.make_k();
  cout << var.get_k();
  cout << "\n";

  var2.f();
  var2.put_ij();

  return 0;
}
```

Since **Y** inherits **X** as **public**, the **protected** elements of **X** become **protected** elements of **Y**, which means that they can be inherited by **Z** and this program compiles and runs correctly. However, changing **X**'s status in **Y** to **private**, as shown in the following program, causes **Z** to be denied access to **i** and **j**, and the functions **get_ij( )** and **put_ij( )** that access them, because they have been made **private** in **Y**:

```
#include <iostream.h>

class X {
protected:
  int i;
  int j;
public:
```

```
  void get_ij() {
    cout << "Enter two numbers: ";
    cin >> i >> j;
  }
  void put_ij() { cout << i << " " << j << "\n"; }
} ;

// Now, i and j are converted to private members of Y.
class Y : private X {
  int k;
public:
  int get_k() { return k; }
  void make_k() { k = i*j; }
} ;

/* Because i and j are private in Y, they
   may not be inherited by Z. */
class Z : public Y {
public:
  void f();
} ;

// This function no longer works.
void Z::f()
{
//  i = 2;  i and j are no longer accessible
//  j = 3;
}

int main()
{
  Y var;
  Z var2;

//  var.get_ij();  no longer accessible
//  var.put_ij();  no longer accessible

  var.make_k();
  cout << var.get_k();
  cout << "\n";

  var2.f();
//  var2.put_ij();  no longer accessible
```

```
  return 0;
}
```

When **X** is inherited as **private** in **Y**'s declaration, it causes **i**, **j**, **get_ij( )**, and **put_ij( )** to be treated as **private** in **Y**, which means they cannot be inherited by **Z**; thus, **Z**'s class can no longer access them.

Constructors and Destructors in Derived Classes

When using derived classes, it is important to understand how and when constructor and destructor functions are executed in both the base and derived classes. Let's begin with constructors.

It is possible for a base class and a derived class to each have a constructor function. (In fact, in the case of a multilayered class hierarchy, it is possible for all involved classes to have constructors, but we will start with the simplest case.) When a base class contains a constructor, that constructor is executed before the constructor in the derived class. For example, consider this short program:

```
#include <iostream.h>

class Base {
public:
  Base() {cout << "\nBase created\n";}
};

class D_class1 : public Base {
public:
  D_class1() {cout << "D_class1 created\n";}
};

int main()
{
  D_class1 d1;

  // do nothing but execute constructors
  return 0;
}
```

This program creates an object of type **D_class1**. It displays this output:

```
Base created
D_class1 created
```

Here, **d1** is an object of type **D_class1**, which is derived using **Base**. Thus, when **d1** is created, first **Base( )** is executed, then **D_class1( )** is called.

It makes sense for constructors to be called in the same order in which the derivation takes place. Because the base class has no knowledge of the derived class, any initialization it needs to perform is separate from and possibly prerequisite to any initialization performed by the derived class, so it must be executed first.

On the other hand, a destructor function in a derived class is executed before the destructor in the base. The reason for this is also easy to understand. Since the destruction of a base class object implies the destruction of the derived class object, the derived object's destructor must be executed before the base object is destroyed. This program illustrates the order in which constructors and destructors are executed:

```
#include <iostream.h>

class Base {
public:
  Base() {cout << "\nBase created\n";}
  ~Base() {cout << "Base destroyed\n\n";}
};

class D_class1 : public Base {
public:
  D_class1() {cout << "D_class1 created\n";}
  ~D_class1() {cout << "D_class1 destroyed\n";}
};

int main()
{
  D_class1 d1;

  cout << "\n";

  return 0;
}
```

This program produces the following output:

```
Base created
D_class1 created
D_class1 destroyed
Base destroyed
```

As you know, it is possible for a derived class to be used as a base class in the creation of another derived class. When this happens, constructors are executed in the order of their derivation and destructors in the reverse order. For example, consider this program, which uses **D_class1** to derive **D_class2**:

```
#include <iostream.h>

class Base {
public:
  Base() {cout << "\nBase created\n";}
  ~Base() {cout << "Base destroyed\n\n";}
};

class D_class1 : public Base {
public:
  D_class1() {cout << "D_class1 created\n";}
  ~D_class1() {cout << "D_class1 destroyed\n";}
};

class D_class2 : public D_class1 {
public:
  D_class2() {cout << "D_class2 created\n";}
  ~D_class2() {cout << "D_class2 destroyed\n";}
};

int main()
{
  D_class1 d1;
  D_class2 d2;

  cout << "\n";

  return 0;
}
```

The program produces this output:

```
Base created
D_class1 created

Base created
D_class1 created
D_class2 created

D_class2 destroyed
D_class1 destroyed
```

```
Base destroyed

D_class1 destroyed
Base destroyed
```

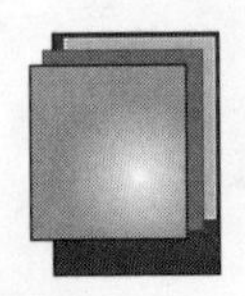

REMEMBER: Constructors are called in order of derivation. Destructors are called in reverse order.

Multiple Inheritance

It is possible for one class to inherit the attributes of two or more classes at the same time. To accomplish this, use a comma-separated inheritance list in the derived class' base class list. The general form is

class *derived-class-name* : *base-class list*
{
  .
  .
  .
};

For example, in this program **Z** inherits both **X** and **Y**:

```
#include <iostream.h>

class X {
protected:
  int a;
public:
  void make_a(int i) { a = i; }
};

class Y {
protected:
  int b;
public:
  void make_b(int i) { b = i; }
} ;

// Z inherits both X and Y
class Z : public X, public Y {
public:
```

```
  int make_ab() { return a*b; }
} ;

int main()
{
  Z i;

  i.make_a(10);
  i.make_b(12);
  cout << i.make_ab();

  return 0;
}
```

Since **Z** inherits both **X** and **Y**, it has access to the **public** and **protected** portions of both **X** and **Y**.

In the preceding example, neither **X**, **Y**, nor **Z** contained constructor functions. However, the situation is more complex when a base class contains a constructor function. For example, let's change the preceding example so that the classes **X**, **Y**, and **Z** each have a constructor:

```
#include <iostream.h>

class X {
protected:
  int a;
public:
  X() {
    a = 10;
    cout << "Initializing X\n";
  }
};

class Y {
protected:
  int b;
public:
  Y() {
    cout << "Initializing Y\n";
    b = 20;
  }
} ;

// Z inherits both X and Y
```

```
class Z : public X, public Y {
public:
  Z() { cout << "Initializing Z\n"; }
  int make_ab() { return a*b; }
} ;

int main()
{
  Z i;

  cout << i.make_ab();

  return 0;
}
```

When this program runs, it displays the following:

```
Initializing X
Initializing Y
Initializing Z
200
```

Notice that the base classes are constructed in the order they appear from left to right in **Z**'s declaration.

In general, when a list of base classes is used, the constructors are called in order from left to right. Destructors are called in order from right to left.

Passing Parameters to a Base Class

So far, none of the examples of inheritance have included a base class constructor that used parameters. As long as no base class constructor requires arguments, a derived class need not do anything special. However, when a base class constructor requires arguments, your derived classes must explicitly handle this situation by passing the necessary arguments to the base class. To accomplish this, you will use an extended form of the constructor function within the derived class that passes arguments to the constructor function of the base class. This extended form is shown here:

derived-constructor(*arg-list*) : *base1*(*arg-list*), base2(*arg-list*), . . ., *baseN*(*arg-list*)
{
.
.
.
}

Here, *base1* through *baseN* are the names of the base classes inherited by the derived class. Notice that the colon is used to separate the derived class' constructor function from the argument lists of the base classes. The argument lists associated with the base classes can consist of constants, global variables, or the parameters to the derived class' constructor function. Since an object's initialization occurs at run time, you can use as an argument any identifier that is defined within the scope of the class.

The following program illustrates how to pass arguments to the base classes of a derived class by modifying the preceding program:

```
#include <iostream.h>

class X {
protected:
  int a;
public:
  X(int i) { a = i; }
};

class Y {
protected:
  int b;
public:
  Y(int i) { b = i; }
} ;

// Z inherits both X and Y
class Z : public X, public Y {
public:
  /* Initialize X and Y via Z's constructor.
     Notice that Z does not actually use x or y
     itself, but it could, if it so chooses. */
  Z(int x, int y) : X(x), Y(y)
  {
    cout << "Initializing\n";
  }
  int make_ab() { return a*b; }
} ;

int main()
{
  Z i(10, 20);

  cout << i.make_ab();
```

```
  return 0;
}
```

Notice how the constructor **Z** does not actually use its parameters directly. Instead, in this example they are simply passed along to the constructor functions for **X** and **Y**. There is no reason, however, that **Z** could not use these or other arguments.

Pointers and References to Derived Types

Before moving on to virtual functions and polymorphism, it is necessary to explain a unique attribute of pointers and references that provides their foundation. We will begin with pointers. In general, a pointer of one type cannot point to an object of a different type. However, there is an important exception to this rule that relates only to derived classes. In C++, a base class pointer may point to an object of a class derived from that base. For example, assume that you have a base type called **B_class** and a type called **D_class** that is derived from **B_class**. In C++, any pointer declared as type **B_class *** can also point to an object of type **D_class**. For example, given

```
B_class *p; // pointer to object of type B_class
B_class B_ob; // object of type B_class
D_class D_ob; // object of type D_class
```

the following is perfectly valid:

```
p = &B_ob; // p points to object of type B_class

p = &D_ob; /* p points to object of type D_class,
              which is an object derived from B_class. */
```

Using **p**, all elements of **D_ob** inherited from **B_ob** can be accessed. However, elements specific to **D_ob** cannot be referenced using **p** (unless a type cast is employed). This is because the pointer only "knows" about the members of its base type even though it can point to derived types.

For a concrete example that uses base class pointers, consider this short program, which defines a base class called **B_class** and a derived class called **D_class**. The derived class implements a simple automated telephone book.

```
// Using pointers on derived class objects.

#include <iostream.h>
#include <string.h>

class B_class {
  char name[80];
public:
```

```
  void put_name(char *s) {strcpy(name, s); }
  void show_name() {cout << name << " ";}
} ;

class D_class : public B_class {
  char phone_num[80];
public:
  void put_phone(char *num) {
    strcpy(phone_num, num);
  }
  void show_phone() {cout << phone_num << "\n";}
};

int main()
{
  B_class *p;
  B_class B_ob;

  D_class *dp;
  D_class D_ob;

  p = &B_ob;  // address of base

  // Access B_class via pointer.
  p->put_name("Thomas Edison");

  // Access D_class via base pointer.
  p = &D_ob;
  p->put_name("Albert Einstein");

  // Show that each name went into proper object.
  B_ob.show_name();
  D_ob.show_name();
  cout << "\n";

  /* Since put_phone and show_phone are not part of the
     base class, they are not accessible via the base
     pointer p and must be accessed either directly,
     or, as shown here, through a pointer to the
     derived type.
  */
  dp = &D_ob;
  dp->put_phone("555 555-1234");
  p->show_name(); // either p or dp can be used in this line
```

```
    dp->show_phone();
    return 0;
}
```

In this example, the pointer **p** is defined as a pointer to **B_class**. However, it can point to an object of the derived class **D_class** and can be used to access those elements of the derived class that are defined by the base class. However, remember that a base pointer cannot access those elements specific to the derived class without the use of a type cast. This is why **show_phone( )** is accessed using the **dp** pointer, which is a pointer to the derived class.

If you want to access elements defined by a derived type using a base type pointer, you must cast it into a pointer of the derived type. For example, this line of code calls the **show_phone( )** function of **D_ob**:

```
((D_class *)p)->show_phone();
```

The outer set of parentheses is necessary to associate the cast with **p** and not with the return type of **show_phone( )**. While there is technically nothing wrong with casting a pointer in this manner, it is best avoided because it simply adds confusion to your code.

While a base pointer can be used to point to any type of derived object, the reverse is not true. That is, you cannot use a pointer to a derived class to access an object of the base type.

One final point: A pointer is incremented and decremented relative to its base type. Therefore, when a pointer to a base class is pointing to a derived class, incrementing or decrementing it does *not* make it point to the next object of the derived class. Therefore, you should consider it invalid to increment or decrement a pointer when it is pointing to a derived object.

References to Derived Types

Similar to the action of pointers just described, a base class reference can be used to refer to an object of a derived type. The most common application of this is found in function parameters. A base class reference parameter can receive objects of the base class as well as any other type derived from that base. You will see an example of this shortly.

Virtual Functions

Run-time polymorphism is achieved through the use of derived types and virtual functions. In short, a *virtual function* is a function that is declared as **virtual** in a base class and redefined in one or more derived classes. Virtual functions are special because when one is called through a base class pointer (or reference) to an object of a derived class, C++ determines which function to call *at run time* based on the type of object *pointed to*. Thus, when different objects are pointed to, different versions of the virtual function are executed. A class that contains one or more virtual functions is called a *polymorphic class*.

A virtual function is declared as **virtual** inside the base class by preceding its declaration with the keyword **virtual**. However, when a virtual function is redefined by a derived class, the keyword **virtual** need not be repeated (although it is not an error to do so).

As a first example of virtual functions, examine this short program:

```
// A short example that uses virtual functions.
#include <iostream.h>

class Base {
public:
  virtual void who() { // specify a virtual function
    cout << "Base\n";
  }
};

class first_d : public Base {
public:
  void who() { // define who() relative to first_d
    cout << "First derivation\n";
  }
};

class second_d : public Base {
public:
  void who() { // define who() relative to second_d
    cout << "Second derivation\n";
  }
};

int main()
{
  Base base_obj;
  Base *p;
  first_d first_obj;
  second_d second_obj;

  p = &base_obj;
  p->who();  // access Base's who

  p = &first_obj;
  p->who(); // access first_d's who
```

```
  p = &second_obj;
  p->who();  // access second_d's who

  return 0;
}
```

This program produces the following output:

```
Base
First derivation
Second derivation
```

Let's examine the program in detail to understand how it works.

As you can see, in **Base**, the function **who( )** is declared as **virtual**. This means that the function can be redefined by a derived class. Inside both **first_d** and **second_d**, **who( )** is redefined relative to each class. Inside **main( )**, four variables are declared. The first is **base_obj**, which is an object of type **Base**; then **p**, which is a pointer to **Base** objects; and then **first_obj** and **second_obj**, which are objects of the two derived classes. Next, **p** is assigned the address of **base_obj**, and the **who( )** function is called. Since **who( )** is declared as **virtual**, C++ determines at run time which version of **who( )** is referred to by the type of object pointed to by **p**. In this case, it is an object of type **Base**, so the version of **who( )** declared in **Base** is executed. Next, **p** is assigned the address of **first_obj**. (Remember that a base class pointer can be used with any derived class.) Now, when **who( )** is called, C++ again examines what type of object is pointed to by **p** to determine what version of **who( )** to call. Since **p** points to an object of type **first_d**, that version of **who( )** is used. Likewise, when **p** is assigned the address of **second_obj**, the version of **who( )** declared inside **second_d** is executed.

The most common way that a base class reference is used to call a virtual function is through a function parameter. For example, consider the following variation on the preceding program:

```
/* Here, a base class reference is used to access
   a virtual function. */
#include <iostream.h>

class Base {
public:
  virtual void who() { // specify a virtual function
    cout << "Base\n";
  }
};

class first_d : public Base {
public:
```

```
  void who() { // define who() relative to first_d
    cout << "First derivation\n";
  }
};

class second_d : public Base {
public:
  void who() { // define who() relative to second_d
    cout << "Second derivation\n";
  }
};

// Use a base class reference parameter.
void show_who(Base &r) {
  r.who();
}

int main()
{
  Base base_obj;
  first_d first_obj;
  second_d second_obj;

  show_who(base_obj); // access Base's who

  show_who(first_obj); // access first_d's who

  show_who(second_obj); // access second_d's who

  return 0;
}
```

This program produces the same output as its preceding version. In this example, the function **show_who( )** defines a reference parameter of type **Base**. Inside **main( )**, the function is called using objects of type **Base**, **first_d**, and **second_d**. Inside **show_who( )**, the specific version of **who( )** that is called is determined by the type of object being referenced when the function is called.

The key point to using virtual functions to achieve run-time polymorphism is that you must access those functions through the use of a base class pointer or reference. Although it is legal to call a virtual function just like you call any other "normal" function (by applying the dot operator to an object), it is only when a virtual function is called through a base class pointer (or reference) that run-time polymorphism is achieved.

At first glance, the redefinition of a virtual function in a derived class looks like a special form of function overloading. But, this is not the case, and the term *overloading* is not applied to virtual function redefinition because several differences exist. First, the prototypes for virtual functions must match. As you know, when overloading normal functions, the number and type of parameters must differ. However, when redefining a virtual function, these elements must be unchanged. If the prototypes of the functions differ, then the function is simply considered overloaded, and its virtual nature is lost. Also, if only the return types of the function differ, an error occurs. (Functions that differ only in their return types are inherently ambiguous.) Another restriction is that a virtual function must be a member, not a **friend**, of the class for which it is defined. However, a virtual function can be a **friend** of another class. Also, destructor functions can be virtual but constructors cannot.

Because of the restrictions and differences between overloading normal functions and redefining virtual functions, the term *overriding* is used to describe the virtual function redefinition.

Once a function is declared as **virtual**, it stays virtual no matter how many layers of derived classes it passes through. For example, if **second_d** is derived from **first_d** instead of **Base**, as shown in the following example, **who( )** is still virtual, and the proper version is still correctly selected:

```
// Derive from first_d, not Base
class second_d : public first_d {
public:
  void who() { // define who() relative to second_d
    cout << "Second derivation\n";
  }
};
```

When a derived class does not override a virtual function, then the version of the function in the base class is used. For example, try this version of the preceding program:

```
#include <iostream.h>

class Base {
public:
  virtual void who() {
    cout << "Base\n";
  }
};

class first_d : public Base {
public:
  void who() {
    cout << "First derivation\n";
  }
};
```

```
class second_d : public Base {
// who() not defined
};

int main()
{
  Base base_obj;
  Base *p;
  first_d first_obj;
  second_d second_obj;

  p = &base_obj;
  p->who();  // access Base's who()

  p = &first_obj;
  p->who(); // access first_d's who()

  p = &second_obj;
  p->who();  /* access Base's who() because
                second_d does not redefine it */

  return 0;
}
```

This program now outputs the following:

```
Base
First derivation
Base
```

Keep in mind that inherited characteristics are hierarchical. To illustrate this point imagine that, in the preceding example, **second_d** is derived from **first_d** instead of **Base**. When **who( )** is referenced relative to an object of type **second_d** (in which **who( )** is not defined), it is the version of **who( )** declared inside **first_d** that is called since it is the class closest to **second_d**. In general, when a class does not override a virtual function, C++ uses the first definition that it finds in reverse order of derivation.

Why Virtual Functions?

As stated at the start of this chapter, virtual functions in combination with derived types allow C++ to support run-time polymorphism. Polymorphism is essential to object-oriented programming because it allows a generalized class to specify those functions that will be common to any derivative of that class while allowing a derived class to specify the exact implementation of some or all of those functions. In other words, the base class dictates the general *interface* that any object derived from that class will have, but lets the derived class define the actual *method.* This is why the phrase "one interface, multiple methods" is often used to describe polymorphism.

Part of the key to successfully applying polymorphism is understanding that base and derived classes form a hierarchy that moves from greater to lesser generalization (base to derived). Hence, when used correctly, the base class provides all elements that a derived class can use directly plus the basis for those functions that the derived class must implement on its own.

Having a consistent interface with multiple implementations is important because it helps the programmer handle increasingly complex programs. For example, when you develop a program, all objects you derive from a particular base class are accessed in the same general way, even if the specific actions vary from one derived class to the next. This means that you need to remember only one interface rather than several. Further, the separation of interface and implementation allows the creation of *class libraries,* which can be provided by a third party. If these libraries are implemented correctly, they provide a common interface that you can use to derive your own specific classes.

To get an idea of the power of the "one interface, multiple methods" concept, examine this short program. It creates a base class called **figure**. This class is used to store the dimensions of various two-dimensional objects and to compute their areas. The function **set_dim( )** is a standard member function because its operation is common to all derived classes. However, **show_area( )** is declared as **virtual** because the way the area of each object is computed varies. The program uses **figure** to derive two specific classes, called **square** and **triangle**.

```
#include <iostream.h>

class figure {
protected:
  double x, y;
public:
  void set_dim(double i, double j) {
    x = i;
    y = j;
  }
  virtual void show_area() {
    cout << "No area computation defined ";
    cout << "for this class.\n";
  }
} ;

class triangle : public figure {
  public:
```

```
    void show_area() {
      cout << "Triangle with height ";
      cout << x << " and base " << y;
      cout << " has an area of ";
      cout << x * 0.5 * y << ".\n";
    }
};

class square : public figure {
  public:
    void show_area() {
      cout << "Square with dimensions ";
      cout << x << "x" << y;
      cout << " has an area of ";
      cout << x *  y << ".\n";
    }
};

int main()
{
  figure *p;  /* create a pointer to base type */

  triangle t;  /* create objects of derived types */
  square s;

  p = &t;
  p->set_dim(10.0, 5.0);
  p->show_area();
  p = &s;
  p->set_dim(10.0, 5.0);
  p->show_area();

  return 0;
}
```

As you can see by examining this program, the interface to both **square** and **triangle** is the same even though both provide their own methods for computing the area of each of their objects.

Given the declaration for **figure**, it is possible to derive a class called **circle** that computes the area of a circle given its radius. To do so, you must create a new derived type that computes the area of a circle. The power of virtual functions is based in the fact that you can easily derive a new type that shares the same common interface as other related objects. For example, here is one way to do it:

```
class circle : public figure {
  public:
    void show_area() {
      cout << "Circle with radius ";
      cout << x;
      cout << " has an area of ";
      cout <<  3.14 * x * x;
    }
} ;
```

Before trying to use **circle**, look closely at the definition of **show_area( )**. Notice that it uses only the value of **x**, which is assumed to hold the radius. (Remember that the area of a circle is computed using the formula πR^2.) However, the function **set_dim( )** as defined in **figure** assumes that it will be passed not just one, but two values. Since **circle** does not require this second value, what is the best course of action?

There are two ways to resolve this problem. First, you can call **set_dim( )** using a dummy value as the second parameter when using a **circle** object. This has the disadvantage of being sloppy as well as requiring you to remember a special exception, which violates the "one interface, many methods" approach.

A better way to resolve this problem is to give the **y** parameter inside **set_dim( )** a default value. In this way, when calling **set_dim( )** for a circle, you need specify only the radius. When calling **set_dim( )** for a triangle or a square, you would specify both values. The expanded program is shown here:

```
#include <iostream.h>

class figure {
protected:
  double x, y;
public:
  void set_dim(double i, double j=0) {
    x = i;
    y = j;
  }
  virtual void show_area() {
    cout << "No area computation defined ";
    cout << "for this class.\n";
  }
} ;

class triangle : public figure {
  public:
    void show_area() {
      cout << "Triangle with height ";
```

```
      cout << x << " and base " << y;
      cout << " has an area of ";
      cout << x * 0.5 * y << ".\n";
    }
};

class square : public figure {
  public:
    void show_area() {
      cout << "Square with dimensions ";
      cout << x << "x" << y;
      cout << " has an area of ";
      cout << x *  y << ".\n";
    }
};

class circle : public figure {
  public:
    void show_area() {
      cout << "Circle with radius ";
      cout << x;
      cout << " has an area of ";
      cout << 3.14 * x * x;
    }
} ;

int main()
{
  figure *p;  /* create a pointer to base type */
  triangle t;  /* create objects of derived types */
  square s;
  circle c;

  p = &t;
  p->set_dim(10.0, 5.0);
  p->show_area();

  p = &s;
  p->set_dim(10.0, 5.0);
  p->show_area();

  p = &c;
  p->set_dim(9.0);
  p->show_area();
```

```
  return 0;
}
```

This example also points out that when defining base classes, it is important to be as flexible as possible. Don't give your program unnecessary restrictions.

Pure Virtual Functions and Abstract Types

When a virtual function that is not overridden in a derived class is called for an object of that derived class, the version of the function as defined in the base class is used. However, in many circumstances there is no meaningful definition of a virtual function inside the base class. For example, in the base class **figure**, used in the preceding example, the definition of **show_area( )** is simply a placeholder. It does not compute and display the area of any type of object. There are two ways you can handle this situation. One way is to simply have it report a warning message, as shown in the example. While this approach can be useful in certain situations, it is not appropriate for all circumstances. There can be virtual functions that must be defined by the derived class in order for the derived class to have any meaning. For example, the **class triangle** has no meaning if **show_area( )** is not defined. In this sort of case, you want some method to ensure that a derived class does, indeed, define all necessary functions. C++'s solution to this problem is the pure virtual function.

A *pure* virtual function is a function declared in a base class that has no definition relative to the base. Since it has no definition relative to the base, any derived type must define its own version—it cannot simply use the version defined in the base. To declare a pure virtual function, use this general form:

virtual *type func_name*(*parameter list*) = 0;

where *type* is the return type of the function and *func_name* is the name of the function. For example, in the following version of **figure**, **show_area( )** is a pure virtual function:

```
class figure {
  double x, y;
public:
  void set_dim(double i, double j=0) {
    x = i;
    y = j;
  }
  virtual void show_area() = 0; // pure
} ;
```

By declaring a virtual function as pure, you force any derived class to define its own implementation. If a class fails to do so, a compile-time error results. For example, if you try to compile this modified version of the **figure** program, in which the definition for **show_area( )** has been removed from the **circle** class, you will see an error message:

```
/*
   This program will not compile because the class
   circle does not override show_area().
*/
#include <iostream.h>

class figure {
protected:
  double x, y;
public:
  void set_dim(double i, double j) {
    x = i;
    y = j;
  }
  virtual void show_area() = 0; // pure
} ;

class triangle : public figure {
  public:
    void show_area() {
      cout << "Triangle with height ";
      cout << x << " and base " << y;
      cout << " has an area of ";
      cout << x * 0.5 * y << ".\n";
    }
};

class square : public figure {
  public:
    void show_area() {
      cout << "Square with dimensions ";
      cout << x << "x" << y;
      cout << " has an area of ";
      cout << x *  y << ".\n";
    }
};
```

```
class circle : public figure {
// no definition of show_area() will cause an error
};

int main()
{
  figure *p;  // create a pointer to base type
  circle c; // attempt to create an object of type circle -- ERROR
  triangle t;  // create objects of derived types */
  square s;

  p = &t;
  p->set_dim(10.0, 5.0);
  p->show_area();

  p = &s;
  p->set_dim(10.0, 5.0);
  p->show_area();

  return 0;
}
```

If a class has at least one pure virtual function, that class is said to be *abstract.* Abstract classes have one important feature: There can be no objects of that class. Instead, an abstract class must be used only as a base that other classes will inherit. The reason that an abstract class cannot be used to declare an object is that one or more of its member functions have no definition. However, even if the base class is abstract, you still can use it to declare pointers or references, which are needed to support run-time polymorphism.

Early Versus Late Binding

There are two terms that are commonly used when discussing object-oriented programming languages: early binding and late binding. Relative to C++, these terms refer to events that occur at compile time and events that occur at run time, respectively.

In object-oriented terms, *early binding* means that an object is bound to its function call at compile time. That is, all information necessary to determine which function will be called is known when the program is compiled. Examples of early binding include standard function calls, overloaded function calls, and overloaded operator function calls. The principal advantage to early binding is efficiency—it is faster and often requires less memory than late binding. Its disadvantage is a lack of flexibility.

Late binding means that an object is bound to its function call only at run time, not before. Late binding is achieved in C++ by using virtual functions and derived types. The advantage to late binding is that it allows greater flexibility. It can be used to support a common interface while allowing various objects that use that interface to define their own implementations. Further, it can be used to help you create class libraries, which can be reused and extended.

Whether your program uses early or late binding depends on what your program is designed to do. (Actually, most large programs use a combination of both.) Late binding is one of C++'s most powerful additions to the C language. However, the price you pay for this power is that your program will run slightly slower. Therefore, it is best to use late binding only when it adds to the structure and manageability of your program. Keep in mind that the loss of performance is small, so when the situation calls for late binding, you should most definitely use it.

Chapter Twenty-Four

The C++ I/O Class Library

Although C++ supports all of C's I/O functions, C++ defines its own object-oriented I/O system. This chapter presents an overview of the C++ I/O class library. It also discusses how to overload the << and >> operators so that you can input or output objects of classes that you design. C++'s I/O system is very large and it isn't possible to cover every function or feature here, but this chapter introduces you to the most important and commonly used functions and features.

Why C++ Has Its Own I/O System

If you have programmed in other languages, you know that C has one of the most flexible, yet powerful I/O systems. (In fact, it may be safe to say that among the world's structured languages, C's I/O system is unparalleled.) In spite of the power of C's I/O functions, the C I/O system provides no support for user-defined objects. This is one reason why C++ defines its own I/O functions. For example, in C, if you create this structure:

```
struct my_struct {
  int count;
  char s[80];
  double balance;
} ;
```

there is no way to customize or extend C's I/O system so that it knows about and can perform I/O operations directly on a variable of type **my_struct**.

However, using C++'s approach to I/O it is possible to overload the << and >> operators so that they know about classes that you create. This includes the console I/O operations you have been using throughout this part of the book as well as file I/O. (As you will see, console and file I/O are linked in C++ as they are in C.)

Although the C and C++ I/O systems contain virtually the same operations, the fact that C++'s system can be made aware of user-defined types greatly increases its flexibility. It can also help prevent bugs. For example, in this call to **scanf( )**:

```
char str[80];
int i;

scanf("%d%s", str, &i);
```

the string and the integer are inverted in the argument list; the **%d** is matched with the string **str** and the **%s** with the integer **i**. However, while this produces peculiar results, a call such as this is not technically an error in C. (It is conceivable that in some highly unusual situation, you might want to use a call to **scanf( )** as shown.) However, it is more likely that this call to **scanf( )** is, indeed, an error. In short, when calling **scanf( )**, C has no means of providing strong type checking. In C++, however, I/O operations for all built-in types are defined relative to the << and >> operators so that there is no way for such an inversion to take place. Instead, the correct operation is automatically determined by the type of the operand. This feature can also be extended to user-defined objects. (If needed, you can still cause something like the unusual **scanf( )** call to be generated in C++ by type casting.)

C++ Streams

The C and C++ I/O systems have one important thing in common: they both operate on streams, which are discussed in Part 1 of this book. The fact that C and C++ streams are similar means that what you already know about streams is completely applicable to C++.

The C++ Predefined Streams

Like C, C++ contains several predefined streams that are opened automatically when your C++ program begins execution. They are **cin**, **cout**, **cerr**, and **clog**. As you know, **cin** is the stream associated with standard input and **cout** is the stream associated with standard output. The streams **cerr** and **clog** are used for error output. The difference between **cerr** and **clog**, which are both linked to standard output, is that **cerr** is not buffered, so any data sent to it is immediately output. Alternatively, **clog** is buffered, and output is only written when a buffer is full.

By default, the C++ standard streams are linked to the console, but they can be redirected to other devices or files by your program. Also, they can be redirected by the operating system.

The C++ Stream Classes

C++ provides support for its I/O system in the header file **iostream.h**. In this file, two class hierarchies are defined that support I/O operations. The lowest level class is called **streambuf**. This class provides the basic input and output operations. Unless you are deriving your own I/O classes, you will not use **streambuf** directly. The second class hierarchy starts with **ios**. It provides support for formatted I/O. From **ios** are derived the classes **istream**, **ostream**, and **iostream**. These classes are used to create streams capable of input, output, and input/output, respectively. As you will see in subsequent chapters, many other classes are derived from **ios** to support disk files and in-RAM formatting.

The **ios** class contains many member functions and variables that control or monitor the fundamental operation of a stream. In the course of this and the next chapter, many references will be made to its members. Just keep in mind that if you are using the C++ I/O system in a normal fashion, the members of **ios** will be available for use with any stream.

Creating Your Own Inserters and Extractors

In the preceding four chapters, member functions were created in order to output or input a class' data, often called something like **show_data( )** or **get_data( )**. While there is nothing technically wrong with this approach, C++ provides a much better way of performing I/O operations on classes by overloading the << and >> operators.

In the language of C++, the << operator is referred to as the *insertion* operator because it inserts characters into a stream. Likewise, the >> operator is called the *extraction* operator because it extracts characters from a stream. The operator functions that overload the insertion and extraction operators are generally called *inserters* and *extractors*, respectively.

The insertion and extraction operators are already overloaded (in **iostream.h**) to perform stream I/O on any of C++'s built-in types. This section explains how to define these operators relative to classes that you define.

Creating Inserters

C++ provides an easy way to create inserters for classes that you create. This simple example creates an inserter for the **three_d** class (first defined in Chapter 22):

```
class three_d {
public:
  int x, y, z; // 3-d coordinates
  three_d(int a, int b, int c) {x=a; y=b; z=c;}
} ;
```

To create an inserter function for an object of type **three_d**, you must define what an insertion operation means relative to the class **three_d**. To do this, you must overload the << operator. One way is shown here.

```
// Display X, Y, Z coordinates (three_d's inserter).
ostream &operator<<(ostream &stream, three_d obj)
{
  stream << obj.x << ", ";
  stream << obj.y << ", ";
  stream << obj.z << "\n";
  return stream; // return the stream
}
```

Many of the features in this function are common to all inserter functions. First, notice that it is declared as returning a reference to an object of type **ostream**. This is necessary to allow several insertion operations to be performed in a single statement. Next, the function has two parameters. The first is the reference to the stream that occurs on the left side of the << operator; the second parameter is the object that occurs on the right side. Inside the function, the three values contained in an object of type **three_d** are output, and **stream** is returned. Here is a short program that demonstrates the inserter:

```
#include <iostream.h>

class three_d {
public:
  int x, y, z; // 3-d coordinates
  three_d(int a, int b, int c) {x=a; y=b; z=c;}
} ;

// Display X, Y, Z coordinates - three_d inserter.
ostream &operator<<(ostream &stream, three_d obj)
{
  stream << obj.x << ", ";
  stream << obj.y << ", ";
  stream << obj.z << "\n";
  return stream;  // return the stream
}

int main()
{
  three_d a(1, 2, 3), b(3, 4, 5), c(5, 6, 7);

  cout << a << b << c;
```

```
  return 0;
}
```

If you eliminate the code that is specific to the **three_d** class, you are left with the general form of an inserter function, as shown here:

```
ostream &operator<<(ostream &stream, class_type obj)
{
  // type specific code goes here
  return stream; // return the stream
}
```

What an inserter function actually does is up to you. Just make sure that you return *stream*. Also, it is perfectly acceptable—indeed, it is common—for the *obj* parameter to be a reference, rather than an object. The advantage of passing a reference to the object being output is twofold. First, if the object is quite large, it will save time to pass only its address. Second, it prevents the object's destructor from being called when the inserter returns.

You might wonder why the **three_d** inserter function was not coded like this:

```
// Limited version - don't use.
ostream &operator<<(ostream &stream, three_d obj)
{
  cout << obj.x << ", ";
  cout << obj.y << ", ";
  cout << obj.z << "\n";
  return stream;  // return the stream
}
```

In this version, the **cout** stream is hard-coded into the function. However, remember that the **<<** operator can be applied to any stream. Therefore, you must use the stream passed to the function if it is to work correctly in all cases.

In the **three_d** inserter program, the overloaded inserter function is not a member of **three_d**. In fact, neither inserter nor extractor functions can be members of a class. This is because when an operator function is a member of a class, the left operand (implicitly passed using the **this** pointer) is an object of the class that generated the call to the operator function. There is no way to change this. However, when overloading inserters, the left argument is a stream and the right argument is an object of the class. Therefore, overloaded inserters cannot be member functions.

The fact that inserters must not be members of the class they are defined to operate on raises a serious question: How can an overloaded inserter access the private elements of a class? In the previous program, the variables **x**, **y**, and **z** were made public so that the inserter could access them. But, hiding data is an important part of object-oriented programming, and forcing all data to be public is inconsistent with the object-oriented approach. However, there is a solution: An inserter can be a friend of a class. As a friend of the class it is defined for, it has access to private data. To see an example of this, the **three_d** class and sample program are reworked here, with the overloaded inserter declared as a **friend**.

```
#include <iostream.h>

class three_d {
  int x, y, z; // 3-d coordinates - - now private
public:
  three_d(int a, int b, int c) {x=a; y=b; z=c;}
  friend ostream &operator<<(ostream &stream, three_d obj);
} ;

// Display X, Y, Z coordinates - three_d inserter.
ostream &operator<<(ostream &stream, three_d obj)
{
  stream << obj.x << ", ";
  stream << obj.y << ", ";
  stream << obj.z << "\n";
  return stream;  // return the stream
}

int main()
{
  three_d a(1, 2, 3), b(3, 4, 5), c(5, 6, 7);

  cout << a << b << c;

  return 0;
}
```

Notice that the variables **x**, **y**, and **z** are now private to **three_d**, but can still be accessed directly by the inserter. Making inserters (and extractors) friends of the classes they are defined for preserves the encapsulation principle of OOP.

Overloading Extractors

To overload an extractor, use the same general approach as when overloading an inserter. For example, this extractor inputs 3-D coordinates. Notice that it also prompts the user.

```
// Get three dimensional values - extractor.
istream &operator>>(istream &stream, three_d &obj)
{
```

```
  cout <<
    "Enter X Y Z values, separating each with a space: ";
  stream >> obj.x >> obj.y >> obj.z;
  return stream;
}
```

Extractors must return a reference to an object of type **istream**. Also, the first parameter must be a reference to an object of type **istream**. The second parameter is a reference to the variable that will be receiving input. Because it is a reference, the second argument can be modified when information is input.

The general form of an extractor is

istream &operator>>(istream &*stream*, *class_type* &*obj*)
{
 // put your extractor code here
 return *stream*;
}

Here is a program that demonstrates the extractor for objects of type **three_d**:

```
#include <iostream.h>

class three_d {
  int x, y, z; // 3-d coordinates
public:
  three_d(int a, int b, int c) {x=a; y=b; z=c;}
  friend ostream &operator<<(ostream &stream, three_d obj);
  friend istream &operator>>(istream &stream, three_d &obj);
} ;

// Display X, Y, Z coordinates - inserter.
ostream &operator<<(ostream &stream, three_d obj)
{
  stream << obj.x << ", ";
  stream << obj.y << ", ";
  stream << obj.z << "\n";
  return stream; // return the stream
}

// Get three dimensional values - extractor.
istream &operator>>(istream &stream, three_d &obj)
{
  cout <<
    "Enter X Y Z values, separating each with a space: ";
```

```
  stream >> obj.x >> obj.y >> obj.z;
  return stream;
}

int main()
{
  three_d a(1, 2, 3);

  cout << a;

  cin >> a;
  cout << a;

  return 0;
}
```

Like inserters, extractor functions cannot be members of the class they are designed to operate upon. As shown in the example, they can be friends or simply independent functions.

Except for the fact that you must return a reference to an object of type **istream**, you can do anything you like inside an extractor function. However, for the sake of structure and clarity, it is best to limit the actions of an extractor to the input operation.

Formatting I/O

As you know, using **printf( )** you can control the format of information displayed on the screen. For example, you can specify field widths and left- or right-justification. You can also accomplish the same type of formatting using C++'s approach to I/O. There are two ways to format output. The first uses member functions of the **ios** class. The second uses a special type of function called a *manipulator*. We will begin by looking at formatting using the member functions of **ios**.

Formatting Using the ios Member Functions

The following enumeration is defined in **iostream.h**:

```
// formatting flags
enum {
  skipws = 0x0001,
  left = 0x0002,
  right = 0x0004,
  internal = 0x0008,
  dec = 0x0010,
  oct = 0x0020,
```

```
  hex = 0x0040,
  showbase = 0x0080,
  showpoint = 0x0100,
  uppercase = 0x0200,
  showpos = 0x0400,
  scientific = 0x0800,
  fixed = 0x1000,
  unitbuf = 0x2000,
  stdio = 0x4000
  boolalpha = 0x8000
};
```

The values defined by this enumeration are used to set or clear flags that control some of the ways information is formatted by a stream.

When the **skipws** flag is set, leading white-space characters (spaces, tabs, and newlines) are discarded when performing input on a stream. When **skipws** is cleared, white-space characters are not discarded.

When the **left** flag is set, output is left-justified. When **right** is set, output is right-justified. When the **internal** flag is set, a numeric value is padded to fill a field by inserting spaces between any sign or base character. (You will learn how to specify a field width shortly.) By default, output is right-justified.

Also by default, numeric values are output in decimal. However, you can override this default. For example, setting the **oct** flag causes output to be displayed in octal. Setting the **hex** flag causes output to be displayed in hexadecimal. To return to decimal, set the **dec** flag.

Setting **showbase** causes the base of numeric values to be shown.

Setting **showpoint** causes a decimal point and trailing zeros to be displayed for all floating-point output—whether needed or not.

By default, when scientific notation is displayed, the 'e' is in lowercase. Also, when a hexadecimal value is displayed, the 'x' is in lowercase. When **uppercase** is set, these characters are displayed in uppercase.

Setting **showpos** causes a leading plus sign to be displayed before positive values.

If the **scientific** flag is set, floating-point numeric values are displayed using scientific notation. When **fixed** is set, floating-point values are displayed using normal notation. By default, when **fixed** is set, six decimal places are displayed. When neither flag is set, the compiler chooses an appropriate method.

When **unitbuf** is set, streams are flushed after each insertion operation.

When **stdio** is set, **stdout** and **stderr** are flushed after each output.

When **boolalpha** is set, Booleans can be input or output.

The format flags are held in a long integer. (The draft ANSI C++ standard specifies this type as **fmtflags**, but it is a **long** in Borland C++ at the time of this writing.)

To set a flag, use the **setf( )** function, whose most common form is shown here:

long setf(long *flags*);

This function returns the stream's previous format flag settings and turns on those flags specified by *flags*. All other flags are unaffected. For example, to turn on the **showbase** flag, you can use the following statement:

```
stream.setf(ios::showbase);
```

Here, **stream** can actually be any stream you wish to affect. For example, this program turns on both the **showpos** and **scientific** flags for **cout**:

```
#include <iostream.h>

int main()
{
  cout.setf(ios::showpos);
  cout.setf(ios::scientific);
  cout << 123 << " " << 123.23 << " ";

  return 0;
}
```

The output produced by this program is

```
+123 +1.232300e+02
```

You can OR together as many flags as you like in a single call. For example, you can change the program so that only one call is made to **setf( )** by ORing together **scientific** and **showpos**, as shown here:

```
cout.setf(ios::scientific | ios::showpos);
```

To turn off a flag, use the **unsetf( )** function. Its prototype is shown here:

long unsetf(long *flags*);

The function returns the previous flag settings and turns off those flags specified by *flags*.

Sometimes it is useful to know the current flag settings. You can retrieve the current flag values using this form of the **flags( )** function:

long flags( );

This function returns the current value of the flags associated with the invoking stream.

The following form of **flags( )** sets the flag values to those specified by *flags* and returns the previous flag values:

long flags(long *flags*);

To see how **flags( )** and **unsetf( )** work, examine this program. It includes a function called **showflags( )** that displays the state of the flags.

```
#include <iostream.h>

void showflags (long f);

int main ()
{
  long f;

  f = cout.flags();

  showflags(f);
  cout.setf(ios::showpos);
  cout.setf(ios::scientific);

  f = cout.flags();
  showflags(f);

  cout.unsetf(ios::scientific);

  f = cout.flags();
  showflags(f);

  return 0;
}

void showflags(long f)
{
  long i;

  for(i=0x8000; i; i = i >> 1)
    if(i & f) cout << "1 ";
    else cout << "0 ";

  cout << "\n";
}
```

When run, the program produces this output:

```
0 0 0 0 0 0 0 0 0 0 0 0 0 0 0 1
0 0 0 0 1 1 0 0 0 0 0 0 0 0 0 1
0 0 0 0 0 1 0 0 0 0 0 0 0 0 0 1
```

In addition to the formatting flags, you can also set a stream's field width, the fill character, and the number of digits displayed after a decimal point using these functions:

int width(int *len*);
char fill(char *ch*);
int precision(int *num*);

The **width( )** function returns the stream's current field width and sets the field width to *len*. By default, the field width varies depending upon the number of characters it takes to hold the data. The **fill( )** function returns the current fill character, which is a space by default, and makes the current fill character the same as *ch*. The fill character is the character used to pad output to fill a specified field width. The **precision( )** function returns the number of digits displayed after a decimal point and sets that value to *num*. Here is a program that demonstrates these three functions:

```
#include <iostream.h>

int main()
{
  cout.setf(ios::showpos);
  cout.setf(ios::scientific);
  cout << 123 << " " << 123.23 << "\n";

  cout.precision(2); // two digits after decimal point
  cout.width(10);   // in a field of ten characters
  cout << 123 << " " << 123.23 << "\n";

  cout.fill('#');   // fill using #
  cout.width(10);   // in a field of ten characters
  cout << 123 << " " << 123.23;

  return 0;
}
```

The program displays this output:

```
+123 +1.232300e+02
      +123 +1.23e+02
######+123 +1.23e+02
```

Remember, each stream maintains its own set of format flags. Changing the flag settings of one stream does not affect another stream.

Using Manipulators

The C++ I/O system includes a second way to alter the format parameters of a stream. This way uses special functions called manipulators, which can be included in an I/O expression. The standard manipulators are shown in Table 24-1. To use the manipulators that take parameters, you must include **iomanip.h** in your program.

NOTE: In addition to these standard manipulators, Borland C++ also defines a set of console-based manipulators that apply only to DOS (or a DOS session in Windows). They do such things as set the text color, clear to end of line, and set high-intensity video. You will want to explore these on your own if you are interested in writing applications for DOS or a DOS-like environment.

Manipulator	Purpose	Input/Output
dec	Input/output data in decimal	Input and output
endl	Output a newline character and flush the stream	Output
ends	Output a null	Output
flush	Flush a stream	Output
hex	Input/output data in hexadecimal	Input and output
oct	Input/output data in octal	Input and output
resetiosflags(long *f*)	Turn off the flags specified in *f*	Input and output
setbase(int *base*)	Set the number base to *base*	Output
setfill(int *ch*)	Set the fill character to *ch*	Output
setiosflags(long *f*)	Turn on the flags specified in *f*	Input and output
setprecision(int *p*)	Set the number of digits of precision	Output
setw(int *w*)	Set the field width to *w*	Output
ws	Skip leading white space	Input

Table 24-1. *The C++ I/O Manipulators*

A manipulator can be used as part of an I/O expression. Here is an example program that uses manipulators to change the format of output:

```
#include <iostream.h>
#include <iomanip.h>

int main()
{
  cout << setiosflags(ios::fixed);
  cout << setprecision(2) << 1000.243 << endl;
  cout << setw(20) << "Hello there.";

  return 0;
}
```

It produces this output.

```
1000.24
        Hello there.
```

Notice how the manipulators occur in the chain of I/O operations. Also, notice that when a manipulator does not take an argument, such as **endl** in the example, it is not followed by parentheses. This is because the address of the manipulator is passed to the overloaded **<<** operator.

This program uses **setiosflags( )** to set **cout**'s **scientific** and **showpos** flags:

```
#include <iostream.h>
#include <iomanip.h>

main()
{
  cout << setiosflags(ios::showpos);
  cout << setiosflags(ios::scientific);
  cout << 123 << " " << 123.23;

  return 0;
}
```

The following program uses **ws** to skip any leading white space when inputting a string into **s**:

```
#include <iostream.h>

int main()
{
  char s[80];
```

```
  cin >> ws >> s;
  cout << s;
}
```

Creating Your Own Manipulator Functions

You can create your own manipulator functions. There are two types of manipulator functions: those that take an argument (parameterized) and those that don't (parameterless). There are some differences between the way each is created. This section discusses how to create each type, starting with parameterless manipulators.

Creating Parameterless Manipulators

All parameterless manipulator output functions have this skeleton:

```
ostream &manip-name(ostream &stream)
{
  // your code here
  return stream;
}
```

Here, *manip-name* is the name of the manipulator. It is important to understand that even though the manipulator has as its single argument a pointer to the stream upon which it is operating, no argument is used when the manipulator is inserted in an output operation.

The following program creates a manipulator called **setup( )** that turns on left-justification, sets the field width to 10, and specifies the dollar sign as the fill character.

```
#include <iostream.h>
#include <iomanip.h>

ostream &setup(ostream &stream)
{
  stream.setf(ios::left);
  stream << setw(10) << setfill('$');
  return stream;
}

int main()
{
  cout << 10 << " " << setup << 10;
```

```
  return 0;
}
```

Custom manipulators are useful for two reasons. First, you might need to perform an I/O operation on a device for which none of the predefined manipulators apply—a plotter, for example. In this case, creating your own manipulators makes it more convenient when outputting to the device. Second, you may find that you are repeating the same sequence of operations many times. You can consolidate these operations into a single manipulator, as the preceding program illustrates.

All parameterless manipulator input functions have this general form:

istream &*manip-name*(istream &*stream*)
{
  // *your code here*
  return *stream*;
}

For example, this program creates the **prompt( )** manipulator to display a prompting message and switches numeric input to hexadecimal:

```
#include <iostream.h>
#include <iomanip.h>

istream &prompt(istream &stream)
{
  cin >> hex;
  cout << "Enter number using hex format: ";

  return stream;
}

int main()
{
  int i;

  cin >> prompt >> i;
  cout << i;

  return 0;
}
```

It is crucial that your manipulator return the stream. If this is not done, then your manipulator cannot be used in a larger I/O statement.

Creating Parameterized Manipulators

Creating a manipulator function that takes an argument is less straightforward than creating one that doesn't. One reason for this is that in Borland C++, parameterized manipulators make use of generic classes. Generic classes are created using the **template** keyword. (Templates and generic classes are discussed in Chapter 26.) If you don't understand how generic classes operate, you will not be able to fully understand the creation of a parameterized manipulator.

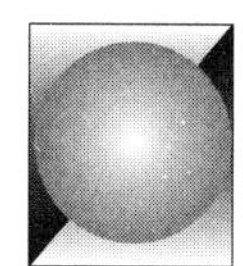

NOTE: At the time of this writing, the exact method of creating parameterized manipulators differs from compiler to compiler. The method described here works for Borland C++, but it may not work for other compilers.

To create a parameterized manipulator, you must include **iomanip.h** in your file. In this header file are defined several generic classes. The two we will use are **omanip** and **imanip**. **omanip** is used to create output manipulators that take an argument. **imanip** is used to create parameterized input manipulators. (You may want to look at the class definitions for these classes in **iomanip.h** to see how they are implemented.)

In general, whenever you need to create a manipulator that takes an argument, you will need to create two overloaded manipulator functions. In one, you need to define two parameters. The first parameter is a reference to the stream, and the second is the parameter that will be passed to the function. The second version of the manipulator defines only one parameter—the one specified when the manipulator is used in an I/O expression. This second version generates a call to the first version. For output manipulators, you will use these general forms for creating parameterized manipulators:

```
ostream &manip-name(ostream &stream, type param)
{
 // your code here
 return stream;
}

// Overload
omanip <type> manip-name(type param) {
 return omanip <type> (manip-name, param);
}
```

Here, *manip-name* is the name of the manipulator and *type* specifies the type of parameter used by the manipulator. Since **omanip** is a generic class, *type* also becomes the type of data operated upon by the specific **omanip** object returned by the manipulator.

The following program creates a parameterized output manipulator called **indent( )**, which indents the specified number of spaces.

```
#include <iostream.h>
#include <iomanip.h>

// Indent length number of spaces.
ostream &indent(ostream &stream, int length)
{
  register int i;

  for(i=0; i<length; i++) cout << " ";
  return stream;
}

omanip<int> indent(int length)
{
  return omanip<int>(indent, length);
}

int main()
{
  cout << indent(10) << "This is a test\n";
  cout << indent(20) << "of the indent manipulator.\n";
  cout << indent(5) << "It works!\n";

  return 0;
}
```

As you can see, **indent( )** is overloaded as previously described. When **indent(10)** is encountered in the output expression, the second version of **indent( )** is executed, with value 10 passed to the **length** parameter. This version then executes the first version with the value 10 again passed in **length**. This process repeats itself for each **indent( )** call.

The type of the parameter you want your manipulator to have is under your control and is determined by the type you specify for the second parameter of the manipulator function. This same type is then used when the generic class is created for the overloaded version of the manipulator. For example, the next program shows how to pass a **double** value to a manipulator function. It then outputs the value by using a dollars-and-cents format.

```
#include <iostream.h>
#include <iomanip.h>
```

```
ostream &dollars(ostream &stream, double amount)
{
  stream.setf(ios::showpoint);
  stream << "$" << setw(10) << setprecision(2)  << amount;

  return stream;
}

omanip <double> dollars(double amount) {
  return omanip<double> (dollars, amount);
}

int main()
{
  cout << dollars(123.123456);
  cout << "\n" << dollars(10.0);
  cout << "\n" << dollars(1234.23);
  cout << "\n" << dollars(0.0);

  return 0;
}
```

Input manipulators may also take a parameter. The following program creates the **getpass( )** manipulator, which is used to obtain a password. It takes an argument that specifies how many tries the user has to enter the password correctly.

```
// This program uses a manipulator to input a password.
#include <iostream.h>
#include <iomanip.h>
#include <string.h>
#include <stdlib.h>

char *password="IlikeC++";
char pw[80];

// Input a password
istream &getpass(istream &stream, int tries)
{
  do {
    cout << "Enter password: ";
    stream >> pw;
    if(!strcmp(password, pw)) return stream;
    cout << "\a"; // bell
    tries--;
```

```
  } while(tries>0);

  cout << "All tries failed!\n";
  exit(1) ; // didn't enter password

  return stream;
}

imanip<int> getpass(int tries) {
  return imanip<int>(getpass, tries);
}

int main()
{
  // give 3 tries to enter password
  cin >> getpass(3);
  cout << "Login Complete!\n";

  return 0;
}
```

Notice that the format is the same as for output manipulators, with two exceptions: The input stream **istream** must be used, and the class **imanip** is specified.

As you work with C++, you will find that custom manipulators can help streamline your I/O statements.

File I/O

You can use the C++ I/O system to perform file I/O. Although the end result is the same, C++'s approach to file I/O differs somewhat from the ANSI C I/O system discussed earlier. For this reason, you should pay special attention to this section.

In order to perform file I/O, you must include the header file **fstream.h** in your program. It defines several important classes and values.

Opening and Closing a File

In C++, a file is opened by linking it to a stream. There are three types of streams: input, output, and input/output. To open an input stream, you must declare the stream to be of class **ifstream**. To open an output stream, it must be declared as class **ofstream**. Streams that will perform both input and output operations must be declared as class **fstream**. For example, this fragment creates one input stream, one output stream, and one stream capable of both input and output:

```
ifstream in;  // input

ofstream out; // output

fstream both; // input and output
```

Once you have created a stream, one way to associate it with a file is by using the **open( )** function. This function is a member of each of the three stream classes. Its prototype is

void open(const char **filename*, int *mode*, int *access*=filebuf::openprot);

Here, *filename* is the name of the file and can include a path specifier. The value of *mode* determines how the file is opened. It must be one (or more) of these values (defined in **fstream.h**):

ios::app
ios::ate
ios::binary
ios::in
ios::nocreate
ios::noreplace
ios::out
ios::trunc

You can combine two or more of these values by ORing them together.

Including **ios::app** causes all the output to that file to be appended to the end. This value can only be used with files capable of output. Including **ios::ate** causes a seek to the end of the file to occur when the file is opened.

The **ios::in** specifies that the file is capable of input. The **ios::out** specifies that the file is capable of output. However, creating a stream using **ifstream** implies input, and creating a stream using **ofstream** implies output, so in these cases it is unnecessary to supply these values.

Including **ios::nocreate** causes the **open( )** function to fail if the file does not already exist. The **ios::noreplace** value causes the **open( )** function to fail if the file already exists and **ios::ate** or **ios::app** is not also specified.

The **ios::trunc** value causes the contents of a preexisting file by the same name to be destroyed and the file is truncated to zero length.

The **ios::binary** mode causes a file to be opened for binary operations. This means that no character translations will occur.

The value of *access* determines how the file can be accessed. In Borland C++, these values correspond to the DOS/Windows file attribute codes. They are

Attribute	Meaning
0	Normal file, open access
1	Read-only file
2	Hidden file
4	System file
8	Archive bit set

You can OR two or more of these together. Normally, you will simply let the file default to **filebuf::openprot**, which is a normal file.

The following fragment opens a normal output file:

```
ofstream out;
out.open("test", ios::out, 0);
```

However, you will seldom (if ever) see **open( )** called as shown because both the *mode* and *access* parameters have default values: For **ifstream**, *mode* defaults to **ios::in**; and for **ofstream**, it defaults to **ios::out**. The *access* parameter defaults to a normal file, as just mentioned. Therefore, the preceding statement will usually look like this:

```
out.open("test");  // defaults to output and normal file
```

To open a stream for both input and output, you must specify both the **ios::in** and the **ios::out** *mode* values, as shown in this example:

```
fstream mystream;
mystream.open("test", ios::in | ios::out);
```

If **open( )** fails, the stream will be null.

Although opening a file using the **open( )** function is perfectly acceptable, most of the time you will not do so because the **ifstream**, **ofstream**, and **fstream** classes include constructor functions that automatically open the file. The constructor functions have the same parameters and defaults as the **open( )** function. Therefore, the most common way to open a file is shown here:

```
ifstream  mystream("myfile"); // open file for input
```

If for some reason the file cannot be opened, the value of the associated stream variable is null. You can use the following code to confirm that the file has actually been opened:

```
ifstream  mystream("myfile"); // open file for input
if(!mystream) {
  cout << "Cannot open file.\n";
  //  process error
}
```

To close a file, use the member function **close( )**. For example, to close the file linked to a stream called **mystream**, use this statement:

```
mystream.close();
```

The **close( )** function takes no parameters and returns no value.

Reading and Writing Text Files

To read from or write to a text file, you simply use the << and >> operators with the stream you opened. For example, the following program writes an integer, a floating-point value, and a string to a file called TEST:

```
#include <iostream.h>
#include <fstream.h>

int main()
{
  ofstream out("test");
  if(!out) {
    cout << "Cannot open file.\n";
    return 1;
    }

  out << 10 << " " << 123.23 << "\n";
  out << "This is a short text file.\n";

  out.close();

  return 0;
}
```

The following program reads an integer, a floating-point number, a character, and a string from the file created by the preceding program:

```
#include <iostream.h>
#include <fstream.h>

int main()
```

```
{
  char ch;
  int i;
  float f;
  char str[80];

  ifstream in("test");
  if(!in) {
    cout << "Cannot open file.\n";
    return 1;
  }

  in >> i;
  in >> f;
  in >> ch;
  in >> str;

  cout << i << " " << f << " " << ch << "\n";
  cout << str;

  in.close();
  return 0;
}
```

When reading text files using the **>>** operator, keep in mind that certain character translations occur. For example, white-space characters are omitted. If you want to prevent any character translations, you must use C++'s binary I/O functions, discussed in the next section.

Binary I/O

There are several ways to write and read binary data to or from a file. We will look at two in this chapter. First, you can write a byte using the member function **put( )** and read a byte using the member function **get( )**. The **get( )** function has many forms, but the most commonly used version is shown here along with **put( )**:

istream &get(char &*ch*);
ostream &put(char *ch*);

The **get( )** function reads a single character from the associated stream and puts that value in *ch*. It returns a reference to the stream. The **put( )** function writes *ch* to the stream and returns a reference to the stream.

*NOTE: Remember, when working with binary files, be sure to open them using the **ios::binary** mode specifier.*

This program displays the contents of any file on the screen. It uses the **get( )** function.

```
#include <iostream.h>
#include <fstream.h>

int main(int argc, char *argv[])
{
  char ch;

  if(argc!=2) {
    cout << "Usage: PR <filename>\n";
    return 1;
  }

  ifstream in(argv[1], ios::in | ios::binary);
  if(!in) {
    cout << "Cannot open file.\n";
    return 1;
  }

  while(in) { // in will be null when eof is reached
    in.get(ch);
    cout << ch;
  }

  in.close();

  return 0;
}
```

When **in** reaches the end of the file, it will become null, causing the **while** loop to stop.

There is a more compact way to code the loop that reads and displays a file, as shown here:

```
while(in.get(ch))
  cout << ch;
```

This works because **get( )** returns the stream **in** which will be null when the end of the file is encountered.

This program uses **put( )** to write a string that includes non-ASCII characters to a file:

```
#include <iostream.h>
#include <fstream.h>

int main()
{
  char *p = "hello there\n\r\xfe\xff";

  ofstream out("test", ios::out | ios::binary);
  if(!out) {
    cout << "Cannot open file.\n";
    return 1;
   }

  while(*p) out.put(*p++);

  out.close();

  return 0;
}
```

The second way to read and write binary data uses C++'s **read( )** and **write( )** member functions. The prototypes for two of their most commonly used forms are

istream &read(unsigned char **buf*, int *num*);
ostream &write(const unsigned char **buf*, int *num*);

The **read( )** function reads *num* bytes from the associated stream and puts them in the buffer pointed to by *buf*. The **write( )** function writes *num* bytes to the associated stream from the buffer pointed to by *buf*.

The following program writes and then reads an array of integers:

```
#include <iostream.h>
#include <fstream.h>

int main()
{
  int n[5] = {1, 2, 3, 4, 5};
  register int i;
```

```
  ofstream out("test", ios::out | ios::binary);
  if(!out) {
    cout << "Cannot open file.\n";
    return 1;
   }

  out.write((unsigned char *) &n, sizeof n);

  out.close();

  for(i=0; i<5; i++) // clear array
    n[i] = 0;

  ifstream in("test", ios::in | ios::binary);
  in.read((unsigned char *) &n, sizeof n);

  for(i=0; i<5; i++) // show values read from file
    cout << n[i] << " ";

  in.close();

  return 0;
}
```

Note that the type casts inside the calls to **read( )** and **write( )** are necessary when operating on a buffer that is not defined as a character array.

If the end of the file is reached before the specified number of characters has been read, **read( )** simply stops and the buffer contains as many characters as were available. You can find out how many characters have been read using another member function called **gcount( )**, which has this prototype:

    int gcount( );

It returns the number of characters read by the last binary input operation.

Detecting EOF

You can detect when the end of the file is reached using the member function **eof( )**, which has the prototype

    int eof( );

It returns nonzero when the end of the file has been reached; otherwise, it returns 0.

Random Access

In C++'s I/O system, you perform random access using the **seekg( )** and **seekp( )** functions. Their most common forms are

istream &seekg(streamoff *offset*, seek_dir *origin*);
ostream &seekp(streamoff *offset*, seek_dir *origin*);

Here, **streamoff** is a type defined in **iostream.h** that is capable of containing the largest valid value that *offset* can have. (**streamoff** is currently **typdef**ed as a **long**.)

The C++ I/O system manages two pointers associated with each file. One is the *get pointer*, which specifies where in the file the next input operation will occur. The other is the *put pointer*, which specifies where in the file the next output operation will occur. Each time an input or an output operation takes place, the appropriate pointer is automatically advanced. However, using the **seekg( )** and **seekp( )** functions, it is possible to access the file in a nonsequential fashion.

The **seekg( )** function moves the associated file's current get pointer *offset* number of bytes from the specified *origin*, which must be one of these three values:

Value	Meaning
ios::beg	Beginning of file
ios::cur	Current location
ios::end	End of file

The **seekp( )** function moves the associated file's current put pointer *offset* number of bytes from the specified *origin*, which must be one of the same three values.

This program demonstrates the **seekp( )** function. It allows you to specify a file name on the command line, followed by the specific byte in the file you want to change. It then writes an "X" at the specified location. Notice that the file must be opened for read/write operations.

```
#include <iostream.h>
#include <fstream.h>
#include <stdlib.h>

int main(int argc, char *argv[])
{
  if(argc!=3) {
    cout << "Usage: CHANGE <filename> <byte>\n";
    return 1;
```

```
  }

  fstream out(argv[1], ios::in | ios::out | ios::binary);
  if(!out) {
    cout << "Cannot open file.\n";
    return 1;
  }

  out.seekp(atoi(argv[2]), ios::beg);

  out.put('X');
  out.close();

  return 0;
}
```

The next program uses **seekg( )** to display the contents of a file beginning with the location you specify on the command line:

```
#include <iostream.h>
#include <fstream.h>
#include <stdlib.h>

int main(int argc, char *argv[])
{
  char ch;

  if(argc!=3) {
    cout << "Usage: NAME <filename> <starting location>\n";
    return 1;
  }

  ifstream in(argv[1], ios::in | ios::binary);
  if(!in) {
    cout << "Cannot open file.\n";
    return 1;
  }

  in.seekg(atoi(argv[2]), ios::beg);

  while(in.get(ch))
    cout << ch;

  in.close();
```

```
  return 0;
}
```

You can determine the current position of each file pointer using these functions:

streampos tellg( );
streampos tellp( );

Here, **streampos** is a type defined in **iostream.h** that is capable of holding the largest value that either function can return. (It is currently **typdef**ed as a **long**.)

As you have seen, C++'s I/O system is both powerful and flexible. Although this chapter discusses some of the most commonly used functions, C++ includes several others. For example, you will want to explore the **getline( )** function (defined by **istream**) and the various overloaded forms of the I/O functions described here.

Chapter Twenty-Five

Array-based I/O

In addition to console and file I/O, C++'s class-based I/O system allows array-based I/O. *Array-based I/O* uses RAM as either the input device or the output device, or both. Array-based I/O is performed through normal C++ streams. In fact, all the information presented in the preceding chapter is applicable to array-based I/O. The only thing that makes array-based I/O unique is that the device linked to the stream is memory.

In some C++ literature, array-based I/O is referred to as *in-RAM I/O.* Also, because the streams are, like all C++ streams, capable of handling formatted information, sometimes array-based I/O is called *in-RAM formatting.* (Sometimes the archaic term *incore formatting* is also used. But since core memory is largely a thing of the past, this book uses the terms "in-RAM" and "array-based.")

C++'s array-based I/O is similar in effect to C's **sprintf( )** and **sscanf( )** functions. Both approaches use memory as an input or output device.

To use array-based I/O in your programs, you must include **strstrea.h**.

The Array-based Classes

The array-based I/O classes are **istrstream**, **ostrstream**, and **strstream**. You use these classes to create input, output, and input/output streams, respectively. All of these classes have **strstreambase** as one of their base classes. This class defines several low-level details that are used by the derived classes. In addition to **strstreambase**, the **istrstream** class also has **istream** as a base. The **ostrstream** class is also derived from **ostream** and the **strstream** class also contains the **iostream** class. Therefore, all array-based classes also have access to the same member functions that the "normal" I/O classes do.

Creating an Array-based Output Stream

To link an output stream to an array, use this **ostrstream** constructor:

ostrstream *ostr*(char **buf*, int *size*, int *mode*=ios::out);

Here, *buf* is a pointer to the array that will be used to collect characters written to the stream *ostr*. The size of the array is passed in the *size* parameter. By default, the stream is opened for normal output, but you can OR various other options (discussed in Chapter 24) with it to create the mode you need. (For example, you might include **ios::app** to cause output to be written at the end of any information already contained in the array.) For most purposes, *mode* will be allowed to default.

Once you have opened an array-based output stream, all output to that stream is put into the array. However, no output will be written outside the bounds of the array. An attempt to do so results in an error.

Here is a simple program that demonstrates an array-based output stream:

```
#include <strstrea.h>
#include <iostream.h>

int main()
{
  char str[80];
  int a = 10;

  ostrstream outs(str, sizeof(str));

  outs << "Hello there ";
  outs << a+44 << hex << " ";
  outs.setf(ios::showbase);
  outs << 100 << ends;

  cout << str;  // display string on console

  return 0;
}
```

This program displays "Hello there 54 0x64". Keep in mind that **outs** is a stream like any other stream and that it has the same capabilities as any of the other types of streams you saw earlier. The only difference is that the device it is linked to is memory. Because **outs** is a stream, manipulators like **hex** and **ends** are perfectly valid. Also, **ostream** member functions, such as **setf( )**, are available for use.

If you want the output array to be null-terminated, you must explicitly write a null. In this program, the **ends** manipulator was used to null-terminate the string, but you could also have used '\0'.

If you're not quite sure what is really happening in the preceding program, compare it to the following C program. This program is functionally equivalent to the C++ version. However, it uses **sprintf( )** to construct an output array.

```
#include <stdio.h>

int main()
{
  char str[80];
  int a = 10;

  sprintf(str, "Hello there %d %#x", a+44, 100);

  printf(str);

  return 0;
}
```

You can determine how many characters are in the output array by calling the **pcount( )** member function. It has this prototype:

int pcount( );

The number returned by **pcount( )** also includes the null terminator, if it exists.

The next program illustrates **pcount( )**. It reports that 17 characters are in **outs**—16 characters plus the null terminator.

```
#include <strstrea.h>
#include <iostream.h>

int main()
{
  char str[80];

  ostrstream outs(str, sizeof(str));

  outs << "Hello ";
  outs << 34 << "  " << 1234.23;
  outs << ends;  // null terminate
```

```
  cout << outs.pcount(); // display how many chars in outs

  cout << " " << str;

  return 0;
}
```

Using an Array as Input

To link an input stream to an array, use this **istrstream** constructor:

istrstream *istr* (*char *buf*);

Here, *buf* is a pointer to the array that will be used as a source of characters each time input is performed on the stream *istr.* The contents of the array pointed to by *buf* must be null-terminated. However, the null terminator is never read from the array.

Here is an example that uses a string as input:

```
#include <iostream.h>
#include <strstrea.h>

int main()
{
  char s[] = "One 2 3.00";

  istrstream ins(s);

  int i;
  char str[80];
  float f;

  // reading: one 2
  ins >> str;
  ins >> i;
  cout << str << " " << i << endl;

  // reading 3.00
  ins >> f;
  cout << f << '\n' ;

  return 0;
}
```

If you wish only part of a string to be used for input, use this form of the **istrstream** constructor:

istrstream *istr*(char **buf*, int *size*);

Here, only the first *size* elements of the array pointed to by *buf* will be used. This string need not be null-terminated since it is the value of *size* that determines the size of the string.

Streams linked to memory behave just like those linked to other devices. For example, the following program illustrates the way that contents of any null-terminated text array may be read. When the end of the array (same as end-of-file) is reached, **ins** will be null.

```
/* This program shows how to read the contents of any
   null-terminated array. */
#include <iostream.h>
#include <strstrea.h>

int main()
{
  char s[] = "C++ arrays are fun! 123.23 0x23\n";

  istrstream ins(s);

  char ch;

  // This will read and display the contents of an array.
  ins.unsetf(ios::skipws); // don't skip spaces
  while (ins) {  // null when end of array is reached
    ins >> ch;
    cout << ch;
  }

  return 0;
}
```

Using ios Member Functions on Array-based Streams

Array-based streams can also be accessed with the standard **ios** member functions, such as **get( )** and **put( )**. You can also use the **eof( )** function to determine when the end of the array has been reached. For example, this program shows how to read the contents of any array by using **get( )**:

```
#include <iostream.h>
#include <strstrea.h>

int main()
{
  char s[] = "This is a test array\23\22\21\a\t\n";

  istrstream ins(s);

  char ch;

  // This will read the contents of any type of array.
  while (!ins.eof()) {
    ins.get(ch);
    cout << ch;
  }

  return 0;
}
```

In this example, the values formed by " \23\22\21" are the nontext control characters CTRL-W, CTRL-V, and CTRL-U. The " \a" is the bell character and the " \t" is a tab. However, any type of data could have been read.

If you need to read buffers of data, you can use the **read( )** member function. To write buffers of data, use the **write( )** function.

Input/Output Array-based Streams

To create an array-based stream that can perform both input and output, use this **strstream** constructor function:

strstream *iostr(char *buf*, int *size*, int *mode)*;

Here, *buf* points to the string that will be used for I/O operations. The value of *size* specifies the size of the array. The value of *mode* determines how the stream operates. For normal input/output operations, *mode* will be **ios::in | ios::out**. For input, the array must be null-terminated.

Here is a program that uses an array to perform both input and output:

```
// Perform both input and output.
#include <iostream.h>
#include <strstrea.h>

int main()
{
  char iostr[80];

  strstream ios(iostr, sizeof(iostr), ios::in | ios::out);

  int a, b;
  char str[80];

  ios << "1734 534abcdefghijklmnopqrstuvwxyz";
  ios >> a >> b >> str;
  cout << a << " " << b << " " << str << endl;

}
```

This program first writes two integers and the alphabet to the array and then reads them back.

Random Access Within Arrays

It is important to remember that all normal I/O operations apply to array-based I/O. This also includes random access using **seekg( )** and **seekp( )**. For example, the next program seeks to the eighth character inside **iostr** and displays it. (It outputs **h**.)

```
#include <iostream.h>
#include <strstrea.h>

int main()
{
  char iostr[80];

  strstream ios(iostr, sizeof(iostr), ios::in | ios::out);

  char ch;

  ios << "abcdefghijklmnopqrstuvwxyz";
  ios.seekg(7, ios::beg);
```

```
  ios >> ch;
  cout << "Character at 7: " << ch;

  return 0;
}
```

You can seek anywhere *inside* the I/O array, but you are not allowed to seek past an array boundary.

You can also apply functions like **tellg( )** and **tellp( )** to array-based streams.

Using Dynamic Arrays

In the first part of this chapter, when you linked a stream to an output array, the array and its size were passed to the **ostrstream** constructor. This approach is fine as long as you know the maximum number of characters you will be outputting to that array. However, what if you don't know how large the output array needs to be? The solution to this problem is to use a second form of the **ostrstream** constructor, shown here:

ostrstream( );

When this constructor is used, **ostrstream** creates and maintains a dynamically allocated array. This array is allowed to grow in length to accommodate the output it must store.

To access the dynamically allocated array requires the use of a second function called **str( )**. Its prototype is shown here.

char *str( );

This function "freezes" the array and returns a pointer to it. Once a dynamic array is frozen, it may not be used for output again. Therefore, you will not want to freeze the array until you are through outputting characters to it.

Here is a program that uses a dynamic output array:

```
#include <strstrea.h>

#include <iostream.h>

int main()
{
  char *p;

  ostrstream outs;  // dynamically allocate array
```

```
  outs << "I like C++ ";
  outs << -10 << hex << " ";
  outs.setf(ios::showbase);
  outs << 100 << ends;

  p = outs.str(); /* Freeze dynamic buffer and return
                     pointer to it. */

  cout << p;

  delete p;  // Free dynamic buffer created by ostrstream().
  return 0;
}
```

As this program illustrates, once a dynamic array has been frozen, it is your responsibility to release its memory back to the system when you are through with it. However, if you never freeze the array, the memory is automatically freed when the stream is destroyed.

You can also use dynamic I/O arrays with the **strstream** class, which may perform both input and output on an array.

Manipulators and Array-based I/O

Since array-based streams are the same as any other stream, manipulators that you create for I/O in general can be used with array-based I/O with no changes whatsoever. For example, in Chapter 24, the output manipulator **setup( )** was created, which turned on left-justification and set the field width to 10 and the fill character to the dollar sign. This manipulator can be used unchanged when using an array as output, as shown here:

```
/* This program uses a custom manipulator with
   array-based I/O. */

#include <strstrea.h>
#include <iostream.h>
#include <iomanip.h>

// Custom output manipulator.
ostream &setup(ostream &stream)
{
  stream.setf(ios::left);
  stream << setw(10) << setfill('$');
  return stream;
}
```

```
int main()
{
  char str[80];

  ostrstream outs(str, sizeof(str));

  outs << setup << 99 << ends;

  cout << str  << '\n';

  return 0;
}
```

Custom Extractors and Inserters

As has been said many times in this chapter, since array-based streams are just that—streams—you can create your own extractor and inserter functions in just the same way you do for other types of streams. For example, the following program creates a class called **plot** that maintains the X,Y coordinates of a point in two-dimensional space. The overloaded inserter for this class displays a small coordinate plane and plots the location of the point. For simplicity, the range of the X,Y coordinates is restricted to 0 through 5.

```
#include <iostream.h>
#include <strstrea.h>

const int size=5;

class plot {
  int x, y;
public:
  plot(int i, int j) {
    // For simplicity, restrict x and y to 0 through size.
    if(i>size) i = size;  if (i<0) i=0;
    if(j>size) j = size;  if (j<0) j=0;
    x=i; y=j;
  }
```

```
  // An inserter for plot.
  friend ostream &operator<<(ostream &stream, plot o);
};

ostream &operator<<(ostream &stream, plot o)
{
  register int i, j;

  for(j=size; j>=0; j--) {
    stream << j;
    if(j == o.y) {
      for(i=0; i<o.x; i++) stream << "  ";
      stream << '*';
    }
    stream << "\n";
  }

  for(i=0; i<=size; i++) stream << " " << i;
  stream << "\n";

  return stream;
}

int main()
{
  plot a(2, 3), b(1, 1);

  // output first using cout
  cout << "Output using cout:\n";
  cout << a << "\n" << b << "\n\n";

  char str[200];  // now use RAM-based I/O
  ostrstream outs(str, sizeof(str));

  // now output using outs and in-RAM formatting
  outs << a << b << ends;

  cout << "Output using in-RAM formatting:\n";
  cout << str;
}
```

This program produces the following output:

```
Output using cout:
5
4
3    *
2
1
0
 0 1 2 3 4 5

5
4
3
2
1  *
0
 0 1 2 3 4 5


Output using in-RAM formatting:
5
4
3    *
2
1
0
 0 1 2 3 4 5
5
4
3
2
1  *
0
 0 1 2 3 4 5
```

Uses for Array-based Formatting

In C, the in-RAM I/O functions **sprintf( )** and **sscanf( )** are particularly useful for preparing output or reading input from nonstandard devices. However, because of C++'s ability to overload inserters and extractors relative to a class and to create custom manipulators, you can handle many exotic devices easily by using these features, making the need for in-RAM formatting less important. Nevertheless, there are still many uses for array-based I/O.

One common use of array-based formatting is to construct a string that will be used as input by either a standard library or a third-party function. For example, you may need to construct a string that will be parsed by the **strtok( )** standard library function. (The **strtok( )** function *tokenizes*—that is, decomposes to its elements—a string.) Another place where you can use array-based I/O is in text editors that perform complex formatting operations. Often, it is easier to use C++'s array-based formatted I/O to construct a complex string than it is to do so by "manual" means.

Chapter Twenty-Six

Templates, Exceptions, and RTTI

This chapter discusses several of C++'s most advanced features: templates, exceptions, run-time type ID (RTTI), and the casting operators.

Using a template, it is possible to create *generic functions* and *generic classes*. In a generic function or class, the type of data upon which the function or class operates is specified as a parameter. Thus, you can use one function or class with several different types of data without having to explicitly recode specific versions for different data types.

Exception handling allows you to handle run-time errors in a structured and controlled manner. The principal advantage of exception handling is that it automates much of the error-handling code that previously had to be implemented "by hand" in any large program.

Run-time type identification (RTTI) lets you determine the type of an object at run time. You may also test if an object is of a particular type or if two objects are of the same type.

Also discussed in this chapter are four new casting operators: **const_cast**, **dynamic_cast**, **reinterpret_cast**, and **static_cast**. These casting operators give you fine-grained control over type casting.

Generic Functions

A generic function defines a general set of operations that will be applied to various types of data. Using this mechanism, the same general procedure can be applied to a wide range of data. As you probably know, many algorithms are logically the same no matter what type of data is being operated upon. For example, the Quicksort sorting algorithm is the same whether it is applied to an array of integers or an array of **floats**. It is just that the type of the data being sorted is different. By creating a generic function, you can define, independent of any data, the nature of the algorithm. Once this is done, the compiler automatically generates the correct code for the type of data that is actually used when you execute the function. In essence, when you create a generic function you are creating a function that can automatically overload itself.

A generic function is created with the keyword **template**. The normal meaning of the word "template" accurately reflects its use in C++. It is used to create a template (or framework) that describes what a function will do, leaving it to the compiler to fill in the details as needed. The general form of a **template** function definition is shown here:

```
template <class Ttype> ret-type func-name(parameter list)
{
  // body of function
}
```

Here, *Ttype* is a placeholder name for a data type used by the function. This name may be used within the function definition. However, it is only a placeholder that the compiler will automatically replace with an actual data type when it creates a specific version of the function.

Here is a short example that creates a generic function that swaps the values of the two variables with which it is called. Because the general process of exchanging two values is independent of the type of the variables, it is a good choice to be made into a generic function.

```
// Function template example.
#include <iostream.h>

// This is a function template.
template <class X> void swap(X &a, X &b)
{
  X temp;

  temp = a;
  a = b;
  b = temp;
}

int main()
{
  int i=10, j=20;
  float x=10.1, y=23.3;
```

```
  char a='x', b='z';

  cout << "Original i, j: " << i << ' ' << j << endl;
  cout << "Original x, y: " << x << ' ' << y << endl;
  cout << "Original a, b: " << a << ' ' << b << endl;

  swap(i, j); // swap integers
  swap(x, y); // swap floats
  swap(a, b); // swap chars

  cout << "Swapped i, j: " << i << ' ' << j << endl;
  cout << "Swapped x, y: " << x << ' ' << y << endl;
  cout << "Swapped a, b: " << a << ' ' << b << endl;

  return 0;
}
```

Let's look closely at this program. The line

```
template <class X> void swap(X &a, X &b)
```

tells the compiler two things: that a template is being created and that a generic definition is beginning. Here, **X** is a generic type that is used as a placeholder. After the **template** portion, the function **swap( )** is declared, using **X** as the data type of the values that will be swapped. In **main( )**, the **swap( )** function is called using three different types of data: integers, **float**s, and **char**s. Because **swap( )** is a generic function, the compiler automatically creates three versions of **swap( )**—one that will exchange integer values, one that will exchange floating-point values, and one that will swap characters.

A Function with Two Generic Types

You may define more than one generic data type in the **template** statement using a comma-separated list. For example, this program creates a generic function that has two generic types:

```
#include <iostream.h>

template <class type1, class type2>
void myfunc(type1 x, type2 y)
{
  cout << x << ' ' << y << endl;
}

int main()
{
```

```
  myfunc(10, "hi");

  myfunc(0.23, 10L);

  return 0;
}
```

In this example, the placeholder types **type1** and **type2** are replaced by the compiler with the data types **int** and **char *** and **double** and **long**, respectively, when the compiler generates the specific instances of **myfunc( )** within **main( )**. Remember: When you create a generic function, you are, in essence, allowing the compiler to generate as many different versions of that function as necessary to handle the various ways that your program calls that function.

Explicitly Overloading a Generic Function

Even though a template function overloads itself as needed, you can explicitly overload one, too. If you overload a generic function, then that overloaded function overrides (or "hides") the generic function relative to that specific version. For example, consider this version of **swap( )**:

```
// Overriding a template function.
#include <iostream.h>

template <class X> void swap(X &a, X &b)
{
  X temp;

  temp = a;
  a = b;
  b = temp;
}

// This overrides the generic version of swap().
void swap(int &a, int &b)
{
  int temp;

  temp = a;
  a = b;
  b = temp;
  cout << "Inside overloaded swap(int &, int &).\n";
}

int main()
```

```
{
  int i=10, j=20;
  float x=10.1, y=23.3;
  char a='x', b='z';

  cout << "Original i, j: " << i << ' ' << j << endl;
  cout << "Original x, y: " << x << ' ' << y << endl;
  cout << "Original a, b: " << a << ' ' << b << endl;

  swap(i, j); // this calls the explicitly overloaded swap()
  swap(x, y); // swap floats
  swap(a, b); // swap chars

  cout << "Swapped i, j: " << i << ' ' << j << endl;
  cout << "Swapped x, y: " << x << ' ' << y << endl;
  cout << "Swapped a, b: " << a << ' ' << b << endl;

  return 0;
}
```

As the comments indicate, when **swap(i, j)** is called, it invokes the explicitly overloaded version of **swap( )** defined in the program. Thus, the compiler does not generate this version of the generic **swap( )** function because the generic function is overridden by the explicit overloading.

Manual overloading of a template, as shown in this example, allows you to specially tailor a version of a generic function to accommodate a special situation. However, in general, if you need to have different versions of a function for different data types, you should use overloaded functions rather than templates.

Generic Function Restrictions

Generic functions are similar to overloaded functions except that they are more restrictive. When functions are overloaded, you may have different actions performed within the body of each function. But a generic function must perform the same general action for all versions—only the type of data may differ. For example, in the following program, the overloaded functions could *not* be replaced by a generic function because they do not do the same thing:

```
#include <iostream.h>
#include <math.h>

void myfunc(int i)
{
  cout << "value is: " << i << "\n";
}
```

```
void myfunc(double d)
{
  double intpart;
  double fracpart;

  fracpart = modf(d, &intpart);
  cout << "Fractional part: " << fracpart;
  cout << "\n";
  cout << "Integer part: " << intpart;
}

int main()
{
  myfunc(1);
  myfunc(12.2);

  return 0;
}
```

Here are some other restrictions to template functions. A virtual function cannot be a template function. A template function must use C++ linkage.

Generic Classes

In addition to generic functions, you can also define a generic class. When you do this, you create a class that defines all algorithms used by that class, but the actual type of data being manipulated will be specified as a parameter when objects of that class are created.

Generic classes are useful when a class contains generalizable logic. For example, the same algorithm that maintains a queue of integers will also work for a queue of characters. Also, the same mechanism that maintains a linked list of mailing addresses will also maintain a linked list of auto part information. By using a generic class, you can create a class that will maintain a queue, a linked list, and so on for any type of data. The compiler will automatically generate the correct type of object based upon the type you specify when the object is created.

The general form of a generic class declaration is shown here:

template <class *Ttype*> class *class-name* {
.
.
.
}

Here, *Ttype* is the placeholder type name that will be specified when a class is instantiated. If necessary, you may define more than one generic data type using a comma-separated list.

Once you have created a generic class, you create a specific instance of that class using the following general form:

class-name <type> ob;

Here, *type* is the type name of the data that the class will be operating upon.

Member functions of a generic class are, themselves, automatically generic. They need not be explicitly specified as such using **template**.

In the following program, a generic **stack** class is created that implements a standard last-in, first-out stack. Thus, it can be used to provide a stack for any type of object. In the example shown here, a character stack, an integer stack, and a floating-point stack are created:

```
// Demonstrate a generic stack class.
#include <iostream.h>

const int SIZE = 100;

// This creates the generic class stack.
template <class SType> class stack {
  SType stck[SIZE];
  int tos;
public:
  stack();
  ~stack();
  void push(SType i);
  SType pop();
};

// stack's constructor function.
template <class SType> stack<SType>::stack()
{
  tos = 0;
  cout << "Stack Initialized\n";
}

/* stack's destructor function.
   This function is not required.  It is included
   for illustration only. */
template <class SType> stack<SType>::~stack()
```

```
{
  cout << "Stack Destroyed\n";
}

// Push an object onto the stack.
template <class SType> void stack<SType>::push(SType i)
{
  if(tos==SIZE) {
    cout << "Stack is full.\n";
    return;
  }
  stck[tos] = i;
  tos++;
}

// Pop an object off the stack.
template <class SType> SType stack<SType>::pop()
{
  if(tos==0) {
    cout << "Stack underflow.\n";
    return 0;
  }
  tos--;
  return stck[tos];
}

int main()
{
  stack<int> a; // create integer stack
  stack<double> b; // create a double stack
  stack<char> c; // create a character stack

  int i;

  // use the integer and double stacks
  a.push(1);
  b.push(99.3);
  a.push(2);
  b.push(-12.23);

  cout << a.pop() << " ";
  cout << a.pop() << " ";
  cout << b.pop() << " ";
```

```
  cout << b.pop() << "\n";

  // demonstrate the character stack
  for(i=0; i<10; i++) c.push((char) 'A'+i);
  for(i=0; i<10; i++) cout << c.pop();
  cout << "\n";

  return 0;
}
```

As you can see, the declaration of a generic class is similar to that of a generic function. The generic data type is used in the class declaration and in its member functions. It is not until an object of the stack is declared that the actual data type is determined. When a specific instance of **stack** is declared, the compiler automatically generates all the necessary functions and data to handle the actual data. In this example, three different types of stacks are declared (one for integers, one for **double**s, and one for characters). Pay special attention to these declarations:

```
stack<int> a; // create integer stack
stack<double> b; // create a double stack
stack<char> c; // create a character stack
```

Notice how the desired data type is passed inside the angle brackets. By changing the type of data specified when **stack** objects are created, you can change the type of data stored in that stack. For example, you could create another stack that stores character pointers by using this declaration:

```
stack<char *> chrptrstck;
```

You can also create stacks to store data types that you create. For example, you might store address information using this structure:

```
struct addr {
  char name[40];
  char street[40];
  char city[30];
  char state[3];
  char zip[12];
}
```

Then, to use **stack** to generate a stack that will store objects of type **addr**, use a declaration like this:

```
stack<addr> obj;
```

An Example with Two Generic Data Types

A template class can have more than one generic data type. Simply declare all the data types required by the class in a comma-separated list within the **template** specification. For example, the following short example creates a class that uses two generic data types:

```
/* This example uses two generic data types in a
   class definition.
*/
#include <iostream.h>

template <class Type1, class Type2> class myclass
{
  Type1 i;
  Type2 j;
public:
  myclass(Type1 a, Type2 b) { i = a; j = b; }
  void show() { cout << i << ' ' << j << '\n'; }
};

int main()
{
  myclass<int, double> ob1(10, 0.23);
  myclass<char, char *> ob2('X', "This is a test");

  ob1.show(); // show int, double
  ob2.show(); // show char, char *

  return 0;
}
```

This program produces the following output:

```
10 0.23
X This is a test
```

The program declares two types of objects. **ob1** uses an integer and **double** data. **ob2** uses a character and a character pointer. For both cases, the compiler automatically generates the appropriate data and functions to accommodate the way the objects are created.

Template functions and classes give you unprecedented power to create reusable code. When you have a generalizable routine, consider making it into a template. Once you have fully debugged and tested it, you can employ it over and over again in different situations without having to incur additional development overhead.

However, resist the temptation to make everything into a generic function or class. Using templates where they do not apply renders your code both confusing and misleading.

Exception Handling

Exception handling allows you to manage run-time errors in an orderly fashion. Using C++ exception handling, your program can automatically invoke an error-handling routine when an error occurs. The principal advantage of exception handling is that it automates much of the error-handling code that previously had to be coded "by hand" in any large program.

Exception-Handling Fundamentals

C++ exception handling is built upon three keywords: **try**, **catch**, and **throw**. In the most general terms, program statements that you want to monitor for exceptions are contained in a **try** block. If an exception (i.e., an error) occurs within the **try** block, it is thrown (using **throw**). The exception is caught, using **catch**, and processed. The following discussion elaborates upon this general description.

As stated, any statement that throws an exception must have been executed from within a **try** block. (Functions called from within a **try** block may also throw an exception.) Any exception must be caught by a **catch** statement that immediately follows the **try** statement that throws the exception. The general form of **try** and **catch** are shown here:

```
try {
  // try block
}
catch (type1 arg) {
  // catch block
}
catch (type2 arg) {
  // catch block
}
catch (type3 arg) {
  // catch block
}
.
.
.
catch (typeN arg) {
  // catch block
}
```

The **try** block can be as short as a few statements within one function or as all-encompassing as enclosing the **main( )** function code within a **try** block (which effectively causes the entire program to be monitored).

When an exception is thrown, it is caught by its corresponding **catch** statement, which processes the exception. There can be more than one **catch** statement associated with a **try**. Which **catch** statement is used is determined by the type of the exception. That is, if the data type specified by a **catch** matches that of the exception, then that **catch** statement is executed (and all others are bypassed). When an exception is caught, *arg* will receive its value. Any type of data may be caught, including classes that you create. If no exception is thrown (that is, no error occurs within the **try** block), then no **catch** statement is executed.

The general form of the **throw** statement is shown here:

throw *exception;*

throw must be executed either from within the **try** block, proper, or from any function called (directly or indirectly) from within the **try** block. *exception* is the value thrown.

If you throw an exception for which there is no applicable **catch** statement, an abnormal program termination may occur. Throwing an unhandled exception causes the **terminate( )** function to be invoked. By default, **terminate( )** calls **abort( )** to stop your program. However, you may specify your own handlers if you like, using **set_terminate( )**. (See the Borland documentation for details on specifying your own termination handlers.)

Here is a simple example that shows the way C++ exception handling operates:

```
// A simple exception handling example.
#include <iostream.h>

int main()
{
  cout << "Start\n";

  try { // start a try block
    cout << "Inside try block\n";
    throw 100; // throw an error
    cout << "This will not execute";
  }
  catch (int i) { // catch an error
    cout << "Caught an exception -- value is: ";
    cout << i << "\n";
  }

  cout << "End";
```

```
  return 0;
}
```

This program displays the following output:

```
Start
Inside try block
Caught an exception -- value is: 100
End
```

Look carefully at this program. As you can see, there is a **try** block containing three statements and a **catch(int i)** statement that processes an integer exception. Within the **try** block, only two of the three statements will execute: the first **cout** statement and the **throw**. Once an exception has been thrown, control passes to the **catch** expression and the **try** block is terminated. That is, **catch** is *not* called. Rather, program execution is transferred to it. (The program's stack is automatically reset as needed to accomplish this.) Thus, the **cout** statement following the **throw** will never execute.

Usually, the code within a **catch** statement attempts to remedy an error by taking appropriate action. If the error can be fixed, then execution will continue with the statements following the **catch**. However, sometimes an error cannot be fixed and a **catch** block will terminate the program with a call to **exit( )** or **abort( )**.

As mentioned, the type of the exception must match the type specified in a **catch** statement. For example, in the preceding example, if you change the type in the **catch** statement to **double**, then the exception will not be caught and abnormal termination will occur. This change is shown here:

```
// This example will not work.
#include <iostream.h>

int main()
{
  cout << "Start\n";

  try { // start a try block
    cout << "Inside try block\n";
    throw 100; // throw an error
    cout << "This will not execute";
  }
  catch (double i) { // Won't work for an int exception
    cout << "Caught an exception -- value is: ";
    cout << i << "\n";
  }

  cout << "End";
```

```
  return 0;
}
```

This program produces the following output because the integer exception will not be caught by the **catch(double i)** statement:

```
Start
Inside try block
Abnormal program termination
```

An exception can be thrown from a statement that is outside the **try** block as long as it is within a function that is called from within the **try** block. For example, this is a valid program:

```
/* Throwing an exception from a function outside the
   try block.
*/
#include <iostream.h>

void Xtest(int test)
{
  cout << "Inside Xtest, test is: " << test << "\n";
  if(test) throw test;
}

int main()
{
  cout << "Start\n";

  try { // start a try block
    cout << "Inside try block\n";
    Xtest(0);
    Xtest(1);
    Xtest(2);
  }
  catch (int i) { // catch an error
    cout << "Caught an exception -- value is: ";
    cout << i << "\n";
  }

  cout << "End";

  return 0;
}
```

This program produces the following output:

```
Start
Inside try block
Inside Xtest, test is: 0
Inside Xtest, test is: 1
Caught an exception -- value is: 1
End
```

A **try** block can be localized to a function. When this is the case, each time the function is entered, the exception handling relative to that function is reset. For example, examine this program:

```
#include <iostream.h>

// A try/catch can be inside a function other than main().
void Xhandler(int test)
{
  try{
    if(test) throw test;
  }
  catch(int i) {
    cout << "Caught Exception #: " << i << '\n';
  }
}

int main()
{
  cout << "Start\n";

  Xhandler(1);
  Xhandler(2);
  Xhandler(0);
  Xhandler(3);

  cout << "End";

  return 0;
}
```

This program displays this output:

```
Start
Caught Exception #: 1
Caught Exception #: 2
```

```
Caught Exception #: 3
End
```

As you can see, three exceptions are thrown. After each exception, the function returns. When the function is called again, the exception handling is reset.

It is important to understand that the code associated with a **catch** statement will only be executed if it catches an exception. Otherwise, execution simply bypasses a **catch** statement.

Using Multiple catch Statements

As stated, you can have more than one **catch** associated with a **try**. In fact, it is common to do so. However, each **catch** must catch a different type of exception. For example, this program catches both integers and strings:

```
#include <iostream.h>

// Different types of exceptions can be caught.
void Xhandler(int test)
{
  try{
    if(test) throw test;
    else throw "Value is zero";
  }
  catch(int i) {
    cout << "Caught Exception #: " << i << '\n';
  }
  catch(char *str) {
    cout << "Caught a string: ";
    cout << str << '\n';
  }
}

int main()
{
  cout << "Start\n";

  Xhandler(1);
  Xhandler(2);
  Xhandler(0);
  Xhandler(3);

  cout << "End";
```

```
  return 0;
}
```

This program produces the following output:

```
Start
Caught Exception #: 1
Caught Exception #: 2
Caught a string: Value is zero
Caught Exception #: 3
End
```

As you can see, each **catch** statement responds only to its own type.

In general, **catch** expressions are checked in the order in which they occur in a program. Only a matching statement is executed. All other **catch** blocks are ignored.

Exception-Handling Options

There are several additional features and nuances to C++ exception handling that make it easier and more convenient to use. These attributes are discussed here.

Catching All Exceptions

In some circumstances you will want an exception handler to catch all exceptions instead of just a certain type. This is easy to accomplish. Simply use this form of **catch**:

catch(...) {
  // *process all exceptions*
}

Here, the ellipsis matches any type of data.

The following program illustrates **catch(...)**:

```
// This example catches all exceptions.
#include <iostream.h>

void Xhandler(int test)
{
  try{
    if(test==0) throw test; // throw int
    if(test==1) throw 'a'; // throw char
    if(test==2) throw 123.23; // throw double
  }
  catch(...) { // catch all exceptions
    cout << "Caught One!\n";
```

```
  }
}

int main()
{
  cout << "Start\n";

  Xhandler(0);
  Xhandler(1);
  Xhandler(2);

  cout << "End";

  return 0;
}
```

This program displays the following output:

```
Start
Caught One!
Caught One!
Caught One!
End
```

As you can see, all three **throw**s were caught using the one **catch** statement.

Restricting Exceptions

When a function is called from within a **try** block, you can restrict what type of exceptions that function can throw. In fact, you can also prevent that function from throwing any exceptions whatsoever. To accomplish these restrictions, you must add a **throw** clause to the function definition. The general form of this is shown here:

ret-type func-name(*arg-list*) throw(*type-list*)
{
  // ...
}

Here, only those data types contained in the comma-separated *type-list* may be thrown by the function. Throwing any other type of expression will cause abnormal program termination. If you don't want a function to be able to throw *any* exceptions, then use an empty list.

Attempting to throw an exception that is not supported by a function will cause the **unexpected( )** function to be called. Generally, this function, in turn, calls

terminate( ). You can specify your own unexpected exception handler using **set_expected( )**. (See the Borland documentation for details.)

The following program shows how to restrict the types of exceptions that can be thrown from a function:

```
// Restricting function throw types.
#include <iostream.h>

// This function can only throw ints, chars, and doubles.
void Xhandler(int test) throw(int, char, double)
{
  if(test==0) throw test; // throw int
  if(test==1) throw 'a'; // throw char
  if(test==2) throw 123.23; // throw double
}

int main()
{
  cout << "start\n";

  try{
    Xhandler(0); // also, try passing 1 and 2 to Xhandler()
  }
  catch(int i) {
    cout << "Caught an integer\n";
  }
  catch(char c) {
    cout << "Caught char\n";
  }
  catch(double d) {
    cout << "Caught double\n";
  }

  cout << "end";

  return 0;
}
```

In this program, the function **Xhandler( )** may only throw integer, character, and **double** exceptions. If it attempts to throw any other type of exception, then an abnormal program termination will occur. (Specifically, the, **unexpected( )** function will be called.) To see an example of this, remove **int** from the list and retry the program.

A function can only be restricted in what types of exceptions it throws back to the **try** block that called it. That is, a **try** block *within* a function may throw any type of exception as long as it is caught *within* that function. The restriction applies only when throwing an exception outside of the function.

The following change to **Xhandler( )** prevents it from throwing any exceptions:

```
// This function can throw NO exceptions!
void Xhandler(int test) throw()
{
  /* The following statements no longer work.  Instead,
     they will cause an abnormal program termination. */
  if(test==0) throw test;
  if(test==1) throw 'a';
  if(test==2) throw 123.23;
}
```

Rethrowing an Exception

If you wish to rethrow an exception from within an exception handler, you may do so by calling **throw**, by itself, with no exception. This causes the current exception to be passed on to an outer **try/catch** sequence. The most likely reason for doing so is to allow multiple handlers access to the exception. For example, perhaps one exception handler manages one aspect of an exception and a second handler copes with another. An exception can only be rethrown from within a **catch** block (or from any function called from within that block). When you rethrow an exception, it will not be recaught by the same **catch** statement. It will propagate to the next outer **catch** statement. The following program illustrates rethrowing an exception. It rethrows a **char** * exception.

```
// Example of "rethrowing" an exception.
#include <iostream.h>

void Xhandler()
{
  try {
    throw "hello"; // throw a char *
  }
  catch(char *) { // catch a char *
    cout << "Caught char * inside Xhandler\n";
    throw ; // rethrow char * out of function
  }
}

int main()
{
  cout << "Start\n";

  try{
```

```
    Xhandler();
  }
  catch(char *) {
    cout << "Caught char * inside main\n";
  }

  cout << "End";

  return 0;
}
```

This program displays this output:

```
Start
Caught char * inside Xhandler
Caught char * inside main
End
```

Applying Exception Handling

Exception handling is designed to provide a structured means by which your program can handle abnormal events. This implies that the error handler must do something rational when an error occurs. For example, consider the following simple program. It inputs two numbers and divides the first by the second. It uses exception handling to manage a divide-by-zero error.

```
#include <iostream.h>

void divide(double a, double b);

int main()
{
  double i, j;

  do {
    cout << "Enter numerator (0 to stop): ";
    cin >> i;
    cout << "Enter denominator: ";
    cin >> j;
    divide(i, j);
  } while(i != 0);

  return 0;
}
```

```
void divide(double a, double b)
{
  try {
    if(!b) throw b; // check for divide-by-zero
    cout << "Result: " << a/b << endl;
  }
  catch (double b) {
    cout << "Can't divide by zero.\n";
  }
}
```

While the preceding program is a very simple example, it does illustrate the essential nature of exception handling. Since division by zero is illegal, the program cannot continue if a zero is entered for the second number. In this case, the exception is handled by not performing the division (which would have caused abnormal program termination) and notifying the user of the error. The program then reprompts the user for two more numbers. Thus, the error has been handled in an orderly fashion and the user may continue on with the program. The same basic concepts will apply to more complex applications of exception handling.

Exception handling is especially useful for exiting from a deeply nested set of routines when a catastrophic error occurs. In this regard, C++'s exception handling is designed to replace the rather clumsy C-based **setjmp( )** and **longjmp( )** functions.

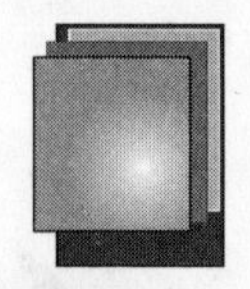

REMEMBER: The key point about using exception handling is to provide an orderly means of handling errors. This means rectifying the situation, if possible.

Run-time Type Identification (RTTI)

Using run-time type identification, you can determine the type of an object during program execution. To obtain an object's type, use **typeid**. You must include the header file **typeinfo.h** in order to use **typeid**. Its general form is shown here:

typeid(*object*)

Here, *object* is the object whose type you will be obtaining. **typeid** returns a reference to an object of type **typeinfo** that describes the type of object defined by *object*. (In the draft standard for C++, this type is call **type_info**. Future versions of Borland C++ will probably be changed to reflect this new name.) The **typeinfo** class defines the following public members:

bool operator==(const typeinfo &*ob*) const;

bool operator!=(const typeinfo &*ob*) const;

bool before(const typeinfo &*ob*) const;

const char *name( ) const;

The overloaded **==** and **!=** provide for the comparison of types. The **before( )** function returns true if the invoking object is before the object used as a parameter in collation order. (This function is mostly for internal use only. Its return value has nothing to do with inheritance or class hierarchies.) The **name( )** function returns a pointer to the name of the type.

When **typeid** is applied to a base class pointer of a polymorphic class, it will automatically return the type of the object being pointed to, including any classes derived from that base. (Remember, a polymorphic class is one that contains at least one virtual function.)

The following program demonstrates **typeid**:

```
// An example that uses typeid.
#include <iostream.h>
#include <typeinfo.h>

class BaseClass {
  int a, b;
  virtual void f() {}; // make BaseClass polymorphic
};

class Derived1: public BaseClass {
  int i, j;
};

class Derived2: public BaseClass {
  int k;
};

int main()
{
  int i;
  BaseClass *p, baseob;
  Derived1 ob1;
  Derived2 ob2;

  // First, display type name of a built in type.
  cout << "Typeid of i is ";
```

```
  cout << typeid(i).name() << endl;

  // Demonstrate typeid with polymorphic types.
  p = &baseob;
  cout << "p is pointing to an object of type ";
  cout << typeid(*p).name() << endl;

  p = &ob1;
  cout << "p is pointing to an object of type ";
  cout << typeid(*p).name() << endl;

  p = &ob2;
  cout << "p is pointing to an object of type ";
  cout << typeid(*p).name() << endl;

  return 0;
}
```

The output produced by this program is shown here:

```
Typeid of i is int
p is pointing to an object of type BaseClass
p is pointing to an object of type Derived1
p is pointing to an object of type Derived2
```

As mentioned, when **typeid** is applied to a base class pointer of a polymorphic type, the type of object pointed to will be determined at run time, as the output produced by the program shows. For an experiment, comment out the virtual function **f( )** in **BaseClass** and observe the results.

RTTI is not something that every program will use. However, when working with polymorphic types, it allows you to know what type of object is being operated upon in any given situation.

New Casting Operators

Although C++ still fully supports the traditional C-like casting operator, described in Part 1, it defines four additional casting operators. They are **const_cast**, **dynamic_cast**, **reinterpret_cast**, and **static_cast**. Their general forms are shown here:

const_cast<*type*> (*object*)

dynamic_cast<*type*> (*object*)

reinterpret_cast<*type*> (*object*)

static_cast<*type*> (*object*)

Here, *type* specifies the target type of the cast and *object* is the object being cast into the new type.

The **const_cast** operator is used to explicitly override **const** and/or **volatile** in a cast. The target type must be the same as the source type except for the alteration of its **const** or **volatile** attributes. The most common use of **const_cast** is to remove **const**-ness.

dynamic_cast performs a run-time cast that verifies the validity of the cast. If the cast cannot be made, the cast fails and the expression evaluates to null. Its main use is for performing casts on polymorphic types. For example, given two polymorphic classes B and D, with D derived from B, a **dynamic_cast** can always cast a D* pointer into a B* pointer. A **dynamic_cast** can cast a B* pointer into a D* pointer only if the object being pointed to actually is a D*. In general, **dynamic_cast** will succeed if the attempted polymorphic cast is permitted (that is, if the target type can legally apply to the type of object being cast). If the cast cannot be made, then **dynamic_cast** evaluates to null.

The **static_cast** operator performs a nonpolymorphic cast. For example, it can be used to cast a base class pointer into a derived class pointer. It can also be used for any standard conversion. No run-time checks are performed. The **reinterpret_cast** operator changes one type into a fundamentally different type. For example, it can be used to change a pointer into an integer. A **reinterpret_cast** should be used for casting inherently incompatible pointer types.

Only **const_cast** can cast away **const**-ness; that is, neither **dynamic_cast**, **static_cast**, nor **reinterpret_cast** can alter the **const**-ness of an object.

The following program demonstrates the use of **dynamic_cast**:

```
#include <iostream.h>

#define NUM_EMPLOYEES 4

class employee {
public:
  employee() { cout << "Constructing employee\n"; }
  virtual void print() = 0;
};

class programmer : public employee {
public:
  programmer() { cout << "Constructing programmer\n"; }
  void print() { cout << "Printing programmer object\n"; }
```

```
};

class salesperson : public employee {
public:
  salesperson() { cout << "Constructing salesperson\n"; }
  void print() { cout << "Printing salesperson object\n"; }
};

class executive : public employee {
public:
  executive() { cout << "Constructing executive\n"; }
  void print() { cout << "Printing executive object\n"; }
};

int main() {
  programmer prog1, prog2;
  executive ex;
  salesperson sp;

  // Initialize the array of employees
  employee *e[NUM_EMPLOYEES];
  e[0] = &prog1;
  e[1] = &sp;
  e[2] = &ex;
  e[3] = &prog2;

  // See which ones are programmers.
  for(int i = 0; i < NUM_EMPLOYEES; i++) {
    programmer *pp = dynamic_cast<programmer*>(e[i]);
    if(pp) {
      cout << "Is a programmer\n";
      pp->print();
    }
    else {
      cout << "Not a programmer\n";
    }
  }
}
```

The array **e** contains pointers to the four employees. The **dynamic_cast** operator is used to identify which of these are programmers. If the **dynamic_cast** operator returns a null, that employee is not a programmer. Otherwise, the **print( )** function for that object is invoked.

The output produced by this program is shown here:

```
Constructing employee
Constructing programmer
Constructing employee
Constructing programmer
Constructing employee
Constructing executive
Constructing employee
Constructing salesperson
Is a programmer
Printing programmer object
Not a programmer
Not a programmer
Is a programmer
Printing programmer object
```

The following program demonstrates the use of **reinterpret_cast**:

```
// An example that uses reinterpret_cast.
#include <iostream.h>

int main()
{
  int i;
  char *p = "This is a string";

  i = reinterpret_cast<int> (p); // cast pointer to integer

  cout << i;

  return 0;
}
```

While the new casting operators are not needed by most simple programs, they will be of value in more complex C++ applications.

Chapter Twenty-Seven

Miscellaneous C++ Topics

This chapter discusses several aspects of C++ not covered in the previous chapters. It also looks at some differences between C and C++ as well as some design philosophy.

Dynamic Allocation Using new and delete

As you know, C uses the functions **malloc( )** and **free( )** (among others) to dynamically allocate memory and to free dynamically allocated memory. However, C++ contains two operators that perform the function of allocating and freeing memory in a more efficient and easier-to-use way. The operators are **new** and **delete**. Their general forms are

pointer_var = new *var_type* ;
delete *pointer_var* ;

Here, *pointer_var* is a pointer of type *var_type*. The **new** operator allocates sufficient memory to hold a value of type *var_type* and returns an address to it. Any data type can be allocated using **new**. The **delete** operator frees the memory pointed to by *pointer_var*.

If an allocation request cannot be filled, the **new** operator throws an exception of type **xalloc**. If your program does not catch this exception, then your program will be terminated. While this default behavior is fine for short sample programs, in real-world programs that you write, you should catch this exception and process it in some rational manner. To watch for this exception, you must include **except.h** in your program.

*NOTE: As just explained, when **new** cannot fulfill a memory request, it throws an exception. At the time of this writing, Borland C++ calls this exception type **xalloc**. However, the current draft of the ANSI C++ standard calls this exception type **bad_alloc**. Frankly, the precise operation of **new** when an allocation failure occurs is still undergoing refinement. This is an area that you will want to watch carefully in the near future.*

Because of the way dynamic allocation is managed, you must use **delete** only with a pointer to memory that was allocated using **new**. Using **delete** with any other type of address will cause serious problems.

There are several advantages to using **new** instead of **malloc( )**. First, **new** automatically computes the size of the type being allocated. You don't have to make use of the **sizeof** operator, which saves you some effort. More important, it prevents the wrong amount of memory from being accidentally allocated. Second, it automatically returns the correct pointer type—you don't need to use a type cast. Third, as you will soon see, it is possible to initialize the object being allocated using **new**. Finally, it is possible to overload **new** (and **delete**) globally or relative to classes you create.

Here is a simple example of **new** and **delete**. Notice how a **try/catch** block is used to monitor for an allocation failure.

```
#include <iostream.h>
#include <except.h>

int main()
{
  int *p;

  try {
    p = new int; // allocate memory for int
  } catch (xalloc xa) {
    cout << "Allocation failure.\n";
    return 1;
  }

  *p = 20; // assign that memory the value 20
  cout << *p; // prove that it works by displaying value

  delete p; // free the memory

  return 0;
}
```

This program assigns to **p** an address in memory that is large enough to hold an integer. It then assigns that memory the value 20 and displays the contents of that memory on the screen. Finally, it frees the dynamically allocated memory.

As stated, you can initialize the memory using the **new** operator. To do this, specify the initial value inside the parentheses after the type name. For example, this program uses initialization to give the memory pointed to by **p** the value 99:

```
#include <iostream.h>
#include <except.h>

int main()
{
  int *p;

  try {
    p = new int (99);  // initialize with 99
  } catch(xalloc xa) {
    cout << "Allocation failure.\n";
    return 1;
  }

  cout << *p;

  delete p;

  return 0;
}
```

You can allocate arrays using **new**. The general form for a singly dimensioned array is

pointer_var = new *var_type* [*size*];

Here, *size* specifies the number of elements in the array. There is one important restriction to remember when allocating an array: you cannot initialize it.

When you free a dynamically allocated array, you must use this form of **delete**:

delete [ ] *pointer_var*;

Here, the **[ ]** informs **delete** that an array is being released.

The following program allocates a 10-element array of **float**s, assigns the array the values 100 to 109, and displays the contents of the array on the screen:

```
#include <iostream.h>
#include <except.h>

int main()
{
  float *p;
  int i;

  try {
    p = new float [10]; // get a 10-element array
  } catch(xalloc xa) {
    cout << "Allocation failure.\n";
    return 1;
  }

  // assign the values 100 through 109
  for(i=0; i<10; i++) p[i] = 100.00 + i;

  // display the contents of the array
  for(i=0; i<10; i++)  cout << p[i] << " ";

  delete [] p; // delete the entire array

  return 0;
}
```

Allocating Objects

As stated, you can allocate memory for any valid type. This includes objects. For example, in this program, **new** allocates memory for an object of type **three_d**:

```
#include <iostream.h>
#include <except.h>

class three_d {
public:
  int x, y, z; // 3-d coordinates
  three_d(int a, int b, int c);
  ~three_d() {cout << "Destructing\n";}
} ;

three_d::three_d(int a, int b, int c)
{
  cout << "Constructing\n";
```

```
  x = a;
  y = b;
  z = c;
}

// Display X, Y, Z coordinates - three_d inserter.
ostream &operator<<(ostream &stream, three_d &obj)
{
  stream << obj.x << ", ";
  stream << obj.y << ", ";
  stream << obj.z << "\n";
  return stream;  // return the stream
}

int main()
{
  three_d *p;

  try {
    p = new three_d (5, 6, 7);
  } catch(xalloc xa) {
    cout << "Allocation failure.\n";
    return 1;
  }

  cout << *p;

  delete p;

  return 0;
}
```

Notice that this program makes use of the inserter function for the **three_d** class to output the coordinate values. When you run the program, you will see that **three_d**'s constructor function is called when **new** is encountered and that its destructor function is called when **delete** is reached. Also note that the initializers are automatically passed to the constructor by **new**.

Here is an example that allocates an array of objects of type **three_d**.

```
#include <iostream.h>
#include <except.h>

class three_d {
public:
```

```
  int x, y, z; // 3-d coordinates
  three_d(int a, int b, int c) ;
  three_d(){cout << "Constructing\n";} // needed for arrays
  ~three_d() {cout << "Destructing\n";}
};

three_d::three_d(int a, int b, int c)
{
  cout << "Constructing\n";
  x = a;
  y = b;
  z = c;
}

// Display X, Y, Z coordinates - three_d inserter.
ostream &operator<<(ostream &stream, three_d &obj)
{
  stream << obj.x << ", ";
  stream << obj.y << ", ";
  stream << obj.z << "\n";
  return stream;  // return the stream
}

int main()
{
  three_d *p;
  int i;

  try {
    p = new three_d [10];
  } catch (xalloc xa) {
    cout << "Allocation failure.\n";
    return 1;
  }

  for(i=0; i<10; i++) {
    p[i].x = 1;
    p[i].y = 2;
    p[i].z = 3;
  }

  for(i=0; i<10; i++) cout << *p;
```

```
  delete [] p;

  return 0;
}
```

Notice that a second constructor function has been added to the **three_d** class. Because allocated arrays cannot be initialized, a constructor function that does not have any parameters is needed. If you don't supply this constructor, a compile-time message will be displayed.

Another Way to Watch for Allocation Failure

When C++ was first invented, the **new** operator did not throw an exception when an allocation error occurred. Instead, it returned null (just like C's **malloc( )** function). If you wish to have **new** work this way instead of throwing an exception, simply call the function **set_new_handler( )** with an argument of zero. After doing so, **new** will return a null if it cannot satisfy a memory request. You must include the file **new.h** when using the **set_new_handler( )** function.

The following program shows this alternative approach to using **new**. It first calls **set_new_handler( )** with an argument of zero, and then allocates memory until it is exhausted.

```
// Demonstrate a new alternative.
#include <new.h>
#include <iostream.h>

int main()
{
  double *p;

  // have new return null on failure
  set_new_handler(0);

  // this will eventually run out of memory
  do {
    p = new double[100000];
    if(p) cout << "Allocation OK\n";
    else cout << "Allocation Error\n";
  } while(p);

  return 0;
}
```

As this program demonstrates, when using this approach you must check the pointer returned by **new** after each allocation request.

Overloading new and delete

It is possible to overload **new** and **delete**. You might want to do this when you want to use some special allocation method. For example, you may want allocation routines that automatically begin using a disk file as virtual memory when the heap has been exhausted. Whatever the reason, it is a very simple matter to overload these operators.

The skeletons for the functions that overload **new** and **delete** are

```
void *operator new(size_t size)
{
  // perform allocation
  return pointer_to_memory;
}

void operator delete(void *p)
{
  // free memory pointed to by p
}
```

The parameter *size* will contain the number of bytes needed to hold the object being allocated. This value is automatically obtained for you. The overloaded **new** function must return a pointer to the memory that it allocates. Beyond this constraint, the overloaded **new** function can do anything else you require.

The **delete** function receives a pointer to the region of memory to free. It must then release the memory pointed to by that pointer.

To overload **new** and **delete** for use with arrays, use these general forms.

```
void *operator new[ ](size_t size)
{
  // perform allocation
  return pointer_to_memory;
}

void operator delete[ ](void *p)
{
  // free memory pointed to by p
}
```

You may overload **new** and **delete** globally or relative to a class. To overload them for a class, simply make their operator functions class members.

static Class Members

The keyword **static** can be applied to members of a class. Its meaning in this context is similar to its original C-like meaning. When you declare a member of a class as **static**, you are telling the compiler that no matter how many objects of the class are created, there is only one copy of the **static** member. A **static** member is *shared* by all objects of the class. All static data is initialized to zero when the first object of its class is created and no other initialization is specified.

When you declare a **static** data member within a class, you are *not* defining it. Instead, you must provide a global definition for it elsewhere, outside the class. You do this by redeclaring the static variable, using the scope resolution operator to identify which class it belongs to. This is necessary for storage to be allocated for the **static** variable.

As an example, examine the following program and try to understand how it works:

```
#include <iostream.h>

class counter {
  static int count;
public:
  void setcount(int i) {count = i;};
  void showcount() {cout << count << "  ";}
};

int counter::count; // define count

int main()
{
  counter a, b;

  a.showcount(); // prints 0
  b.showcount(); // prints 0

  a.setcount(10); // set static count to 10

  a.showcount(); // prints 10
  b.showcount(); // also prints 10

  return 0;
}
```

Notice first that the static integer **count** is both declared inside the **counter** class and then defined as a global variable. Borland C++ initializes **count** to zero since no other initialization is given. This is why the first calls to **showcount( )** both display zero. Next, object **a** sets **count** to 10. Then, both **a** and **b** use **showcount( )** to display its value. Because there is only one copy of **count** shared by both **a** and **b**, both cause the value 10 to be displayed.

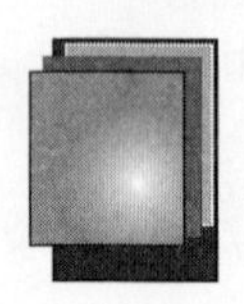

REMEMBER: When you declare a member of a class as ***static****, you are causing only one copy of that member to be created and then shared by all objects of that class.*

You can also have **static** member functions. Static member functions cannot refer directly to nonstatic data and nonstatic functions declared in their class. This is because a **static** member function does not have a **this** pointer; it has no way of knowing which object's nonstatic data to access. For example, if there are two objects of a class that contain a **static** function called **f( )**, and if **f( )** attempts to access a nonstatic variable called **var** (defined by its class), which copy of **var** is being referred to? The compiler has no way of knowing. This is why **static** functions can access only other **static** functions or data directly. Also, a **static** function cannot be virtual or declared as **const** or **volatile**. A **static** function can be called using either an object of its class or by using the class name and the scope resolution operator. However, remember, even when called using an object, the function is still not passed a **this** pointer.

The following short program illustrates one of the many ways you can use **static** functions. It is not uncommon for an object to require access to some scarce resource, such as a shared file in a network. As the program illustrates, the use of **static** data and functions provides a method by which an object can check on the status of the resource and access it if it is available.

```
#include <iostream.h>

enum access_t {shared, in_use, locked, unlocked};

// a scarce resource control class
class access {
  static enum access_t acs;
  // ...
public:
  static void set_access(enum access_t a) {acs = a;}
  static enum access_t get_access()
  {
    return acs;
  }
  // ...
};

enum access_t access::acs; // define acs
```

```
int main()
{
  access  obj1, obj2;

  access::set_access(locked); // call using class name

  // ... intervening code

  // see if obj2 can access resource
  if(obj2.get_access()==unlocked) { // call using object
    access::set_access(in_use);  // call using class name
    cout << "Access resource.\n";
  }
  else cout << "Locked out.\n";

  // ...

  return 0;
}
```

When you compile this skeleton, "locked out" is displayed. Notice that **set_access( )** is called using the class name and the scope resolution operator. The function **get_access( )** is called using an object and the dot operator. Either form may be used when calling a **static** member function and both forms have the same effect. You might want to play with the program a little to make sure you understand the effect of **static** on both data and functions.

As stated, **static** functions can directly access only other **static** functions or **static** data within the same class. To prove this, try compiling this version of the program:

```
// This program contains an error and will not compile.
#include <iostream.h>

enum access_t {shared, in_use, locked, unlocked};

// a scarce resource control class
class access {
  static enum access_t acs;
  int i;  // non-static
  // ...
public:
  static void set_access(enum access_t a) {acs = a;}
  static enum access_t get_access()
  {
    i = 100; // this will not compile
```

```
    return acs;
  }
  // ...
};

enum access_t access::acs; // define acs

int main()
{
  access obj1, obj2;

  access::set_access(locked); // call using class name

  // ... intervening code

  // see if obj2 can access resource
  if(obj2.get_access()==unlocked) { // call using object
    access::set_access(in_use); // call using class name
    cout << "Access resource.\n";
  }
  else cout << "Locked out.\n";

  // ...
}
```

This program does not compile because **get_access( )** is attempting to access a non**static** variable.

You may not see an immediate need for **static** members, but as you continue to write programs in C++, you will find them very useful in certain situations because they allow you to avoid the use of global variables.

Virtual Base Classes

As you know, in C++, the **virtual** keyword is used to declare **virtual** functions that will be overridden by a derived class. However, **virtual** also has another use that enables you to specify a *virtual base class.* To understand what a virtual base class is and why the keyword **virtual** has a second meaning, let's begin with the short, incorrect program shown here:

```
// This program contains an error and will not compile.
#include <iostream.h>

class base {
public:
```

```
  int i;
};

// d1 inherits base.
class d1 :  public base {
public:
  int j;
};

// d2 inherits base.
class d2 : public base {
public:
  int k;
};

/* d3 inherits both d1 and d2. This means that there
   are two copies of base in d3! */
class d3 : public d1, public d2 {
public:
  int m;
};

int main()
{
  d3 d;

  d.i = 10;  // this is ambiguous, which i???
  d.j = 20;
  d.k = 30;
  d.m = 40;


  // also ambiguous, which i???
  cout << d.i << " ";
  cout << d.j << " " << d.k << " ";
  cout << d.m;

  return 0;
}
```

As the comments in the program indicate, both **d1** and **d2** inherit **base**. However, **d3** inherits both **d1** and **d2**. This means there are two copies of **base** present in an object of type **d3**. Therefore, in an expression like

```
d.i = 20;
```

which **i** is being referred to—the one in **d1** or the one in **d2**? Since there are two copies of **base** present in object **d**, there are two **d.i**'s. As you can see, the statement is inherently ambiguous.

There are two ways to remedy the preceding program. The first is to apply the scope resolution operator to **i** and manually select one **i**. For example, this version of the program does compile and run as expected:

```
#include <iostream.h>

class base {
public:
  int i;
};

// d1 inherits base.
class d1 :  public base {
public:
  int j;
};

// d2 inherits base.
class d2 : public base {
public:
  int k;
};

/* d3 inherits both d1 and d2. This means that there
   are two copies of base in d3! */
class d3 : public d1, public d2 {
public:
  int m;
};

int main()
{
  d3 d;

  d.d2::i = 10; // scope resolved, using d2's i
  d.j = 20;
  d.k = 30;
  d.m = 40;
```

```
  // scope resolved, using d2's i
  cout << d.d2::i << " ";
  cout << d.j << " " << d.k << " ";
  cout << d.m;

  return 0;
}
```

As you can see, by applying the ::, the program has manually selected **d2**'s version of **base**. However, this solution raises a deeper issue: What if only one copy of **base** is actually required? Is there some way to prevent two copies from being included in **d3**? The answer, as you probably have guessed, is yes. And this solution is achieved by using virtual base classes.

When two or more classes are derived from a common base class, you can prevent multiple copies of the base class from being present in an object derived from those classes by declaring the base class as **virtual** when it is inherited. For example, here is another version of the example program in which **d3** contains only one copy of **base**:

```
#include <iostream.h>

class base {
public:
  int i;
};

// d1 inherits base as virtual.
class d1 : virtual public base {
public:
  int j;
};

// d2 inherits base as virtual.
class d2 : virtual public base {
public:
  int k;
};

/* d3 inherits both d1 and d2. However, now there is
   only one copy of base in d3. */
class d3 : public d1, public d2 {
public:
  int m;
};
```

```
int main()
{
  d3 d;

  d.i = 10; // no longer ambiguous
  d.j = 20;
  d.k = 30;
  d.m = 40;

  cout << d.i << " "; // no longer ambiguous
  cout << d.j << " " << d.k << " ";
  cout << d.m;

  return 0;
}
```

As you can see, the keyword **virtual** precedes the rest of the inherited class' specification. Now that both **d1** and **d2** have inherited **base** as **virtual**, any multiple inheritance involving them will cause only one copy of **base** to be present. Therefore, in **d3**, there is only one copy of **base**, so **d.i = 10** is perfectly valid and unambiguous.

One further point to keep in mind: Even though both **d1** and **d2** specify **base** as **virtual**, **base** is still present in any objects of either type. For example, the following sequence is perfectly valid:

```
// define a class of type d1
d1 myclass;

myclass.i = 100;
```

Virtual base classes and normal ones differ only when an object inherits the base more than once. If virtual base classes are used, only one base class is present in the object. Otherwise, multiple copies will be found.

const and volatile Member Functions

Class member functions may be declared as **const**, **volatile**, or both. A few rules apply. First, objects declared as **volatile** may call only member functions also declared as **volatile**. A **const** object may not invoke a non**const** member function. However, a **const** member function can be called by either **const** or non**const** objects. A **const** member function cannot modify the object that invokes it. The rules combine for functions that are both **const** and **volatile**.

To specify a member function as **const** or **volatile**, use the forms shown in the following example:

```
class X {
public:
  int f1() const; // const member function
  void f2(int a) volatile; // volatile member function
  char *f3() const volatile; // const volatile member function
};
```

Using the asm Keyword

In Borland C++, you can embed assembly language directly into your program by using the **asm** keyword. The **asm** keyword has three slightly different general forms:

> asm *instruction* ;
> asm *instruction newline*
> asm {
>   *instruction sequence*
> }

Here, *instruction* is any valid 80*x*86 assembly language instruction. Unlike any other Borland C++ statement, an **asm** statement does not have to end with a semicolon; it can end with either a semicolon or a newline.

As a first simple example, this program uses **asm** to execute an **INT 5** instruction, which invokes the PC's print screen function. (This is a 16-bit example that assumes a DOS execution environment.)

```
// Print the screen.
#include <iostream.h>

int main()
{
  asm int 5;
  return 0;
}
```

If you want to use a sequence of assembly language statements, surround them with braces, as shown in this do-nothing (but harmless) example:

```
#include <iostream.h>

int main()
{
  // this effectively does nothing
  asm {
```

```
    push ds
    pop ds
  }

  return 0;
}
```

If you want to put a comment on the same line as an assembly language statement, use C++-like comments.

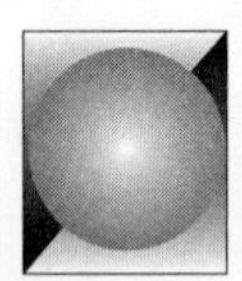

NOTE: A thorough working knowledge of assembly language programming is required to use the asm statement. If you are not proficient at assembly language, it is best to avoid using it because nasty errors may result.

Linkage Specification

In C++, you can specify how a function is linked. Specifically, you can tell Borland C++ to link a function as a C function or as a C++ function. By default, functions are linked as C++ functions. However, by using a *linkage specification* you can cause a function to be linked as a different type of language function. The general form of a linkage specifier is

extern "*language* " *function-prototype*

where *language* denotes the desired language. In Borland C++, *language* must be either C or C++, but other implementations may allow other language types.

This program causes **myCfunc( )** to be linked as a C function:

```
#include <iostream.h>

extern "C" void myCfunc(void);

int main()
{
  myCfunc();

  return 0;
}

// This will link as a C function.
void myCfunc(void)
{
```

```
  cout << "This links as a C function.\n";
}
```

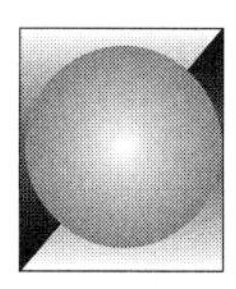

*NOTE: The **extern** keyword is a necessary part of the linkage specification. Further, the linkage specification must be global; it cannot be used inside a function.*

You can specify more than one function at a time by using this form of the linkage specification:

extern "*language*" {
  prototypes
}

The use of a linkage specification is rare; you will probably not need to use one.

The .* and –>* Operators

The **.*** and **–>*** are called *pointer-to-member* operators. Their job is to allow you to "point to" a member of a class generically rather than to a specific instance of that member within some object. These two operators are needed because a pointer to a member does not fully define an address. Instead, it provides an offset at which that member can be found within any object of its class. Since member pointers are not true pointers, the normal **.** and **–>** operators cannot be used. Instead, the **.*** and **–>*** operators must be employed.

Let's begin with an example. The following program displays the summation of the number 7. It accesses the function **sum_it( )** and the variable **sum** using member pointers.

```
#include <iostream.h>

class myclass {
public:
  int sum;
  void myclass::sum_it(int x);
};

void myclass::sum_it(int x) {
  int i;

  sum = 0;
  for(i=x; i; i--) sum += i;
}
```

```
int main()
{
  int myclass::*dp;  // pointer to an integer class member
  void (myclass::*fp)(int x); // pointer to member function
  myclass c;

  dp = &myclass::sum;  // get address of data
  fp = &myclass::sum_it; // get address of function

  (c.*fp)(7);  // compute summation of 7
  cout << "summation of 7 is " << c.*dp;

  return 0;
}
```

Inside **main( )**, this program creates two member pointers: **dp**, which points to the variable **sum**; and **fp**, which points to the function **sum_it( )**. Note carefully the syntax of each declaration. The scope resolution operator is used to specify which class is being referred to. The program also creates an object of **myclass** called **c**.

The program then obtains the addresses of **sum** and **sum_it( )**. As stated earlier, these addresses are really just offsets into an object of **myclass** where **sum** and **sum_it( )** are found. Next, the program uses a function pointer **fp** to call the **sum_it( )** function of **c**. The extra parentheses are necessary in order to correctly associate the **.*** operator. Finally, the summed value is displayed by accessing **c**'s **sum** through **dp**.

When you are accessing a member of an object using an object or a reference, you must use the **.*** operator. However, if you are using a pointer to the object, you need to use the **–>*** operator, as illustrated in this version of the preceding program:

```
#include <iostream.h>

class myclass {
public:
  int sum;
  void myclass::sum_it(int x);
};

void myclass::sum_it(int x) {
  int i;

  sum = 0;
  for(i=x; i; i--) sum += i;
}
```

```
int main()
{
  int myclass::*dp;   // pointer to an integer class member
  void (myclass::*fp)(int x); // pointer to member function
  myclass *c, d; // c is now a pointer to an object

  c = &d; // give c the address of an object

  dp = &myclass::sum;   // get address of data
  fp = &myclass::sum_it; // get address of function

  (c->*fp)(7);   // now, use ->* to call function
  cout << "summation of 7 is " << c->*dp; // use ->*

  return 0;
}
```

In this version, **c** is now a pointer to an object of type **myclass** and the **–>*** operator is used to access **sum** and **sum_it( )**.

Creating Conversion Functions

Sometimes you will create a class that you want to be able to freely mix in an expression with other types of data. While overloaded operator functions can provide a means of mixing types, sometimes a simple conversion is all that you want. In these cases, you can use a type conversion function to convert your class into a type compatible with that of the rest of the expression. The general form of a type conversion function is

operator (*type*)( ) {return *value* ;}

Here, *type* is the target type that you are converting your class to and *value* is the value of the class after conversion. A conversion function must be a member of the class for which it is defined.

To illustrate how to create a conversion function, let's use the **three_d** class once again. Suppose you want to be able to convert an object of type **three_d** into an integer so it can be used in an integer expression. Further, the conversion will take place by using the product of the three dimensions. To accomplish this, you use a conversion function that looks like this:

```
operator int() { return x * y * z; }
```

Here is a program that illustrates how the conversion function works:

```
#include <iostream.h>

class three_d {
  int x, y, z; // 3-d coordinates
public:
  three_d(int a, int b, int c) {x=a; y=b, z=c;}

  three_d operator+(three_d op2) ;
  friend ostream &operator<<(ostream &stream, three_d &obj);

  operator int() {return x*y*z;}
} ;

// Display X, Y, Z coordinates - three_d inserter.
ostream &operator<<(ostream &stream, three_d &obj)
{
  stream << obj.x << ", ";
  stream << obj.y << ", ";
  stream << obj.z << "\n";
  return stream;  // return the stream
}

three_d three_d::operator+(three_d op2)
{
  three_d temp(0, 0, 0);

  temp.x = x+op2.x;  // these are integer additions
  temp.y = y+op2.y;  // and the + retains its original
  temp.z = z+op2.z;  // meaning relative to them
  return temp;
}

int main()
{
  three_d a(1, 2, 3), b(2, 3, 4);

  cout << a << b;

  cout <<  b+100;  // displays 124 because of conversion to int
  cout << "\n";
  cout << a+b;  // displays 3, 5, 7 - no conversion
```

```
  return 0;
}
```

This program displays the output

```
1, 2, 3
2, 3, 4
124
3, 5, 7
```

As the program illustrates, when a **three_d** object is used in an integer expression, such as **cout << b+100**, the conversion function is applied to the object. In this specific case, the conversion function returns the value 24, which is then added to 100. However, when no conversion is needed, as in **cout << a+b**, the conversion function is not called.

Remember that you can create different conversion functions to meet different needs. You could define one that converts to **double** or **long**, for example. Each is applied automatically.

Copy Constructors

By default, when one object is used to initialize another, C++ performs a bitwise copy. That is, an identical copy of the initializing object is created in the target object. Although this is perfectly adequate for many cases—and generally exactly what you want to happen—there are situations in which a bitwise copy cannot be used. One of the most common situations in which you must avoid a bitwise copy is when an object allocates memory when it is created. For example, assume two objects, *A* and *B*, of the same class, called *ClassType*, which allocates memory when creating objects, and assume that *A* is already in existence. This means that *A* has already allocated its memory. Further, assume that *A* is used to initialize *B*, as shown here:

```
ClassType B = A;
```

If a simple bitwise copy is performed, then *B* will be an exact copy of *A*. This means that *B* will be using the same piece of allocated memory that *A* is using, instead of allocating its own. Clearly, this is not the desired outcome. For example, if *ClassType* includes a destructor that frees the memory, then the same piece of memory will be freed twice when *A* and *B* are destroyed!

The same type of problem can occur in two additional ways. The first way is when a copy of an object is made when it is passed as an argument to a function. The second way is when a temporary object is created as a return value from a function. (Remember, temporary objects are automatically created to hold the return value of a function, and they may also be created in certain other circumstances.)

To solve the type of problem just described, C++ allows you to create a *copy constructor*, which the compiler uses when one object is used to initialize another. When a copy constructor exists, the bitwise copy is bypassed. The general form of a copy constructor is

classname (const *classname &o*) {
// *body of constructor*
}

Here, *o* is a reference to the object on the right side of the initialization. It is permissible for a copy constructor to have additional parameters if they have default arguments defined for them. However, in all cases the first parameter must be a reference to the object doing the initializing.

Initialization occurs three ways: when on object initializes another, when a copy of an object is made to be passed to a function, or when a temporary object is generated (most commonly, as a return value). For example, each of the following statements involves initialization:

```
myclass x = y; // initialization
func(x); // parameter passing
y = func();  // receiving temporary object
```

Following is an example where an explicit copy constructor function is needed. This program creates a very simple "safe" integer array type that prevents array boundaries from being overrun. Storage for each array is allocated by the use of **new**, and a pointer to the memory is maintained within each array object.

```
/* This program creates a "safe" array class.  Since space
   for the array is allocated using new, a copy constructor
   is provided to allocate memory when one array object is
   used to initialize another.
*/
#include <iostream.h>
#include <stdlib.h>

class array {
  int *p;
  int size;
public:
  array(int sz) {
    p = new int[sz];
    size = sz;
```

```
  }
  ~array() {delete [] p;}

  // copy constructor
  array(const array &a);

  void put(int i, int j) {
    if(i>=0 && i<size) p[i] = j;
  }
  int get(int i) {
    return p[i];
  }
};

// copy constructor
array::array(const array &a) {
  int i;

  p = new int[a.size];
  for(i=0; i<a.size; i++) p[i] = a.p[i];
}

int main()
{
  array num(10);
  int i;

  for(i=0; i<10; i++) num.put(i, i);
  for(i=9; i>=0; i--) cout << num.get(i);
  cout << "\n";

  // create another array and initialize with num
  array x(num);  // invokes copy constructor
  for(i=0; i<10; i++) cout << x.get(i);

  return 0;
}
```

When **num** is used to initialize **x**, the copy constructor is called, memory for the new array is allocated and stored in **x.p**, and the contents of **num** are copied to **x**'s array. In this way, **x** and **num** have arrays that have the same values, but each array is separate and distinct. (That is, **num.p** and **x.p** do not point to the same piece of memory.) If the copy constructor had not been created, the default bitwise initialization would have resulted in **x** and **num** sharing the same memory for their arrays. (That is, **num.p** and **x.p** would have, indeed, pointed to the same location.)

The copy constructor is called only for initializations. For example, this sequence does not call the copy constructor defined in the preceding program:

```
array a(10);
  .
  .
  .
array b(10);

b = a; // does not call copy constructor
```

In this case, **b = a** performs the assignment operation. If = is not overloaded (as it is not here), a bitwise copy will be made. Therefore, in some cases you may need to overload the = operator as well as create a copy constructor to avoid problems.

Granting Access

When you inherit a base class as **private**, all elements (including **public** elements) of the base class become **private** elements of the derived class. However, in some instances you may wish to grant certain **public** elements of the base class **public** status in the derived class. To accomplish this, you must use an *access declaration*. An access declaration has the general form

base-class-name::element;

The access declaration is put under the appropriate heading in the derived class' declaration.

Here is a simple example that illustrates how to use an access declaration:

```
#include <iostream.h>

class B_class {
public:
  int i, j;
};

class D_class : private B_class {
public:
  // access declaration
  B_class::i;  // i from B_class is now public again

  int k;
```

```
} ;

int main()
{
  D_class d;

  d.i = 10;  // legal because i is made public in D_class
  d.k = 20;
// d.j = 30; // illegal because j is private in D_class

  cout << d.i * d.k;

  return 0;
}
```

In this example, **B_class** is inherited by **D_class** as **private**. This means that both **i** and **j** become **private** elements of **D_class**. However, inside **D_class**, an access declaration specifies that **i** should become **public** again.

You can also use an access declaration to grant **protected** elements in the base class **protected** status in a derived class. Keep in mind, however, that you cannot raise or lower an element's access status. For example, a **private** element of the base cannot become a **public** element in a derived class.

Using Namespaces

As names with global scope are added to a system, the probability of collisions among these names increases. This becomes especially true as you make use of libraries that are developed by multiple, independent vendors. The **namespace** feature in C++ allows you to partition the global namespace so that this problem is avoided. In essence, a **namespace** defines a scope.

The general form of **namespace** is shown here:

```
namespace name {
  // object declarations
}
```

In addition, you may have anonymous namespaces as shown here:

```
namespace {
  // object declarations
}
```

Anonymous namespaces allow you to establish unique identifiers that are known only within the scope of a single file.

Here is an example of a **namespace**:

```
namespace MyNameSpace {
  int i, k;
  void myfunc(int j) { cout << j; }
}
```

Here, **i**, **k**, and **myfunc( )** are part of the scope defined by the **MyNameSpace** namespace.

Since a namespace defines a scope, you need to use the scope resolution operator to refer to objects defined within a namespace. For example, to assign the value 10 to **i**, you must use this statement:

```
MyNameSpace::i = 10;
```

If the members of a namespace will be frequently used, you can use a **using** directive to simplify their access. The **using** statement has these two general forms:

using namespace *name*;

using *name::member*;

In the first form, *name* specifies the name of the namespace you want to access. All of the members defined within the specified namespace may be used without qualification. In the second form, only a specific member of the namespace is made visible. For example, assuming **MyNameSpace** as shown above, the following **using** statements and assignments are valid:

```
using MyNameSpace::k; // only k is made visible
k = 10; // OK because k is visible

using namespace MyNameSpace; // all members of MyNameSpace are visible
i = 10; // OK because all members of MyNameSpace are now visible
```

Some Recent Changes

Some recent changes to C++ have been incorporated into Borland C++. They are described here.

New Headers

The draft ANSI C++ standard has defined a new way to specify header files and Borland C++ now allows this new approach. However, the traditional style (which is used by this book) is still fully supported and, indeed, commonplace. The new style does not require the use of an actual file name. Instead, a standard header identifier is used, which will be mapped to a file name by the compiler, if necessary. For example, the new-style header that includes the header file for the I/O system is

```
#include <iostream>
```

As you can see, the **.h** has been left off. This example can be generalized. For instance, using the new-style header format, the following statement includes the header for file I/O:

```
#include <fstream>
```

You can use the new header style if you like. It has not been used in this book because, currently, few compilers other than Borland C++ support it. Thus, using it may reduce the portability of your code in the near future. Of course, this header style will be universally accepted once the ANSI C++ standard has been formally adopted (which should occur sometime within the next few years).

Explicit Constructors

The keyword **explicit** is used to create "nonconverting constructors." For example, given the following class:

```
class MyClass {
  int i;
public:
  MyClass(int j) {i = j;}
  // ...
};
```

MyClass objects can be declared as shown here:

```
MyClass ob1(1);
MyClass ob2 = 10;
```

In this case, the statement

```
MyClass ob2 = 10;
```

is automatically converted into the form

```
MyClass ob2(10);
```

However, by declaring the **MyClass** constructor as **explicit**, this automatic conversion will not be supplied. Here is **MyClass** shown using an **explicit** constructor:

```
class MyClass {
  int i;
public:
```

```
  explicit MyClass(int j) {i = j;}
  // ...
};
```

Now, only constructors of the form

```
MyClass ob(110);
```

will be allowed.

Using mutable

C++ defines the keyword **mutable**. It is used to allow a member of an object to override **const**ness. That is, a **mutable** member of a **const** object is not **const** and can be modified.

typename

C++ supports the **typename** keyword. It may be used in place of the keyword **class** in a **template** declaration or to signify an undefined type.

The Standard Template Library

The standardization efforts for C++ are still continuing. Part of the activity involves defining a standard set of classes and libraries for all ANSI-conforming C++ compilers. In addition to the standard I/O class library described in Chapter 24, C++ also defines several other class libraries. Some of these provide support for containers, algorithms, and iterators. These libraries implement what is commonly known as the *standard template library* or STL. At the time of this writing, the final form of these libraries had not yet been determined. However, included with Borland C++ 5.0 is an implementation of the Standard C++ Library by Rogue Wave Software, Inc. This section provides a very brief introduction to this feature.

REMEMBER: The standard C++ class library is still undergoing development and is subject to change. The only part of the C++ library that should be considered stable are the I/O classes and functions described in Chapter 24.

The standard C++ library includes several types of containers. Containers are classes that create objects that hold other objects. There are classes such as **vector** (a dynamic array), **deque** (a double-ended queue), and **list** (a linear list). These provide different tradeoffs in terms of update and access efficiency. **queue** and **stack** provide first-in, first-out and last-in, first-out functionality, respectively. A **priority_queue** removes elements according to their individual priority.

The containers library also defines associative containers, which allow efficient retrieval of values based on keys. A **map** provides access to values from unique keys. Thus, a **map** stores a key/value pair and allows a value to be retrieved given its key. In a map, a key must be associated with only one value A **multimap** allows you to use one key to refer to multiple values. Also supported are sets, using either **set** or **multiset**.

The algorithms include capabilities for initializing, searching, and transforming the contents of containers. Some examples of how you can apply these algorithms are

- A sequence may be filled with an initial value or a set of values generated by a function.
- A sequence may be searched for an individual element or subsequence that satisfies certain properties.
- Two sequences may be checked for pairwise equality.
- A function may be applied to each element of a collection.
- The union, intersection, or difference between two sequences may be calculated.

Here, the term *sequence* refers to the elements of a container. The algorithms are designed to operate with a wide variety of containers.

Also included are iterators. These are objects that are, more or less, pointers. They give you the ability to cycle through the contents of a container in much the same way that you would use a pointer to cycle through an array. Different iterators provide alternative mechanisms for traversing a container (e.g., forward, backward, random access, bidirectional).

Here is an example that demonstrates the **vector** container. As mentioned, a **vector** is similar to an array. However, it has the advantage that it automatically handles its own storage management. A **vector** provides methods so that you can determine its size and add or remove elements.

The following program illustrates the use of a **vector** class:

```
// A short example that demonstrates vector.
#include <iostream.h>
#include <vector.h>

// must use std namespace for vector
using namespace std;

int main()
{
  vector<int> v; // create zero-length vector

  cout << "size = " << v.size() << endl;
```

```
  /* put values onto end of vector
     vector will grow as needed. */
  for(int i=0; i<10; i++) v.push_back(i);

  cout << "size now = " << v.size() << endl;

  // can access vector contents using subscripting
  for(int i=0; i<10; i++) cout << v[i] << " ";
  cout << endl;

  // Can access vector's first and last element
  cout << "front = " << v.front() << endl;
  cout << "back = " << v.back() << endl;

  // access via iterator
  vector<int>::iterator p = v.begin();
  while(p != v.end()) {
    cout << *p << " ";
    p++;
  }

  return 0;
}
```

The output from this program is

```
size = 0
size now = 10
0 1 2 3 4 5 6 7 8 9
front = 0
back = 9
0 1 2 3 4 5 6 7 8 9
```

In this program, the vector is initially created with zero length. The **push_back( )** member function puts values onto the end of the vector, expanding its size as needed. The **size( )** function displays the size of the vector. The vector may be indexed like a normal array. It may also be accessed using an iterator. The function **begin( )** returns a pointer to the start of the vector. The function **end( )** returns a pointer to the end of the vector.

The C++ standard library classes that support containers, algorithms, and iterators are some of its most exciting features. Once these items have become fully stable, you will want to use them in all your programming tasks. Don't be intimidated by the rather complex syntax. Once you grasp the basic concept, these items are extremely easy to use.

Differences Between C and C++

For the most part, C++ is a superset of ANSI-standard C, and virtually all C programs are also C++ programs. However, a few differences do exist, the most important of which are discussed here.

One of the most important yet subtle differences between C and C++ is the fact that in C, a function declared like this:

```
int f();
```

says *nothing* about any parameters to that function. That is, when there is nothing specified between the parentheses following the function's name, in C this means that nothing is being stated, one way or the other, about any parameters to that function. It might have parameters and it might not have parameters. However, in C++, a function declaration like this means that the function does *not* have parameters. That is, in C++, these two declarations are equivalent:

```
int f();
int f(void):
```

In C++, the **void** is optional. Many C++ programmers include the **void** as a means of making it completely clear to anyone reading the program that a function does not have any parameters, but this is technically unnecessary.

In C++, all functions must be prototyped. This is an option in C (although good programming practice suggests full prototyping be used in a C program).

A small, but potentially important, difference between C and C++ is that in C, a character constant is automatically elevated to an integer. In C++, it is not.

In C, it is not an error to declare a global variable several times, even though it is bad programming practice. In C++, this is an error.

In C, an identifier will have at least 31 significant characters. In C++, all characters are considered significant. However, from a practical point of view, extremely long identifiers are unwieldy and are seldom needed.

In C, although unusual, you can call **main( )** from within a program. In C++, this is not allowed.

In C, you cannot take the address of a **register** variable. In C++, you can.

Final Thoughts

If you are new to object-oriented programming but want to become proficient, the best approach is to write many object-oriented programs. Programming is best learned by doing. Also, look at examples of C++ programs written by other people. If possible, study the C++ code written by several different programmers, paying attention to how each program is designed and implemented. Look for shortcomings as well as strong points. This will broaden the way you think about programming. (Several extended examples of C++ are found in my book *Expert C++* (Berkeley, CA: Osborne/McGraw-Hill, 1996.) Finally, experiment. Push your limits. You will be surprised at how quickly you become an expert C++ programmer!

PART FOUR

The Borland C++ Integrated Development Environment

Part 4 of this book covers the Borland C++ development environment. This includes the integrated development environment (IDE), the editor, and the debugger.

Chapter Twenty-Eight

The Integrated Development Environment

Borland C++ has two separate modes of operation. The first is called its integrated development environment, or IDE. Using the IDE, editing, compilation, and execution are controlled by single keystrokes, mouse clicks, and easy-to-use menus. In fact, the IDE is so easy to use that its operation is almost intuitive. The other method of operation uses the traditional command-line approach. When using the command line, you first use an editor to create a program source file and then you compile it, link it, and run it. Many programmers still favor the command-line method of program development. However, most find that the conveniences offered by the IDE speed up and simplify development.

This chapter provides a brief overview of the Borland C++ IDE. If you are new to Borland C++ and have never used an integrated development environment before, then you will find this tour helpful. For detailed information about using the IDE, consult Borland's online help system.

NOTE: Since the Borland C++ IDE executes under Windows, it is assumed that you know how to make menu selections, use dialog boxes, and otherwise manage a Windows environment. This rudimentary information is not presented here.

The IDE Main Window

When you first execute the IDE you see the window shown in Figure 28-1. It consists of these, in order from top to bottom:

- The Menu bar
- The SpeedBar
- The window area
- The Status bar

The window area is where the various windows (such as edit and message windows) associated with your project are displayed. The remainder of this chapter briefly examines the other three items.

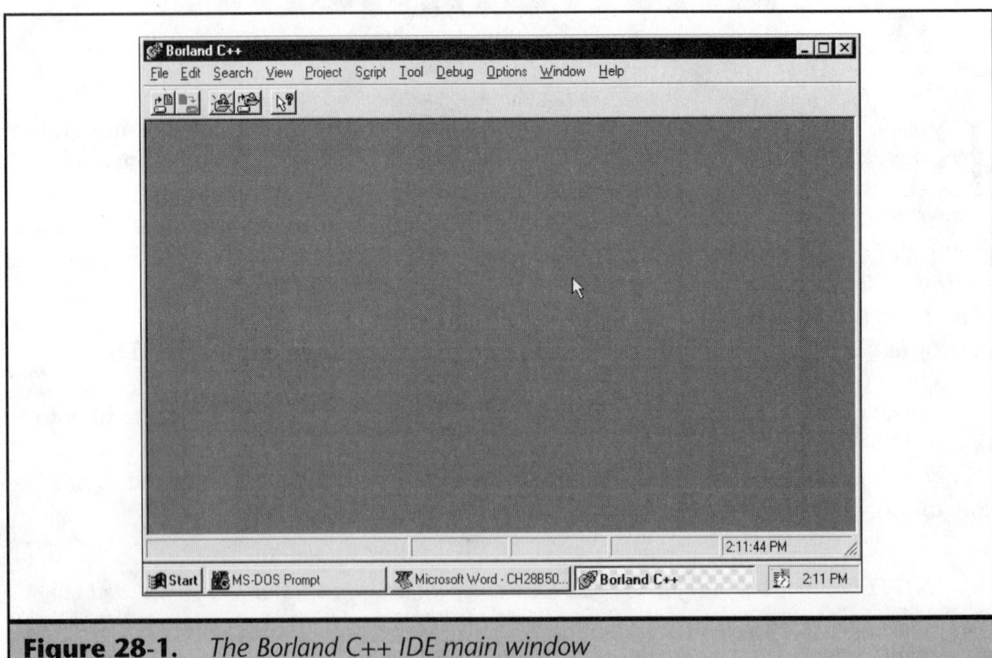

Figure 28-1. *The Borland C++ IDE main window*

The Menu Bar

The Menu bar is used either to tell the IDE to do something, such as load a file or compile a program, or to set an option. Table 28-1 summarizes the purpose of each menu.

When you select a Menu bar item, a pull-down menu is displayed that contains a list of choices. Some pull-down menu selections produce another pull-down menu that displays additional options relating to the first menu. Secondary pull-down menus operate just like primary pull-down menus. When one menu will generate another, it is shown with a dark arrow to its right. If a pull-down menu item is followed by three periods, it means that selecting this item will cause a dialog box to be displayed that relates to the item.

Let's take a closer look at the Menu bar options.

Item	Purpose
File	Load and save projects and files, handle printing, and exit the IDE
Edit	Perform various editing functions
Search	Perform various text searches and replacements
View	Display project, class, message, and debugging information
Project	Open, close, and build projects
Script	Define and execute scripts
Tool	Run programs, tools, and utilities
Debug	Access the integrated debugger
Options	Modify the settings for the IDE and projects
Window	Manage the IDE windows
Help	Access online help

Table 28-1. *Summary of the Menu Bar Items*

Exploring the Menu Bar

This section examines each entry of the Menu bar. To follow along, position the highlight on the appropriate menu selection, and press ENTER. As each option is discussed, move the highlight to that option.

File

Highlighting the **File** option activates the **File** pull-down menu, as shown in Figure 28-2.

Selecting **New** opens another pull-down menu that has entries for **Text Edit**, **Project**, **AppExpert**, and **Resource Project**. **Text Edit** gives you a new window in which to enter a program source file. **Project** allows you to establish a new project. **AppExpert** helps you create Windows programs based upon Borland's ObjectWindows class library. A **Resource Project** is a collection of one or more resources.

The **Open** option prompts you for a file name and then loads that file into the IDE. If the file does not exist, it is created. The **Open** option also displays a list of files from which you can choose. Use the arrow keys to move the highlight until it is on the file you wish to load and press ENTER to load the file, or double-click on the desired file name. Note that the file type is not limited to a C or C++ source file. Makefiles, bitmap images, project files, and resource files are some of the possible file types.

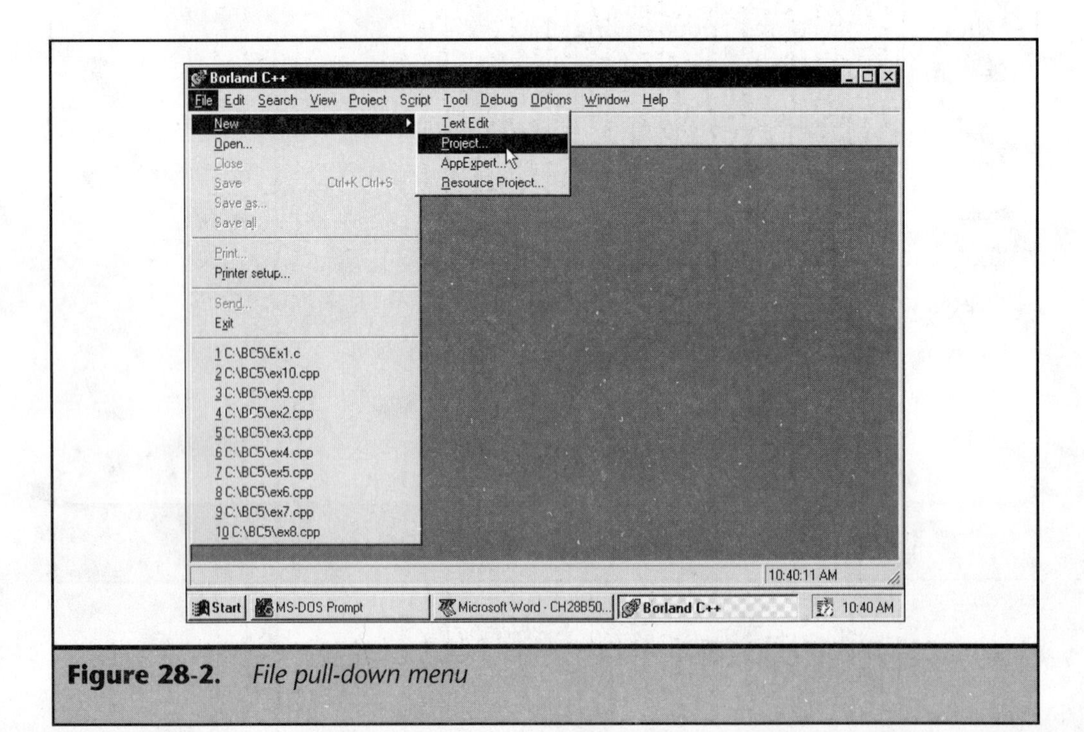

Figure 28-2. *File pull-down menu*

The **Close** option closes and removes the current file and/or project.

The **Save** option saves the file in the active window. The **Save as** option lets you save a file using a different file name. The **Save all** option saves the files in all open windows.

The **Print** option prints the file in the active window. The **Printer setup** option lets you choose and/or configure the printer.

Exit exits the IDE.

Finally, note that there is a history list of the most recently used files. You may click on one of these to open it.

Edit

The **Edit** option allows you to perform several editor operations. These commands and the operation of the editor are discussed at length in Chapter 29.

Search

The **Search** Main menu entry allows you to perform various types of searches and search-and-replace operations on the text in the active window. Since the **Search** options relate to the editor, they are discussed in Chapter 29.

View

Highlighting the **View** option activates the **View** pull-down menu. It allows you to display various windows.

ClassExpert helps you manage classes when using the **AppExpert**. **Project** presents a graphical hierarchy showing the various files that comprise your current project. **Message** displays a window that contains the various messages generated by the IDE, such as warnings and errors, that occur when compiling your program. **Classes** displays a graphical hierarchy showing the various classes in your application. **Globals** displays the global variables used by your application. **CPU** presents low-level debugging information. **Process** lists all running processes and threads. **Watch** is used during debugging activities to obtain the current values of any watched expressions you have defined. **Breakpoint** lists all breakpoints. (Breakpoints are used when debugging.) Finally, the **Call Stack** displays the current call stack, which is useful when debugging.

Project

Highlighting the **Project** option activates the **Project** pull-down menu.

Open project loads an existing project. **Close project** closes and removes the current project. **New target** adds new components to a project. **Compile** compiles the currently selected file. **Make all** compiles and links those parts of your project that are out of date. **Build all** compiles and links all parts of your project even if they are not out of date. **Generate makefile** constructs a makefile for the current project. (This makefile can be executed using Borland's command-line utility MAKE.EXE.)

Script

Highlighting the **Script** option activates the **Script** pull-down menu. This option relates to Borland's new **cScript** language. Scripting allows you to enhance the operation of the IDE. (It is briefly described later in this chapter.)

Run opens a window in which you can enter a script command. **Commands** opens a dialog box listing the script commands and variables. **Modules** lists all active script modules. **Compile file** compiles and runs the script in the currently selected window. **Run file** executes the script in the currently selected window. **Install/Uninstall examples** is used to obtain access to the sample scripts that are provided with Borland C++.

Tool

The **Tool** pull-down menu provides a convenient way to access preinstalled or user-installed tools without leaving the context of the IDE. You may install additional tools into this pull-down menu by selecting **Tools** in the **Options** menu.

Debug

The **Debug** option lets you use and control the integrated debugger. The operation of the debugger and its options are discussed in Chapter 30.

Options

Highlighting the **Options** entry activates the **Options** pull-down menu.

The **Project** option determines how your program is compiled and linked. The **Environment** option lets you control the behavior of IDE components such as the editor, browser, debugger, and resource editor. It is also possible to choose fonts and syntax highlighting. The **Tools** option lets you install, remove, and manage the tools that are accessible via the **Tool** option from the Main menu.

A style sheet is a group of option settings that control how parts of a project are built. The **Style Sheets** selection allows you to define these.

Finally, the **Save** option allows you to save the environment, desktop, project, and message options that you select.

Window

The **Window** option allows you to manage various aspects of the IDE's windows. The IDE allows several windows to be open at the same time. There are two ways that multiple windows may be displayed: tiled or cascaded. By default, windows are cascaded; this means that each time a new one is created, it partially overlays one or more other windows. For example, Figure 28-3 shows an example of several cascaded windows. By contrast, if you select the **Tile horizontal** or **Tile vertical** option, no window overlays another. Tiling vertically optimizes the vertical dimension. Tiling horizontally optimizes the horizontal dimension. Each is given a reduced part of the

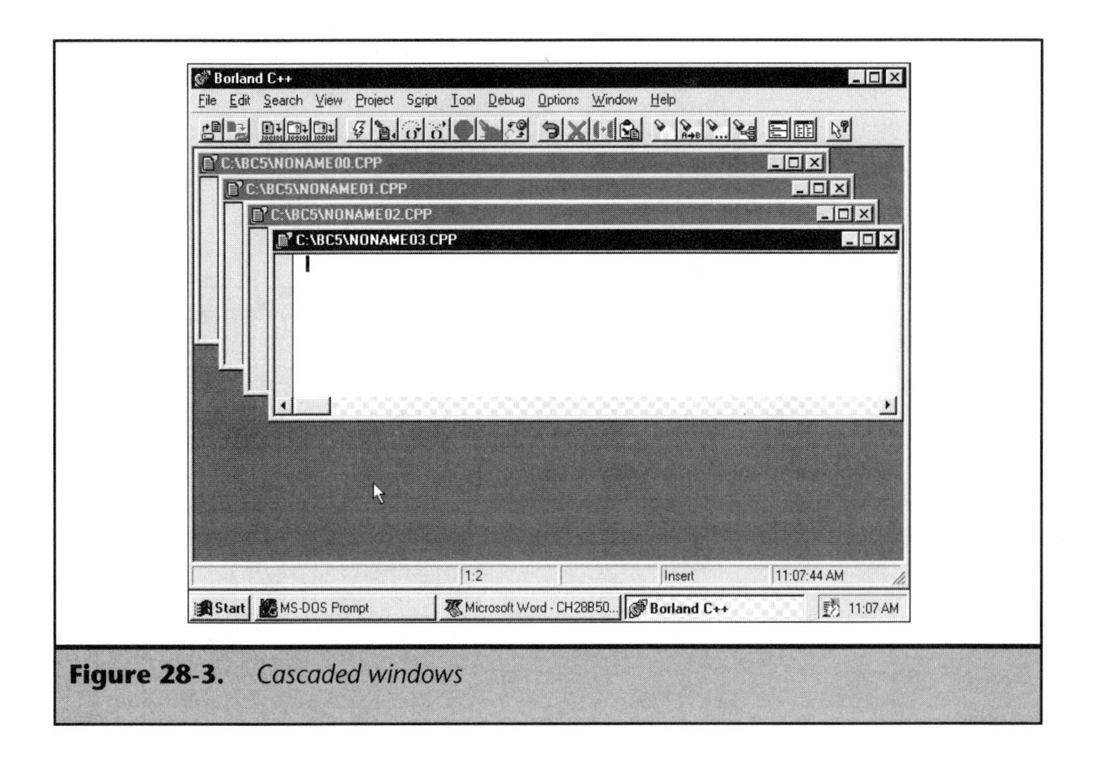

Figure 28-3. *Cascaded windows*

screen. Figure 28-4 shows the same windows as those in Figure 28-3, but in tiled vertical format.

Arrange icons neatly spaces the icons on your desktop. **Close all** or **Minimize all** can be used to close or minimize one or more of the various windows. Some of the windows that may exist are the message, editor, project, browser, debugger, and resource workshop. These will become familiar to you as you work with Borland C++. **Restore all** restores any previously minimized windows

Help

Highlighting the **Help** entry activates the **Help** pull-down menu.

The **Contents** option displays an index of the contents of the help system. The **Keyword search** option lets you get help about a specific keyword. To do so, highlight the keyword and then select **Keyword search**. Alternatively, you may select the keyword and then press F1. In either case, you will then see information relating to the keyword you selected.

The **Keyboard** option describes how to define shortcuts for your keyboard. **Using help** tells about the organization of the help files. **Windows API** gives information about the Windows application programming interface functions. **OWL API** presents information about Borland's Object Windows Library. The **About** option displays the version of Borland C++ you are using.

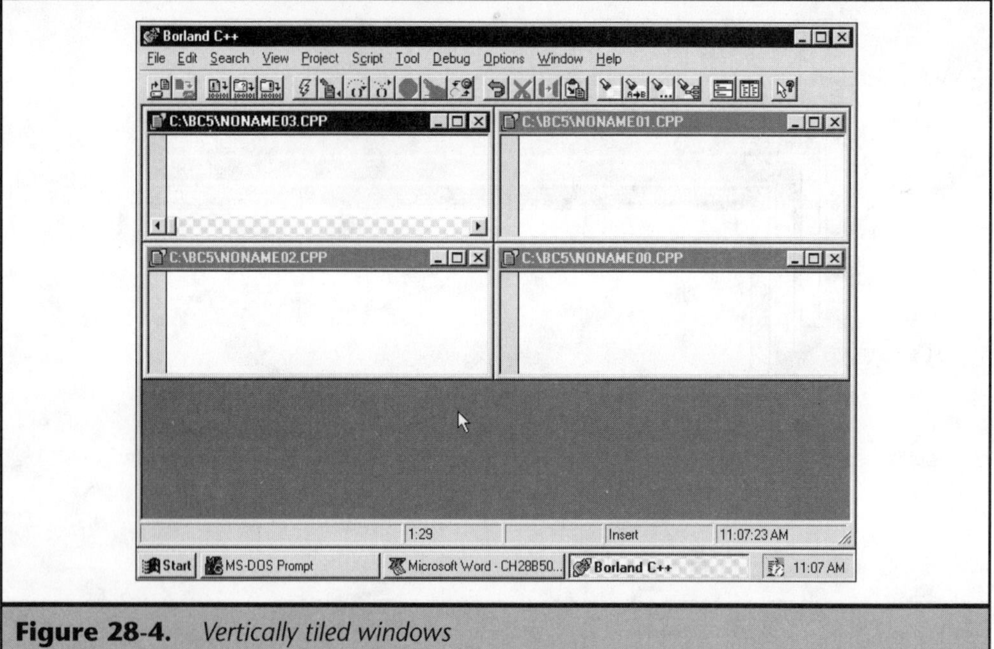

Figure 28-4. *Vertically tiled windows*

Using Context-Sensitive Help

The IDE contains *context-sensitive* help that allows you to obtain information about any feature of Borland C++ by simply pressing the F1 key. This means it displays help information that relates to what you are doing at the time. More specifically, it displays information that relates to the current focus of activity. For example, if you highlight **Save** under the **File** option in the Menu bar and then activate the help system by pressing F1, you will see information about the **Save** option. Also, if the cursor is positioned over the name of a library function, keyword, or preprocessor directive, pressing F1 gives you information about that item.

Before moving on, you might want to try the context-sensitive help feature on your own. As you will see, it is a powerful aid.

The SpeedBar

The row of icons immediately below the Menu bar is the *SpeedBar*. The SpeedBar provides a fast way to immediately select an option, bypassing the menus. The icons that are present in the SpeedBar depend upon what you are currently doing and how you have configured the IDE. You can customize the SpeedBar by selecting **Environment** in the **Options** menu and then selecting **SpeedBar**.

The Status Bar

The line at the bottom of the main window is called the *Status bar*. It displays information relating to whatever you are currently doing. For example, when you are working in the editor window, the status line includes the current row and column position of the cursor in that window and whether insert or overstrike mode is in effect. In general, the information displayed on the Status bar provides clues about the meaning of whatever is the current focus of the IDE.

Using SpeedMenus

Borland C++ includes special menus called *SpeedMenus* that are activated by pressing the right mouse button when it is over certain items. For example, to compile a C++ program, position the mouse pointer over the name of the source file in your project window and then press the right mouse button. A SpeedMenu will pop up. One of the options in this menu will be **C++ Compile**. SpeedMenus save several keystrokes and are generally quite useful.

Scripting

Borland C++ allows you to customize and enhance the operation of the IDE. This is done by writing small programs, or *scripts*. A special object-oriented programming language called **cScript** has been provided for this purpose. Many of the elements that comprise the IDE are represented as classes and, therefore, can be manipulated by **cScript**. It is a language that has some similarities to C++ and, therefore, you should find it easy to learn.

A set of sample scripts has been provided by Borland. To enable convenient access to these programs, choose the **Install/Uninstall examples** option in the **Script** menu. You'll notice that a new entry labeled **Example scripts** is now included in the Menu bar.

The sample scripts demonstrate the power of **cScript** to customize and enhance the IDE. They also provide starting points for your own optimizations. Here are just a few of the types of operations provided by the sample scripts:

- Search and replace within multiple files
- Convert a block of text into a comment
- Open the header files associated with a source file
- Automatically save files at predetermined intervals
- Obtain additional help from known sites on the Internet

If you will be using Borland C++ for high-powered development, **cScript** is something that you will definitely want to look into.

A Short Word on Creating Projects and Compiling Programs

Although Borland's online help information fully describes the creation of projects and the compilation of programs, a few words are in order. When using the IDE, you will normally create a project for every program that you write. When creating the project, you must select the target type. The target you select determines what type of operating environment your program is designed to run under. For example, using Borland C++ you can create programs for Windows 3.1, Windows 95/NT, and DOS (which includes the command-prompt interface provided by Windows). Many first-time users find the target options intimidating. Here are three tips that might help:

1. When compiling simple, non-Windows programs, such as those shown in Parts 1, 2, and 3 of this book, select Application as the target type and DOS as the platform.
2. When creating programs for Windows, you must decide if you will be using the Windows API (as is used by the Windows examples in Part 5 of this book), Borland's Object Windows Library (OWL), or Microsoft's Foundation Classes (MFC). When compiling a Windows application that uses the API functions, select Application as the target type and then select a version of Windows. For Windows 95/NT, select Win32.
3. When creating Java programs, select Java as the target type.

If you don't make the target selections correctly, then your program will either fail to compile or fail to run correctly. Without a doubt, failure to properly set the target options is a major source of trouble for newcomers. If you encounter problems attempting to compile or run any of the programs in this book, make sure that you have your target options set correctly.

To actually run a program from within the IDE, select the **Run** option from within the **Debug** menu. One more thing: When you run a DOS program, a temporary DOS session is created in which the program is executed. This session is destroyed as soon as your program terminates. If the DOS session is terminating before you have time to observe the results of your program, try adding an input statement as the last line of your program. This way the program will not terminate until you have entered something from the keyboard.

Chapter Twenty-Nine

Using the Editor

This chapter discusses the IDE text editor. This is the editor that you will use to create your program's source files. Although the editor contains many commands, you will not have to learn all of them at once. The most important deal with insertion, deletion, block moves, searching, and replacement. Once you have mastered these basic areas, you will easily be able to learn the rest of the editor commands and put them to use as you need them. Actually, learning to use the editor is surprisingly simple because you have the online context-sensitive help system at your disposal.

Invoking the Editor and Entering Text

You create a new editor window by

1. Selecting **File** on the Menu bar
2. Selecting **New** from the first pull-down menu
3. Selecting **Text Edit** from the second pull-down menu

The top line of the editor window displays the name of the file currently being edited, which is also the title of the editor window. When an editor window has input focus, the Status bar at the bottom of the IDE window displays information about the state of the editor, including the current line and column position of the cursor.

When the editor window is active and you are not in the middle of giving it a command, it is ready to accept input. This means that when you strike keys on the keyboard, they will appear in the editor at the current cursor location.

By default, the editor is in *insert mode*. This means that as you enter text, it is inserted in the middle of what (if anything) is already there. The opposite, *overwrite mode*, overwrites existing text with new text. You can toggle between these two modes by pressing the INS key. You can tell which mode is currently active by the shape of the cursor. When in insert mode, the cursor is represented as a blinking vertical bar. In overwrite mode, it is a blinking rectangle. The insert/overwrite mode is also displayed in the Status window.

Make sure the editor window is active and type the following lines:

```
This is a
test of the
Borland C++ IDE editor.
```

Press ENTER at the end of the last line. If you make a mistake, you can use the BACKSPACE key to correct it. Your screen now looks like the one in Figure 29-1. Notice that the row and column position of the cursor is displayed in the Status bar of the IDE window. Also, notice that now there is an indication that the editor window has been modified.

When editing text, you can use the arrow keys to move the cursor around the text at random. Also, when you click the mouse, the cursor moves to the position of the mouse pointer. At this time, use either the arrow keys or the mouse to position the cursor at the far left of the line "test of the". Now, type **very small** and press ENTER. As you do so, watch the way the existing line is moved to the right instead of being overwritten. This is what happens when the editor is in insert mode. Had you toggled

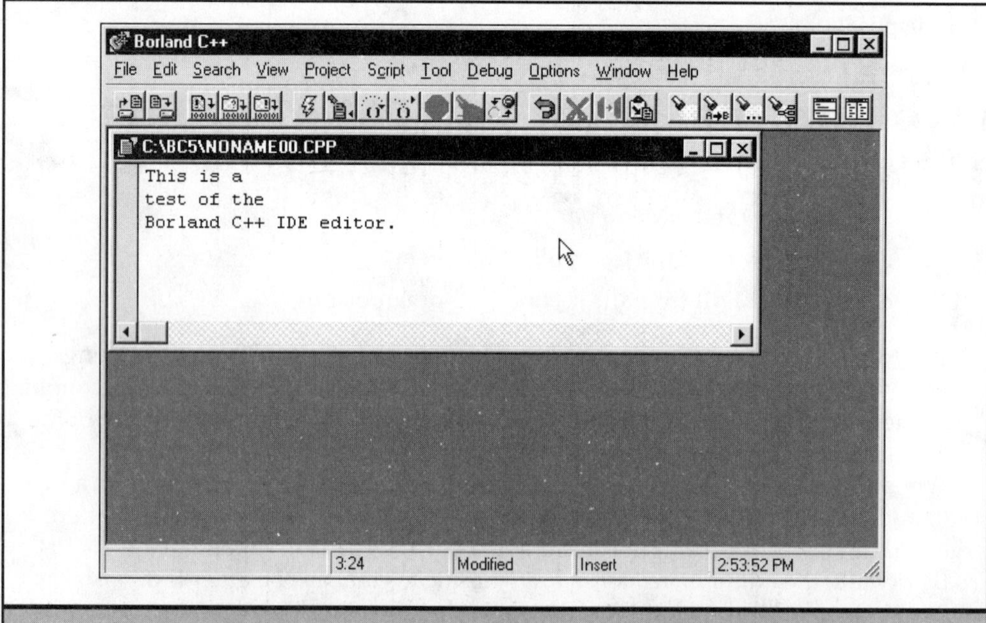

Figure 29-1. *Editor window with text entered*

the editor into overwrite mode, the original line would have been overwritten. Your screen now looks like the one in Figure 29-2.

Deleting Characters, Words, and Lines

You can delete a single character two ways: with the BACKSPACE key or with the DEL key. The BACKSPACE key deletes the character immediately to the left of the cursor, while the DEL key deletes the character immediately to the right of the cursor.

You can delete an entire word that is to the right of the cursor by pressing CTRL-T.

You can remove an entire line by pressing CTRL-Y. It does not matter where the cursor is positioned in the line; the entire line is deleted.

Moving, Copying, and Deleting Blocks of Text

The IDE editor allows you to manipulate a block of text by moving or copying it to another location or deleting it altogether. In order to do any of these things, you must first define a block. A *block* can be as short as a single character or as large as your entire file. However, a block is typically somewhere between these two extremes. To

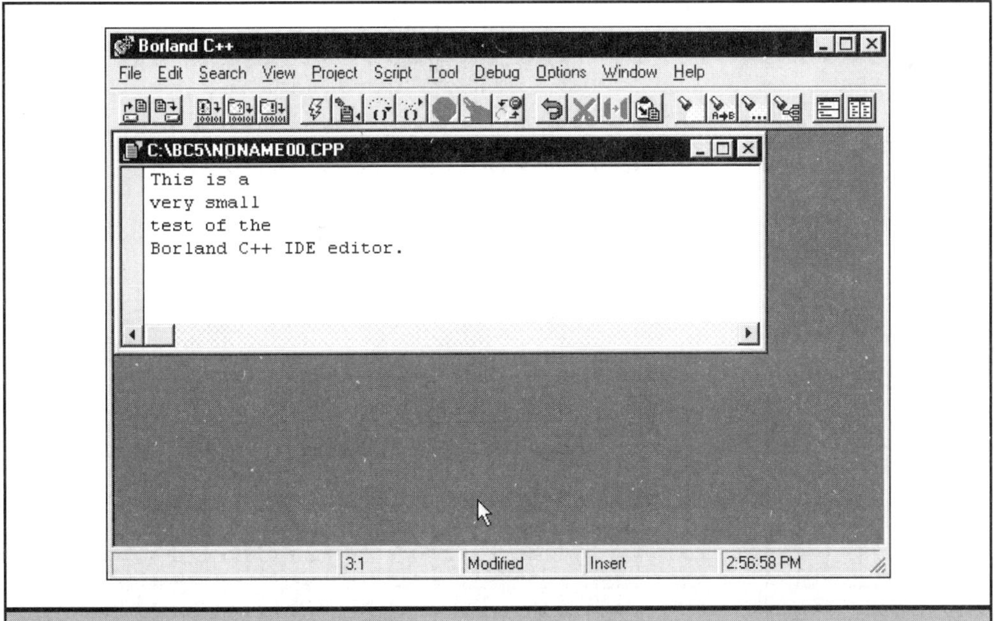

Figure 29-2. *Editor window after inserting a line*

define a block by using the mouse, first position the mouse pointer at the start of the block. Next, press and hold down the left mouse button and move the mouse pointer to the end of the block. Finally, release the button. The block you have defined is highlighted.

You can also define a block with the keyboard by holding down the SHIFT key and using the arrow keys and the PGUP, PGDN, HOME, and END keys. As you move the cursor with the SHIFT key down, the area the cursor moves over becomes highlighted. By pressing SHIFT-CTRL-END, you define a block that begins at the current cursor location and stops at the end of the file. By pressing SHIFT-CTRL-HOME, you define a block that begins at the current cursor location and stops at the start of the file.

Try defining a block from the start of the third line to the end of the last line. Your screen should look like the one in Figure 29-3.

To copy a block, first define the block. Next, select **Copy** from the **Edit** menu. Then, position the cursor at the point where you want the block copied. Finally, select **Paste** from the **Edit** menu. The block you highlighted appears immediately after the point where you positioned the cursor. Alternatively, you may use the keyboard commands CTRL-C for **Copy** and CTRL-V for **Paste**.

Copy the block you defined earlier (as shown in Figure 29-3) to the beginning of the file. Your screen should now look like the one in Figure 29-4.

You can move a block with the **Edit** menu by first deleting the block using **Cut** and then restoring it at the desired location by using **Paste**.

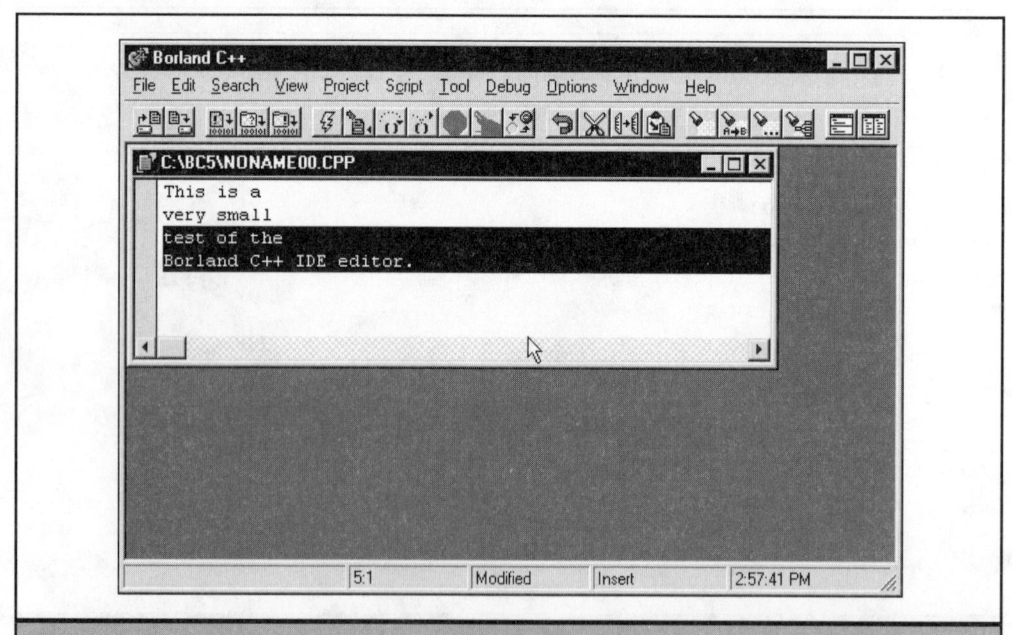

Figure 29-3. *Editor window after defining a block*

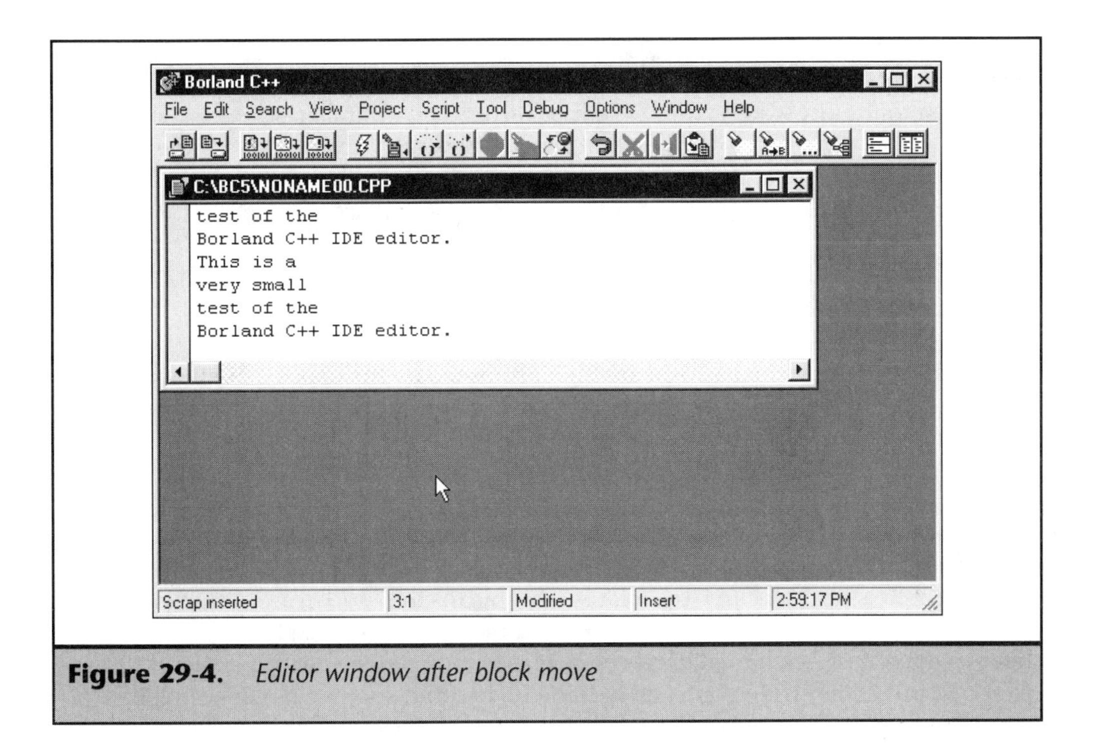

Figure 29-4. *Editor window after block move*

To delete the currently marked block, also use **Cut**. The block you delete is automatically put into the *clipboard*. You will see how to use the clipboard in the next section.

Using the Clipboard

The clipboard is a temporary depository for fragments of text. To move text into the clipboard, you need to mark the region and then either delete that block or, using the **Edit** menu, select the **Copy** option. If you select **Copy**, the block is not deleted from the file, but it is still copied into the clipboard.

To retrieve a block of text from the clipboard, use the **Edit** menu's **Paste** command. This causes the current contents of the clipboard to be copied into the current editor window at the current cursor location.

If you wish to delete a block without having it copied into the clipboard, select the block and execute the **Clear** option in the **Edit** menu. This removes the block but does not copy it to the clipboard. You can also clear a block by pressing the DEL key.

You can edit more than one file at a time simply by loading another file or creating another new one. Each file you edit will be in its own editor window. To copy text from one window to another, define the block you want in the source window, copy it to the clipboard, and then paste it into the target window.

More on Cursor Movement

In addition to the arrow keys, the IDE editor recognizes a number of special keyboard commands that allow you to move about the file. Several of the most common are summarized in Table 29-1. You might want to experiment with these commands now. Of course, you can also position the cursor by using the mouse.

Find and Replace

To find a specific sequence of characters, use the **Search** menu's **Find** command. This is accessed from the Menu bar. You are then prompted by the dialog box shown in Figure 29-5 for the string you wish to find. You can also specify various search options to alter the way the search is conducted.

By default, the search for the string proceeds from the current cursor location forward in the file. To change this so the search moves in the opposite direction, select the **Backward** direction. You can also have the search cover the entire file by selecting the **Entire scope** option.

The search is case-sensitive by default. This means that uppercase and lowercase characters, such as "A" and "a", are treated as different characters. However, you can choose to have the search treat these characters as though they are the same.

By default, if the string you enter is contained within another, larger string, this produces a match. (This is called a substring match.) For example, if you enter "is" for

Command	Action
PGUP	Moves the cursor up one full window.
PGDN	Moves the cursor down one full window.
HOME	Moves the cursor to the start of the line.
END	Moves the cursor to the end of the line.
CTRL-PGUP	Moves the cursor to the top of the window.
CTRL-PGDN	Moves the cursor to the bottom of the window.
CTRL-HOME	Moves the cursor to the beginning of the file.
CTRL-END	Moves the cursor to the end of the file.

Table 29-1. *Common Cursor Commands*

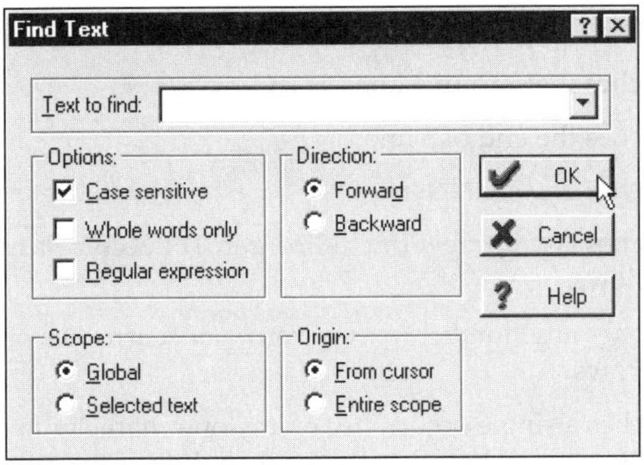

Figure 29-5. *The Find Text dialog box*

the search string, the editor will find a match in the word "this". You can cause the search to match only whole words by checking the **Whole words only** box.

You can confine the search to a block by selecting the **Selected text** option.

If you check the **Regular Expression** box, you can use the wildcard characters shown in Table 29-2 in your search string. Here are some examples of how the wildcard characters work:

Expression	**Matches**
h..lo	hello (and others)
^test	test (at start of line)
test$	test (at end of line)
[two]	t, w, or o
x*	x, xx, xxx, etc.

Remember, to use regular expressions, you must check the **Regular expression** box in the **Find Text** dialog box.

You can substitute one string for another using the **Replace** option in the **Search** menu. When you select **Replace**, you see the dialog box shown in Figure 29-6. As you can see, the options available in the **Replace Text** dialog box are similar to those available with **Find**. But, notice one addition. By default, the editor asks you before making a change. You can turn off this feature by deselecting **Prompt on replace**.

Character	Purpose
^	Matches the start of a line.
$	Matches the end of a line.
.	Matches any character.
*	Matches any number (including zero) of occurrences of the character it follows.
+	Matches any number (except zero) of occurrences of the character it follows.
[*string*]	Matches a single occurrence of any one character in *string*. You can specify a range by using the hyphen. If the first character in the string is a ^, the construct will match any characters except those in the string.
\	Causes the character it precedes to be treated literally and not as a wildcard.

Table 29-2. *The Regular Expression Wildcard Characters*

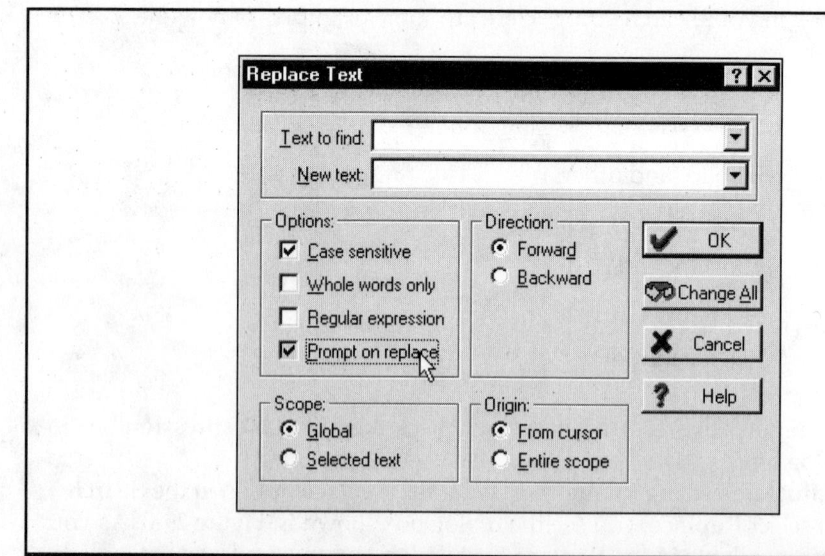

Figure 29-6. *The Replace Text dialog box*

Saving and Loading Your File

There are two ways to save your file. The first saves it to a file that has the same name as that shown in the title of the editor window. The second way allows you to save your file under a different name and makes that the current name of your file. Let's look at how each works.

To save the current contents of the editor window to a disk file with the name shown in the window title, select **File** from the Menu bar followed by **Save**. If you wish to save the contents of the editor into a file with a name other than that shown on the editor status line, select **File** from the Menu bar followed by **Save as**. This allows you to enter the name of the file to which you wish to write the current contents of the editor. It also becomes the file's name.

To load a file, select **File,** then **Open**. This displays a dialog box, and you are prompted for the name of the file you wish to load. There are two ways to specify the file name. First, you can type it. Second, you can make a selection from the list of files shown in the dialog box. By default, all files with the C, CPP, H, or HPP extension are displayed, but you can change this.

When you save a file that already exists on disk, the old version of the file is not overwritten. Instead, it is kept as a backup file and its extension is changed to .BAK.

Understanding Autoindentation

As you most likely know, good programmers use indentation to help make the programs they write clearer and easier to understand. To assist in this practice, after you press ENTER, the editor automatically places the cursor at the same indentation level as the line that was previously entered. You can toggle this feature on and off. To do so, first select **Options** from the Menu bar, followed by **Environment**. Then click the **Editor** entry and then **Options**. A dialog box is then presented that allows you to access the editor options. To turn off autoindenting, simply remove the check from this option.

To see how autoindentation works, enter the following lines exactly as they are shown here:

```
This is an illustration
  of the autoindentation
  mechanism
    of the Borland C++
    editor.
```

As you enter the text, notice that the editor automatically maintains the last indentation level. You will find this feature quite handy when entering C++ source code.

Moving Blocks of Text to and from Disk Files

It is possible to move a block of text into a disk file for later use. You do this by first defining a block and then pressing CTRL-K W. You are then prompted for the name of the file in which you wish to save the block. The original block of text is not removed from your program.

To read a block into a file, use the command CTRL-K R. You are prompted for the file name. The contents of that file will be read in at the current cursor location.

These two commands are most useful when you are moving text between two or more files, as is often the case during program development.

Pair Matching

There are several delimiters in C/C++ that work in pairs—for example, the { }, the [ ], and the ( ). In very long or complex programs, it is sometimes difficult to find the proper companion to a delimiter. It is possible to have the editor automatically find the companion delimiter for the following delimiter pairs:

```
{ }
[ ]
( )
< >
" "
' '
```

To find the matching delimiter, place the cursor before the delimiter you wish to match and press CTRL-Q [for a forward match or CTRL-Q] for a backward match. The editor moves the cursor to the position before the matching delimiter.

Some delimiters are nestable and some are not. The nestable delimiters are { }, [ ], ( ), and < >. The editor finds the proper matching delimiter in accordance with C/C++ syntax. If for some reason the editor cannot find a proper match, the cursor does not move.

Miscellaneous Commands

You can abort any command that requests input by pressing ESC at the prompt or by clicking the mouse on the **Cancel** button, if one exists. For example, if you execute the **Find** command and then change your mind, simply press ESC or click the mouse on **Cancel**.

To undo an edit, select the **Undo** option in the **Edit** menu. To undo an undo, select **Redo** in the **Edit** menu.

To print the file, select the **Print** command in the **File** menu.

Using the SpeedMenu

Many of the editing commands are available on the SpeedMenu. For example, **Find** and **Replace** can be activated using the SpeedMenu. The SpeedMenu is usually the fastest way to activate these commands when using the mouse.

Changing the Editor Defaults

You can change some aspects of the way the editor operates by selecting **Options** from the Menu bar, followed by **Environment.** Next, click on the **Editor** entry in the list of topics, and select the line labeled **Options**. This activates a dialog box that lets you set several editor options.

Keyboard Command Summary

Table 29-3 shows several of the most commonly used editor keyboard commands. If you plan on making extensive use of the keyboard commands when editing, you might want to look at the information presented when you select **Keyboard** in the **Help** menu. It shows the key mappings for all of the editor commands.

Cursor Commands

Command	Action
LEFT ARROW	Moves left one character.
RIGHT ARROW	Moves right one character.
UP ARROW	Moves up one line.
DOWN ARROW	Moves down one line.
PGUP	Moves up one page.
PGDN	Moves down one page.
HOME	Moves to start of line.
END	Moves to end of line.

Table 29-3. *Commonly Used Editor Keyboard Commands*

Insert Commands

Command	Action
INS	Toggles insert mode.
ENTER or CTRL-N	Inserts a line.

Delete Commands

Command	Action
CTRL-Y	Deletes entire line.
BACKSPACE	Deletes character to left of cursor.
DEL	Insert mode: deletes character to right of cursor.
	Overwrite mode: deletes character under cursor.
CTRL-T	Deletes word to the right.

Block Commands

Command	Action
CTRL-K W	Writes a block to disk.
CTRL-K R	Reads a block from disk.
CTRL-K I	Indents a block.
CTRL-K U	Extends a block.
CTRL-K P	Prints a block.
CTRL-INS	Copies to clipboard.
SHIFT-DEL	Cuts to clipboard.
SHIFT-INS	Pastes from clipboard.

Table 29-3. *Commonly Used Editor Keyboard Commands* (continued)

Pair Matching

Command	Action
CTRL-Q [	Matches pair forward.
CTRL-Q]	Matches pair reverse.

Miscellaneous Commands

Command	Action
CTRL-C	Copies to the clipboard.
CTRL-V	Copies from the clipboard.
CTRL-X	Deletes and copies to the clipboard.
CTRL-Z	Undoes last operation.
SHIFT-CTRL-Z	Redo last undo.

Table 29-3. *Commonly Used Editor Keyboard Commands* (continued)

Chapter Thirty

Using Borland C++'s Integrated Debugging Environment

Borland C++ includes a built-in source-level debugger in its integrated development environment. This chapter introduces the debugger and explores some of its most important features.

NOTE: The integrated debugger is not available for 16-bit programs.

Preparing Your Programs for Debugging

Although Borland C++'s debugger is available for use at the press of a key, you must make sure that your programs are compiled for a debugging session. This means that you must compile and link your program with debugging information. By default, this is automatically the case. But, if you need to turn on these options, here is how.

To add debugging information to your .obj files, choose **Options**, then **Project**. Next, expand the compiler data by clicking on the **+** symbol to the left of the **Compiler** entry in the list box and select the checkbox labeled **Debug information in OBJs**.

To add debugging information to your .exe files, choose **Options**, then **Project**. Next, expand the linker data by clicking on the **+** symbol to the left of the **Linker** entry in the list box and then choose **General**. Finally, select the checkbox labeled **Include debug information**.

What Is a Source-Level Debugger?

To understand what a source-level debugger is and why it is so valuable, it is best to compare it to an old-style, traditional debugger. A traditional debugger is designed to provide object-code debugging, in which you monitor the contents of the CPU's registers or memory. To use a traditional debugger, the linker generates a symbol table that shows the memory address of each function and variable in memory. To debug a program, you use this symbol table and begin executing your program, monitoring the contents of various registers and memory locations. Most debuggers allow you to step through your program one instruction at a time, and to set breakpoints in the object code. However, the biggest drawback to a traditional debugger is that the object code of your program bears little resemblance to the source code. This makes it difficult, even with the use of a symbol table, to know exactly what is happening.

A source-level debugger offers a vast improvement over the older, traditional form in that it allows you to debug your program using the original source code. The debugger automatically links the compiled object code associated with each line in your program with its corresponding source code. You no longer need to use a symbol table. You can control the execution of your program by setting breakpoints in the source code. You can watch the values of various variables using the variables' names. You can step through your program one statement at a time and watch the contents of the program's call stack. Also, communication with Borland C++'s debugger is accomplished using C/C++-like expressions, so there is nothing new to learn.

Debugger Basics

This section introduces the most common debugging commands. To follow along, you need to create a new project. When the **New Target** dialog box is displayed, set **Target Type** to **Application**, **Platform** to **Win32**, and **Target Model** to **Console**. Call the project **test**. Next, press the **Advanced** button. In the **Advanced Options** dialog box, uncheck the boxes labeled **.rc** and **.def**. These items are not needed by the programs in this chapter. In the **Project** window, double-click the line with the .cpp file. In the editor window, enter the following source code.

```
#include <iostream.h>

void sqr_it(int n);

int main() {
  int i;
```

```
  for(i=0; i<10; i++) {
    cout << i << " ";
    sqr_it(i);
  }
  return 0;
}

void sqr_it(int n)
{
  cout << n*n << " ";
}
```

After you have entered the program, compile and run it to make sure that you entered it correctly. It prints the values 0 through 9 along with their squares.

Single-Stepping

Single-stepping is the process by which you execute your program one statement at a time. To accomplish this, press the F7 key. Notice that the line containing the **main( )** function declaration is highlighted. This is where your program begins execution. Note also that the line **#include <iostream.h>** and **sqr_it( )**'s prototype are skipped over. Statements that do not generate code, such as the preprocessor directives, obviously cannot be executed, so the debugger automatically skips them. Variable declaration statements without initializers are also skipped when single-stepping as they are not action statements that can be traced.

There are two other ways you can execute a single step. You can choose the **Statement step into** icon on the SpeedBar. You can also select the **Statement Step Into** option in the SpeedMenu that appears when you right-click the mouse in the edit window that contains your source code.

Press F7 several times. Notice how the highlight moves from line to line. Also notice that when the function **sqr_it( )** is called, the highlight moves into the function and then returns from it. The F7 key causes the execution of your program to be traced into function calls.

There can be times when you only want to watch the performance of the code within one function. To accomplish this, use the F8 key. Each time this key is pressed, another statement is executed, but calls to functions are not traced. Pressing F8 is the same as clicking the **Statement step over** icon on the SpeedBar or selecting the **Statement Step Over** option in the SpeedMenu. Experiment with the F8 key at this time. Notice that the highlight never enters the **sqr_it( )** function.

Figure 30-1 shows the appearance of the edit window SpeedMenu. It provides numerous debugging functions, including the **Statement Step Into** and **Statement Step Over** functions just discussed.

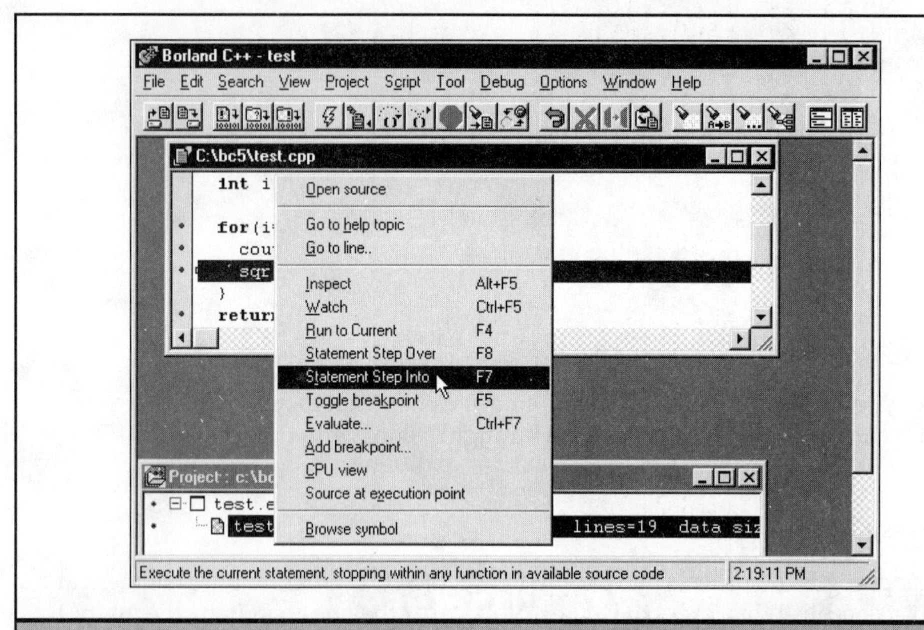

Figure 30-1. *Edit window SpeedMenu*

Breakpoints

As useful as single-stepping is, it can be very tedious in a large program—especially if the piece of code that you want to debug is deep in the program. Instead of pressing F7 or F8 repeatedly to get to the section you want to debug, it is easier to set a breakpoint at the beginning of the critical section. A *breakpoint* is, as the name implies, a break in the execution of your program. When execution reaches the breakpoint, your program stops running before that line is executed. Control returns to the debugger, allowing you to check the value of certain variables or to begin single-stepping the routine.

The Borland C++ debugger allows you to define the various different types of breakpoints shown here:

Type	Operation
Source	Stops execution when a line in your source code is executed.
Address	Stops execution when the machine instruction at a specified address is executed.
Data Watch	Stops execution when the data at a specified location is changed.

Type	Operation
C++ Exception	Stops execution when a C++ exception is thrown or caught.
OS Exception	Stops execution when an exception is caused by the operating system.
Thread	Stops execution when a specified type of thread is created.
Module	Stops execution when a specified dynamic link library (DLL) is loaded.

Here, we will examine only the source breakpoint because it is the most important and frequently used. (After understanding source breakpoints, you can easily explore the others on your own.)

There are two basic flavors of breakpoints: conditional and unconditional. Each is examined next.

Setting Unconditional Source Breakpoints

An unconditional source breakpoint always stops execution each time it is encountered. There are several ways to add this type of breakpoint. First, position your cursor at the line where you want to place the breakpoint. Then, you may do any of the following:

- Press F5.
- Click the **Toggle breakpoint** icon on the SpeedBar.
- Select the **Toggle breakpoint** option in the edit window SpeedMenu.
- Click the left margin of the edit window at the line where you want to add a breakpoint.

The line of code at which the breakpoint is set is highlighted. You can have several active breakpoints in a program.

Once you have defined one or more breakpoints, execute your program by choosing **Run** from the **Debug** menu. Your program runs until it encounters the first breakpoint. As an example, set a breakpoint at the line

```
cout << n*n << " ";
```

inside **sqr_it( )**, and then run the program. As you can see, execution stops at that line. Figure 30-2 shows both the editor and **Breakpoints** windows in the IDE. You may select **Breakpoint** from the **View** menu to obtain this display. The **Breakpoints** window lists all of the breakpoints and also indicates which of these was the last encountered.

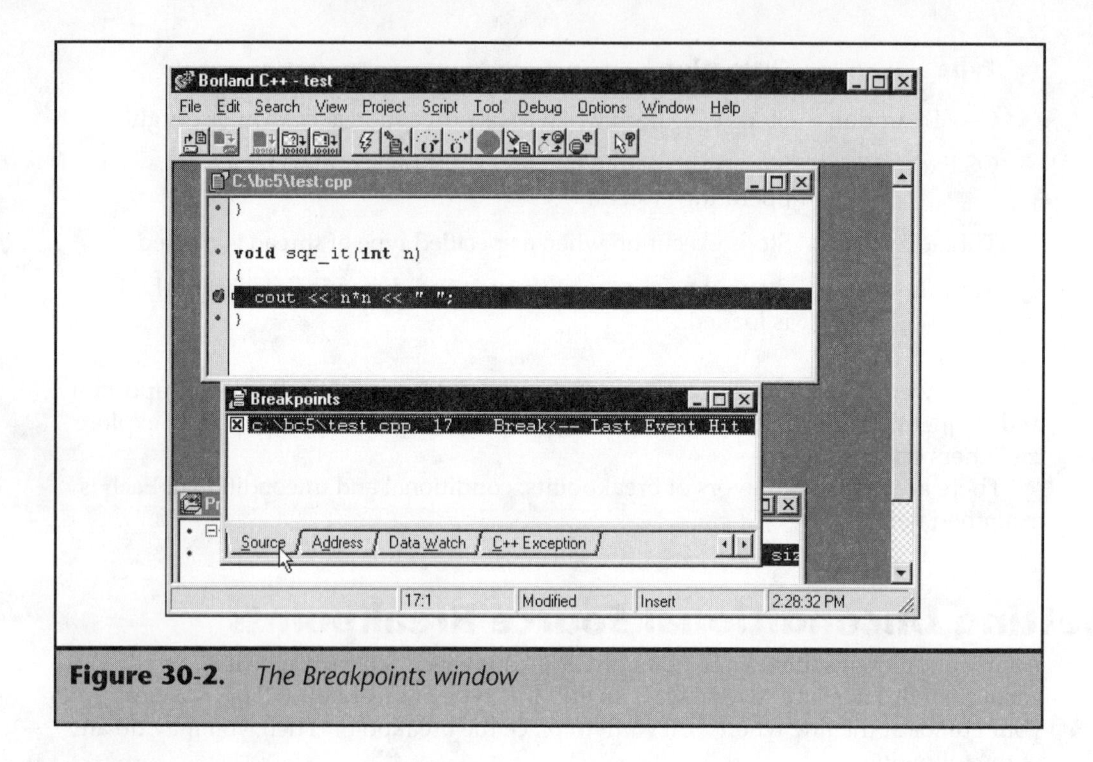

Figure 30-2. *The Breakpoints window*

There are several ways to remove a breakpoint. You may do any one of the following:

- Press F5.
- Click the right side of the editor window.
- Click the **Toggle breakpoint** icon on the SpeedBar.
- Select the **Toggle breakpoint** option in the edit window SpeedMenu.
- Highlight a breakpoint entry in the **Breakpoint** window and then press the DEL key.

Setting Conditional Source Breakpoints

A conditional source breakpoint allows you to specify the conditions under which a breakpoint stops execution and the actions that occur when it does. Let's look at an example, using the program from the preceding section. To add a conditional source breakpoint, position your cursor in the editor window at the line where you want to establish the breakpoint. For example, position it in the **main( )** function at the line where the **sqr_it( )** function is called. Choose **Add Breakpoint** from the **Debug** menu. This action causes the dialog box shown in Figure 30-3 to appear.

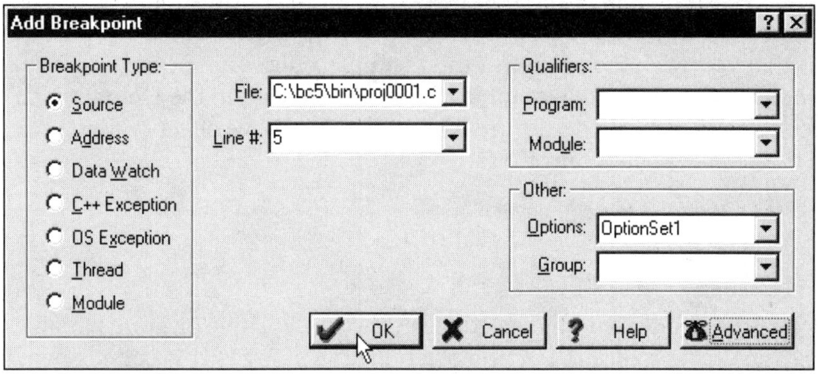

Figure 30-3. *Add Breakpoint dialog box*

Now click on the **Advanced** button in the lower right corner of this dialog box. This activates the dialog box shown in Figure 30-4.

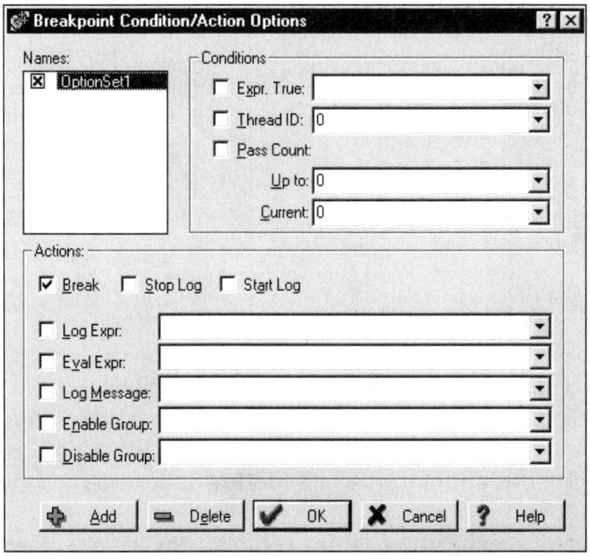

Figure 30-4. *Breakpoint Condition/Action dialog box*

Sometimes you will want to establish a breakpoint so that it stops execution only after a specified number of iterations through a loop. This threshold is defined by checking the **Pass Count** checkbox and setting the **Up to** field equal to the number of iterations that you wish to ignore. For this example, enter **4**.

To see the conditional breakpoint in action, choose **Run** in the **Debug** menu. The program begins execution and the breakpoint does not have effect until the **sqr_it( )** function has been executed four times.

Watching Variables

While debugging, you commonly need to see the value of one or more variables as your program executes. Using Borland's debugger, this is easily accomplished. First, activate the **Watches** window by selecting **Watch** from the **View** menu. To add a watch, first activate the **Add Watch** dialog box. Here are three ways you may do this:

- Press CTRL-F5.
- Click in the **Watches** window to make it active and then click the **Add watch** icon on the SpeedBar.
- Select the **Watch** option in the edit window's SpeedMenu.

Once the **Add Watch** dialog box is displayed, enter the name of the variable you want to watch. The debugger automatically displays the value of the variable in the **Watches** window as the program executes. If the variable is global, its value is always available. However, if the variable is local, its value is reported only when the function containing that variable is being executed. When execution moves to a different function, the variable's value is unknown. Keep in mind that if two functions both use the same name for a variable, the value displayed relates to the function currently executing.

As an example, activate the **Add Watch** dialog box and enter **i**. If you are not currently running the program or if execution has been stopped inside the **sqr_it( )** function, you will first see the message

Undefined symbol 'i'

However, when execution is inside the **main( )** function, the value of **i** is displayed.

Figure 30-5 shows the appearance of the editor and **Watches** windows when execution is suspended at a breakpoint. Notice that the editor window indicates the location of the breakpoints and the **Watches** window indicates the value of any watched variables.

You are not limited to watching only the contents of variables. You can watch any valid C/C++ expression involving variables. However, it cannot use any **#define** values or variables that are not in the scope of the function that is being executed.

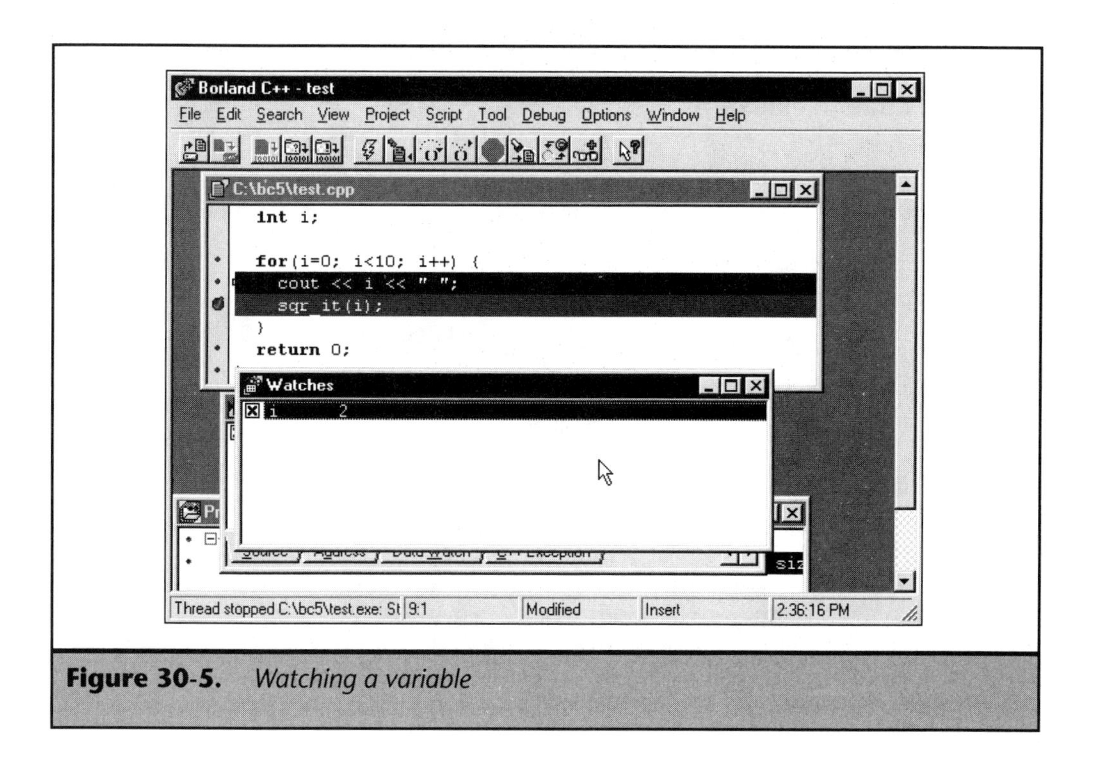

Figure 30-5. *Watching a variable*

Watched-Expression Format Codes

Borland C++'s debugger allows you to format the output of a watched expression by using format codes. To specify a format code, use this general form:

expression,format-code;

The format codes are shown in Table 30-1. If you don't specify a format code, the debugger automatically provides a default format.

You can display integers in either decimal or hexadecimal. The debugger automatically knows the difference between **long** and **short** integers because it has access to the source code.

When specifying a floating-point format, you can tell the debugger to show a certain number of significant digits after the decimal point by adding a number to the **F** format. For example, if **average** is a **float**, then this tells the debugger to show five significant digits:

```
average,F5
```

When a structure or a union is displayed, the values associated with each field are shown using an appropriate format. By including the **R** format command, the name of

Format Code	Meaning
C	Display as a character with no translation.
D	Display in decimal.
F	Display in floating point.
H	Display in hexadecimal.
M	Show memory.
P	Display as a pointer.
R	Display class, structure, or union member names and values.
S	Display as a character with appropriate character translations.
X	Display in hexadecimal (same as H).

Table 30-1. *Debugger Format Codes*

each field is also shown. To see an example, enter the following program. Try watching both **sample** and **sample,R**.

```
#include <string.h>

struct inventory {
  char item[10];
  int  count;
  float cost;
} sample;

int main()
{
  strcpy(sample.item, "hammer");
  sample.count = 100;
  sample.cost = 3.95;

  return 0;
}
```

After the three assignments have taken place, the output shown in the **Watches** window looks like this:

```
sample: {"hammer", 100, 3.95}
sample,R: {item: "hammer", count: 100, cost: 3.95}
```

As you might expect, you can also watch an object of a **class**. When you watch an object, you are shown the current value of any data that is contained within the object. As with structures and unions, if you use the **R** format specifier, the names of each data item are also displayed. When watching an object of a class, all **private**, **protected**, and **public** data is displayed. For example, if the previous program is changed as shown here:

```
#include <string.h>

class inventory {
  int i;   // private data
public:
  inventory() {i=100;}
  char item[10];
  int  count;
  float cost;
} sample;

int main()
{
  strcpy(sample.item, "hammer");
  sample.count = 100;
  sample.cost = 3.95;

  return 0;
}
```

the following output is obtained when watching **sample,R**:

```
sample,R: {i: 100, item: "hammer", count: 100, cost: 3.95}
```

As you can see, even though **i** is **private** to **inventory**, for the purposes of debugging, it is accessible to the debugger.

Figure 30-6 shows the options that are available via the SpeedMenu of the **Watches** window. As indicated, you may modify, add, remove, or disable watches.

Qualifying a Variable's Name

You can watch the value of a local variable no matter what function is currently executing by qualifying its name using this format:

filename.function-name.variable-name;

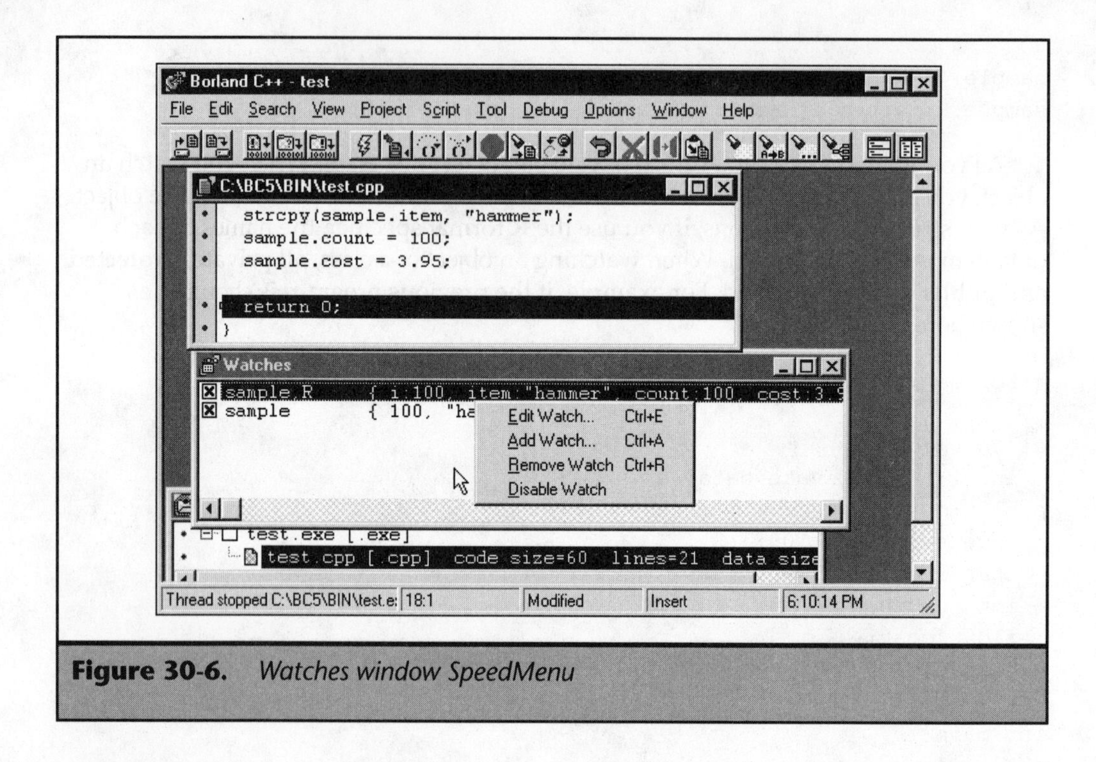

Figure 30-6. *Watches window SpeedMenu*

The *filename* is optional in single-file programs, and the *function-name* is optional when there is only one variable by the specified name.

As an example, assume that you want to watch both the **count** in **f1( )** and the **count** in **f2( )**, given this fragment:

```
void f1()
{
  int count;
  .
  .
  .
}

void f2()
{
  int count;
  .
  .
  .
}
```

To specify these variables, use

```
f1.count
f2.count
```

Watching the Stack

During the execution of your program, you can display the contents of the call stack by

- Selecting the **Call Stack** option in the View menu.
- Pressing CTRL-F3.

This option displays the order in which the various functions in your program are called. It also displays the value of any function parameters at the time of the call.

To see how this feature works, enter this program:

```
#include <iostream.h>
void f1(), f2(int i);

int main()
{
  f1();
  return 0;
}

void f1()
{
  int i;

  for(i=0; i<10; i++) f2(i);
}

void f2(int i)
{
  cout << "in f2, value is " << i << " ";
}
```

Set a breakpoint at the line containing the **cout** statement in **f2( )**, and then inspect the call stack. The first time the breakpoint is reached, the call stack looks like that shown in Figure 30-7.

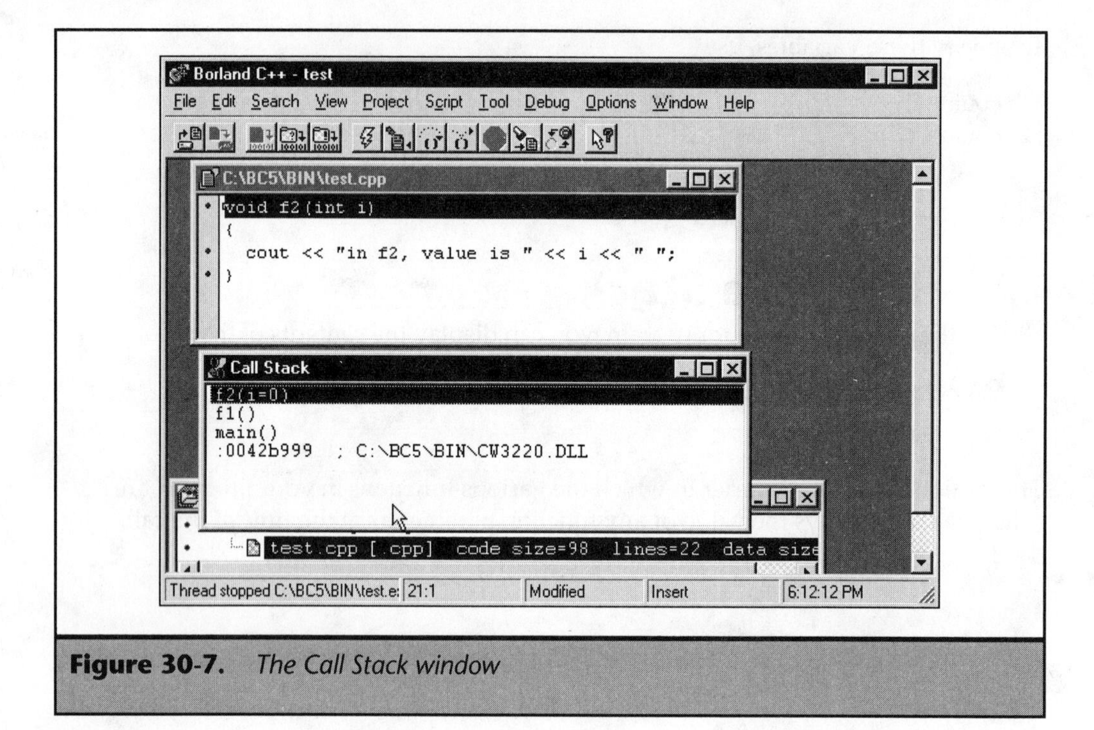

Figure 30-7. *The Call Stack window*

Evaluating an Expression

You can evaluate any legal C/C++ expression by using the **Evaluator** window. This is shown in Figure 30-8. To obtain this window, you may do any one of the following:

- Press CTRL-F7.
- Select **Evaluate** from the SpeedMenu.
- Select **Evaluate** from the **Debug** menu.

To evaluate an expression, enter it in the **Expression** field. You will see its value in the **Result** field. Expressions can contain constants and variables defined in the program you are debugging. They may also call functions. However, you cannot use any #**define** value.

Modifying a Variable

By changing a variable's value using the debugger, you can quickly get past a simple bug so that you can continue your debugging session. Also, in some situations you

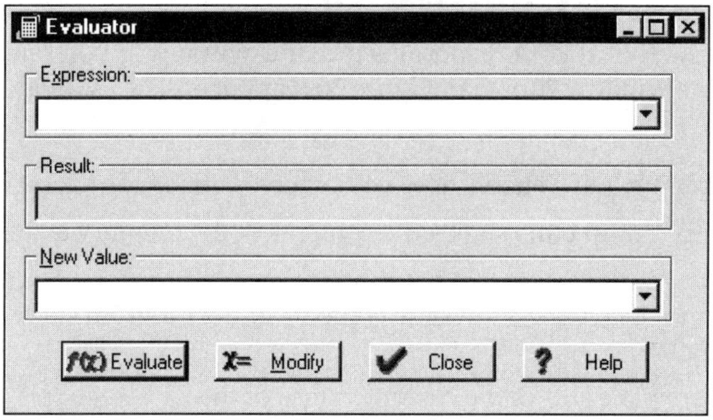

Figure 30-8. *The Evaluator window*

may have a loop that iterates a great number of times. To get past it, change the loop control variable so that the loop exits. Remember, of course, that changing a variable's value using the debugger is only a temporary fix. To change a variable, assign it a value in the **Evaluate** dialog box.

Inspecting a Variable

Although watching a variable using the **Watch** option is generally sufficient, in the most demanding of circumstances you may need to monitor more closely what happens to a variable. To do this, use the **Inspect** option in the **Debug** menu and enter the name of the variable in the **Inspect** dialog box. This option displays the contents and address of a variable. Knowing a variable's address can be of value when bugs involving things like wild pointers occur. Keep in mind that you can inspect any type of variable, including structures, unions, and classes. In the case of these types of objects, the names of members are displayed along with each value.

Pausing a Program

You may pause a program by choosing the **Pause process** option in the **Debug** menu. Execution of your program is suspended and you may then use any of the facilities that have already been discussed to troubleshoot a problem. To resume execution, select **Run** in the **Debug** menu.

Using the CPU Window

One final debugging tool at your disposal is the CPU window. If you select **CPU** from the **View** menu, the window shown in Figure 30-9 appears. This is divided into five separate panes:

- The disassembly pane shows how your source code maps to assembly code.
- The memory dump pane shows the contents of the memory available to your program.
- The machine stack pane shows the contents of the program stack in hexadecimal.
- The registers pane shows the current values of the CPU registers.
- The flags pane shows the current values of the CPU flags.

To make good use of the **CPU** window requires an intimate knowledge of assembly language programming and the architecture of your machine. However, for really difficult bugs, careful analysis of the **CPU** window may be your only resort.

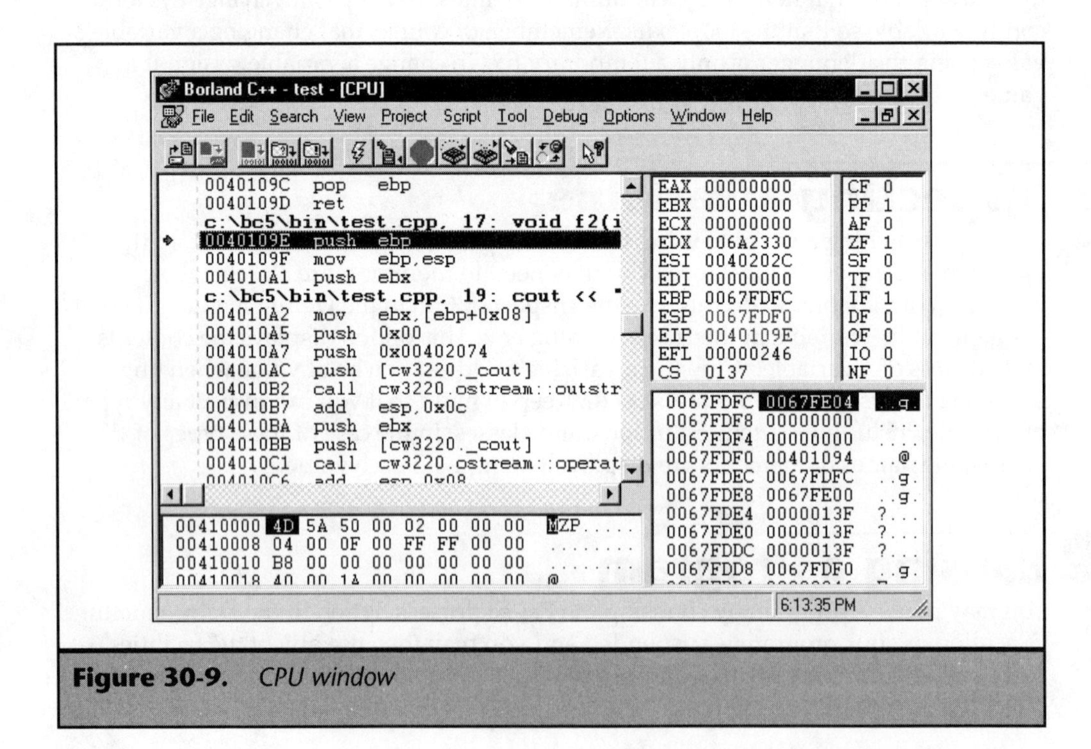

Figure 30-9. *CPU window*

A Debugging Tip

Before concluding this chapter, one piece of advice must be offered: Don't rely too heavily on the debugger. While great debuggers, such as that provided with Borland C++, are an indispensable part of any programmer's arsenal, they should never be a substitute for good design and good coding practices. If you are using the debugger on a daily (or even weekly) basis, then you are probably using it too much. Frankly, a poor implementation that is "fixed" through extensive debugging is almost always inferior.

PART FIVE

Windows 95 Programming Overview

Part 5 of this book shows you how to use Borland C++ to create Windows 95 applications. As you will see, writing a Windows application is not as easy as writing console-based programs such as those for DOS. However, programming for Windows is also not as difficult as you may have been led to believe. To create a successful Windows program, you simply follow a well-defined set of rules.

While this section contains all information necessary for you to write simple yet useful Windows 95 applications, it does not come close to describing all aspects of the Windows 95 operating system. Windows is simply too large a system. (In fact, several large books are required to fully document the Windows 95 programming environment.) The purpose of this section is to introduce the basics of Windows 95 programming and explain how to use Borland C++ to accomplish it. It also serves as a starting point for your further study of Windows programming.

There are three ways to approach the creation of a Windows program:

1. Using the Windows API (Application Program Interface) Functions
2. Using Borland's ObjectWindows Library (OWL)
3. Using Microsoft's Foundation Classes (MFC)

This section teaches Windows programming using the API. The reason for this is simple: you cannot effectively use either of the other two methods without a firm understanding of the Windows API. The information presented here will give you a firm foundation on which to pursue your further study of Windows programming no matter which way you choose.

Part 5 assumes that you are an accomplished C/C++ programmer. Windows programs are more complex than the types of programs shown in the beginning of this book.

NOTE: *Although the material presented here is for Windows 95, for the most part it also applies to Windows NT. Further, the essential elements of a Windows 95 program are the same as those for any version of Windows, including Windows 3.1.*

Chapter Thirty-One

Windows 95 Fundamentals

Before you can begin programming for Windows 95, you must understand in a general way how Windows 95 operates, how it interacts with your programs, what constitute the basic elements of any Windows 95 application, and what rules your programs must follow. It is also important to know how Windows 95 differs from its predecessor: Windows 3.1. Toward these ends, this chapter presents an overview of Windows 95, discusses ways in which it relates to and differs from its forerunners, and concludes with a Windows 95 skeleton program. This skeleton will be used as the foundation for the rest of the programs presented in Part 5.

What Is Windows 95?

Windows 95 is part of the next generation of operating systems intended to operate PCs well into the next century. As you probably know, Windows 95 features a graphical user interface (GUI) that uses the desktop model. It fully supports the mouse and keyboard as input devices. Windows 95 was specifically designed to overcome several of the limitations imposed by its earlier incarnation: Windows 3.1. It also adds a substantial number of new features and provides a new (and improved) user interface. (These differences and enhancements will be discussed shortly.)

Perhaps the single most important characteristic of Windows 95 is that it is a 32-bit operating system. By moving to a 32-bit implementation, Windows 95 has left behind many of the quirks and problems associated with the older 16-bit systems. Although the move to 32 bits is largely transparent to the user, it makes programming Windows 95 easier.

A primary design goal of Windows 95 was compatibility with both Windows 3.1 and with DOS—and the programs designed to run under them. That is, Windows 95 was designed to be upwardly compatible with the large base of existing PC applications. Toward this end, Windows 95 can run three types of programs: those written for DOS, those written for Windows 3.1, and those written specifically for Windows 95. Windows 95 automatically creates the right environment for the type of program you run. For example, when you execute a DOS program, Windows 95 automatically creates a windowed command prompt in which the program runs.

Let's look at a few of the more important features of Windows 95.

Windows 95 Uses Thread-based Multitasking

As you almost certainly know, Windows 95 is a multitasking operating system. As such, it can run two or more programs concurrently. Of course, the programs share the CPU and do not, technically, run simultaneously; but, because of the speed of the computer, they appear to. Windows 95 supports two forms of multitasking: process-based and thread-based. A process is a program that is executing. Because Windows 95 can multitask processes, it means that Windows 95 can run more than one program at a time. Thus, Windows 95 supports the traditional, process-based multitasking you are probably familiar with.

Windows 95's second form of multitasking is thread-based. A thread is a dispatchable unit of executable code. The name comes from the concept of a "thread of execution." All processes have at least one thread. However, a Windows 95 process may have several.

Since Windows 95 multitasks threads and each process can have more than one thread, this implies that it is possible for one process to have two or more pieces of itself executing simultaneously. As it turns out, this implication is correct. Therefore, when working with Windows 95, it is possible to multitask both programs and pieces of a single program.

The Windows 95 Call-based Interface

If you come from a DOS background then you know that a program accesses DOS using various software interrupts. For example, the standard DOS interrupt is 0x21. While using a software interrupt to access DOS services is perfectly acceptable (given the limited scope of the DOS operating system), it is completely inadequate as a means of interfacing to a full-featured, multitasking operating system like Windows 95. Instead, Windows 95, like Windows 3.1 before it, uses a *call-based interface.*

The Windows 95 call-based interface uses a rich set of system-defined functions to access operating system features. Collectively, these functions are called the Application Programming Interface, or API for short. The API contains several hundred functions that your application program calls in order to communicate with Windows 95. These functions include all necessary operating system-related activities, such as memory allocation, outputting to the screen, creating windows, and the like.

Dynamic Link Libraries (DLLs)

Because the API consists of several hundred functions, you might be thinking that a large amount of code is linked into every program that is compiled for Windows 95, causing each program to contain much duplicate code. However, this is not the case. Instead, the Windows 95 API functions are contained in *dynamic link libraries*, or DLLs for short, which each program has access to when it is executed. Here is how dynamic linking works.

The Windows 95 API functions are stored in a relocatable format within a DLL. During the compilation phase, when your program calls an API function, the linker does not add the code for that function to the executable version of your program. Instead, it adds loading instructions for that function, such as what DLL it resides in and its name. When your program is executed, the necessary API routines are also loaded by the Windows 95 loader. In this way, each application program does not need to contain the actual API code. The API functions are added only when the application is loaded into memory for execution.

Dynamic linking has some very important benefits. First, since virtually all programs will use the API functions, DLLs prevent disk space from being wasted by the significant amount of duplicated object code that would be created if the API functions were actually added to each program's executable file on disk. Second, updates and enhancements to Windows 95 can be accomplished by changing the dynamic link library routines. Existing application programs do not need to be recompiled.

Windows 95 Versus Windows 3.1

Since many readers of this book will already be familiar with Windows 3.1, a brief comparison with Windows 95 is in order. Although Windows 95 is the next step in the Windows product line, which began with Windows' original release in 1985, it also represents a major step forward in operating system design.

The good news is that if you are familiar with Windows 3.1, you will have no trouble learning to use or program Windows 95. From the user's point of view, Windows 95 adds an improved interface and has moved toward a document-centered organization. Specifically, such fundamental items as the Program Manager and the File Manager have been replaced with the Start menu and the Explorer. However, if you can run Windows 3.1, you will feel at home with Windows 95. Things still work essentially the same way.

From the programmer's point of view, the more important good news is that you program for Windows 95 in much the same way that you did for Windows 3.1. Windows 95 preserves the name space of the original Windows API functions. When Windows 95 added functionality, it generally did so by adding new functions. While there are some differences between Windows 3.1 and Windows 95, for the most part these differences are easy to accommodate. Also, old Windows 3.1 programs run fine under Windows 95, so you won't have to port all of your applications at once.

The following sections look at the differences between Windows 3.1 and Windows 95 in more detail.

User Differences

From the user's point of view, Windows 95 differs from Windows 3.1 in four major ways:

1. The desktop interface has changed.
2. The style of a window has been altered.
3. New control elements are available to applications.
4. DOS is no longer required.

As mentioned, the Program Manager found in Windows 3.1 has been replaced by the Start menu. Further, the desktop now contains the Task bar. The Task bar displays a list of all active tasks in the system and allows you to switch to a task by clicking on it. Most users will find the Start menu and Task bar a significant improvement over the Program Manager.

The visual look of windows under Windows 95 has been redesigned. To most users, the new look will seem more stylish and "snappy." One of the criticisms of Windows 3.1 was its rather "clunky" look. Windows 95 has changed its look for the better. Also, when you use Windows 95 applications, you will notice that several new control elements, such as toolbars, spin controls, tree views, and Status bars, will appear quite frequently. These modern controls give the user a more convenient means of setting the various attributes associated with a program.

Windows 95 does not require DOS. As you probably know, Windows 3.1 was not a completely stand-alone operating system. It ran on top of DOS, which provided support for the file system. Windows 95 is a complete operating system and DOS is no longer needed. However, Windows 95 still provides support for DOS programs. (In fact, some DOS programs run better under Windows 95 than they do under DOS!) Also, using Windows 95, you may have multiple "DOS" sessions.

Windows 95 also adds substantial functionality, including the ability to transparently run DOS programs. When you run a DOS program, a windowed command prompt interface is automatically created. Further, this windowed command prompt is fully integrated into the overall Windows 95 graphical interface. For example, you can now execute Windows programs directly from the prompt. (Under Windows 3.1, you had to execute Windows programs from within Windows.)

Another new feature of Windows 95 is its support for long filenames. As you probably know, DOS and Windows 3.1 only allowed eight-character filenames followed by a three-character extension. Windows 95 allows filenames to be up to 255 characters long.

Programming Differences

From the programmer's point of view there are two main differences between Windows 3.1 and Windows 95. First, Windows 95 supports 32-bit addressing and uses virtual memory. Windows 3.1 uses a 16-bit segmented addressing mode. For many application programs, this difference will have little effect. For others, the effect will be substantial. Frankly, while the transition may not be painless, you will find the Windows 95 32-bit memory model much easier to program for.

The second difference concerns the way that multitasking is accomplished. Windows 3.1 uses a nonpreemptive approach to task switching. This means that a Windows 3.1 task must manually return control to the scheduler in order for another task to run. In other words, a Windows 3.1 program retains control of the CPU until it decides to give it up. Therefore, an ill-behaved program could monopolize the CPU. By contrast, Windows 95 uses preemptive, time-slice–based tasking. In this scheme, tasks are automatically preempted by Windows 95 and the CPU is then assigned to the next task (if one exists). Preemptive multitasking is generally the superior method because it allows the operating system to fully control tasking and prevents one task from dominating the system. Most programmers view the move to preemptive multitasking as a step forward.

In addition to the two major changes just described, Windows 95 differs from Windows 3.1 in some other, less dramatic ways, which are described here.

Input Queues

One difference between Windows 3.1 and Windows 95 is found in the input queue. (Input queues hold messages, such as a keypress or mouse activity, until they can be sent to your program.) In Windows 3.1, there is just one input queue for all tasks running in the system. However, Windows 95 supplies each thread with its own input queue. The advantage to each thread having its own queue is that no one process can reduce system performance by responding to its messages slowly.

Although multiple input queues are an important addition, this change has no direct impact on how you program for Windows 95.

Threads and Processes

Windows 3.1 only supports process-based multitasking. That is, the process is Windows 3.1's smallest dispatchable unit. As mentioned earlier, Windows 95 multitasks both threads and processes. While older Windows 3.1 programs will not require changes to run fine under Windows 95, you may want to enhance them to take advantage of thread-based multitasking.

Consoles

In the past, text-based (i.e., nonwindowed) applications were fairly inconvenient to use from Windows. However, Windows 95 supports a special type of window called a *console*. A console window provides a standard text-based interface, command-prompt environment. However, aside from being text-based, a console acts and can be manipulated like other windows. The addition of the text-based console not only allows nonwindowed applications to run in a full Windows environment, but also makes it more convenient for you to create short, throwaway utility programs. Perhaps more importantly, the inclusion of consoles in Windows 95 is a final acknowledgment that some text-based applications make sense and now they can be managed as part of the overall Windows environment. In essence, the addition of console windows completes the Windows application environment.

Flat Addressing and Virtual Memory

Windows 95 applications have available to them 4 gigabytes of virtual memory in which to run! Further, this address space is *flat*. Unlike Windows 3.1, DOS, and other 8086-family operating systems that use segmented memory, Windows 95 treats memory as linear. And, because it virtualizes it, each application has as much memory as it could possibly (and reasonably) want. While the change to flat addressing is mostly transparent to the programmer, it does relieve much of the tedium and frustration of dealing with the old, segmented approach.

Because of the move to flat, 32-bit addressing (and other enhancements), each Windows 95 process runs in its own address space and is insulated from other processes. This means that if one process crashes, the other processes are unaffected. (That is, one misbehaving program cannot take down the entire system.)

Changes to Messages and Parameter Types

Because of Windows 95 shift to 32-bit addressing, some messages passed to a Windows 95 program will be organized differently than they are when passed to a Windows 3.1 program. Also, the parameter types used to declare a window function have changed because of the move to 32-bit addressing.

New Common Controls

As mentioned earlier, Windows 95 supports a rich and expanded set of control elements. Like Windows 3.1, Windows 95 still supports the standard controls, such as pushbuttons, checkboxes, radio buttons, edit boxes, and the like. To these standard controls, Windows 95 adds support for several new ones. The new controls added by Windows 95 are called *common controls*. The common controls include such things as toolbars, tooltips, status bars, progress bars, track bars, and tree views (to name just a few). Using the new common controls gives your application the modern look and feel that will clearly identify it as a Windows 95 program.

Installable File System

Under DOS and Windows 3.1, the file system is accessed via interrupt 0x21. This file system uses 16-bit code and operates in real mode. However, Windows 95 uses a 32-bit, protected-mode, installable file system and provides an installable file system manager to coordinate accesses to the file system and its devices. Because the new file system operates in protected mode, no time is wasted switching to 16-bit real mode to access it. (Windows 3.1 had to switch between the two modes.) This means greater overall file system performance is achieved. Since the file system is generally accessed using high-level functions provided by Windows 95-compatible C/C++ compilers, this improvement will not alter the way you handle files in your programs. However, it will improve the performance of programs that you write.

The NT Connection

Windows NT is Microsoft's high-end Windows-based operating system. Windows NT has much in common with Windows 95. Both support 32-bit, flat addressing. Both support thread-based multitasking. And, both support the console-based interface. However, Windows 95 is *not* Windows NT. For example, Windows NT uses a special approach to operating system implementation based on the client/server model. Windows 95 does not. Windows NT supports a full security system, Windows 95 does not. While there is no doubt that much of the basic technology developed for use in Windows NT eventually found its way into Windows 95, they are not the same.

Windows 95 Programs Are Unique

If you have never written a Windows program before, then you may be in for a surprise. Windows programs are structured differently from programs that you are probably used to writing. The unique structure of a Windows-style program is dictated by two constraints. The first is determined by the way your program interacts with Windows. The second is governed by the rules that must be followed to create a standard, Windows-style application interface (that is, to make a program that "looks like" a Windows program).

The goal of Windows 95 (and Windows in general) is to enable a person who has basic familiarity with the system to sit down and run virtually any application without prior training. Toward this end, Windows provides a consistent interface to the user. In theory, if you can run one Windows-based program, you can run them all. Of course, in actuality, most useful programs will still require some sort of training in order to be used effectively, but at least this instruction can be restricted to *what* the program *does*, not *how* the user must *interact* with it. In fact, much of the code in a Windows application is there just to support the user interface.

Although creating a consistent Windows-style interface is a crucial part of writing any Windows 95 program, it does not happen automatically. That is, it is possible to write Windows programs that do not take advantage of the Windows interface elements. To create a Windows-style program, you must purposely do so using the techniques described in this book. Only those programs written to take advantage of Windows will look and feel like Windows programs. While you can override the basic Windows design philosophy, you had better have a good reason to do so, otherwise the users of your programs will most likely be very disturbed. In general, if you are writing application programs for Windows 95, they should utilize the normal Windows interface and conform to the standard Windows design practices.

How Windows 95 and Your Program Interact

When you write a program, for many operating systems it is your program that initiates interaction with the operating system. For example, in a DOS program, it is the program that requests such things as input and output. Put differently, programs written in the "traditional way" call the operating system. The operating system does not call your program. However, in a large measure, Windows 95 works in the opposite way. It is Windows 95 that calls your program. The process works like this: A Windows 95 program waits until it is sent a *message* by Windows. The message is passed to your program through a special function that is called by Windows. Once a message is received, your program is expected to take an appropriate action. While your program may call one or more Windows 95 API functions when responding to a message, it is still Windows 95 that initiates the activity. More than anything else, it is the message-based interaction with Windows 95 that dictates the general form of all Windows 95 programs.

There are many different types of messages that Windows 95 may send your program. For example, each time the mouse is clicked on a window belonging to your program, a mouse-clicked message will be sent. Another type of message is sent each time a window belonging to your program must be redrawn. Still another message is sent each time the user presses a key when your program is the focus of input. Keep one fact firmly in mind: as far as your program is concerned, messages arrive randomly. This is why Windows 95 programs resemble interrupt-driven programs. You can't know what message will be next.

Win32: The Windows 95 API

As mentioned earlier, the Windows environment is accessed through a call-based interface called the API (Application Program Interface). The API consists of several hundred functions that your program calls as needed. The API functions provide all the system services performed by Windows 95. A subset to the API, called the GDI (Graphics Device Interface), provides device-independent graphics support. It is the GDI functions that make it possible for a Windows application to run on a variety of hardware.

Window 95 programs use the Win32 API. For the most part, Win32 is a superset of the older Windows 3.1 API (Win16). Indeed, for the most part the functions are called by the same names and are used in the same way. However, even though similar in spirit and purpose, the two APIs differ because Windows 95 supports 32-bit, flat addressing while Win16 supports only the 16-bit, segmented memory model. This difference has caused several API functions to be widened to accept 32-bit arguments and return 32-bit values. Also, a few API functions have had to be altered to accommodate the 32-bit architecture. API functions have also been added to support the new approach to multitasking, its new interface elements, and the other enhanced Windows 95 features. If you are new to Windows programming in general, then these changes will not affect you significantly. However, if you will be porting code from Windows 3.1 to Windows 95, then you will need to carefully examine the arguments you pass to each API function.

Because Windows 95 supports full 32-bit addressing, it makes sense that integers are also 32 bits long. This means that types **int** and **unsigned** will be 32 bits, not 16 bits long as is the case for Windows 3.1. If you want to use a 16-bit integer, it must be declared as **short**. (Portable **typedef** names are provided by Windows 95 for these types, as you will see shortly.) If you will be porting code from the 16-bit environment, you will need to check your use of integers because they will automatically be expanded from 16 to 32 bits and side effects may result.

Another result of 32-bit addressing is that pointers no longer need to be declared as **near** or **far**. Any pointer can access any part of memory. In Windows 95, both **far** and **near** are defined as nothing. This means you can leave **far** and **near** in your programs when porting to Windows 95, but they will have no effect.

The Components of a Window

Before moving on to specific aspects of Windows 95 programming, a few important terms need to be defined. Figure 31-1 shows a standard window with each of its elements pointed out.

All windows have a border that defines the limits of the window and is used to resize the window. At the top of the window are several items. On the far left is the system menu icon (also called the title bar icon). Clicking on this box displays the system menu. To the right of the system menu box is the window's title. At the far right are the minimize, maximize, and close icons. (Previous versions of Windows did not include a close icon. This is a Windows 95 innovation.) The client area is the part of the window in which your program activity takes place. Most windows also have horizontal and vertical scroll bars that are used to move text through the window.

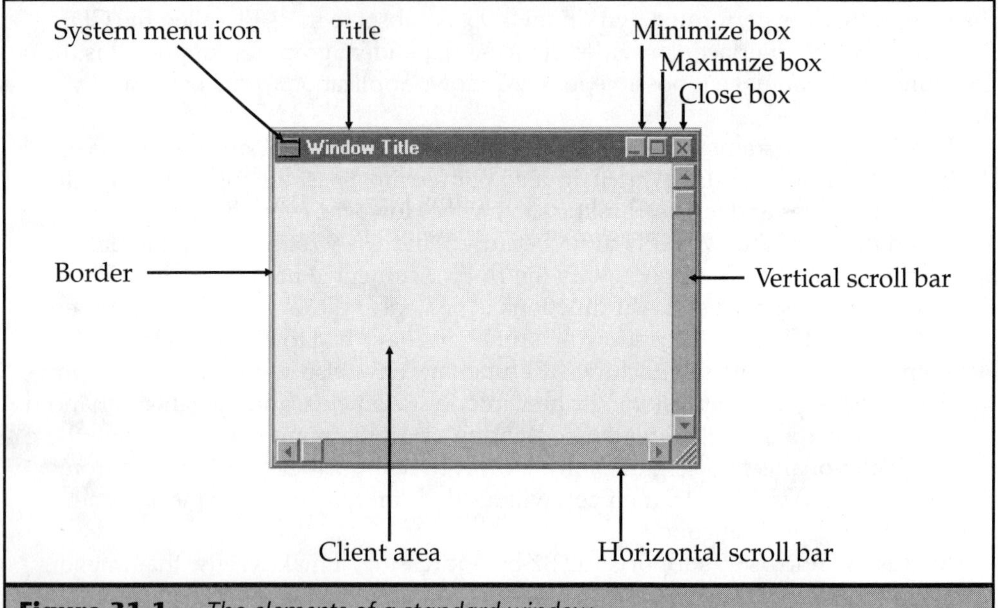

Figure 31-1. *The elements of a standard window*

Some Windows 95 Application Fundamentals

Before developing a Windows 95 application skeleton, some fundamental concepts common to all Windows 95 programs need to be discussed. If you already know how to write programs for Windows 3.1, then this and the next few sections contain material with which you are already familiar. (In fact, Windows 3.1 and Windows 95 programs are, on the surface, almost identical.) However, you should at least skim through this material because there are some important differences between Windows 3.1 and Windows 95.

WinMain( )

All Windows 95 programs begin execution with a call to **WinMain( )**. (As a general rule, Windows programs do not have a **main( )** function.) **WinMain( )** has some special properties that differentiate it from other functions in your application. First, it must be compiled using the **WINAPI** calling convention. (You will see **APIENTRY** used as well. They both mean the same thing.) By default, functions in your C or C++ programs use the C calling convention. However, it is possible to compile a function so that it uses a different calling convention. For example, a common alternative is to use the Pascal calling convention. For various technical reasons, the calling convention Windows 95 uses to call **WinMain( )** is **WINAPI**. The return type of **WinMain( )** should be **int**.

The Window Function

All Windows 95 programs must contain a special function that is *not* called by your program but is called by Windows 95. This function is generally called the *window function* or the *window procedure*. The window function is called by Windows 95 when it needs to pass a message to your program. It is through this function that Windows 95 communicates with your program. The window function receives the message in its parameters. All window functions must be declared as returning type **LRESULT CALLBACK**. The type **LRESULT** is a **typdef** that (at the time of this writing) is another name for a long integer. The **CALLBACK** calling convention is used with those functions that will be called by Windows 95. In Windows terminology, any function that is called by Windows is referred to as a callback function.

In addition to receiving the messages sent by Windows 95, the window function must initiate any actions indicated by a message. Typically, a window function's body consists of a **switch** statement that links a specific response to each message that the program will respond to. Your program need not respond to every message that Windows 95 will send. For messages that your program doesn't care about, you can let Windows 95 provide default processing of them. Since there are hundreds of different messages that Windows 95 can generate, it is common for most messages to simply be processed by Windows 95 and not your program.

All messages are 32-bit integer values. Further, all messages are linked with any additional information that the message requires.

Window Classes

When your Windows 95 program first begins execution, it will need to define and register a *window class*. (Here, the word *class* is not being used in its C++ sense. Rather, it means *style* or *type*.) When you register a window class, you are telling Windows 95 about the form and function of the window. However, registering the window class does not cause a window to come into existence. To actually create a window requires additional steps.

The Message Loop

As explained earlier, Windows 95 communicates with your program by sending it messages. All Windows 95 applications must establish a *message loop* inside the **WinMain( )** function. This loop reads any pending message from the application's message queue and dispatches that message back to Windows 95, which then calls your program's window function with that message as a parameter. This may seem to be an overly complex way of passing messages, but it is nevertheless the way that all Windows programs must function. (Part of the reason for this is to return control to Windows 95 so that the scheduler can allocate CPU time as it sees fit rather than waiting for your application's time slice to end.)

Windows Data Types

As you will soon see, Windows 95 programs do not make extensive use of standard C/C++ data types, such as **int** or **char** *. Instead, all data types used by Windows 95 have been **typdef**ed within the **windows.h** file and/or its related files. This file is supplied by Borland C++ and must be included in all Windows 95 programs. Some of the most common types are **HANDLE, HWND, BYTE, WORD, DWORD, UINT, LONG, BOOL, LPSTR,** and **LPCSTR. HANDLE** is a 32-bit integer that is used as a handle. As you will see, there are a number of handle types, but they all are the same size as **HANDLE**. A *handle* is simply a value that identifies some resource. For example, **HWND** is a 32-bit integer that is used as a window handle. Also, all handle types begin with an H. **BYTE** is an 8-bit unsigned character. **WORD** is a 16-bit unsigned short integer. **DWORD** is an unsigned long integer. **UINT** is an unsigned 32-bit integer. **LONG** is another name for **long. BOOL** is an integer. This type is used to indicate values that are either true or false. **LPSTR** is a pointer to a string and **LPCSTR** is a **const** pointer to a string.

In addition to the basic types described above, Windows 95 defines several structures. The two that are needed by the skeleton program are **MSG** and **WNDCLASSEX**. The **MSG** structure holds a Windows 95 message and **WNDCLASSEX** is a structure that defines a window class. These structures will be discussed later in this chapter.

A Windows 95 Skeleton

Now that the necessary background information has been covered, it is time to develop a minimal Windows 95 application. As stated, all Windows 95 programs have certain things in common. In this section, a Windows 95 skeleton is developed that provides these necessary features. In the world of Windows programming, application skeletons are commonly used because there is a substantial "price of admission" when creating a Windows program. Unlike DOS programs that you may have written, in which a minimal program is about 5 lines long, a minimal Windows program is approximately 50 lines long.

A minimal Windows 95 program contains two functions: **WinMain( )** and the window function. The **WinMain( )** function must perform the following general steps:

1. Define a window class.
2. Register that class with Windows 95.
3. Create a window of that class.
4. Display the window.
5. Begin running the message loop.

The window function must respond to all relevant messages. Since the skeleton program does nothing but display its window, the only message that it must respond to is the one that tells the application that the user has terminated the program.

Before discussing the specifics, examine the following program, which is a minimal Windows 95 skeleton. It creates a standard window that includes a title. The window also contains the system menu and is, therefore, capable of being minimized, maximized, moved, resized, and closed. It also contains the standard minimize, maximize, and close boxes.

```
/* A minimal Windows 95 skeleton. */

#include <windows.h>

LRESULT CALLBACK WindowFunc(HWND, UINT, WPARAM, LPARAM);

char szWinName[] = "MyWin"; /* name of window class */

int WINAPI WinMain(HINSTANCE hThisInst, HINSTANCE hPrevInst,
                   LPSTR lpszArgs, int nWinMode)
{
  HWND hwnd;
  MSG msg;
  WNDCLASSEX wcl;

  /* Define a window class. */
  wcl.hInstance = hThisInst; /* handle to this instance */
  wcl.lpszClassName = szWinName; /* window class name */
  wcl.lpfnWndProc = WindowFunc; /* window function */
  wcl.style = 0; /* default style */

  wcl.cbSize = sizeof(WNDCLASSEX); /* set size of WNDCLASSEX*/

  wcl.hIcon = LoadIcon(NULL, IDI_APPLICATION); /* large icon */
  wcl.hIconSm = LoadIcon(NULL, IDI_WINLOGO); /* small icon */

  wcl.hCursor = LoadCursor(NULL, IDC_ARROW); /* cursor style */
  wcl.lpszMenuName = NULL; /* no menu */

  wcl.cbClsExtra = 0; /* no extra */
  wcl.cbWndExtra = 0; /* information needed */
```

```
  /* Make the window background white. */
  wcl.hbrBackground = (HBRUSH) GetStockObject(WHITE_BRUSH);

  /* Register the window class. */
  if(!RegisterClassEx(&wcl)) return 0;

  /* Now that a window class has been registered, a window
     can be created. */
  hwnd = CreateWindow(
    szWinName, /* name of window class */
    "Windows 95 Skeleton", /* title */
    WS_OVERLAPPEDWINDOW, /* window style - normal */
    CW_USEDEFAULT, /* X coordinate - let Windows decide */
    CW_USEDEFAULT, /* Y coordinate - let Windows decide */
    CW_USEDEFAULT, /* width - let Windows decide */
    CW_USEDEFAULT, /* height - let Windows decide */
    HWND_DESKTOP, /* no parent window */
    NULL, /* no menu */
    hThisInst, /* handle of this instance of the program */
    NULL /* no additional arguments */
  );

  /* Display the window. */
  ShowWindow(hwnd, nWinMode);
  UpdateWindow(hwnd);

  /* Create the message loop. */
  while(GetMessage(&msg, NULL, 0, 0))
  {
    TranslateMessage(&msg); /* allow use of keyboard */
    DispatchMessage(&msg); /* return control to Windows */
  }
  return msg.wParam;
}

/* This function is called by Windows 95 and is passed
   messages from the message queue.
*/
LRESULT CALLBACK WindowFunc(HWND hwnd, UINT message,
                            WPARAM wParam, LPARAM lParam)
{
  switch(message) {
    case WM_DESTROY: /* terminate the program */
```

```
      PostQuitMessage(0);
      break;
    default:
      /* Let Windows 95 process any messages not specified in
         the preceding switch statement. */
      return DefWindowProc(hwnd, message, wParam, lParam);
  }
  return 0;
}
```

Compiling the Skeleton

To compile the Windows 95 skeleton (or any Windows program), you must first create a project. In the **New Target** dialog box, for target type select **Application**, for platform select **Win32**, and for target model select **GUI**. You can call the project **Skel**. Next, press the **Advanced** button. In the **Advanced Options** dialog box, turn off the **.rc** and **.def** options. The skeleton program does not require these files. (Briefly, a file using the extension .RC is a resource file, which is described in Chapter 33, and a file using the extension .DEF is a definition file, which is no longer needed by Windows 95 programs.) Next, enter the code for the skeleton program. To compile and run the skeleton, select **Run** from the **Debug** menu.

Depending upon how your compiler is configured, you might see these two warning messages when you compile the skeleton:

Parameter 'hPrevInst' is never used.

Parameter 'lpszArgs' is never used.

You should ignore these errors. These parameters are not generally used by short, example Windows 95 programs. In fact, as explained below, **hPrevInst** is no longer used by Windows 95 at all, but it is still required in the parameter list to **WinMain( )**.

A Closer Look at the Skeleton

When you run this program, you will see a window similar to that shown in Figure 31-2. Let's go through this program step by step.

First, all Windows 95 programs must include the header file **windows.h**. As stated, this file (along with its support files) contains the API function prototypes and various types, macros, and definitions used by Windows 95. For example, the data types **HWND** and **WNDCLASSEX** are defined by including **windows.h**.

The window function used by the program is called **WindowFunc( )**. It is declared as a callback function because this is the function that Windows 95 calls to communicate with the program.

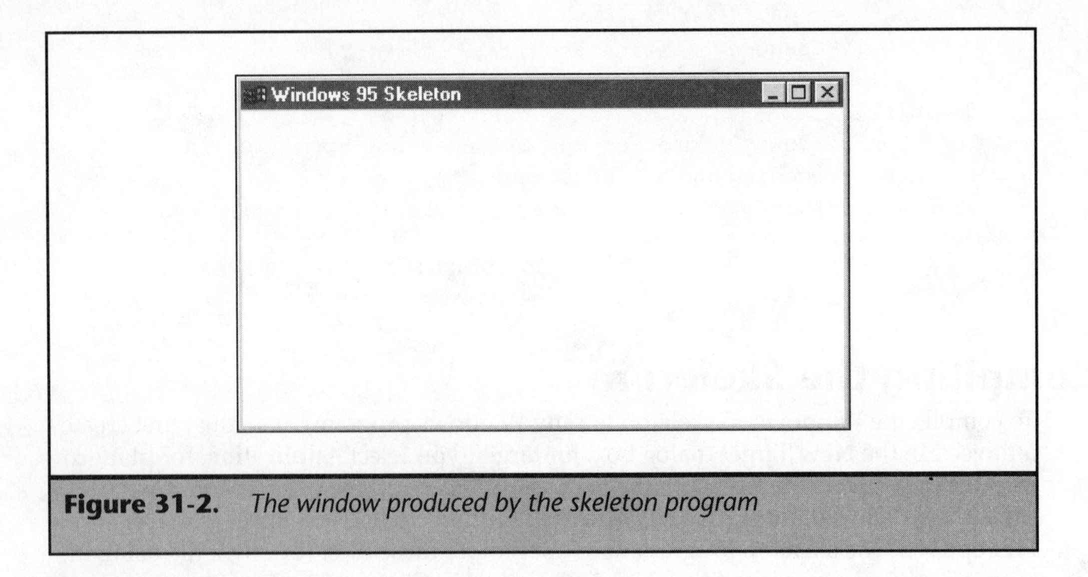

Figure 31-2. *The window produced by the skeleton program*

Program execution begins with **WinMain( )**. **WinMain( )** is passed four parameters. **hThisInst** and **hPrevInst** are handles. **hThisInst** refers to the current instance of the program. Remember, Windows 95 is a multitasking system, so it is possible that more than one instance of your program may be running at the same time. **hPrevInst** will always be **NULL** and is generally not used. (In Windows 3.1 programs, **hPrevInst** would be nonzero if there were other instances of the program currently executing, but this no longer applies to Windows 95.) The **lpszArgs** parameter is a pointer to a string that holds any command-line arguments specified when the application was begun. No parameters are used by the skeleton, so this parameter is ignored. The **nWinMode** parameter contains a value that determines how the window will be displayed when your program begins execution.

Inside the function, three variables are created. The **hwnd** variable will hold the handle to the program's window. The **msg** structure variable will hold window messages and the **wcl** structure variable will be used to define the window class.

Defining the Window Class

The first two actions that **WinMain( )** takes is to define a window class and then register it. A window class is defined by filling in the fields defined by the **WNDCLASSEX** structure. Its fields are shown here:

```
UINT cbSize; /* size of the WNDCLASSEX structure */
UINT style; /* type of window */
WNDPROC lpfnWndProc; /* address to window func */
int cbClsExtra; /* extra class info */
int cbWndExtra; /* extra window info */
HINSTANCE hInstance; /* handle of this instance */
```

```
HICON hIcon; /* handle of large icon */
HICON hIconSm; /* handle of small icon */
HCURSOR hCursor; /* handle of mouse cursor */
HBRUSH hbrBackground; /* background color */
LPCSTR lpszMenuName; /* name of main menu */
LPCSTR lpszClassName; /* name of window class */
```

As you can see by looking at the program, **cbSize** is assigned the size of the **WNDCLASSEX** structure. The **hInstance** field is assigned the current instance handle as specified by **hThisInst**. The name of the window class is pointed to by **lpszClassName**, which points to the string "MyWin" in this case. The address of the window function is assigned to **lpfnWndProc**. No default style is specified. No extra information is needed.

All Windows applications need to define a default shape for the mouse cursor and for the application's icons. An application can define its own custom version of these resources or it may use one of the built-in styles, as the skeleton does. In either case, handles to these resources must be assigned to the appropriate members of the **WNDCLASSEX** structure. To see how this is done, let's begin with icons.

A Windows 95 application has two icons associated with it: one large and one small. The small icon is used when the application is minimized, and it is also the icon that is used for the system menu. The large icon is displayed when you move or copy an application to the desktop. Typically, large icons are 32×32 bitmaps and small icons are 16×16 bitmaps. The style of each icon is loaded by the API function **LoadIcon( )**, whose prototype is shown here:

HICON LoadIcon(HINSTANCE *hInst*, LPCSTR *lpszName*);

This function returns a handle to an icon. Here, *hInst* specifies the handle of the module that contains the icon and its name is specified in *lpszName*. However, to use one of the built-in icons, you must use **NULL** for the first parameter and specify one of the following macros for the second:

Icon Macro	**Shape**
IDI_APPLICATION	Default icon
IDI_ASTERISK	Information icon
IDI_EXCLAMATION	Exclamation point icon
IDI_HAND	Stop sign
IDI_QUESTION	Question mark icon
IDI_WINLOGO	Windows 95 Logo

In the skeleton, **IDI_APPLICATION** is used for the large icon and **IDI_WINLOGO** is used for the small icon.

To load the mouse cursor, use the API **LoadCursor( )** function. This function has the following prototype:

```
HCURSOR LoadCursor(HINSTANCE hInst, LPCSTR lpszName);
```

This function returns a handle to a cursor resource. Here, *hInst* specifies the handle of the module that contains the mouse cursor and its name is specified in *lpszName*. However, to use one of the built-in cursors, you must use **NULL** for the first parameter and specify one of the built-in cursors using its macro for the second parameter. Some of the most common built-in cursors are shown here:

Cursor Macro	Shape
IDC_ARROW	Default arrow pointer
IDC_CROSS	Cross hairs
IDC_IBEAM	Vertical I-beam
IDC_WAIT	Hourglass

The background color of the window created by the skeleton is specified as white and a handle to this *brush* is obtained using the API function **GetStockObject( )**. A brush is a resource that paints the screen using a predetermined size, color, and pattern. The function **GetStockObject( )** is used to obtain a handle to a number of standard display objects, including brushes, pens (which draw lines), and character fonts. It has this prototype:

```
HGDIOBJ GetStockObject(int object);
```

The function returns a handle to the object specified by *object*. (The type **HGDIOBJ** is a GDI handle.) Here are some of the built-in brushes available to your program:

Brush Macro	Background Type
BLACK_BRUSH	Black
DKGRAY_BRUSH	Dark gray
HOLLOW_BRUSH	See-through window
LTGRAY_BRUSH	Light gray
WHITE_BRUSH	White

You may use these macros as parameters to **GetStockObject( )** to obtain a brush.

Once the window class has been fully specified, it is registered with Windows 95 using the API function **RegisterClassEx( )**, whose prototype is shown here:

```
ATOM RegisterClassEx(CONST WNDCLASSEX *lpWClass);
```

The function returns a value that identifies the window class. **ATOM** is a **typedef** that means **WORD**. Each window class is given a unique value. *lpWClass* must be the address of a **WNDCLASSEX** structure.

Creating a Window

Once a window class has been defined and registered, your application can actually create a window of that class using the API function **CreateWindow( )**, whose prototype is shown here:

```
HWND CreateWindow(
  LPCSTR lpClassName, /* name of window class */
  LPCSTR lpWinName, /* title of window */
  DWORD dwStyle, /* type of window */
  int X, int Y, /* upper-left coordinates */
  int Width, int Height, /* dimensions of window */
  HWND hParent, /* handle of parent window */
  HMENU hMenu, /* handle of main menu */
  HINSTANCE hThisInst, /* handle of creator */
  LPVOID lpszAdditional /* pointer to additional info */
);
```

As you can see by looking at the skeleton program, many of the parameters to **CreateWindow( )** may be defaulted or specified as **NULL**. In fact, most often the *X*, *Y*, *Width*, and *Height* parameters will simply use the macro **CW_USEDEFAULT**, which tells Windows 95 to select an appropriate size and location for the window. If the window has no parent, which is the case in the skeleton, then *hParent* must be specified as **HWND_DESKTOP**. (You may also use **NULL** for this parameter.) If the window does not contain a main menu, then *hMenu* must be **NULL**. Also, if no additional information is required, as is most often the case, then *lpszAdditional* is **NULL**. (The type **LPVOID** is **typedef**ed as **void ***. Historically, **LPVOID** stands for long pointer to **void**.)

The remaining four parameters must be explicitly set by your program. First, *lpszClassName* must point to the name of the window class. (This is the name you gave it when it was registered.) The title of the window is a string pointed to by *lpszWinName*. This can be a null string, but usually a window will be given a title.

The style (or type) of window actually created is determined by the value of *dwStyle*. The macro **WS_OVERLAPPEDWINDOW** specifies a standard window that has a system menu; a border; and minimize, maximize, and close boxes. While this style of window is the most common, you can construct one to your own specifications. To accomplish this, you simply OR together the various style macros that you want. Some other common styles are shown here:

Style Macros	**Window Feature**
WS_OVERLAPPED	Overlapped window with border
WS_MAXIMIZEBOX	Maximize box
WS_MINIMIZEBOX	Minimize box
WS_SYSMENU	System menu
WS_HSCROLL	Horizontal scrollbar
WS_VSCROLL	Vertical scrollbar

The *hThisInst* parameter must contain the current instance handle of the application.

The **CreateWindow( )** function returns the handle of the window it creates or **NULL** if the window cannot be created.

Once the window has been created, it is still not displayed on the screen. To cause the window to be displayed, call the **ShowWindow( )** API function. This function has the following prototype:

BOOL ShowWindow(HWND *hwnd*, int *nHow*);

The handle of the window to display is specified in *hwnd*. The display mode is specified in *nHow*. The first time the window is displayed, you will want to pass **WinMain( )**'s **nWinMode** as the *nHow* parameter. Remember, the value of **nWinMode** determines how the window will be displayed when the program begins execution. Subsequent calls can display (or remove) the window as necessary. Some common values for *nHow* are shown here:

Display Macros	**Effect**
SW_HIDE	Removes the window
SW_MINIMIZE	Minimizes the window into an icon
SW_MAXIMIZE	Maximizes the window
SW_RESTORE	Returns a window to normal size

The **ShowWindow( )** function returns the previous display status of the window. If the window was displayed, then nonzero is returned. If the window was not displayed, zero is returned.

Although not technically necessary for the skeleton, a call to **UpdateWindow( )** is included because it is needed by virtually every Windows 95 application that you will create. It tells Windows 95 to send a message to your application that the main window needs to be updated. (This message will be discussed in the next chapter.)

The Message Loop

The final part of the skeletal **WinMain( )** is the *message loop*. The message loop is a part of all Windows applications. Its purpose is to receive and process messages sent by Windows 95. When an application is running, it is continually being sent messages. These messages are stored in the application's message queue until they can be read and processed. Each time your application is ready to read another message, it must call the API function **GetMessage( )**, which has this prototype:

BOOL GetMessage(LPMSG *msg*, HWND *hwnd*, UINT *min*, UINT *max*);

The message will be received by the structure pointed to by *msg*. All Windows messages are of structure type **MSG**, shown here:

```
/* Message structure */
typedef struct tagMSG
{
  HWND hwnd; /* window that message is for */
  UINT message; /* message */
  WPARAM wParam; /* message-dependent info */
  LPARAM lParam; /* more message-dependent info */
  DWORD time; /* time message posted */
  POINT pt; /* X,Y location of mouse */
} MSG;
```

In **MSG**, the handle of the window for which the message is intended is contained in **hwnd**. All Windows 95 messages are 32-bit integers. The message itself is contained in **message**. Additional information relating to each message is passed in **wParam** and **lParam.** The type **WPARAM** is a **typedef** for **UINT** and **LPARAM** is a **typedef** for **LONG**.

The time the message was sent (posted) is specified in milliseconds in the **time** field.

The **pt** member will contain the coordinates of the mouse when the message was sent. The coordinates are held in a **POINT** structure, which is defined like this:

```
typedef struct tagPOINT {
  LONG x, y;
} POINT;
```

If there are no messages in the application's message queue, then a call to **GetMessage( )** will pass control back to Windows 95. (We will explore messages in greater detail in the next chapter.)

The *hwnd* parameter to **GetMessage( )** specifies the window for which messages will be obtained. It is possible (even likely) that an application will contain several windows and you may only want to receive messages for a specific window. If you want to receive all messages directed at your application, this parameter must be **NULL**.

The remaining two parameters to **GetMessage( )** specify a range of messages that will be received. Generally, you want your application to receive all messages. To accomplish this, specify both *min* and *max* as 0, as the skeleton does.

GetMessage( ) returns zero when the user terminates the program, causing the message loop to terminate. Otherwise, it returns nonzero.

Inside the message loop, two functions are called. The first is the API function **TranslateMessage( )**. This function translates virtual key codes generated by Windows 95 into character messages. (Virtual keys are discussed in Chapter 33.) Although it is not necessary for all applications, most call **TranslateMessage( )** because it is needed to allow full integration of the keyboard into your application program.

Once the message has been read and translated, it is dispatched back to Windows 95 using the **DispatchMessage( )** API function. Windows 95 then holds this message until it can pass it to the program's window function.

Once the message loop terminates, the **WinMain( )** function ends by returning the value of **msg.wParam** to Windows 95. This value contains the return code generated when your program terminates.

The Window Function

The second function in the application skeleton is its window function. In this case, the function is called **WindowFunc( )**, but it could have any name you like. The window function is passed the first four members of the **MSG** structure as parameters. For the skeleton, the only parameter that is used is the message itself. However, in the next chapter you will learn more about the parameters to this function.

The skeleton's window function responds to only one message explicitly: **WM_DESTROY**. This message is sent when the user terminates the program. When this message is received, your program must execute a call to the API function **PostQuitMessage( )**. The argument to this function is an exit code that is returned in **msg.wParam** inside **WinMain( )**. Calling **PostQuitMessage( )** causes a **WM_QUIT** message to be sent to your application, which causes **GetMessage( )** to return false and thus stops your program.

Any other messages received by **WindowFunc( )** are passed along to Windows 95 via a call to **DefWindowProc( )** for default processing. This step is necessary because all messages must be dealt with in one fashion or another.

What About Definition Files?

If you are familiar with Windows 3.1 programming, then you have used *definition files*. For Windows 3.1, all programs need to have a definition file associated with them. A definition file is simply a text file that specifies certain information and settings needed by your Windows 3.1 program. Definition files use the file extension .DEF. However, because of the 32-bit architecture of Windows 95 (and other improvements), definition files are not needed for Windows 95 programs. Frankly, definition files were always an inelegant kludge and it is a good thing that they are gone.

Although definition files are not required for Windows 95 programs, there is also no harm in supplying one, either. For example, if you want to include one for the sake of downward compatibility with Windows 3.1, then you are free to do so.

Naming Conventions

Before finishing this chapter, a short comment on naming functions and variables needs to be made. If you are new to Windows programming, several of the variable and parameter names in the skeleton program and its description probably seemed rather unusual. The reason for this is that they follow a set of naming conventions that was invented by Microsoft for Windows programming. For functions, the name consists of a verb followed by a noun. The first character of the verb and noun are capitalized.

For variable names, Microsoft chose to use a rather complex system of embedding the data type into a variable's name. To accomplish this, a lowercase type prefix is added to the start of the variable's name. The name itself is begun with a capital letter. The type prefixes are shown in Table 31-1. The use of type prefixes is controversial and is not universally supported. Many Windows programmers use this method, many do not. You are free to use any naming convention you like.

Prefix	Data Type
b	Boolean (one byte)
c	Character (one byte)
dw	Long unsigned integer
f	16-bit bit-field (flags)
fn	Function
h	Handle
l	Long integer
lp	Long pointer
n	Short integer
p	Pointer
pt	Long integer holding screen coordinates
w	Short unsigned integer
sz	Pointer to null-terminated string
lpsz	Long pointer to null-terminated string
rgb	Long integer holding RGB color values

Table 31-1. *Variable Prefix Characters*

Chapter Thirty-Two

Application Essentials: Messages and Basic I/O

Although the skeleton developed in Chapter 31 forms the framework for a Windows 95 program, by itself it is useless. To be useful, a program must be capable of performing two fundamental operations. First, it must be able to respond to various messages sent by Windows 95. As explained in Chapter 31, Windows 95 communicates with your application by sending it messages. As you will see, the processing of these messages is at the core of all Windows 95 applications. Second, your program must provide some means of outputting information to the user (that is, displaying information on the screen). Unlike programs that you may have written for other operating systems, outputting information to the user is a nontrivial task in Windows 95. Without the ability to process messages and display information, no useful Windows program can be written. For this reason, message processing and the basic I/O operations are the subject of this chapter.

We will begin with a discussion of one of Windows' easiest to use output mechanisms: the message box.

Message Boxes

Before you can develop useful programs, you will need some way for your program to communicate with you. That is, you will need some mechanism to output information to the screen. Although this was probably a simple task for the other types of programs that you have written, it takes some effort when working with Windows. In fact, managing output forms a large part of any Windows 95 application. Fortunately, Windows does provide one fairly easy (but limited) means of displaying information: the message box. As you will see, many of the examples in this section make use of message boxes.

A message box is a simple window that displays a message to the user and waits for an acknowledgment. Unlike other types of windows that you must create, a message box is a system-defined window that you may use. In general, the purpose of a message box is to inform the user that some event has taken place. However, it is possible to construct a message box that allows the user to select from among a few basic alternatives as a response to the message. For example one common form of message box allows a user to select Abort, Retry, or Ignore.

NOTE: In the term message box, *the word* message *refers to human-readable text that is displayed on the screen. It does not refer to Windows 95 messages that are sent to your program's window function. Although the terms sound similar,* message boxes *and* messages *are two entirely separate concepts.*

To create a message box, use the **MessageBox( )** API function. Its prototype is shown here:

int MessageBox(HWND *hwnd*, LPCSTR *lpText*, LPCSTR *lpCaption*, UINT *wMBType*);

Here, *hwnd* is the handle to the parent window. The *lpText* parameter is a pointer to a string that will appear inside the message box. The string pointed to by *lpCaption* is used as the title for the box. The value of *wMBType* determines the exact nature of the message box, including what type of buttons will be present. Some of its most common values are shown in Table 32-1. These macros are defined by including **windows.h** and you can OR together two or more of these macros as long as they are not mutually exclusive.

MessageBox( ) returns the user's response to the box. The possible return values are shown here:

Button Pressed	**Return Value**
Abort	IDABORT
Retry	IDRETRY
Ignore	IDIGNORE
Cancel	IDCANCEL
No	IDNO
Yes	IDYES
OK	IDOK

Value	Effect
MB_ABORTRETRYIGNORE	Displays Abort, Retry, and Ignore pushbuttons
MB_ICONEXCLAMATION	Displays exclamation-point icon
MB_ICONHAND	Displays a stop sign icon
MB_ICONINFORMATION	Displays an information icon
MB_ICONQUESTION	Displays a question mark icon
MB_ICONSTOP	Same as MB_ICONHAND
MB_OK	Displays OK button
MB_OKCANCEL	Displays OK and Cancel pushbuttons
MB_RETRYCANCEL	Displays Retry and Cancel pushbuttons
MB_YESNO	Displays Yes and No pushbuttons
MB_YESNOCANCEL	Displays Yes, No, and Cancel pushbuttons

Table 32-1. *Some Common Values for* wMBType

These macros are defined by including **windows.h**. Remember, depending upon the value of *wMBType*, only certain buttons will be present. Quite often, message boxes are simply used to display an item of information and the only response offered to the user is the OK button. In these cases, the return value of a message box is ignored by the program.

To display a message box, simply call the **MessageBox( )** function. Windows 95 will display it at its first opportunity. **MessageBox( )** automatically creates a window and displays your message in it. For example, this call to **MessageBox( )**

```
i = MessageBox(hwnd, "This is Caption", "This is Title", MB_OKCANCEL);
```

produces the message box shown in Figure 32-1. Depending upon which button the user presses, **i** will contain either **IDOK** or **IDCANCEL**.

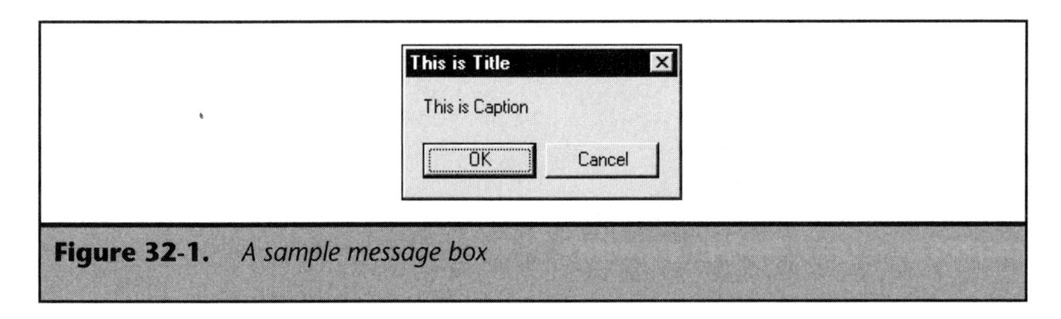

Figure 32-1. *A sample message box*

Message boxes are typically used to notify the user that some event has occurred. However, because message boxes are so easy to use, they make excellent debugging tools when you need a simple way to output something to the screen. As you will see, subsequent examples will use a message box whenever a simple means of displaying information is required.

Understanding Windows 95 Messages

As it relates to Windows 95, a message is a unique 32-bit integer value. Windows 95 communicates with your program by sending it messages. Each message corresponds to some event. For example, there are messages to indicate that the user has pressed a key, that the mouse has moved, or that a window has been resized.

Although you could, in theory, refer to each message by its numeric value, in practice this is seldom done. Instead, there are macro names defined for all of Windows 95 messages. Typically, you will use the macro name, not the actual integer value, when referring to a message. The standard names for the messages are defined by including **windows.h** in your program. Here are some common Windows 95 message macros:

WM_CHAR	WM_PAINT	WM_MOVE	WM_CLOSE
WM_LBUTTONUP	WM_LBUTTONDOWN	WM_COMMAND	WM_HSCROLL

Two other values accompany each message and contain information related to each message. One of these values is of type **WPARAM**, the other is of type **LPARAM**. For Windows 95, both of these types translate into 32-bit integers. These values are commonly called **wParam** and **lParam**, respectively. The contents of **wParam lParam** are determined by which message is received. They typically hold things like mouse coordinates or the value of a keypress, or a system-related value such as character size. As each message is discussed, the meaning of the values contained in **wParam** and **lParam** will be described.

As mentioned in Chapter 31, the function that actually processes messages is your program's window function. As you should recall, this function is passed four parameters: the handle of the window that the message is for; the message itself; and the last two parameters, which are **wParam** and **lParam**.

Sometimes two pieces of information are encoded into the two words that comprise the **wParam** and **lParam** parameters. To provide easy access to each half of **wParam** and **lParam**, Windows defines two macros called **LOWORD** and **HIWORD**. They return the low-order and high-order words of a long integer, respectively. They are used like this:

```
x = LOWORD(lParam);
x = HIWORD(lParam);
```

You will see these macros in use soon.

Although it is not possible to examine every message used by Windows 95, this chapter discusses some of the most common. Other messages are described throughout the remainder of Part 5 as the need arises.

Responding to a Keypress

One of the most common Windows 95 messages is generated when a key is pressed. This message is called **WM_CHAR**. It is important to understand that your application never receives, per se, keystrokes directly from the keyboard. Instead, each time a key is pressed, a **WM_CHAR** message is sent to the active window. To see how this process works, this section extends the skeletal application developed in Chapter 31 so that it processes keystroke messages.

Each time **WM_CHAR** is sent, **wParam** contains the ASCII value of the key pressed. **LOWORD(lParam)** contains the number of times the key has been repeated as a result of the key being held down. The bits of **HIWORD(lParam)** are encoded as shown here:

15: Set if the key is being released; cleared if the key is being pressed.

14: Set if the key was pressed before the message sent; cleared if it was not pressed.

13: Set if the ALT key is also being pressed; cleared if ALT is not pressed.

12: Used by Windows 95

11: Used by Windows 95

10: Used by Windows 95

9: Used by Windows 95

8: Set if the key pressed is a function key or an extended key; cleared otherwise.

7–0: Manufacturer-dependent key code (i.e., the scan code)

For our purposes, the only value that is important at this time is **wParam**, since it holds the key that was pressed. However, notice how detailed the information is that Windows 95 supplies about the state of the system. Of course, you are free to use as much or as little of this information as you like.

To process a **WM_CHAR** message, you must add it to the **switch** statement inside your program's window function. For example, here is a program that processes a keystroke by displaying the character on the screen using a message box:

```
/* Processing WM_CHAR messages. */

#include <windows.h>
#include <string.h>
#include <stdio.h>

LRESULT CALLBACK WindowFunc(HWND, UINT, WPARAM, LPARAM);

char szWinName[] = "MyWin"; /* name of window class */

char str[255] = ""; /* holds output string */

int WINAPI WinMain(HINSTANCE hThisInst, HINSTANCE hPrevInst,
                   LPSTR lpszArgs, int nWinMode)
{
  HWND hwnd;
  MSG msg;
  WNDCLASSEX wcl;

  /* Define a window class. */
  wcl.hInstance = hThisInst; /* handle to this instance */
  wcl.lpszClassName = szWinName; /* window class name */
  wcl.lpfnWndProc = WindowFunc; /* window function */
  wcl.style = 0; /* default style */

  wcl.cbSize = sizeof(WNDCLASSEX); /* set size of WNDCLASSEX */

  wcl.hIcon = LoadIcon(NULL, IDI_APPLICATION); /* large icon */
  wcl.hIconSm = LoadIcon(NULL, IDI_APPLICATION); /* small icon */

  wcl.hCursor = LoadCursor(NULL, IDC_ARROW); /* cursor style */
  wcl.lpszMenuName = NULL; /* no menu */

  wcl.cbClsExtra = 0; /* no extra */
  wcl.cbWndExtra = 0; /* information needed */

  /* Make the window white. */
  wcl.hbrBackground = (HBRUSH) GetStockObject(WHITE_BRUSH);
```

```
  /* Register the window class. */
  if(!RegisterClassEx(&wcl)) return 0;

  /* Now that a window class has been registered, a window
     can be created. */
  hwnd = CreateWindow(
    szWinName, /* name of window class */
    "Processing WM_CHAR Messages", /* title */
    WS_OVERLAPPEDWINDOW, /* window style - normal */
    CW_USEDEFAULT, /* X coordinate - let Windows decide */
    CW_USEDEFAULT, /* Y coordinate - let Windows decide */
    CW_USEDEFAULT, /* width - let Windows decide */
    CW_USEDEFAULT, /* height - let Windows decide */
    HWND_DESKTOP, /* no parent window */
    NULL, /* no menu */
    hThisInst, /* handle of this instance of the program */
    NULL /* no additional arguments */
  );

  /* Display the window. */
  ShowWindow(hwnd, nWinMode);
  UpdateWindow(hwnd);

  /* Create the message loop. */
  while(GetMessage(&msg, NULL, 0, 0))
  {
    TranslateMessage(&msg); /* allow use of keyboard */
    DispatchMessage(&msg); /* return control to Windows */
  }
  return msg.wParam;
}

/* This function is called by Windows 95 and is passed
   messages from the message queue.
*/
LRESULT CALLBACK WindowFunc(HWND hwnd, UINT message,
                            WPARAM wParam, LPARAM lParam)
{
  switch(message) {
    case WM_CHAR: /* process keystroke */
      sprintf(str, "Character is %c", (char) wParam);
      MessageBox(hwnd, str, "WM_CHAR Received", MB_OK);
```

```
      break;
    case WM_DESTROY: /* terminate the program */
      PostQuitMessage(0);
      break;
    default:
      /* Let Windows 95 process any messages not specified in
         the preceding switch statement. */
      return DefWindowProc(hwnd, message, wParam, lParam);
  }
  return 0;
}
```

Sample output produced by this program is shown in Figure 32-2. In the program, look carefully at these lines of code from **WindowFunc( )**:

```
case WM_CHAR: /* process keystroke */
      sprintf(str, "Character is %c", (char) wParam);
      MessageBox(hwnd, str, "WM_CHAR Received", MB_OK);
      break;
```

As you can see, the **WM_CHAR** message has been added to the **case** statement. When you run the program, each time you press a key, a **WM_CHAR** message is generated and sent to **WindowFunc( )**. Inside the **WM_CHAR** case, the character received in **wParam** is displayed using a message box.

Outputting Text to a Window

Although the message box is the easiest means of displaying information, it is obviously not suitable for all situations. Although a little more complicated than using a message box, there is another way for your program to output information: it can write directly to the client area of its window. In this section, you will learn the basics of text output.

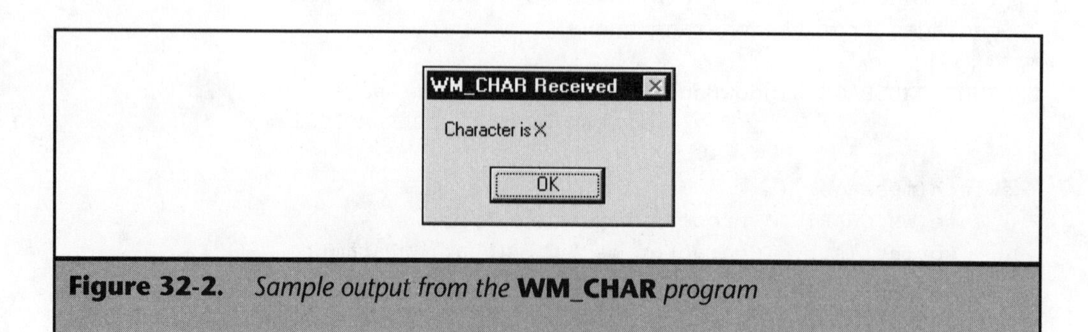

Figure 32-2. *Sample output from the* **WM_CHAR** *program*

The first thing to understand about outputting text to a window is that you cannot use the standard C or C++ I/O system. The reason for this is easy to understand: The standard C/C++ I/O functions and operators direct their output to standard output. However, in a Windows program, output is directed to a window. To see how text can be written to a window, let's begin with an example. Specifically, let's change the preceding program so that it outputs each character that you type to the program's window instead of using a message box. To do this, change the **WindowFunc( )** so that it looks like this:

```
LRESULT CALLBACK WindowFunc(HWND hwnd, UINT message,
                            WPARAM wParam, LPARAM lParam)
{
  HDC hdc;
  static unsigned j=0;

  switch(message) {
    case WM_CHAR: /* process keystroke */
      hdc = GetDC(hwnd); /* get device context */
      sprintf(str, "%c", (char) wParam); /* stringize character */
      TextOut(hdc, j*10, 0, str, strlen(str)); /* output char */
      j++; /* try commenting-out this line */
      ReleaseDC(hwnd, hdc); /* release device context */
      break;
    case WM_DESTROY: /* terminate the program */
      PostQuitMessage(0);
      break;
    default:
      /* Let Windows 95 process any messages not specified in
         the preceding switch statement. */
      return DefWindowProc(hwnd, message, wParam, lParam);
  }
  return 0;
}
```

Look carefully at the code inside the **WM_CHAR** case. It simply echoes each character that you type to the program's window. Compared to using the standard C/C++ I/O functions or operators, this code probably seems overly complex. The reason for this is that Windows must establish a link between your program and the screen. This is called a device context (DC for short) and it is acquired by calling **GetDC( )**. For now, don't worry about precisely what a device context is. It will be discussed in the next section. However, once you obtain a device context, you may write to the window. At the end of the process, the device context is released using **ReleaseDC( )**. Your program must release the device context when it is done with it. There are a finite number of device contexts. If your program doesn't release the DC, eventually the available DCs will be exhausted and a subsequent call to **GetDC( )** will fail. Both **GetDC( )** and **ReleaseDC( )** are API functions. Their prototypes are shown here:

HDC GetDC(HWND *hwnd*);

int ReleaseDC(HWND *hwnd*, HDC *hdc*);

GetDC( ) returns a device context associated with the window whose handle is specified by *hwnd*. The type **HDC** specifies a handle to a device context. If a device context cannot be obtained, the function returns **NULL**.

ReleaseDC( ) returns true if the device context was released and false otherwise. The *hwnd* parameter is the handle of the window for which the device context is released. The *hdc* parameter is the handle of device context obtained through the call to **GetDC( )**.

The function that actually outputs the character is the API function **TextOut( )**. Its prototype is shown here:

BOOL TextOut(HDC *hdc*, int *x*, int *y*, LPCSTR *lpstr*, int *nlength*);

The **TextOut( )** function outputs the string pointed to by *lpstr* at the window coordinates specified by *x,y*. (By default, these coordinates are in terms of pixels.) The length of the string is specified in *nlength*. The **TextOut( )** function returns nonzero if successful and zero otherwise.

In the **WindowFunc( )** function, each time a **WM_CHAR** message is received the character that is typed by the user is converted, using **sprintf( )**, into a string that is one character long and then displayed in the window using **TextOut( )**. The first character is displayed at location 0, 0. Remember, in a window, the upper left corner of the client area is location 0, 0. Window coordinates are always relative to the window, not the screen. Therefore, the first character is displayed in the upper left corner no matter where the window is physically located on the screen. The reason for the variable j is to allow each character to be displayed to the right of the preceding character. That is, the second character is displayed at 10,0, the third at 20,0, and so on. Windows does not support any concept of a text cursor that is automatically advanced. Instead, you must explicitly specify where each **TextOut( )** string will be written. Also, **TextOut( )** does not advance to the next line when a newline character is encountered, nor does it expand tabs. You must perform all these activities yourself.

Before moving on, you might want to try one simple experiment: comment out the line of code that increments **j**. This will cause all characters to be displayed at location 0, 0. Next, run the program and try typing several characters. Specifically, try typing a **W** followed by an **i**. Because Windows is a graphics-based system, characters are of different sizes and overwriting one character by another does not necessarily cause all of the previous character to be erased. For example, when you type a **W** followed by an **i**, part of the **W** is still displayed. The fact that characters are not proportional also explains why the spacing between characters that you type is not even.

Understand that the method used in this program to output text to a window is quite crude. In fact, no real Windows 95 application would use this approach. Windows 95 provides the means by which you can fully manage text output to a window. However, a description of these features is beyond the scope of this book. (For coverage of text output to a window, see my book *Windows 95 Programming from the Ground Up*, Osborne/McGraw-Hill, 1997.)

No Windows 95 API function will allow output beyond the borders of a window. Output will automatically be clipped to prevent the boundaries from being crossed. To confirm this for yourself, try typing characters past the border of the window. As you will see, once the right edge of the window has been reached, no further characters are displayed.

At first you might think that using **TextOut( )** to output a single character is not an efficient application of the function. The fact is that Windows 95 (and Windows, in general) does not contain a function that simply outputs a character. Since Windows 95 performs much of its user interaction through dialog boxes, menus, toolbars, etc., it only contains a few functions that output text to the client area.

Here is the entire program that echoes keystrokes to the window. Figure 32-3 shows sample output.

```
/* Displaying text using TextOut(). */

#include <windows.h>
#include <string.h>
#include <stdio.h>

LRESULT CALLBACK WindowFunc(HWND, UINT, WPARAM, LPARAM);

char szWinName[] = "MyWin"; /* name of window class */

char str[255] = ""; /* holds output string */

int WINAPI WinMain(HINSTANCE hThisInst, HINSTANCE hPrevInst,
                   LPSTR lpszArgs, int nWinMode)
{
  HWND hwnd;
  MSG msg;
  WNDCLASSEX wcl;

  /* Define a window class. */
  wcl.hInstance = hThisInst; /* handle to this instance */
  wcl.lpszClassName = szWinName; /* window class name */
```

```
wcl.lpfnWndProc = WindowFunc; /* window function */
wcl.style = 0; /* default style */

wcl.cbSize = sizeof(WNDCLASSEX); /* set size of WNDCLASSEX */

wcl.hIcon = LoadIcon(NULL, IDI_APPLICATION); /* large icon */
wcl.hIconSm = LoadIcon(NULL, IDI_APPLICATION); /* small icon */

wcl.hCursor = LoadCursor(NULL, IDC_ARROW); /* cursor style */
wcl.lpszMenuName = NULL; /* no menu */

wcl.cbClsExtra = 0; /* no extra */
wcl.cbWndExtra = 0; /* information needed */

/* Make the window white. */
wcl.hbrBackground = (HBRUSH) GetStockObject(WHITE_BRUSH);

/* Register the window class. */
if(!RegisterClassEx(&wcl)) return 0;

/* Now that a window class has been registered, a window
   can be created. */
hwnd = CreateWindow(
  szWinName, /* name of window class */
  "Display WM_CHAR Messages Using TextOut", /* title */
  WS_OVERLAPPEDWINDOW, /* window style - normal */
  CW_USEDEFAULT, /* X coordinate - let Windows decide */
  CW_USEDEFAULT, /* Y coordinate - let Windows decide */
  CW_USEDEFAULT, /* width - let Windows decide */
  CW_USEDEFAULT, /* height - let Windows decide */
  HWND_DESKTOP, /* no parent window */
  NULL, /* no menu */
  hThisInst, /* handle of this instance of the program */
  NULL /* no additional arguments */
);

/* Display the window. */
ShowWindow(hwnd, nWinMode);
UpdateWindow(hwnd);

/* Create the message loop. */
while(GetMessage(&msg, NULL, 0, 0))
{
  TranslateMessage(&msg); /* allow use of keyboard */
  DispatchMessage(&msg); /* return control to Windows */
```

```
  }
  return msg.wParam;
}

/* This function is called by Windows 95 and is passed
   messages from the message queue.
*/
LRESULT CALLBACK WindowFunc(HWND hwnd, UINT message,
                            WPARAM wParam, LPARAM lParam)
{
  HDC hdc;
  static unsigned j=0;

  switch(message) {
    case WM_CHAR: /* process keystroke */
      hdc = GetDC(hwnd); /* get device context */
      sprintf(str, "%c", (char) wParam); /* stringize character */
      TextOut(hdc, j*10, 0, str, strlen(str)); /* output char */
      j++; /* try commenting-out this line */
      ReleaseDC(hwnd, hdc); /* release device context */
      break;
    case WM_DESTROY: /* terminate the program */
      PostQuitMessage(0);
      break;
    default:
      /* Let Windows 95 process any messages not specified in
         the preceding switch statement. */
      return DefWindowProc(hwnd, message, wParam, lParam);
  }
  return 0;
}
```

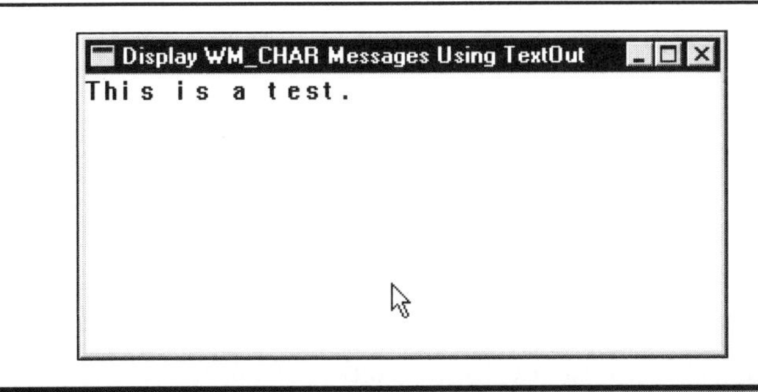

Figure 32-3. *Sample window produced using* **TextOut( )**

Device Contexts

The program in the previous section had to obtain a device context prior to outputting to the window. It is now time to understand what a device context is. A device context is an output path from your Windows 95 application, through the appropriate device driver, to the client area of your window. The device context also fully defines the state of the device driver.

Before your application can output information to the client area of the window, a device context must be obtained. Until this is done, there is no linkage between your program and the window relative to output. Since **TextOut( )** and other output functions require a handle to a device context, this is a self-enforcing rule.

Processing the WM_PAINT Message

One of the most important messages that your program will receive is **WM_PAINT**. This message is sent when your program needs to restore the contents of its window. To understand why this is important, run the program from the previous section and enter a few characters. Next, minimize and then restore the window. As you will see, the characters that you typed are not displayed after the window is restored. Also, if the window is overwritten by another window and then redisplayed, the characters are not redisplayed. The reason for this is simple: in general, Windows does not keep a record of what a window contains. Instead, it is your program's job to maintain the contents of a window. To help your program accomplish this, each time the contents of a window must be redisplayed, your program will be sent a **WM_PAINT** message. (This message will also be sent when your window is first displayed.) Each time your program receives this message it must redisplay the contents of the window.

Before explaining how to respond to a **WM_PAINT** message, it might be useful to explain why Windows does not automatically rewrite your window. The answer is short and to the point. In many situations, it is easier for your program, which has intimate knowledge of the contents of the window, to rewrite it than it would be for Windows to do so. While the merits of this approach have been much debated by programmers, you should simply accept it because it is unlikely to change.

The first step in processing a **WM_PAINT** message is to add it to the **switch** statement inside the window function. For example, here is one way to add a **WM_PAINT** case to the previous program:

```
case WM_PAINT: /* process a repaint request */
  hdc = BeginPaint(hwnd, &paintstruct); /* get DC */
  TextOut(hdc, 0, 0, str, strlen(str));
  EndPaint(hwnd, &paintstruct); /* release DC */
  break;
```

Let's look at this closely. First, notice that a device context is obtained using a call to **BeginPaint( )** instead of **GetDC( )**. For various reasons, when you process a

WM_PAINT message, you must obtain a device context using **BeginPaint( )**, which has this prototype:

HDC BeginPaint(HWND *hwnd*, PAINTSTRUCT **lpPS*);

BeginPaint( ) returns a device context if successful or **NULL** on failure. Here, *hwnd* is the handle of the window for which the device context is being obtained. The second parameter is a pointer to a structure of type **PAINTSTRUCT**. The structure pointed to by *lpPS* will contain information that your program can use to repaint the window. **PAINTSTRUCT** is defined like this:

```
typedef struct tagPAINTSTRUCT {
  HDC hdc; /* handle to device context */
  BOOL fErase; /* true if background must be erased */
  RECT rcPaint; /* coordinates of region to redraw */
  BOOL fRestore;  /* reserved */
  BOOL fIncUpdate; /* reserved */
  BYTE rgbReserved[32]; /* reserved */
} PAINTSTRUCT;
```

Here, **hdc** will contain the device context of the window that needs to be repainted. This DC is also returned by the call to **BeginPaint( )**. **fErase** will be nonzero if the background of the window needs to be erased. However, as long as you specified a background brush when you created the window, you can ignore the **fErase** member. Windows 95 will erase the window for you.

The type **RECT** is a structure that specifies the upper left and lower right coordinates of a rectangular region. This structure is shown here:

```
typedef tagRECT {
  LONG left, top; /* upper left */
  LONG right, bottom; /* lower right */
} RECT;
```

In **PAINTSTRUCT**, the **rcPaint** element contains the coordinates of the region of the window that needs to be repainted. For now, you will not need to use the contents of **rcPaint** because you can assume that the entire window must be repainted. However, real programs that you write will probably need to utilize this information.

Once the device context has been obtained, output can be written to the window. Once the window has been repainted, you must release the device context using a call to **EndPaint( )**, which has this prototype:

BOOL EndPaint(HWND *hwnd*, CONST PAINTSTRUCT **lpPS*);

EndPaint( ) returns nonzero. (It cannot fail.) Here, *hwnd* is the handle of the window that was repainted. The second parameter is a pointer to the **PAINTSTRUCT** structure used in the call to **BeginPaint( )**.

It is critical to understand that a device context obtained using **BeginPaint( )** must be released only through a call to **EndPaint( )**. Further, **BeginPaint( )** must only be used when a **WM_PAINT** message is being processed.

Here is the full program that now processes **WM_PAINT** messages:

```
/* Process WM_PAINT Messages */

#include <windows.h>
#include <string.h>
#include <stdio.h>

LRESULT CALLBACK WindowFunc(HWND, UINT, WPARAM, LPARAM);

char szWinName[] = "MyWin"; /* name of window class */

char str[255] = "Sample Output"; /* holds output string */

int WINAPI WinMain(HINSTANCE hThisInst, HINSTANCE hPrevInst,
                   LPSTR lpszArgs, int nWinMode)
{
  HWND hwnd;
  MSG msg;
  WNDCLASSEX wcl;

  /* Define a window class. */
  wcl.hInstance = hThisInst; /* handle to this instance */
  wcl.lpszClassName = szWinName; /* window class name */
  wcl.lpfnWndProc = WindowFunc; /* window function */
  wcl.style = 0; /* default style */

  wcl.cbSize = sizeof(WNDCLASSEX); /* set size of WNDCLASSEX */

  wcl.hIcon = LoadIcon(NULL, IDI_APPLICATION); /* large icon */
  wcl.hIconSm = LoadIcon(NULL, IDI_APPLICATION); /* small icon */

  wcl.hCursor = LoadCursor(NULL, IDC_ARROW); /* cursor style */
  wcl.lpszMenuName = NULL; /* no menu */

  wcl.cbClsExtra = 0; /* no extra */
  wcl.cbWndExtra = 0; /* information needed */
```

```
  /* Make the window white. */
  wcl.hbrBackground = (HBRUSH) GetStockObject(WHITE_BRUSH);

  /* Register the window class. */
  if(!RegisterClassEx(&wcl)) return 0;

  /* Now that a window class has been registered, a window
     can be created. */
  hwnd = CreateWindow(
    szWinName, /* name of window class */
    "Process WM_PAINT Messages", /* title */
    WS_OVERLAPPEDWINDOW, /* window style - normal */
    CW_USEDEFAULT, /* X coordinate - let Windows decide */
    CW_USEDEFAULT, /* Y coordinate - let Windows decide */
    CW_USEDEFAULT, /* width - let Windows decide */
    CW_USEDEFAULT, /* height - let Windows decide */
    HWND_DESKTOP, /* no parent window */
    NULL, /* no menu */
    hThisInst, /* handle of this instance of the program */
    NULL /* no additional arguments */
  );

  /* Display the window. */
  ShowWindow(hwnd, nWinMode);
  UpdateWindow(hwnd);

  /* Create the message loop. */
  while(GetMessage(&msg, NULL, 0, 0))
  {
    TranslateMessage(&msg); /* allow use of keyboard */
    DispatchMessage(&msg); /* return control to Windows */
  }
  return msg.wParam;
}

/* This function is called by Windows 95 and is passed
   messages from the message queue.
*/
LRESULT CALLBACK WindowFunc(HWND hwnd, UINT message,
                            WPARAM wParam, LPARAM lParam)
{
  HDC hdc;
  static unsigned j=0;
  PAINTSTRUCT paintstruct;
```

```
  switch(message) {
    case WM_CHAR: /* process keystroke */
      hdc = GetDC(hwnd); /* get device context */
      sprintf(str, "%c", (char) wParam); /* stringize character */
      TextOut(hdc, j*10, 0, str, strlen(str)); /* output char */
      j++; /* try commenting-out this line */
      ReleaseDC(hwnd, hdc); /* release device context */
      break;
    case WM_PAINT: /* process a repaint request */
      hdc = BeginPaint(hwnd, &paintstruct); /* get DC */
      TextOut(hdc, 0, 0, str, strlen(str));
      EndPaint(hwnd, &paintstruct); /* release DC */
      break;
    case WM_DESTROY: /* terminate the program */
      PostQuitMessage(0);
      break;
    default:
      /* Let Windows 95 process any messages not specified in
         the preceding switch statement. */
      return DefWindowProc(hwnd, message, wParam, lParam);
  }
  return 0;
}
```

Before continuing, enter, compile, and run this program. Try typing a few characters and then minimizing and restoring the window. As you will see, each time the window is redisplayed, the last character you typed is automatically redrawn. The reason that only the last character is redisplayed is because **str** only contains the last character that you typed. You might find it fun to alter the program so that it adds each character to a string and then redisplays that string each time a **WM_PAINT** message is displayed. (You will see one way to do this in the next example.) Notice that the global array **str** is initialized to **Sample Output** and that this is displayed when the program begins execution. The reason for this is that when a window is created, a **WM_PAINT** message is automatically generated.

While the handling of the **WM_PAINT** message in this program is quite simple, it must be emphasized that most real-world applications will be more complex because most windows contain considerably more output. Since it is your program's responsibility to restore the window if it is resized or overwritten, you must always provide some mechanism to accomplish this. In real-world programs, this is usually done in one of three ways. First, your program can simply regenerate the output by computational means. This is most feasible when no user input is used. Second, in some instances you can keep a record of events and replay the events when the window needs to be redrawn. Finally, your program can maintain a virtual window that you simply copy to the window each time it must be redrawn. This is the most general method. Which approach is best depends completely upon the application. Most of the examples in this book won't bother to redraw the window because doing so typically involves substantial additional code that often just muddies the point of an example. However, your programs will need to restore their windows in order to be conforming Windows 95 applications.

Generating a WM_PAINT Message

It is possible for your program to cause a **WM_PAINT** message to be generated. At first, you might wonder why your program would need to generate a **WM_PAINT** message since it seems that it can repaint its window whenever it wants. However, this is a false assumption. Remember, updating a window is a costly process in terms of time. Because Windows is a multitasking system that might be running other programs that are also demanding CPU time, your program should simply tell Windows that it wants to output information, but let Windows decide when it is best to actually perform that output. This allows Windows to better manage the system and efficiently allocate CPU time to all the tasks in the system. Using this approach, your program simply holds all output until a **WM_PAINT** message is received.

In the previous example, the **WM_PAINT** message was only received when the window was resized or uncovered. However, if all output is held until a **WM_PAINT** message is received, then to achieve interactive I/O, there must be some way to tell Windows that it needs to send a **WM_PAINT** message to your window whenever output is pending. As expected, Windows 95 includes such a feature. Thus, when your program has information to output, it simply requests that a **WM_PAINT** message be sent when Windows is ready to do so.

To cause Windows to send a **WM_PAINT** message, your program will call the **InvalidateRect( )** API function. Its prototype is shown here:

BOOL InvalidateRect(HWND *hwnd*, CONST RECT **lpRect*, BOOL *bErase*);

Here, *hwnd* is the handle of the window to which you want to send the **WM_PAINT** message. The **RECT** structure pointed to by *lpRect* specifies the coordinates within the window that must be redrawn. If this value is **NULL**, then the entire window will be specified. If *bErase* is true, then the background will be erased. If it is zero, then the background is left unchanged. The function returns nonzero if successful and zero otherwise. (In general, this function will always succeed.)

When **InvalidateRect( )** is called, it tells Windows that the window is invalid and must be redrawn. This, in turn, causes Windows to send a **WM_PAINT** message to the program's window function.

Here is a reworked version of the previous program that routes all output through the **WM_PAINT** message. The code that responds to a **WM_CHAR** message simply stores each character and then calls **InvalidateRect( )**. In this version of the program, notice that inside the **WM_CHAR** case, each character you type is added to the string **str**. Thus, each time the window is repainted, not just the last character, but the entire string, containing all the characters you typed, is output.

```
/* A Windows skeleton that routes output through
   the WM_PAINT message. */

#include <windows.h>
#include <string.h>
#include <stdio.h>

LRESULT CALLBACK WindowFunc(HWND, UINT, WPARAM, LPARAM);

char szWinName[] = "MyWin"; /* name of window class */

char str[255] = ""; /* holds output string */

int WINAPI WinMain(HINSTANCE hThisInst, HINSTANCE hPrevInst,
                   LPSTR lpszArgs, int nWinMode)
{
  HWND hwnd;
  MSG msg;
  WNDCLASSEX wcl;

  /* Define a window class. */
  wcl.hInstance = hThisInst; /* handle to this instance */
  wcl.lpszClassName = szWinName; /* window class name */
  wcl.lpfnWndProc = WindowFunc; /* window function */
  wcl.style = 0; /* default style */

  wcl.cbSize = sizeof(WNDCLASSEX); /* set size of WNDCLASSEX */

  wcl.hIcon = LoadIcon(NULL, IDI_APPLICATION); /* large icon */
  wcl.hIconSm = LoadIcon(NULL, IDI_APPLICATION); /* small icon */

  wcl.hCursor = LoadCursor(NULL, IDC_ARROW); /* cursor style */
  wcl.lpszMenuName = NULL; /* no menu */

  wcl.cbClsExtra = 0; /* no extra */
  wcl.cbWndExtra = 0; /* information needed */

  /* Make the window white. */
  wcl.hbrBackground = (HBRUSH) GetStockObject(WHITE_BRUSH);
```

```
  /* Register the window class. */
  if(!RegisterClassEx(&wcl)) return 0;

  /* Now that a window class has been registered, a window
     can be created. */
  hwnd = CreateWindow(
    szWinName, /* name of window class */
    "Routing Output Through WM_PAINT", /* title */
    WS_OVERLAPPEDWINDOW, /* window style - normal */
    CW_USEDEFAULT, /* X coordinate - let Windows decide */
    CW_USEDEFAULT, /* Y coordinate - let Windows decide */
    CW_USEDEFAULT, /* width - let Windows decide */
    CW_USEDEFAULT, /* height - let Windows decide */
    HWND_DESKTOP, /* no parent window */
    NULL, /* no menu */
    hThisInst, /* handle of this instance of the program */
    NULL /* no additional arguments */
  );

  /* Display the window. */
  ShowWindow(hwnd, nWinMode);
  UpdateWindow(hwnd);

  /* Create the message loop. */
  while(GetMessage(&msg, NULL, 0, 0))
  {
    TranslateMessage(&msg); /* allow use of keyboard */
    DispatchMessage(&msg); /* return control to Windows */
  }
  return msg.wParam;
}

/* This function is called by Windows 95 and is passed
   messages from the message queue.
*/
LRESULT CALLBACK WindowFunc(HWND hwnd, UINT message, WPARAM wParam,
                            LPARAM lParam)
{
  HDC hdc;
  PAINTSTRUCT paintstruct;
  char temp[2];

  switch(message) {
```

```
    case WM_CHAR: /* process keystroke */
      sprintf(temp, "%c", (char) wParam); /* stringize character */
      strcat(str, temp); /* add character to string */
      InvalidateRect(hwnd, NULL, 1); /* paint the screen */
      break;
    case WM_PAINT: /* process a repaint request */
      hdc = BeginPaint(hwnd, &paintstruct); /* get DC */
      TextOut(hdc, 0, 0, str, strlen(str)); /* output char */
      EndPaint(hwnd, &paintstruct); /* release DC */
      break;
    case WM_DESTROY: /* terminate the program */
      PostQuitMessage(0);
      break;
    default:
       /* Let Windows 95 process any messages not specified in
         the preceding switch statement. */
      return DefWindowProc(hwnd, message, wParam, lParam);
  }
  return 0;
}
```

Many Windows applications route all (or most) output to the client area through **WM_PAINT** for the reasons already stated. However, there is nothing wrong in outputting text or graphics as needed. Which method you use will depend upon the exact nature of each situation.

Responding to Mouse Messages

Since Windows is, to a great extent, a mouse-based operating system, all Windows 95 programs should respond to mouse input. Because the mouse is so important, there are several different types of mouse messages. This section examines the two most common. These are **WM_LBUTTONDOWN** and **WM_RBUTTONDOWN**, which are generated when the left button and right buttons are pressed, respectively.

When either the **WM_LBUTTONDOWN** or **WM_RBUTTONDOWN** message is received, the mouse's current X, Y location is specified in **LOWORD(lParam)** and **HIWORD(lParam)**, respectively. The following program uses this fact when it responds to the mouse messages. Each time you press a mouse button, a message will be displayed at the current location of the mouse pointer.

Here is the complete program that responds to the mouse messages.

```
/* Process Mouse Messages. */

#include <windows.h>
#include <string.h>
```

```
#include <stdio.h>

LRESULT CALLBACK WindowFunc(HWND, UINT, WPARAM, LPARAM);

char szWinName[] = "MyWin"; /* name of window class */

char str[255] = ""; /* holds output string */

int WINAPI WinMain(HINSTANCE hThisInst, HINSTANCE hPrevInst,
                   LPSTR lpszArgs, int nWinMode)
{
  HWND hwnd;
  MSG msg;
  WNDCLASSEX wcl;

  /* Define a window class. */
  wcl.hInstance = hThisInst; /* handle to this instance */
  wcl.lpszClassName = szWinName; /* window class name */
  wcl.lpfnWndProc = WindowFunc; /* window function */
  wcl.style = 0; /* default style */

  wcl.cbSize = sizeof(WNDCLASSEX); /* set size of WNDCLASSEX */

  wcl.hIcon = LoadIcon(NULL, IDI_APPLICATION); /* large icon */
  wcl.hIconSm = LoadIcon(NULL, IDI_APPLICATION); /* small icon */

  wcl.hCursor = LoadCursor(NULL, IDC_ARROW); /* cursor style */
  wcl.lpszMenuName = NULL; /* no menu */

  wcl.cbClsExtra = 0; /* no extra */
  wcl.cbWndExtra = 0; /* information needed */

  /* Make the window white. */
  wcl.hbrBackground = (HBRUSH) GetStockObject(WHITE_BRUSH);

  /* Register the window class. */
  if(!RegisterClassEx(&wcl)) return 0;

  /* Now that a window class has been registered, a window
     can be created. */
  hwnd = CreateWindow(
    szWinName, /* name of window class */
    "Processing Mouse Messages", /* title */
    WS_OVERLAPPEDWINDOW, /* window style - normal */
```

```
    CW_USEDEFAULT, /* X coordinate - let Windows decide */
    CW_USEDEFAULT, /* Y coordinate - let Windows decide */
    CW_USEDEFAULT, /* width - let Windows decide */
    CW_USEDEFAULT, /* height - let Windows decide */
    HWND_DESKTOP, /* no parent window */
    NULL, /* no menu */
    hThisInst, /* handle of this instance of the program */
    NULL /* no additional arguments */
  );

  /* Display the window. */
  ShowWindow(hwnd, nWinMode);
  UpdateWindow(hwnd);

  /* Create the message loop. */
  while(GetMessage(&msg, NULL, 0, 0))
  {
    TranslateMessage(&msg); /* allow use of keyboard */
    DispatchMessage(&msg); /* return control to Windows */
  }
  return msg.wParam;
}

/* This function is called by Windows 95 and is passed
   messages from the message queue.
*/
LRESULT CALLBACK WindowFunc(HWND hwnd, UINT message,
                            WPARAM wParam, LPARAM lParam)
{
  HDC hdc;

  switch(message) {
    case WM_RBUTTONDOWN: /* process right button */
      hdc = GetDC(hwnd); /* get DC */
      sprintf(str, "Right button is down at %d, %d",
              LOWORD(lParam), HIWORD(lParam));
      TextOut(hdc, LOWORD(lParam), HIWORD(lParam),
              str, strlen(str));
      ReleaseDC(hwnd, hdc); /* Release DC */
      break;
```

```
    case WM_LBUTTONDOWN: /* process left button */
      hdc = GetDC(hwnd); /* get DC */
      sprintf(str, "Left button is down at %d, %d",
              LOWORD(lParam), HIWORD(lParam));
      TextOut(hdc, LOWORD(lParam), HIWORD(lParam),
              str, strlen(str));
      ReleaseDC(hwnd, hdc); /* Release DC */
      break;
    case WM_DESTROY: /* terminate the program */
      PostQuitMessage(0);
      break;
    default:
       /* Let Windows 95 process any messages not specified in
         the preceding switch statement. */
      return DefWindowProc(hwnd, message, wParam, lParam);
  }
  return 0;
}
```

Figure 32-4 shows sample output from this program.

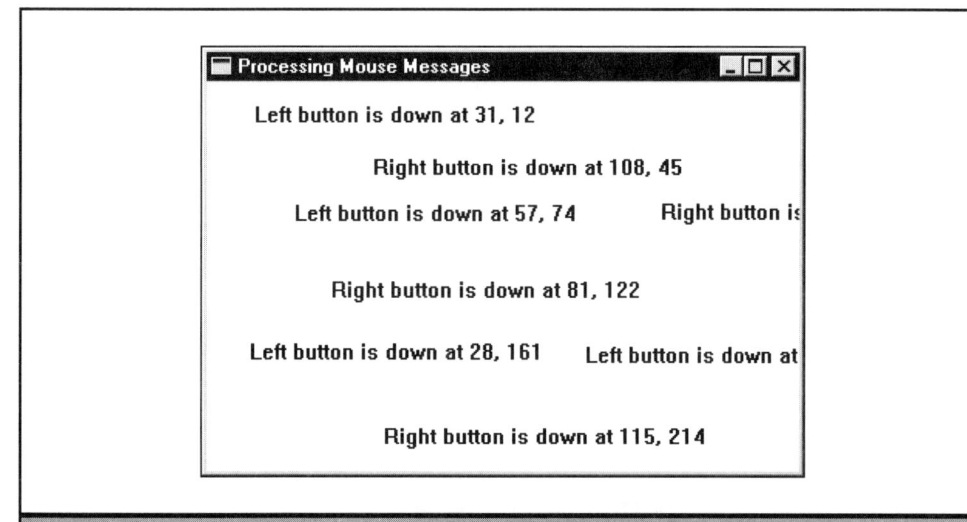

Figure 32-4. *Sample output from the mouse message program*

More About Mouse Messages

Each time a **WM_LBUTTONDOWN** or a **WM_RBUTTONDOWN** message is generated, several pieces of information are also supplied in the **wParam** parameter. It may contain any combination of the following values:

MK_CONTROL
MK_SHIFT
MK_MBUTTON
MK_RBUTTON
MK_LBUTTON

If the control key is pressed when a mouse button is pressed, then **wParam** will contain **MK_CONTROL**. If the SHIFT key is pressed when a mouse button is pressed, then **wParam** will contain **MK_SHIFT**. If the right button is down when the left button is pressed, then **wParam** will contain **MK_RBUTTON**. If the left button is down when the right button is pressed, then **wParam** will contain **MK_LBUTTON**. If the middle button (if it exists) is down when one of the other buttons is pressed, then **wParam** will contain **MK_MBUTTON**. Before moving on, you might want to try experimenting with these messages.

Chapter Thirty-Three

Using Menus

Now that you know the basic constituents of a Windows 95 application, it is time to begin exploration of its user interface components. If you are learning to program Windows for the first time, it is important to understand that your application will most often communicate with the user through one or more predefined interface components. There are several different types of interface elements supported by Windows 95. This chapter discusses its most fundamental: the menu. Virtually any program you write will use one. As you will see, the basic style of the menu is predefined. You need only supply the specific information that relates to your application.

This chapter also introduces the resource. A resource is essentially an object defined outside your program but used by your program. Icons, cursors, menus, and bitmaps are common resources. Resources are a crucial part of nearly all Windows applications.

Introducing Menus

In Windows the most common element of control is the menu. Virtually all main windows have some type of menu associated with them. Because menus are so common and important in Windows applications, Windows provides substantial built-in support for them. As you will see, adding a menu to a window involves these relatively few steps:

1. Define the form of the menu in a resource file.
2. Load the menu when your program creates its main window.
3. Process menu selections.

In a Windows application, the main (top-level) menu is displayed across the top of the window. Submenus are displayed as popup menus. (You should be accustomed to this approach, because it is used by virtually all Windows programs.)

Before beginning, it is necessary to explain what resources and resource files are.

Using Resources

Windows defines several common types of objects as *resources*. As mentioned at the beginning of this chapter, resources are essentially objects that are used by your program but are defined outside your program. They include things such as menus, icons, dialog boxes, and bitmapped graphics. Since a menu is a resource, you need to understand resources before you can add a menu to your program.

A resource is created separately from your program, but is added to the .EXE file when your program is linked. Resources are contained in *resource files* (also called *resource script files*), which have the extension .RC. In general, the resource filename should be the same as that of your program's .EXE file. For example, if your program is called PROG.EXE, then its resource file should be called PROG.RC.

Depending upon the resource, some are text files that you create using a standard text editor. Text resources can be defined within a normal text file. Others, such as icons, are most easily generated using a resource editor, such as the one provided by Borland C++. In either case, they still must be referred to in the .RC file that is associated with your application.

The example resource files in this chapter are shown as text files. To use them, simply open an edit window, enter the resource script, and then save the file using the .RC extension. Keep in mind that normally you will want to use Borland's resource editors for creating resource files. It's just that text files are the only way to represent resources in a printed form.

Resource files do not contain C or C++ statements. Instead, resource files consist of special resource statements. In the course of this chapter, the resource commands needed to support menus are discussed. Other resource commands are described in the following chapter.

One last point: When creating projects that use resource files, you will need to reenable the **.rc** option in the **Advanced Options** dialog box (activated from the **New Target** dialog box). If you forget, just add the resource file that you create to your project by selecting **Add Node** from the project SpeedMenu. To follow along with the examples in this chapter, create a new project now, called Menu. This project should have two nodes: MENU.CPP and MENU.RC.

Compiling .RC files

Resource files are not used directly by your program. Instead, they must be converted into a linkable format. Once you have created an .RC file, it must be compiled into an .RES file using a *resource compiler*. Fortunately, Borland C++ handles this phase for you automatically when you compile your project. The resulting .RES file is linked with the rest of your program to build the final Windows 95 application.

Creating a Simple Menu

Before a menu can be included, you must define its content in a resource file. All menu definitions have this general form

```
MenuName MENU [options]
{
  menu items
}
```

Here, *MenuName* is the name of the menu. (It may also be an integer value identifying the menu, but all examples in this book will use a name when referring to the menu.) The keyword **MENU** tells the resource compiler that a menu is being created. There are several options that can be specified when creating the menu. They are shown in Table 33-1. (These macros are defined by including **windows.h**.) The examples in this book simply use the default settings and specify no options.

There are two types of items that can be used to define the menu: **MENUITEM**s and **POPUP**s. A **MENUITEM** specifies a final selection. A **POPUP** specifies a popup submenu, which may in itself contain other **MENUITEM**s or **POPUP**s. The general form of these two statements is shown here:

```
MENUITEM "ItemName", MenuID [,Options]

POPUP "PopupName" [,Options]
```

Here, *ItemName* is the name of the menu selection, such as "Help" or "File". *MenuID* is a unique integer associated with a menu item that will be sent to your application

Option	Meaning
DISCARDABLE	Menu may be removed from memory when no longer needed.
FIXED	Menu is fixed in memory.
LOADONCALL	Menu is loaded when used.
MOVEABLE	Menu may be moved in memory.
PRELOAD	Menu is loaded when your program begins execution.

Table 33-1. *The* **MENU** *Options*

Option	Meaning
CHECKED	A check mark is displayed next to the name (not applicable to top-level menus.)
GRAYED	The name is shown in gray and may not be selected.
HELP	May be associated with a help selection. This applies to MENUITEMs only.
INACTIVE	The option may not be selected.
MENUBARBREAK	For menu bar, causes the item to be put on a new line. For popup menus, causes the item to be put in a different column. In this case, the item is separated using a bar.
MENUBREAK	Same as MENUBARBREAK except that no separator bar is used.

Table 33-2. *The* **MENUITEM** *and* **POPUP** *Options*

when a selection is made. Typically, these values are defined as macros inside a header file that is included in both your application code and in its resource file. *PopupName* is the name of the popup menu. For both cases, the values for *Options* (defined by including **windows.h**) are shown in Table 33-2.

Here is a simple menu that will be used by subsequent example programs. You should enter it at this time into a text file called MENU.RC. To do this, do *not* click on MENU.RC in the project window. Rather, create a new text file, enter the resource command shown below, and then save the file, calling MENU.RC. (If you click on MENU.RC in the project window, you will activate Borland's resource editor, which is not what you want to use at this time.)

```
; Sample menu resource file.
#include "menu.h"

MYMENU MENU
{
  POPUP "&File"
  {
    MENUITEM "&Open", IDM_OPEN
    MENUITEM "&Close", IDM_CLOSE
    MENUITEM "&Exit", IDM_EXIT
  }
  POPUP "&Options"
```

```
  {
    MENUITEM "&Colors", IDM_COLORS
    POPUP "&Response Time"
    {
      MENUITEM "&Slow", IDM_SLOW
      MENUITEM "&Fast", IDM_FAST
    }
    MENUITEM "&Sound", IDM_SOUND
    MENUITEM "&Video", IDM_VIDEO
  }
  MENUITEM "&Help", IDM_HELP
}
```

This menu, called **MYMENU**, contains three top-level menu bar options: File, Options, and Help. The File and Options entries contain popup submenus. The Response Time option activates a popup submenu of its own. Notice that options that activate submenus do not have menu ID values associated with them. Only actual menu items have ID numbers. In this menu, all menu ID values are specified as macros beginning with **IDM**. (These macros are defined in the header file **menu.h**.) What names you give these values is arbitrary.

An **&** in an item's name causes the key that it precedes to become the shortcut key associated with that option. That is, once that menu is active, pressing that key causes that menu item to be selected. It doesn't have to be the first key in the name, but it should be unless a conflict with another name exists.

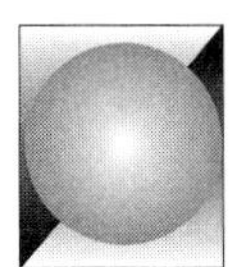

NOTE: You can embed comments into a resource file on a line-by-line basis by beginning them with a semicolon, as the first line of the resource file shows. You may also use C- and C++-style comments.

The MENU.H header file, which is included in MENU.RC, contains the macro definitions of the menu ID values. It is shown here. Enter it at this time.

```
#define IDM_OPEN     100
#define IDM_CLOSE    101
#define IDM_EXIT     102
#define IDM_COLORS   103
#define IDM_SLOW     104
#define IDM_FAST     105
#define IDM_SOUND    106
#define IDM_VIDEO    107
#define IDM_HELP     108
```

This file defines the menu ID values that will be returned when the various menu items are selected. This file will also be included in the program that uses the menu.

Remember, the actual names and values you give the menu items are arbitrary. But each value must be unique. Also, the valid range for ID values is 0 through 65,565.

Including a Menu in Your Program

Once you have created a menu, you include that menu in a program by specifying its name when you create the window's class. Specifically, you assign **lpszMenuName** a pointer to a string that contains the name of the menu. For example, to load the menu **MYMENU**, you would use this line when defining the window's class:

```
wcl.lpszMenuName = "MYMENU"; /* main menu */
```

Responding to Menu Selections

Each time the user makes a menu selection, your program's window function is sent a **WM_COMMAND** command message. When that message is received, the value of **LOWORD(wParam)** contains the menu item's ID value. (That is, **LOWORD(wParam)** contains the value you associate with the item when you defined the menu in its .RC file.) You will need to use a nested **switch** statement to determine which item was selected. For example, this fragment responds to a selection made from MYMENU:

```
switch(message) {
    case WM_COMMAND:
      switch(LOWORD(wParam)) {
        case IDM_OPEN: MessageBox(hwnd, "Open File", "Open", MB_OK);
          break;
        case IDM_CLOSE: MessageBox(hwnd, "Close File", "Close", MB_OK);
          break;
        case IDM_EXIT:
          response = MessageBox(hwnd, "Quit the Program?",
                                "Exit", MB_YESNO);
          if(response == IDYES) PostQuitMessage(0);
          break;
        case IDM_COLORS: MessageBox(hwnd, "Set Colors", "COLORS", MB_OK);
          break;
        case IDM_SLOW: MessageBox(hwnd, "Slow Speed", "Slow", MB_OK);
          break;
        case IDM_FAST: MessageBox(hwnd, "Fast Speed", "Fast", MB_OK);
          break;
        case IDM_SOUND: MessageBox(hwnd, "Sound Options", "Sound", MB_OK);
          break;
        case IDM_VIDEO: MessageBox(hwnd, "Video Options", "Video", MB_OK);
          break;
        case IDM_HELP: MessageBox(hwnd, "No Help", "Help", MB_OK);
```

```
        break;
      }
      break;
```

For the sake of illustration, the response to each selection simply displays an acknowledgment of that selection on the screen. Of course, in a real application the response to menu selections will perform the specified operations.

A Sample Menu Program

Here is a program that demonstrates the previously defined menu. Enter it at this time, calling it MENU.CPP. Sample output from the program is shown in Figure 33-1.

```
/* Demonstrate menus. */

#include <windows.h>
#include <string.h>
#include <stdio.h>
#include "menu.h"

LRESULT CALLBACK WindowFunc(HWND, UINT, WPARAM, LPARAM);

char szWinName[] = "MyWin"; /* name of window class */

int WINAPI WinMain(HINSTANCE hThisInst, HINSTANCE hPrevInst,
                   LPSTR lpszArgs, int nWinMode)
{
  HWND hwnd;
  MSG msg;
  WNDCLASSEX wcl;

  /* Define a window class. */
  wcl.hInstance = hThisInst; /* handle to this instance */
  wcl.lpszClassName = szWinName; /* window class name */
  wcl.lpfnWndProc = WindowFunc; /* window function */
  wcl.style = 0; /* default style */

  wcl.cbSize = sizeof(WNDCLASSEX); /* set size of WNDCLASSEX */

  wcl.hIcon = LoadIcon(NULL, IDI_APPLICATION); /* large icon */
  wcl.hIconSm = LoadIcon(NULL, IDI_APPLICATION); /* small icon */

  wcl.hCursor = LoadCursor(NULL, IDC_ARROW); /* cursor style */
```

```
  /* specify name of menu resource */
  wcl.lpszMenuName = "MYMENU"; /* main menu */

  wcl.cbClsExtra = 0; /* no extra */
  wcl.cbWndExtra = 0; /* information needed */

  /* Make the window white. */
  wcl.hbrBackground = (HBRUSH) GetStockObject(WHITE_BRUSH);

  /* Register the window class. */
  if(!RegisterClassEx(&wcl)) return 0;

  /* Now that a window class has been registered, a window
     can be created. */
  hwnd = CreateWindow(
    szWinName, /* name of window class */
    "Using Menus", /* title */
    WS_OVERLAPPEDWINDOW, /* window style - normal */
    CW_USEDEFAULT, /* X coordinate - let Windows decide */
    CW_USEDEFAULT, /* Y coordinate - let Windows decide */
    CW_USEDEFAULT, /* width - let Windows decide */
    CW_USEDEFAULT, /* height - let Windows decide */
    HWND_DESKTOP, /* no parent window */
    NULL, /* no menu */
    hThisInst, /* handle of this instance of the program */
    NULL /* no additional arguments */
  );

  /* Display the window. */
  ShowWindow(hwnd, nWinMode);
  UpdateWindow(hwnd);

  /* Create the message loop. */
  while(GetMessage(&msg, NULL, 0, 0))
  {
    TranslateMessage(&msg); /* allow use of keyboard */
    DispatchMessage(&msg); /* return control to Windows */
  }
  return msg.wParam;
}

/* This function is called by Windows 95 and is passed
```

```
   messages from the message queue.
*/
LRESULT CALLBACK WindowFunc(HWND hwnd, UINT message,
                            WPARAM wParam, LPARAM lParam)
{
  int response;

  switch(message) {
    case WM_COMMAND:
      switch(LOWORD(wParam)) {
        case IDM_OPEN: MessageBox(hwnd, "Open File", "Open", MB_OK);
          break;
        case IDM_CLOSE: MessageBox(hwnd, "Close File", "Close", MB_OK);
          break;
        case IDM_EXIT:
          response = MessageBox(hwnd, "Quit the Program?",
                                "Exit", MB_YESNO);
          if(response == IDYES) PostQuitMessage(0);
          break;
        case IDM_COLORS: MessageBox(hwnd, "Set Colors", "COLORS", MB_OK);
          break;
        case IDM_SLOW: MessageBox(hwnd, "Slow Speed", "Slow", MB_OK);
          break;
        case IDM_FAST: MessageBox(hwnd, "Fast Speed", "Fast", MB_OK);
          break;
        case IDM_SOUND: MessageBox(hwnd, "Sound Options", "Sound", MB_OK);
          break;
        case IDM_VIDEO: MessageBox(hwnd, "Video Options", "Video", MB_OK);
          break;
        case IDM_HELP: MessageBox(hwnd, "No Help", "Help", MB_OK);
          break;
      }
      break;
    case WM_DESTROY: /* terminate the program */
      PostQuitMessage(0);
      break;
    default:
      /* Let Windows 95 process any messages not specified in
         the preceding switch statement. */
      return DefWindowProc(hwnd, message, wParam, lParam);
  }
  return 0;
}
```

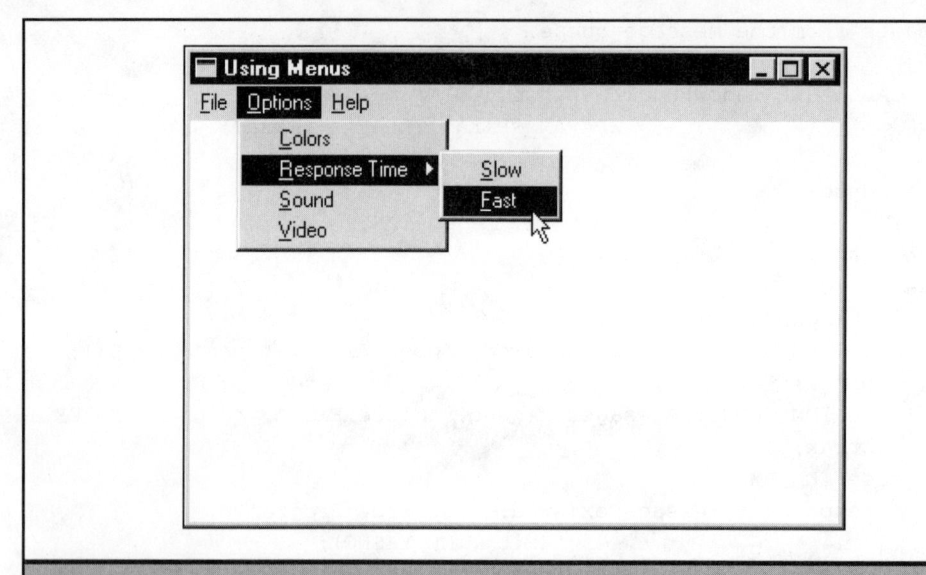

Figure 33-1. *Sample output from the menu example*

A Short Word About Borland's Resource Editor

As mentioned, Borland C++ provides a complete resource editor. This editor is activated when you click on an .RC file in the project window or when you create a new resource project. It may be used to create any type of resource. This editor is very easy to use and Borland's online instructions walk you through its operation. Therefore there is no need to repeat those instructions here.

You will need to learn to use the resource editor because it is the way you will create most resource script files. Remember, these files are shown as text in this chapter because it is the only way they can be represented in a book. This is not the way you will normally create resource files. It is worth pointing out, however, that using the resource editor you can edit your resource files as text files if you like. To do so, simply select the **Edit as Text** option from the resource editor's SpeedMenu.

Adding Menu Accelerator Keys

There is one feature of Windows that is commonly used in conjunction with a menu. This feature is the accelerator key. *Accelerator keys* are special keystrokes that you define, which, when pressed, automatically select a menu option even though the menu in which that option resides is not displayed. Put differently, you can select an item directly by pressing an accelerator key, bypassing the menu entirely. The term *accelerator keys* is an accurate description because pressing one is generally a faster way to select a menu item than first activating its menu and then selecting the item.

To define accelerator keys relative to a menu you must add an accelerator key table to your resource file. All accelerator table definitions have this general form:

```
TableName ACCELERATORS
{
  Key1, MenuID1 [,type] [option]
  Key2, MenuID2 [,type] [option]
  Key3, MenuID3 [,type] [option]
  .
  .
  .
  KeyN, MenuIDn [,type] [option]
}
```

Here, *TableName* is the name of the accelerator table. *Key* is the keystroke that selects the item and *MenuID* is the ID value associated with the desired item. The *type* specifies whether the key is a standard key (the default) or a virtual key (discussed shortly). The options may be one of the following macros: **NOINVERT**, **ALT**, **SHIFT**, or **CONTROL**. **NOINVERT** prevents the selected menu item from being highlighted when its accelerator key is pressed. **ALT** specifies an ALT key. **SHIFT** specifies a SHIFT key. **CONTROL** specifies a CONTROL key.

The value of *Key* will be a quoted character, an ASCII integer value corresponding to a key, or a virtual key code. If it is a quoted character, then it is assumed to be an ASCII character. If it is an integer value, then you must tell the resource compiler explicitly that this is an ASCII character by specifying *type* as **ASCII**. If it is a virtual key, then *type* must be **VIRTKEY**.

If the key is an uppercase quoted character, then its corresponding menu item will be selected if it is pressed while holding down SHIFT. If it is a lowercase character, then its menu item will be selected if the key is pressed by itself. If the key is specified as a lowercase character and **ALT** is specified as an option, then pressing ALT and the character will select the item. (If the key is uppercase and **ALT** is specified, then you must press SHIFT and ALT to select the item.) Finally, if you want the user to press CTRL and the character to select an item, precede the key with a **^**.

A virtual key is a system-independent code for a variety of keys. Virtual keys include the function keys F1 through F12, the arrow keys, and various non-ASCII keys. They are defined by macros in the header file **windows.h** (or one of its derivatives). All virtual key macros begin with **VK_**. The functions keys are **VK_F1** through **VK_F12**, for example. You should refer to **windows.h** for the other virtual key code macros. To use a virtual key as an accelerator, simply specify its macro for the *key* and specify **VIRTKEY** for its *type*. You may also specify **ALT**, **SHIFT**, or **CONTROL** to achieve the desired key combination.

Here are some examples of accelerator keys:

```
"A", IDM_x     ; select by pressing Shift-A
"a", IDM_x     ; select by pressing a
"^A", IDM_x   ; select by pressing Ctrl-A
"a", IDM_x, ALT   ; select by pressing Alt-a
VK_F2, IDM_x     ; select by pressing F2
VK_F2, IDM_x, SHIFT ; select by pressing Shift-F2
```

Here is the MENU.RC resource file that also contains accelerator key definitions for the menu specified in the previous section:

```
; Sample menu resource file
#include <windows.h>
#include "menu.h"

MYMENU MENU
{
  POPUP "&File"
  {
    MENUITEM "&Open\tF2", IDM_OPEN
    MENUITEM "&Close\tF3", IDM_CLOSE
    MENUITEM "&Exit\tCtrl-X", IDM_EXIT
  }
  POPUP "&Options"
  {
    MENUITEM "&Colors\tCtrl-C", IDM_COLORS
    POPUP "&Response Time"
    {
      MENUITEM "&Slow\tF4", IDM_SLOW
      MENUITEM "&Fast\tCtrl-F4", IDM_FAST
    }
    MENUITEM "&Sound\tCtrl-S", IDM_SOUND
    MENUITEM "&Video\tCtrl-V", IDM_VIDEO
  }
  MENUITEM "&Help", IDM_HELP
}

; Define menu accelerators
MYMENU ACCELERATORS
{
  VK_F2, IDM_OPEN, VIRTKEY
  VK_F3, IDM_CLOSE, VIRTKEY
  "^X", IDM_EXIT
  "^C", IDM_COLORS
```

```
  VK_F4, IDM_FAST, VIRTKEY, CONTROL
  VK_F4, IDM_SLOW, VIRTKEY
  "^S", IDM_SOUND
  "^V", IDM_VIDEO
  VK_F1, IDM_HELP, VIRTKEY
}
```

Notice that the menu definition has been enhanced to display which accelerator key selects which option. Each item is separated from its accelerator key using a tab. The header file **windows.h** is included because it defines the virtual key macros.

Loading the Accelerator Table

Even though the accelerators are contained in the same resource file as the menu, they must be loaded separately using another API function called **LoadAccelerators( )**, whose prototype is shown here:

HACCEL LoadAccelerators(HINSTANCE *ThisInst*, LPCSTR *Name*);

where *ThisInst* is the handle of the application and *Name* is the name of the accelerator table. The function returns a handle to the accelerator table or **NULL** if the table cannot be loaded.

You must call **LoadAccelerators( )** soon after the window is created. This shows how to load the **MYMENU** accelerator table:

```
HACCEL hAccel;

hAccel = LoadAccelerators(hThisInst, "MYMENU");
```

The value of **hAccel** will be used later to help process accelerator keys.

Although the **LoadAccelerators( )** function loads the accelerator table, your program can still not process them until you add another API function to the message loop. This function is called **TranslateAccelerator( )**, and its prototype is shown here:

int TranslateAccelerator(HWND *hwnd*, HACCEL *hAccel*, LPMSG *lpMess*);

Here, *hwnd* is the handle of the window for which accelerator keys will be translated. *hAccel* is the handle to the accelerator table that will be used. This is the handle returned by **LoadAccelerator( )**. Finally, *lpMess* is a pointer to the message. The **TranslateAccelerator( )** function returns true if an accelerator key was pressed and false otherwise. This function translates accelerator keystrokes into the proper **WM_COMMAND** message and sends that message to the window.

When using **TranslateAccelerator( )**, your message loop should look like this:

```
while(GetMessage(&msg, NULL, 0, 0))
{
  if(!TranslateAccelerator(hwnd, hAccel, &msg)) {
    TranslateMessage(&msg); /* allow use of keyboard */
    DispatchMessage(&msg); /* return control to Windows */
  }
}
```

To try using accelerators, substitute the following version of **WinMain()** into the preceding application and add the accelerator table to your resource file:

```
/* Process accelerator keys. */

#include <windows.h>
#include <string.h>
#include <stdio.h>
#include "menu.h"

LRESULT CALLBACK WindowFunc(HWND, UINT, WPARAM, LPARAM);

char szWinName[] = "MyWin"; /* name of window class */

int WINAPI WinMain(HINSTANCE hThisInst, HINSTANCE hPrevInst,
                   LPSTR lpszArgs, int nWinMode)
{
  HWND hwnd;
  MSG msg;
  WNDCLASSEX wcl;
  HACCEL hAccel;

  /* Define a window class. */
  wcl.hInstance = hThisInst; /* handle to this instance */
  wcl.lpszClassName = szWinName; /* window class name */
  wcl.lpfnWndProc = WindowFunc; /* window function */
  wcl.style = 0; /* default style */

  wcl.cbSize = sizeof(WNDCLASSEX); /* set size of WNDCLASSEX */

  wcl.hIcon = LoadIcon(NULL, IDI_APPLICATION); /* large icon */
  wcl.hIconSm = LoadIcon(NULL, IDI_APPLICATION); /* small icon */

  wcl.hCursor = LoadCursor(NULL, IDC_ARROW); /* cursor style */

  /* specify name of menu resource */
```

```
  wcl.lpszMenuName = "MYMENU"; /* main menu */

  wcl.cbClsExtra = 0; /* no extra */
  wcl.cbWndExtra = 0; /* information needed */

  /* Make the window white. */
  wcl.hbrBackground = (HBRUSH) GetStockObject(WHITE_BRUSH);

  /* Register the window class. */
  if(!RegisterClassEx(&wcl)) return 0;

  /* Now that a window class has been registered, a window
     can be created. */
  hwnd = CreateWindow(
    szWinName, /* name of window class */
    "Using Menus", /* title */
    WS_OVERLAPPEDWINDOW, /* window style - normal */
    CW_USEDEFAULT, /* X coordinate - let Windows decide */
    CW_USEDEFAULT, /* Y coordinate - let Windows decide */
    CW_USEDEFAULT, /* width - let Windows decide */
    CW_USEDEFAULT, /* height - let Windows decide */
    HWND_DESKTOP, /* no parent window */
    NULL, /* no menu */
    hThisInst, /* handle of this instance of the program */
    NULL /* no additional arguments */
  );

  /* load the keyboard accelerators */
  hAccel = LoadAccelerators(hThisInst, "MYMENU");

  /* Display the window. */
  ShowWindow(hwnd, nWinMode);
  UpdateWindow(hwnd);

  /* Create the message loop. */
  while(GetMessage(&msg, NULL, 0, 0))
  {
    if(!TranslateAccelerator(hwnd, hAccel, &msg)) {
      TranslateMessage(&msg); /* allow use of keyboard */
      DispatchMessage(&msg); /* return control to Windows */
    }
  }
  return msg.wParam;
}
```

Dynamically Managing a Menu

Although most simple Windows 95 applications fully define their menus in their resource file, more sophisticated applications frequently need to add or delete menu items dynamically, during run time, in response to changing program conditions. For example, an accounting program may add a Purge option to its file menu when year-end reports are generated. Or, a computer-aided design program might add or delete certain drawing tools depending upon what type of object is being designed. Whatever the reason, it is easy to add or delete menu items during the execution of a program.

Windows 95 includes several menu management API functions. The ones used in this chapter are **AppendMenu( )**, **EnableMenuItem( )**, **DeleteMenu( )**, **GetMenu( )**, and **GetSubMenu( )**. Before an example is developed, these functions are described.

Adding an Item to a Menu

To add an item to a menu, use **AppendMenu( )**, shown here:

BOOL AppendMenu(HMENU *hMenu*, UINT *flags*, UINT *ItemID*,
    LPCSTR *lpContent*);

AppendMenu( ) adds an item to the menu whose handle is specified by *hMenu*. The ID value associated with the new item is passed in *ItemID*. The description of the new item that will be displayed in the menu is pointed to by *lpContent*. The value of *flags* specifies various attributes associated with the new menu item. It can be one or more of the values shown in Table 33-3. **AppendMenu( )** returns nonzero if successful and zero on failure.

Deleting a Menu Item

To remove a menu item, use the **DeleteMenu( )** function, shown here:

BOOL DeleteMenu(HMENU *hMenu*, UINT *ItemID*, UINT *How*);

Here, *hMenu* specifies the handle of the menu to be affected. The item to be removed is specified in *ItemID*. The value of *How* determines how *ItemID* is interpreted. If *How* is **MF_BYPOSITION**, then the value in *ItemID* must be the index of the item to be deleted. This index is the position of the item within the menu, with the first menu item being zero. If *How* is **MF_BYCOMMAND**, then *ItemID* is the command ID associated with the menu item. **DeleteMenu( )** returns nonzero if successful and zero on failure.

Value	Meaning
MF_BITMAP	*lpContent* specifies a bitmap handle.
MF_CHECKED	Checks the new menu item.
MF_DISABLED	Disables the new menu item.
MF_ENABLED	Enables the new menu item.
MF_GRAYED	Disables the menu item and turns it gray.
MF_MENUBARBREAK	For menu bar, causes the item to be put on a new line. For popup menus, causes the item to be put in a different column. In this case, the item is separated using a bar.
MF_MENUBREAK	Same as **MF_MENUBARBREAK** except that no separator bar is used.
MF_OWNDERDRAW	Owner drawn item.
MF_POPUP	New item is a popup menu. In this case, *ItemID* must contain a handle to a popup menu.
MF_SEPARATOR	Places a horizontal dividing line between menu items. The values in *ItemID* and *lpContent* are ignored.
MF_STRING	*lpContent* is a pointer to a string that describes the menu item. (This is the default if neither **MF_BITMAP** nor **MF_OWNERDRAW** is specified.)
MF_UNCHECKED	Does not check the new menu item.

Table 33-3. *Valid Values for the flags Parameter of* **AppendMenu( )**

Obtaining a Handle to a Menu

As you have just seen, to add or delete a menu item requires a handle to the menu. To obtain the handle of the Main menu, use **GetMenu( )**, shown here:

HMENU GetMenu(HWND *hwnd*);

GetMenu( ) returns the handle of the menu associated with the window specified by *hwnd*. It returns **NULL** on failure.

Given a handle to a window's main menu, you can easily obtain the handles of the popup submenus contained in the main menu by using **GetSubMenu( )**. Its prototype is shown here:

HMENU GetSubMenu(HMENU *hMenu*, int *ItemPos*);

Here, *hMenu* is the handle of the parent menu and *ItemPos* is the position of the desired popup menu within the parent window. (The first position is zero.) The function returns the handle of the specified popup menu or **NULL** on failure.

Obtaining the Size of a Menu

Frequently, when working with menus dynamically, you will need to know how many items are in a menu. To obtain the number of menu items, use **GetMenuItemCount( )**, shown here:

int GetMenuItemCount(HMENU *hMenu*);

Here, *hMenu* is the handle of the menu in question. It returns –1 on failure.

Enabling and Disabling a Menu Item

Sometimes a menu item will only apply to certain situations and not to others. In such cases, you may wish to temporarily disable an item, enabling it later. To accomplish this, use the **EnableMenuItem( )** function, shown here:

BOOL EnableMenuItem(HMENU *hMenu*, UINT *ItemID*, UINT *How*);

The handle of the menu is passed in *hMenu*. The item to be enabled or disabled is specified in *ItemID*. The value of *How* determines two things. First, it specifies how *ItemID* is interpreted. If *How* contains **MF_BYPOSITION**, then the value in *ItemID* must be the index of the item to be deleted. This index is the position of the item within the menu, with the first menu item being zero. If *How* contains **MF_BYCOMMAND**, then *ItemID* is the command ID associated with the menu item. The value in *How* also determines whether the item will be enabled or disabled, based upon which of the following values are present:

MF_DISABLED	Disables the new menu item
MF_ENABLED	Enables the new menu item
MF_GRAYED	Disables the menu item and turns it gray

To construct the desired value of *How*, OR together the appropriate values. **EnableMenuItem( )** returns the previous state of the item or –1 on failure.

Demonstrating Dynamic Menu Management

The following program demonstrates how an item may be added to or deleted from a menu. In the process, it utilizes the menu management functions just described. This program allows a new menu option to be added to or deleted from the File menu of the previous example. Pay special attention to the **IDM_ADDITEM** and **IDM_DELITEM** cases inside **WindowFunc( )**. This is the code that adds or deletes a menu item:

```
/* Dynamically managing menus. */

#include <windows.h>
#include <string.h>
#include <stdio.h>
#include "menu.h"

LRESULT CALLBACK WindowFunc(HWND, UINT, WPARAM, LPARAM);

char szWinName[] = "MyWin"; /* name of window class */

int WINAPI WinMain(HINSTANCE hThisInst, HINSTANCE hPrevInst,
                   LPSTR lpszArgs, int nWinMode)
{
  HWND hwnd;
  MSG msg;
  WNDCLASSEX wcl;
  HACCEL hAccel;

  /* Define a window class. */
  wcl.hInstance = hThisInst; /* handle to this instance */
  wcl.lpszClassName = szWinName; /* window class name */
  wcl.lpfnWndProc = WindowFunc; /* window function */
  wcl.style = 0; /* default style */

  wcl.cbSize = sizeof(WNDCLASSEX); /* set size of WNDCLASSEX */

  wcl.hIcon = LoadIcon(NULL, IDI_APPLICATION); /* large icon */
  wcl.hIconSm = LoadIcon(NULL, IDI_APPLICATION); /* small icon */

  wcl.hCursor = LoadCursor(NULL, IDC_ARROW); /* cursor style */

  /* specify name of menu resource */
  wcl.lpszMenuName = "MYMENU"; /* main menu */
```

```
  wcl.cbClsExtra = 0; /* no extra */
  wcl.cbWndExtra = 0; /* information needed */

  /* Make the window white. */
  wcl.hbrBackground = (HBRUSH) GetStockObject(WHITE_BRUSH);

  /* Register the window class. */
  if(!RegisterClassEx(&wcl)) return 0;

  /* Now that a window class has been registered, a window
     can be created. */
  hwnd = CreateWindow(
    szWinName, /* name of window class */
    "Dynamically Managing Menus", /* title */
    WS_OVERLAPPEDWINDOW, /* window style - normal */
    CW_USEDEFAULT, /* X coordinate - let Windows decide */
    CW_USEDEFAULT, /* Y coordinate - let Windows decide */
    CW_USEDEFAULT, /* width - let Windows decide */
    CW_USEDEFAULT, /* height - let Windows decide */
    HWND_DESKTOP, /* no parent window */
    NULL, /* no menu */
    hThisInst, /* handle of this instance of the program */
    NULL /* no additional arguments */
  );

  /* load the keyboard accelerators */
  hAccel = LoadAccelerators(hThisInst, "MYMENU");

  /* Display the window. */
  ShowWindow(hwnd, nWinMode);
  UpdateWindow(hwnd);

  /* Create the message loop. */
  while(GetMessage(&msg, NULL, 0, 0))
  {
    if(!TranslateAccelerator(hwnd, hAccel, &msg)) {
      TranslateMessage(&msg); /* allow use of keyboard */
      DispatchMessage(&msg); /* return control to Windows */
    }
  }
  return msg.wParam;
}

/* This function is called by Windows 95 and is passed
```

```
   messages from the message queue.
*/
LRESULT CALLBACK WindowFunc(HWND hwnd, UINT message,
                            WPARAM wParam, LPARAM lParam)
{
  int response;
  HMENU hmenu, hsubmenu;
  int count;

  switch(message) {
    case WM_COMMAND:
      switch(LOWORD(wParam)) {
        case IDM_OPEN: MessageBox(hwnd, "Open File", "Open", MB_OK);
          break;
        case IDM_CLOSE: MessageBox(hwnd, "Close File", "Close", MB_OK);
          break;
        case IDM_ADDITEM: /* dynamically add menu item */
          /* get handle of main menu */
          hmenu = GetMenu(hwnd);

          /* get handle of 1st popup menu */
          hsubmenu = GetSubMenu(hmenu, 0);

          /* append a separator and a new menu item */
          AppendMenu(hsubmenu, MF_SEPARATOR, 0, "");
          AppendMenu(hsubmenu, MF_ENABLED, IDM_NEW, "&New Item");

          /* deactivate the Add Item option */
          EnableMenuItem(hsubmenu, IDM_ADDITEM,
                         MF_BYCOMMAND | MF_GRAYED);

          /* activate the Delete Item option */
          EnableMenuItem(hsubmenu, IDM_DELITEM,
                         MF_BYCOMMAND | MF_ENABLED);
          break;
        case IDM_DELITEM: /* dynamically delete menu item */
          /* get handle of main menu */
          hmenu = GetMenu(hwnd);

          /* get handle of 1st popup menu */
          hsubmenu = GetSubMenu(hmenu, 0);

          /* delete the new item and the separator */
```

```
          count = GetMenuItemCount(hsubmenu);
          DeleteMenu(hsubmenu, count-1, MF_BYPOSITION | MF_GRAYED);
          DeleteMenu(hsubmenu, count-2, MF_BYPOSITION | MF_GRAYED);

          /* reactivate the Add Item option */
          EnableMenuItem(hsubmenu, IDM_ADDITEM,
                         MF_BYCOMMAND | MF_ENABLED);

          /* deactivate the Delete Item option */
          EnableMenuItem(hsubmenu, IDM_DELITEM,
                         MF_BYCOMMAND | MF_GRAYED);
          break;
        case IDM_EXIT:
          response = MessageBox(hwnd, "Quit the Program?",
                                "Exit", MB_YESNO);
          if(response == IDYES) PostQuitMessage(0);
          break;
        case IDM_NEW: MessageBox(hwnd, "New Item", "New Item", MB_OK);
          break;
        case IDM_COLORS: MessageBox(hwnd, "Set Colors", "COLORS", MB_OK);
          break;
        case IDM_SLOW: MessageBox(hwnd, "Slow Speed", "Slow", MB_OK);
          break;
        case IDM_FAST: MessageBox(hwnd, "Fast Speed", "Fast", MB_OK);
          break;
        case IDM_SOUND: MessageBox(hwnd, "Sound Options", "Sound", MB_OK);
          break;
        case IDM_VIDEO: MessageBox(hwnd, "Video Options", "Video", MB_OK);
          break;
        case IDM_HELP: MessageBox(hwnd, "No Help", "Help", MB_OK);
          break;
      }
      break;
    case WM_DESTROY: /* terminate the program */
      PostQuitMessage(0);
      break;
    default:
      /* Let Windows 95 process any messages not specified in
         the preceding switch statement. */
      return DefWindowProc(hwnd, message, wParam, lParam);
  }
  return 0;
}
```

The resource file required by the program is shown here:

```
; Sample menu resource file
#include <windows.h>
#include "menu.h"

MYMENU MENU
{
  POPUP "&File"
  {
    MENUITEM "&Open\tF2", IDM_OPEN
    MENUITEM "&Close\tF3", IDM_CLOSE
    MENUITEM "&Add Item\tCtrl-A", IDM_ADDITEM
    MENUITEM "&Delete Item\tCtrl-D", IDM_DELITEM, GRAYED
    MENUITEM "&Exit\tCtrl-X", IDM_EXIT
  }
  POPUP "&Options"
  {
    MENUITEM "&Colors\tCtrl-C", IDM_COLORS
    POPUP "&Response Time"
    {
      MENUITEM "&Slow\tF4", IDM_SLOW
      MENUITEM "&Fast\tCtrl-F4", IDM_FAST
    }
    MENUITEM "&Sound\tCtrl-S", IDM_SOUND
    MENUITEM "&Video Ctrl-V", IDM_VIDEO
  }
  MENUITEM "&Help", IDM_HELP
}

; Define menu accelerators
MYMENU ACCELERATORS
{
  VK_F2, IDM_OPEN, VIRTKEY
  VK_F3, IDM_CLOSE, VIRTKEY
  "^A", IDM_ADDITEM
  "^D", IDM_DELITEM
  "^X", IDM_EXIT
  "^C", IDM_COLORS
  VK_F4, IDM_FAST, VIRTKEY, CONTROL
  VK_F4, IDM_SLOW, VIRTKEY
  "^S", IDM_SOUND
  "^V", IDM_VIDEO
```

```
  VK_F1, IDM_HELP, VIRTKEY
}
```

As you can see, the File menu now contains two new options: Add Item and Delete Item. These options are used to dynamically add or delete a menu item.

The modified MENU.H header file is shown here:

```
#define IDM_OPEN      100
#define IDM_CLOSE     101
#define IDM_EXIT      102
#define IDM_COLORS    103
#define IDM_SLOW      104
#define IDM_FAST      105
#define IDM_SOUND     106
#define IDM_VIDEO     107
#define IDM_HELP      108

#define IDM_ADDITEM   200
#define IDM_DELITEM   201

#define IDM_NEW       300
```

Sample output is shown in Figure 33-2. Initially, Delete Item is grayed and therefore may not be selected. After the new item has been dynamically added to the menu, the Delete Item option is activated and the Add Item option is grayed. When Delete Item is selected, the new item is deleted, Add Item is reactivated, and Delete Item is once again grayed. This procedure prevents the new menu item from being added or deleted more than once.

Creating Dynamic Menus

In addition to adding new items to an existing menu, you can dynamically create an entire popup menu. (That is, you can create a popup menu at run time.) Once you have created the menu, it can then be added to an existing menu. To dynamically create a popup menu, you first need to create one using the API function **CreatePopupMenu( )**, shown here:

```
HMENU CreatePopupMenu(void);
```

This function creates an empty menu and returns a handle to it. After you have created a menu, you add items to it using **AppendMenu( )**. Once the menu is fully constructed, you can add it to an existing menu, also using **AppendMenu( )**.

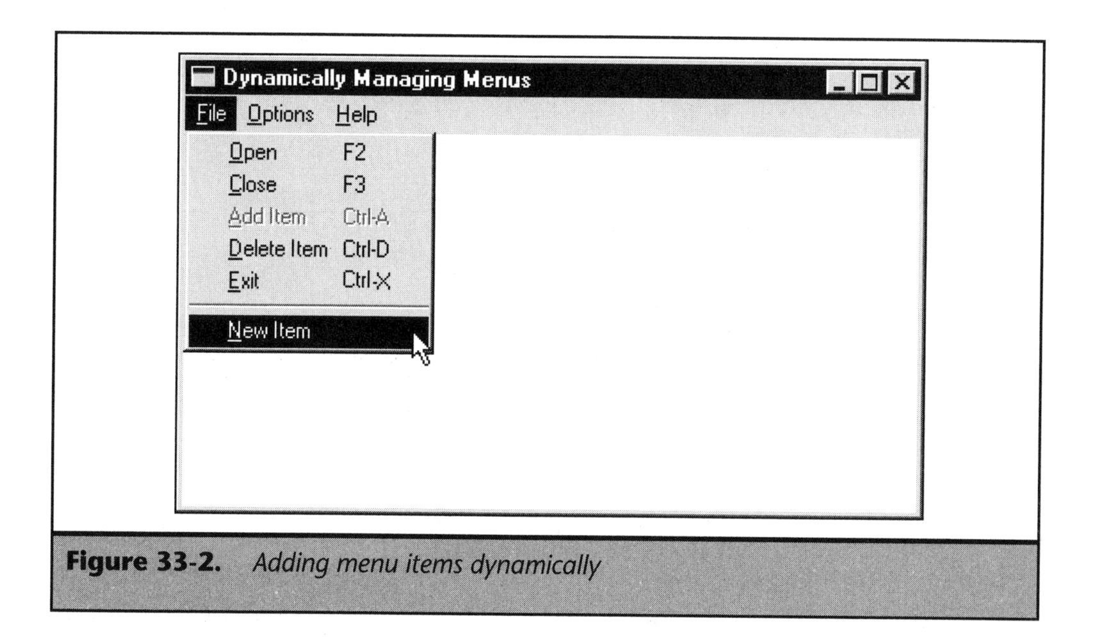

Figure 33-2. *Adding menu items dynamically*

Menus created using **CreatePopupMenu( )** must be destroyed. If the menu is attached to a window, then it will be destroyed automatically. A menu is also automatically destroyed when it is removed from a parent menu by a call to **DeleteMenu( )**. Dynamic menus can be destroyed explicitly by calling **DestroyMenu( )**.

The following **WindowFunc( )** dynamically creates a popup menu. To see its effect, substitute it into the preceding program.

```
/* This function is called by Windows 95 and is passed
   messages from the message queue.
*/
LRESULT CALLBACK WindowFunc(HWND hwnd, UINT message,
                            WPARAM wParam, LPARAM lParam)
{
  int response;
  HMENU hmenu, hsubmenu;
  static HMENU hpopup;
  int count;

  switch(message) {
    case WM_COMMAND:
      switch(LOWORD(wParam)) {
        case IDM_OPEN: MessageBox(hwnd, "Open File", "Open", MB_OK);
          break;
```

```
case IDM_CLOSE: MessageBox(hwnd, "Close File", "Close", MB_OK);
  break;
case IDM_ADDITEM: /* dynamically add menu */
  /* get handle of main menu */
  hmenu = GetMenu(hwnd);

  /* get handle of 1st popup menu */
  hsubmenu = GetSubMenu(hmenu, 0);

  /* create new popup menu */
  hpopup = CreatePopupMenu();

  /* add items to dynamic popup menu */
  AppendMenu(hpopup, MF_ENABLED, IDM_NEW,
             "&First New Item");
  AppendMenu(hpopup, MF_ENABLED, IDM_NEW,
             "&Second New Item");

  /* add new menu to File menu */
  AppendMenu(hsubmenu, MF_SEPARATOR, 0, "");
  AppendMenu(hsubmenu, MF_POPUP, (UINT) hpopup, "&New Popup");

  /* deactivate the Add Menu option */
  EnableMenuItem(hsubmenu, IDM_ADDITEM,
                 MF_BYCOMMAND | MF_GRAYED);

  /* activate the Delete Menu option */
  EnableMenuItem(hsubmenu, IDM_DELITEM,
                 MF_BYCOMMAND | MF_ENABLED);
  break;
case IDM_DELITEM: /* dynamically delete menu */
  /* get handle of main menu */
  hmenu = GetMenu(hwnd);

  /* get handle of 1st popup menu */
  hsubmenu = GetSubMenu(hmenu, 0);

  /* delete the new menu and the separator */
  count = GetMenuItemCount(hsubmenu);
  DeleteMenu(hsubmenu, count-1, MF_BYPOSITION | MF_GRAYED);
  DeleteMenu(hsubmenu, count-2, MF_BYPOSITION | MF_GRAYED);

  /* reactivate the Add Menu option */
  EnableMenuItem(hsubmenu, IDM_ADDITEM,
```

```
                        MF_BYCOMMAND | MF_ENABLED);

          /* deactivate the Delete Menu option */
          EnableMenuItem(hsubmenu, IDM_DELITEM,
                         MF_BYCOMMAND | MF_GRAYED);
          break;
        case IDM_EXIT:
          response = MessageBox(hwnd, "Quit the Program?",
                                "Exit", MB_YESNO);
          if(response == IDYES) PostQuitMessage(0);
          break;
        case IDM_NEW: MessageBox(hwnd, "New Item", "New Item", MB_OK);
          break;
        case IDM_COLORS: MessageBox(hwnd, "Set Colors", "COLORS", MB_OK);
          break;
        case IDM_SLOW: MessageBox(hwnd, "Slow Speed", "Slow", MB_OK);
          break;
        case IDM_FAST: MessageBox(hwnd, "Fast Speed", "Fast", MB_OK);
          break;
        case IDM_SOUND: MessageBox(hwnd, "Sound Options", "Sound", MB_OK);
          break;
        case IDM_VIDEO: MessageBox(hwnd, "Video Options", "Video", MB_OK);
          break;
        case IDM_HELP: MessageBox(hwnd, "No Help", "Help", MB_OK);
          break;
      }
      break;
    case WM_DESTROY: /* terminate the program */
      PostQuitMessage(0);
      break;
    default:
      /* Let Windows 95 process any messages not specified in
         the preceding switch statement. */
      return DefWindowProc(hwnd, message, wParam, lParam);
  }
  return 0;
}
```

This program uses the same **menu.h** as the preceding program, but requires the following resource file:

```
; Sample menu resource file
#include <windows.h>
#include "menu.h"
```

```
MYMENU MENU
{
  POPUP "&File"
  {
    MENUITEM "&Open\tF2", IDM_OPEN
    MENUITEM "&Close\tF3", IDM_CLOSE
    MENUITEM "&Add Menu\tCtrl-A", IDM_ADDITEM
    MENUITEM "&Delete Menu\tCtrl-D", IDM_DELITEM, GRAYED
    MENUITEM "&Exit\tCntl-X", IDM_EXIT
  }
  POPUP "&Options"
  {
    MENUITEM "&Colors\tCntl-C", IDM_COLORS
    POPUP "&Response Time"
    {
      MENUITEM "&Slow\tF4", IDM_SLOW
      MENUITEM "&Fast\tCntl-F4", IDM_FAST
    }
    MENUITEM "&Sound\tCntl-S", IDM_SOUND
    MENUITEM "&Video Cntl-V", IDM_VIDEO
  }
  MENUITEM "&Help", IDM_HELP
}

; Define menu accelerators
MYMENU ACCELERATORS
{
  VK_F2, IDM_OPEN, VIRTKEY
  VK_F3, IDM_CLOSE, VIRTKEY
  "^A", IDM_ADDITEM
  "^D", IDM_DELITEM
  "^X", IDM_EXIT
  "^C", IDM_COLORS
  VK_F4, IDM_FAST, VIRTKEY, CONTROL
  VK_F4, IDM_SLOW, VIRTKEY
  "^S", IDM_SOUND
  "^V", IDM_VIDEO
  VK_F1, IDM_HELP, VIRTKEY
}
```

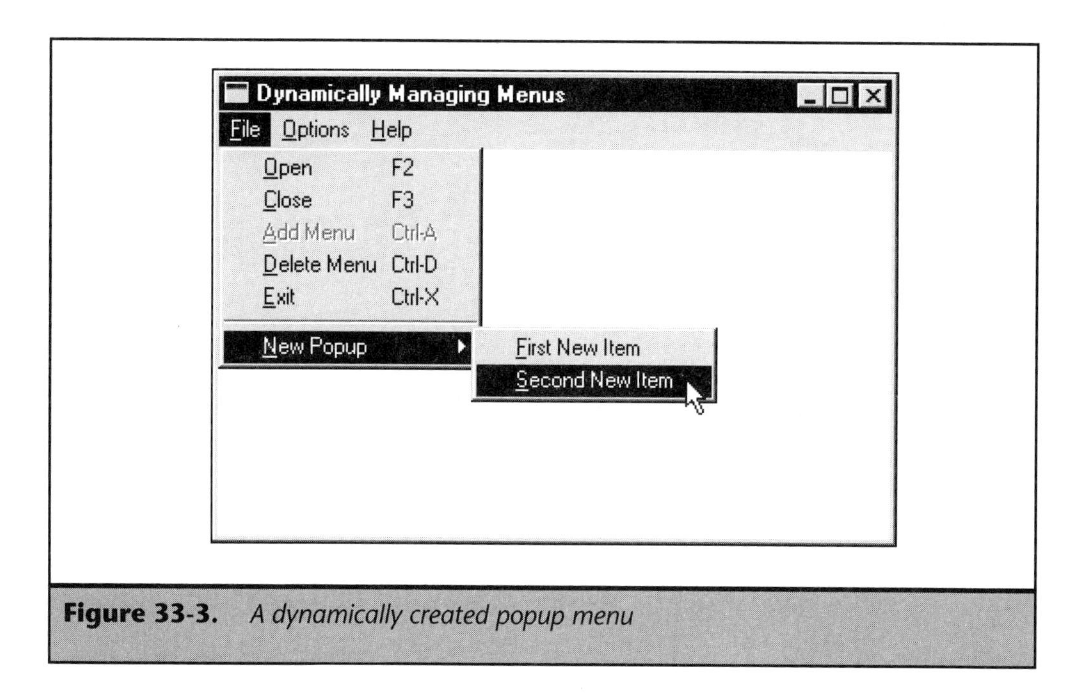

Figure 33-3. *A dynamically created popup menu*

Sample output from this program is shown in Figure 33-3.

One final thought: Since menus are the gateway to your application, their design and implementation deserve significant care and attention to detail. A well thought-out set of menus will make your program easier to use and more appealing.

Chapter Thirty-Four

Dialog Boxes

Although menus are an important part of nearly every Windows 95 application, they cannot be used to handle all types of user responses. For example, it would be difficult to use a menu to input the time or date. To handle all types of input, Windows provides the *dialog box*. A dialog box is a special type of window that provides a flexible means by which the user can interact with your application. In general, dialog boxes allow the user to select or enter information that would be difficult or impossible to enter using a menu. In this chapter, you will learn how to create and manage a dialog box.

Also discussed in this chapter are three of Windows' standard controls. Within a dialog box, interaction with the user is performed through a control. In a sense, a dialog box is simply a container that holds various control elements.

As a means of illustrating the dialog box and several of its control elements, a very simple database application will be developed. The database contains a list of several American cities along with their populations, state, and time zone. The dialog box created in this chapter will allow you to select a city and obtain its information. While the database example is necessarily quite simple, it will give you the flavor of how a real application can effectively use a dialog box.

Dialog Boxes Use Controls

By itself, a dialog box does nothing. Instead, it is the controls within the dialog box that interact with the user. Technically, the dialog box is simply a management device. Formally stated, a *control* is a special type of input or output window. A control is owned by its parent window, which, for the examples presented in this chapter, is the dialog box. Windows 95 supports several standard controls, including pushbuttons, checkboxes, radio buttons, list boxes, edit boxes, combination boxes, scrollbars, and static controls. (Windows 95 also supports several enhanced controls called *common controls,* which are beyond the scope of this book.) In the course of explaining how to use dialog boxes, the examples in this chapter illustrate three of these controls: pushbuttons, the list box, and the edit box.

A *pushbutton* is a control that the user "pushes on" to activate some response. You have already been using pushbuttons in message boxes. For example, the OK button that we have been using in most message boxes is a pushbutton.

A *list box* displays a list of items from which the user selects one (or more). List boxes are commonly used to display things such as file names.

An *edit box* allows the user to enter a string. Edit boxes provide all necessary text editing features required by the user. Therefore, to input a string, your program simply displays an edit box and waits until the user has finished typing in the string. A combination box is a combination of a list box and an edit box.

It is important to understand that controls both generate messages (when accessed by the user) and receive messages (from your application). A message generated by a control indicates what type of interaction the user has had with the control. A message sent to the control is essentially an instruction to which the control must respond. You will see examples of this type of message passing later in this chapter.

Modal Versus Modeless Dialog Boxes

There are two types of dialog boxes: *modal* and *modeless*. The most common dialog boxes are modal. A modal dialog box demands a response before the parent program will continue. That is, a modal dialog box will not allow the user to refocus input to another part of the parent application without first responding to the dialog box.

A modeless dialog box does not prevent the parent program from running. That is, it does not demand a response before input can be refocused to another part of the program.

We will examine modal dialog boxes first, since they are the most common. A modeless dialog box example concludes this chapter.

Receiving Dialog Box Messages

A dialog box is a type of window. Events that occur within it are sent to your program using the same message-passing mechanism that the main window uses. However, dialog box messages are not sent to your program's main window function. Instead, each dialog box that you define will need its own window function, which is generally called a *dialog function*. This function must have this prototype. (Of course, the name of the function may be anything that you like.)

```
BOOL CALLBACK DFunc(HWND hdwnd, UINT message, WPARAM wParam,
                    LPARAM lParam);
```

As you can see, a dialog function receives the same parameters as your program's main window function. However, it differs from the main window function in that it returns a true or false result. Like your program's main window function, the dialog box window function will receive many messages. If it processes a message, then it must return true. If it does not respond to a message, it must return false.

In general, each control within a dialog box will be given its own resource ID. Each time that control is accessed by the user, a **WM_COMMAND** message will be sent to the dialog function, indicating the ID of the control and the type of action the user has taken. That function will then decode the message and take appropriate actions. This process parallels the way messages are decoded by your program's main window function.

Activating a Dialog Box

To activate a modal dialog box (that is, to cause it to be displayed), you must call the **DialogBox( )** API function, whose prototype is shown here:

```
int DialogBox(HINSTANCE hThisInst, LPCSTR lpName, HWND hwnd,
              DLGPROC lpDFunc);
```

Here, *hThisInst* is a handle to the current application that is passed to your program in the instance parameter to **WinMain( )**. The name of the dialog box as defined in the resource file is pointed to by *lpName*. The handle to the parent window that activates the dialog box is passed in *hwnd*. The *lpDFunc* parameter contains a pointer to the dialog function described in the preceding section. If **DialogBox( )** fails, then it returns –1. Otherwise, the return value is that specified by **EndDialog( )**, discussed next.

Deactivating a Dialog Box

To deactivate (that is, destroy and remove from the screen) a modal dialog box, use **EndDialog( )**. It has this prototype:

```
BOOL EndDialog(HWND hdwnd, int nStatus);
```

Here, *hdwnd* is the handle to the dialog box and *nStatus* is a status code returned by the **DialogBox( )** function. (The value of *nStatus* may be ignored if it is not relevant to your program.) This function returns nonzero if successful and zero otherwise. (In normal situations, the function is successful.).

Creating a Simple Dialog Box

To illustrate the basic dialog box concepts, we will begin with a simple dialog box. This dialog box will contain four pushbuttons called Size, State, Zone, and Cancel.

When the Size, State, or Zone button is pressed, it will activate a message box indicating the choice selected. (Later these pushbuttons will be used to obtain information from the database. For now, the message boxes are simply placeholders.) The dialog box will be removed from the screen when the Cancel button is pressed.

The Dialog Box Resource File

A dialog box is another resource that is contained in your program's resource file. Before developing a program that uses a dialog box, you will need a resource file that specifies one. Although it is possible to specify the contents of a dialog box using a text editor and enter its specifications as you do when creating a menu, this is seldom done. Instead, most programmers use Borland's dialog editor. The main reason for this is that dialog box definitions involve the positioning of the various controls inside the dialog box, which is best done interactively. However, since the complete .RC files for the examples in this chapter are supplied in their text form, you should simply enter them as text. Just remember that when creating your own dialog boxes, you will want to use Borland's dialog editor.

Since in practice most dialog boxes are created using a dialog editor, only a brief explanation of the dialog box definition in the resource file is given for the examples in this chapter.

Dialog boxes are defined within your program's resource file using the **DIALOG** statement. Its general form is shown here:

Dialog-name DIALOG [DISCARDABLE] *X*, *Y*, *Width*, *Height*
Features
{
  Dialog-items
}

The *Dialog-name* is the name of the dialog box. The box's upper left corner will be at *X*,*Y* and the box will have the dimensions specified by *Width* × *Height*. If the box may be removed from memory when not in use, then specify it as **DISCARDABLE**. One or more features of the dialog box may be specified. As you will see, two of these are the caption and the style of the box. The *Dialog-items* are the controls that comprise the dialog box.

The following resource file defines the dialog box that will be used by the first example program. It includes a menu that is used to activate the dialog box, the menu accelerator keys, and then the dialog box itself. You should enter it into your computer at this time, calling it DIALOG.RC.

```
; Sample dialog box and menu resource file.
#include <windows.h>
#include "dialog.h"
```

```
MYMENU MENU
{
  POPUP "&Dialog"
  {
    MENUITEM "&Dialog", IDM_DIALOG
    MENUITEM "&Exit", IDM_EXIT
  }
  MENUITEM "&Help", IDM_HELP
}

MYMENU ACCELERATORS
{
  VK_F2, IDM_DIALOG, VIRTKEY
  VK_F3, IDM_EXIT, VIRTKEY
  VK_F1, IDM_HELP, VIRTKEY
}

MYDB DIALOG 10, 10, 140, 110
CAPTION "Cities Dialog Box"
STYLE DS_MODALFRAME | WS_POPUP | WS_CAPTION | WS_SYSMENU
{
  DEFPUSHBUTTON "Size", IDD_SIZE, 11, 10, 32, 14,
             WS_CHILD | WS_VISIBLE | WS_TABSTOP
  PUSHBUTTON "State", IDD_STATE, 11, 34, 32, 14,
             WS_CHILD | WS_VISIBLE | WS_TABSTOP
  PUSHBUTTON "Zone", IDD_ZONE, 11, 58, 32, 14,
             WS_CHILD | WS_VISIBLE | WS_TABSTOP
  PUSHBUTTON "Cancel", IDCANCEL, 8, 82, 38, 16,
             WS_CHILD | WS_VISIBLE | WS_TABSTOP
}
```

This defines a dialog box called **MYDB** that has its upper left corner at location 10, 10. Its width is 140 and its height is 110. The string after **CAPTION** becomes the title of the dialog box. The **STYLE** statement determines what type of dialog box is created. Some common style values, including those used in this chapter, are shown in Table 34-1. You can OR together the values that are appropriate for the style of dialog box that you desire. These style values may also be used by other controls.

Within the **MYDB** definition are defined four pushbuttons. The first is the default pushbutton. This button is automatically highlighted when the dialog box is first displayed. The general form of a pushbutton declaration is shown here:

PUSHBUTTON "*string*", *PBID*, *X*, *Y*, *Width*, *Height* [, *Style*]

Value	Meaning
DS_MODALFRAME	Dialog box has a modal frame. This style can be used with either modal or modeless dialog boxes.
WS_BORDER	Include a border.
WS_CAPTION	Include title bar.
WS_CHILD	Create as child window.
WS_POPUP	Create as popup window.
WS_MAXIMIZEBOX	Include maximize box.
WS_MINIMIZEBOX	Include minimize box.
WS_SYSMENU	Include system menu.
WS_TABSTOP	Control may be tabbed to.
WS_VISIBLE	Box is visible when activated.

Table 34-1. *Some Common Dialog Box Style Options*

Here, *string* is the text that will be shown inside the pushbutton. *PBID* is the value associated with the pushbutton. It is this value that is returned to your program when this button is pushed. The button's upper left corner will be at *X,Y* and the button will have the dimensions specified by *Width* × *Height*. *Style* determines the exact nature of the pushbutton. To define a default pushbutton, use the **DEFPUSHBUTTON** statement. It has the same parameters as the regular pushbuttons.

The header file DIALOG.H, which is also used by the example program, is shown here:

```
#define IDM_DIALOG    100
#define IDM_EXIT      101
#define IDM_HELP      102

#define IDD_SIZE      200
#define IDD_STATE     201
#define IDD_ZONE      202
```

Enter this file now.

The Dialog Box Window Function

As stated earlier, events that occur with a dialog box are passed to the window function associated with that dialog box and not to your program's main window function. The following dialog box window function responds to the events that occur within the **MYDB** dialog box:

```
/* A simple dialog function. */
BOOL CALLBACK DialogFunc(HWND hdwnd, UINT message,
                         WPARAM wParam, LPARAM lParam)
{
  switch(message) {
    case WM_COMMAND:
      switch(LOWORD(wParam)) {
        case IDCANCEL:
          EndDialog(hdwnd, 0);
          return 1;
        case IDD_SIZE:
          MessageBox(hdwnd, "Size", "Size", MB_OK);
          return 1;
        case IDD_STATE:
          MessageBox(hdwnd, "State", "State", MB_OK);
          return 1;
        case IDD_ZONE:
          MessageBox(hdwnd, "Zone", "Zone", MB_OK);
          return 1;
      }
  }
  return 0;
}
```

Each time a control within the dialog box is accessed, a **WM_COMMAND** message is sent to **DialogFunc( )**, and **LOWORD(wParam)** contains the ID of the control affected.

DialogFunc( ) processes the four messages that can be generated by the box. If the user presses **Cancel**, then **IDCANCEL** is sent, causing the dialog box to be closed using a call to the API function **EndDialog( )**. (**IDCANCEL** is a standard ID defined by including **windows.h**.) Pressing any one of the other three buttons causes a message box to be displayed that confirms the selection. As mentioned, these buttons will be used by later examples to display information from the database.

A First Dialog Box Sample Program

Here is the entire dialog box example. When the program begins execution, only the top-level menu is displayed on the menu bar. By selecting **Dialog**, the user causes the dialog box to be displayed. Once the dialog box is displayed, selecting a pushbutton causes the appropriate response. A sample screen is shown in Figure 34-1. Notice that the cities database is included in this program, but is not used. It will be used by subsequent examples, however.

```
/* Demonstrate a Modal Dialog box. */

#include <windows.h>
#include <string.h>
#include <stdio.h>
#include <time.h>
#include "dialog.h"

#define NUMCITIES 6

LRESULT CALLBACK WindowFunc(HWND, UINT, WPARAM, LPARAM);
BOOL CALLBACK DialogFunc(HWND, UINT, WPARAM, LPARAM);

char szWinName[] = "MyWin"; /* name of window class */

HINSTANCE hInst;

/* cities database -- this will be used by later examples */
struct citiesTag {
  char name[30];
  unsigned long size;
  char state[3];
  char timezone[30];
} cities[NUMCITIES] = {
  {"New York", 7322564, "NY", "Eastern"},
  {"Atlanta", 394017, "GA", "Eastern"},
  {"Chicago", 2783726, "IL", "Central"},
  {"Houston", 1630553, "TX", "Central"},
  {"Denver", 467610, "CO", "Mountain"},
  {"Los Angeles", 3485398, "CA", "Pacific"}
};

int WINAPI WinMain(HINSTANCE hThisInst, HINSTANCE hPrevInst,
                   LPSTR lpszArgs, int nWinMode)
{
  HWND hwnd;
  MSG msg;
  WNDCLASSEX wcl;
  HACCEL hAccel;
```

```
/* Define a window class. */
wcl.hInstance = hThisInst; /* handle to this instance */
wcl.lpszClassName = szWinName; /* window class name */
wcl.lpfnWndProc = WindowFunc; /* window function */
wcl.style = 0; /* default style */

wcl.cbSize = sizeof(WNDCLASSEX); /* set size of WNDCLASSEX */

wcl.hIcon = LoadIcon(NULL, IDI_APPLICATION); /* Large icon */
wcl.hIconSm = LoadIcon(NULL, IDI_APPLICATION); /* Small icon */

wcl.hCursor = LoadCursor(NULL, IDC_ARROW); /* cursor style */

/* specify name of menu resource */
wcl.lpszMenuName = "MYMENU"; /* main menu */

wcl.cbClsExtra = 0; /* no extra */
wcl.cbWndExtra = 0; /* information needed */

/* Make the window white. */
wcl.hbrBackground = (HBRUSH) GetStockObject(WHITE_BRUSH);

/* Register the window class. */
if(!RegisterClassEx(&wcl)) return 0;

/* Now that a window class has been registered, a window
   can be created. */
hwnd = CreateWindow(
  szWinName, /* name of window class */
  "Demonstrate Dialog Boxes", /* title */
  WS_OVERLAPPEDWINDOW, /* window style - normal */
  CW_USEDEFAULT, /* X coordinate - let Windows decide */
  CW_USEDEFAULT, /* Y coordinate - let Windows decide */
  CW_USEDEFAULT, /* width - let Windows decide */
  CW_USEDEFAULT, /* height - let Windows decide */
  HWND_DESKTOP, /* no parent window */
  NULL, /* no menu */
  hThisInst, /* handle of this instance of the program */
  NULL /* no additional arguments */
);

hInst = hThisInst; /* save the current instance handle */
```

```
  /* load accelerators */
  hAccel = LoadAccelerators(hThisInst, "MYMENU");

  /* Display the window. */
  ShowWindow(hwnd, nWinMode);
  UpdateWindow(hwnd);

  /* Create the message loop. */
  while(GetMessage(&msg, NULL, 0, 0))
  {
    if(!TranslateAccelerator(hwnd, hAccel, &msg)) {
      TranslateMessage(&msg); /* allow use of keyboard */
      DispatchMessage(&msg); /* return control to Windows */
    }
  }
  return msg.wParam;
}

/* This function is called by Windows 95 and is passed
   messages from the message queue.
*/
LRESULT CALLBACK WindowFunc(HWND hwnd, UINT message,
                            WPARAM wParam, LPARAM lParam)
{
  int response;

  switch(message) {
    case WM_COMMAND:
      switch(LOWORD(wParam)) {
        case IDM_DIALOG:
          DialogBox(hInst, "MYDB", hwnd, (DLGPROC) DialogFunc);
          break;
        case IDM_EXIT:
          response = MessageBox(hwnd, "Quit the Program?",
                                "Exit", MB_YESNO);
          if(response == IDYES) PostQuitMessage(0);
          break;
        case IDM_HELP:
          MessageBox(hwnd, "No Help", "Help", MB_OK);
          break;
      }
      break;
```

```
    case WM_DESTROY: /* terminate the program */
      PostQuitMessage(0);
      break;
    default:
      /* Let Windows 95 process any messages not specified in
         the preceding switch statement. */
      return DefWindowProc(hwnd, message, wParam, lParam);
  }
  return 0;
}

/* A simple dialog function. */
BOOL CALLBACK DialogFunc(HWND hdwnd, UINT message,
                         WPARAM wParam, LPARAM lParam)
{
  int i;  /* these vars are used by later examples */
  char str[80];

  switch(message) {
    case WM_COMMAND:
      switch(LOWORD(wParam)) {
        case IDCANCEL:
          EndDialog(hdwnd, 0);
          return 1;
        case IDD_SIZE:
          MessageBox(hdwnd, "Size", "Size", MB_OK);
          return 1;
        case IDD_STATE:
          MessageBox(hdwnd, "State", "State", MB_OK);
          return 1;
        case IDD_ZONE:
          MessageBox(hdwnd, "Zone", "Zone", MB_OK);
          return 1;
      }
  }
  return 0;
}
```

Notice the global variable **hInst**. This variable is assigned a copy of the current instance handle passed to **WinMain( )**. The reason for this variable is that the dialog box needs access to the current instance handle. However, the dialog box is not created in **WinMain( )**. Instead, it is created in **WindowFunc( )**. Therefore, a copy of the instance parameter must be made so that it can be accessible outside of **WinMain( )**.

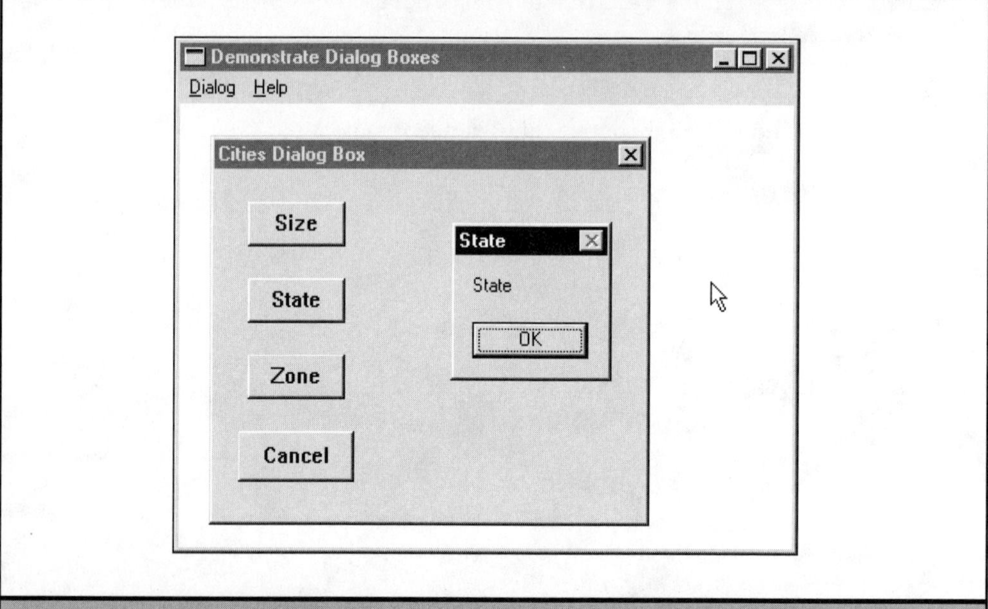

Figure 34-1. *Sample output from the first dialog box program*

Adding a List Box

To continue exploring dialog boxes, let's add another control to the dialog box defined in the previous program. One of the most common controls after the pushbutton is the list box. We will use the list box to display a list of the cities in the database and allow the user to select one. The **LISTBOX** statement has this general form:

LISTBOX LBID, *X*, *Y*, *Width*, *Height* [,*Style*]

Here, *LBID* is the value that identifies the list box. The box's upper left corner will be at *X*,*Y* and the box will have the dimensions specified by *Width* × *Height*. *Style* determines the exact nature of the list box.

To add a list box, you must change the dialog box definition in DIALOG.RC. First, add this list box description to the dialog box definition:

```
LISTBOX IDD_LB1, 66, 5, 63, 33, LBS_NOTIFY |
          WS_VISIBLE | WS_BORDER | WS_VSCROLL | WS_TABSTOP
```

Second, add this pushbutton to the dialog box definition:

```
PUSHBUTTON "Select City", IDD_SELECT, 72, 41, 54, 14,
             WS_CHILD | WS_VISIBLE | WS_TABSTOP
```

After these changes, your dialog box definition should now look like this:

```
MYDB DIALOG 10, 10, 140, 110
CAPTION "Cities Dialog Box"
STYLE DS_MODALFRAME | WS_POPUP | WS_CAPTION | WS_SYSMENU
{
  DEFPUSHBUTTON "Size", IDD_SIZE, 11, 10, 32, 14,
             WS_CHILD | WS_VISIBLE | WS_TABSTOP
  PUSHBUTTON "State", IDD_STATE, 11, 34, 32, 14,
             WS_CHILD | WS_VISIBLE | WS_TABSTOP
  PUSHBUTTON "Zone", IDD_ZONE, 11, 58, 32, 14,
             WS_CHILD | WS_VISIBLE | WS_TABSTOP
  PUSHBUTTON "Cancel", IDCANCEL, 8, 82, 38, 16,
             WS_CHILD | WS_VISIBLE | WS_TABSTOP
  LISTBOX IDD_LB1, 66, 5, 63, 33, LBS_NOTIFY |
             WS_VISIBLE | WS_BORDER | WS_VSCROLL | WS_TABSTOP
  PUSHBUTTON "Select City", IDD_SELECT, 72, 41, 54, 14,
             WS_CHILD | WS_VISIBLE | WS_TABSTOP
}
```

You will also need to add these macros to **DIALOG.H**:

```
#define IDD_LB1       203
#define IDD_SELECT    204
```

IDD_LB1 identifies the list box specified in the dialog box definition in the resource file. **IDD_SELECT** is the ID value of the Select City pushbutton.

List Box Basics

When using a list box, you must perform two basic operations. First, you must initialize the list box when the dialog box is first displayed. This consists of sending the list box the list that it will display. (By default, the list box will be empty.) Second, once the list box has been initialized, your program will need to respond to the user selecting an item from the list.

List boxes generate various types of messages. The only one we will use is **LBN_DBLCLK**. This message is sent when the user has double-clicked on an entry in the list. This message is contained in **HIWORD(wParam)** each time a **WM_COMMAND** is generated for the list box. (The list box must have the **LBS_NOTIFY** style flag included in its definition in order to generate **LBN_DBLCLK** messages.) Once a selection has been made, you will need to query the list box to find out which item has been selected.

Unlike a pushbutton, a list box is a control that receives messages as well as generating them. You can send a list box several different messages. To send a message to the list box (or any other control) use the **SendDlgItemMessage( )** API function. Its prototype is shown here:

```
LONG SendDlgItemMessage(HWND hdwnd, int ID, UINT IDMsg,
                        WPARAM wParam, LPARAM lParam);
```

SendDlgItemMessage( ) sends to the control (within the dialog box) whose ID is specified by *ID* the message specified by *IDMsg*. The handle of the dialog box is specified in *hdwnd*. Any additional information required by the message is specified in *wParam* and *lParam*. The additional information, if any, varies from message to message. If there is no additional information to pass to a control, the *wParam* and the *lParam* arguments should be 0. The value returned by **SendDlgItemMessage( )** contains the information requested by *IDMsg*.

Here are a few of the most common messages that you can send to a list box:

Macro	**Purpose**
LB_ADDSTRING	Adds a string (selection) to the list box
LB_GETCURSEL	Requests the index of the selected item
LB_SETCURSEL	Selects an item
LB_FINDSTRING	Finds a matching entry
LB_SELECTSTRING	Finds a matching entry and selects it
LB_GETTEXT	Obtains the text associated with an item

Let's take a closer look at these messages now.

LB_ADDSTRING adds a string to the list box. That is, the specified string becomes another selection within the box. The string must be pointed to by *lParam*. (*wParam* is unused by this message.) The value returned by the list box is the index of the string in the list. If an error occurs, **LB_ERR** is returned.

The **LB_GETCURSEL** message causes the list box to return the index of the currently selected item. All list box indexes begin with 0. Both *lParam* and *wParam* are unused. If an error occurs, **LB_ERR** is returned. If no item is currently selected, then an error results.

You can set the current selection inside a list box using the **LB_SETCURSEL** command. For this message, *wParam* specifies the index of the item to select. *lParam* is not used. On error, **LB_ERR** is returned.

You can find an item in the list that matches a specified prefix using **LB_FINDSTRING**. That is, **LB_FINDSTRING** attempts to match a partial string with an entry in the list box. *wParam* specifies the index at which point the search begins and *lParam* points to the string that will be matched. If a match is found, the index of the matching item is returned. Otherwise, **LB_ERR** is returned. **LB_FINDSTRING** does not select the item within the list box.

If you want to find a matching item and select it, use **LB_SELECTSTRING**. It takes the same parameters as **LB_FINDSTRING** but also selects the matching item.

You can obtain the text associated with an item in a list box using **LB_GETTEXT**. In this case, *wParam* specifies the index of the item and *lParam* points to the character array that will receive the null-terminated string associated with that index. The length of the string is returned if successful, or **LB_ERR** is returned on failure.

Initializing the List Box

As mentioned, when a list box is created, it is empty. This means that you will need to initialize it each time the dialog box that contains it is displayed. This is easy to accomplish because each time a dialog box is activated, its window function is sent a **WM_INITDIALOG** message. Therefore, you will need to add this case to the outer **switch** statement in **DialogFunc( )**:

```
case WM_INITDIALOG: /* initialize list box */
  /* initialize list box */
  for(i=0; i<NUMCITIES; i++)
    SendDlgItemMessage(hdwnd, IDD_LB1,
               LB_ADDSTRING, 0, (LPARAM)cities[i].name);

  /* select first item */
  SendDlgItemMessage(hdwnd, IDD_LB1, LB_SETCURSEL, 0, 0);
  return 1;
```

This code loads the list box with the names of cities as defined in the **cities** array. Each string is added to the list box by calling **SendDlgItemMessage( )** with the **LB_ADDSTRING** message. The string to add is pointed to by the *lParam* parameter. (The type cast to **LPARAM** is necessary in this case to convert a pointer into a unsigned integer.) In this example, each string is added to the list box in the order it is sent. (However, depending upon how you construct the list box, it is possible to have the items displayed in alphabetical order.) If the number of items you send to a list box exceeds what it can display in its window, vertical scrollbars will be added automatically.

This code also selects the first item in the list box. When a list box is first created, no item is selected. While this might be desirable under certain circumstances, it is not in this case. Most often, you will want to automatically select the first item in a list box as a convenience to the user.

REMEMBER: ***WM_INITDIALOG*** *is sent to a dialog box each time it is activated. You should perform all initializations required by the dialog box when this message is received.*

Processing a Selection

After the list box has been initialized, it is ready for use. There are essentially two ways a user makes a selection from a list box. First, the user may double-click on an item in the list box. This causes a **WM_COMMAND** message to be passed to the dialog box's window function. In this case, **LOWORD(wParam)** contains the ID associated with the list box and **HIWORD(wParam)** contains the **LBN_DBLCLK** message. Double-clicking causes your program to be immediately aware of the user's selection. The other way to use a list box is to simply highlight a selection (either by single-clicking or by using the arrow keys to move the highlight). This does *not* cause a message to be sent to your program, but the list box remembers the selection and waits until your program requests the selection. Both methods are demonstrated in the example program.

Once an item has been selected in a list box, you determine which item was chosen by sending the **LB_GETCURSEL** message to the list box. The list box then returns the index of the selected item. Remember, if this message is sent before an item has been selected, the list box returns **LB_ERR**. (This is one reason that it is a good idea to select a list box item when it is initialized.)

To demonstrate how to process a list box selection, add these cases to the inner switch inside **DialogFunc( )**. Your dialog box will now look like that shown in Figure 34-2. Each time a selection is made because of a double-click, or when the user presses the "Select City" pushbutton, the currently selected city has its information displayed.

```
case IDD_LB1: /* process a list box LBN_DBLCLK */
  /* see  if user made a selection */
  if(HIWORD(wParam)==LBN_DBLCLK) {
    i = SendDlgItemMessage(hdwnd, IDD_LB1,
            LB_GETCURSEL, 0, 0);  /* get index */
    sprintf(str, "%s, %s\n%s Time Zone\nPop.:%lu",
            cities[i].name, cities[i].state,
            cities[i].timezone, cities[i].size);

    MessageBox(hdwnd, str, "Selection Made", MB_OK);
  }
  return 1;
case IDD_SELECT: /* Select City button has been pressed */
  i = SendDlgItemMessage(hdwnd, IDD_LB1,
          LB_GETCURSEL, 0, 0);  /* get index */
  sprintf(str, "%s, %s\n%s Time Zone\nPop.:%lu",
          cities[i].name, cities[i].state,
          cities[i].timezone, cities[i].size);

  MessageBox(hdwnd, str, "Selection Made", MB_OK);
  return 1;
```

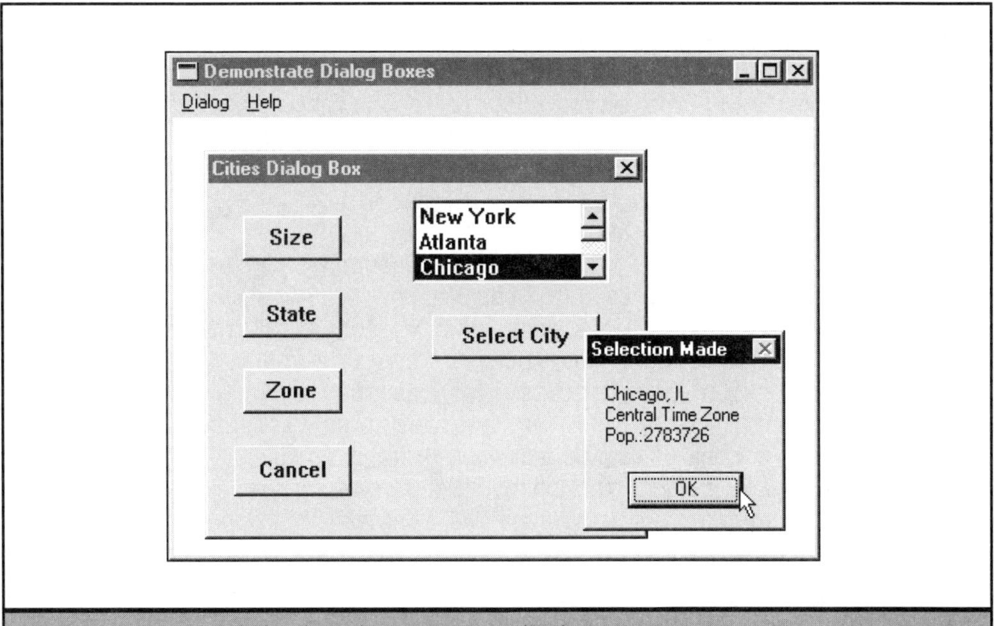

Figure 34-2. *A dialog box that contains a list box*

Notice the code under the **IDD_LB1** case. Since the list box can generate several different types of notification messages, it is necessary to examine the high-order word of **wParam** to determine if the user double-clicked on an item. That is, just because the control generates a notification message, does not mean that it is a double-click message.

Adding an Edit Box

In this section, we will add an edit control to the dialog box. Edit boxes are particularly useful because they allow users to enter a string of their own choosing. The edit box in this example will allow the user to enter the name of a city. If the city is in the list, then that city will be selected and information about the city can be obtained. Although the addition of an edit box enhances our simple database application, it also serves another purpose. It will illustrate how two controls can work together.

Before you can use an edit box, you must define one in your resource file. For this example, change **MYDB** so that it looks like this:

```
MYDB DIALOG 10, 10, 140, 110
CAPTION "Cities Dialog Box"
STYLE DS_MODALFRAME | WS_POPUP | WS_CAPTION | WS_SYSMENU
```

```
{
  DEFPUSHBUTTON "Size", IDD_SIZE, 11, 10, 32, 14,
           WS_CHILD | WS_VISIBLE | WS_TABSTOP
  PUSHBUTTON "State", IDD_STATE, 11, 34, 32, 14,
           WS_CHILD | WS_VISIBLE | WS_TABSTOP
  PUSHBUTTON "Zone", IDD_ZONE, 11, 58, 32, 14,
           WS_CHILD | WS_VISIBLE | WS_TABSTOP
  PUSHBUTTON "Cancel", IDCANCEL, 8, 82, 38, 16,
           WS_CHILD | WS_VISIBLE | WS_TABSTOP
  LISTBOX IDD_LB1, 66, 5, 63, 33, LBS_NOTIFY |
           WS_VISIBLE | WS_BORDER | WS_VSCROLL | WS_TABSTOP
  PUSHBUTTON "Select City", IDD_SELECT, 72, 41, 54, 14,
           WS_CHILD | WS_VISIBLE | WS_TABSTOP
  EDITTEXT IDD_EB1, 65, 73, 63, 12, ES_LEFT | WS_VISIBLE |
           WS_BORDER | ES_AUTOHSCROLL | WS_TABSTOP
  PUSHBUTTON "Enter City", IDD_DONE, 73, 91, 46, 14,
           WS_CHILD | WS_VISIBLE | WS_TABSTOP
}
```

This version adds a pushbutton called Enter City, which will be used to tell the program that you entered the name of a city into the edit box. It also adds the edit box itself. The ID for the edit box is **IDD_EB1**. This definition causes a standard edit box to be created.

The **EDITTEXT** statement has this general form:

EDITTEXT *EDID, X, Y, Width, Height* [,*Style*]

Here, *EDID* is the value that identifies the edit box. The box's upper left corner will be at *X,Y* and its dimensions are specified *Width* and *Height*. *Style* determines the exact nature of the list box.

Next, add these macro definitions to DIALOG.H:

```
#define IDD_EB1       205
#define IDD_DONE      206
```

Edit boxes recognize many messages and generate several of their own. However, for the purposes of this example, there is no need for the program to respond to any messages. As you will see, edit boxes perform the editing function on their own. There is no reason for program interaction when text is edited. Your program simply decides when it wants to obtain the current contents of the edit box.

To obtain the current contents of the edit box, use the API function **GetDlgItemText( )**. It has this prototype:

UINT GetDlgItemText(HWND *hdwnd*, int *nID*, LPSTR *lpstr*, int *nMax*);

This function causes the edit box to copy the current contents of the box to the string pointed to by *lpstr*. The handle of the dialog box is specified by *hdwnd*. The ID of the edit box is specified by *nID*. The maximum number of characters to copy is specified by *nMax*. The function returns the length of the string.

Although not required by all applications, it is possible to initialize the contents of an edit box using the **SetDlgItemText( )** function. Its prototype is shown here:

BOOL SetDlgItemText(HWND *hdwnd*, int *nID*, LPSTR *lpstr*);

This function sets the contents of the edit box to the string pointed to by *lpstr*. The handle of the dialog box is specified by *hdwnd*. The ID of the edit box is specified by *nID*. The function returns nonzero if successful or zero on failure.

To add an edit box to the sample program, add this case statement to the inner **switch** of the **DialogFunc( )** function. Each time the Enter City button is pressed, the list box is searched for a city that matches the string that is currently in the edit box. If a match is found, then that city is selected in the list box. Remember that you only need to enter the first few characters of the city. The list box will automatically attempt to match them with a city.

```
case IDD_DONE: /* Enter City button pressed */
  /* get current contents of edit box */
  GetDlgItemText(hdwnd, IDD_EB1, str, 80);

  /* find a matching string in the list box */
  i = SendDlgItemMessage(hdwnd, IDD_LB1, LB_FINDSTRING,
          0, (LPARAM) str);

  if(i != LB_ERR) { /* if match is found */
    /* select the matching city in list box */
    SendDlgItemMessage(hdwnd, IDD_LB1, LB_SETCURSEL, i, 0);

    /* get string associated with that index */
    SendDlgItemMessage(hdwnd, IDD_LB1, LB_GETTEXT,
        i, (LPARAM) str);

    /* update text in edit box */
    SetDlgItemText(hdwnd, IDD_EB1, str);
  }
  else  MessageBox(hdwnd, str, "No Match With", MB_OK);
  return 1;
```

This code obtains the current contents of the edit box and looks for a match with the strings inside the list box. If it finds one, it selects the matching item in the list box and then copies the string from the list box back into the edit box. In this way, the two controls work together, complementing each other. As you become a more experienced Windows 95 programmer, you will find that there are often instances in which two or more controls can work together.

You will also need to add this line of code to the **INITDIALOG** case. It causes the edit box to be initialized each time the dialog box is activated.

```
/* initialize the edit box */
SetDlgItemText(hdwnd, IDD_EB1, "New York");
```

In addition to these changes, the code that processes the list box will be enhanced so that it automatically copies the name of the city selected in the list box into the edit box. These changes are reflected in the full program listing that follows. You should have no trouble understanding them.

The Entire Modal Dialog Box Program

The entire modal dialog box sample program that includes pushbuttons, a list box, and an edit box, is shown here. Notice that the code associated with the pushbuttons now displays information about the city currently selected in the list box.

```
/* A modal dialog box example. */

#include <windows.h>
#include <string.h>
#include <stdio.h>
#include "dialog.h"

#define NUMCITIES 6

LRESULT CALLBACK WindowFunc(HWND, UINT, WPARAM, LPARAM);
BOOL CALLBACK DialogFunc(HWND, UINT, WPARAM, LPARAM);

char szWinName[] = "MyWin"; /* name of window class */

HINSTANCE hInst;

/* cities database */
struct citiesTag {
  char name[30];
  unsigned long size;
  char state[3];
  char timezone[30];
```

```
} cities[NUMCITIES] = {
  {"New York", 7322564, "NY", "Eastern"},
  {"Atlanta", 394017, "GA", "Eastern"},
  {"Chicago", 2783726, "IL", "Central"},
  {"Houston", 1630553, "TX", "Central"},
  {"Denver", 467610, "CO", "Mountain"},
  {"Los Angeles", 3485398, "CA", "Pacific"}
};


int WINAPI WinMain(HINSTANCE hThisInst, HINSTANCE hPrevInst,
                   LPSTR lpszArgs, int nWinMode)
{
  HWND hwnd;
  MSG msg;
  WNDCLASSEX wcl;
  HACCEL hAccel;

  /* Define a window class. */
  wcl.hInstance = hThisInst; /* handle to this instance */
  wcl.lpszClassName = szWinName; /* window class name */
  wcl.lpfnWndProc = WindowFunc; /* window function */
  wcl.style = 0; /* default style */

  wcl.cbSize = sizeof(WNDCLASSEX); /* set size of WNDCLASSEX */

  wcl.hIcon = LoadIcon(NULL, IDI_APPLICATION); /* Large icon */
  wcl.hIconSm = LoadIcon(NULL, IDI_APPLICATION); /* Small icon */

  wcl.hCursor = LoadCursor(NULL, IDC_ARROW); /* cursor style */

  /* specify name of menu resource */
  wcl.lpszMenuName = "MYMENU"; /* main menu */

  wcl.cbClsExtra = 0; /* no extra */
  wcl.cbWndExtra = 0; /* information needed */

  /* Make the window white. */
  wcl.hbrBackground = (HBRUSH) GetStockObject(WHITE_BRUSH);

  /* Register the window class. */
  if(!RegisterClassEx(&wcl)) return 0;

  /* Now that a window class has been registered, a window
```

```
     can be created. */
  hwnd = CreateWindow(
    szWinName, /* name of window class */
    "Demonstrate Dialog Boxes", /* title */
    WS_OVERLAPPEDWINDOW, /* window style - normal */
    CW_USEDEFAULT, /* X coordinate - let Windows decide */
    CW_USEDEFAULT, /* Y coordinate - let Windows decide */
    CW_USEDEFAULT, /* width - let Windows decide */
    CW_USEDEFAULT, /* height - let Windows decide */
    HWND_DESKTOP, /* no parent window */
    NULL, /* no menu */
    hThisInst, /* handle of this instance of the program */
    NULL /* no additional arguments */
  );

  hInst = hThisInst; /* save the current instance handle */

  /* load accelerators */
  hAccel = LoadAccelerators(hThisInst, "MYMENU");

  /* Display the window. */
  ShowWindow(hwnd, nWinMode);
  UpdateWindow(hwnd);

  /* Create the message loop. */
  while(GetMessage(&msg, NULL, 0, 0))
  {
    if(!TranslateAccelerator(hwnd, hAccel, &msg)) {
      TranslateMessage(&msg); /* allow use of keyboard */
      DispatchMessage(&msg); /* return control to Windows */
    }
  }
  return msg.wParam;
}

/* This function is called by Windows 95 and is passed
   messages from the message queue.
*/
LRESULT CALLBACK WindowFunc(HWND hwnd, UINT message,
                            WPARAM wParam, LPARAM lParam)
{
  int response;

  switch(message) {
```

```
    case WM_COMMAND:
      switch(LOWORD(wParam)) {
        case IDM_DIALOG:
          DialogBox(hInst, "MYDB", hwnd,(DLGPROC) DialogFunc);
          break;
        case IDM_EXIT:
          response = MessageBox(hwnd, "Quit the Program?",
                                "Exit", MB_YESNO);
          if(response == IDYES) PostQuitMessage(0);
          break;
        case IDM_HELP:
          MessageBox(hwnd, "No Help", "Help", MB_OK);
          break;
      }
      break;
    case WM_DESTROY: /* terminate the program */
      PostQuitMessage(0);
      break;
    default:
      /* Let Windows 95 process any messages not specified in
         the preceding switch statement. */
      return DefWindowProc(hwnd, message, wParam, lParam);
  }
  return 0;
}

/* A simple dialog function. */
BOOL CALLBACK DialogFunc(HWND hdwnd, UINT message,
                         WPARAM wParam, LPARAM lParam)
{
  long i;
  char str[80];

  switch(message) {
    case WM_COMMAND:
      switch(LOWORD(wParam)) {
        case IDCANCEL:
          EndDialog(hdwnd, 0);
          return 1;
        case IDD_SIZE:
          i = SendDlgItemMessage(hdwnd, IDD_LB1,
                  LB_GETCURSEL, 0, 0);  /* get index */
          sprintf(str, "%lu", cities[i].size);
          MessageBox(hdwnd, str, "Size", MB_OK);
```

```
          return 1;
        case IDD_STATE:
          i = SendDlgItemMessage(hdwnd, IDD_LB1,
                  LB_GETCURSEL, 0, 0);  /* get index */
          sprintf(str, "%s", cities[i].state);
          MessageBox(hdwnd, str, "State", MB_OK);

          return 1;
        case IDD_ZONE:
          i = SendDlgItemMessage(hdwnd, IDD_LB1,
                  LB_GETCURSEL, 0, 0);  /* get index */
          sprintf(str, "%s", cities[i].timezone);
          MessageBox(hdwnd, str, "Zone", MB_OK);
          return 1;
        case IDD_DONE: /* Enter City button pressed */
          /* get current contents of edit box */
          GetDlgItemText(hdwnd, IDD_EB1, str, 80);

          /* find a matching string in the list box */
          i = SendDlgItemMessage(hdwnd, IDD_LB1, LB_FINDSTRING,
                  0, (LPARAM) str);

          if(i != LB_ERR) { /* if match is found */
            /* select the matching city in list box */
            SendDlgItemMessage(hdwnd, IDD_LB1, LB_SETCURSEL, i, 0);

            /* get string associated with that index */
            SendDlgItemMessage(hdwnd, IDD_LB1, LB_GETTEXT,
                i, (LPARAM) str);

            /* update text in edit box */
            SetDlgItemText(hdwnd, IDD_EB1, str);
          }
          else  MessageBox(hdwnd, str, "No Match With", MB_OK);
          return 1;
       case IDD_LB1: /* process a list box LBN_DBLCLK */
          /* see  if user made a selection */
          if(HIWORD(wParam)==LBN_DBLCLK) {
            i = SendDlgItemMessage(hdwnd, IDD_LB1,
                    LB_GETCURSEL, 0, 0);  /* get index */
            sprintf(str, "%s, %s\n%s Time Zone\nPop.:%lu",
                    cities[i].name, cities[i].state,
                    cities[i].timezone, cities[i].size);
```

```
          MessageBox(hdwnd, str, "Selection Made", MB_OK);

          /* get string associated with that index */
          SendDlgItemMessage(hdwnd, IDD_LB1, LB_GETTEXT,
              i, (LPARAM) str);

          /* update edit box */
          SetDlgItemText(hdwnd, IDD_EB1, str);
        }
        return 1;
      case IDD_SELECT: /* Select City button has been pressed */
        i = SendDlgItemMessage(hdwnd, IDD_LB1,
                LB_GETCURSEL, 0, 0);  /* get index */
        sprintf(str, "%s, %s\n%s Time Zone\nPop.:%lu",
                cities[i].name, cities[i].state,
                cities[i].timezone, cities[i].size);

        MessageBox(hdwnd, str, "Selection Made", MB_OK);

        /* get string associated with that index */
        SendDlgItemMessage(hdwnd, IDD_LB1, LB_GETTEXT,
            i, (LPARAM) str);

        /* update edit box */
        SetDlgItemText(hdwnd, IDD_EB1, str);
        return 1;
    }
    break;
  case WM_INITDIALOG: /* initialize list box */
    for(i=0; i<NUMCITIES; i++)
      SendDlgItemMessage(hdwnd, IDD_LB1,
                LB_ADDSTRING, 0, (LPARAM)cities[i].name);

    /* select first item */
    SendDlgItemMessage(hdwnd, IDD_LB1, LB_SETCURSEL, 0, 0);

    /* initialize the edit box */
    SetDlgItemText(hdwnd, IDD_EB1, "New York");

    return 1;
  }
  return 0;
}
```

Figure 34-3 shows sample output created by the complete modal dialog box program.

Using a Modeless Dialog Box

To conclude this chapter, the modal dialog box used by the preceding program will be converted into a modeless dialog box. As you will see, using a modeless dialog box requires a little more work than does using a modal one. The main reason for this is that a modeless dialog box is a more independent window than is a modal dialog box. Specifically, the rest of your program is still active when a modeless dialog box is displayed. Also, both it and your application's window function continue to receive messages. Thus, some additional overhead is required in your application's message loop to accommodate the modeless dialog box.

To create a modeless dialog box, you do not use **DialogBox( )**. Instead, you must use the **CreateDialog( )** API function. Its prototype is shown here:

HWND CreateDialog(HINSTANCE *hThisInst*, LPCSTR *lpName*, HWND *hwnd*,
DLGPROC *lpDFunc*)

Here, *hThisInst* is a handle to the current application that is passed to your program in the instance parameter to **WinMain( )**. The name of the dialog box as defined in the

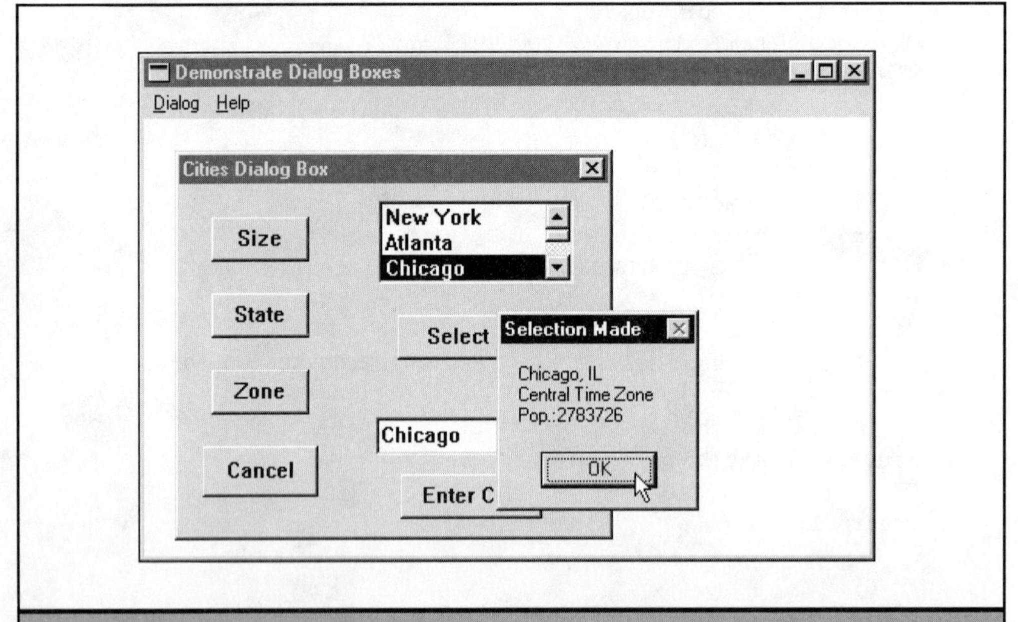

Figure 34-3. *Sample output produced by the complete modal dialog box program*

resource file is pointed to by *lpName*. The handle to the parent window that activates the dialog box is passed in *hwnd*. The *lpDFunc* parameter contains a pointer to the dialog function. The dialog function is of the same type as that used for a modal dialog box. **CreateDialog( )** returns a handle to the dialog box. If the dialog box cannot be created, **NULL** is returned.

Unlike a modal dialog box, a modeless dialog box is not automatically visible, so you may need to call **ShowWindow( )** to cause it to be displayed after it has been created. However, if you add **WS_VISIBLE** to the dialog box's definition in its resource file, then it will be automatically displayed.

To close a modeless dialog box your program must call **DestroyWindow( )** rather than **EndDialog( )**. The prototype for **DestroyWindow( )** is shown here:

BOOL DestroyWindow(HWND *hwnd*);

Here, *hwnd* is the handle to the window (in this case, dialog box) being closed. The function returns nonzero if successful and zero on failure.

Since your application's window function will continue receiving messages while a modeless dialog box is active, you must make a change to your program's message loop. Specifically, you must add a call to **IsDialogMessage( )**. This function routes dialog box messages to your modeless dialog box. It has this prototype:

BOOL IsDialogMessage(HWND *hdwnd*, LPMSG *msg*);

Here, *hdwnd* is the handle of the modeless dialog box and **msg** is the message obtained from **GetMessage( )** within your program's message loop. The function returns nonzero if the message is for the dialog box. It returns false otherwise. If the message is for the dialog box, then it is automatically passed to the dialog box function. Therefore, to process modeless dialog box messages, your program's message loop must look something like this:

```
while(GetMessage(&msg, NULL, 0, 0))
  {
    if(!IsDialogMessage(hDlg, &msg)) {
      /* not dialog box message */
      if(!TranslateAccelerator(hwnd, hAccel, &msg)) {
        TranslateMessage(&msg); /* allow use of keyboard */
        DispatchMessage(&msg); /* return control to Windows */
      }
    }
  }
```

As you can see, the message is only processed by the rest of the message loop if it is not a dialog box message.

Creating a Modeless Dialog Box

To convert the modal dialog box shown in the preceding example into a modeless one, surprisingly few changes are needed. The first change that you need to make is to the dialog box definition in the DIALOG.RC resource file. Since a modeless dialog box is not automatically visible, add **WS_VISIBLE** to the dialog box definition. Also, although not technically necessary, you can remove the **DS_MODALFRAME** style, if you like. After making these adjustments, your dialog box definition should look like the one shown here:

```
MYDB DIALOG 10, 10, 140, 110
CAPTION "Cities Dialog Box"
STYLE WS_POPUP | WS_CAPTION | WS_SYSMENU | WS_VISIBLE
{
  DEFPUSHBUTTON "Size", IDD_SIZE, 11, 10, 32, 14,
             WS_CHILD | WS_VISIBLE | WS_TABSTOP
  PUSHBUTTON "State", IDD_STATE, 11, 34, 32, 14,
             WS_CHILD | WS_VISIBLE | WS_TABSTOP
  PUSHBUTTON "Zone", IDD_ZONE, 11, 58, 32, 14,
             WS_CHILD | WS_VISIBLE | WS_TABSTOP
  PUSHBUTTON "Cancel", IDCANCEL, 8, 82, 38, 16,
             WS_CHILD | WS_VISIBLE | WS_TABSTOP
  LISTBOX IDD_LB1, 66, 5, 63, 33, LBS_NOTIFY |
             WS_VISIBLE | WS_BORDER | WS_VSCROLL | WS_TABSTOP
  PUSHBUTTON "Select City", IDD_SELECT, 72, 41, 54, 14,
             WS_CHILD | WS_VISIBLE | WS_TABSTOP
  EDITTEXT IDD_EB1, 65, 73, 63, 12, ES_LEFT | WS_VISIBLE |
             WS_BORDER | ES_AUTOHSCROLL | WS_TABSTOP
  PUSHBUTTON "Enter City", IDD_DONE, 73, 91, 46, 14,
             WS_CHILD | WS_VISIBLE | WS_TABSTOP
}
```

Next, you must make the following changes to the program:

1. Create a global handle called **hDlg**.
2. Add **IsDialogMessage( )** to the message loop.
3. Create the dialog box using **CreateDialog( )** rather than **DialogBox( )**.
4. Close the dialog box using **DestroyWindow( )** instead of **EndDialog( )**.

The entire listing (which incorporates these changes) for the modeless dialog box example is shown here. Sample output from this program is shown in Figure 34-4. (You should experiment with this program on your own to fully understand the difference between modal and modeless dialog boxes.)

```
/* Demonstrate a Modeless Dialog Box */

#include <windows.h>
#include <string.h>
#include <stdio.h>
#include "dialog.h"

#define NUMCITIES 6

LRESULT CALLBACK WindowFunc(HWND, UINT, WPARAM, LPARAM);
BOOL CALLBACK DialogFunc(HWND, UINT, WPARAM, LPARAM);

char szWinName[] = "MyWin"; /* name of window class */

HINSTANCE hInst;

HWND hDlg; /* dialog box handle */

/* cities database */
struct citiesTag {
  char name[30];
  unsigned long size;
  char state[3];
  char timezone[30];
} cities[NUMCITIES] = {
  {"New York", 7322564, "NY", "Eastern"},
  {"Atlanta", 394017, "GA", "Eastern"},
  {"Chicago", 2783726, "IL", "Central"},
  {"Houston", 1630553, "TX", "Central"},
  {"Denver", 467610, "CO", "Mountain"},
  {"Los Angeles", 3485398, "CA", "Pacific"}
};


int WINAPI WinMain(HINSTANCE hThisInst, HINSTANCE hPrevInst,
                   LPSTR lpszArgs, int nWinMode)
{
  HWND hwnd;
  MSG msg;
  WNDCLASSEX wcl;
  HACCEL hAccel;

  /* Define a window class. */
```

```
wcl.hInstance = hThisInst; /* handle to this instance */
wcl.lpszClassName = szWinName; /* window class name */
wcl.lpfnWndProc = WindowFunc; /* window function */
wcl.style = 0; /* default style */

wcl.cbSize = sizeof(WNDCLASSEX); /* set size of WNDCLASSEX */

wcl.hIcon = LoadIcon(NULL, IDI_APPLICATION); /* Large icon */
wcl.hIconSm = LoadIcon(NULL, IDI_APPLICATION); /* Small icon */

wcl.hCursor = LoadCursor(NULL, IDC_ARROW); /* cursor style */

/* specify name of menu resource */
wcl.lpszMenuName = "MYMENU"; /* main menu */

wcl.cbClsExtra = 0; /* no extra */
wcl.cbWndExtra = 0; /* information needed */

/* Make the window white. */
wcl.hbrBackground = (HBRUSH) GetStockObject(WHITE_BRUSH);

/* Register the window class. */
if(!RegisterClassEx(&wcl)) return 0;

/* Now that a window class has been registered, a window
   can be created. */
hwnd = CreateWindow(
  szWinName, /* name of window class */
  "Demonstrate a Modeless Dialog Box", /* title */
  WS_OVERLAPPEDWINDOW, /* window style - normal */
  CW_USEDEFAULT, /* X coordinate - let Windows decide */
  CW_USEDEFAULT, /* Y coordinate - let Windows decide */
  CW_USEDEFAULT, /* width - let Windows decide */
  CW_USEDEFAULT, /* height - let Windows decide */
  HWND_DESKTOP, /* no parent window */
  NULL, /* no menu */
  hThisInst, /* handle of this instance of the program */
  NULL /* no additional arguments */
);

hInst = hThisInst; /* save the current instance handle */

/* load accelerators */
hAccel = LoadAccelerators(hThisInst, "MYMENU");
```

```
  /* Display the window. */
  ShowWindow(hwnd, nWinMode);
  UpdateWindow(hwnd);

  /* Create the message loop. */
  while(GetMessage(&msg, NULL, 0, 0))
  {
    if(!IsDialogMessage(hDlg, &msg)) {
      /* not dialog box message */
      if(!TranslateAccelerator(hwnd, hAccel, &msg)) {
        TranslateMessage(&msg); /* allow use of keyboard */
        DispatchMessage(&msg); /* return control to Windows */
      }
    }
  }

  return msg.wParam;
}

/* This function is called by Windows 95 and is passed
   messages from the message queue.
*/
LRESULT CALLBACK WindowFunc(HWND hwnd, UINT message,
                            WPARAM wParam, LPARAM lParam)
{
  int response;

  switch(message) {
    case WM_COMMAND:
      switch(LOWORD(wParam)) {
        case IDM_DIALOG:
          /* create modeless dialog box */
          hDlg = CreateDialog(hInst, "MYDB", hwnd, (DLGPROC) DialogFunc);
          break;
        case IDM_EXIT:
          response = MessageBox(hwnd, "Quit the Program?",
                                "Exit", MB_YESNO);
          if(response == IDYES) PostQuitMessage(0);
          break;
        case IDM_HELP:
          MessageBox(hwnd, "No Help", "Help", MB_OK);
          break;
      }
```

```
      break;
    case WM_DESTROY: /* terminate the program */
      PostQuitMessage(0);
      break;
    default:
      /* Let Windows 95 process any messages not specified in
         the preceding switch statement. */
      return DefWindowProc(hwnd, message, wParam, lParam);
  }
  return 0;
}

/* A simple dialog function. */
BOOL CALLBACK DialogFunc(HWND hdwnd, UINT message,
                         WPARAM wParam, LPARAM lParam)
{
  long i;
  char str[80];

  switch(message) {
    case WM_COMMAND:
      switch(LOWORD(wParam)) {
        case IDCANCEL:
          DestroyWindow(hdwnd);
          return 1;
        case IDD_SIZE:
          i = SendDlgItemMessage(hdwnd, IDD_LB1,
                  LB_GETCURSEL, 0, 0);  /* get index */
          sprintf(str, "%lu", cities[i].size);

          MessageBox(hdwnd, str, "Size", MB_OK);
          return 1;
        case IDD_STATE:
          i = SendDlgItemMessage(hdwnd, IDD_LB1,
                  LB_GETCURSEL, 0, 0);  /* get index */
          sprintf(str, "%s", cities[i].state);
          MessageBox(hdwnd, str, "State", MB_OK);
          return 1;
        case IDD_ZONE:
```

```
    i = SendDlgItemMessage(hdwnd, IDD_LB1,
            LB_GETCURSEL, 0, 0);  /* get index */
    sprintf(str, "%s", cities[i].timezone);
    MessageBox(hdwnd, str, "Zone", MB_OK);
    return 1;
  case IDD_DONE: /* Enter Cities button pressed */
    /* get current contents of edit box */
    GetDlgItemText(hdwnd, IDD_EB1, str, 80);

    /* find a matching string in the list box */
    i = SendDlgItemMessage(hdwnd, IDD_LB1, LB_FINDSTRING,
            0, (LPARAM) str);

    if(i != LB_ERR) { /* if match is found */
      /* select the matching city in list box */
      SendDlgItemMessage(hdwnd, IDD_LB1, LB_SETCURSEL, i, 0);

      /* get string associated with that index */
      SendDlgItemMessage(hdwnd, IDD_LB1, LB_GETTEXT,
          i, (LPARAM) str);

      /* update text in edit box */
      SetDlgItemText(hdwnd, IDD_EB1, str);
    }
    else  MessageBox(hdwnd, str, "No Match With", MB_OK);
    return 1;
 case IDD_LB1: /* process a list box LBN_DBLCLK */
    /* see  if user made a selection */
    if(HIWORD(wParam)==LBN_DBLCLK) {
      i = SendDlgItemMessage(hdwnd, IDD_LB1,
              LB_GETCURSEL, 0, 0);  /* get index */
      sprintf(str, "%s, %s\n%s Time Zone\nPop.:%lu",
              cities[i].name, cities[i].state,
              cities[i].timezone, cities[i].size);

      MessageBox(hdwnd, str, "Selection Made", MB_OK);

      /* get string associated with that index */
      SendDlgItemMessage(hdwnd, IDD_LB1, LB_GETTEXT,
          i, (LPARAM) str);
```

```
          /* update edit box */
          SetDlgItemText(hdwnd, IDD_EB1, str);
        }
        return 1;
      case IDD_SELECT: /* Select City button has been pressed */
        i = SendDlgItemMessage(hdwnd, IDD_LB1,
              LB_GETCURSEL, 0, 0);  /* get index */
        sprintf(str, "%s, %s\n%s Time Zone\nPop.:%lu",
              cities[i].name, cities[i].state,
              cities[i].timezone, cities[i].size);

        MessageBox(hdwnd, str, "Selection Made", MB_OK);

        /* get string associated with that index */
        SendDlgItemMessage(hdwnd, IDD_LB1, LB_GETTEXT,
            i, (LPARAM) str);

        /* update edit box */
        SetDlgItemText(hdwnd, IDD_EB1, str);
        return 1;
    }
    break;
  case WM_INITDIALOG: /* initialize list box */
    for(i=0; i<NUMCITIES; i++)
      SendDlgItemMessage(hdwnd, IDD_LB1,
              LB_ADDSTRING, 0, (LPARAM)cities[i].name);

    /* select first item */
    SendDlgItemMessage(hdwnd, IDD_LB1, LB_SETCURSEL, 0, 0);

    /* initialize the edit box */
    SetDlgItemText(hdwnd, IDD_EB1, "New York");

    return 1;
  }
  return 0;
}
```

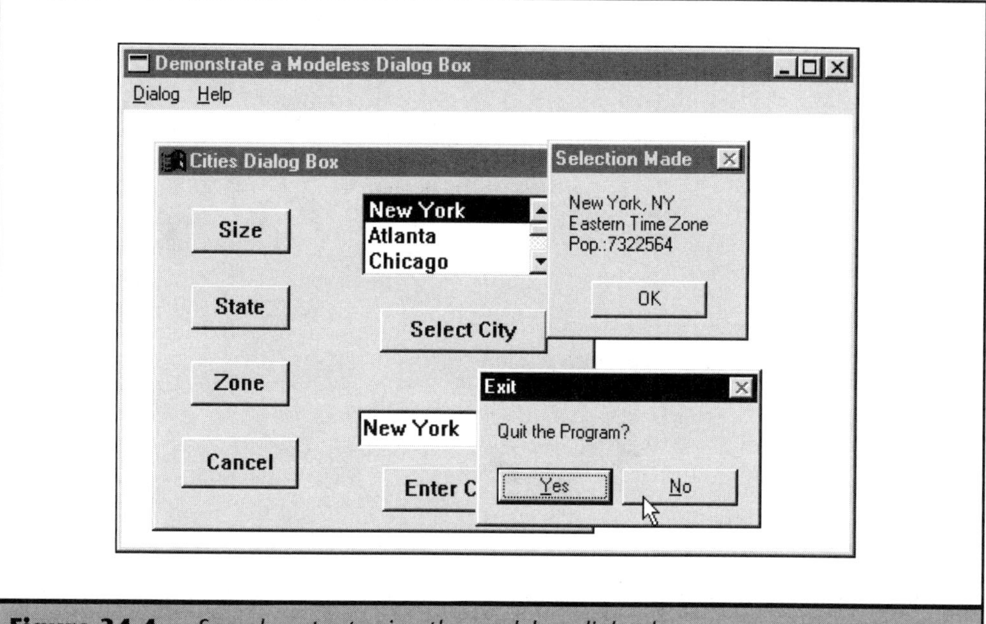

Figure 34-4. *Sample output using the modeless dialog box*

What Next?

While the chapters in this section introduce you to Windows 95 programming using Borland C++ and explain several of Windows' essential principles, they only scratch the surface of Windows programming. If you want to become an excellent Windows programmer, you will need to spend a lot more time reading about and experimenting with Windows programs. However, be persistent—your efforts will be richly rewarded.

PART SIX

A Jump-Start to Java

Part 6 introduces the Java programming language. As you know, beginning with version 5, Borland C++ has included an add-on for Java programming. At the time of this writing, the Java compiler and run-time system supplied by Borland is Sun's Java Development Kit, usually called the Java SDK. This SDK is Sun's standard development environment for Java. Thus, Borland C++ provides an industry-standard way to write and run Java code. If you have not yet installed the Java add-on, do so now.

Part 6 begins an overview of Java, including its key differences with C++. Chapter 36 discusses inheritance, packages, and interfaces. Some of the concepts are similar to C++, but there are also important differences. Chapter 37 describes how to write simple Java applets.

The description of Java that follows assumes that you are an accomplished C/C++ programmer and are familiar with object-oriented concepts. (Everything you need to know is covered in Parts 1 and 3 of this book.) Part 6 builds upon this knowledge base and describes the similarities and differences between Java and C++.

The description of Java presented here is sufficient to get you started. However, due to space limitations, it cannot fully describe the Java language and its libraries. (In fact, a complete description of Java requires a very thick book of its own!) Part 6 will, however, give you a jump-start in learning this important new language. If you will be doing a significant amount of Java development, you will need a good reference book on Java. One such book is *Java: The Complete Reference* by Naughton and Schildt (Berkeley, CA: Osborne/McGraw-Hill, 1997). This book provides an in-depth look at Java, its libraries, and its application.

NOTE: *Portions of the material in Part 6 are adapted by permission from* Java: The Complete Reference *by Naughton and Schildt (Berkeley, CA: Osborne/McGraw-Hill, 1997).*

Chapter Thirty-Five

Overview of Java

As anyone involved with computers knows, the World Wide Web and the Internet have become part and parcel of our computing universe. The Internet has moved from being simply an information distribution system into what amounts to a vast, distributed computing environment. And this change has prompted the invention of the latest evolution of C++: Java. Here is why.

As you know, in a network there are two very broad categories of objects that are transmitted between the server and your personal computer: passive information and dynamic, active programs. For example, when you read your e-mail, you are viewing passive data. Even when you download a program, the program's code is still only passive data until you execute it. However, there is a second type of object that can be transmitted to your computer: a dynamic, self-executing program. For example, such a program might be provided by a server to properly display the data that it is sending to you. While their appeal is great, dynamic, networked programs have also been greeted with concern because of the security and portability problems involved. As you will see, Java is an attempt to answer those concerns.

What Is Java?

Java is the language of the Internet. To understand the importance of Java, consider the following analogy: Java is to Internet programming what C/C++ is to systems programming. Java is that fundamental.

Java was conceived by James Gosling, Patrick Naughton, Chris Warth, Ed Frank, and Mike Sheridan at Sun Microsystems, Inc., in 1991. It took 18 months to develop the first working version. This language was initially called Oak, but was renamed Java in 1995. Between the initial implementation of Oak in the fall of 1992 and the public announcement of Java in the spring of 1995, many more people contributed to the design and evolution of the language. Bill Joy, Arthur van Hoff, Jonathan Payne,

Frank Yellin, and Tim Lindholm were key contributors to the maturing of the original prototype.

Although somewhat surprising, the original impetus for Java was not the Internet! Instead, the primary motivation was the need for a platform- and CPU-independent language that could be used to create software to be embedded in various consumer electronic devices, such as microwave ovens and remote controls. Java was initially designed as a means of providing portable code that could be run in a variety of different types of controllers.

About the time that the details of Java were being worked out, a second, and ultimately more important, factor was emerging that would play a crucial role in the future of Java. This second force was, of course, the World Wide Web. It too, needed a means of providing portable code. Had the Web not taken shape at about the same time that Java was being implemented, Java might have remained a useful but obscure language for programming consumer electronic products. However, with the emergence of the World Wide Web, Java was propelled to the forefront of computer language design.

Java relates to C++ in two important ways. First, it uses the same syntax as C++. For example, the general forms of the **for**, **while**, and **do** loops are the same. Second, it supports object-oriented programming in much the same way as C++. Because of the surface similarities between Java and C++, it is easy to simply think of Java as the Internet version of C++. However, this statement is not quite true because Java also has significant differences from C++ that fundamentally alter its character. But don't worry. As a C++ programmer, you will feel right at home with Java.

Why Java?

Since C and C++ are powerful, well-defined, professional programming languages, you might be wondering why another computer language is needed. The answer to this question can be summarized in two words: safety and portability. Let's look at each.

Safety

As you are almost certainly aware, every time you download a "normal" program you are risking a viral infection. Prior to Java, most users did not download executable programs frequently, and those that did scanned them for viruses prior to execution. Even so, most users still worried about the possibility of infecting their systems with a virus or allowing a malicious program to run wild in their systems. (A malicious program might gather private information—such as credit card numbers, bank account balances, and passwords—by searching the contents of your computer's local file system.) Java answers these concerns by providing a "firewall" between a networked application and your computer.

When using a Java-compatible Web browser, it is possible to safely download Java applets without fear of viral infection. The way that Java achieves this is by confining a Java program to the Java execution environment and not allowing it access to other parts of the computer. (You will see how this is accomplished shortly.) Frankly, the ability to download applets with confidence that no harm will be done to the client computer is the single most important aspect of Java.

Portability

There are many different types of computers and operating systems in use throughout the world—and many are connected to the Internet. In order for programs to be dynamically downloaded to all of the various types of platforms connected to the Web, some means of generating portable executable code is needed. As you will see, the means by which Java achieves portability is both elegant and efficient.

Java's Magic: The Bytecodes

The key that allows Java to solve many problems is that the output of a Java compiler is not executable code. Rather, it is *bytecode*. Bytecode is a highly optimized set of instructions designed to be executed by a virtual machine that the Java run-time system emulates. That is, the Java run-time system is an *interpreter for bytecode*. This may come as a bit of a surprise. As you know, C++ is compiled to executable code. In fact, most modern languages are designed to be compiled, not interpreted—mostly because of performance concerns. However, the fact that a Java program is interpreted helps solve the major problems associated with downloading programs over the Internet. Here is why.

By interpreting Java bytecode, it is much easier to allow Java programs to run in a wide variety of environments. The reason for this is straightforward: only the Java run-time system needs to be implemented for each platform. Once the run-time package exists for a given system, any Java program can run on it. Remember, although the details of the Java run-time system will differ from platform to platform, they will all interpret the same Java bytecode. If Java were a compiled language, then different versions of the same program would have to exist for each different type of CPU connected to the Internet. This is, of course, not a feasible solution. Thus, interpretation is the easiest way to create truly portable programs.

The fact that Java is interpreted also helps make it secure. Because the execution of every Java program is under the control of the run-time system, the run-time system can contain the program and not allow it to generate side effects outside the system. As you will see, safety is also enhanced by certain restrictions that exist in the Java language.

As you may know, when a program is interpreted, it generally runs substantially slower than the same program would run if compiled to executable code. However, with Java, the differential between the two is not so great. The use of bytecode makes it possible for the Java run-time system to execute programs much faster than one would ordinarily expect.

One other point: Although Java was designed to be interpreted, there is nothing about Java that technically prevents "on the fly" compilation of bytecode into native code. However, even if dynamic compilation is applied to bytecode, the portability and safety features will still apply because the run-time system will still be in charge of the execution environment.

Key Advantages of Java

No discussion of the genesis of Java is complete without a look at the Java "buzzwords." Although the fundamental forces that necessitated the invention of Java are portability and security, there are other factors that played an important role in molding the final form of the language. These other considerations were summed up by the Java team as the list of "buzzwords" shown here:

- Simple
- Secure
- Portable
- Object-oriented
- Robust
- Multithreaded
- Architecture-neutral
- Interpreted
- High-performance
- Distributed
- Dynamic

Security and portability have already been discussed. The others are examined here.

Simple

Java was designed to be easy for the professional programmer to learn and use effectively. This is especially true if you are an experienced C++ programmer—moving to Java will require very little effort. Since Java inherits the C/C++ syntax and many of the object-oriented features of C++, most programmers will have little trouble learning Java. Also, some of the more confusing concepts from C++ are either left out of Java or implemented in a cleaner, more approachable manner.

Object-Oriented

The designers of Java built upon and refined the object-oriented concepts of existing object-oriented languages, such as C++. However, they did not need to carry with them any baggage from the past. Instead, they were able to create an object model from the ground up that provides a clean, easy-to-use approach to objects. However, even though Java implements a strong object model, it can deliver high performance. For example, primitive types such as integers and characters are elemental types, not objects, in the interest of efficiency.

Robust

There are several features of Java that help you write robust software. First, it is a strongly typed language. Every variable and expression has a type, and this information is used to catch problems at compile time. Any type mismatches are reported to you as a compile error. Second, memory management is much easier in Java than in C++. You do not need to write code to deallocate memory. Automatic garbage collection takes care of this. Third, object-oriented exception handling provides a clean way to structure your code so that run-time error conditions are caught and handled.

Multithreaded

Java was designed to meet the real-world requirement of creating interactive, networked programs. To accomplish this, Java supports multithreaded programming, which allows you to write programs that do many things at once. The Java run-time comes with an elegant yet sophisticated solution for multiprocess synchronization that makes it possible to construct smoothly running interactive systems. Java's easy-to-use approach to multithreading allows you to think about the specific behavior of your program, not the multitasking subsystem.

Architecture-Neutral

One of the major achievements of the Java team is that it is now possible to write software once and run it on a variety of heterogeneous platforms. As new hardware and software become available, the Java virtual machine must be ported to those environments. However, the bytecodes that are generated from Java source code remain unchanged.

Interpreted and High Performance

Interpreted languages frequently suffer from slow run-time performance. This is especially apparent on low-power CPUs. However, it is possible to do "just-in-time" compilation. This means that bytecodes generated by the Java compiler are translated into native code just before they must be executed for the first time. The bytecode instruction set was designed so that this translation would be straightforward. Further, the bytecode itself has been optimized for interpretation, so the performance problems usually associated with interpreted languages are not as significant with Java.

Distributed

Java was designed for the distributed environment of the Internet because it handles TCP/IP protocols. In fact, accessing a resource using a URL is not much different than accessing a file.

Dynamic

Java programs carry with them substantial amounts of run-time type information that is used to verify and resolve accesses to objects at run time. This makes it possible to dynamically link code in a safe and expedient manner. This is crucial to the robustness of the applet environment where small fragments of bytecode may be dynamically updated on a running system.

Differences Between Java and C++

Although the Java language is modeled on C++, it has several fundamental differences. Some of these differences are simply that—just slight alterations. Others are major design decisions that profoundly affect how you write programs. Several of the most important differences are highlighted here. Before beginning, it is important to keep in mind one important fact: Java was designed to allow portable applications to be safely downloaded over a network. In its current form, it is not designed to replace C or C++ as a systems programming language. With this firmly in mind, let's take a look at some of the differences between C++ and Java.

What Java Removed from C++

There are a number of C++ features that Java does not support. In some cases, a specific C++ feature simply didn't relate to the Java environment. In other cases, the designers of Java eliminated some of the duplication of features that exists in C++. In still other instances, a feature of C++ is not supported by Java because it was deemed too dangerous for Internet applets. Here are a few of the most important "deletions."

Perhaps the single biggest difference between Java and C++ is that Java does not support pointers. As a C++ programmer, you know that the pointer is one of C++'s most powerful and important language features. It is also one of its most dangerous when used improperly. Pointers don't exist in Java for two reasons. First, pointers are inherently insecure. For example, using a C++-style pointer, it is possible to gain access to memory addresses outside a program's code and data. A malicious program could make use of this fact to damage the system, perform unauthorized accesses (such as obtaining passwords), or otherwise violate security restrictions. Second, even if pointers could be restricted to the confines of the Java run-time system (which is theoretically possible since Java programs are interpreted), the designers of Java believed that they were inherently troublesome. Since pointers don't exist in Java, neither does the –> operator.

Java does not include structures or unions. These were felt to be redundant since the class encompasses them.

Java does not support operator overloading. Operator overloading is sometimes a source of ambiguity in a C++ program and the Java design team felt that it causes more trouble than it does benefit.

Java does not include a preprocessor or support the preprocessor directives. As you may know, the preprocessor plays a less important role in C++ than it does in C. The designers of Java felt that it was time to eliminate it entirely.

Java does not perform any automatic type conversions that result in a loss of precision. For example, a conversion from long integer to integer must be explicitly cast.

All the code in a Java program is encapsulated within one or more classes. Therefore, Java does not have what you normally think of as global variables or global functions.

Java does not allow default arguments. In C++, you may specify a value that a parameter will have when there is no argument corresponding to that parameter when the function is invoked. This is not allowed in Java.

Java does not support the inheritance of multiple superclasses by a subclass.

Although Java supports constructors, it does not have destructors. It does, however, add the **finalize( )** function.

Java does not support **typedef**.

It is not possible to declare unsigned integers.

Java does not allow the **goto**.

It does not have the **delete** operator.

The << and >> are not overloaded for I/O operations.

In Java, objects are passed by reference only. In C++, objects may be passed by value or by reference.

New Features Added by Java

There are several features in Java that have no equivalent in C++. Perhaps the three most important are packages, interfaces, and multithreading. There are also several others that enrich the Java programming environment.

In Java, a package defines a name space and is a way to group related classes together. There is no feature in C++ that directly corresponds to a Java package. The closest similarity is a set of library functions that use a common header file. However, constructing and using a library in C++ is completely different from constructing and using a package in Java. (Packages are described in Chapter 36.)

The Java **interface** is somewhat similar to a C++ abstract class. (An abstract class in C++ is a class that contains at least one pure virtual function.) For example, it is not possible to create an instance of a C++ abstract class or a Java **interface**. Both are used to specify a consistent interface that subclasses will implement. The main difference is that an **interface** more cleanly represents this concept. (Interfaces are also described in Chapter 36.)

Multithreading allows two or more pieces of the same program to execute concurrently. Further, this approach to concurrency is supported at the language level. There is no parallel for this in C++. If you need to multithread a C++ program, you will need to do so manually, using operating system functions. While both methods allow for concurrent execution of two or more threads, Java's approach is cleaner and easier to use. While it is beyond the scope of this book to describe Java's multitasking subsystem, you will want to learn about it if you plan to do a significant amount of Java programming.

Another way that Java differs from C++ is its approach to memory allocation. Like C++, it supports the **new** keyword. However, it does not have **delete**. Instead, when the last reference to an object is destroyed, the object itself is automatically deleted the next time that garbage collection occurs.

Java "removes" the C/C++ standard library, replacing it with its own set of API classes. While there is a substantial amount of functional similarity, there are significant differences in the names and parameters. Also, since all the Java API library is object-oriented, and only a portion of the C++ library is, there will be differences in the way library routines are invoked.

The **break** and **continue** statements have been enhanced to accept labels as targets.

The **char** type declares 16-bit-wide Unicode characters. This makes them similar to C++'s **wchar_t** type. The use of Unicode helps ensure portability.

Java adds the >>> operator, which performs an unsigned right shift.

In addition to supporting single line and multiline comments, Java adds a third comment form: the documentation comment. Documentation comments begin with a /** and end with a */.

Java contains a built-in string type called **String**. **String** is somewhat similar to the standard **string** class type provided by C++. Of course, in C++ **string** is only available if you include its class declarations in your program. It is not a built-in type.

Features That Differ

There are some features common to both C++ and Java that each language handles a bit differently.

While both C++ and Java support a Boolean data type, Java does not implement true and false in the same way as C++. In C++, true is any nonzero value. False is zero. In Java, **true** and **false** are predefined literals, and these are the only values that a **boolean** expression may have. While C++ also defines **true** and **false**, which may be assigned to a **bool** variable, C++ automatically converts nonzero values into **true** and zero values into **false**. This does not occur in Java.

When you create a C++ **class**, the access specifiers apply to groups of statements. In Java, access specifiers apply only to the declarations that they immediately precede.

C++ supports exception handling that is fairly similar to Java's. However, in C++ there is no requirement that a thrown exception be caught. In Java, most exceptions must be caught.

Java Applications and Applets

Java can be used to create two types of programs: applications and applets. An application is a program that runs on your computer, under the operating system of that computer. That is, an application created by Java is (more or less) like one created using C or C++. When used to create applications, Java is not much different than any other computer language. Rather, it is Java's ability to create applets that makes it important. An *applet* is a small application that is designed to be transmitted over the Internet and executed by a Java-compatible Web browser. Through the use of applets, Web-based content can be actively engaged in how that content is displayed. The ability to create portable, dynamically downloadable applets is the single greatest reason for Java's success.

Methods Versus Functions

Before moving on, an important term that is used by Java programmers must be defined. In the language of Java, the word *function* is seldom used. Instead, what a C++ programmer normally calls a member function, a Java programmer calls a *method*. One reason for the different terms is to emphasize the fact that Java does not support global functions. All functions (that is, methods) are members of a class.

A Simple Java Application

Now that the foundation of Java has been discussed, we will look at some actual Java programs. Let's start by compiling and running the short sample program shown here. As you will see, this involves a little more work than you might imagine.

```
/*
   This is a simple Java program.
   Call this file "Demo.java".
*/
class Demo {
  // Your program begins with a call to main().
  public static void main(String args[]) {
    System.out.println("This is my first Java program!");
  }
}
```

Entering the Program

For most computer languages, the name of the file that holds the source code to a program is arbitrary. However, this is not the case with Java. The first thing that you must learn about Java is that the name you give to a source file is very important. For this example, the name of the source file should be **Demo.java**. Let's see why.

In Java, a source file is officially called a *compilation unit*. It is a text file that contains one or more class definitions. The Java compiler requires that a source file use the **.java** filename extension. Notice that the file extension is four characters long. As you might guess, your operating system must be capable of supporting long file names. This means that DOS or Windows 3.1 are not capable of supporting Java (at least at this time). However, Windows 95 and Windows NT work just fine.

As you can see by looking at the program, the name of the class defined by the program is also called **Demo**. This is not a coincidence. In Java, all code must reside inside a class. By convention, the name of that class should match the name of the file that holds the program. You should also make sure that the capitalization of the file name matches the class name. The reason for this is that Java is case-sensitive. At this point, the convention that file names correspond to class names may seem arbitrary. However, doing so makes it easier to maintain and organize your programs.

Compiling and Running a Java Program

There are two ways to compile and run a Java program using Borland C++. First, you can use the IDE. There are online instructions provided by Borland that walk you through this process and they are not duplicated here. Second, you can use the command-line tools. Frankly, in many ways using the command-line tools is the easiest way to compile and run Java programs.

Using the command-line tools to compile the **Demo** program, execute the compiler, **javac**, specifying the name of the source file on the command line, as shown here:

```
javac Demo.java
```

A new file called **Demo.class** is created if the compilation is successful. This contains the bytecodes that the Java interpreter can execute.

To actually run the program, you must use the Java interpreter, called **java**. To do so, pass the class name **Demo** as a command-line argument. For example,

```
java Demo
```

When the program is run, the following output is displayed:

```
This is my first Java program!
```

One more point: When Java source code is compiled, each individual class is put into its own output file named after the class and using the **.class** extension. This is why it is a good idea to give your Java source files the same name as the class they contain—the name of the source file will match the name of the **.class** file. When you execute the Java interpreter as just shown, you are actually specifying the name of the class that you want the interpreter to execute. It will automatically search for a file by that name that has the **.class** extension. If it finds the file, it will execute the code contained in the specified class.

A Closer Look at The First Application

Although **Demo.java** is quite short, it includes several key features that are common to all Java programs. Let's closely examine each part of the program.

The program begins with the following lines:

```
/*
   This is a simple Java program.
   Call this file "Demo.java".
*/
```

As in C++, this is a comment. Java supports both multiline and single-line comments in just the same way as C++.

The next line of code in the program is shown here:

```
class Demo {
```

This line uses the keyword **class** to declare that a new class is being defined. **Demo** is the name of the class. The entire class definition, including all of its members, will be between the opening curly brace { and the closing curly brace }. (The use of the curly braces in Java is identical to the way they are used in C and C++.) For the moment, we won't worry too much about the details of a class except to say that in Java, all program activity occurs within one. This is one reason why all Java programs are (at least a little bit) object-oriented.

Next is a single-line comment followed by the line of code shown here:

```
public static void main(String args[]) {
```

This line begins the **main( )** method. As the comment preceding it suggests, this is the line at which the program will begin executing. Like C++, all Java applications begin execution by calling **main( )**. However, Java's **main( )** method is somewhat different from C++'s **main( )** function. Let's take a closer look at each part.

The **public** keyword has essentially the same meaning in Java as it does in C++. When a class member is preceded by **public**, then that member may be accessed by code outside the class in which it is declared. (Java also includes the **private** and **protected** specifiers.) In this case, **main( )** must be declared as **public** since it must be called by code outside of its class when the program is started. The keyword **static** allows **main( )** to be called without having to instantiate a particular instance of the class. This is necessary since **main( )** is called by the Java interpreter before any objects are made. The keyword **void** simply tells the compiler that **main( )** does not return a value and means the same thing as it does in C++.

Any information that you need to pass to a method is received by parameters specified within the set of parentheses that follow the name of the method. If there are no parameters required for a given method, you still need to include the empty parentheses. In **main( )**, there is only one parameter, albeit a complicated one. **String args[ ]** declares a parameter named **args**, which is an array of instances of the class **String**. Objects of type **String** store character strings. These strings receive any command-line arguments present when the program is executed. This program does not make use of this information.

The last character on the line is the {. This signals the start of **main( )**'s body. All of the code that comprises a method will occur between the method's opening curly brace and its closing curly brace.

One other point: **main( )** is simply a starting place for the interpreter to begin. A complex program will have dozens of classes, only one of which will need to have a **main( )** method to get things started. When we begin creating applets—Java programs that are embedded in Web browsers—we won't use **main( )** at all, since the Web browser uses a different means of starting the execution of applets.

The next line of code is shown here. Notice that it occurs inside **main( )**.

```
System.out.println("This is my first Java program!");
```

This line outputs the string "This is my first Java program!" followed by a newline on the screen. Output is actually accomplished by the built-in **println( )** method. In this case, **println( )** displays the string that is passed to it. As you will see, **println( )** can be used to display other types of information, too. The line begins with **System.out**. **System** is a predefined class that provides access to the system and **out** is the output stream that is connected to the console. Thus, **out** is, more or less, Java's equivalent of **cout.**

As you have probably guessed, console output (and input) is not used frequently in real Java programs and applets. Since most modern computing environments are windowed and graphical in nature, console I/O is used mostly for simple utility programs and for demonstration programs.

Notice that the **println( )** statement ends with a semicolon. Like C++, all statements in Java end with a semicolon.

The lone curly brace on line 4 ends **main( )** and the curly brace on line 5 ends the **Demo** class definition.

A Second Example

Before moving on, let's look at another simple program. The following example demonstrates the expanded features of **break** in Java and performs simple console input:

```
/* Here is an example that illustrates the expanded
   capabilities of break and performs simple input.
*/
class JavaTest {
```

```
  public static void main(String strargs[])
        throws java.io.IOException
  {
    int i, j, k;

    System.out.println("Display ASCII codes.");

lab1: for(;;) {
      System.out.println("Enter a character: ");
      do {
        k = System.in.read();
      } while((char) k == '\n');
      i = k;
      j = 1;
lab2:
      while(i>0) {
        while(i>0) {
          j++;
          if((j%20)==0) break;
          if((char) k == 'q') break lab1;
          if((char) k == '\n') break lab2;
          System.out.print(i+" ");
          i--;
        }
        System.out.println();
        j = 1;
      }
    }
  }
}
```

This program prompts for a character to be entered by the user. It then displays all the ASCII codes beginning with that character and counting down to zero. Sample output is shown here:

```
Display ASCII codes.
Enter a character: 1
49 48 47 46 45 44 43 42 41 40 39 38 37 36 35 34 33 32
31 30 29 28 27 26 25 24 23 22 21 20 19 18 17 16 15 14
13 12 11 10 9 8 7 6 5 4 3 2 1
Enter a character: 2
50 49 48 47 46 45 44 43 42 41 40 39 38 37 36 35 34 33
32 31 30 29 28 27 26 25 24 23 22 21 20 19 18 17 16 15
14 13 12 11 10 9 8 7 6 5 4 3 2 1
```

```
Enter a character: 3
51 50 49 48 47 46 45 44 43 42 41 40 39 38 37 36 35 34
33 32 31 30 29 28 27 26 25 24 23 22 21 20 19 18 17 16
15 14 13 12 11 10 9 8 7 6 5 4 3 2 1
Enter a character: q
```

In Java, the **break** command may take a label as a target. When no label is present, it works like its equivalent in C++ by breaking out of the innermost block. However, when a label is present, then execution is transferred out of the specified block. In the preceding program, **break**, by itself, breaks out of the inner **while** loop. **break lab2** breaks out of the outer **while** loop. **break lab1** breaks out of the outer **for** loop, causing program termination when a **q** is entered. As you can guess, the ability to target a specific block greatly expands the uses for **break**. In fact, one of the reasons that Java does not support the **goto** is because of the expanded capabilities of **break**.

The use of a labeled **break** can also be applied to breaking out of a **switch** statement. The **continue** statement may also continue to a labeled block. Remember, the target label of either the **break** or **continue** must be at the start of a block.

Before leaving this example, there are a few other points of interest worth mentioning. First, notice that characters are read by calling **System.in.read( )**. This function reads characters from standard input. By default, standard input is line-buffered, so you must press ENTER before any characters you type will be sent to your program. This situation is similar to C++, and you are probably already familiar with this style of input.

One other point: Because input is being performed, the program must tell the compiler that the function **main( )** might throw a **java.io.IOException** exception. In general, in a Java program, exceptions must be explicitly handled in one form or another. In this case, the **throws** clause tells the compiler that an I/O exception might be thrown out of **main( )**. This is one way that Java exception handling differs from C++. If an exception might be thrown in a method that does not handle it, you must explicitly declare this fact. In C++, no such requirement exists.

Some Java Basics

Here, we will look at some of the fundamental elements and features of Java.

Java Is a Strongly Typed Language

Java is a more strongly typed language than is C++. Indeed, part of Java's safety and robustness comes from this fact. Let's see what this means. First, every variable has a type, every expression has a type, and every type is strictly defined. Second, all assignments, whether explicit or via parameter passing in method calls, are checked for type compatibility. There are no automatic coercions or conversions of conflicting types as in some languages. The Java compiler checks all expressions and parameters to ensure that the types are compatible. Any type mismatches are errors that must be corrected before the compiler will finish compiling the class.

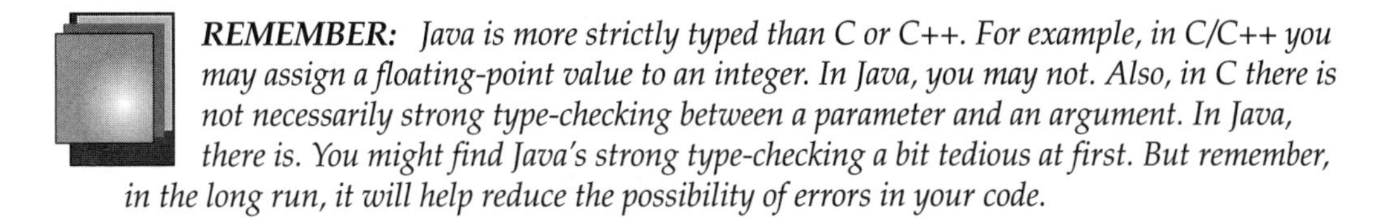

REMEMBER: *Java is more strictly typed than C or C++. For example, in C/C++ you may assign a floating-point value to an integer. In Java, you may not. Also, in C there is not necessarily strong type-checking between a parameter and an argument. In Java, there is. You might find Java's strong type-checking a bit tedious at first. But remember, in the long run, it will help reduce the possibility of errors in your code.*

Java's Built-in Simple Types

Java defines the following eight simple (or, elemental) types of data.

Type	**Meaning**	**Width in Bits**
byte	A small integer	8
short	A short integer	16
int	An integer	32
long	An integer	64
char	A character	16
float	Single-precision floating point	32
double	Double-precision floating point	64
boolean	True/false values	N/A

These simple, or atomic, types have essentially the meaning in Java that they do in C++. They represent single values—not objects. Although Java is otherwise completely object-oriented, the simple types are not. The reason for this is efficiency. Making the simple types into objects would have degraded performance too much.

The simple types are defined to have an explicit range and mathematical behavior. As you may know, languages such as C and C++ allow the size of an integer to vary based upon the dictates of the execution environment. However, Java is different. Because of Java's portability requirement, all data types have a strictly defined range. For example, an **int** is always 32 bits, regardless of the particular platform.

Java does not support unsigned integer values. In Java, all integers are signed. However, Java does define an unsigned right-shift operator that overcomes this limitation.

In Java, the data type used to store characters is **char**. However, C/C++ programmers beware: **char** in Java is not the same as **char** in C or C++. In C/C++, **char** is an integer type that is 8 bits wide. This is *not* the case in Java. Instead, Java uses *Unicode* to represent characters. Unicode defines a fully international character set that can represent all of the characters found in all human languages. This requires 16 bits. Thus, the range of a **char** is 0 to 65536. Of course, **char** variables can still be used to hold 8-bit ASCII character values.

Character literals are represented inside single quotes such as 'a' or '%'. Java supports a set of *escape sequences*, shown here, that are similar to C++'s backslash character constants:

Escape Sequence	Description
\ddd	Octal character (ddd)
\uxxxx	Hexadecimal Unicode character (xxxx)
\'	Single quote
\"	Double quote
\\	Backslash
\r	Carriage return
\n	Newline
\f	Formfeed
\t	Tab
\b	Backspace

Like C++, Java defines a Boolean data type. Its keyword is **boolean**. It can have only one of two possible values, **true** or **false**, which are literals defined by Java.. This is the type returned by all relational operators and logical operators.

String Literals

String literals are a sequence of characters enclosed by a pair of double quotes. As you may know, in most other languages, including C/C++, strings are implemented as arrays of characters. However, this is not the case in Java. Strings are actually object types. Because Java implements strings as objects, it includes extensive string-handling capabilities that are both powerful and easy to use.

Type Conversion and Casting

When assigning one type of data to another type of variable, an *automatic type conversion* will take place if the following two conditions are met:

- The two types are compatible
- The destination type is larger than the source type

When these two conditions are met, a *widening conversion* takes place. For example, the **long** type is always large enough to hold all valid **byte** values, so no explicit cast statement is required.

For widening conversions, the numeric types, including integer and floating-point types, are compatible with each other. However, the numeric types are not compatible with **char** or **boolean**. Also, **char** and **boolean** are not compatible with each other.

Java also performs an automatic type conversion when storing a literal integer constant into variables of type **byte**, **short**, or **long**.

Although the automatic type conversions are helpful, they will not answer all needs. For example, what if you want to assign an **int** value to a **byte** variable? This conversion will not be performed automatically because a **byte** is smaller than an **int**. This kind of conversion is sometimes called a *narrowing conversion*, since you are explicitly making the value narrower so that it will fit into the target type. To create a conversion between two incompatible types, you must use a cast. A cast is simply an explicit type conversion. A cast in Java is syntactically the same as it is in C++.

Operators

Java supports essentially the same set of operators as does C++. For example, it includes the assignment operators, such as **+=** and **%=**. It also includes the same arithmetic, bitwise, logical, and relational operators as C++. There are a few minor differences, however. As mentioned earlier, since Java has no pointers, it does not define the **–>**, **&**, or * pointer operators. It also does not define the **delete** memory deallocation operator, since it is not needed.

Java also adds a few operators not defined by C++. First, in Java, the **>>** operator automatically fills the high-order bit with its previous contents each time a shift occurs. This preserves the sign of the value. However, sometimes this is undesirable. For example, if you are shifting something that does not represent a numeric value, you may not want sign extension to take place. In these cases, you will generally want to shift a zero into the high-order bit when a right shift occurs. In Java, this is known as an *unsigned shift*. To accomplish this, you will use Java's unsigned, shift-right operator, **>>>**, which always shifts zeros into the high-order bit.

Java defines the two "short-circuit" bitwise operators shown here:

||	Short-circuit OR
&&	Short-circuit AND

As you know, in an OR operation, if either operand is true, the outcome of the OR is true. Conversely, in an AND operation, if either operand is false, the outcome of the AND is false. The short-circuit operators take advantage of this fact. They begin by evaluating the left-hand operand. If the outcome of that operand can determine the final outcome, the right-hand operand is not evaluated.

Control Statements

If you know C/C++, Java's control statements will be very familiar. The selection statements **if** and **switch** are supported. Iteration is available via the **for**, **while**, and **do-while** constructs. The **break**, **continue**, and **return** statements affect control flow.

As mentioned, the **break** and **continue** statements have some expanded capabilities, which allow them to be used with labels.

Class Fundamentals

Java shares many similarities with C++ as it relates to classes, but there are also several differences. Several of the more important aspects of classes in Java will be examined here. Let's start by stating the similarities between C++ classes and Java classes. Java classes may contain both member variables and member functions (called *methods* in Java). Given an object, members of its class are accessed using the "dot" operator. Java classes may include constructors. Constructors may be overloaded. In fact, any member function may be overloaded. Overloading works in Java more or less the same as it works in C++. Each object that you create will have its own copy of its member variables (again, just like in C++).

Although Java classes are similar to C++ classes, they do have some important differences that we will examine here. As in C++, a class is a template for an object. You declare a class by using the **class** keyword. The general form of a **class** definition is shown here:

```
class classname {
  type instance-variable1;
  type instance-variable2;
  // ...
  type instance-variableN;

  type methodname1(parameter-list) {
     // body of method
  }
  type methodname2(parameter-list) {
     // body of method
  }
  // ...
  type methodnameN(parameter-list) {
     // body of method
  }
}
```

The data, or variables, defined within a **class** are called *instance variables*. The code is contained within *methods*.

An optional *access specifier* may precede each member to indicate how that member may be accessed. When a member of a class is modified by the **public** specifier, then that member may be accessed by any other code in your program. When a member of a class is specified as **private**, then that member may only be accessed by other members of its class. This is why **main( )** must always be preceded by the **public** specifier. It is called by code that is outside the program—i.e., the Java run-time system. When no access specifier is used, then by default the member of a class is public within its own package but cannot be accessed outside of its package.

An access specifier precedes the rest of a member's type specification. That is, it must begin a member's declaration statement. For example,

```
public int i;
private double j;

private int myMethod(int a, char b) { // ...
```

There are three important differences between classes in C++ and classes in Java:

1. In C++, it is possible to write code that is not a class method. This is not possible in Java.
2. In Java, all methods are defined inside of their class. It is not possible to declare them outside their class.
3. An access specifier only applies to the item that it precedes. In C++, access specifiers designate an access heading that applies to all items under the heading until the next access specifier is encountered.

A Simple Java Class

Let's look at an example that uses a simple Java class. Here is a class called **Box** that defines three instance variables: **width**, **height**, and **depth**. Currently, **Box** does not contain any methods.

```
class Box {
  double width;
  double height;
  double depth;
}
```

As stated, a class defines a new type of data. In this case, the new data type is called **Box**. You will use this name to declare objects of type **Box**. It is important to remember that a **class** declaration only creates a template, it does not create an actual object. Thus, the preceding code does not cause any objects of type **Box** to come into existence.

To actually create a **Box** object, you will use a statement like the following:

```
Box mybox = new Box(); // create a Box object called mybox
```

After this statement executes, **mybox** will be an instance of **Box**. Thus, it will have "physical" reality. For the moment, don't worry about the details of this statement.

Here is a complete program that uses the **Box** class:

```
/* A program that uses the Box class.

   Call this file BoxDemo.java
*/
class Box {
  double width;
  double height;
  double depth;
}

// This class declares an object of type Box.
class BoxDemo {
  public static void main(String args[]) {
    Box mybox = new Box();
    double vol;

    // assign values to mybox's instance variables
    mybox.width = 10;
    mybox.height = 20;
    mybox.depth = 15;

    // compute volume of box
    vol = mybox.width * mybox.height * mybox.depth;

    System.out.println("Volume is " + vol);
  }
}
```

You should call the file that contains this program **BoxDemo.java** because the **main( )** method is in the class called **BoxDemo**, not the class called **Box**. When you compile this program, you will find that two **.class** files have been created, one for **Box** and one for **BoxDemo**. The Java compiler automatically puts each class into its own **.class** file. It is not necessary for both the **Box** and the **BoxDemo** class to actually be in the same source file. You could put each class in its own file, called **Box.java** and **BoxDemo.java**, respectively. To run this program, you must execute **BoxDemo.class**. When you do, you will see the following output:

```
Volume is 3000
```

Declaring Objects

As just explained, when you create a class, you are creating a new data type. You can use this type to declare objects of that type. However, obtaining objects of a class is actually a two-step process. First, you must declare a variable of the class type. This variable does not define an object itself. Instead, it is simply a variable that can *refer to an object*. Second, you must acquire an actual physical copy of the object and assign it to that variable. This is accomplished using the **new** operator. The **new** operator dynamically allocates (i.e., allocates at run time) memory for an object and returns a reference to it. This reference is, more or less, the address in memory of the object allocated by **new**. This reference is then stored in the variable. Thus, in Java, all class objects must be dynamically allocated. Let's look at the details of this procedure.

In the preceding sample programs, a line similar to the following is used to declare an object of type **Box**:

```
Box mybox = new Box();
```

This statement combines the two steps just described. It can be rewritten like this to show each step more clearly:

```
Box mybox; // declare reference to object
mybox = new Box(); // allocate a box object
```

The first line declares **mybox** as a reference to an object of type **Box**. After this line executes, **mybox** contains the value **null**, which indicates that it does yet point to an actual object. Any attempt to use **mybox** at this point will result in a compile-time error. The next line allocates an actual object and assigns a reference to it to **mybox**. After the second line executes, you can use **mybox** as if it were a **Box** object itself. But in reality, **mybox** simply holds the memory address of the actual **Box** object.

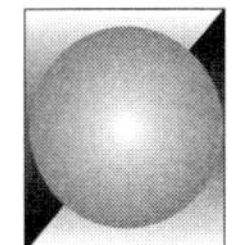

NOTE: You may have noticed that object references appear to be similar to pointers. This suspicion is essentially correct. An object reference is similar to a memory pointer. The main difference—and the key to Java's safety—is that you cannot manipulate references as you can actual pointers. Thus, you cannot cause an object reference to point to an arbitrary memory location or manipulate it like an integer.

Assigning Object Reference Variables

Object reference variables act differently than you might expect when an assignment takes place. For example, what do you think the following fragment does?

```
Box b1 = new Box();
Box b2 = b1;
```

You might think that **b2** is being assigned a reference to a copy of the object referred to by **b1**. That is, you might think that **b1** and **b2** refer to separate and distinct objects. However, this would be wrong. Instead, after this fragment executes, **b1** and **b2** will both refer to *the same object*. The assignment of **b1** to **b2** does not allocate any memory or copy any part of the original object. It simply makes **b2** refer to the same object as does **b1**. Thus, any changes made to the object through **b2** will affect the object to which **b1** is referring since they are the same object.

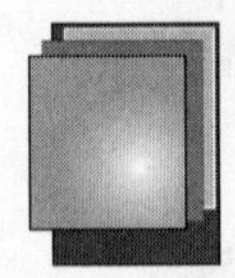

REMEMBER: When you assign one object reference variable to another object reference variable, you are not creating a copy of the object, you are only making a copy of the reference.

Although **b1** and **b2** both refer to the same object, they are not linked in any other way. For example, a subsequent assignment to **b1** will simply *unhook* **b1** from the original object without affecting the object or affecting **b2**. For example:

```
Box b1 = new Box();
Box b2 = b1;
// ...
b1 = null;
```

Here, **b1** has been set to **null**, but **b2** still points to the original object.

Adding a Method and a Constructor

Like C++, Java classes usually contain methods and constructors. Both of these work in Java essentially the same way that they work in C++. For example, the following version of **Box** adds a parameterized constructor that initializes a box when it is created and a method called **volume( )** that displays the volume of a box:

```
/* Here, Box uses a parameterized constructor to
   initialize the dimensions of a box and volume()
   to display the volume of the box.
*/
class Box {
  double width;
  double height;
  double depth;

  // This is the constructor for Box.
  Box(double w, double h, double d) {
    width = w;
    height = h;
    depth = d;
  }

  // compute and return volume
  double volume() {
    return width * height * depth;
```

```
  }
}

class BoxDemo2 {
  public static void main(String args[]) {
    // declare, allocate, and initialize Box objects
    Box mybox1 = new Box(10, 20, 15);
    Box mybox2 = new Box(3, 6, 9);

    double vol;

    // get volume of first box
    vol = mybox1.volume();
    System.out.println("Volume is " + vol);

    // get volume of second box
    vol = mybox2.volume();
    System.out.println("Volume is " + vol);
  }
}
```

The output from this program is shown here:

```
Volume is 3000
Volume is 162
```

As you can see, each object is initialized as specified in the parameters to its constructor. For example, in the line

```
Box mybox1 = new Box(10, 20, 15);
```

the values 10, 20, and 15 are passed to the **Box( )** constructor when **new** creates the object. Thus, **mybox1**'s copy of **width**, **height**, and **depth** will contain the values 10, 20, and 15, respectively. Again, this works in Java just the way it does in C++.

Notice that the code for both **Box( )** and **volume( )** is fully defined within the **Box** class. This is necessary. You cannot define methods outside their class.

In general, when you don't explicitly define a constructor for a class, then Java creates a default constructor for the class. This is why the first version of **Box** did not need to explicitly define a constructor. The default constructor takes no arguments and automatically initializes all instance variables to zero. The default constructor is often sufficient for simple classes, but it usually won't do for more sophisticated ones. Once you define your own constructor, the default constructor is no longer available for use.

Arrays

On the surface, arrays appear to work in Java the way they work in C++. But be careful. Arrays in Java have some subtle yet important differences. For this reason, they are briefly examined here.

One-Dimensional Arrays

To create an array, you first must create an array variable of the desired type. The general form of a one-dimensional array declaration is

type var-name[ ];

Here, *type* declares the base type of the array. Notice that the **[ ]** does not contain a dimension. As you will see, the dimension of an array is determined later. The base type determines the data type of each element that comprises the array. Thus, the base type for the array determines what type of data the array will hold. For example, the following declares an array named **numbers** with the type "array of **int**":

```
int numbers[];
```

Although this declaration establishes the fact that **numbers** is an array variable, no array actually exists. In fact, the value of **numbers** is set to **null**, which represents an array with no value. To link **numbers** with an actual physical array of integers, you must allocate one using **new** and assign it to **numbers**. The general form of **new** as it applies to one-dimensional arrays is shown here:

array-var = new *type*[*size*];

Here, *type* specifies the type of data being allocated, *size* specifies the number of elements in the array, and *array-var* is the array variable that is linked to the array. That is, to use **new** to allocate an array, you must specify the type and number of elements to allocate. The elements in the array allocated by **new** will automatically be initialized to zero. This example allocates an array of integers and links them to **numbers**:

```
numbers = new int[100];
```

After this statement executes, **numbers** will refer to an array of 100 integers. Further, all elements in the array will be initialized to zero.

Let's review. Obtaining an array is a two-step process. First, you must declare a variable of the desired array type. Second, you must allocate the memory that will hold the array, using **new**, and assign it to the array variable. Thus, in Java all arrays are dynamically allocated.

Once you have allocated an array, it will behave like the C++ arrays with which you are familiar. For example, all array indexes start at zero and you access a specific element in the array by specifying its index within square brackets. For example, this statement assigns the value 28 to the second element of **numbers**:

```
numbers[1] = 28;
```

The next line displays the value stored at index 3.

```
System.out.println(numbers[3]);
```

Here is a program that demonstrates the preceding discussion. It creates a 100-element array and stores the square of the values from zero to 99.

```
// Demonstrate Arrays
class ArrayDemo {
  public static void main(String args[]) {
    int numbers[];
    numbers = new int[100];
    int i;

    for(i=0; i<100; i++) numbers[i] = i*i;

    for(i=0; i<100; i++)
      System.out.println(i + " squared is " + numbers[i]);
  }
}
```

It is possible to combine the declaration of the array variable with the allocation of the array itself, as shown here:

```
int numbers[] = new int[100];
```

This is the way that you will normally see it done in professionally written Java programs.

Arrays can be initialized when they are declared. The process is much the same as that used by C++. The array will automatically be created large enough to hold the number of initializers that you specify. There is no need to use **new**. For example, the following code initializes an array of integers:

```
// Demonstrate Arrays
class InitArray {
  public static void main(String args[]) {
    int numbers[] = {0, 1, 2, 3, 4, 5, 6, 7, 8, 9};
    int i;
```

```
    for(i=0; i<10; i++) System.out.println(numbers[i]);
  }
}
```

This program prints the numbers 0 through 9 on the screen.

Java prevents array boundaries from being exceeded. That is, Java provides a run-time boundary check on array operations. (In this regard, Java is fundamentally different than C/C++, which provides no run-time boundary checks.) For example, in the preceding program, Java will check the value of each index into **numbers** to make sure that it is within its range. If you try to access elements outside the range of the array an error will occur.

Multidimensional Arrays

In Java, multidimensional arrays are actually arrays of arrays. Although they are similar to multidimensional arrays in C++, there are a couple of subtle differences. To declare a multidimensional array variable, specify each additional index using another set of square brackets. For example, this declares a two-dimensional array variable called **twoD**:

```
int twoD[][] = new int[4][5];
```

This allocates a 4 × 5 array and assigns it to **twoD**. Internally this matrix is implemented as an *array* of *arrays* of **int**.

When you allocate memory for a multidimensional array, you need only specify the memory for the first (leftmost) dimension. You can allocate the remaining dimensions separately. For example, this next code allocates memory for the first dimension of **twoD** when it is declared. It allocates the second dimension manually.

```
int twoD[][] = new int[4][];
twoD[0] = new int[5];
twoD[1] = new int[5];
twoD[2] = new int[5];
twoD[3] = new int[5];
```

While there is no advantage to individually allocating the second dimension arrays in this situation, there may be in others. For example, when you allocate dimensions manually, you do not need to allocate the same number of elements for each dimension. As stated earlier, since multidimensional arrays are actually arrays of arrays, the length of each array is under your control. The following program creates a two-dimensional array in which the sizes of the second dimension are unequal:

```
// Manually allocate differing size second dimensions.
class TwoD {
```

```
    public static void main(String args[]) {
      int twoD[][] = new int[4][];
      twoD[0] = new int[1];
      twoD[1] = new int[2];
      twoD[2] = new int[3];
      twoD[3] = new int[4];

      int i, j, k = 0;

      for(i=0; i<4; i++)
        for(j=0; j<i+1; j++) {
          twoD[i][j] = k;
          k++;
        }

      for(i=0; i<4; i++) {
        for(j=0; j<i+1; j++)
          System.out.print(twoD[i][j] + " ");
        System.out.println();
      }
    }
}
```

This program produces the following output:

```
0
1 2
3 4 5
6 7 8 9
```

Frankly, the use of uneven (or, irregular) multidimensional arrays is not recommended for most applications because it runs contrary to what one expects to find when a multidimensional array is encountered. However, it can be effective in some situations. For example, if you need a very large two-dimensional array that is sparsely populated (that is, one in which not all of the elements will be used), then an irregular array might be a perfect solution.

Garbage Collection

Since objects and arrays are dynamically allocated using the **new** operator, you might be wondering how such objects are destroyed and their memory released for later reallocation. In some languages, such as C++, dynamically allocated objects must be manually released by using a **delete** operator. Java takes a different approach; it handles deallocation for you automatically. The technique that accomplishes this is called *garbage collection*. It works like this: When no references to an object exist, that object is assumed to be no longer needed and the memory occupied by the object can be reclaimed. There is no explicit need to destroy objects as in C++. Garbage collection only occurs sporadically (if at all) during the execution of your program. It will not occur simply because one or more objects exist that are no longer used. Furthermore, different Java run-time implementations will take varying approaches to garbage collection, but, for the most part, you should not have to think about it while writing your programs.

The finalize( ) Method

Sometimes an object will need to perform some action when it is destroyed. For example, if an object is holding some non-Java resource such as a file handle or window character font, then you might want to make sure these resources are freed before an object is destroyed. To handle these types of situations, Java provides a mechanism called *finalization*. Using finalization, you can define specific actions that will occur when an object is just about to be reclaimed by the garbage collector.

To add a finalizer to a class, you simply define the **finalize( )** method. The Java run-time calls that method whenever it is about to recycle an object of that class. Inside the **finalize( )** method, you will specify those actions that must be performed before an object is destroyed.

The **finalize( )** method has this general form:

```
protected void finalize( )
{
  // finalization code here
}
```

It is important to understand that **finalize( )** is only called just prior to garbage collection. It is not called when an object goes out-of-scope, for example. This means that you cannot know when—or even if—**finalize( )** will be executed. Therefore, your program should provide other means of releasing system resources, etc., used by the object. It must not rely on **finalize( )** for normal program operation.

Chapter Thirty-Six

Inheritance, Packages, and Interfaces

This chapter describes three key features of Java: inheritance, packages, and interfaces. Inheritance is implemented in Java in more or less the same way as it is in C++. Packages and interfaces have no direct parallel in C++.

Although the general mechanism of inheritance in Java is the same as it is in C++, the specifics differ. For example, Java only supports single inheritance. (That is, inheritance of multiple base classes by a single derived class is not allowed.) Related to inheritance is dynamic method dispatch, which is the mechanism by which Java achieves run-time polymorphism. Like C++, run-time polymorphism is implemented using class hierarchies.

Packages partition the class name space. Using a package, you can avoid collisions between the names of your classes and the names of classes in other packages—including third-party packages. Related to packages is the **import** statement.

An interface defines a set of methods that other classes must implement. That is, an interface specifies the form of a class but not its implementation. Java programmers use interfaces to accomplish what is often done using abstract classes and multiple inheritance in C++. In Java, a class may implement several interfaces and an interface may be implemented by several classes.

Each of these topics is examined, in turn.

Inheritance

Before beginning, it is necessary to define some terminology. What a C++ programmer calls a base class, a Java programmer calls a *superclass*. What a C++ programmer calls a derived class, a Java programmer calls a *subclass*. Of course, there is no rule that mandates the use of these terms. However, it is the way you will see inheritance written about in other Java literature.

In Java, one class inherits another by use of the keyword **extends**. The general form of a **class** declaration that inherits another **class** is shown here:

class *subclass-name* extends *superclass-name* {
  // ...
}

Here, *subclass-name* specifies the name of the inheriting class and *superclass-name* specifies the name of the class being inherited. As in C++, the subclass has access to all the members of the superclass except those specified as **private**.

The following program creates a superclass called **A** and a subclass called **B**. Notice how the keyword **extends** is used to create a subclass of **A**.

```
// A simple example of inheritance.

// Create a superclass.
class A {
  int i, j;

  void showij() {
    System.out.println("i and j: " + i + " " + j);
  }
}

// Create a subclass by extending class A.
class B extends A {
  int k;

  void showk() {
    System.out.println("k: " + k);
  }
  void sum() {
    System.out.println("i+j+k: " + (i+j+k));
  }
}

class SimpleInheritance {
```

```
  public static void main(String args[]) {
    A superOb = new A();
    B subOb = new B();

    // The superclass may be used by itself.
    superOb.i = 10;
    superOb.j = 20;
    System.out.println("Contents of superOb: ");
    superOb.showij();
    System.out.println();

    /* The subclass has access to all public members of
       its superclass. */
    subOb.i = 7;
    subOb.j = 8;
    subOb.k = 9;
    System.out.println("Contents of subOb: ");
    subOb.showij();
    subOb.showk();
    System.out.println();

    System.out.println("Sum of i, j and k in subOb:");
    subOb.sum();
  }
}
```

The output from this program is shown here:

```
Contents of superOb:
i and j: 10 20

Contents of subOb:
i and j: 7 8
k: 9

Sum of i, j and k in subOb:
i+j+k: 24
```

As the example shows, the subclass **B** includes all of the members of its superclass, **A**. This is why **subOb** may access **i** and **j** and call **showij( )**. Also, inside **sum( )**, **i** and **j** may be referred to directly, as if they were part of **B**.

Even though **A** is a superclass for **B**, it is also a completely independent, stand-alone class. Being a superclass for some subclass does not necessarily mean that the superclass cannot be used by itself. Further, a subclass can be a superclass for another subclass.

You may only specify one superclass for any subclass that you create. Java does not support the inheritance of multiple superclasses into a single subclass. (This differs from C++, in which you may inherit multiple base classes.)

When Constructors Are Called

In a class hierarchy, constructors are called in order of derivation, from superclass to subclass. (This is the same as it is for C++.) The following program illustrates this fact:

```
// Demonstrate when constructors are called.

// Create a super class.
class A {
  A() {
    System.out.println("Inside A's constructor.");
  }
}

// Create a subclass by extending class A.
class B extends A {
  B() {
    System.out.println("Inside B's constructor.");
  }
}

// Create another subclass by extending B.
class C extends B {
  C() {
    System.out.println("Inside C's constructor.");
  }
}

class CallingCons {
  public static void main(String args[]) {
    C c = new C();
  }
}
```

The output from this program is shown here:

```
Inside A's constructor.
Inside B's constructor.
Inside C's constructor.
```

As you can see, the constructors are called in order of derivation.

Using super

Whenever a subclass needs to refer to its immediate superclass, it may do so using the keyword **super**, which has two forms. The first calls the superclass constructor. The second is used to access a member of the superclass that has been hidden by a member of a subclass.

Using super to Call Superclass Constructors

A subclass may call a constructor defined by its superclass using the following form of **super**:

super(*parameter-list*);

Here, *parameter-list* specifies any parameters needed by the constructor in the superclass. **super( )** must always be the first statement executed inside a subclass' constructor.

To see how **super( )** is used, consider the following example, which expands the **Box** class developed in the preceding chapter. Here, the class **BoxWeight** extends the class **Box** by including a fourth component called **weight**. Thus, **BoxWeight** describes a box's width, height, depth, and weight. The **BoxWeight** constructor uses **super** to call **Box**'s constructor.

```
// An example that uses super.
class Box {
  private double width;
  private double height;
  private double depth;

  // This is the constructor for Box.
  Box(double w, double h, double d) {
    width = w;
    height = h;
    depth = d;
  }

  // compute and return volume
  double volume() {
    return width * height * depth;
  }
}

/* BoxWeight extends Box.  It uses super to
   initialize its Box attributes. */
```

```
class BoxWeight extends Box {
  private double weight; // weight of box

  // initialize width, height, and depth using super()
  BoxWeight(double w, double h, double d, double m) {
    super(w, h, d); // call superclass constructor
    weight = m;
  }

  double getWeight() { return weight; }
}

class BoxWeightDemo {
  public static void main(String args[]) {
    BoxWeight mybox1 = new BoxWeight(10, 20, 15, 100);
    BoxWeight mybox2 = new BoxWeight(29, 33, 8, 60);

    // get volume of first box
    System.out.println("Volume of mybox1 is " + mybox1.volume());
    System.out.println("Its weight is " + mybox1.getWeight());

    System.out.println();

    // get volume of second box
    System.out.println("Volume of mybox2 is " + mybox2.volume());
    System.out.println("Its weight is " + mybox2.getWeight());
  }
}
```

The program produces the following output:

```
Volume of mybox1 is 3000
Its weight is 100

Volume of mybox2 is 7656
Its weight is 60
```

In the program, **BoxWeight( )** calls **super( )** with the parameters **w**, **h**, and **d**. This causes the **Box( )** constructor to be called, which initializes width, height, and depth using these values. This leaves **Box** free to make these values private because **BoxWeight** does not need access to them directly. **BoxWeight( )** only needs access to the member it adds: **weight**.

In the preceding example, **super( )** was called using three arguments since this is the form of the constructor defined by **Box( )**. In general, **super( )** can be called using any form that matches a constructor defined by the superclass. The constructor executed will be the one that has the same argument list. For example, here is an expanded implementation of **Box** and **BoxWeight** that provides constructors for the various ways that a box can be constructed. It includes a constructor for a cube (in which only one argument is passed), for duplicating a box, and for creating an uninitialized **Box** object. In each case, **super( )** is called using the appropriate arguments.

```
// A complete implementation of Box and BoxWeight.
class Box {
  private double width;
  private double height;
  private double depth;

  // construct clone of an object
  Box(Box ob) { // pass object to constructor
    width = ob.width;
    height = ob.height;
    depth = ob.depth;
  }

  // constructor used when all dimensions specified
  Box(double w, double h, double d) {
    width = w;
    height = h;
    depth = d;
  }

  // constructor used when no dimensions specified
  Box() {
    width = -1;  // use -1 to indicate
    height = -1; // an uninitialized
    depth = -1;  // box
  }

  // constructor used when cube is created
  Box(double len) {
    width = height = depth = len;
  }

  // compute and return volume
  double volume() {
    return width * height * depth;
  }
```

```
}

// BoxWeight now fully implements all constructors.
class BoxWeight extends Box {
  private double weight; // weight of box

  // construct clone of an object
  BoxWeight(BoxWeight ob) { // pass object to constructor
    super(ob);
    weight = ob.weight;
  }

  // constructor when all parameters are specified
  BoxWeight(double w, double h, double d, double m) {
    super(w, h, d); // call superclass constructor
    weight = m;
  }

  // default constructor
  BoxWeight() {
    super();
    weight = -1;
  }

  // constructor used when cube is created
  BoxWeight(double len, double m) {
    super(len);
    weight = m;
  }

  double getWeight() { return weight; }
}

class DemoSuper {
  public static void main(String args[]) {
    BoxWeight mybox1 = new BoxWeight(10, 20, 15, 34.3);
    BoxWeight mybox2 = new BoxWeight(2, 3, 4, 0.076);
    BoxWeight mybox3 = new BoxWeight(); // default
    BoxWeight mycube = new BoxWeight(3, 2);
    BoxWeight myclone = new BoxWeight(mybox1);

    System.out.println("Volume of mybox1 is " + mybox1.volume());
    System.out.println("Its weight is " + mybox1.getWeight());
```

```
    System.out.println();

    System.out.println("Volume of mybox2 is " + mybox2.volume());
    System.out.println("Its weight is " + mybox2.getWeight());
    System.out.println();

    System.out.println("Volume of mybox3 is " + mybox3.volume());
    System.out.println("Its weight is " + mybox3.getWeight());
    System.out.println();

    System.out.println("Volume of myclone is " + myclone.volume());
    System.out.println("Its weight is " + myclone.getWeight());
    System.out.println();

    System.out.println("Volume of mycube is " + mycube.volume());
    System.out.println("Its weight is " + mycube.getWeight());
    System.out.println();
  }
}
```

This program produces the following output:

```
Volume of mybox1 is 3000
Its weight is 34.3

Volume of mybox2 is 24
Its weight is 0.076

Volume of mybox3 is -1
Its weight is -1

Volume of myclone is 3000
Its weight is 34.3

Volume of mycube is 27
Its weight is 2
```

Pay special attention to this constructor in **BoxWeight( )**:

```
// construct clone of an object
BoxWeight(BoxWeight ob) { // pass object to constructor
  super(ob);
  weight = ob.weight;
}
```

Notice that **super( )** is called with an object of type **BoxWeight**—not of type **Box**. This still invokes the constructor **Box(Box ob)**. A superclass variable can be used to reference any object derived from that class. Thus, we are able to pass a **BoxWeight** object to the **Box** constructor. Of course, **Box** only has knowledge of its own members.

Before moving on, let's review the key concepts behind **super( )**. When a subclass calls **super( )**, it is calling the constructor of its immediate superclass. Thus, **super( )** always refers to the superclass immediately above the calling class. This is true even in a multileveled hierarchy. Also, **super( )** must always be the first statement executed inside a subclass constructor.

A Second Use for super

The second form of **super** acts somewhat like **this** except that it always refers to the superclass of the subclass in which it is used. (**this** in Java has the same meaning as it has in C++.) This form of **super** has the following general form:

super.*member*

Here, *member* can be either a method or an instance variable.

This form of **super** is most applicable to situations in which member names of a subclass hide members by the same name in the superclass. Consider the following simple class hierarchy:

```
// Using super to overcome name hiding.
class A {
  int i;
}

// Create a subclass by extending class A.
class B extends A {
  int i; // this i hides the i in A

  B(int a, int b) {
    super.i = a; // i in A
    i = b; // i in B
  }

  void show() {
    System.out.println("i in superclass: " + super.i);
    System.out.println("i in subclass: " + i);
  }
}

class UseSuper {
```

```
  public static void main(String args[]) {
    B subOb = new B(1, 2);

    subOb.show();
  }
}
```

This program displays the following:

```
i in superclass: 1
i in subclass: 2
```

Although the instance variable **i** in **B** hides the **i** in **A**, **super** allows access to the **i** defined in the superclass. **super** may also be used to call methods that are hidden by a subclass.

Method Overriding and Dynamic Dispatch

In C++, functions declared as **virtual** in a base class may be overridden by functions in a derived class. Java supports a similar mechanism, but the keyword **virtual** is not needed. In fact, Java does not even define the **virtual** keyword. In Java, whenever a method in a subclass has the same name and type signature (i.e., same parameter list) as a method in its superclass, then the method in the subclass overrides the method defined by the superclass. Thus, in Java, unless explicitly specified to the contrary, all methods are "virtual."

When a method is overridden in a subclass, the version of the method defined by the superclass will be hidden. This means that the subclass' version is automatically used whenever a subclass object invokes an overridden method. Consider the following:

```
// Method overriding.
class A {
  int i, j;

  A(int a, int b) {
    i = a;
    j = b;
  }

  // display i and j
  void show() {
    System.out.println("i and j: " + i + " " + j);
```

```
    }
  }

  class B extends A {
    int k;

    B(int a, int b, int c) {
      super(a, b);
      k = c;
    }

    // display k -- this overrides show() in A
    void show() {
      System.out.println("k: " + k);
    }
  }

  class Override {
    public static void main(String args[]) {
      B subOb = new B(1, 2, 3);

      subOb.show(); // this calls show() in B
    }
  }
```

The output produced by this program is shown here:

```
k: 3
```

When **show( )** is invoked on an object of type **B**, the version of **show( )** defined within **B** is used. That is, the version of **show( )** inside **B** overrides the version declared in **A**.

Dynamic Dispatch

While the example in the preceding section demonstrates the mechanics of method overriding, it does not show its power. Indeed, if there were nothing more to method overriding than a namespace convention, then it would be, at best, an interesting curiosity, but of little real value. However, this is not the case. Method overriding forms the basis for one of Java's most powerful concepts: *dynamic method dispatch*. Dynamic method dispatch is the mechanism by which a call to an overridden function is resolved at run time rather than compile time. Dynamic method dispatch is important because this is how Java implements run-time polymorphism.

Let's begin by stating an important principle: a superclass reference variable can refer to a subclass object. Java uses this fact to resolve calls to overridden methods at run time. Here is how. When an overridden method is called through a superclass reference, Java determines which version of that method to execute based upon the type of the object being referred to at the time the call occurs. Thus, this determination is made at run time. When different types of objects are referred to, different versions of an overridden method will be called. In other words, *it is the type of the object being referred to* that determines which version of an overridden method will be executed—not the type of the reference variable. Therefore, if a superclass contains a method that is overridden by a subclass, then when different types of objects are referred to through a superclass reference variable, different versions of the method are executed.

Here is an example:

```
// Use Dynamic Method Dispatch.
class A {
  int i, j;

  A(int a, int b) {
    i = a;
    j = b;
  }

  // display i and j
  void show() {
    System.out.println("i and j: " + i + " " + j);
  }
}

class B extends A {
  int k;

  B(int a, int b, int c) {
    super(a, b);
    k = c;
  }

  // display k -- this overrides show() in A
  void show() {
    super.show(); // show values in A
    System.out.println("k: " + k);
  }
}

class C extends B {
  int m;
```

```
  C(int a, int b, int c, int d) {
    super(a, b, c);
    m = d;
  }

  // display m -- this overrides show() in B
  void show() {
    super.show(); // show values in B
    System.out.println("m: " + m);
  }
}

class DynDispatch {
  public static void main(String args[]) {
    A Aob;
    B Bob = new B(1, 2, 3);
    C Cob = new C(5, 6, 7, 8);

    Aob = Bob; // refer to B object
    Aob.show(); // calls B's show()

    System.out.println();

    Aob = Cob; // refer to C object
    Cob.show(); // call's C's show()
  }
}
```

In **main( )**, the method **show( )** is called twice through the base class reference variable **Aob**. The first time, **Aob** is pointing to an object of type **B**. The second time, **Aob** is pointing to an instance of **C**. In each case, the version of **show( )** called is determined by the object being referred to. This program displays the following output:

```
i and j: 1 2
k: 3

i and j: 5 6
k: 7
m: 8
```

One other point: Inside **B** and **C**, notice how **super** is used to invoke the superclass version of **show( )**. It will always refer to the immediate superclass, even when called from within an overridden method.

Abstract Methods and Classes

As you know from your C++ experience, sometimes a virtual function defined by a base class will have no meaningful implementation. When this happens, such a function is typically made into a pure virtual function. Pure virtual functions must be overridden by a derived class. That is, since a pure virtual function has no implementation defined for it within the base class, each derived class must define one for itself. Java supports a similar feature called the *abstract method.*

An abstract method is declared using the **abstract** specifier and has no implementation defined for it. Thus, when a superclass contains an abstract method, any subclass must override the abstract method—it cannot simply use the version defined by the superclass, since it doesn't exist. To declare an abstract method, use this general form:

abstract *type name*(*parameter-list*);

As you can see, no method body is present.

Any class that contains one or more abstract methods must also be declared abstract. This is called an *abstract class*. To declare a class abstract, simply put the **abstract** keyword in front of the **class** keyword at the beginning of the class declaration.

Here is a very simple example that uses an abstract method and class:

```
// Demonstrate abstract method and class.
abstract class Square {
  abstract int square(int i); // abstract method
}

/* SqrIt must implement square.  If it doesn't a
    compile-time error will occur. */
class SqrIt extends Square {
  int square(int i) { return i*i; }
}

class AbstractDemo {
  public static void main(String args[]) {
    SqrIt ob = new SqrIt();
    System.out.println("10 squared is " + ob.square(10));
  }
}
```

As the comments indicate, since **square( )** is an abstract method, its class **Square** must also be abstract. This means that **SqrIt**, which extends **Square**, must implement

square( ). Failure to do so would prevent the program from compiling. To prove this to yourself, try removing the implementation for **square( )** in **SqrIt**.

There can be no objects of an abstract class. That is, an abstract class cannot be directly instantiated with the **new** operator. The reason for this is easy to understand. Such objects would be useless, because an abstract class is not fully defined. Also, you cannot declare abstract constructors or abstract static methods. Any subclass of an abstract class must either implement all of the abstract methods in the superclass or be itself declared **abstract**.

Using final

Java defines the keyword **final**, which has three uses. Two relate directly to inheritance. The third allows you to create named constants. All three uses are examined here.

Using final to Prevent Overriding

While method overriding is one of Java's most powerful features, there will be times when you will want to prevent it from occurring. To disallow a method from being overridden, specify **final** as a modifier at the start of its declaration. The following fragment illustrates **final**:

```
class A {
  final void meth() {
    System.out.println("This is a final method.");
  }
}

class B extends A {
  void meth() { // ERROR! Can't override.
    System.out.println("Illegal!");
  }
}
```

Because **meth( )** is declared as **final**, it cannot be overridden in **B**. If you attempt to do so, a compile-time error will result. Also, methods declared as **final** can have their code generated inline, thus avoiding the overhead of the normal call and return mechanism. (In this regard, a **final** method is similar to an **inline** function in C++.)

Using final to Prevent Inheritance

Sometimes you will want to prevent a class from being inherited. To do this, precede the class declaration with **final**. Declaring a class as **final** implicitly declares all of its methods as **final**, too. As you might expect, it is illegal to declare a class as both

abstract and **final** since an abstract class is incomplete by itself and relies upon its subclasses to provide complete implementations.

Here is an example of a **final** class:

```
final class A {
  // ...
}

// The following class is illegal.
class B extends A { // ERROR! Can't subclass A
  // ...
}
```

As the comments imply, it is illegal for **B** to inherit **A** since **A** is declared as **final**.

Using final to Create Named Constants

The third use of **final** creates the equivalent of a named constant. If you precede a variable declaration with **final**, it cannot be modified. This means that you must initialize a **final** variable when it is declared. (In this usage, **final** is similar to **const** in C/C++.) For example:

```
final int COUNT = 100;
```

Here, **COUNT** is a constant that has the value 100.

The Object Class

Before leaving the topic of inheritance, it is necessary to mention one special class defined by Java: **Object**. The reason **Object** is important is that all other classes are subclasses of it. Or, put differently, **Object** is a superclass of all other classes. This means that a reference variable of type **Object** can refer to an object of any other class. Also, since arrays are implemented as classes, a variable of type **Object** can also refer to any array.

Packages

Packages allow you to partition the class name space. Packages are especially important when you create class libraries. They prevent the names of the classes defined by a library from colliding with other names used in a program. Packages also provide a way to limit the visibility of components in a class library. You can define a package so that only a subset of its classes are accessible to software outside that package. You can also define a class so that only a subset of its members are accessible to software outside that package.

Because a package partitions the name space, you might think that it is somewhat similar to a C++ **namespace**. However, except in the most general way, this is false. As you will see, both the syntax and semantics of packages differ fundamentally from those of a **namespace**.

Defining a Package

To create a package is quite easy: simply include a **package** command as the first statement in a Java source file. Any classes declared within that file will belong to the specified package. The **package** statement defines a name space in which classes are stored. If you omit the **package** statement, the class names are put into the default package, which has no name. (This is why we haven't had to worry about packages before now.) While the default package is fine for short, sample programs, it is inadequate for real applications. Most of the time, you will define a package for your code.

Here is the general form of the **package** statement:

package *pkg;*

Here, *pkg* is the name of the package. For example, the following statement creates a package called **GraphPackage**:

```
package GraphPackage;
```

Java uses file system directories to store packages. For example, the **.class** files for any classes you declare to be part of **GraphPackage** must be saved in a directory called **GraphPackage**. The directory name must match the package name exactly.

More than one file may include the same **package** statement. The **package** statement simply specifies to which package the classes defined in a file belong. It does not exclude other classes in other files from being part of that same package. Most real-world packages are spread across many files.

You can create a hierarchy of packages. To do so, simply separate each package name from the one above it using a period. The general form of a multileveled package statement is shown here:

package *pkg1*[.*pkg2*[.*pkg3*]];

Your package hierarchy must mirror your directory hierarchy. For example, a package declared as

```
package java.awt.image;
```

needs to be stored in the **java\awt\image** directory. Be sure to choose your package names carefully. You cannot rename a package without renaming the directory in which the classes are stored.

Understanding CLASSPATH

Before looking at an example that uses a package, a short but important discussion of the **CLASSPATH** environmental variable is required. The **CLASSPATH** environmental variable contains an ordered list of paths that the Java compiler and run-time system search for packages and classes.

For example, assume that **CLASSPATH** has been set to

```
.;c:\bc5\java\classes\java;c:\bc5\java\mystuff
```

and the compiler needs to find a class named **airplane.instrument.Altimeter**. The search for **Altimeter.class** proceeds in the following sequence:

.\airplane\instrument\Altimeter.class

\bc5\java\classes\java\airplane\instrument\Altimeter.class

\bc5\java\mystuff\airplane\instrument\Altimeter.class

The compiler uses the first instance of the file it locates. If the file is in none of these locations, you will receive an error message.

The reason **CLASSPATH** is important is that if it is not set correctly, then when you try to run a program that uses a package, you will receive an error. For simple test programs, you don't always need to change the setting of **CLASSPATH.** Usually, you can simply make sure that you execute your program from one directory above the directory that holds your package. (We will look at an example in which this approach can be used shortly.) However, for real applications, you must store your packages in a path defined in **CLASSPATH**.

NOTE: For further instructions relating to CLASSPATH, see Borland's online help information.

A Short Package Example

Keeping the preceding discussion of **CLASSPATH** in mind, here is a simple package that you can try:

```
// A simple package.
package MyPack;

class Balance {
  String name;
```

```
  double bal;

  Balance(String n, double b) {
    name = n;
    bal = b;
  }

  void show() {
    if(bal<0)
      System.out.print("--> ");
    System.out.println(name + ": $" + bal);
  }
}

class AccountBalance {
  public static void main(String args[]) {
    Balance current[] = new Balance[3];

    current[0] = new Balance("K. J. Fielding", 123.23);
    current[1] = new Balance("Will Tell", 157.02);
    current[2] = new Balance("Tom Jackson", -12.33);

    for(int i=0; i<3; i++) current[i].show();
  }
}
```

Call this file **MyPack.java.** Next, create a directory called **MyPack**, which should be an immediate subdirectory of your current working directory. Next, compile the file. Then, put the resulting **.class** files into the **MyPack** directory. Finally, try executing the **AccountBalance** class using this command line:

```
java MyPack.AccountBalance
```

Remember, you will need to be in the directory directly above **MyPack** when you execute this command or have your **CLASSPATH** environmental variable set appropriately.

As explained, **AccountBalance** is now part of the package **MyPack**. This means that it cannot be executed by itself. That is, you cannot use this command line:

```
java AccountBalance
```

AccountBalance must be qualified with its package name.

Importing Packages

There are two ways to refer to a class that is contained within another package. First, you can specify its full name, which includes its package. For example, assume a class called **Altimeter** that is part of the **instrument** package, which, in turn, is part of the **airplane** package. To extend **Altimeter**, you would use something like this:

```
class B747Altimeter extends airplane.instrument.Altimeter {
...
}
```

As you can guess, it can become tedious to type the long version of a class name with the complete package hierarchy. It can also make the source code harder to read. This leads to the second way to access code in another package: the **import** statement.

The **import** statement has this general form:

import *package-name.class-name*;

Here, *package-name* is the name of the package and *class-name* is the name of the class to which you wish to have access. The **import** statement causes the compiler to bring the specified class into the current name space. To import all classes in a package, use a * for the *class-name.* Once a class has been imported, you may refer to it directly without using its fully qualified package name.

For example, here, the entire contents of the **airplane.instrument** are imported:

```
import airplane.instrument.*;
...
class B747Altimeter extends Altimeter {
...
}
```

Now, **Altimeter** can be referred to directly.

When you import an entire package using the * format, the **import** statement notifies the compiler that it should search the package whenever it encounters a name that is not defined by the current program. However, if you know that you only need one or two classes from a package, you can simply import those classes. For example, to use **airplane.instrument**, you can also use the following **import** statement:

```
import airplane.instrument.Altimeter;
...
class B747Altimeter extends Altimeter {
...
}
```

This format explicitly names the class to be imported. Importing only the classes you need may save you some time when you are compiling a program that uses packages that contain many classes, because it is not necessary for the compiler to search through the entire package to find a matching class. However, usually the time differential is quite small and it is simply easier to import the entire package.

The Standard Packages

Perhaps the most common use of **import** is to gain access to Java's standard classes. Like C++, Java defines an extensive set of standard classes that you may use in your programs. These standard classes are contained in the packages shown here:

Package	Purpose
java.applet	Support for applets
java.awt	Support for Windows-based I/O
java.awt.image	Support for imaging
java.awt.peer	A support class for java.awt
java.io	Console and file I/O
java.lang	Basic language support
java.util	General utilities, such as vectors and stacks
java.net	Networking support

The package most frequently used by a Java program is **java.lang**. However, you don't have to import it. Since it is fundamental to all Java programs, it is automatically imported into every source file.

Access Control and Packages

In general, Java implements access control in more or less the same way as C++, using the keywords **public**, **private**, and **protected**. However, Java's access control mechanism is more complicated than C++ for two reasons. First, Java defines a default access level that is distinct from **public**. Second, classes and packages, which both provide access control, interact with each other. Thus, Java provides these four categories of visibility for class members relative to packages:

- Subclasses in the same package
- Non-subclasses in the same package
- Subclasses in different packages
- Classes that are neither in the same package nor subclasses

Table 36-1 shows how the various access levels apply to the various elements of Java. The columns indicate the different access specifiers that may be applied to a member of a class. The rows specify the places from which each type of member can or cannot be accessed. The entry at the intersection of that row and column indicates if access is permitted.

In general, **public** grants access to anyone. **private** denies access to everyone except code within that same class. **protected** provides access to all code in the same package and to subclasses in different packages. The default access restricts access to the same package.

Table 36-1 applies only to members of classes. For classes, there are only two possible access levels: default and public. When a class is declared as **public**, it is accessible by any other code. If a class has default access, then it may only be used by other code within its same package.

Interfaces

The **interface** is one of Java's most exciting features. It allows you to fully abstract a class's interface from its implementation. That is, using **interface**, you can specify what a class must do but not how it does it. Interfaces are syntactically similar to classes, but their methods are declared without any body. Thus, in many ways an **interface** is similar to an abstract class.

	private member	**default member**	**protected member**	**public member**
Visible within same class	Yes	Yes	Yes	Yes
Visible within same package by subclass	No	Yes	Yes	Yes
Visible within same package by non-subclass	No	Yes	Yes	Yes
Visible within different package by subclass	No	No	Yes	Yes
Visible within different package by non-subclass	No	No	No	Yes

Table 36-1. *Class Member Access*

Once defined, any number of classes may implement an **interface**. Also, one class may implement any number of interfaces. To implement an interface, a class must create the complete set of methods defined by the interface. However, each class is free to determine the details of its own implementation. By providing **interface**, Java allows you to fully utilize the "one interface, multiple methods" aspect of polymorphism.

Defining an Interface

An interface is defined much like a class. The general form of an interface is shown here:

```
access interface name {
   return-type method-name1(parameter-list);
   return-type method-name2(parameter-list);
   type final-varname1 = value;
   type final-varname2 = value;
   // ...
   return-type method-nameN(parameter-list);
   type final-varnameN = value;
}
```

Here, *access* is either **public** or not used. When no access specifier is included, then default access results and the interface is only available to other members of the package in which it is declared. When it is declared as **public**, the interface may be used by any other code. *name* is the name of the interface and may be any valid identifier. Notice that the methods that are declared have no bodies. They end with a semicolon after the parameter list. They are essentially abstract methods; there can be no default implementation of any method specified within an interface. Each class that implements an interface must implement all of the methods. Variables may be declared inside of interface declarations. They are implicitly **final** and **static**, meaning they cannot be changed by the implementing class. They must also be initialized with a constant value. All methods and variables are implicitly public if the interface itself is declared as **public**.

To summarize, when you define an interface, you must specify the prototypes to all methods that are required by the interface. Each class that implements the interface must create actual methods for each prototype contained in the interface.

Implementing an Interface

To implement an interface, you must include an **implements** clause in the implementing class and then implement each method defined by the interface. The general form of a class that includes the **implements** clause looks like this:

access class *classname* implements *interface* {
  // *class-body*
}

Here, *access* is either **public** or not used. If a class implements more than one interface, the interfaces are separated with a comma. If a class implements two interfaces that declare the same method, then the same method will be used by clients of either interface. The methods that implement an interface must be declared **public**. Also, the type signature of the implementing method must match exactly the type signature specified in the **interface** definition.

Here is a short example. The **Series** interface defines the form of a number generator. The **nextNumber( )** method returns the next number in the series. **setStart( )** defines the starting point for the series. However, precisely what kind of series will be generated and how the starting point is set is not determined by the interface. This is left to each implementing class.

```
// A simple interface example.
interface Series {
  int nextNumber(); // get next number in series
  void setStart(int i); // set starting point
}

class MySeries implements Series {
  int num;

  public int nextNumber() {
    num += 2;
    return num;
  }

  public void setStart(int i) { num = i; }
}

class IFaceDemo {
  public static void main(String args[]) {
    MySeries ob = new MySeries();

    ob.setStart(10);

    for(int i=0; i<10; i++)
      System.out.println(ob.nextNumber() + " ");
  }
}
```

This program prints the numbers 12 through 30. Here, **MySeries** implements the **Series** interface. Each time **nextNumber( )** is called, it increases **num** by 2 and returns the result. However, another class could have implemented **nextNumber( )** in a completely different way. The point is that how an interface is implemented is your concern. The interface itself only defines what must be implemented.

Interfaces Can Be Extended

One interface can inherit another using the keyword **extends**. The syntax is the same as for inheriting classes. When a class implements an interface that inherits another interface, it must provide implementations for all methods defined within the interface inheritance chain.

Accessing Implementations Through Interface References

You can declare variables as object references that use an interface rather than a class type. Any instance of any class that implements the declared interface may be stored in such a variable. When you call a method through one of these references, the correct version will be called based on the actual instance of the interface being referred to. This is one of the key features of interfaces. The method to be executed is looked up dynamically at run time. This is another way that Java supports run-time polymorphism, and it is similar to using a superclass reference to access a subclass object, as described earlier. The following example makes use of this feature.

Applying Interfaces

To understand the power of interfaces, let's look at a practical example. There are many ways to implement a stack. For example, the stack can be of a fixed size or it can be "growable." The stack can also be held in an array, a linked list, a binary tree, etc. No matter how the stack is implemented, the interface to the stack remains the same. That is, the methods **push( )** and **pop( )** define the interface to the stack independently of the details of the implementation. Because the interface to a stack is separate from its implementation, it is easy to define a stack interface, leaving it to each implementation to define the specifics. Let's look at two examples.

First, here is the interface that defines an integer stack. Put this in a file called **IntStack.java**. This interface will be used by both stack implementations.

```
// Define an integer stack interface.
interface IntStack {
  void push(int item); // store an item
  int pop(); // retrieve an item
}
```

The following program creates a class called **FixedStack** that implements a fixed-length version of an integer stack:

```
// An implementation of IntStack that uses fixed storage.
class FixedStack implements IntStack {
  private int stck[];
  private int tos;

  // allocate and initialize stack
  FixedStack(int size) {
    stck = new int[size];
    tos = -1;
  }

  // Push an item onto the stack.
  public void push(int item) {
    if(tos==stck.length-1) // use length member
      System.out.println("Stack is full.");
    else
      stck[++tos] = item;
  }

  // Pop an item from the stack.
  public int pop() {
    if(tos < 0) {
      System.out.println("Stack underflow.");
      return 0;
    }
    else
      return stck[tos--];
  }
}

class IFTest {
  public static void main(String args[]) {
    FixedStack mystack1 = new FixedStack(5);
    FixedStack mystack2 = new FixedStack(8);

    // push some numbers onto the stack
    for(int i=0; i<5; i++) mystack1.push(i);
    for(int i=0; i<8; i++) mystack2.push(i);
```

```
    // pop those numbers off the stack
    System.out.println("Stack in mystack1:");
    for(int i=0; i<5; i++)
       System.out.println(mystack1.pop());

    System.out.println("Stack in mystack2:");
    for(int i=0; i<8; i++)
       System.out.println(mystack2.pop());
  }
}
```

Using the same **interface** definition, here is another implementation of **IntStack** that creates a dynamic stack. In this implementation, each stack is constructed with an initial length. If this initial length is exceeded, then the stack is increased in size. Each time more room is needed, the length of the stack is doubled.

```
// Implement a "growable" stack.
class DynStack implements IntStack {
  private int stck[];
  private int tos;

  // allocate and initialize stack
  DynStack(int size) {
    stck = new int[size];
    tos = -1;
  }

  // Push an item onto the stack.
  public void push(int item) {
    // if stack is full, allocate a larger stack
    if(tos==stck.length-1) {
      int temp[] = new int[stck.length * 2]; // double size
      for(int i=0; i<stck.length; i++) temp[i] = stck[i];
      stck = temp;
      stck[++tos] = item;
    }
    else
      stck[++tos] = item;
  }

  // Pop an item from the stack.
  public int pop() {
    if(tos < 0) {
      System.out.println("Stack underflow.");
```

```
      return 0;
    }
    else
      return stck[tos--];
  }
}

class IFTest2 {
  public static void main(String args[]) {
    DynStack mystack1 = new DynStack(5);
    DynStack mystack2 = new DynStack(8);

    // these loops cause each stack to grow
    for(int i=0; i<12; i++) mystack1.push(i);
    for(int i=0; i<20; i++) mystack2.push(i);

    System.out.println("Stack in mystack1:");
    for(int i=0; i<12; i++)
       System.out.println(mystack1.pop());

    System.out.println("Stack in mystack2:");
    for(int i=0; i<20; i++)
       System.out.println(mystack2.pop());
  }
}
```

The following class uses both the **FixedStack** and **DynStack** implementations. It does so through an interface reference. This means that calls to **push( )** and **pop( )** are resolved at run time rather than compile time.

```
/* Create an interface variable and
   access stacks through it.
*/
class IFTest3 {
  public static void main(String args[]) {
    IntStack mystack; // create an interface reference variable
    DynStack ds = new DynStack(5);
    FixedStack fs = new FixedStack(8);

    mystack = ds; // load dynamic stack
    // push some numbers onto the stack
    for(int i=0; i<12; i++) mystack.push(i);

    mystack = fs; // load fixed stack
```

```
        for(int i=0; i<8; i++) mystack.push(i);

        mystack = ds;
        System.out.println("Values in dynamic stack:");
        for(int i=0; i<12; i++)
            System.out.println(mystack.pop());

        mystack = fs;
        System.out.println("Values in fixed stack:");
        for(int i=0; i<8; i++)
            System.out.println(mystack.pop());
    }
}
```

In the program, **mystack** is a reference to the **IntStack** interface. Thus, when it refers to **ds**, it uses the versions of **push( )** and **pop( )** defined by the **DynStack** implementation. When it refers to **fs**, it uses the versions of **push( )** and **pop( )** defined by **FixedStack**. As explained, these determinations are made at run time. Accessing multiple implementations of an interface through an interface reference variable is the most powerful way that Java achieves run-time polymorphism.

Because of the constraints of space, only the most important and commonly used features of inheritance, packages, and interfaces have been described in this chapter. If you will be doing a significant amount of Java development, you will need to explore these topics further.

Chapter Thirty-Seven

Introducing Applets

The examples in the preceding two chapters have been Java applications. However, applications only constitute one class of Java programs. The other type of program is the *applet*. As explained in Chapter 35, an applet is a small Java program that is designed to be transmitted over the Internet and executed by a Web browser. Although Java is useful for writing applications, it is the applet for which Java is optimized. As you will see, applets differ from applications in several key areas.

This chapter presents an overview of applet programming. In the process, it introduces Java's largest package: the *Abstract Window Toolkit* (AWT). While it is far beyond the scope of this book to fully discuss all of the aspects related to applets or the AWT, the material in this chapter will help you get started.

A Simple Applet

Let's begin with the very simple example shown here:

```
// A very simple applet.
import java.awt.*;
import java.applet.*;

public class SimpleApplet extends Applet {
  public void paint(Graphics g) {
    g.drawString("A Simple Applet", 20, 20);
  }
}
```

The first thing you should notice is that the applet begins with two **import** statements. The first imports the Abstract Window Toolkit (AWT) classes. Applets interact with the user through the AWT, not through the console-based I/O classes. The AWT contains support for a window-based, graphical interface. The AWT is quite sophisticated and a complete description of its features easily fills several hundred pages. Fortunately, the simple applets in this chapter use only a very small portion of the AWT. The next **import** statement imports the **applet** package. This package contains the class **Applet**. Every applet that you create will be a subclass of **Applet**.

The next line in the program declares the class **SimpleApplet**. This class must be declared as **public** because it will be accessed by code outside the program.

Inside **SimpleApplet**, **paint( )** is declared. This method is defined by the AWT and must be overridden by the applet. **paint( )** is called each time the applet must redisplay its output. This situation can occur for several reasons. For example, the window in which the applet is running may be overwritten by another window and then uncovered. Or the applet window may be minimized and then restored. **paint( )** is also called when the applet begins execution. Whatever the cause, whenever the applet must redraw its output, **paint( )** is called. The **paint( )** method has one parameter of type **Graphics**. This parameter will contain the graphics context, which describes the graphics environment in which the applet is running. This context is used whenever output to the applet is required.

Inside **paint( )**, there is a call to **drawString( )**, which is a member of the **Graphics** class. This method outputs a string beginning at the specified X,Y location. Its prototype is shown here:

void drawString(String *message*, int *x*, int *y*)

Here, *message* is the string to be output beginning at *x,y*. In a Java window, the upper left corner is location 0,0. The call to **drawString( )** in the applet causes the message "A Simple Applet" to be displayed beginning at location 20,20.

Notice that the applet does not have a **main( )** method. Unlike Java programs, applets do not begin execution at **main( )**. In fact, most applets don't even have a **main( )** method. Instead, an applet begins execution when the name of its class is passed to an applet viewer or to a network browser.

Compiling and Viewing the Applet

There are two ways to compile and run a Java applet using Borland C++. First, you may use the integrated development environment (IDE). Second, you may use the command-line tools. Each way is described here.

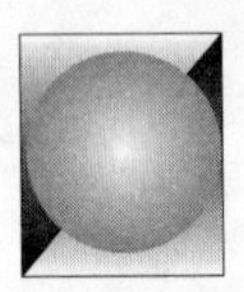

NOTE: Since Borland's Java add-on is quite new, it is possible that the exact procedure that you use to compile and run an applet will change over time. Be sure to consult your user's manual and Borland C++'s online instructions.

Using the IDE

If you are using Borland's IDE to create and test Java applets, then the easiest way to create and run an applet is to create a Java project that uses the same name as the main applet class. For example, the name of the project for the example applet should be **SimpleApplet**. The IDE will automatically create a project that has two files called **SimpleApplet.java** and **SimpleApplet.html**. Enter the source code for the applet into the **SimpleApplet.java** file.

After you have entered the source code for **SimpleApplet**, you compile in just the same way that you have been compiling Java applications. (Highlight **SimpleApplet.java**, press the right mouse button to activate the Speed menu, and then select JavaCompile.) However, running **SimpleApplet** involves a different process. In fact, there are two ways in which you can run an applet. The first way is to execute the applet within a Java-compatible Web browser, such as Netscape Navigator. The second way is to use an applet viewer, such as the **appletviewer** tool provided with the Borland Java add-on. An applet viewer executes your applet in a window. Using the applet viewer is probably the fastest and easiest way to test your applet. But let's look at each method.

To execute an applet in a Web browser, you need to write a short HTML text file that contains the appropriate APPLET tag. You will put this HTML into the **.html** file defined by your project. In this case, the file is called **SimpleApplet.html**. Here is the HTML file that will execute **SimpleApplet**:

```
<applet code="SimpleApplet" width=240 height=60>
</applet>
```

The **width** and **height** statements specify the dimensions of the display area used by the applet. After you have created this file, you can execute your browser and then load this file. Doing so causes **SimpleApplet** to be executed.

To execute **SimpleApplet** with an applet viewer, you may also execute the HTML file shown above. To do this using the IDE, just highlight **SimpleApplet.html** in the project window, press the right mouse button (which activates a Speed menu), select View from the menu, and then Select Java View. This causes the applet viewer to display your applet in a stand-alone window.

Using the Command-Line Tools

While using the IDE is a good way to develop Java applets, you might prefer using the command-line tools. To compile and run an applet from the command line, follow these steps. First, compile the applet in the same way that you compiled the applications shown in the preceding two chapters, by using **javac**. Next, write an HTML file, like that shown above, that loads the applet. Then, to execute the applet in your browser, simply load the HTML file and the applet will automatically be executed. Alternatively, you can execute the applet using the applet viewer, using the same HTML file. For example, if the HTML file is called **SimpleApplet.html**, then the following command line will run **SimpleApplet** under the applet viewer:

```
appletviewer SimpleApplet.html
```

When using the command line and the applet viewer, there is a "trick" that you can use that will speed up the edit, compile, test cycle when developing applets. Simply include a comment at the head of your Java source code file that contains the APPLET tag that loads your applet. This way you can test your compiled applet by starting the applet viewer using your Java source code file for input. Using this method, the **SimpleApplet** source file looks like this:

```
import java.awt.*;
import java.applet.*;
/*
  <applet code="SimpleApplet" width=240 height=60>
  </applet>
*/

public class SimpleApplet extends Applet {
  public void paint(Graphics g) {
    g.drawString("A Simple Applet", 20, 20);
  }
}
```

Now, using the command line, you can view the applet using the following command:

```
appletviewer SimpleApplet.java
```

The applet viewer will encounter the HTML startup code and execute your applet. In addition to speeding up development, embedding the HTML necessary to load an applet into the applet's source code also provides a secondary benefit: it documents the necessary HTML statements required by your applet. For your convenience, the HTML code necessary to load each applet is contained in a comment at the top of the example applets shown in this chapter.

The window produced by **SimpleApplet** when run using the applet viewer is shown in Figure 37-1.

Before continuing, here are the three key points that you should remember about applets:

1. Applets do not need a **main( )** method.
2. Applets must be run under an applet viewer or a Java-compatible browser.
3. User I/O is not accomplished using the Java's console I/O system. Instead, applets use the interface provided by the AWT.

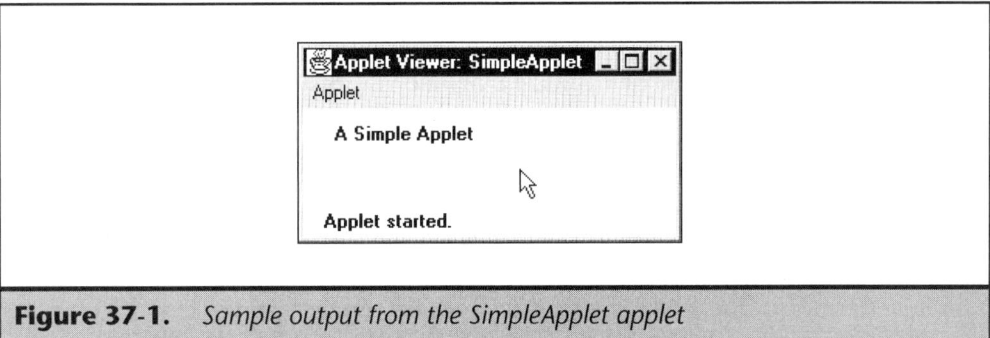

Figure 37-1. *Sample output from the SimpleApplet applet*

The Applet Class

The **Applet** class provides all necessary support for applet execution, such as starting and stopping. It also provides methods that load and display images and load and play audio clips. **Applet** extends a class defined by the AWT called **Panel**, which encapsulates a simple window. Thus, **Applet** provides all of the necessary support for window-based activities.

Applet Architecture

Since an applet is a window-based program, its architecture is different from the "normal," console-based programs used earlier. If you are familiar with Windows programming (which is described in Part 5), you will be right at home writing applets. However, be forewarned: Although conceptually similar to Windows programs, applets differ significantly in the specifics. If you are not familiar with Windows programming, then the architecture of an applet will seem strange at first. But be patient. Applet programming is really quite easy once you have mastered the basics.

The single most important aspect of an applet is that it is event-driven. In this regard, the architecture of an applet resembles that of a set of interrupt service routines. Here is how the process works. An applet waits until an event occurs. The AWT notifies the applet about an event by calling an event handler defined by the applet. Once this happens, the applet must take appropriate action and then quickly return control to the AWT. This is a crucial point. For the most part, your applet should not enter a "mode" of operation in which it maintains control for an extended period of time. Instead, it must perform specific actions in response to events and then return control to the AWT run-time system. In those situations in which your applet needs to perform a repetitive task on its own (for example, displaying a scrolling message across its window), you must start an additional thread of execution.

A second point to understand is that it is the user that initiates interaction with an applet—not the other way around. As you know, in a nonwindowed program, when the program needs input, it will prompt the user and then call some input method, such as **readLine( )**. This is not the way it works in an applet. Instead, the user interacts with the applet as he or she wants, when he or she wants. These interactions are sent to the applet as events to which the applet must respond. For example, when the user clicks a mouse inside the applet's window, a mouse-clicked event is generated. If the user presses a key while the applet's window has input focus, a keypress event is generated. Applets can contain various controls, such as pushbuttons and checkboxes. When the user interacts with one of these controls, an event is generated.

While the architecture of an applet is not as easy to understand as that of a console-based program, Java's AWT makes it as simple as possible. If you have written programs for Windows, you know how intimidating that environment can be. Fortunately, Java's AWT provides a much cleaner approach that is more quickly mastered.

An Applet Skeleton

All but the most trivial applets override a set of methods that provide the basic mechanism by which the browser or applet viewer interfaces to the applet and controls its execution. Four of these methods—**init( )**, **start( )**, **stop( )**, and **destroy( )**—are defined by **Applet**. Another, **paint( )**, is defined by the AWT **Component** class. Default implementations for all of these methods are provided. Applets do not need to override those methods that they do not use. However, only very simple applets will not need to define all of them. These five methods can be assembled into the skeleton shown here:

```
// An Applet skeleton.
import java.awt.*;
import java.applet.*;
/*
  <applet code="AppletSkel" width=300 height=100>
  </applet>
*/

public class AppletSkel extends Applet {
  // Called first.
  public void init() {
    // initialization
  }

  /* Called second, after init().  Also called whenever
     the applet is restarted. */
  public void start() {
    // start or resume execution
```

```
  }

  // Called when the applet is stopped.
  public void stop() {
    // suspends execution
  }

  /* Called when applet is terminated.  This is the last
     method executed. */
  public void destroy() {
    // perform shutdown activities
  }

  // Called when an applet's window must be restored.
  public void paint(Graphics g) {
    // redisplay contents of window
  }
}
```

Although this skeleton does not do anything, it can be compiled and run. When run using the applet viewer, the applet skeleton produces the window shown in Figure 37-2.

Order of Applet Initialization and Termination

It is important to understand the order in which the various methods shown in the skeleton are called. When an applet begins, the AWT calls the following methods in this sequence:

1. **init( )**
2. **start( )**
3. **paint( )**

When an applet is terminated, the following sequence takes place:

1. **stop( )**
2. **destroy( )**

Let's look more closely at these methods.

init( )

When an applet begins execution, **init( )** is the first method called. This is where you will perform any initializations required by your applet. It is called only once during the run time of your applet.

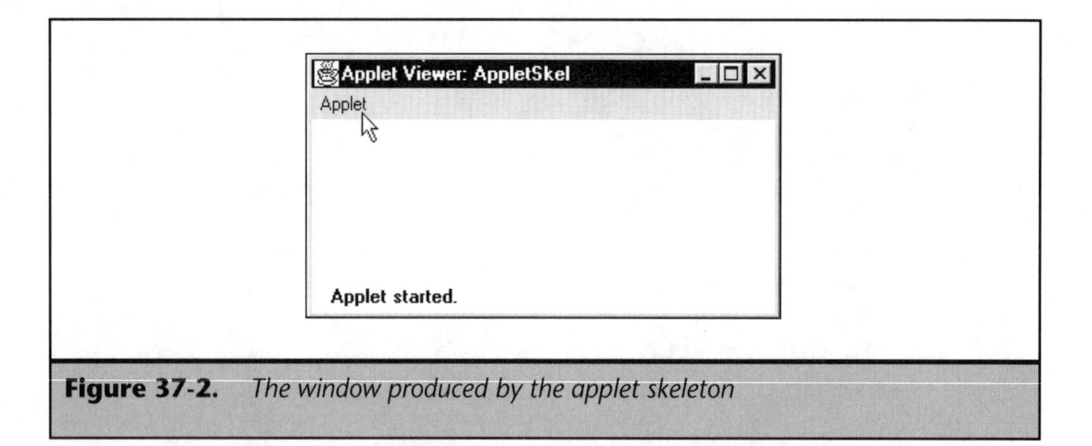

Figure 37-2. *The window produced by the applet skeleton*

start( )

The **start( )** method is used to start or restart your applet. It is called immediately after **init( )**. But, it may be invoked several times during the execution of an applet because it is called to restart an applet that has been stopped. The most common way that an applet is stopped is when the user moves on to another page. When the user returns to the page that contains the applet, **start( )** is called to restart the applet.

paint( )

The **paint( )** method is called each time your applet's output must be redrawn. **paint( )** is also called when the applet begins execution.

stop( )

The **stop( )** method may be invoked several times during the execution of an applet. For example, it is called each time a user leaves the page that contains the applet. Consider an applet that is calculating a long-running simulation and presenting results to the user. If the user leaves the page, the **stop( )** method is called. Inside **stop( )** you should take whatever steps are necessary to suspend the activity of your simulation when it is not being displayed. For example, you may wish to suspend any threads that are executing at that time. If the user returns to that page, the **start( )** method is automatically called and that code can resume the threads. This strategy avoids wasting CPU time when the applet is not visible. Also, the user might miss important results if the simulation continued when he or she was not viewing it.

destroy( )

The **destroy( )** method is invoked only once during the execution of an applet—when your applet needs to be removed from memory. This is the place at which you should perform any shutdown actions required by the applet.

The update( ) Method

In some situations, your applet may need to override another method defined by the AWT, called **update( )**. This method is called when your applet has requested that a portion of its window be redrawn. The default version of **update( )** first fills an applet with the default background color and then calls **paint( )**. In some situations, such as when you do not want the background redrawn, your applet may need to override this default behavior. For the simple examples in this chapter, the default behavior of **update( )** is fine. But sophisticated applets commonly override **update( )**.

Requesting Repainting

As a general rule, an applet writes to its window only when its **update( )** or **paint( )** methods are called by the AWT. This raises an interesting question: How can the applet, itself, cause its window to be updated when its information changes? For example, if an applet is displaying a moving banner, what mechanism does the applet use to update the window each time this banner scrolls? Remember, one of the fundamental architectural constraints imposed on an applet is that it must quickly return control to the AWT run-time system. You cannot create a loop inside **paint( )** that repeatedly scrolls the banner, for example. This would prevent control from passing back to the AWT. Given this constraint, it may seem that output to your applet's window will be difficult, at best. Fortunately, this is not the case. Whenever your applet needs to update the information displayed in its window, it simply calls **repaint( )**.

The **repaint( )** method is defined by **Applet**. It causes the AWT run-time system to execute a call to your applet's **update( )** method, which in its default implementation calls **paint( )**. Thus, for another part of your applet to output to its window, simply store the output and then call **repaint( )**. The AWT will then execute a call to **paint( )**, which can display the stored information. For example, if part of your applet needs to output a string, it can store this string in a **String** variable and then call **repaint( )**. Inside **paint( )**, you will output the string using **drawString( )**. The **repaint( )** method has several forms. Its two most common are described here.

The simplest version of **repaint( )** is:

void repaint( )

This version causes the entire window to be repainted. The next version specifies a region that will be repainted:

void repaint(int *left*, int *top*, int *width*, int *height*)

Here, the coordinates of the upper left corner of the region are specified by *left* and *top* and the width and height of the region are passed in *width* and *height*. These dimensions are specified in pixels. By specifying a region to repaint, you save time. Window updates are costly in terms of time. If you only need to update a small portion of the window, it is more efficient to repaint only that region.

You will see examples that use **repaint( )** later in this chapter.

Using the Status Window

In addition to displaying information in its window, an applet can also output a message to the status window of the browser or applet viewer on which it is running. To do so, call **showStatus( )** with the string that you want displayed. The status window is a good place to give the user feedback about what is occurring in the applet, suggest options, or possibly report some types of errors. The status window also makes an excellent debugging aid because it gives you an easy way to output information about your applet.

The following applet demonstrates **showStatus( )**:

```
// Using the Status Window.
import java.awt.*;
import java.applet.*;
/*
  <applet code="StatusWindow" width=300 height=50>
  </applet>
*/

public class StatusWindow extends Applet{
  public void paint(Graphics g) {
    g.drawString("This is in the applet window.", 10, 20);
    showStatus("This is shown in the status window.");
  }
}
```

This applet produces the window shown in Figure 37-3.

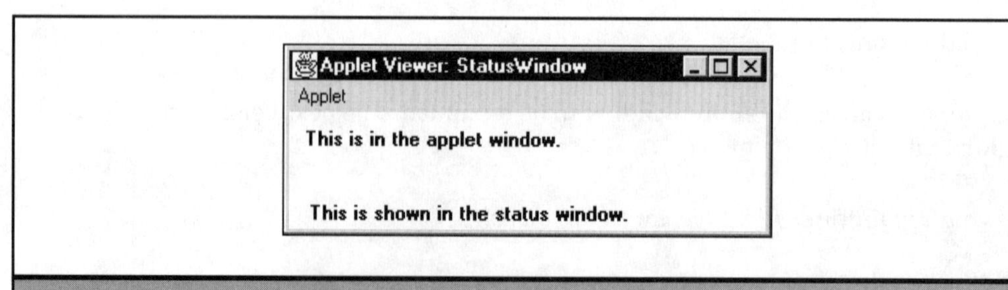

Figure 37-3. *Sample output from the StatusWindow applet*

Handling Events

As explained earlier, applets are event-driven programs. Most events to which your applet will respond are generated by the user. These events are passed to your applet in a variety of different ways, with the specific method depending upon the actual event. There are several types of events. Here, you will see how to handle two of the most common: those generated by the mouse and the keyboard.

The Event Class

All events are encapsulated within an **Event** object. The **Event** class is part of the AWT. It defines several variables that describe the event. For example, the location of the mouse when a mouse event occurs is stored in the variables **x** and **y**. When a key is pressed, the key is stored in the **key** variable. **Event** also defines several methods and constants. Although the information contained in an **Event** object is always available to your program when an event occurs, for many events you will not need to access it directly. This is because the AWT automatically routes mouse and keyboard events to a set of predefined methods that your applet will override.

Processing Mouse Events

The methods that process mouse events are shown in Table 37-1. The **Applet** class inherits these methods from the **Component** class in the AWT. These methods can be overridden by your applet. When doing so, the method must return **true** if it handles the event. If it does not handle the event, then it must return **false**. This causes the event to be passed on to the event handler of a parent window, should one exist. Generally, if you are overriding an event handler, you should handle the event and return **true**. The two most important methods are **mouseDown( )** and **mouseUp( )**. The **mouseDown( )** handler is called whenever any mouse button is pressed. The **mouseUp( )** handler is called whenever any mouse button is released. Java does not distinguish between mouse buttons. This is because not all systems have the same number of mouse buttons. In essence, Java is designed for the lowest common denominator: a one-button mouse.

Here is an applet that demonstrates the mouse event handlers. It displays the current coordinates of the mouse in the applet's status window. Each time a button is pressed, the word "Down" is displayed at the location of the mouse pointer. Each time the button is released, the word "Up" is shown. When dragging the mouse, a "*" is shown that tracks with the mouse pointer as it is dragged. Notice that the two variables, **mouseX** and **mouseY**, store the location of the mouse when a button down, button up, or dragging event occurs. These coordinates are then used by **paint( )** to display output at the point of these occurrences. Also, notice that the program uses **repaint( )** to update the window each time an event occurs.

Method	Description
boolean mouseDown(Event *evtObj*, int *x*, int *y*)	Called when a mouse button is pressed. The event object that describes the event is passed in *evtObj*. The coordinates of the mouse pointer at the time the event was generated are passed in *x* and *y*. This method must return **true** if it handles the event.
boolean mouseDrag(Event *evtObj*, int *x*, int *y*)	Called when the mouse is moved when a button is pressed. The event object that describes the event is passed in *evtObj*. The coordinates of the mouse pointer at the time the event was generated are passed in *x* and *y*. This method must return **true** if it handles the event. Mouse drag events continue to occur as long as the mouse is being moved within the window and a button is pressed.
boolean mouseEnter(Event *evtObj*, int *x*, int *y*)	Called when the mouse moves into the window. The event object that describes the event is passed in *evtObj*. The coordinates of the mouse pointer at the time the event was generated are passed in *x* and *y*. This method must return **true** if it handles the event.
boolean mouseExit(Event *evtObj*, int *x*, int *y*)	Called when the mouse moves out of the window. The event object that describes the event is passed in *evtObj*. The coordinates of the mouse pointer at the time the event was generated are passed in *x* and *y*. This method must return **true** if it handles the event.
boolean mouseMove(Event *evtObj*, int *x*, int *y*)	Called when the mouse is moved. The event object that describes the event is passed in *evtObj*. The coordinates of the mouse pointer at the time the event was generated are passed in *x* and *y*. This method must return **true** if it handles the event. Mouse move events continue to occur as long as the mouse is being moved within the window and no button is pressed.
boolean mouseUp(Event *evtObj*, int *x*, int *y*)	Called when a mouse button is released. The event object that describes the event is passed in *evtObj*. The coordinates of the mouse pointer at the time the event was generated are passed in *x* and *y*. This method must return **true** if it handles the event.

Table 37-1. *Mouse Event Handlers*

```
// Demonstrate the mouse event handlers.
import java.awt.*;
import java.applet.*;
/*
  <applet code="MouseEvents" width=300 height=100>
  </applet>
*/

public class MouseEvents extends Applet{
  String msg = "";
  int mouseX = 0, mouseY = 0; // coordinates of mouse

  // Handle button press.
  public boolean mouseDown(Event evtObj, int x, int y) {
    // save coordinates
    mouseX = x;
    mouseY = y;
    msg = "Down";
    repaint();

    return true;
  }

  // Handle button release.
  public boolean mouseUp(Event evtObj, int x, int y) {
    // save coordinates
    mouseX = x;
    mouseY = y;
    msg = "Up";
    repaint();

    return true;
  }

  // Handle mouse move.
  public boolean mouseMove(Event evtObj, int x, int y) {
    // save coordinates
    showStatus("Moving mouse at " + x + ", " + y);

    return true;
  }

  // Handle mouse drag.
```

```
  public boolean mouseDrag(Event evtObj, int x, int y) {
    // save coordinates
    mouseX = x;
    mouseY = y;
    msg = "*";
    showStatus("Dragging mouse at " + x + ", " + y);
    repaint();

    return true;
  }

  // Handle mouse enter.
  public boolean mouseEnter(Event evtObj, int x, int y) {
    // save coordinates
    mouseX = 0;
    mouseY = 10;
    msg = "Mouse just entered.";
    repaint();

    return true;
  }

  // Handle mouse exit.
  public boolean mouseExit(Event evtObj, int x, int y) {
    // save coordinates
    mouseX = 0;
    mouseY = 10;
    msg = "Mouse just left.";
    repaint();

    return true;
  }

  // Display msg in applet window at current X,Y location.
  public void paint(Graphics g) {
    g.drawString(msg, mouseX, mouseY);
  }
}
```

Sample output produced when this applet is run is shown in Figure 37-4.

One last thing: the **MouseEvent** applet makes use of a Java **String** object to hold the message that is displayed each time the window is repainted. As you will see when you learn more about Java, the **String** type provides both a flexible and powerful way of handling strings.

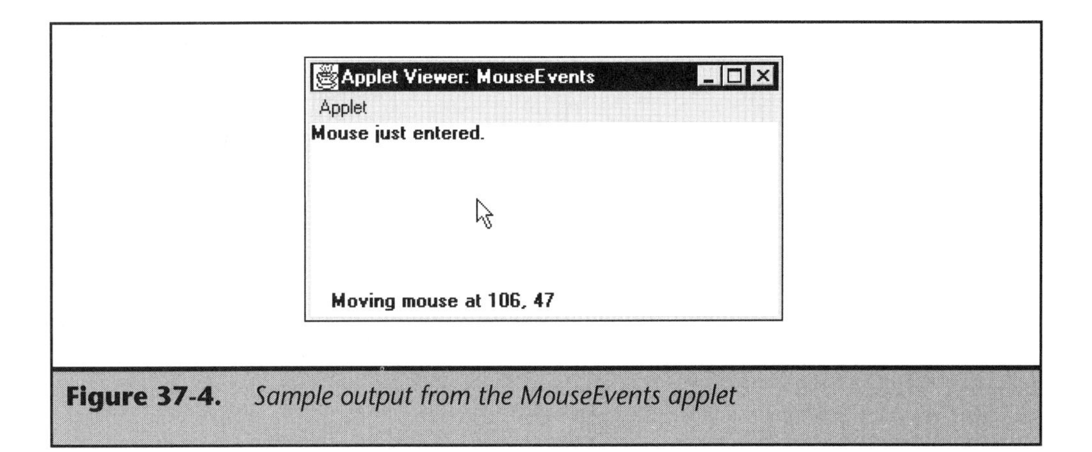

Figure 37-4. *Sample output from the MouseEvents applet*

Handling Keyboard Events

If the user presses a key when your applet has input focus, a keyboard event is generated. Keyboard events are handled by the **keyDown( )** and **keyUp( )** methods, shown here:

boolean keyDown(Event *evtObj*, int *key*)

boolean keyUp(Event *evtObj*, int *key*)

Here, *evtObj* is the object that describes the event and *key* contains the key that was pressed. For key values corresponding to letters, digits, and punctuation, the value contained in *key* can be cast into a **char**. As with the mouse handlers, when overriding these methods, they must return **true** if your applet handles the event, and **false** otherwise.

Here is a simple program that echoes keystrokes to the applet's window. The Status window shows the pressed/released status of each key.

```
// Demonstrate a keyboard event handler.
import java.awt.*;
import java.applet.*;
/*
  <applet code="SimpleKey" width=300 height=100>
  </applet>
*/

public class SimpleKey extends Applet{
  String msg = "";
```

```
  // Handle key press events.
  public boolean keyDown(Event evtObj, int key) {
    msg += (char) key;
    repaint();
    showStatus("Key Down");

    return true;
  }

  // Handle key release events.
  public boolean keyUp(Event evtObj, int key) {
    showStatus("Key Up");

    return true;
  }

  // Display keystrokes.
  public void paint(Graphics g) {
    g.drawString(msg, 10, 20);
  }
}
```

Sample output produced when this applet is run is shown in Figure 37-5.

More Events

While mouse and keyboard events are probably the most common, applets can generate several other types of events. For example, when an applet contains a control,

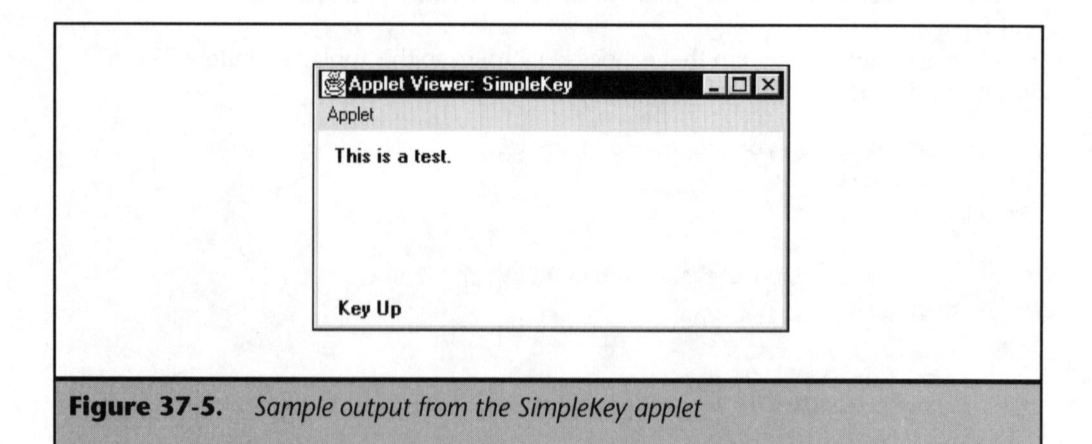

Figure 37-5. *Sample output from the SimpleKey applet*

such as a pushbutton or scrollbar, user interactions with that control are sent to your applet as an event. The same is true for menus. When a user selects from a menu, an event is generated that must be processed by the applet. In many applets, event processing constitutes a majority of the applet's code. Frankly, event handling is fundamental to successful applet programming.

Things to Explore

While this chapter has explained the basics of applets, it only scratches the surface of what you need to know in order to write effective ones. Here are a few of the features used by applets that you will need to explore:

- Controls, such as pushbuttons, checkboxes, and scrollbars
- Text fonts
- Graphics
- Network interfacing

Applets present an intriguing challenge to the programmer because they must be compact, yet still be useful. Fortunately, they are as enjoyable to write as they are demanding.

Learning More About Java

Java is a rich programming environment—easily as varied and complex as C and C++. If Java programming is in your future, you will need to take some time to learn more about it. However, it will be time well spent. Java is the C++ frontier.

Index

&
- bitwise operator, 37, 38
- menu shortcut key, 947
- pointer operator, 41-43, 134-136, 698
- reference parameter, 693, 694

&&, 35-36, 1027

< >, 793

<, 35, 36

<<
- left shift operator, 37, 39-40
- output operator, 623-624, 632, 742, 743-746

<=, 35, 36

>, 35, 36

>=, 35, 36

>>
- input operator, 624, 632, 742, 743, 746-748
- right shift operator, 37, 39-40

>>>, 1018, 1027

*
- multiplication operator, 32, 33
- pointer operator, 41-43, 134-136, 694, 698
- printf( ) placeholder, 198

|, 37, 38

||, 35, 36, 1027

^
- bitwise operator, 37, 38, 39
- used in scanset, 203

:, 626

::, 627, 840

, (comma operator), 44

{ }, 6
. (dot operator), 44-45, 158, 170, 627, 669
.* (pointer-to-member operator), 831-833
!, 35, 36
!=, 35, 36
=, 28
==, 35, 36
-, 32, 33
–> (arrow operator), 44-45, 168, 170, 669
–>* (pointer-to-member operator), 831-833
—, 33-34, 685, 687
( ), 45, 48-49
%, 32, 33
+, 32, 33
++, 32, 33-34, 685-687
#
  preprocessor directive, 225
  preprocessor operator, 240
  printf( ) modifier, 198
##, preprocessor operator, 240-241
? ternary operator, 41, 51, 55-57, 684
; (semicolon), 156, 947
/, 32, 33
/* */, 243
/** */, 1018
//, 624
[ ], 45, 702-705
~, 37, 39-41, 637

A

abort( ), 186, 485-486, 796
abs( ), 574
absread( ), 377-378
abstract type modifier, 1053
Abstract Window Toolkit (AWT), 1069, 1070, 1074
abswrite( ), 377-378
Accelerator keys, 952-957
ACCELERATORS resource statement, 953
Access
  declaration (C++), 838-839
  modifiers (C), 17
  specifiers in C++, 712-717
  specifiers in Java, 1018, 1028-1029, 1060-1061
access( ), 254
acos( ), 356
acosl( ), 356
Addressing
  32-bit and 16-bit, 897
  flat, 898
Algorithms, 843, 844
alloca( ), 447-448
alloc.h header file, 444
allocmem( ), 448
AND
  & bitwise operator, 37, 38
  && Java short-circuit, 1027
  && logical operator, 35, 36
anon_struct directive, 237
ANSI
  C standard, 1, 3
  C++ draft standard, 1, 619-620
API (Application Programming Interface)
  Java, 1018
  Windows, 892, 894, 900-901
APIENTRY calling convention, 902
AppendMenu( ), 958, 966
Applet, 1019, 1069-1085
  architecture, 1073-1074

compiling and viewing, 1070-1073
initialization and termination, 1075-1076
I/O, 1070, 1072
window, requesting repaint of, 1077-1078
Applet class, 1070, 1073
applet package, 1070
APPLET tag, HTML, 1071
arc( ), 496-497
arccoordstype structure, 510
argc, 88, 91-93
argsused directive, 236
Arguments, function
arrays as, 84-88
and call by reference, 82, 83-84, 693
and call by value, 82, 692
default, 650-654, 678-679
to main( ), 88-93
variable number of, 97
argv, 88-93, 147
Arithmetic operators, 32, 35
precedence of, 35
Array(s), 109-132
access with pointers, 121-122, 143-144
bounds checking on, 4, 110
of characters, pointers to, 144-146
dynamically allocated, 122-126, 815
to functions, passing, 84-88, 111-112, 116, 120
generating pointer to, 110-111
indexing versus pointer arithmetic, 121, 143-144
initialization, 126-128
in Java, 1034-1037
multidimensional, 119-120
of objects, 664-668
of pointers, 104-105, 146-147
single dimension, 109-110
of strings, 118-119
of structures, 159-166
within structures, 172
two-dimensional, 114-118
unsized, 128
Array-based I/O (C++), 771-783
classes, 771
creating an input stream for, 774-775
creating an input/output stream for, 776-777
creating an output stream for, 772-774
custom extractors and inserters and, 780-782
formatting, uses for, 783
manipulators and, 779
random access, 777-778
using dynamic arrays and, 778-779
using ios member functions with, 775-776
Arrow (–>) operator, 44-45, 168, 170, 669
asctime( ), 379
asin( ), 356-357
asinl( ), 356-357
asm, 829-830
Assembly language, 4
C used in place of, 6-7
in program using asm, embedding, 829-830
assert( ), 574-575
assert.h header file, 574
Assignment
functions used in, 696

multiple, 28
object, 664
pointer, 123, 136-137
shorthand notation for, 49
statements, 28-31
structure, 158-159
type conversion in, 29-30
atan( ), 357-358
atanl( ), 357-358
atan2( ), 358
atan2l( ), 358
atexit( ), 486
atof( ), 575-576
atoi( ), 89, 576
atol( ), 577
_atold( ), 575-576
ATOM data type, 911
auto keyword, 19, 22

B

Background color (WIndows 95), creating, 910
bad_alloc, 814
bar( ), 497-498
bar3d( ), 497-498
Base class
access control, 714-717
constructors, passing parameters to, 722-724
definition of, 632
general form for inheriting, 714
pointers to derived class objects, 724-726
virtual, 824-828
bdos( ), 380
bdosptr( ), 380
before( ), 807
BeginPaint( ), 930-931
Binary code, 7
BIOS interfacing functions, 375, 377
bioscom( ), 380-383
biosdisk( ), 384
_bios_disk( ), 384-385
biosequip( ), 385-386
_bios_equiplist( ), 385-386
bios.h header file, 377
bioskey( ), 387-388
_bios_keybrd( ), 387-388
biosmemory( ), 388
_bios_memsize( ), 388
biosprint( ), 389-390
_bios_printer( ), 389-390
_bios_serialcom( ), 380-383
biostime( ), 390
_bios_timeofday( ), 390-391
Bit-fields, 155, 172-175
Bitwise operators, 37-41
BOOL data type, 904
bool data type, 640
boolean data type, 1018
boolalpha format flag, 749
break statement, 51, 58, 59, 60, 70-71
in Java, 1018, 1022-1024
brk( ), 448-449
Broken-down time, 376
Brushes, 910
bsearch( ), 577-579
Buffer, 185-186
BYTE data type, 904
Bytecode, 1013-1014, 1015
BYTEREGS structure, 376-377

C

C
- origins of, 3
- overview of, 3-12
- standard, ANSI, 1, 3

C Programming Language, The (Kernighan and Ritchie), 3

C++
- differences between C and, 845
- origins of, 619
- standard, draft ANSI, 1, 619-620

cabs( ), 359
cabsl( ), 359
Calendar time, 375
Call by reference, 82, 83-84, 693
Call by value, 82, 692
Call-based interface, 894
CALLBACK calling convention, 893
Callback function, 903
calloc( ), 444, 449
case, 58, 59
Case sensitivity
- in C, 8, 14
- in Java, 1020

Cast, 48, 1027
- used in pointer assignments, 123, 141

Casting operators, 785, 808-811
catch statement, 795
- using multiple, 800-801

catch(...) statement, 801-802
ceil( ), 360
ceill( ), 360
cerr predefined stream, 742
_cexit( ), 487
_c_exit( ), 487
_chain_intr( ), 391
char data type
- in C, 14
- in Java, 1018, 1025

Character(s)
- in C console I/O, 187-189, 191, 200
- in C file I/O, 207-209
- functions, 321
- literals, 1026

Character translations
- in C I/O streams, 185, 207
- in C++ file I/O, 764

chdir( ), 467
_chdrive( ), 468
chmod( ), 255
chsize( ), 255
cin predefined stream, 624, 742
circle( ), 498
Class(es)
- abstract, 738, 1053-1054
- base. *See* Base class
- declaration, general form for, 626
- derived. *See* Derived class
- forward reference to, 647
- generic, 757, 790-795
- Java, 1021, 1028-1033
- libraries, 732
- overview of, 625-629
- polymorphic, 727, 807-808
- string, developing a, 705-710
- structures and, 654-655
- unions and, 656-657

.class file, 1020
class keyword, 625, 1021
CLASSPATH, 1057
cleardevice( ), 499-500
_clear87( ), 579
clearerr( ), 256-257
clearviewport( ), 499-500

CLK_TCK macro, 671
clock( ), 391-392, 671
clog predefined stream, 742
close( ), 257-258, 763
closedir( ), 468-469
closegraph( ), 500
clreol( ), 500-501
clrscr( ), 171, 500-501
Code
 blocks, 6
 compartmentalization of, 5, 6, 22
 object, 7, 11
 relocatable, 247, 248
 source, 7, 11, 1020
codeseg directive, 237
Comma operator, 44
Command line arguments, 88-93
comment directive, 237
Comments
 in C, 243-244
 in C++, 244, 624
 in Java, 1018
 in resource files, 921
Compilation
 conditional,230-234
 separate, 9-10
 unit, 1020
Compile time, 8, 12, 738
Compiler(s), 7-8, 247
 compiling C programs with Borland C++, 2, 625
 compiling C++ programs with Borland C++, 625
 Java, 1020
Component class, 1074, 1079
conio.h header file, 171, 187, 253, 495
Consoles, definition of, 898
const keyword, 17, 142
Constants
 backslash character (in C), 31-32
 definition of, 31
const_cast, 808-809
Constructor functions, 636-639
 copy, 662, 673, 835-838
 execution order for, 717-722
 explicit, 841-842
 in Java, 1032-1033, 1042-1048
 overloading, 668, 671-673
 parameterized, 641-645
 passing parameters to base class, 722-724
Containers, 842-844
continue statement, 51, 73-74
 in Java, 1018, 1024
Controls
 common, 898, 973-974
 standard, 973-974
_control87( ), 579-580
Copy constructor, 662, 673, 835-838
coreleft( ), 450
cos( ), 360
cosh( ), 361
coshl( ), 361
cosl( ), 360
COUNTRY structure, 392-393
country( ), 392-393
cout predefined stream, 623-624, 742
cprintf( ), 501-502
cputs( ), 502-503
creat( ), 258-260
CreateDialog( ), 998, 1000
CreatePopupMenu( ), 966
CreateWindow( ), 911-912
creatnew( ), 258-260
creattemp( ), 258-260
_cs type modifier, 446

cscanf( ), 503-504
cScript language, 857
ctime( ), 394
ctrlbrk( ), 394-395
ctype.h header file, 218, 321
Cursor, mouse, 910
CW_USEDEFAULT macro, 911

D

Data, compartmentalization of, 5, 22
Data type(s), 4, 14
  16-bit, table of, 15
  32-bit, table of, 16
  creating custom, 155
  Java, 1025-1026
  modifiers, 14-17
  windows, 904
__DATE__ predefined macro, 241, 242
Date. *See* Time and date functions
date structure, 376
Debugger, Borland C++
  source-level, 873-889
    and the CPU window, 888
    setting breakpoints in, 876-880
    and single-stepping, 875
    versus traditional debugger, 874
    and watching the stack, 885
    and watching variables, 880-885
dec format flag, 749
Decrement operator, 33-34
  overloading for prefix and postfix, 685-687
default statement, 58
#define directive, 225, 226-229
  and function-like macros, 227-229
  and preprocessor operators # and ##, 240-241
defined compile-time operator, 235
Definition (.DEF) file, 915
delay( ), 395-396
delete, 813-820
DeleteMenu( ), 958, 967
deque class, 842
delline( ), 504
Derived class
  definition of, 632
  inheriting multiple base classes, 720-722
  objects, base class pointers to, 724-726
Desktop model, 893
destroy( ), 1075, 1076
DestroyMenu( ), 967
DestroyWindow( ), 999, 1000
Destructor functions, 637-639
  execution order for, 717-722
detectgraph( ), 505
Device context, 925, 930
Dialog box
  activating and deactivating, 975
  and controls, 973-974
  creating, 974-979
  definition of, 973
  messages, receiving, 974-975
  modal vs. modeless, 974
  modeless, using, 998-1007
  sample program, 979-983, 992-998, 1001-1007
  window function, 979
Dialog editor, 976
Dialog function, 974-975
DIALOG resource statement, 976

DialogBox( ), 975
difftime( ), 396-397
direct.h header file, 468
Directory manipulation functions, 467-483
dirent structure, 468
dirent.h header file, 468
dir.h header file, 467
disable( ), 397
_disable( ), 397
diskfree_t structure, 400-401
DispatchMessage( ), 914
div( ), 580
div_t structure, 573, 580
DLLs (Dynamic link libraries), 895
do/while loop, 5, 51, 69-70
DOS and Windows 95, 894, 896
DOS interfacing functions, 375, 376
_dos_allocmem( ), 450-451
_dos_close( ), 397
_dos_creatnew( ), 398
_dos_creat( ), 398
dosdate_t structure, 399, 407
DOSERROR structure, 399
dosexterr( ), 399
_dos_findfirst( ), 469-470
_dos_findnext( ), 469-470
_dos_freemem( ), 451
_dos_getdate( ), 399-400
_dos_getdiskfree( ), 400-401
_dos_getdrive( ), 401-402
_dos_getfileattr( ), 402
_dos_getftime( ), 403-404
_dos_getvect( ), 404
dos.h header file, 253, 376, 444
_dos_keep( ), 427-428
_dos_open( ), 405-406
_dos_read( ), 406-407
_dos_setblock( ), 452
_dos_setdate( ), 407-408
_dos_setdrive( ), 408
_dos_setfileattr( ), 408-409
_dos_setftime( ), 409-411
_dos_settime( ), 407-408
_dos_setvect( ), 411
dostime_t structure, 399-400, 407
dostounix( ), 411
_dos_write( ), 412
Dot (.) operator, 44-45, 158, 170, 627, 669
double data type, 14
drawpoly( ), 505-506
drawString( ), 1070
_ds type modifier, 446
DS_MODALFRAME style macro, 1000
dup( ), 260
dup2( ), 260
DWORD data type, 904
Dynamic allocation
    functions, 443-465
    using new and delete, 813-820
Dynamic link libraries (DLLs), 895
Dynamic method dispatch, 1039, 1050-1052
dynamic_cast operator, 808-811

E

Early binding, 738-739
ecvt( ), 580-581
Edit box
    adding, 989-992
    definition of, 974
EDITTEXT resource statement, 990
EDOM macro, 355
#elif directive, 225, 232, 235
ellipse( ), 506-507
else, 52

#else directive, 225, 231-232
_ _emit_ _( ), 581
enable( ), 412
_enable( ), 412
EnableMenuItem( ), 960
Encapsulation, 621
how to achieve, 625
#endif, 225, 231-233
EndDialog( ), 975, 979
EndPaint( ), 931-932
enum keyword, 177
Enumerations, 155, 177-180
env, 91-93
eof( ), 260-261, 767-768
EOF macro, 187, 205
ERANGE macro, 355
errno global variable, 253, 355
errno.h header file, 253
#error directive, 225, 229
_es type modifier, 446
Event class, 1079
Event handling (Java)
keyboard, 1082-1084
mouse, 1079-1082
except.h header file, 813
Exception handling
in C++, 785, 795-806
in Java, 1015, 1024
exec...( ) functions, 487-489
exit( ), 51, 71-73, 490, 797
_exit( ), 490
exit directive, 237-238
EXIT_FAILURE macro, 72, 573
EXIT_SUCCESS macro, 72, 573
exp( ), 361
Expert C++ (Schildt), 846
expl( ), 361
explicit keyword, 841
Expressions, 46-49
type conversion in, 46-48
extends, 1040, 1064
extern storage class specifier, 22, 23-24, 650, 831
Extractors, 743, 746-748

F

fabs( ), 362
fabsl( ), 362
false, 640, 1018
far pointer type modifier, 444, 445-446, 901
farcalloc( ), 452
farcoreleft( ), 452-453
farfree( ), 453-454
farheapcheck( ), 456
farheapcheckfree( ), 456-457
farheapchecknode( ), 457-458
farheapfillfree( ), 459
farheapinfo structure, 461
farheapwalk( ), 460-462
farmalloc( ), 454
farrealloc( ), 454
fcb structure, 431
fclose( ), 186, 206, 209-211, 261-262
fcloseall( ), 261-262
fcntl.h header file, 207
fcvt( ), 581-582
fdopen( ), 262
feof( ), 206, 211-212, 263
ferror( ), 206, 222-223, 263-264
ffblk structure, 471
fflush( ), 206, 264
fgetc( ), 206, 209, 265
fgetchar( ), 265
fgetpos( ), 266
fgets( ), 190, 213-214, 267
File(s), C

in C I/O system, 184, 185-186, 205
checking for EOF in binary, 211-212
closing, 209-210
erasing, 222
opening, 206-207
pointer, 206
File(s), C++
detecting EOF in, 767-768
get and put pointers, 768
opening and closing, 761-763
pointer position, obtaining, 770
reading and writing binary, 764-767
reading and writing text, 763-764
FILE data type, 186, 205, 206
File position indicator, 185
_ _FILE_ _ predefined macro, 235-236, 241, 242
filebuf::openprot, 762
filelength( ), 268
fileno( ), 268
fill( ), 752
fillellipse( ), 507-508
fillpoly( ), 508-509
final, 1054-1055
finalize( ), 1017, 1038
findfirst( ), 471-472
findnext( ), 471-472
find_t structure, 469-470
fixed format flag, 749
flags( ), 750-751
float data type, 14
float.h header file, 579
floodfill( ), 509
floor( ), 362
floorl( ), 362
flushall( ), 269
_fmemccpy( ), 330
_fmemchr( ), 330-331
_fmemcmp( ), 331-332
_fmemcpy( ), 332-333
_fmemicmp( ), 331-332
_fmemmove( ), 333-334
_fmemset( ), 334
fmod( ), 363
_fmode global variable, 207
fmodl( ), 363
_fmovmem( ), 389
fmtflags type, 749
fnmerge( ), 473-474
fnsplit( ), 473-474
fopen( ), 206-207, 210-211, 269-270
FOPEN_MAX macro, 205
for loops, 5, 51, 62-67
Forward reference
class, 647
functions, 94-97
FP_OFF( ), 413
fpos_t data type, 205
_fpreset( ), 582
fprintf( ), 206, 218-222, 271-272
FP_SEG( ), 413
fputc( ), 206, 207, 272-273
fputchar( ), 273
fputs( ), 213-214, 273-274
fread( ), 214-216, 274-275
free( ), 122-123, 140-141, 443, 454-455
freemem( ), 455
freopen( ), 275-276
frexp( ), 363-364
frexpl( ), 363-364
Friend functions, 645-650
friend keyword, 645
fscanf( ), 206, 218-222, 276
fseek( ), 205, 206, 216-218, 277-278

fsetpos( ), 278-279
_fsopen( ), 279-280
fstat( ), 280
_fstrcat( ), 336-337
_fstrchr( ), 337-338
_fstrcspn( ), 339-340
_fstrdup( ), 340
fstream class, 760, 762
fstream.h, 760
_fstricmp( ), 342
_fstrlen( ), 343
_fstrlwr( ), 343-344
_fstrncat( ), 344-345
_fstrncmp( ), 345-346
_fstrncpy( ), 346-347
_fstrnicmp( ), 345-346
_fstrnset( ), 347
_fstrpbrk( ), 347-348
_fstrrchr( ), 348
_fstrrev( ), 349
_fstrset( ), 349-350
_fstrspn( ), 350
_fstrstr( ), 351
_fstrtok( ), 351-352
_fstrupr( ), 352-353
ftell( ), 281
ftime structure, 419
ftime( ), 413-414
_fullpath( ), 474-475
Function(s), 5-6
  arguments. *See* Arguments, function
  conversion, creating, 833-835
  dialog, 974-975
  formal parameters of. *See* Parameters, formal
  general form of, 77
  general-purpose, 106
  generic, 785-790
  inline. *See* Inline functions
  inline code versus, 106-107
  member. *See* Member functions
  passing arrays to, 84-88, 111-112, 116, 120
  passing entire structures to, 167-168
  passing objects to, 660-662
  passing structure members to, 166-167
  pointers to, 103-105, 150-152
  prototypes, 95-99
  recursive, 101-103
  returning from, 77-80
  returning non-integer values from, 93-95
  returning objects from, 663-664
  returning pointers from, 99-100
  scope rules of, 81
  type declaration statement, old-style, 94-95
  used in assignment statement, 696
  virtual. *See* Virtual functions
Function overloading, 629-632, 671-681
  and ambiguity, 676-679
  and constructor functions, 671-673
  and default arguments, 678-679
  and function pointers, 679-680
  versus overriding, 729-730
fwrite( ), 79, 176, 214-216, 281-282

G

Garbage collection, 1015, 1018, 1037
gcount( ), 767
gcvt( ), 582
Generic class, 757, 790-795
Generic functions, 785-790
geninterrupt( ), 414
get( ), 764-765
Get pointer, 768
getarccoords( ), 510
getaspectratio( ), 511
getbkcolor( ), 511-512
getc( ), 206, 209, 210-211, 282-283
getcbrk( ), 415
getch( ), 188-189, 191, 283
getchar( ), 187, 188, 191, 284
getche( ), 187-188, 191, 283
getcolor( ), 512
getcurdir( ), 475
getcwd( ), 476
_getcwd( ), 476-477
getdate( ), 415-416
GetDC( ), 925-926
getdefaultpalette( ), 512-513
getdfree( ), 416-417
getdisk( ), 477-478
GetDlgItemText( ), 990-991
_getdrive( ), 478
getdrivername( ), 513-514
getdta( ), 417
getenv( ), 583
getfat( ), 417-418
getfatd( ), 417-418
getfillpattern( ), 514-515
getfillsettings( ), 515-516
getftime( ), 418-419
getgraphmode( ), 516-517
getimage( ), 517-519
getline( ), 770
getlinesettings( ), 519-520
getmaxcolor( ), 520-521
getmaxmode( ), 521
getmaxx( ), 521-522
getmaxy( ), 521-522
GetMenu( ), 959-960
GetMenuItemCount( ), 960
GetMessage( ), 913-914, 999
getmodename( ), 522
getmoderange( ), 523
getpalette( ), 524-526
getpalettesize( ), 526-527
getpass( ), 583-584
getpid( ), 584
getpixel( ), 527
getpsp( ), 420
gets( ), 87, 189-190, 191, 284-285
GetStockObject( ), 910
GetSubMenu( ), 960
gettext( ), 527-528
gettextinfo( ), 528
gettextsettings( ), 528-530
gettime( ), 415-416
getvect( ), 420
getverify( ), 420-421
getviewsettings( ), 530-531
getw( ), 213, 285-286
getx( ), 531
gety( ), 531
gmtime( ), 421-422
goto, 5, 51, 74-75, 81
gotoxy( ), 171, 531-532, 650, 651
graphdefaults( ), 532
grapherrormsg( ), 532
_graphfreemem( ), 533
_graphgetmem( ), 533
Graphical User Interface (GUI), 893
Graphics driver, 535
Graphics class, 1070

Graphics Device Interface (GDI), 901
Graphics functions, 495-496
graphics.h header file, 495
graphics.lib library, 495
graphresult( ), 533-534

H

HANDLE data type, 904
Handle, definition of, 904
harderr( ), 422-423
_harderr( ), 422-423
hardresume( ), 422-423
_hardresume( ), 422-423
hardretn( ), 422-423
_hardretn( ), 422-423
HDC data type, 926
hdrfile directive, 238
hdrstop directive, 238
Header files, 97-98, 249-251
  commonly used C/C++, table of, 251
  new style, 840-841
Heap, 10, 122, 140, 443
heapcheck( ), 456
heapcheckfree( ), 456-457
heapchecknode( ), 457-458
_heapchk( ), 458-459
heapfillfree( ), 459
heapinfo structure, 461
_heapinfo structure, 461
_heapmin( ), 459-460
_heapset( ), 460
heapwalk( ), 460-462
hex format flag, 749
HGDIOBJ data type, 910
highvideo( ), 534
HIWORD macro, 920
Hoare, C.A.R., 596
HTML file, 1071-1072
huge pointer type modifier, 444, 445-446
HUGE_VAL macro, 355
HWND data type, 894
HWND_DESKTOP, 911
hypot( ), 364
hypotl( ), 364

I

Icons, windows application, 909
IDE (Integrated Development Environment), 847-858, 1070
  context-sensitive help, 856
  menu bar options, 851-855
  scripting, 857
  SpeedBar, 856
  SpeedMenus, 856
  status bar, 857
  target types, 858
IDE text editor, 859-871
  autoindentation feature, 867
  clipboard, using, 863
  cursor commands, 864
  and deleting blocks of text, 861-863
  and entering text, 859-861
  find and replace, 864-866
  keyboard commands, table of, 869-871
  and moving and copying blocks of text, 861-863
  pair matching, 868
  and saving and loading files, 867
Identifiers, 13-14
#if directive, 225, 231-232, 235

if-else-if ladder, 54-55
if statement, 51-57
#ifdef directive, 225, 233-234
#ifndef directive, 225, 233-234
ifstream class, 760, 762
imagesize( ), 534-535
imanip class, 757
implements clause, 1062-1063
import statement, 1039, 1059, 1060
#include directive, 225, 229-230
Increment operator, 33-34
    overloading for prefix and postfix, 685-687
Inheritance, 622, 632-636, 712-726
    access specifiers and, 712-717
    constructors, destructors, and, 717-722
    in Java, 1039-1055
    multiple base class, 720-722
init( ), 1075-1076
initgraph( ), 535-537
Inline assembly code, 238
Inline code, 106-107
    using function-like macros, 227-229
inline
    modifier, 658
    #pragma directive, 238
Inline functions, 658-660
    generating, 238
    within a class, creating, 659-660
Inline Intrinsic Function option (IDE), 238
inp( ), 423-424
inport( ), 423-424
inportb( ), 423-424
Input operator (>>), 624, 632, 742, 743, 746-748
inpw( ), 423-424
Inserters, 743-746
insline( ), 537-538
installuserdriver( ), 538
installuserfont( ), 538-539
int data type, 14
    as default function return type, 77
int86( ), 424-425
int86x( ), 424-425
intdos( ), 425-426
intdosx( ), 425-426
Integers, effect of 32-bit addressing on, 901
Integrated Development Environment. *See* IDE
Interface, 1017, 1039, 1061-1068
    general form of, 1062
    implementing, 1062-1064
    reference variables, 1064
interface keyword, 1062
internal format flag, 749
Internet, 1011, 1012
Interpreters, 7-8
intr( ), 426-427
intrinsic directive, 238
InvalidateRect( ), 935
I/O, ANSI C, 253
I/O, C console, 187-205
    basic functions for, table of, 191
    characters, 187-189, 191, 200
    connection with file I/O, 223-224
    formatted, 190-205
    strings, 189-190, 191, 201
I/O, C file, 205-224
    and blocks of data, 214-215
    and characters, 207-209
    common functions for, table of, 206

connection with console I/O, 223-224
formatted with fprintf( ) and fscanf( ), 218-222
random access, 216-218
and strings, 213-214
See also Streams
See also File(s), C
I/O, C++, 741-770
array-based. *See* Array-based I/O
formatted, 748-760
manipulators. *See* Manipulators
operators. *See* Operators, I/O
stream classes, 743
streams, 742
I/O, C++ file, 760-770
random access, 768-770
See also File(s), C++
I/O, UNIX-like, 253
ioctl( ), 427
io.h header file, 253
iomanip.h header file, 753, 757
ios class, 743
formatted I/O using members of, 748-753
ios::app, 761
ios::ate, 761
ios::beg, 768
ios::binary, 761, 765
ios::cur, 768
ios::end, 768
ios::in, 761
ios::nocreate, 761
ios::noreplace, 761
ios::out, 761
ios::trunc, 761
iostream class, 743, 771
iostream.h header file, 623, 743, 748
isalnum( ), 322
isalpha( ), 322-323
isascii( ), 323
isatty( ), 286
iscntrl( ), 324
IsDialogMessage( ), 999, 1000
isdigit( ), 324-325
isgraph( ), 325
islower( ), 326
isprint( ), 218, 326-327
ispunct( ), 327
isspace( ), 328
istream class, 743, 771
istrstream class, 771
isupper( ), 328-329
isxdigit( ), 581
itoa( ), 584-585
Iterators, 843, 844

J

Java
and C++, differences between, 1016-1018
control statements, 1027-1028
design features, 1012-1013, 1014-1016
and DOS and Windows 3.1, 1020
history of, 1011-1012
as interpreted language, 1013, 1015
and Windows95/Windows NT, 1020
.java file, 1020
javac (Java compiler), 1020
java (Java interpreter), 1020
Java: The Complete Reference (Naughton and Schildt), 1010

jmp_buf data type, 589
Jump statements, 51

K

kbhit( ), 71, 417
keep( ), 427-428
Kernighan, Brian, 3
KeyDown( ), 1083
Keypress, responding to, 921-924
Keys
  accelerator, 952-957
  shortcut, 947
  virtual, 953
KeyUp( ), 1083
Keywords,
  Borland C++, table of, 620
  C, 4, 8, 9

L

Label
  identifier for goto statement, 74
  as target for break and continue, 1024
labs( ), 585
Late binding, 738-739
LB_ADDSTRING message, 986
LB_ERR macro, 986
LB_FINDSTRING message, 986-987
LB_GETCURSEL message, 986
LB_GETTEXT message, 987
LB_SELECTSTRING message, 987
LB_SETCURSEL message, 986
LBN_DBLCLK message, 985, 988
lconv structure, 588-589
ldexp( ), 364
ldexpl( ), 364
ldiv( ), 586
ldiv_t structure, 573, 586
left format flag, 749
lfind( ), 586-588
_LHUGE_VAL macro, 355
Library
  C standard, 8, 249
  C++ I/O class, 741
  C++ standard template library, 842-844
  creating class, 732
  definition of, 12
  header files and functions, 97-98, 249-251
line( ), 539-540
#line directive, 225, 235-236
_ _LINE_ _ predefined macro, 235-236, 241, 242
linerel( ), 539-540
linesettingtype structure, 519
lineto( ), 539-540
Linkage specification, 830-831
Linker, 8-9, 11, 247-248, 249
List boxes
  definition of, 974
  initializing, 987
  messages and, 985-987
  processing selection in, 988
list class, 842
LISTBOX resource statement, 984
LoadAccelerators( ), 955
LoadCursor( ), 909
LoadIcon( ), 909
localeconv( ), 588-589
localtime( ), 428
lock( ), 287
locking( ), 287-288
log( ), 365

Logical operators, 35-36
logl( ), 365
log10( ), 365-366
log10l( ), 365-366
LONG data type, 904
long modifier, 14
longjmp( ), 589-590
Loops
    do/while, 5, 69-70
    for, 51, 62-67
    infinite, 66
    and structured languages, 5
    time delay, 67
    while, 5, 51, 67-69
    with no bodies, 67
LOWORD macro, 920
lowvideo( ), 540
LPARAM data type, 913, 920
lParam message parameter, 920
LPCSTR data type, 904
LPSTR data type, 904
LPVOID data type, 911
LRESULT data type, 903
_lrotl( ), 591-592
_lrotr( ), 591-592
lsearch( ), 586-588
lseek( ), 288-289
ltoa( ), 591

M

Machine code, 7
main( ), 260, 623, 629
    arguments to, 88-93
    in Java, 1021-1022, 1070
    returning value from, 80
_makepath( ), 478-479
malloc( ), 122-124, 140-141, 443, 462-463
malloc.h header file, 444
Manipulators
    creating custom, 755-760
    table of standard, 753
    using standard, 748, 753-755
map container, 843
Mathematical functions, 355-373
_matherr( ), 366-367
_matherrl( ), 366-367
math.h, 355
max( ), 592-593
MB_CUR_MAX macro, 573
mblen( ), 593
mbstowcs( ), 593-594
mbtowc( ), 594
Member functions, 626, 629
    const and volatile, 828-829
    of generic classes, 791
    and scope resolution operator, 627
    static, 822-824
Member variables, 626
    static, 821-824
memccpy( ), 330
memchr( ), 330-331
memcmp( ), 331-332
memcpy( ), 332-333
mem.h header file, 321
memicmp( ), 331-332
memmove( ), 333-334
Memory
    flat, 444, 446, 898
    management, 1015
    manipulation functions, 321
    map, C program, 10-11
    models, 444-447
    segmented, 444-445
    virtual, 898
memset( ), 334

Menu(s), 943-944
  accelerator keys and, 952-957
  creating, 945-948
  creating dynamic, 966-971
  dynamically managing, 958-965
  ID values for items in, 947
  in program, including, 948
  program example, 949-951
  responding to selections from, 948-949
MENU resource statement, 945
menu.h header file, 947
MENUITEM resource statement, 945-946
Message(s), 920-921
  loop, 903, 913-914
  responding to mouse, 938-942
  and the window function, 903
  and Windows programs, 900
Message boxes, 917-920
message directive, 238-239
MessageBox( ), 918-919
Method(s), 1018, 1028, 1029
  abstract, 1053-1054
  dispatch, dynamic, 1039, 1050-1052
  overriding, 1049-1050
min( ), 592-593
MK_CONTROL mouse message, 942
mkdir( ), 479
MK_FP( ), 429-430
MK_RBUTTON mouse message, 942
MK_SHIFT mouse message, 942
MK_LBUTTON mouse message, 942
MK_MBUTTON mouse message, 942
mktemp( ), 480
mktime( ), 429
modf( ), 367
modfl( ), 367
mouseDown( ), 1079, 1080
mouseUp( ), 1079, 1080
movedata( ), 334-335
movemem( ), 335
moverel( ), 540
movetext( ), 541
moveto( ), 541
MSG structure, 904, 913
multimap container, 843
multiset container, 843
Multitasking
  non-preemptive versus preemptive, 897
  process-based, 894
  thread-based, 894, 1015, 1018
mutable keyword, 842

N

name( ), 807
Namespace, 839-840
namespace statement, 839
Naming conventions, Windows, 915-916
Naughton, Patrick, 1010, 1011
near pointer type modifier, 444, 445-446, 901
new, 813-820, 1031
new.h header file, 819
normvideo( ), 541-542
nosound( ), 594-595
NOT
  ! logical operator, 35, 36
  ~ bitwise operator (one's complement), 37, 39-41, 637

- Null, definition of, 112
- NULL macro, 141, 205, 573

O

- Oak, 1011
- O_BINARY, 207
- Object(s)
  - allocating, 816-819
  - arrays of, 664-668
  - assignment, 664
  - base class pointers to derived class, 724-726
  - using class name, creating, 621
  - definition of, 621
  - to functions, passing, 660-662
  - from functions, returning, 663-664
  - initialization, 674-676
  - in Java, 1030-1031
  - passing references to, 695-696
  - pointers to, 668-670
- Object class, 1055
- Object code, 7, 11
- Object-oriented programming, 620-622
  - and Java, 1014-1015
- oct format flag, 749
- Offset (memory), 444-445
- ofstream class, 760, 762
- -Oi command line switch, 238
- omanip class, 757
- One's complement operator (~), 37, 39-41
- OOP. *See* Object-oriented programming
- open( ), 290-292, 761-762
- opendir( ), 468-469
- Operator(s)
  - arithmetic, 33-35
  - arrow (–>), 44-45
  - assignment, 28
  - bitwise, 37-40
  - casting, 785, 808-811
  - comma (,), 44
  - compile-time, 43-44
  - dot (.), 44-45
  - Java, 1027
  - pointer, 41-43, 134-136
  - pointer-to-member (.* and–>*), 831-833
  - precedence summary table of C, 46
  - relational and logical, 35-36
  - scope resolution (::), 627, 840
  - ternary, 41, 51, 55-57
- operator functions
  - creating member, 681-688
  - using friend, 688-692, 699-702
- Operator overloading, 632, 681-710
  - [ ], 702-705
  - increment and decrement, 685-687
  - restrictions, 687-688
  - references and unary, 699-702
- Operators, I/O (<< and >>), 623-624, 632
  - overloading, 743-748
- option directive, 239
- OR
  - | bitwise operator, 37, 38
  - || Java short-circuit, 1027
  - || logical operator, 35, 36
- ostream class, 743, 771
- ostrstream class, 771
- O_TEXT, 207
- outp( ), 430
- outport( ), 430

outportb( ), 430
Output operator (<<), 624, 632, 742, 743-746
outpw( ), 430
outtext( ), 542-543
outtextxy( ), 542-543
Overloading functions. *See* Function overloading
Overloading operators. *See* Operator overloading
Overriding versus function overloading, 729-730
_OvrInitEms( ), 595-596
_OvrInitExt( ), 595-596

P

Package(s), 1017, 1039, 1055-1060
 access control and, 1060-1061
 creating, 1056
 executing classes created in, 1058
 importing, 1059-1060
 Java standard, 1060
package statement, 1056
paint( ), 1070, 1075, 1076
PAINTSTRUCT structure, 931
palettetype structure, 524
Parameters, formal, 20, 81-82
 array, 84-85
 declarations, classic versus modern, 100-101
 pointer, 83
 reference, 692-695
parsfnm( ), 430-431
PATH string, 92
pcount( ), 773
peek( ), 431-432
peekb( ), 432-432
perror( ), 292
pieslice( ), 543-544
POINT structure, 914
Pointer(s), 133-154
 accessing arrays with, 121-122, 143-144
 arithmetic, 137
 arrays of, 104-105, 146-147
 assignments, 123, 136-137
 base type of, 134
 C file, 206
 to character arrays, 144-146
 comparisons, 138-140
 const, 142-143
 definition of, 41, 133
 to derived class objects, 724-726
 dynamic allocation and, 140-141
 to functions, 103-105, 150-152, 679-680
 indexing, 87, 120-121
 initializing, 148-149, 152-153
 and Java, 1031
 member, 831-833
 multiple indirection with, 147-148
 null, 124, 148-149
 to objects, 668-670
 operators, 41-43, 134-136, 698
 problems with, 152-154
 returned from functions, 99-100
 _seg, 446
 structure, 168-171
 this, 680-681, 684, 685, 688, 690
poke( ), 431-432
pokeb( ), 431-432
poly( ), 368
polyl( ), 368

Polymorphism, 621-622, 636, 1039, 1062
through operator and function overloading, 629, 711
through virtual functions and derived types, run time, 726, 729, 731-736
POPUP resource statement, 945-946
Portability
and Java, 1013
using sizeof to ensure, 180-181
using typedef to aid, 182
using a union to help with, 176
PostQuitMessage( ), 915
pow( ), 368-369
powl( ), 368-369
pow10( ), 369-370
pow10l( ), 369-370
#pragma directive, 225, 236-240
precision( ), 752
Preprocessor directives, ANSI C, 225-240
Preprocessor operators, 240-241
printf( ), 80, 97, 190-198, 292-295, 623-624
format specifiers, table of, 192, 293
return value of, 191
println( ), 1022
priority_queue class, 842
private access specifier, 633, 712-717
Process, definition of, 894
Process control functions, 485-494
process.h header file, 485
Programming
object-oriented, 620-622, 1014-1015
structured, 5-6, 620-621
protected access specifier, 712-717
Prototypes, function, 95-99, 626
public access specifier, 626, 712-717
Pushbutton
declaring, 977-978
definition of, 974
PUSHBUTTON resource statement, 977-978
put( ), 764, 766
Put pointer, 768
putc( ), 206, 207-209, 210-211, 295-296
putch( ), 296
putchar( ), 187, 191, 296-297
putenv( ), 596
putimage( ), 544-546
putpixel( ), 546
puts( ), 143-144, 189-190, 191, 297
puttext( ), 546
putw( ), 213, 297-298

Q

qsort( ), 596-598
queue class, 842
Quicksort algorithm, 596, 786

R

raise( ), 598-599
rand( ), 79, 599
randbrd( ), 432-433
randbwr( ), 432-433
RAND_MAX macro, 573
random( ), 599-600

1107

), 599-600
rce) files, 944
alog box, 976-977
embedding comments in, 947
d( ), 298-299, 766-767
readdir( ), 468-469
realloc( ), 444, 463-465
RECT structure, 931
rectangle( ), 547
Recursion, 101-103
Reference(s), 692-702
    base class, 726, 728, 729
    independent, 697-699
    to objects, passing, 695-696
    to overload unary operator, 699-702
    parameters, 692-695
    restrictions on, 695
    returning, 696-697
    variables in Java, object, 1031-1032
register storage class specifier, 22, 27-28
registerbgidriver( ), 547-548
registerbgifont( ), 547-548
RegisterClassEx( ), 911
REGPACK structure, 426
REGS union, 376, 377
reinterpret_cast, 808-809, 811
Relational operators, 35-36
ReleaseDC( ), 925-926
Relocatable format, 9, 248
remove( ), 206, 222, 299
rename( ), 300
repaint( ), 1077-1078
.RES file, 944
Resource
    definition of, 943, 944
    editor, Borland's, 952
restorecrtmode( ), 548
return statement, 51, 77-80
rewind( ), 206, 222-223, 300-301
rewinddir( ), 468-469
Richards, Martin, 3
right format flag, 749
Ritchie, Dennis, 3
rmdir( ), 480-481
_rotl( ), 600-601
_rotr( ), 600-601
_rtl_chmod( ), 301-302
_rtl_close( ), 257
_rtl_creat( ), 258-260
_rtl_heapwalk( ), 460-462
_rtl_open( ), 290-292
_rtl_read( ), 298-299
_rtl_write( ), 318-319
_ _rtti keyword, 640
Run time, 8, 12, 738-739
    system, Java, 1013
Run-time type identification (RTTI), 785, 806-808

S

saveregs directive, 239
sbrk( ), 465
scanf( ), 166, 198-205, 302-305, 624
    format specifiers, table of, 199, 303
Scanset, 202-203, 304-305
scientific format flag, 749
Scope resolution operator (::), 627, 840
Scope rules, 5, 81
_searchenv( ), 603
searchpath( ), 481
sector( ), 548-549
SEEK_CUR macro, 205, 216
SEEK_END macro, 205, 216

seekg( ), 768-769
seekp( ), 768-769
SEEK_SET macro, 205, 216
_seg modifier, 446
Segment (memory), 444-445
specifiers, 446
segread( ), 433
Selection statements, 51-61
SendDlgItemMessage( ), 986
set container, 843
setactivepage( ), 550
setallpalette( ), 550-551
setaspectratio( ), 551
setbkcolor( ), 551-553
setblock( ), 465
setbuf( ), 305-306
setcbrk( ), 433-434
setcolor( ), 553-554
_setcursortype( ), 601
setdate( ), 434
SetDlgItemText( ), 991
setdisk( ), 481-482
setdta( ), 434-435
set_expected( ), 803
setf( ), 749-750
setfillpattern( ), 554
setfillstyle( ), 555-556
setftime( ), 435-436
setgraphbufsize( ), 556
setgraphmode( ), 556
setjmp( ), 601-602
setjmp.h header file, 589
setlinestyle( ), 557-558
setlocale( ), 603-604
setmem( ), 336
setmode( ), 306
set_new_handler( ), 604, 819
setpalette( ), 558-560
setrgbpalette( ), 560
set_terminate( ), 796
settextjustify( ), 560-561
settextstyle( ), 561-562
settime( ), 434
setusercharsize( ), 563-564
setvbuf( ), 306-307
setvect( ), 436
setverify( ), 436-437
setviewport( ), 564
setvisualpage( ),564-565
setwritemode( ), 565-566
short modifier, 14
showbase format flag, 749
showpoint format flag, 749
showpos format flag, 749
showStatus( ), 1078
ShowWindow( ), 912-913, 999
Sign flag, 14
signal( ), 605
signal.h signals, 598, 605
signed modifier, 14
sin( ), 79, 370
sinh( ), 370-371
sinhl( ), 370-371
sinl( ), 370
sizeof operator, 43-44, 180-181, 573
size_t data type, 113, 122, 205, 322, 573
skipws format flag, 749
sleep( ), 437
sopen( ), 307-309
sound( ), 606-607
Source code, 7, 11, 1020
spawn...( ) functions, 491-494
_splitpath( ), 482-483
sprintf( ), 309-310
sqr( ), 79
sqrt( ), 371
sqrtl( ), 371
srand( ), 79, 606
SREGS structure, 377

_ss type modifier, 446
sscanf( ), 310
Stack, 10, 102
    and local variables, 20
stack class, 842
Standard template library (STL), 842
start( ), 1075, 1076
startup directive, 237-238
stat( ), 310-311
Statements, program control, 51-75
static storage class specifier, 22, 24-27, 650
static_cast, 808-809
_status87( ), 607
stdarg.h header file, 613
stdaux stream, 186
_ _STDC_ _ predefined macro, 241, 242
stderr standard stream, 186
stdin standard stream, 186
stdio format flag, 749
stdio.h header file, 97, 183, 205, 253
stdlib.h header file, 122, 141, 444, 485, 573
stdout standard stream, 186
stdprn stream, 186
stime( ), 437-438
stop( ), 1075, 1076
Storage class specifiers, 22-28
stpcpy( ), 336
str( ), 778
strcat( ), 113, 336-337
strchr( ), 337-338
strcmp( ), 64, 113-114, 144, 338
strcmpi( ), 342
strcoll( ), 339
strcpy( ), 339
strcspn( ), 339-340
_strdate( ), 438-439
strdup( ), 340
Stream(s)
    binary, 185
    C++, 742
    for C++ array-based I/O, 771
    for C++ file I/O, 760-761
    classes, 743
    predefined, 186, 223
    text, 185
streambuf class, 743
streamoff data type, 768
streampos data type, 770
strerror( ), 341
_strerror( ), 341
strftime( ), 439
stricmp( ), 342
String(s)
    as array, 112
    arrays of, 118-119
    in console I/O, 189-190, 191, 201
    in file I/O, 213-214
    functions, 321
    literals, 1026
    table, 149
string (Borland C++ class), 705
String class (Java), 1018
string.h header file, 113, 321
strlen( ), 68, 113, 343
strlwr( ), 343-344
strncat( ), 344-345
strncmp( ), 345-346
strncmpi( ), 345-346
strncpy( ), 346-347
strnicmp( ), 345-346
strnset( ), 347
Stroustrup, Bjarne, 619-620
strpbrk( ), 347-348
strrchr( ), 348
strrev( ), 349

strset( ), 349-350
strspn( ), 350
strstr( ), 92-93, 351
strstrea.h header file, 771
strstream class, 771
strstreambase class, 771
_strtime( ), 438-439
strtod( ), 607-608
strtok( ), 351-352, 783
strtol( ), 609
_strtold( ), 607-608
strtoul( ), 609
struct keyword, 156
Structure(s), 155-172,
    accessing, 158
    arrays and structures within, 172
    arrays of, 159-166
    assignments, 158-159
    and classes, 654-655
    declaration, 156-157
    to functions, passing entire, 167-168
    to functions, passing members of, 166-167
    pointers, 168-171
strupr( ), 352-353
strxfrm( ), 353
Subclass, 1040
super
    and constructors, 1043-1048
    and instance variables and hidden methods, 1048-1049
Superclass, 1040
swab( ), 610
switch statement, 51, 58-61
    versus function pointer array, 150
system( ), 610
System.out standard output stream, 1022
Systems program, 7
sys\timeb.h header file, 413

T

Tag, structure, 156
tan( ), 372
tanh( ), 372-373
tanhl( ), 372-373
tanl( ), 372
TCP/IP, 1016
tell( ), 311-312
tellg( ), 770
tellp( ), 770
template keyword, 786, 791
Templates, 785, 786, 794-795
terminate( ), 796
Ternary operator (?), 41, 51, 55-57, 684, 688
Text functions, 495-496
textattr( ), 566-567
textbackground( ), 567
textcolor( ), 568
textheight( ), 569
text_info structure, 528
textmode( ), 569-570
TextOut( ), 926-927
textsettingstype structure, 529
textwidth( ), 570-571
this pointer, 680-681, 684, 685, 688, 690
Thompson, Ken, 3
Thread, definition of, 894
throw, 795-800
    clause, restricting exceptions thrown with, 802-804
    to rethrow, using, 804-805

throws, 1024
time( ), 439-441
Time and date functions, 375-376
Time delay loops, 67
_ _TIME_ _ predefined macro, 241, 242
time structrure, 376
timeb structure, 412-414
time.h, 375, 671
time_t type, 375
tm structure, 375-376
tmpfile( ), 312
tmpnam( ), 312-313
toascii( ), 611
tolower( ), 353-354
_tolower( ), 353-354
toupper( ), 354
_toupper( ), 354
TranslateAccelerator( ), 955-956
TranslateMessage( ), 914
true, 640, 1018
True and false
    in C, 35, 51
    in Java, 1018
try block, 795-800
Two's complement, 16
Type
    cast, 48, 123, 141, 1027
    checking and prototypes, 95
    checking in Java, strong, 1024-1025
    conversion, 29-30, 46-48, 677-678, 1026-1027
    conversion functions, 833-835
typedef, 155, 181-182
typeid, 806-808
typeinfo class, 806-807
typeinfo.h header file, 806
typename keyword, 842
tzset( ), 441

U

UINT data type, 904
ultoa( ), 591
#undef directive, 225, 234
unexpected( ), 802-803
ungetc( ), 313-314
ungetch( ), 314
Unicode, 1018, 1025
Unions, 155, 175-177
    anonymous, 657
    and classes, 656-657
unitbuf format flag, 749
unixtodos( ), 441-442
unlink( ), 315
unlock( ), 315-316
unmask( ), 611-612
unsetf( ), 750, 751
unsigned modifier, 14
update( ), 1077
UpdateWindow( ), 913
uppercase format flag, 749
URL, 1016
using directive, 840
utimbuf structure, 612
utime( ), 612-613

V

va_arg( ), 97, 613-614
va_end( ), 613-614
Variables, 17-28
    access modifiers for, 17
    automatic, 18
    declaration versus definition, 24
    declaring, 17-18
    initializing, 30-31
    instance, 1028

member. *See* Member variables
object reference, 1031-1032
pointer, 134
register, 845
storage class specifiers for, 22-28
Variables, global, 5, 20-22
extern used with, 23-24
static, 26-27
Variables, local, 5, 18-20, 22
differences between C and C++, declaring, 673-674
static, 24-26
va_start( ), 613-614
vector class, 842, 843-844
vfprintf( ), 316-317
vfscanf( ), 317-318
Viewport, 496
Virtual functions, 726-738
and class libraries, 732
overloading versus overriding, 729-730
pure, 736-738
virtual keyword, 726, 727, 824, 828
void data type, 14
in parameter list, 77, 98, 623, 845
volatile, 17
vprintf( ), 316-317
vscanf( ), 317-318
vsprintf( ), 316-317
vsscanf( ), 317-318

W

warn directive, 240
wchar_t data type, 573, 640
wcstombs( ), 615
wctomb( ), 615
wherex( ), 571, 650
wherey( ), 571, 650
while loop, 5, 51, 67-69
width( ), 752
WILDARGS.OBJ, 91
Win32, 900
WINAPI calling convention, 902
Window
components of, 901-902
displaying, 912-913
outputting text to, 924-929
redisplaying, 930-935
style macros, common, 912
text and grahics functions and, 495-496
Window class, 903
defining, 908-910
registering, 911
Window function, 903, 904-905, 914-915
window( ), 571-572
Windows 95
application fundamentals, 902-904
data types, common, 904
general definition of, 893-895
and program interaction, 900
programs, structure of, 899
skeleton, 904-915
versus Windows 3.1, 895-899
versus Windows NT, 899
Windows 95 Programming from the Ground Up (Schildt), 927
windows.h header file, 904, 907
WinMain( ), 902, 904, 908
WM_CHAR message, 921-924
WM_COMMAND message, 948, 975
WM_DESTROY message, 915

WM_INITDIALOG message, 987
WM_LBUTTONDOWN message, 938, 942
WM_PAINT message
 generating, 935-938
 responding to, 930-935
WM_QUIT message, 915
WM_RBUTTONDOWN message, 938, 942
WNDCLASSEX structure, 904, 908-909
WORD data type, 904
WORDREGS structure, 376
World Wide Web, 1011, 1012
WPARAM data type, 913, 920
wParam message parameter, 920
write( ), 318-319, 766-767
WS_OVERLAPPEDWINDOW macro, 912
WS_VISIBLE style, 999, 1000

xalloc, 813, 814
XOR (exclusive OR) bitwise operator (^), 37, 38, 39

GET IT RIGHT THE FIRST TIME WITH THE LATEST PROGRAMMING BOOKS FROM OSBORNE/MCGRAW-HILL

KNOW the CODE

The Java Handbook
by Patrick Naughton
Founder of the Java Team
at Sun Microsystems

$27.95 U.S.A.
ISBN 0-07-882199-1

"This book kicks butt... so fun, it makes me want to go write a Java Applet myself!"

—**Scott McNealy**
Chairman, CEO, and President
Sun Microsystems, Inc.

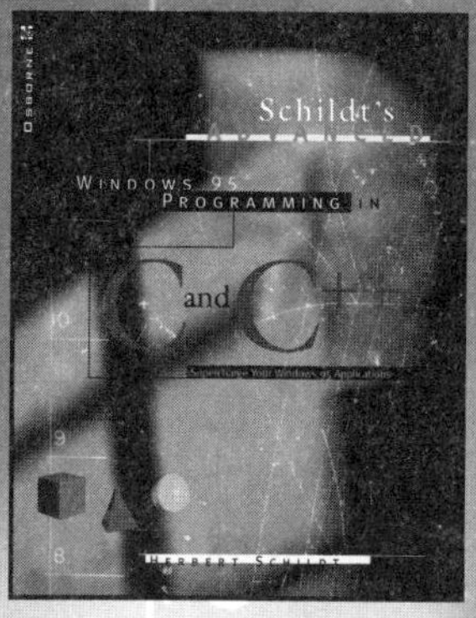

Schildt's Advanced Windows 95 Programming in C and C++
by Herbert Schildt

$29.95 U.S.A.
ISBN 0-07-882174-6

Schildt's Expert C++
by Herbert Schildt

$34.95 U.S.A.
ISBN 0-07-882209-2

Delphi Nuts and Bolts: For Experienced Programmers, Second Edition
by Gary Cornell

$24.95 U.S.A.
ISBN 0-07-882203-3

Delphi In Depth
by Cary Jensen,
Loy Anderson, et al.

$42.95 U.S.A.
ISBN 0-07-882211-4
Includes One CD-ROM

OSBORNE
http://www.osborne.com
A Division of The McGraw-Hill Companies

DIGITAL DESIGN FOR THE 21ST CENTURY

You can count on Osborne/McGraw-Hill and its expert authors to bring you the inside scoop on digital design, production, and the best-selling graphics software.

Digital Images: A Practical Guide
by Adele Droblas Greenberg
and Seth Greenberg
$26.95 U.S.A.
ISBN 0-07-882113-4

Scanning the Professional Way
by Sybil Ihrig and Emil Ihrig
$21.95 U.S.A.
ISBN 0-07-882145-2

Preparing Digital Images for Print
by Sybil Ihrig and Emil Ihrig
$21.95 U.S.A.
ISBN 0-07-882146-0

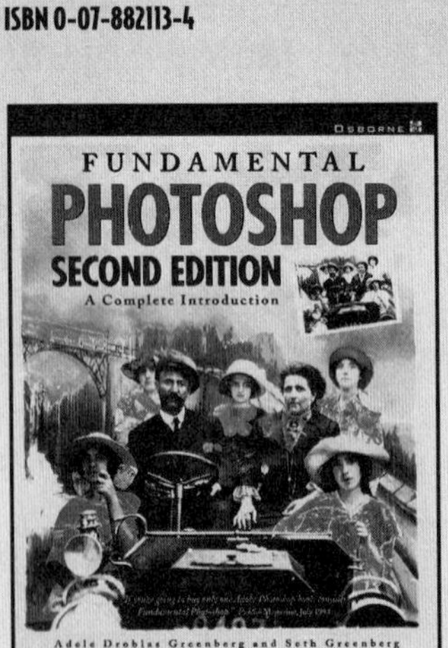

Fundamental Photoshop: A Complete Introduction, Second Edition
by Adele Droblas Greenberg
and Seth Greenberg
$29.95 U.S.A.
ISBN 0-07-882093-6

The Official Guide to CorelDRAW!™6 for Windows 95
by Martin S. Matthews and Carole Boggs Matthews
$34.95 U.S.A.
ISBN 0-07-882168-1

The Official Guide to Corel PHOTO-PAINT 6
by David Huss
$34.95 U.S.A.
ISBN 0-07-882207-6

Bigger and better than ever...each copy is

ONE OF A MILLION!

The hugely successful original ***Internet Yellow Pages*** *is back in its totally updated and revised 1996 edition.*

With more than one million copies in print, it is the undisputed reference of choice for professionals, hobbyists, families, and academic users the world over. Harley Hahn takes readers on a guided tour of the Internet, providing thousands of the best sites including art, games, humor, movies, pets, sports, and much, much more. **The Internet Yellow Pages, Third Edition** is the one Net book—with its humorous style, original phonebook design, and easy-to-reference alphabetical format—that will keep all Internet users happy.

The Internet Yellow Pages, Third Edition
by Harley Hahn
$29.95 U.S.A., 880 pages
ISBN 0-07-882182-7

The Internet
Kids Yellow Pages,
Special Edition
by Jean Armour Polly
$19.95 U.S.A.
ISBN 0-07-882197-5

The Internet
Science, Research, & Technology
Yellow Pages,
Special Edition
by Rick Stout and
Morgan Davis
$22.95 U.S.A.
ISBN 0-07-882187-8

The Internet
Health, Fitness, & Medicine
Yellow Pages,
Special Edition
by Matthew Naythons, M.D.
with Anthony Catsimatides
$22.95 U.S.A.
ISBN 0-07-882188-6

Available at Local Book and Computer Stores or Call 1-800-822-8158

http://www.osborne.com

A Division of The **McGraw-Hill** *Companies*

FUTURE CLASSICS FROM

THE WEB SERVER HANDBOOK

by Cynthia Chin-Lee and Comet

Learn how to set up and maintain a dynamic and effective Web site with this comprehensive guide that focuses on Oracle's new Web solutions.

ISBN: 0-07-882215-7
Price: $39.95 U.S.A.
Includes One CD-ROM

ORACLE MEDIA OBJECTS HANDBOOK

by Dan Shafer

The power, flexibility, and ease of Oracle Media Objects (the cross-platform multimedia authoring tools) are within your reach with this definitive handbook.

ISBN: 0-07-882214-9
Price: $39.95 U.S.A.
Includes One CD-ROM

ORACLE DEVELOPER'S GUIDE

by David McClanahan

Loaded with code for common tasks, developers will find all the information they need to create applications and build a fast, powerful, and secure Oracle database.

ISBN: 0-07-882087-1
Price: $34.95 U.S.A.

ORACLE: THE COMPLETE REFERENCE

Third Edition

by George Koch and Kevin Loney

ISBN: 0-07-882097-9
Price: $34.95 U.S.A.

ORACLE DBA HANDBOOK

by Kevin Loney

ISBN: 0-07-881182-1
Price: $34.95 U.S.A.

ORACLE: A BEGINNER'S GUIDE

by Michael Abbey and Michael J. Corey

ISBN: 0-07-882122-3
Price: $29.95 U.S.A.

TUNING ORACLE

by Michael J. Corey, Michael Abbey, and Daniel J. Dechichio, Jr.

ISBN: 0-07-881181-3
Price: $29.95 U.S.A.

ORACLE® *Oracle Press*™

ORACLE DEVELOPER/2000 HANDBOOK

by Robert J. Muller

This comprehensive resource guides experienced programmers, step by step, through an application development cycle using Oracle Developer/2000's robust tools.

ISBN: 0-07-882180-0
Price: $39.95 U.S.A.
Includes One CD-ROM

ORACLE NETWORKING

by Hugo Toledo, Jr.

Covering topics from Windows 95 workstations to Oracle Internet databases and more, this authoritative guide shows you how to create a fully-realized, networked Oracle database environment.

ISBN: 0-07-882165-7
Price: $34.95 U.S.A.

ORACLE PL/SQL PROGRAMMING

by Scott Urman

Discover the ins and outs of PL/SQL programming with this guide that shows how to develop, test, debug, and tune Oracle applications with a variety of programming tools.

ISBN: 0-07-882176-2
Price: $34.95 U.S.A.

ORACLE POWER OBJECTS HANDBOOK

by Bruce Kolste and David Petersen

ISBN: 0-07-882089-8
Price: $32.95 U.S.A.

ORACLE POWER OBJECTS DEVELOPER'S GUIDE

by Richard Finkelstein, Kasu Sista, and Rick Greenwald

ISBN: 0-07-882163-0
Price: $39.95 U.S.A.
Includes One CD-ROM

ORACLE BACKUP AND RECOVERY HANDBOOK

by Rama Velpuri

ISBN: 0-07-882106-1
Price: $29.95 U.S.A.

ORACLE WORKGROUP SERVER HANDBOOK

by Thomas B. Cox

ISBN: 0-07-881186-4
Price: $27.95 U.S.A.

ORDER BOOKS DIRECTLY FROM OSBORNE/McGRAW-HILL

For a complete catalog of Osborne's books, call 510-549-6600 or write to us at 2600 Tenth Street, Berkeley, CA 94710

Call Toll-Free, *24 hours a day, 7 days a week, in the U.S.A.*
U.S.A.: 1-800-262-4729 ***Canada: 1-800-565-5758***

Mail ***in the U.S.A. to:***

McGraw-Hill, Inc.
Customer Service Dept.
P.O. Box 182607
Columbus, OH 43218-2607

Canada
McGraw-Hill Ryerson
Customer Service
300 Water Street
Whitby, Ontario L1N 9B6

Fax ***in the U.S.A. to:***
1-614-759-3644

Canada
1-800-463-5885
Canada
orders@mcgrawhill.ca

SHIP TO:

Name ______________________

Company ______________________

Address ______________________

City / State / Zip ______________________

Daytime Telephone *(We'll contact you if there's a question about your order.)*

ISBN #	BOOK TITLE	Quantity	Price	Total
0-07-88				
0-07-88				
0-07-88				
0-07-88				
0-07-88				
0-07088				
0-07-88				
0-07-88				
0-07-88				
0-07-88				
0-07-88				
0-07-88				
0-07-88				
0-07-88				
	Shipping & Handling Charge from Chart Below			
	Subtotal			
	Please Add Applicable State & Local Sales Tax			
	TOTAL			

Shipping & Handling Charges

Order Amount	U.S.	Outside U.S.
$15.00 - $24.99	$4.00	$6.00
$25.00 - $49.99	$5.00	$7.00
$50.00 - $74.99	$6.00	$8.00
$75.00 - and up	$7.00	$9.00
$100.00 - and up	$8.00	$10.00

Occasionally we allow other selected companies to use our mailing list. If you would prefer that we not include you in these extra mailings, please check here: ☐

METHOD OF PAYMENT

☐ Check or money order enclosed (payable to Osborne/McGraw-Hill)

☐ AMERICAN EXPRESS ☐ DISCOVER ☐ MasterCard ☐ VISA

Account No. ______________________

Expiration Date ______________________

Signature ______________________

In a hurry? Call with your order anytime, day or night, or visit your local bookstore.

Thank you for your order

Code BC640SL